ROCOCO ARCHITECTURE IN SOUTHERN GERMANY

HENRY-RUSSELL HITCHCOCK

PHAIDON

Henry-Russell Hitchcock

Rococo Architecture in Southern Germany

PHAIDON

FIRST PUBLISHED 1968

PHAIDON PUBLISHERS INC · NEW YORK

DISTRIBUTORS IN THE UNITED STATES: FREDERICK A. PRAEGER INC

111 FOURTH AVENUE · NEW YORK · N.Y. 10003

LIBRARY OF CONGRESS CATALOG CARD NUMBER: 68-27420

SBN 7148 1339 7

MADE IN ENGLAND

TEXT PRINTED BY BELL AND BAIN LTD · GLASGOW

PLATES PRINTED BY HUNT BARNARD AND CO LTD · AYLESBURY · BUCKS

CONTENTS

PREFACE

DURING the preparation of this book for publication it carried the tentative title *Studies in Rococo Architecture* since the first, third and fourth chapters had earlier appeared in print as articles. To the editors of the *Journal of the Society of Architectural Historians*, the *Art Bulletin*, and the Wittkower Festschrift I must express my gratitude for permission to reprint here, if with many emendations, these articles. But as the work proceeded, with the inclusion of Chapter II—written originally in honour of the seventieth birthday of Richard Krautheimer but never published as an independent article—and the addition of an Introduction and a terminal chapter dealing with the Rococo aspects of the *œuvres* of J. M. Fischer and J. B. Neumann, it became apparent that the book would cover most of the significant aspects of the architecture that can be considered Rococo in southern Germany. What is necessarily missing is a consecutive account of the work of the brothers Zimmermann. With that I deal in a separate publication appearing at almost the same time as this book.

In the Preface to *German Rococo: The Zimmermann Brothers* I wrote that Rococo architecture was but the subsidiary theme of the book and that elsewhere I was returning to the subject again. I expressed also there the opinion that 'the history of styles, their recognition and their morphology, [are] always controversial', and noted my belief that stylistic history is generally less useful than the study of the work of particular artists considered in their own particular contexts. The publication as separate articles of the material included here on the Asams, the Schmuzers and Thumb, as also the original form of the chapter on J. G. Fischer, reflected that principle. By bringing together and correlating those articles and by adding a further chapter on two men of at least equal importance, J. M. Fischer and J. B. Neumann, I have yet hoped that the resultant work might be greater than the sum of its parts.

In my study of 18th-century German architecture I have had considerable assistance, especially from Lala Aufsberg and Robert Schmitt, both of whom took many photographs especially for this book. I must also express my gratitude to several scholars, most notably Professor Norbert Lieb of the University of Munich, Dr. Gerhard Hojer of Bonn, Dr. Max Gruber of Bergkirchen, and not least to Dr. Johannes Steiner and Dr. Hugo Schnell of Munich, who have obliged me in many ways.

The *Kunstführer* produced in such amazing quantity by the firm of Schnell & Steiner are an even more valuable resource for anyone interested in German architecture, particularly church architecture, than the post-war editions of Dehio's guide-books for Upper Bavaria and Eastern and Western Swabia as edited by Ernst Gall. Unfortunately no new Dehio–Gall volume has appeared as yet for Lower Bavaria; but volume I of *Reclams Kunstführer*, edited by Alexander von Reitzenstein und Herbert Brunner, covers quite adequately the whole of present-day Bavaria. The parallel volume II for Baden-Württemberg, Pfalz and Saarland, edited by Brunner alone, is also excellent. Even more detailed are the volumes of the series *Bayerische Kunstdenkmäler*, published by the Deutscher Kunstverlag, that deal with particular administrative districts of Bavaria. Of these the ones for Kreis Marktoberdorf and for Kreis Füssen, both by Michael Petzet, were especially useful. Although largely concerned with current religious art and architecture, the periodical *Das Münster*, edited by Dr. Schnell, has from time to time published valuable articles on 18th-century churches and their architects. There are also many useful and well-illustrated monographs on various regions, architects, and individual monuments.

An outsider, entering belatedly this field of study, has available to him, thanks to the work of generations of German scholars, a vast amount of factual material derived from meticulous examination of archival material. Thus he can focus on the subject without the need to lose himself in the pursuit of precise dates and such matters, since these are for the most part readily discoverable in authoritative writings of the present century. I make no apology, therefore, for my reliance on the guide-books, monographs, and theoretical studies of which a remarkable profusion continues to appear all the time. But I will point out the curious fact that, although late publications such as those of Lieb have enormously facilitated study by the remarkable accumulation and correlation of facts that have been unearthed in archival research, it is doubtful whether the interpretation of the material by Feulner in his *Bayerisches Rokoko* of forty years ago has yet been improved on, not even in the extensive article on the international Rococo that Sedlmayer and Bauch contributed to the *Encyclopedia of World Art*. The thirty-eight columns of text and six columns of bibliography of that, however, constitute a very solid treatise, though with sadly limited illustration. Unfortunately the other most available late account in English, found in the eighty-two pages of Part Five of Hempel's *Baroque Art and Architecture in Central Europe* in the Pelican History of Art, is only somewhat better illustrated and much less persuasive as a stylistic study of the Rococo. Thus one may hope that the present work, dealing with most of the major figures of the Rococo period in southern Germany, will at the least amplify for English and American readers what is already available.

There should be a word here as to the geographical area treated in this book as 'southern Germany'. The great majority of the works discussed and illustrated are in the two present-day states of Bavaria and Baden-Württemberg. A certain amount of building activity in western Baden and the Rhineland, mostly for prelates of the Wittelsbach and Schönborn families, is covered as well; and the *oeuvre* of Peter Thumb includes one major church west of the Rhine in Alsace. Several Swiss churches south of the Bodensee are also discussed, most notably the big churches of the Benedictine Abbeys of Einsiedeln and St. Gallen. A few earlier Austrian works enter the argument peripherally as well; and one of J. G. Fischer's less important works is, in fact, across the present Italian border near Merano.

H. R. HITCHCOCK

Northampton, Massachusetts
May 1968

INTRODUCTION

TODAY the Rococo is universally recognized as having been, at the least, an idiosyncratic mode of decoration employed by the middle decades of the eighteenth century throughout the civilized world—even to some extent in the Far East and the Americas. Moreover, many now consider that the Rococo was a rather general phase of style, if not a style in its own right, and one perhaps more characteristic for the period than other contemporary currents in the arts.[1] Initiated as a novel sort of decoration in the office of Louis XIV's *premier architecte*, J. H. Mansart, by the *dessinateur* Pierre Lepautre, and first employed at Versailles about 1700,[2] the Rococo had already begun to spread by the time of Lepautre's death in 1716, even though it had not yet fully matured in France. Nowhere was it sooner or more enthusiastically adopted than in the regions neighbouring the Rhine and the Isar.

The early spread of the Rococo in the second and third decades of the century (Pl. 1)[2a] to certain German states in the south and the west owed a good deal to the political situation. During most of the War of the Spanish Succession—not from 1701 when that war began, but from 1704 to 1714—two German princes, both members of the Wittelsbach family, the Elector Max Emanuel (1662–1726) of Bavaria, whose second wife was a Bourbon, and his brother Joseph Clemens (1671–1723), Elector as well as Archbishop of Cologne, were in exile in France while Allied troops occupied their territories after the Battle of Blenheim.[3] This alien occupation largely halted building construction in Bavaria and the Rhineland. Throughout these years, however, the two princely exiles were in much closer touch with the leading French architects of the day than they might otherwise have been.

A member of another branch of the Wittelsbachs, married long before Max Emanuel into the French Royal family and long resident in Paris, Elisabeth Charlotte von der Pfalz,[4] duchesse d'Orléans (1652–1722), was an even earlier patroness of the Rococo. For a slightly later phase of the Rococo, moreover, her son's more extensive patronage, while he was Regent of France from 1715 to 1723 between the death of Louis XIV and the majority of Louis XV, provides the name 'Régence'. In her salons at the Hotel du Petit Luxembourg, several of them already decorated about 1710 in the Early Rococo mode from the designs of Germain Boffrand (1667–1754) according to Fiske Kimball,[5] there gathered most of those Germans who were in Paris, whether as exalted exiles or as young noblemen making the grand tour. Boffrand, moreover, had already worked a few years earlier for Max Emanuel at Bouchefort near Brussels while the latter was for some years Stadtholder of the Austrian Netherlands thanks to his first Habsburg marriage.

In 1706 the Bavarian Elector had also arranged that Joseph Effner (1687–1745),[6] a son of his court-gardener at Schloss Dachau north-west of Munich, should come to Paris to study garden-design. Effner's interests soon shifted to architecture, however, and he began working under and with Boffrand. (Eventually, Max Emanuel employed the Frenchman Dominique Girard (d. 1738) for his gardens in Bavaria.)

Even before Effner returned to Munich with the Elector after the signing of the Treaty of Rastatt in 1714, the latter had charged him, rather than Boffrand, with the remodelling of the house he had bought in 1713 at Saint-Cloud.[7] Then, on 1 April 1715, back once more in Munich, Max Emanuel appointed the 28-year-old Effner *Hofbaumeister*. In effect, this Paris-trained Bavarian was thenceforth the Elector's court-architect, despite the continuance of the Italian-Swiss Enrico Zuccalli (*c.* 1642–1724) as nominally superior (*Oberhofbaumeister*) down to his death.

Throughout the years of exile Max Emanuel's brother Joseph Clemens was in continuous correspondence with Robert de Cotte (1656–1735), J. H. Mansart's brother-in-law and, after 1708 when Mansart died, his successor as Louis XIV's *premier architecte*, concerning building projects both ecclesiastical and secular at Bonn, his principal seat just south of Cologne. In 1714, moreover, Max Emanuel commissioned designs from de Cotte for the completion of his own Schloss at Schleissheim, to the north of Munich, on which construction under Zuccalli's direction had come to a halt ten years before. In 1716 Joseph Clemens also obtained at least one design for a chimney-piece from G.-M. Oppenord (1672–1742), the architect of the French Regent. Oppenord was a far more advanced artist than the *dessinateurs* who were working under de Cotte after the death of Lepautre in that year.[8]

Too much weight should not, however, be given to the direct contacts of these two German princes with Boffrand, de Cotte, and Oppenord. It was not such leading French architects and designers, content for the most part merely to supply projects that would be executed abroad by others, who effectively brought the Rococo to Germany in the way that the Louis XVI mode, forty or fifty years later, was introduced mainly by French architects who had settled permanently in various princely courts.[9] Specifically, for example, it was Paris-trained craftsmen who were not French—though not Bavarian either—that formed the team working with Effner for Max Emanuel over the years 1716–19 on the earliest surviving Rococo interiors in Germany.[10] These (Pls. 2, 4) are in the Pagodenburg in the gardens of Schloss Nymphenburg,[11] just outside Munich to the west, that Girard was then extending. Soon a few rooms in the Schloss itself and, in Max Emanuel's last years, whole suites of apartments for himself and the Electress (Pl. 2) along the garden front at Schleissheim provided more sumptuous examples of the new mode, rivalling contemporary Parisian interiors of the later Régence both before and after 1723.

Already, moreover, a development was beginning that would increasingly differentiate the German from the French Rococo, even in its still transitional phase in the twenties. In the octagonal lower room at the Pagodenburg the walls are lined with blue-and-white Dutch tiles in the tradition of Louis XIV's Trianon de porcelaine of a generation earlier (Pl. 2). Thus there is no place, as in the principal room above (Pl. 4), for the up-to-date French gold-and-white *boiseries* of J. A. Pichler.[12] More significantly, on the walls of the lobbies of the lower room there are mouldings executed in stucco[13] as they would hardly have been at that time in France.

Very soon the native craft of decoration in stucco, maintained by generations of craftsmen from Wessobrunn in Upper Bavaria, but already much chastened in design (Pls. 15, 18) after the provincial exuberance of the years around 1700 (Pls. 118–123),[14] began to be modified by the introduction of some formal elements from the repertory of the Early Rococo, by this time well established in France. With stuccoers in the court circle such decoration retained for a while a certain French delicacy, moreover, as in the ceiling that J. B. Zimmermann (1680–1758)[15] executed in the mid-twenties in the Kammerkapelle at Schleissheim and even that of 1725 over the library at the Abbey of Benediktbeuern in Upper Bavaria.

Away from Munich, and especially in church interiors, the French influence was at first much more dilute. But it was most notably in the churches built or redecorated by the brothers Asam—whose foreign training had been Roman, not French—that a remarkable stylistic modulation now got under way.[16] Characteristically, the French Rococo at Versailles and in Paris in the early decades of the century, as first emulated in Bavaria for Max Emanuel, was a mode of secular decoration used chiefly for rooms of moderate size.[17] In the chapel at Versailles and at Notre-Dame in Paris, Lepautre, the 'father of the Rococo', and others had already exploited in 1709–10 the new Rococo mode for fittings carved in wood such as doors, choir-stalls, and so forth. But the architectonic aspects of these French churches, whether old or new, were hardly at all affected.

The large-scale Rococo interiors that were first created during the twenties in German churches never had their parallels in France, and rarely elsewhere in Europe. Yet the question is recurrently asked whether a true Rococo *architecture* was then initiated in Germany, and further developed to maturity in the thirties and forties; or whether these notable examples of *Gesamtkunstwerk*, in which collaborating stuccoers and fresco-painters played as great a part as the architects, are not merely examples of Late Baroque architecture, however richly decorated they may be with Rococo ornament. That, indeed, is certainly true up to a point of some of the biggest and most gorgeous churches by J. M. Fischer and others in the second quarter of the century.[18]

In the many-volumed *Geschichte der neueren Baukunst*, edited by Jacob Burckhardt, Wilhelm Lübke and Cornelius Gurlitt, which appeared in the 1880s and was intended to cover architecture from the Renaissance through the Neoclassicism of 1800, the fifth volume (which actually appeared in two parts) was devoted to the *Geschichte des Barockstiles, des Rococo, und des Klassicismus* throughout Europe. The second part by Gurlitt, published in Stuttgart in 1889, dealt nominally only with the Baroque and the Rococo in Germany, though it touched in fact on the beginnings of Neoclassicism as well. However, Gurlitt, who subdivided his complicated subject by region and also by religion—Protestant versus Catholic—rather than chronologically, made no serious attempt to set the Rococo apart from the Baroque. A year earlier Heinrich Wölfflin in his still-influential critical study of *Renaissance und Barock* had also made little or no distinction between the Baroque and the Rococo. Indeed, in defining the major differences between the 'classical' architecture of the High Renaissance of the early sixteenth century—or sometimes the

Neoclassic architecture of the late eighteenth century—and the Baroque, his examples were as often as not Rococo, and so identified in the text.

A good many twentieth-century scholars have sought, at least, to delimit the German Rococo chronologically, though few have persuasively characterized it as a style. Yet, after two generations of research and interpretation, even the chronology is a matter that remains—and perhaps always will remain—somewhat unsettled. Because the answer depends so much, not on discoverable facts, but on the taste, the training, and the breadth of first-hand experience of each writer, it is difficult, perhaps impossible, to resolve objectively or finally how the sub-periods preceding the arrival of international Neoclassicism in Germany fairly late in the third quarter of the eighteenth century should be demarcated, especially as, in fact, they often overlap one another. Norbert Lieb, in the introduction to the book on the Baroque architects from the Vorarlberg for which he shares credit with Franz Dieth, summarized some years ago the conclusions of nearly half a century.[19]

To Hans Rose, writing in 1922, everything was still *Spätbarock* (Late Baroque) over the entire hundred years from 1660 to 1760. That had at least the merit of applying loosely to several other countries beside Germany, but is too broad to be very helpful. Max Hauttmann, the year before, in dealing with the more extended span 1580–1780, had already broken the middle and later portions of this long period, beginning with the years following the end of the Thirty Years' War when building activity revived after a generation of non-production, into a *Hochstufe* or 'high' phase, 1650–1720, and a *Spätstufe*—'late' phase—1720–80, thus fixing his terminal date twenty years beyond that of Rose. Neither set apart the Rococo. Wilhelm Pinder in 1926, however, saw a series of five stylistic 'waves' following one another after 1660. That was a somewhat more realistic initial date than Hauttmann's 1650 and a rather appropriate metaphor, since it implies some overlapping. For him it was the fourth wave that represented specifically the Rococo.

Hans Sedlmayr's triple subdivision of 1930 for Austria—1690–1720, 1720–45, and 1745–80—is broader than Pinder's. His break in 1745, however, perhaps meaningful in Habsburg territories where the uncontested rule of Maria Theresia and her husband began in that year, makes little sense in southern Germany. There the accession of Max III Joseph as Elector of Bavaria was an event of far less artistic significance than the return of his grandfather Max Emanuel from France thirty years before. Moreover, Sedlmayr's further subdivision of the earliest period—the breakdown is 1690–1705, 1705–15, and *c.* 1720—seems much too fragmented to be very useful outside Austria; nor does it recognize as such the proto-Rococo decoration carried out in and near Vienna[20] in the second decade of the century.

In 1958 John Bourke, neither a German nor an art-historian, sensibly if brutally simplified the pattern by noting only a single major dividing line between 1650 and 1770. This he placed at 1710, though with some mention of the onset of the Rococo in Germany, which he put—a bit late it seems to me—about 1730. Hanspeter Landolt, writing in 1948 on the churches of Switzerland, would not have the Rococo begin there until 1740, and refers to Rococo *stucchi* as late as the nineties. Most satisfactory seems Oskar Sandner's proposal of 1950, primarily for architects from the Vorarlberg, which is quite close to Hauttmann's. His 'early' phase, 1650–80, is followed by a 'high' phase, 1680–1720 (this divided into two equal parts at 1700), a 'transitional' phase, 1720–30, and a 'late' phase, extending—more than a bit excessively, I believe, at least north of Switzerland—down to Hauttmann's terminal date of 1780.

Lieb himself would modify this to a five-part sequence: 1650–80, 'High Baroque'; 1680–1700, 'Late Baroque' (in a narrow sense); 1700–25, 'Régence'; 1730–60, 'Rococo'; and 1760-80, 'Proto-Neoclassicism'—the clumsy term is a too literal translation of *Vorklassicismus*; 'Louis XVI', or even the old German tag 'Pigtail Style', would be better. But to use the French name Régence for a period beginning in 1700 is rather inaccurate historically: Régence has a specific historical meaning in reference to the regency of the duc d'Orléans during the minority of Louis XV—1715–23—even though it has also been extended as a stylistic term by some French writers to cover the rest of the twenties. But the gap Lieb leaves between 1725 and 1730, though opening some years later, corresponds well enough with Sandner's 'transitional' phase covering the whole of the decade.

Because of the Pagodenburg at Nymphenburg of 1716–19, if not certain interiors that were decorated two or three years earlier in Franconia,[20a] I would carry this 'transitional' phase a few years further back even than Sandner, calling it 'proto-Rococo'; and I would extend the true Rococo phase further than Lieb, well into, indeed through, the sixties. Such chopping and changing, however, only makes it more difficult to coordinate these brief style-phases in Germany with what was going on in other parts of Europe. In France, for example, the transition to the Rococo may be considered to have started as early as 1700[21] since the Rococo had its international beginnings there; yet the Rococo in that country was barely over by 1760.

In England there is no overall Rococo period. It is rather the reign of George II and, in architecture, the rule of the Anglo-Palladians led by Lord Burlington—that is the decades 1720–60—which correspond with the German Rococo chronologically, if hardly at all stylistically except, in a quite special sense, in garden design. The transition to this period actually started several years earlier; and its termination is marked rather by the opening of Robert Adam's English career on his return from Italy in 1759 than by the accession of George III.

Since the architecture of these decades in southern Germany is, at the least, distinctly Germanic, not just a French import, whether or not it should be sharply distinguished as Rococo from the Late Baroque, various conditions peculiar to Germany, and more particularly to the southern portion, should be noted. Family teams, usually teams of brothers as in the case of Dominikus and Johann Baptist Zimmermann[22] or Cosmas Damian and Egid Quirin Asam,[23] were responsible for much of the finest early and mid eighteenth-century church architecture and decoration in southern Germany. Septs of architects, stuccoers and sculptors—if not so much of painters—especially those with Italian names who originated in the Swiss Grigioni (Graubünden) and those from the Austrian Vorarlberg[24]—among architects Rivas, Viscardis and Zuccallis, on the one hand, and Beers, Thumbs and Moosbruggers on the other—had long been prominent in the south

German and Swiss building scene; while from Wessobrunn[25] in Upper Bavaria came several related groups of stuccoers and stuccoer-architects, notably the Zimmermanns, the Schmuzers[26] and one family of Feichtmayrs.[27]

Stuccoers and architects whose careers began as virtuoso workers in this flourishing south German craft played an especially important part both in the rapid acclimatization of the Rococo in Germany and in the characteristic change in interiors from the domestic scale of French—and even of most of the earlier German—secular work to the monumental scale of the great abbey and pilgrimage churches of the second quarter of the eighteenth century. Even in those edifices which most consistently retained Baroque aspects of planning and tectonic structural expression Rococo *stucchi* can have a considerable effect on the character of the interiors, so that they differ as much from Italian churches of the day as from French ones (Pls. 192, 198). On the other hand, the large frescoes overhead in the German churches, all but unknown on the cut-stone vaults of French churches of the seventeenth and eighteenth centuries, maintain a kinship with an Italian tradition that had all but died out in France by this period. Even so, there are important differences in the way the frescoes are framed or vignetted, in close association with other architectural characteristics quite alien to the Baroque, from what was current south of the Alps.

The origins of these extensive ceiling frescoes in Germany are, of course, Italian. Influences from Andrea Pozzo and even Baccicia are very evident in C. D. Asam's frescoes of 1718–20 at Weingarten (Pls. 32, 33), to mention but one especially conspicuous example. These, however, do not extend beyond single bays, nor do they have the scalloped framing that the Asams would so soon be introducing at large scale on the vaults of Aldersbach in 1720 (Pl. 40). This pregnant innovation in German ceiling decoration was not without prototypes north of the Alps. Though it is unlikely that the Asams had direct knowledge of Austrian interiors of the previous decade, Vienna was the source for this new development—certainly not Paris. Relevant models existed, however, just to the north of Bavaria in Franconia and, on a small scale, even nearer than those to Munich.

Schloss Weissenstein, at Pommersfelden near Bamberg, was built in 1711–18 for Lothar Franz Graf von Schönborn (1655–1729), Archbishop and Elector of Mainz and Prince-Bishop of Bamberg, by Johann Dientzenhofer (1665–1726).[28] Here the Grosse Galerie (Pl. 6), intended and still used for the display of the Schönborn collection of pictures, has a vaulted ceiling stuccoed in 1714 by Daniel Schenk (d. 1737) for which Lothar Franz obtained in that year a design from Vienna.[29] This is a longitudinal interior, comparable to the nave of a church in length, if not in width. It is not divided by an order into bays, however, since the walls were to be even more thickly hung with heavily framed pictures than they are today. Overhead, three relatively large frescoes—or more accurately, in this case, oil paintings—by the Italian Carlo Cignani (1628–1719), set in scalloped stucco frames, interrupt the continuity of the delicate surface decoration on the vault. The monumental Marmorsaal on the garden side of the Schloss, in the principal story behind the stair-hall, is a room as large and as tall as a good-sized church and, in effect, has bays defined by the engaged columns and pilasters that subdivide the walls. In this, rich *stucchi* by Schenk surround a very large ceiling fresco of 1717 by the Austrian-born but Venice-trained J. F. M. Rottmayr (1660–1730), then the leading fresco-painter in Vienna.

The Weissenstein chapel occupying the ground floor of the east wing beside the court, one of the first interiors to be completed—in the autumn of 1714, though consecration followed only in 1718—has a relatively large fresco of the Assumption of the Virgin by J. J. Gebhardt. This is set in a rather broad scalloped stucco frame extending through all three bays of its shallow vault and surrounded by Schenk's *stucchi* (Pl. 5). However, the modest dimensions of this room—for it is a moderate-sized room rather than a monumental interior—and the extremely firm framing of the ceiling fresco make it less premonitory of what was to come in large churches than the treatment overhead of the Marmorsaal or, above all, the Grosse Galerie. Yet the flattened warping of the vault here and the complicated treatment of the corners, with niches on the bias flanking the eastern windows, also have a somewhat proto-Rococo character.

Larger than any of the Pommersfelden ceiling paintings that have been illustrated[30] is the scalloped oval painting by A. C. Lünenschloss (*c.* 1685–1762), surrounded by stucco-work that is either by Schenk or by Georg Hennicke (d. 1739), over the Kaisersaal in the great monastery not far away at Ebrach[31] (Pl. 8). This probably dates from 1718. Although the ceiling here is flat even if coved round the edge not vaulted, the architectural resemblance to a monumental church interior is considerably closer. The wall-bays either side are flanked by engaged columns set against pilaster clusters, while between them are galleried recesses somewhat like the side chapels with tribunes above often present in eighteenth-century churches. That Ebrach was an abbey, and a Cistercian one at that—like Aldersbach, which was actually settled by monks from Ebrach, though in the twelfth century!—makes it a more likely source than Schloss Weissenstein at Pommersfelden (on which Ebrach must in turn depend) for C. D. Asam's large frescoes of 1720 on the vaults at Aldersbach (Pls. 38–40).

The Austrian F. J. Roth's work of 1718–20 in the Deutschordensschloss at Ellingen, southwest of Dinkelsbühl, is another comparable example. The Festsaal there has, on the ceiling, a large scalloped oval fresco by Johann Pinck surrounded by Roth's stucco-work. The decoration of the stair-hall there is equally relevant and in better condition (Pl. 7).

The Franconian innovations certainly derived from Vienna, but relevant Austrian examples of earlier date are not easy to find. Comparable in character to the ceilings that the Austrian J. A. Gumpp painted in the Pagodenburg in these same years (Pls. 2, 4), dependent not on current Parisian work but rather on the engravings of ornament by Berain that had for some years been available internationally, are certain aspects of the interiors in the city and country mansions that Hildebrandt erected or enlarged in the second decade of the century in Austria. In these a Viennese Early Rococo, parallel to what had lately developed in France but not dependent on the new French mode, seems to have been immanent, even if never fully realized.[32] The surviving Groteskensaal, the Goldkabinett (Pl. 10) and the Marmorgalerie in the Lower Belvedere were decorated for Prince Eugene in 1714–16; but even more relevant to the present story must have been some of the rooms in Schloss Schönborn near Göllersdorf, in Lower Austria north of Vienna, which Hildebrandt had been remodelling and enlarging since 1712 for the Vice-Chancellor of the Empire, Friedrich Carl Graf von Schönborn (1674–1746), a nephew of the builder of Schloss Weissenstein.[33]

As early as June 1713, just when interior work was getting under way at Pommersfelden, Friedrich Carl wrote to his uncle that the *stucchi* in the saloon of his own Schloss were completed and that by September twelve more rooms would be stuccoed. In 1714–15 he paid Jonas Drentwett (*c.* 1650–*c.* 1720) 1600 florins for frescoes in his Sala Terrena, his chapel, and his library. The next year it was the same painter who covered the entire walls and ceiling of Prince Eugene's Groteskensaal with polychrome arabesque decorations, based on either Berain's plates of ornament or, possibly, his own brother's versions of such ornament. Thus, although work in the principal interiors at Schloss Weissenstein continued for several years, the campaigns of decoration of the two Schönborn prelates overlapped, as did also that at the Lower Belvedere.

Nevertheless, the ceiling of the saloon at Schloss Schönborn, with its *stucchi* of early 1713, must have been remarkably similar to those in the Elector's apartments at Pommersfelden stuccoed by Schenk after his visit to Vienna in that year. This room at Schloss Schönborn is shown in an engraving after a drawing by Salomon Kleiner[34] to have had Bérainesque bandwork on the coved vault and a figural panel in the centre of irregular, not to say scalloped, outline. Was this frescoed by Drentwett, one wonders, or filled with a stucco relief as in the Marmorgalerie of the Lower Belvedere? The Pommersfelden rooms, as decorated overhead in 1713–14, all have small frescoed panels in the centres of their ceilings surrounded by delicate near-Rococo *stucchi* by Schenk in white and gold against pale-tinted grounds.[35] Unfortunately Hermann Grimschitz, the biographer of Hildebrandt, gives no name or provenance for the stuccoer who worked at Schloss Schönborn.[36]

It is clear that proto-Rococo influence from Vienna preceded in southern Germany the work of Max Emanuel's Paris-trained craftsmen at Nymphenburg by several years. There is also evidence somewhat later of Austrian influence—and specifically from Hildebrandt—in Bavaria in the secular field. The two private mansions that Effner and François Cuvilliés (1695–1768),[36a] both Paris-trained, built in Munich in the twenties followed Viennese rather than Parisian models in their general conception and in the style of their façades. The resemblance of the exterior of the former's Palais Preysing of 1723–28 (Pl. 9), beside the Residenz, to Hildebrandt's Palais Daun-Kinsky[37] of 1713–16 in Vienna is certainly very close. Both have tapered and panelled pilasters dividing the three middle bays and also concave-pointed pediments over some of the windows, though the latter are used on the Viennese mansion in the side bays and on the Munich one in those in the centre. The irregular squarish site in Munich, however, made impossible the symmetrical arrangement of the plan around long and narrow courts in Hildebrandt's more formal way;[38] nor are the attic windows in the Palais Preysing pinched horizontally to fit them into the frieze of a complete entablature. At the same time, it is interesting to note, Prince Eugene in Vienna was borrowing from Max Emanuel his French garden-designer Girard.

Considering the very much greater importance overall of French, as compared to Austrian, sources for the mature German Rococo, it is surprising that French architects played so little direct part in the transplantation of the new mode in the second and third decades of the century.[39] To this there were a few exceptions now known only from drawings. The interiors designed by Robert de Cotte that once existed in the Buen Retiro wing of the Elector Joseph Clemens's Residenz at Bonn, mentioned earlier, have not survived; and the exterior of the Residenz, most of it from his plans, is irrelevant here. What might be called Joseph Clemens's 'Grand Trianon' at Bonn, the still extant Schloss Clemensruhe in the western suburb of Poppelsdorf,[40] is not very relevant either. This was carried out, as regards the exterior, chiefly in 1718–23 from a project supplied by de Cotte in 1715. The *Palier*, or supervising architect, was a minor Frenchman, Guillaume Hauberat,[41] called to Bonn in 1716 on de Cotte's recommendation. The interiors at Poppelsdorf, which might well have received Early Rococo decoration at this point, were in fact only executed for Joseph Clemens's nephew and successor Clemens August in a campaign that began as late as 1744.

The designs for rooms that Boffrand provided in 1724 for the Würzburg Residenz of the Prince-Bishop Johann Philipp Franz von Schönborn, Carl Friedrich's brother, are still, for that date, not very advanced according to French or even German standards.[42] Indeed they are quite similar to those de Cotte supplied in 1716–17 for the Buen Retiro, though not as conservative as his designs for the exteriors of the Poppelsdorf Schloss and the Bonn Residenz.

Even among the craftsmen who had been trained in Paris few, if any, were French by birth, at least among those who worked in Bavaria. Similarly, the Italians and the Italian-Swiss from the Grigioni, who had had such an important part to play through the preceding two or three generations, were no longer of quite so much consequence after 1720.[43] A major exception is J. B. Neumann's collaborating stuccoer, Antonio Bossi (d. 1764), who came from Lugano. Without his major contributions (Pls. 208–210) hardly any of Neumann's works would be considered Rococo.

Moreover, not many of the German architects who were most active through the first half of the century had studied in France. The principal exceptions are Effner and Cuvilliés, who later sent his son to Paris as did certain others in the mid-century. Several of the artists, however, especially the painters, had had some training in Rome or Venice. An Italian background that included two years of study in Rome was certainly important for the Asams.[44] It was considerably less significant in the case of J. G. Fischer, though he probably also spent several years in Italy in his early youth and certainly made a briefer visit much later in his life.[45]

After the twenties and into the sixties—throughout the Rococo period, indeed—the building arts were preponderantly in native German hands, and the hands of Germans who had been trained in their own land. This would not seem so notable but for the fact that it had not been true in the earlier High Baroque period[46] and would not be true to the same extent when imported French architects assumed leadership in the reaction against the Rococo in the later 1760s and 1770s.[47] Yet, in painting, the links with Italy were never to the same extent loosened and, as a result, eighteenth-century German frescoes often seem somewhat out of harmony with their settings. They maintain distinctly Baroque characteristics, especially in *quadratura* and other painted architectural settings, well into the 1750s and then, in the sixties, begin quite early to reflect the Neoclassicism that was already under way in Rome after the middle of the century. In that development, indeed, Germans played an important part, both in the realm of theory—the critic J. J. Winkelmann—and in practice—the painter A. R. Mengs (1728–89).

In the context of the German Baroque the architects from the Vorarlberg, contiguous to Bavarian Swabia, if not those from Graubünden (Grigioni), need hardly be considered foreigners. The importance of the Graubünden architects, like that of the artists who came from north Italy, diminished through the decades of the Rococo. There was no Swiss-born architect of consequence practising in German lands after Zuccalli; and J. C. Bagnato in Baden, like Santini in Bohemia, was Italian only by descent. The peak of the Vorarlbergers' activity came in 1719,[48] but thenceforth they were of less importance and by the sixties hardly identifiable as a group. Yet the Moosbruggers—Andreas and Peter Anton I—were still producing Rococo *stucchi* in Switzerland in the 1770s and even the 1780s,[49] while as late as 1845–46 Hierononymus Moosbrugger carried out the already rather Neo-Baroque ceiling of the Hall of Sessions in the Lower Austrian Landhaus in Vienna.[50]

So extensive and so sumptuous was building production in the eighteenth century in southern Germany that it is difficult to understand how the construction and the decoration of so many churches, monasteries, and palaces could have been possible in districts not, for the period, especially prosperous. The principal explanation must be sought in the continuance of medieval economic conditions. The south German monasteries were, unlike those in most other parts of Europe, still enormously rich. Moreover, the pilgrimages they sponsored were unbelievably popular —are, indeed, so popular today that the great churches are still at least as much visited for religious as for aesthetic reasons—and the contributions of the pilgrims provided ample funds for building. The secular rulers, often contributors to the building of churches as well as very active on their own account, were still handling the income of their states as if it were their own. Their palaces, however, were in fact not much larger or more costly than the mansions of the Whig magnates in Georgian England despite the great difference in style between the German Rococo and the Anglo-Palladian. Many of the grander palaces, moreover, had been begun earlier in more or less direct emulation of Versailles and were, in the half-century 1720–70, merely completed, remodelled and redecorated. Even more frequently, they were provided with subsidiary structures in the gardens, or nearby, that imitated the Grand or (much later) the Petit Trianon.

Most of the monasteries had inherited large churches of medieval date; of these—as, indeed, of smaller village churches also—portions, particularly the choirs and the towers, were in many cases allowed to survive structurally. From Freising Cathedral (Pl. 45), elaborately redecorated in the early 1720s, to Ettal (Pl. 147), 'restored' after a fire in the late 1740s, many immense churches of Romanesque or Gothic construction provided the shells within which Rococo stuccoers and fresco-painters worked to create wholly new ensembles, and these hybrid interiors have unusual importance in southern Germany in the eighteenth century.

There are, of course, instances in many periods of the transformation of older churches by drastic remodelling or recasing of their exteriors or interiors. These have sometimes been pregnant examples of stylistic change. In its early development, even at its initiation, a new style may be markedly influenced by problems imposed by pre-existing construction. As regards exteriors, one thinks of Alberti's Tempio Malatestiano at Rimini. There the earlier medieval walls were entirely hidden by new front and side façades that all but adumbrated the High Renaissance more than a generation *avant la lettre*. In the preceding century the transformation of the Norman choir in Gloucester Cathedral by a reticulated grid of moulded mullions and transoms, covering evenly both the old broad piers and the openings between, was certainly a major step in the early development of the Perpendicular.

The decorative transformation of medieval churches in southern Germany in the eighteenth century played an especially effective part in the initiation and in the maturing of a large-scale Rococo interior *architecture*. The conditions imposed by existing plans and structure were here as elsewhere limiting factors on the freedom of the eighteenth-century artists; yet these limitations seem in Bavaria also to have provided circumstances that were positively conducive to original creation—as, indeed, artistic limitations have often done. But the great interest of these transformed interiors is the very high quality of the results. Even if a Rococo architecture could, in them, be only partially achieved, many rival in distinction all but the finest new churches of the time. In most, moreover, the formal links with the preceding Baroque were more decisively broken in the twenties and early thirties than in other contemporary interiors, except for the relatively modest secular examples that were directly based on French models. Only much later, in the fifties and sixties, would some of the larger German secular interiors rival churches of the period as examples of Rococo interior architecture (Pl. 12).[51]

It was not easy to 'baroquize' a medieval church except by rebuilding it. But total reconstruction was often avoided for reasons of sentiment as well as considerations of expense and inconvenience.[52] The very great length characteristic of many of the old cathedrals and abbeys in Germany and their generally tall and narrow proportions; the multiplicity of supports required by narrow vaulting bays, and usual even where there had originally been no vaulting; the heavy or intricate rib-patterns of Romanesque or Gothic vaults; the broad fields of unbroken wall usual between nave arcade and clerestory; and, not least, the pointed form of the arches and vaults in Gothic churches—all of these features were difficult to disguise, or even to modify, in a way that could satisfy standard Baroque taste anywhere in Europe.

Where, early in the eighteenth century, vaults were merely clothed with a new decorative inner lining of stucco, as by Dominikus Zimmermann in the Carthusian church[53] at Buxheim outside Memmingen in Bavarian Swabia in 1711–13 for example, the discord between the earlier structure, with its plain surfaces and dominant pointed forms, and the plastic *stucchi*, not to speak of the somewhat illusionistic 'skylights' provided by small frescoed panels, was certainly very awkward. Not very many large or important medieval churches were, in fact, remodelled or redecorated before the twenties. The centrally planned Benedictine church at Ettal, already from its original Gothic construction unusual because of its shape, had been something of an exception; but what Zuccalli may have done in the interior in 1710–26 was quite obscured by Josef Schmuzer's superb redecoration after the fire of 1744.

In the twenties and early thirties, thanks in considerable part to the problems and the opportunities that the transformation of medieval churches provided, the shift away from the Baroque not only was more drastic in German ecclesiastical work than in secular work, but also more independent of French influence. Chapter I of this book deals in large part with the earlier stages of this transformation as represented by the Asam brothers' redecoration of such medieval churches as Freising Cathedral (Pl. 45) in 1723–24 and St. Emmeram at Regensburg (Pl. 63) ten years later. It was between these two major campaigns, it should be noted, that the first great new churches were built and decorated which may be considered, at the very least, significantly proto-Rococo—if not, indeed, actually Early Rococo—notably the Zimmermann brothers' Steinhausen (Pl. 11) of 1727–31 and J. M. Fischer's almost precisely contemporary Osterhofen (Pl. 58) as frescoed and stuccoed by the Asams. Three more old churches, redecorated by members of the Schmuzer family in the thirties and forties, are discussed and illustrated in Chapter III (Pls. 137, 144, 147).

Drastic remodelling of earlier churches was, by the eighteenth century, a very old story. Yet in the thirty years or so following the Asams' redecoration of Freising such programmes in southern Germany were unusually successful in the quality and, indeed, the originality of the architectural entities thus created. This is true even in comparison with the more important new churches designed and executed by such leading architects among the Asams' contemporaries as Neumann and J. M. Fischer[54] or even Dominikus Zimmermann. In such work, moreover, artists like the Asams and Dominikus's brother Johann Baptist, who were active principally as stuccoers and fresco-painters, often had a more important role than professional architects, if architects as such were employed at all. Indeed, the one who was perhaps most successful at this work, Joseph Schmuzer, had been trained by his father Johann as much to be a stuccoer as an architect.

The interiors of such abbey churches in southern Bavaria as those at Rottenbuch (Pl. 137), at Steingaden (Pl. 144), and above all at Ettal (Pl. 147)—the first and last redecorated by Joseph Schmuzer, the second by his son Franz Xaver II—all created, like that at Freising, within Romanesque or Gothic shells, are among the near-masterpieces of monumental Rococo interiors. But because of their relatively late dates—1737–47, 1740–50, and 1744–52, respectively—they played no part in the early development of the German Rococo. Freising, on the other hand, was certainly of prime importance in that development, regardless of whether the Asams' work there be considered still proto-Rococo or already Early Rococo.[55] Particularly significant is the fact that their decoration owes so little to direct influence from Paris, or even from the Paris-trained artists with whom C. D. Asam, at least, must have been in contact at Schleissheim for two or three years before he began to work at Freising.[56]

This book is not a formal treatise concerning Rococo architecture even in southern Germany and need offer no exact definition of what is Rococo and what is not.[57] Rather, the first four of the succeeding chapters, two devoted to family teams—the Asams and the Schmuzers—and two to individual architects, are intended to present major examples of south German Rococo in the context of their designers' whole careers. Thus, the approach is not inductive, from supposed principles to more or less perfect examples, but deductive. Yet what is common to the major works of these men, most of them continuously active as mature artists from the twenties to the sixties, may well be considered to constitute the essence of German Rococo architecture.

The account in the first half of Chapter V of a large proportion of the work of J. M. Fischer should support the proposition that the Rococo was a sort of enclave in the Late Baroque rather than its successor. Fischer was close to the main line of the developing Rococo when he worked with the Asams in the late twenties at Osterhofen; but in most of his major works after Osterhofen, from Diessen to Rott-am-Inn, he was predominantly Baroque in his architectonic conceptions, despite all the wealth of Rococo decoration that the brothers F. X. and J. M. Feichtmayr and other stuccoers supplied in his churches. The same is true of J. B. Neumann, whose works which can be—or have been—considered more Rococo than Late Baroque are also discussed in the final chapter.

Certainly no inexorable stylistic sequence leads from the Baroque, through the Rococo, to the Neoclassic.[58] The major historical break, as has long been recognized, came not at the beginning but at the end of the Rococo. Indeed, the earlier steps, especially in theory, leading up to that break—steps that have been studied in great detail in the last decade—took place during the florescence of the Rococo.[59] Even in Germany—though not in the south before d'Ixnard's St. Blasien as designed about 1770—very early evidence of proto-Neoclassic reaction against the Baroque is not entirely lacking: the Neo-Palladian Opera in Berlin by G. W. von Knobelsdorff (1699–1753) and the nearby Hedwigskirche, modelled on the Pantheon by the Rome-trained Frenchman J.-L. Legeay, both built in the forties, are well-known examples. Both, moreover, were executed for a client, Frederick the Great, whose own rooms of the mid-century decades in the Charlottenburg Schloss and in his palaces at Potsdam are masterpieces of Late Rococo decoration carried out under Knobelsdorff's direction, yet with external adjuncts designed though not executed by Legeay that are not Rococo at all.[60]

In the literature in English on German eighteenth-century architecture,[61] the Rococo as a quasi-independent entity tends to get lost in the complexity of the total story. Although there are few important churches, at least, among those to be discussed in the following chapters that are not touched on by John Bourke, these receive relatively shorter shrift from Eberhard Hempel. Indeed, he mentions many of them not at all, since the purview of his book is so much wider both chronologically and geographically. Hempel deals with two hundred years of building in areas now part of six modern countries.[62] The great majority of monuments described and illustrated in this book were produced in the fifty years between 1715 and 1765 and are all in the present-day German states (*Länder*) of Bavaria and Baden-Württemberg, in northern Switzerland, in western Austria and—somewhat unexpectedly—west of the Rhine in Alsace.

Since the careers of the various architects are in each case considered here as a whole, there is much chronological overlap between the chapters. Moreover, two of the most relevant works of J. M. Fischer, one of the two protagonists of the final chapter, are first discussed at length in the opening chapter because of their decoration by the Asams. There is, nonetheless, a certain sequence as regards the most consummate productions of these seven or eight men. C. D. Asam's first important work, Weltenburg, was begun in 1716 and he died relatively young in 1739. J. G. Fischer's finest and latest churches date from the mid-thirties (Pls. 107, 111), despite the fact that his independent architectural career began in 1717, only a year after Asam's. The Schmuzers' best work falls in the forties; Thumb's extends through the fifties; while the latest church by J. M. Fischer, that at Altomünster (Pl. 204), was only begun in 1763, the year of his death. Thanks to such a succession, the course of the Rococo from the second decade of the century to its full maturity in the later thirties, forties and fifties should be fairly clear.

There will be no attempt to discuss at length the terminal stage in the late sixties and seventies, nor the first significant echoes of rising international Neoclassicism in southern Germany which were contemporary with that stage. The international story of the third quarter of the century has often been told primarily, if not solely, in its forward-looking aspects. It is a pity that the appealing aura of immanent success characteristic of an on-coming style has, as is so often the case, tended to obscure the continuing vitality of the one that was approaching its end. In this book Thumb's late work at St. Gallen (Pls. 169–171) and J. M. Fischer's at Rott-am-Inn and Altomünster (Pls. 195, 204) must serve to illustrate—though somewhat peripherally, I fear—the semi-final stage in the history of the Rococo church architecture in southern Germany. By that time, as had been true earlier around 1720, secular commissions were becoming again more truly representative. At least, therefore, one especially splendid terminal example of the great Rococo secular interiors of the sixties, the Festsaal in the Schäzler Haus in Augsburg, should be shown (Pl. 12). The mansion was built in 1765–67 for the ennobled banker von Liebert by Cuvilliés's follower K. A. von Lespilliez (?1728–96). The stucco-work by J. M. Feichtmayr (or his nephew Franz Xaver II) is much richer than that at Vierzehnheiligen (Pls. 214–216), which is of much the same date. The *boiseries* are by Placidus Verhelst (1727–78). He was a son of Egijd Verhelst (1686–1749), a Flemish-born sculptor who had worked in many of the great Rococo churches. That the decoration of the Festsaal was completed as late as 1770 provides an excellent reminder that the Rococo ended in Germany in the way it had begun half a century earlier, as a mode especially suitable for festive and palatial interiors. Significantly, moreover, the client here was neither an abbot nor a prince but a *bourgeois* banker.

The chronological framework of the Rococo in southern Germany was discussed earlier in this Introduction,[63] but thus far little has been said about its character during the long period of its high florescence over the decades 1730–60. My own ideas about the character of the Rococo as exemplified in large-scale church architecture will receive rather explicit—though, I trust, not too doctrinaire—expression in later chapters in relation to a succession of major monuments extending from pre-Rococo Weltenburg of 1716–18 to St. Gallen, completed in the sixties. In the latter, ideals alien to the Rococo had already begun to find expression; that, at all events, is how many scholars besides myself interpret Thumb's great Swiss abbey church.

In this Introduction categorical statements concerning the peculiar characteristics of Rococo, as distinguished from Late Baroque, architecture of this period in Germany have thus far been largely avoided. So well, however, has the Belgian Philippe Minguet, a professor at Liège who is neither Francophile nor Germanophile, lately analysed German Rococo architecture in the relevant chapter of his *Esthétique du rococo* that a few of his subheadings to that chapter may be quoted here.[64] These words and phrases indicate very succinctly some, at least, of the specific differentials of the German Rococo: 'Le rococo joue à dissimuler l'effort constructif. Procédès d'atectonicité . . . [in handling interior space] le rococo vise une homogenéité synthétique, designée, mais non manifestée. L'envelope devient allusive . . . La suavité rococo . . . Valeurs d'intimité et suggestions oniriques . . . [and finally, quite categorically] Le rococo est irréductible au baroque.' If these highly suggestive notations have not been translated here, it is because several of the key words do not even exist in English—in particular 'atectonicité', though the more or less coined adjective 'a-tectonic' will be frequently used in later chapters.

One aspect of the 'a-tectonic', more specifically the way in which, to translate Minguet literally, 'the Rococo plays at obscuring constructive effort', deserves further comment here. In many, some would say most, of the great periods of the past, expression of particular modes of construction and particular building materials is of the very essence of what is significant in any recognized style of architecture as distinguished from other characteristics that are more generally manifest in all the arts of the period. This is least true of that succession of styles and style-phases between the beginning of the Renaissance in the fifteenth century and the introduction of iron as a major structural element in the later eighteenth century. In the Rococo, above all, expression of structure was consistently minimized; and in monumental interiors the real building materials are always completely covered with a skin of stucco that carries the characteristic decoration—a decoration that would have been extremely difficult to execute with comparable virtuosity in carved marble or stone. Furthermore, real marble was generally replaced in interiors by scagliola, wood was often painted white, gilding very extensively employed, and only iron grillwork allowed to express its own 'nature' (as Frank Lloyd Wright would call it), though ironwork was somewhat less extensively used in Germany than in contemporary France.

An exception to these basic principles might seem to be the general use of vaults in monumental German interiors, even though the tectonic effect of projecting ribs is, in them, generally avoided. In small churches, however, flat ceilings framed in the secular French way by coves are quite as common. Such flat ceilings are necessarily of wooden construction, though the construction is entirely masked, as in France, by the plaster coating of the under surface. Very often, moreover, vault-forms were emulated in wooden construction, especially as the style matured. At Steinhausen in the late twenties Dominikus Zimmermann built his oval dome of masonry; at Die Wies twenty years later he made his 'dome' of wood.[65]

Generally, though not always, it is fairly easy to tell whether the vaults in an eighteenth-century German church are real or simulated. Churches with wall-pillars at the sides of the nave—most of J. M. Fischer's best-known works, for example—obviously have masonry vaults, for which the wall-pillars provide direct support and also buttressing. Over large churches without aisles, side-chapels, or external buttresses—several of J. G. Fischer's and Joseph Schmuzer's St. Martin at

Garmisch, for example—the 'barrel' ceilings had to be of wooden construction. Generally this is quite evident thanks to the flattened or semi-elliptical sectional curves that are employed. This seems like a definite approach, whether conscious or not, to the more quintessentially Rococo flat ceilings framed by coves that J. G. Fischer's uncle J. J. Herkomer, for one, had employed at least as early as 1717 (Pl. 84). When, a good deal later in the century, plastered wooden vaults were substituted at Neresheim for the masonry vaults that J. B. Neumann had intended and for which his son actually provided working drawings, the semicircular curve originally proposed was very much lowered, inappropriate though that flattening was to the post-Rococo—not to say proto-Neoclassic—character of the decorations.

What can be considered the 'unreality' of German Rococo wooden 'vaults', and often of true vaults also, with their shapes warped well away from the simple geometrical shapes of more or less semicircular barrel or cross-vaults and semicircular domes—no large dome of full hemispheric section seems to have been erected after that over the crossing of Weingarten built by the Italian-Swiss D. G. Frisoni (1683–1735) in 1718–20—was much enhanced by the character of the decoration on the surfaces. In most cases, the greater part of the vaults or vault-shaped ceilings overhead was opened up illusionistically by great frescoes. These frescoes were only very rarely framed by tectonic ribs. Instead they were surrounded by scalloped borders of stucco or vignetted by lacy ornament. Occasionally, even, such ornament was, presumably as an economy, painted rather than moulded in stucco with a less happy result.

While few contemporary worshippers, however much they were moved by the sermons, would have believed that they were able actually to look up in these churches into Heaven, the illusionism of the frescoes overhead—at first thanks to perspectives of *quadratura* architecture, later more loosely and naturalistically—disguises the real upper boundary of the interior space. For instance, the 'dome' of Die Wies, as the section reveals, is actually flat at the top, but because of the domical organization of the painted space of the heavens in J. B. Zimmermann's fresco this is not at all apparent to the observer below. Already, more than twenty years earlier, the fresco C. D. Asam executed in 1721, some years after the church was built, on the quite flat upper ceiling above the lower coved shell at Weltenburg appears domical because of the effective illusionism of the colonnaded drum and coffered dome he provided in paint as background for his crowd of saintly figures (Pl. 25).

Thus this aspect of German eighteenth-century church interiors, even of those by J. M. Fischer and J. B. Neumann that remain most tectonically Baroque in the treatment of the supporting elements underneath (Pls. 192, 198, 215), is somewhat paradoxical and to many, indeed, even disturbingly ambiguous. Elsewhere, moreover, the vault-forms, even when constructed of wood, still at least suggest Renaissance or Baroque structure, though in many cases their lowered sectional curvature and lack of adequate support make evident the fact that they cannot be of masonry. But these forms should not be 'read' by the observer as structural, as still in most Baroque interiors, but rather as playing a major role in creating that 'synthetic homogeneity' of an 'allusive envelope', or container, which Minguet mentions. Moreover, this is true even where there is, in fact, a masonry vault, as over J. B. Neumann's most totally Rococo interior, the Weisser Saal in the Würzburg Residenz (Pl. 209). There, however, Antonio Bossi's large-scale Rococo *stucchi* on the vault serve to dematerialize the vault, just as Neumann at one point intended that similar stucco-decoration should lighten visually the enormous vault over the stair-hall.[66] Eventually, however, that vault was entirely painted out, so to say, by Tiepolo's largest fresco. There Tiepolo abolished by the illusionism of his art any sense of structure in the vault even more completely than Bossi had done in the Weisser Saal.

Generally vaults received as their principal decoration a sort of treatment that was all but unknown in French Rococo interiors but in direct continuity with the Italian High Baroque. Vast illusionistic frescoes like Tiepolo's play a major role in creating the special qualities of German Rococo interior space. Despite their Italian origin and the Italian birth or training of those responsible for most of them in the earlier decades of the Rococo—Amigoni, for example, and C. D. Asam—such frescoes were already of importance in the early twenties. They continued to be painted into the sixties and even the seventies, moreover, as often as not by artists such as Christian Wenziger (1710–97) and Martin Knoller (1725–1804) who had studied abroad, or even still, as at Vierzehnheiligen and Brühl, by Italians.

The German creation was much more positive and idiosyncratic in character than can be indicated by the over-simple proposition that it was merely a combination of Baroque structure, real or imitated, and Baroque fresco-painting superficially modified by a flood of ornament borrowed from the French Rococo. How this came about should not be merely generalized. The development must rather be seen to proceed step by step from specific monument to specific monument in the *œuvres* of the more significant individual architects and their associates. All of these men, of course, had begun as Baroque designers in the first decades of the century; several of them knew the Italian High Baroque at first hand; and none, at least among those responsible for major church interiors, had studied or—except for J. B. Neumann—even travelled in France. Not inappropriately the stylistic term for their mature work has often been spelt *Rokoko* by Germans[67] rather than Rococo, but that would be rather pointless in English, even in a book such as this.

CHAPTER I

The Brothers Cosmas Damian and Egid Quirin Asam

ALTHOUGH one was primarily a fresco-painter and the other a sculptor, the brothers Asam were responsible for the architecture as well as the decoration with frescoes, stucco-work, and sculpture of two of the most admired German churches of the eighteenth century.[1] Cosmas Damian, the elder brother, signed his fresco at Weltenburg (Pl. 25) 'pictor et architectus A^0 1721'; Egid Quirin designed the church of St. Johann Nepomuk in Munich (Pl. 72), built from 1733 onwards largely at his own expense and usually known as the 'Asamkirche'. Their names are to most people even more synonymous with the Bavarian Late Baroque and Rococo than those of another nearly contemporary pair of brothers, Dominikus and Johann Baptist Zimmermann, who were responsible for the great pilgrimage churches at Steinhausen (Pl. 11) and Die Wies. Although the Asams were somewhat younger—Cosmas Damian was born in 1688, six years after J. B. Zimmermann and a year after his brother Dominikus, Egid Quirin only in 1692—their careers began as early as those of the Zimmermanns.

C. D. Asam's Weltenburg church (Pl. 20), for a Benedictine abbey set in an almost secret spot on the Danube south of Regensburg and a little above Kelheim, was begun in 1716 at just the same time that Dominikus Zimmermann must have designed his first rather modest church for the Dominican nuns at Mödingen (often called Maria-Medingen), near Dillingen in Bavarian Swabia, and both were complete physically by 1718.[2] The major decorative work of E. Q. as well as C. D. Asam at Weltenburg is somewhat later (*c.* 1721) as are J. B. Zimmermann's frescoes at Mödingen, the earliest signed one above the nuns' gallery dated 1719 and another 1722. It was ten years before Dominikus Zimmermann received from the Premonstratensian monks of Schussenried, not far from Biberach in western Swabia, the commission to build the pilgrimage church at nearby Steinhausen, his first work comparable in importance to Weltenburg, and another four years before his brother's frescoes there were painted.

C. D. Asam's earliest fresco, signed and dated 1714, fills the shallow-domed ceiling over the 'crossing'—usually, but not correctly, called the choir—of the church of the Benedictine Abbey of Ensdorf near Amberg in the Upper Palatinate (northern Bavaria today). It is not especially notable (Pl. 17). Yet if this be considered in relation to the very similar one of some score or more years before on the domical vault over the crossing in the church of the Benedictine Abbey of Tegernsee in southern Bavaria (Pl. 16) one very good reason for the employment here of the twenty-eight-year-old Asam suggests itself. The Tegernsee fresco is by Hans Georg Asam (1649–1711), the father of C. D. and E. Q. Asam, and the Abbot of Ensdorf who carried that church to completion had come from the Tegernsee monastery.

At least as relevant, however, is the fact that both the Asams were known to have studied for some two years in Rome, still generally recognized as the artistic capital of the western world. They were, moreover, among the few even of their generation in Germany who had had such an opportunity. (H. G. Asam visited Venice only rather briefly in 1682.) The young men were sent to Italy, after their father's death in 1711, by Abbot Quirin Millon of Tegernsee.[3] In Rome Cosmas Damian studied with Pierleone Ghezzi (1674–1755) not, at first thought, a very appropriate master for an ecclesiastical fresco-painter-to-be; significantly, however, Ghezzi was the godson of Carlo Maratti (1625–1713), who had maintained his position as the leading Roman painter of church frescoes well beyond the opening of the new century.[4] On 23 May 1713 Cosmas Damian was awarded a prize for a painting by the Accademia di San Luca. His brother's particular artistic connections in Rome are uncertain. But on Egid Quirin's return to Germany he is known to have continued his studies until 1716 under the Austrian-born sculptor Andreas Faistenberger (1647–1736), then a leading artistic figure in Munich.

Among the reasons for the early employment of the brothers, their descent was doubtless as important as their excellent training. Unlike the Zimmermanns, whose father and stepfather were no more than modest masons and stuccoers at Wessobrunn, but like Joseph and Franz Schmuzer, whose father Johann had been an important architect, the Asams' father had been the leading fresco-painter of his generation in Bavaria. Moreover, their maternal grandfather (who had been their father's master), Nikolaus Prugger (*c.* 1620–94), had earlier been of some importance in his day as an electoral *Hofmaler* in Munich.

Except perhaps for certain details of the decoration of the cove-like dome-shell to be discussed later (p. 47), there can be no question of considering the Asams' Weltenburg, as it was built and decorated in 1716–21, at all a Rococo work any more than the Zimmermann's contemporaneous Mödingen. With the Rococo, which was just making its appearance in Bavaria as an importation from France in the interiors of the Pagodenburg at Schloss Nymphenburg, neither the Asams nor the Zimmermanns seem to have had contact until J. B. Zimmermann—but not Dominikus—and C. D. Asam—but not E. Q.—were called to work with Max Emanuel's Paris-trained architect Joseph Effner in the Neues Schloss at Schleissheim in 1720 in preparation for the marriage in 1722 of the Elector's son Carl Albrecht, later the Emperor Karl VII, to Maria Amalia of Austria.[5]

The situation would be quite different by the time the Asamkirche in Munich was being built and decorated. Though begun in 1733 as has been said, and probably designed a year or two earlier shortly after St. John Nepomuk's canonization in 1729, this was not entirely complete as regards its decoration and furnishing even at E. Q. Asam's death in 1750, despite the fact that it had already been consecrated in 1746.[6]

Of a less famous earlier work, Santa Maria de Victoria, which was not a normal church but a Jesuit 'praying hall' at Ingolstadt, begun the year before the Asamkirche and completed within three or four years,[7] one may already say that its interior (Pl. 70) is *architecturally* a Rococo work. There is here little if any surviving trace of the Roman Baroque in which the Asams had been trained in Italy in the years round 1712, except for the great ceiling fresco, if that be considered strictly as painting. Even so, the generally Rococo character of Santa Maria de Victoria was undoubtedly much intensified by the introduction of the elaborate high altar in the early sixties that is attributed to the sculptor (not the architect of the same name) J. M. Fischer (d. 1801), not to speak of the tall carved wooden stalls along the walls and the interior doorways executed in 1748 by Michael Vogl and Anton Hofkofler. The same may be said, moreover, of the Asams' remodelling of the interior of the big Romanesque church of the Benedictine Abbey of St. Emmeram at Regensburg (Pl. 63),[8] which seems to have been carried out about 1732, just before the Ingolstadt hall was decorated.

These two prime examples of the early maturity of Bavarian Rococo church architecture may not improperly be compared in certain respects to the superb Rococo secular work of these same years in the Munich Residenz by the Paris-trained Walloon François Cuvilliés and his team of artist craftsmen—of whom J. B. Zimmermann as stuccoer, but not as fresco-painter, was one—or the latter's Neuer Festsaal in the Abbey of Benediktbeuern (Pl. 13).

But the differences from such French-inspired work are very significant. St. Emmeram and Santa Maria de Victoria are rather more advanced in style than Steinhausen (Pl. 11), begun by Dominikus Zimmermann in 1727 and completed in 1730–31 with his own stuccos and his brother's frescoes as noted earlier. But that and Osterhofen (Pls. 58, 59), on the Danube above Passau in northeastern Bavaria, where the Asams were still busy in the early thirties are grander, if still rather transitional, examples of the beginnings of the German Rococo in monumental church architecture. The same can hardly be said of any of the work of Cuvilliés round 1730, and only up to a point of Zimmermann's decorations at Weyarn and Beyharting of 1729 and 1730.

A crucial cycle of the Asams' work falls within the twenties. This period concluded with their decoration of the above-mentioned church for the Premonstratensian abbey at Osterhofen-Altenmarkt, which was built by the architect J. M. Fischer in 1726–28. E. Q. Asam probably began to execute the stuccos there as early as 1729, even though the chronogram over the choir-arch gives the date 1731 and the painting by his brother over the high altar is signed and dated 1732.[9] The cycle seems to have begun with their decoration of the Cistercian abbey church at Aldersbach in or a little before 1720; there the nave had just been rebuilt by Domenico Magzin from nearby Landau, with the earlier choir retained (Pls. 38, 39).[10] Like Osterhofen this lies south of the Danube above Passau. During this decade, so significant for the introduction and early assimilation of the French Rococo in Germany—or at least in Bavaria—the Asams made a contribution towards the creation of a new sort of German interior architecture that was in considerable degree independent of both France and Italy. What they then produced is, on the one hand, markedly different from Italian Baroque church architecture, even in its latest stages—the Baroque that they had known so well in Rome and which Cosmas Damian emulated so successfully in the interior architecture of Weltenburg and Egid Quirin in that of Rohr[11] the preceding decade—and equally remote from the secular Rococo of these years of the late Régence in France.

Freystadt

To make evident the significance of the changes that the Asams gradually introduced into German church interiors in the transitional years between 1720 and the mid-thirties it will be well to start with the first decorative project in which they were involved, as assistants to their father, at Freystadt in 1708 when C. D. Asam was twenty-two and his brother only sixteen. (In eighteenth-century Germany artist-craftsmen often began their apprentice training at fourteen, and may still so do today.) Something should first be said concerning their father, however, dipping back a little into the High Baroque period in German architecture when Germans began collaborating as equals with Italian and Italian-Swiss artists and already sometimes rivalled them. The surviving *œuvre* of H. G. Asam is not extensive. After his major fresco cycles of the 1680s and 1690s at Benediktbeuren and at Tegernsee (Pl. 16) in southern Bavaria, that at Freystadt in what is now north-eastern Bavaria is the most important. The church, considered as an architectural monument, is the masterpiece of the Swiss-born G. A. Viscardi (1645–1713), long Zuccalli's rival on the Munich architectural scene.[12]

Internally the pilgrimage church of Mariahilf at Freystadt, commissioned in 1699 by Ferdinand Lorenz Franz X. Graf von Tilly (for whom Viscardi had since 1691 been building the Cistercian Abbey of Fürstenfeldbruck west of Munich), follows the model of the Rainaldi-Borromini church of Sant'Agnese in Agone in Rome, although here it is the east and west, rather than the north and south, arms of the Greek cross that are prolonged an extra bay, much as in the late sixteenth-century Gesù Nuovo in Naples.[13] H. G. Asam's frescoes play a less important part in the general effect of the interior than at Benediktbeuern or Tegernsee (Pl. 16). The larger fields occupy those segments between the eight ribs of the dome in which there are no window openings (Pl. 14). The smaller fields on the barrel vaults of the arms are all but lost in the rich stucco-work that still provides the chief decoration of the interior. The *stucchi*, as befits their date late in the first decade of the new century, are rather lower in relief and fussier in detail than those by unknown hands (Italian or Italian-Swiss in all probability) that surround H. G. Asam's frescoes in the two Benedictine abbey churches. Of both of these the architect was Antonio Riva (d. 1713) from Roveredo in the Grigioni. The stuccoer at Freystadt was P. F. Appiani, a north Italian with whom C. D. Asam would again be associated in the choir of Fürstenfeldbruck in 1722–23. It is quite characteristic of the opening years of the century that a German artist collaborated here with an Italian-Swiss architect and an Italian stuccoer. It is only a little surprising that it was the painter who was German at this point.

For the young Asams the impression of their early experience at Freystadt must have been largely cancelled by what they saw a year or two later in Rome. As regards frescoes, at least, even their father's finest work could hardly hold a candle to the seventeenth-century cycles in the churches of Rome by the leading Baroque painters from Lanfranco and Pietro da Cortona to Pozzo and Maratti; while the rich polychromy of such marble-lined interiors as Sant'Agnese and Sant'Andrea al Quirinale must have dimmed for some years their memories of the pale stucco-work at Freystadt.[14]

Cosmas Damian's Earliest Frescoes

On the return of the brothers to Bavaria from their Roman sojourn one may assume that E. Q. Asam, still in his early twenties, decided very soon to continue his studies under Faistenberger, even though only the date of termination of that presumably two or three-year relationship in 1716 is recorded. His choice of vocation will surely have been notably influenced by admiration for the work of the great Baroque sculptors, and above all that of Bernini, which he had seen in Rome.

C. D. Asam, by now in his late twenties, was employed at once, as has been mentioned, in the Benedictine abbey church at Ensdorf not far from Freystadt. Designed in 1694 by Wolfgang Dientzenhofer (1648–1706) from nearby Amberg, this had been begun somewhat later by Martin Funk for Abbot Bonaventura Oberhuber (who came from Tegernsee) and completed early in the new century by Christoph Grantauer (b. 1661), a relative of Dientzenhofer. The stucco-work was undertaken in 1708 by Mathias, Thomas, and Martin Ehamb.[15]

The interior of this conventional wall-pillar church is perhaps more remarkable for the delicacy of the Ehambs' stucco-work in the nave—clean white on pink and other light-coloured grounds as lately restored—and the relatively large size of the fresco fields than for C. D. Asam's frescoes as such. Those in the nave are simply framed and, like most of H. G. Asam's, remain essentially independent paintings set into the surface of the vault with little effect on the spatial character of the rather broad, low interior (Pl. 18). The crossing, however, has a domical ceiling; and the fresco, signed and dated 1714, attempts to create an illusionistic extension upwards of the real space (Pl. 17). This H. G. Asam had already done, at least as successfully, over the crossing at Tegernsee (Pl. 16) in an old tradition that goes back to Correggio. Hordes of figures, interlocking and overlapping, lead up to a small oculus-like clear space in the centre. There the Holy Spirit appears—almost more like a Barberini bee than a dove!—in triangular relationship to the figures of Christ and God the Father to left and right below.

Cosmas Damian's next commission, following closely after Ensdorf, was very important, not so much for what he achieved as for the prestige resulting from that employment. The Dreifaltigkeitskirche in Munich, designed and begun by Viscardi, was effectively this architect's last work. It was built as a votive church during the War of the Spanish Succession by the Bavarian (*Landstände*) and Munich (*Burgenschaft*) authorities, not by the Elector Max Emanuel who was then in exile in France. The cornerstone was laid on 27 October 1711 and it was roofed by the time of Viscardi's death in 1713. The structure was completed the next year under the supervision of J. G. Ettenhofer (1688–1741), Viscardi's assistant, and of Enrico Zuccalli, his successor as electoral *Oberhofbauintendant*, and blessed on 6 October 1714.[16] Although not consecrated until 29 October 1718, when the altars executed in 1716–18 were finally in place, the major work of decoration was carried out in 1714–15 by J. G. Bader, who provided the *stucchi*, and by C. D. Asam. The latter received his first payment for the frescoes on 24 September 1714 and completed the job the following year.[17]

Smaller than Freystadt, which it somewhat resembles internally but not externally, the Munich church is in general effect more delicate and intimate.[18] As at Freystadt, the dome over the crossing is broken by four large windows above the circular cornice at its base. C. D. Asam's painting, though overlapped by and also slightly overlapping here and there the stucco-work framing the windows, fills the whole centre much as at Ensdorf even though there is here a small lantern at the apex (Pl. 15). The subject, like the treatment, is not dissimilar to that at Ensdorf: the Glorification of the Trinity, with certain iconographic peculiarities appropriate to the Carmelite religious, to whom charge of the new church was assigned. (Those who supervise Freystadt today are Franciscans.)

The close connection between stucco-work and frescoes evident in the spaces between the windows at the base of the dome extends to the treatment of the pendentives and the vault surfaces of the arms of the Greek cross, here as at Freystadt slightly prolonged to ritual east (north) and ritual west (south)—for example, the hands of the Evangelists in the cartouche-like panels on the pendentives overlap the stucco frames. If the frescoed areas are still relatively small except on the upper surface of the dome, their freer shapes harmonize better with the surrounding stucco decoration; and their colours, mostly quite light and bright, relate more harmoniously to the scheme of white scroll-work on pink and yellow grounds that Bader used to decorate the vaults as well as the panels between the sunken columns along the walls.

Weltenburg

The next year there came to Cosmas Damian a very much greater opportunity. In 1714 Abbot Maurus Bächl had begun to rebuild the Benedictine monastery at Weltenburg, employing designs by the obscure Franciscan lay-brother F. Ph. Blank (d. 1720) and Michael Wolf as mastermason. Bächl, before coming to Weltenburg in 1713, had been prior at Ensdorf and would have known the frescoes there even though they were executed after his promotion. All the same it is surprising he should have called on a thirty-year-old painter to design, as architect, a new church to replace the old one which was then just being demolished. Wolf continued as mastermason, however. The cornerstone was laid on 28 June 1716 and the church, physically complete internally but presumably quite undecorated, was consecrated on 9 October 1718, as was noted above, by the prelate who had earlier laid the cornerstone, Johann Franz Ecker von Kapfing und Lichteneck, Prince-Bishop of Freysing, who was destined later to be a very important client of the Asam brothers.[19] The church as known today, however, with its striking high altar and ceiling fresco, not to speak of its quadrantal altars of the mid-1730s and its vestibule as decorated at that time and later, is very different from what it must have been in those early years of the century (Pl. 24). Here one realizes the importance of Cosmas Damian's Italian training. Hitherto he had been quite as much his father's son as a direct emulator of the Roman High Baroque. Egid Quirin, more Faistenberger's pupil than a late disciple of Bernini at this point, probably did not work here before 1721.

Weltenburg, in plan, is a longitudinal oval 21.15 × 15 m. and 22.37 m. high, with an oblong choir 13.5 m. high and rounded apse to the east, and an irregularly oval vestibule to the west (Fig. 1). The two projections, although of the same width (about 7.30 m.), are not precisely balanced. The eastern end of the choir is about the same distance from that end of the nave as the inside of the front façade from the other—about 10 m.—but the apse projects a good bit further eastward. Moreover, the handling of these subsidiary spaces is quite different. At the sides of the barrel-vaulted choir balconettes of semi-elliptical plan are carried on a sub-order of columns in front of arches similar to those of the half-domed quadrantal chapels in the nave. These features constrict the area of the choir before the dominating high altar (Pls. 24, 36).

At the other end (Fig. 1, Pl. 26) the irregular oval of the projection is subdivided vertically into the vestibule below and a barrel-vaulted organ gallery above. The lower space, with flat ceiling coved at the edges, is partially screened from the nave by two columns of the same sub-order as the pilasters on the walls of the vestibule. These are considerably shorter than those that support the balconettes flanking the choir and they carry an entablature that completes the irregular oval of the vestibule in a continuous curved line tangent to the larger oval of the nave. The corresponding curve at the front, however, is flattened where it meets the straight front wall of the church. Above this, and largely blocking the light from the big west window over the main entrance, is the organ by Kasper Mayr, with a case for which the builder J. K. Brandenstein's contract is dated 1728.

The interior of the vestibule is of advanced Rococo character.[20] Much of the stucco-work is by E. Q. Asam and dates from 1734–36, like the altars in the quadrantal chapels, but that framing the confessionals is as late as 1751 and by F. A. Neu (d. 1758). The oil painting in the centre of the ceiling is by Cosmas Damian's son Franz Erasmus Quirin (1720–95) and dated 1745, six years after his father's death in 1739 and two years even after Bächl's.

Leaving aside the eastward and westward projections, the oval nave must be recognized as more Roman Baroque, indeed, specifically Berninian, than German or even Austrian in inspiration. Yet oval plans for churches or parts of churches had been projected in this part of Europe as early as the several schemes by Caspar Moosbrugger (1656–1723) of the 1680s and later for the choir of the church of the

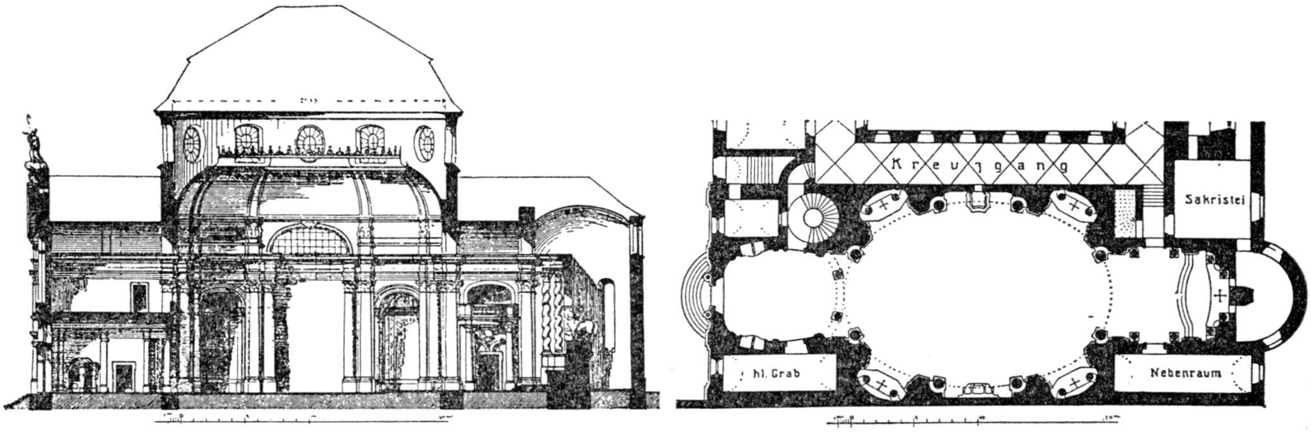

Fig. 1. Weltenburg, Abbey Church. Section and plan

Benedictine Abbey of Einsiedeln in Switzerland. Moreover, they had several times been executed in Habsburg territories since the last years of the seventeenth century by Lukas von Hildebrandt and Fischer von Erlach. Indeed Fischer's most famous work, the Karlskirche in Vienna, had just been begun on an oval plan in 1715.

It is much too simple to describe the oval nave as being merely that of Bernini's Sant'Andrea al Quirinale with the axis shifted from the exceptional transverse to the more usual longitudinal. At Sant'Andrea, for example, the entablature of the pilaster order is without breaks except for the pedimented projection over the pairs of free-standing and engaged columns flanking the entrance to the shallow choir (Pl. 23) and its omission below the arch in the corresponding entrance bay. Those columns, moreover, are the only ones in the interior. But at Weltenburg single free-standing columns not only frame the opening into the deep choir in the plane of the pilasters (Pl. 24), over which the entablature consistently breaks forward, but are also set on either side of the shallow chapels at the middle of each side. These last project considerably further into the interior than do the pilasters, which are throughout clustered and not single as in Sant'Andrea.

Still more notably different at Weltenburg are the broad arches rising above the entablature level at the four cardinal points, as earlier in Rome at San Giacomo degli Incurabili, but at Sant'Andrea only in the entrance bay. Sant'Andrea, moreover, has no cross-axis since the sides each have two, not three, chapels; but here at Weltenburg the middle chapels, while shallower than those on the diagonals—themselves not so deep as in the Roman church—are as broad as the openings to east and west. On the outer walls of these chapels there are large oil paintings by Cosmas Damian set above marble confessionals. The paintings have heavy gilded frames rising in broken curves across the entablature below the lunettes; to the arches of the latter they are linked by stucco clouds. In the middle of the painting on the left, rather curiously, is placed the modest marble pulpit, its sounding board crowned by a polychromed statue of St. Benedict.[21]

A minor point, yet undoubtedly serving to make the German church less academic than Bernini's, is the absence of round arches. Here the higher arches at the cardinal points are segmental and the lower ones over the diagonal chapels elliptical. This need hardly, in 1716–18, be considered evidence of French influence, even though Effner was also using both forms at the Pagodenburg in those years.

The sumptuous and for Germany almost unique use throughout the interior of marbles—mostly golden-toned—worked by F. P. Giorgioli[22] and Sebastian Rothenfelder resembles closely in value, if not in colour, the pink and grey marble interior of Sant'Andrea below the gold and white stucco-work that is common to both. But the Weltenburg interior—most exceptionally for Germany, yet true also of the Asams' own church in Munich of twenty years later (Pl. 72)—is much darker than the Roman one and such natural lighting as there is, is more dramatically controlled.[23] Although the high altar of Sant'Andrea is lighted from a small concealed source behind the pediment over the choir entrance (Pl. 23), the nave there is strongly lit by the lunette over the entrance, the range of segmental-topped windows at the base of the dome, and the largely invisible side-lights of the small lantern above. At Weltenburg most of the major light sources are invisible, or effectively so. As has been noted, it is unlikely that in the original scheme of 1716–18 the light coming from the west window was meant to be quite so much blocked by the organ as it is now (Pl. 26). But the way the side-lights of the terminal drum over the nave are completely hidden by the broad lower cove, and the high altar lit from behind and above (Pl. 36)—much more strongly than at Sant'Andrea—must have been intended from the first. The only more or less direct light—that coming from the two segmental lunettes in the cross-axial bays—is naturally less than what comes from the lunettes in the four side chapels at Sant'Andrea and barely noticeable.

As with the coloured marble lining of the interior, it is impossible to say how far the idea for the high altar had matured during the early campaign of construction. One must presumably consider, as do most scholars, that the executed high altar composition was designed in 1721.[24] But the cove overhead, which is so important to the particular spatial quality of the church and also to the character of the lighting in the nave, is original, even though Cosmas Damian's fresco on the flat upper ceiling was not executed until 1721, as indicated by the inscription. Various unlikely prototypes for this arrangement have been suggested, all the way to J. H. Mansart's Dôme des Invalides in Paris and even Wren's St. Paul's in London! Although considerably smaller, a more plausible prototype seems at first thought to be Hildebrandt's chapel, structurally complete by 1715, in the Palais Schwarzenberg in Vienna (Pl. 21).[25] Even though the oval lower shell rises there on pendentives over a rectangle with cut-off corners, not over a nave of oval plan, the fashion in which its surface is panelled by stucco mouldings with C-scrolls in the concave corners of the broader panels at the cardinal points is certainly very similar to the treatment of the cove at Weltenburg—yet the stucco-work in Vienna must be very considerably later than 1715.[26]

It seems likely, therefore, considering Cosmas Damian's years in Rome, that the source was the oval chapel of Santa Cecilia built by Antonio Gherardi (1644–1702) in San Carlo ai Catinari in Rome in 1691 (Pl. 22). (This may well also be the source of Hildebrandt's chapel, for that matter.) Another possible Italian prototype is the oval saloon of the Palazzo Carignano in Turin by Guarini, planned in 1679. This is more nearly of the same dimensions, though secular; and there is the parallel hypothesis that, somewhat later, the *atrio* below in the Turin palace provided the prototype for Dominikus Zimmermann's arcaded oval nave at Steinhausen. Generally, however, Guarinian influence up to this point had been largely restricted to Bohemia and the Dientzenhofers.

The frescoing of the flat upper ceiling, though not executed until later, was doubtless planned from the first. The idea for this may possibly derive from another interior by Hildebrandt, the rectangular stair-hall in the Palais Daun-Kinsky of 1713–16 in Vienna with its invisibly lighted fresco overhead, above the mezzanine gallery, by the Bolognese painter Marcantonio Chiarini and his brother-in-law Gaetano Fanti. Perhaps more probably, that could be the prototype for the Schleissheim stair-hall, where Asam had just frescoed the upper ceiling in a rather similar way for Effner in 1720–21; but the idea there must have been the architect's, not Asam's.

Although surely in large part the necessary result of the exiguous site, the character of the exterior of Weltenburg, so different from Viscardi's completely plastic treatment of free-standing Freystadt, seems Roman; for the church externally has no real existence except as an ornamented front. That was brought to completion, apparently, only after the execution of the main west portal by Vitus Filler in 1735 and is not necessarily at all what Cosmas Damian may originally have intended (Pl. 19). This sort of façade also appears on the Asams' own later church in Munich that Egid Quirin designed, St. Johann-Nepomuk, and on their last joint work, the Ursulinenkirche at Straubing, also designed by Egid Quirin, indicating perhaps a real preference for this treatment, at least on that brother's part. The location of these two later churches on narrow streets, however, would suggest or require such a treatment even more than did the confined site at Weltenburg.

In an account of the Asams' work that aims at chronological sequence the discussion of Weltenburg must be broken off at the consecration of 1718. Not surprisingly, considering the date, nothing at all probably of 1716–18 at Weltenburg has any real Rococo, or even proto-Rococo, flavour—one must assume that the decoration of the cove is of the period three years later when the ceiling fresco above it was executed.[27] The years preceding 1721 were busy ones both for Cosmas Damian as painter and for the sculptor-stuccoer, Egid Quirin, who now like his brother at Weltenburg began to practise also as an architectural designer. At this point, moreover, came Cosmas Damian's earliest known contact with Effner's team of French-trained artists working for the electoral court. That contact was presumably responsible for the first faint reflections in the Asams' work at Rohr and Aldersbach of the French Rococo those craftsmen had, since their arrival in 1716, been introducing into Bavaria in the Pagodenburg at Nymphenburg and in the Nymphenburg Schloss itself.

Amberg and Michelfeld

In June 1716, at the time the cornerstone of Weltenburg was being laid, negotiations had already begun with Cosmas Damian to carry out an extensive set of frescoes in the pilgrimage church of Maria-Hilf above Amberg, the largest town near Ensdorf. The contract dates from 28 June 1716, but the work—twenty-nine large and small frescoes in the nave and five in the choir—was executed only the following summer (30 June to 25 July 1717) following a detailed programme provided by the church authorities in a letter of 11 December 1716. Three more frescoes under the organ gallery and one in each of the six side chapels were carried out in 1718. Asam received 800 gulden for the work and free lodging for himself and his helpers.[28]

Despite the special interest these frescoes have because of the survival of the iconographic programme of late 1716 they require no more than a bare mention here. The stuccos with which they are associated, and which dominate the decorative ensemble, were begun by G. B. Carlone, an Italian-Swiss from the Ticino—or F. A. Carlone, according to Hanfstaengl—in 1702–3 and completed by his pupil Paolo d'Aglio—Decallio according to Hanfstaengl—who had previously worked together in the Cathedral of Passau in 1678–86 and later in several important Austrian churches. The effective period of the decorative scheme of this interior, then, with its high altar of 1703 and its side altars of 1710–12, is not those years when Asam was working here but the first decade of the century, just after it was built by

Georg Peimbl and Philipp Plankh in 1697–1701. Thus the general impression, even with the Asam frescoes, is less advanced than at Freystadt where Cosmas Damian had assisted his father ten years before.[29]

It was while work was still proceeding in the nave of Maria-Hilf that C. D. Asam and also his brother, who had finished his training as a sculptor the previous year under Faistenberger, were called in 1717 to decorate the Benedictine abbey church at Michelfeld, north of Amberg, for Abbot Wolfgang Rinswerger who, like the Abbot of Ensdorf, came from the Tegernsee monastery. It seems very probable that here we have the earliest joint work of the brothers, working together for the first time since they both assisted their father at Freystadt (Pl. 14).[30] Doubtless on the strength of these commissions at Amberg and Michelfeld, Cosmas Damian married on 8 February 1717 the daughter of the engraver F. A. Mörl.

What is Cosmas Damian's work at Michelfeld is clear enough. But unfortunately the inscribed dates—1717 on the fresco of the Adoration of the Shepherds over the westernmost bay of the nave and 1721 on the Last Supper, the oil painting at the high altar—provide an awkward spread of four years. Within those years, moreover, when Cosmas Damian was still employed on the original campaign of construction at Weltenburg into 1718, fall the completion of the work at Maria-Hilf and a modest fresco at nearby Walderbach which is no longer extant; his much more important frescoes at Weingarten of 1718–20; the destroyed chapel at St. Corbinian's Spring near Weihenstephan, on which he was busy with his brother in the spring of 1720;[31] almost certainly the frescoes at Aldersbach; and certainly that dated 1721 on the nave ceiling at Weltenburg. There is even more difficulty with his brother's contribution, not merely as regards the dating of its different elements within the same span of four years, but as to what, other than the high altar with its statuary, the flanking figures of St. Otto and St. Wolfgang, and fourteen others of saints in the nave,[32] is really by him.

It will be well first to give the earlier history of the church and a general description of the interior. As at Ensdorf, Wolfgang Dientzenhofer seems to have provided the plans for the rebuilding of this church. The work was carried out in the 1690s by the same master builder, Grantauer—actually an Ensdorfer—and the church consecrated in 1697. But the decoration of the interior was not initiated until nearly twenty years later during Rinswerger's rule as abbot (1707–21). Michelfeld is a relatively modest wall-pillar church. It has galleries set awkwardly high above shallow chapels between the piers and is covered by flattened cross-vaults over the rectangular bays of the nave.[33] Architecturally it is chiefly of interest for its domically ceiled square choir, dominated to the east by Egid Quirin's high altar (Pl. 30). This is flanked by diagonally-set Salomonic columns and crowned by a broken pediment framing Cosmas Damian's Last Supper, signed and dated 1721 as has been noted. The oil painting, which is of very high quality in composition, command of chiaroscuro, and colouring, gives evidence that Cosmas Damian learned more than fresco technique in Rome, as his prize at the Accademia di San Luca implies. A curious feature of the choir is the diagonal setting of the free-standing marbled columns at the four corners. Pendants visually to the Salomonic columns of the altar, but rather confusedly related to the pilaster order behind them, these may well have been introduced only in 1720–21 by the Asams.

The ceiling of the choir has no stucco-work; instead, a higher dome is represented in fresco, though not very convincingly. The perspective is so handled that the illusion is persuasive only from the nave, not inside the choir. In this ceiling painting Cosmas Damian emulated the ribbed design of the Freystadt dome. But he executed the ribs only in fresco and overlapped them freely with the clouds on which are poised the angels surrounding St. John the Evangelist's vision of the Holy Trinity and the Seven Gifts of the Holy Ghost. Here the collaboration is not so much the already conventional South German one between fresco-painter and stuccoer/decorator as between fresco-painter and sculptor/altar-designer; for the high altar is crowned not only with sculptured figures—admittedly executed in stucco rather than in wood like most of Faistenberger's work—but also flanked by St. Otto and St. Wolfgang in stucco on the wall between the low sacristy doors and the small windows over them at either side. These last open into the retrochoir. But the decoration of the ceiling of that upper chamber is not visible even from the east end of the church, and this terminal element of the plan plays no part in the spatial organization of the building.

The frescoes in the nave, one of them signed and dated 1717 as has been said, represent scenes from the Life of Christ. These seem somewhat less accomplished, and hence probably earlier by a year or two, than that over the choir (Pl. 31). Predominantly rectangular in shape and heavily framed with roll mouldings, they are more independent of the surrounding stucco decoration than those in the Munich Dreifaltigkeitskirche. However, the character of this decoration in the first and third bays of the nave, which consists of delicate white scroll-work in low relief against a pale green ground, is very similar to Bader's in Munich, even though the foliage here may seem somewhat flimsy and underscaled. The bolder architectural and figural motifs in the second bay are more effective, but the most striking features are the cartouche-like frames of the smaller frescoes at the four corners of the central bay (Pl. 29). The area of the main fresco of Christ on the Mount of Olives in this bay is increased by wide bulges at the sides, and its frame is linked by smaller blank cartouches to the arches on either side and to the simpler panels to east and west.

The major questions which arise concerning Michelfeld are two. Is the 'dome' fresco of about the same date, 1717 or a year or so later, as those in the nave, or is it closer in date to the altarpiece, forming an essential part of an architectural entity of 1720–21 in which stucco decoration—as distinguished from stucco figural sculpture—plays practically no part? And is the stucco decoration over the nave wholly, or only in part, by E. Q. Asam and of the same date as the frescoes there? Although the documents provide no evidence of C. D. Asam's actual presence at Michelfeld after 1718, it seems just possible that the choir fresco is of approximately the date of the altar—that is towards 1720—despite its inferiority to his frescoes at Weingarten.

The decoration of the nave is notable because of the unusually large size, for 1717–18, and the close visual relationship to one another of C. D. Asam's three frescoes. It differs markedly from that in the retrochoir (*Psallierchor*) over the sacristy behind the altar. There the *stucchi* are dated by a chronogram 1716 and the fields available for C. D. Asam's frescoes are multiple and very tiny. The stucco-work in the nave, then, is likely to be at least slightly later than that in the retrochoir and by a different hand, hence not too improbably Egid Quirin's. Yet, while working under Faistenberger just before this—and *a fortiori* in Italy—Egid Quirin would hardly have had much contact with the German tradition in stucco decoration of the Wessobrunners. This question must also remain open.

Weingarten

By 1718, the latest year his presence is actually recorded at Michelfeld[34]—as also at Amberg—Cosmas Damian was busy with a much more important commission far to the south, that for the frescoes on the vaults in the great new Benedictine abbey church at Weingarten. This had been begun in 1715 for Abbot Sebastian Hyller. He had come there in 1697 from Salzburg, and lived to see the work on the church—but not the monastery—completed well before his death in 1730.

The architectural history of this vast edifice, associated with an even vaster and partially incomplete monastery that still dominates the town of Weingarten, just north of Ravensburg in southern Württemberg, is very complicated. The architect in charge at this point was D. G. Frisoni, who had come originally from Laino between the Lakes of Como and Lugano. He had been called to Württemberg in 1709 from Prague, where he had settled the year before, to work as a stuccoer under the German-born architect J. F. Nette (1672–1714) on the Versailles-like palace of Duke Eberhard Ludwig at Ludwigsburg.[35] In 1715, a year after Nette's death, Frisoni succeeded him as architect of the Ludwigsburg Schloss and by 1717 was *Landesbaudirektor* of Württemberg. The associated stuccoer at Weingarten was, however, Franz Schmuzer, a member of the middle generation of the Wessobrunn family (whose work is discussed in some detail in Chapter IV), rather than one of Frisoni's compatriots, colleagues, and assistants at Ludwigsburg such as Diego Carlone (1674–1750), a son of G. B. Carlone, who had worked at Maria-Hilf, Amberg, or Riccardo Retti (1687–1741), like Frisoni from Laino and actually a relative of his.

Whoever was responsible for the original project for the grandiose church at Weingarten it was certainly not Frisoni. He had come into supervisory control only in 1717, two years after the church was begun, despite his already important position at Ludwigsburg. Alternatives, all specifically mentioned in the records, are: the Bavarian court architect Zuccalli, in 1679; the Benedictine monk Caspar Moosbrugger from Einsiedeln, in 1684; Heinrich Baader, in 1687—all before Hyller's time; then J. J. Herkomer in 1711–13; the Weingarten monk Andreas Schreck (1659–1730), in 1715; Franz II Beer (1660–1726) and also Christian Thumb (*c.* 1640–1726), in 1716; and C. D. Lucchese. Once the vaulting of the nave had been completed, probably under Beer's direction,[36] Frisoni began to provide designs for finishing various parts of the church: for the dome, in February 1718; for the interior, the following month; from May 1719, for the façade and towers, and finally for the altars.[37]

Schmuzer's contract for the stucco-work is dated the last day of March 1718 and in May he began to carry it out. C. D. Asam was first commissioned the following month—the contract is dated 30 June 1718—but that contract was only for the fresco in the easternmost bay of the choir; in the autumn, on 3 October, he received a further contract for the rest of the frescoes.[38] The first service was held in the new church on 16 April 1719; but the date 1720 over the crossing arch indicates more plausibly the date by which the *stucchi* and frescoes were probably completed, just within the two years specified in Asam's contract. By that time, at least, he was almost certainly working on the more significant, if rather less attractive, frescoes that are surrounded, not by Schmuzer's, but by his brother Egid Quirin's stucco-work at Aldersbach, if not once more at Michelfeld also.

Since Frisoni had been himself first a stuccoer and continued as an architect at Ludwigsburg to work closely with stuccoers and fresco-painters, a question must arise as to what extent his designs of March 1718 provided the decorative programme for Schmuzer's and Asam's contributions to Weingarten. The construction and the decoration of the Hofkapelle at Ludwigsburg and of the church at Weingarten, both begun in 1715, both structurally complete by 1717–18, and both stuccoed and frescoed in the years immediately following, ran parallel, and in 1717 the architect of the former took over the completion of the latter. There are, however, notable differences between the two. For one thing, the Ludwigsburg edifice, a court chapel attached to a vast palace as is the one at Versailles, was destined for Lutheran use. (It was consecrated to the Catholic faith only in 1743 after Carl Alexander, Eberhard Ludwig's cousin, succeeded—he had been converted on his marriage in 1727 to Maria Augusta von Thurn und Taxis. However, it became Protestant once more in 1799.) The Hofkapelle has a centrally planned circular interior of modest size with a rectangular western arm and three semi-elliptical ones, those to the north and south containing galleries. The most notably Protestant feature was the original placing of the pulpit in the eastern lobe behind and above the altar—that is right in front of Carlone's altarpiece, which was an enlarged copy of a Last Supper by Luca Giordano that Frisoni had bought in Augsburg but found too small for this position.

There was thus one good reason why Frisoni's designs for the decoration of the Hofkapelle might not have been considered a proper model for the decoration of the big monastic church at Weingarten that followed the well-established German variant with flanking wall-pillars of the Counter-Reformation churches of Rome. Even though there is nothing strictly stylistic about the Hofkapelle that is unsuitable for Catholic worship, the tone and spirit of the architecture and the decoration is wholly different—chiefly because of the relative up-to-dateness of their character by Italian and Austrian standards—from the almost sixteenth-century combination of grandeur and severity at Weingarten (Pl. 32). In contrast to the predominantly white walls and piers of Weingarten, the columns, pilasters, entablatures, and even the intervening wall surfaces in the Hofkapelle are all of warm-coloured scagliola executed by Antonio Corbellini (1674–1742), while the capitals and other ornaments are richly gilded. *Quadratura* painting rather than stucco decoration frames Carlo Carlone's dome fresco between and above the oval oculi in the four pendentives; and a profusion of three-dimensional white stucco angels and putti by Diego Carlone, riding on puffs of cloud, lead up to the gilded cross over the choir-arch.

In two things only is there some similarity to Weingarten: in the great size of the frescoes, no novelty in the secular interiors at Ludwigsburg; and in the flat, proto-Rococo character of Diego Carlone's interlaced bandwork in stucco on the intradoses of the main arches, which is surely there of Viennese rather than direct French inspiration. Little more true collaboration between architect and fresco-painter at Weingarten may have existed than at Maria-Hilf, Amberg; yet Frisoni presumably approved—if indeed he did not suggest—the relative novelty, for an early eighteenth-century German church interior, of the expansive handling of the frescoes in the Weingarten nave (Pl. 33). Though modest in width, the frescoes of 1716 by L. C. Colomba (1661–1737) in the eastern Spiegelgalerie at Ludwigsburg had already filled far more completely the long barrel-vault and are less interrupted by transverse ribs than Asam's at Weingarten; while his apse fresco in the Hofkapelle fills the entire conch of the apse above the entablature. That, at least, was impossible at Weingarten. There the clerestory windows intersecting the apse vault had required a complex type of radial cross-vaulting which led to the nearly complete omission of this portion of the church from the general fresco programme.

A corollary of the increase in the size of the frescoes at Weingarten, as also in the Hofkapelle, is the reduction in the space available for stucco decoration on the vaults. There is, moreover, little interrelationship in either case between the stucco decoration, evidently underway at Weingarten two months before Asam came on the scene, and the frescoes. Schmuzer's stucco-work—mostly in white on a dove-grey ground, with almost no gilding—is most noticeable and most similar to that at Ludwigsburg, where it fills the intradoses of the transverse arches, here architecturally much more tectonic than in the Hofkapelle. The low relief of the additional *stucchi* on the exiguous 'pendentives' at the corners of the handkerchief vaults of the nave and choir around Asam's fresco panels (Pls. 32, 33), in contrast to the free use of stucco figure-sculpture in the round at the Hofkapelle, is consonant with specifically Bavarian tendencies in this direction evident as early as Appiani's stucco-work of ten years before at Freystadt and again in the lately completed Munich Dreifaltigkeitskirche (Pls. 14, 15).

Despite the close contemporaneity of the stucco-work and the frescoes at Weingarten and the presumptive agreement of both with Frisoni's ideas of March 1718 for the decoration of the interior of a church whose basic architectural character had been established before he arrived on the scene, this impressive vessel cannot be considered a coherent step in the architectural and decorative development of the south German church interior in these crucial years. It is a climactic conclusion rather than a beginning, and the work of Frisoni, Schmuzer, and Asam there does not lead at all directly to the more novel entity that C. D. Asam and his brother were so soon to create within the structural shell provided by Magzin at Aldersbach.

Nonetheless, Asam's Weingarten frescoes deserve some comment here. They are, first of all, notable in his development, and even in the general south German development, for their relatively great size, though no bigger absolutely than Carlone's and Colomba's of the same date in the Hofkapelle. The early one over the eastern half-bay of the choir and its pendant over the westernmost half-bay above the organ are still little larger than those over the nave at Michelfeld (Pls. 29–31). The increase in the size of the fresco fields would seem to date not from Asam's first employment here in the summer of 1718 but rather from the contract of that autumn.

Among the larger frescoes those over the crossing require the least description. The giant figures of the Evangelists filling the pendentives, with clouds and even limbs overflowing the frames, resemble those in the Munich Dreifaltigkeitskirche (Pl. 15) and are quite in the Roman Baroque tradition. On the dome itself—here, by exception in Germany at this late date, raised by Frisoni almost out of sight above a tall, windowed drum as the architects involved earlier must always have intended—the resemblance of the composition to that of 1714 on the flatter domical ceiling at Ensdorf is close (Pl. 17). So also, not surprisingly, is the subject—the Holy Trinity adored by the Church Triumphant—though the execution, four or five years later in Asam's career, is somewhat superior.

More striking is the fresco representing the Pentecost over the next bay to the east, that is, the square westernmost bay of the choir; for here on the handkerchief vault a high dome is simulated in perspective in such a way that, from the proper position below and to the west, one seems to see overhead a colonnaded drum, much more strongly tectonic than the real drum nearby over the crossing, with the figures of the Apostles in the intercolumniations and a ribbed and richly coffered hemisphere above (Pl. 32). This is rather like the Baroque domes in Rome that Pietro da Cortona probably initiated at Santi Luca e Martina well before Bernini's of the 1650s and 1660s. At the centre is a simulated oculus from which clouds and angels float downwards, apparently into the real space over the observer's head. The superiority to the choir fresco at Michelfeld is very great, and the model here must certainly have been the illusionistic fresco of the 1690s over the low-domed crossing in Sant'Ignazio in Rome by Andrea Pozzo, which Asam would surely have known. Of this, in any case, a useful plate was now readily available in the German translation of Pozzo's treatise, *Perspectivae pictorum*, that had appeared at Augsburg in two volumes in 1706 and in 1709, the year Pozzo died in Vienna.

It is rather surprising, and evidence perhaps of the Asams' lack of contact with Vienna,[39] where Pozzo had settled in 1702, that influence from Pozzo had not been very evident before this. At Ludwigsburg Frisoni had called Carlo Carlone from Vienna to fresco the dome of the Hofkapelle. But Austrian influence is generally more evident in these years in southern Germany in secular than in religious works as, for example, at Pommersfelden.

More handsome at Weingarten than the frescoes of the dome and the pseudo-dome, and more characteristic of Asam's approaching maturity, are the roughly square ones that occupy the three main bays of the nave (Pl. 33). Those in the first and third bays are slightly smaller than that in the middle bay, though not as much smaller as at Michelfeld. These have cut-off concave corners and, therefore, rather more of Schmuzer's stucco-work at the corners and the sides. Most interesting is the one devoted to the Glorification of St. Benedict in the middle bay. Here, as in the choir bay, *quadratura* architecture seems to carry up the space of the nave a further story, much as does Pozzo's fresco over the nave at Sant'Ignazio in Rome, with heavy clusters of painted pilasters echoing the clusters of real pilasters forming the ponderous wall-pillars below and a 'gold'-framed circular opening above revealing St. Benedict in Heaven. Out of this both clouds and figures float downwards, not only into the illusionary space created by the *quadratura* architecture but also, by overlapping slightly the strongly defined rib that closes the bay to the east, into the real space of the church as in Baccicia's fresco on the ceiling of the Gesù in Rome.[40]

Here, as in seventeenth-century Roman examples, is fresco painting that has a quite definite architectural effect, especially as regards the space composition, in this massively tectonic interior. Otherwise the church recalls, like the splendid exterior of Viscardi's Freystadt, the Italian sixteenth century almost more than the seventeenth. Yet the means and the result are wholly Baroque as with the decorations carried out during the seventeenth century in the late sixteenth-century churches of the Jesuits, the Oratorians, and the Theatines in Rome. Schmuzer's bandwork, with its slightly proto-Rococo flavour, on the broad transverse and longitudinal rib-bands actually seems underscaled in juxtaposition to the painted as well as the real architecture of the church (Pls. 32, 33).[41]

Rohr

For the construction and decoration of Rohr, E. Q. Asam's first and largest architectural work, which is located not far to the south of Weltenburg, documented dates are in shorter supply than at Weingarten. The Augustinian monastery there was rebuilt about 1690 for Prior Patritius Freiherr von Heydon by Riva, the Italian-Swiss who was the architect of the contemporary abbey churches at Benediktbeuern and Tegernsee that H. G. Asam had decorated with frescoes. In 1717 Heydon ordered the old church to be demolished and that year the cornerstone of the new one was laid.[42] The date 1721 over the arch at the entrance to the choir and on C. D. Asam's signed altar painting of St. Joseph in the transept seems to provide a *terminus* for the stucco decoration even though the church was not consecrated until 22 September the following year. But the principal feature of the church, the sculptural Assumption of the Virgin above and behind the high altar, carries on one of the figures the date 1723 with the signature of an Italian assistant of Egid Quirin, Giovanni Cloudy from Como, while the altars in the side chapels were not all finished until 1725. Yet the general character of the high altar composition and its dominant relationship to the interior as a whole may well have been planned from the first—it would be the natural and, indeed, the expected result of employing a sculptor as designing architect.

It seems plausible to suppose that the church, begun in 1717, was structurally complete in 1719 or 1720; that the stucco decoration came next in 1720–21; and that the final design, and certainly the execution, of the high altar dates from 1721–23. If this dating is correct, the architectural design of the church, at least, must have followed quite shortly after Cosmas Damian's for Weltenburg. However, it resembles Weltenburg only in its Roman inspiration and in the great importance given in both to the sculptural composition above the high altar.

The construction of the church, under the supervision of Joseph Bader (d. 1721) from Wessobrunn, who had heightened the tower of the old church in 1696, overlapped the years of C. D. Asam's employment at Weingarten. The suggested date of 1720–21 for the stucco-work would make that almost exactly contemporary not only with E. Q. Asam's high altar at Michelfeld, but more significantly with his stucco-work at Aldersbach; yet this dating still leaves the precise sequence to be worked out hypothetically by stylistic analysis. The date 1721–23 for the high altar probably implies that its execution, at least, follows rather than precedes—as some scholars have supposed—that of the high altar at Weltenburg. Cosmas Damian's employment at Weingarten perhaps into the year 1720, at Aldersbach presumably in 1720, and in 1720–21 at Schleissheim might explain why the Rohr frescoes, for which his brother provided big framed fields, were not executed.

Externally the church at Rohr is very simple and dominated by the tall medieval tower which was topped with its present dome only in 1739 after Heydon's death; doubtless Bader, rather than E. Q. Asam, had full responsibility for the exterior. The interior (Pl. 35), like that of Weingarten, follows the so-called 'Vorarlberg scheme' (Fig. 2).[43] Wall-pillars divide the nave into three and a half bays, the half bay at the west end being occupied by the choir gallery and organ (Pl. 34).[44] Between the wall-pillars are side chapels, here linked by arched openings to provide the equivalent of aisles, somewhat as in the Oratorians' Chiesa Nuova in Rome. The nave arcade is relatively low and over the chapels between the pillars there are no side galleries as at Michelfeld and Weingarten. Somewhat exceptionally for Germany, large clerestory windows above the entablature flood the nave with light as in the big Roman churches of the late sixteenth century and the seventeenth-century churches of Paris. Beyond the square-crossing the choir, lined with stalls forming a horseshoe-shaped termination of the floor plan, consists of a half bay and one full bay, that lead almost abruptly to the rich dark screen backing the high altar in the semi-circular apse above and behind the stalls (Fig. 2, Pl. 35). The transept arms are only half a bay deep, with curved corners at their ends as in Carlo Rainaldi's Santa Maria in Campitelli in Rome. The treatment of the walls of this interior, telescopic in effect despite the short, transeptal arms, is strongly tectonic. The nave piers carry pilaster clusters in high relief over which the entablature breaks boldly

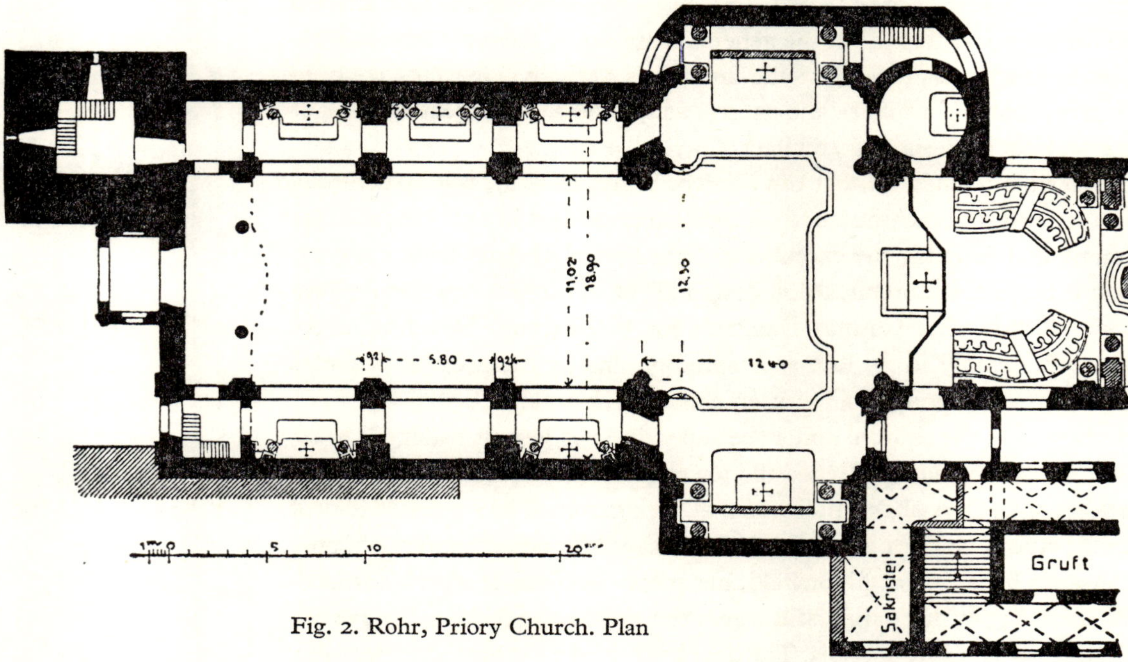

Fig. 2. Rohr, Priory Church. Plan

forward, while the crossing piers are further strengthened visually by pairs of engaged three-quarter columns (Pl. 35).

Above the entablature, however, the character of the expression changes notably. Analysis tends to exaggerate this shift. It is not quite so striking when the interior is seen as a whole. Though four deep ribs frame the handkerchief dome over the crossing—so much less Roman than Frisoni's tall-drummed dome at Weingarten—and shallower ribs set off the half bay to the west and similarly frame the first full bay of the choir to the east, the emphasis in the decoration of the vaulting is not on structure but on continuity of surface, an effect actually enhanced by the absence of the intended frescoes (Pl. 34). Here, or at Aldersbach,[45] depending on which was first designed as regards the treatment of the vaults, the Asams initiated something that would later be a constituent element of most German Rococo church architecture; for the fresco field on the nave vault is, to use a mouth-filling German word, *jochverschleifend*—that is, it occupies the vault from end to end through all three main bays of the nave.

Frescoes occupying whole bays, especially domed bays, were no novelty in Germany, as has several times been noted earlier; nor, in secular architecture, were very large, rectangular vaulted areas, without structural subdivision into bays and carrying very extensive framed or unframed frescoes. Dating from two or three years before this are those, described in the Introduction, over the stair-hall and the Marmorsaal at Schloss Weissenstein at Pommersfelden in Franconia carried out for the Elector of Mainz, Lothar Franz Graf von Schönborn, respectively by the painters J. R. Byss and J. F. M. Rottmayr whom he had brought from Vienna, the one Swiss-born, the other Bavarian.[46] At almost this very moment Jacopo Amigoni, Neapolitan-born but trained in Venice and active after 1729 in England, was providing such a fresco over the dining-hall of the Badenburg in the gardens of Schloss Nymphenburg designed by the Paris-trained Joseph Effner for the Bavarian Elector Max Emanuel. Cosmas Damian himself, as has been noted, was executing in 1720–21 the fairly extensive fresco above the Schleissheim stair-hall, seen somewhat as is that in Hildebrandt's Palais Daun-Kinsky in Vienna through a good-sized opening in the ceiling of the main story. He was also covering almost the whole barrel-vault of the adjacent Maximilianskapelle with a single fresco.[47]

A literally *jochverschleifend* framed fresco field in a large church, however, was at this time new in Germany and examples before 1720 are infrequent even in small churches and chapels (Pl. 5).[48] As regards its sidewise extension and its outline, moreover, the framed field was handled here at Rohr in such a way as to minimize the tectonic aspect of the vault, opening upwards, seemingly, the entire central space of the nave and reducing the vaulting conoids at the sides visually to subsidiary elements without structural significance. These are, in fact, largely masked on their inner faces by rich, cartouche-like stucco decoration (Pl. 34) surrounding small areas of 'gold' *mosaïque* like that used even more extensively on the transverse severies here as also, at just this point, in the Schleissheim chapel. The stucco-work dissolves at the top into clouds that overlap the gilded frame of the main fresco field, a reversal of the more usual overlapping of fresco across a decorative frame of stucco that C. D. Asam had employed just before this in the middle bay of the nave of Weingarten (Pl. 33). At the ends, the frame of the fresco at Rohr has double-S curves, suggesting the crowning mouldings of Early Rococo *boiserie* panels, with elaborate central ornaments that touch the still quite tectonic transverse ribs to east and west.

The detailing of the stucco-work, from the full Corinthianesque capitals of the main order to the scrolls and foliage surrounding the cartouches above, is somewhat fat and heavy in distinct contrast to the real delicacy of that at Michelfeld in the first and third bays of the nave or Franz Schmuzer's at Weingarten, as executed in both cases two or three years earlier (Pls. 32, 33). A comparable elegance is found here only in the painted tendrils scrolling round the large central monogram of the Madonna that takes the place of the absent fresco (Pl. 34). There is, however, in the nave much less figural work in relief than in the middle bay of the nave at Michelfeld; but there is more—and fully three-dimensional as in the Ludwigsburg Hofkapelle—in the crossing, both at the corners and over the choir-arch.

Otherwise the treatment of the crossing (Pl. 35) is more like what Cosmas Damian and Franz Schmuzer had carried out, perhaps at Frisoni's suggestion, in the bays of the nave at Weingarten (Pl. 33). The fresco field, heavily framed by a reeded moulding made still richer and more plastic by recurrent foliage, is drawn so far down into the pendentives that there is room for little but the standing stucco figures of cherubim. These perch rather precariously on round brackets above the scrolled foliage that laps up and across the entablature below. There are also floating angels above the choir-arch carrying a wavy banderole inscribed with the chronogram below a gilded glory. The decoration of the crossing has a rather earlier character than the treatment of the nave ceiling. Still earlier, seemingly, indeed little advanced beyond the decoration in the first and third bays of the nave of Michelfeld (Pl. 29), is the handling of the surfaces of the vaults in the choir and the apse. On these the rather small oval and circular fresco fields, respectively, are tightly bound by the transverse ribs and the surrounding stucco foliage is quite small in scale (Pl. 35). A chronological sequence in design, as well as in execution, for the stucco-work of the vaults from east to west perhaps provides the best explanation for this disparity. Stylistically it also seems probable—and the known dates do not make it unlikely—that the decoration of Aldersbach by the two brothers working together may be interpolated within this suggested sequence at Rohr and not dated either before or after what Egid Quirin did alone there.

Aldersbach

Despite its Italian or Italian-Swiss architect, Domenico Magzin, concerning whom little is known beyond his presumptive responsibility for the parish church at nearby Landau—begun in 1713 but not consecrated until 1726—the interior architecture of the Cistercian Abbey of Aldersbach, as rebuilt for Abbot Theobald I Grad from 1718 on, seems far less Roman than Rohr (Pl. 38).[49] There is no crossing here and the earlier choir, dating from 1617 as has been said and possibly built on Gothic foundations, is much deeper and narrower; while in the new, four-bay nave the piers, or wall-pillars, are somewhat wider. In section the nave has no clerestory so that the light is less intense on the vault than at Rohr. It enters only through the tall, arched windows in the side walls which are more or less masked to the observer by the depth of the piers. The corners of the piers are rounded and the single pilasters between these convex elements provide little more than flat surface decoration, with none of the tectonic vigour of those at Rohr (Pl. 34).

As a result the sides of the nave seem more continuous and there is also less contrast here between the treatment of the wall-pillars and that of the vault. Indeed, the decoration on the frieze of the entablature, in contrast to the multiplicity of sharp undecorated mouldings at Rohr, serves as a link to the stucco ornamentation below, which includes curvilinear moulded heads on the panels at the sides of the wall-pillars above and behind the later side altars, rich pilaster capitals with pendants, and garlands hanging on the convex corners of the piers. Above, there is rather similar scroll-work on such areas of the vault surface as are not occupied by fresco. In some places this principally outlines and defines the severies in the spirit of the wall panels; in others it fills them more evenly, rather in the manner of Michelfeld (Pl. 29).

This seems to confirm what the few established dates indicate—that the architecture of Rohr, as distinct from its decoration, is almost certainly earlier than the decoration of Aldersbach. In any case, the building of the former began a year sooner. When it comes to the dating of the individual frescoes and their settings, moreover, a sequence from east to west, as with the *stucchi* at Rohr, seems probable also at Aldersbach (Pl. 38). The round fields of the frescoes in the apse and the easternmost bay of the nave are hardly larger, and are even simpler in shape, than those at Michelfeld (Pl. 31). But the main fresco in the choir is not only bigger—it occupies two of the admittedly narrow bays of the seventeenth-century (or earlier) structure—the straight sides and the double-S-curved ends of the frame are not unlike those of the empty fresco field over the nave at Rohr (Pl. 39). Yet the overall shape is more nearly square, and thus similar to the fresco fields in the nave of Weingarten (Pl. 33), whose shape and size were very likely determined in March 1718 by Frisoni.

The question of the relative priority of the large fresco field over the nave at Aldersbach (Pl. 40) and that at Rohr is not easy to answer even hypothetically. Because of the absence of an executed fresco at Rohr to compare with that of the Christmas Vision of St. Bernard on the Aldersbach vault, there is no possibility of finding clues in the actual painting. The Aldersbach fresco retains and extends the balustrade of the middle nave fresco at Weingarten (Pl. 33); indeed, this is here used a good deal more effectively to direct the gaze upward as one advances into the nave. But the rich and monumental *quadratura* architecture of Weingarten, extending illusionistically the space of the nave a further story upward, gives way to a looser and more episodic handling of the simple, even rustic, architectural elements that provide the setting for the saint and his vision of the Nativity; while it is towards the west, at what is compositionally the top of the fresco rather than at its centre, that the surface opens to Heaven and to God the Father in Glory.

If the Aldersbach fresco cannot be compared with the one at Rohr, its framing may be (Pls. 34, 40); but the conclusion cannot be very definite. At Rohr the longitudinal edges of the frame are straight, as at Aldersbach over the choir (Pl. 39), cutting across the transverse severies, while the tops of the cartouches on the vaulting conoids overlap them; at Aldersbach the edges of the fresco frame bow inwards in the central bay and the small inward scallops on either side avoid any contact with the coarse palmettes that crown the cartouches so that there is here no overlap of either element by the other. Only occasional puffs of stucco cloud and a fairly broad inscribed riband carried by stucco putti, winding irregularly in and out, break the continuity of the frame of the fresco-panel. Overall the shape approaches a longitudinal oval with pinched waist, while that of the Rohr field is more nearly rectangular and emphasizes breadth rather than length.

Thus the latter already resembles the remarkably extensive ceiling fresco over the nave, which had been widened in 1720 by Benedikt Schöttl (1688–1742), of the church of the Benedictine Abbey of Metten on the Danube by Ignaz Waräthi (*c.* 1690–1758), vignetted in stucco-work by F. J. Holzinger (1691–1775). This was probably designed as early as 1722, the date of Holzinger's contract, although it was not painted until several years later. A drawing by C. D. Asam in the Staatliche Graphische Sammlung in Munich may perhaps be an earlier project for this ceiling (Pl. 41) since the subject is the Triumph of St. Michael, the patron of the Metten church. If so, that certainly marks an important stage in the development of *jochverschleifend* ceiling frescoes. It was clearly intended to cover the full length of a nave; it is so broad that it must impinge on the presumptive vaulting conoids at the sides; and it is slightly 'ovalized' by curved corners.[50]

The stylistic evidence seems again to support the plain interpretation of the inscribed dates: 1720 for the decoration of the nave of Aldersbach, 1721 for Rohr, despite the presumptive priority of the architecture of Rohr to the decoration of Aldersbach that was noted above. Yet the general effect of the Aldersbach interior is certainly more proto-Rococo than that of Rohr. In part this is because Rohr is still architecturally so Roman. The basic difference, moreover, is reinforced by the handling of the altars. At Rohr the interior is dominated by the very tectonically constructed high altar (Pl. 35). (Because of its probable date, a little later than the decoration of the vaults, this has not yet been described.) The modest side altars there are incorporated architecturally into the outer walls of the chapels flanking the nave below small circular windows quite in the Roman way.

At Aldersbach, however, the side altars, despite their size—and above all their height—which largely masks the western sides of the wall piers they are set against, look essentially like pieces of rich furniture, relatively dark, thanks to the reddish, yellowish, and greenish scagliola and the oil paintings, in contrast to the white piers and vaults with their raised decoration in pink and putty colour. These altars are all later than the decoration of the walls and the vault, however. The high altar that fills the eastern end of the choir is by J. M. Götz and of 1723–25; the side altars, also by Götz, date from the following years 1726–29. Neither their fairly advanced character, approaching the mature Rococo, nor even their height were probably envisaged by the Asams in 1720, although their location—common in German wall-pillar churches—probably was (Pl. 38). It would be some years still before Egid Quirin's altars became so intricate and so delicate in scale.

What is far more significant in the present context is that Egid Quirin's stucco-work at Aldersbach, above all that on vertical surfaces, already offers more apparent evidence of familiarity with the decoration characteristic of French Rococo *boiseries*, such as he or his brother might have seen at Nymphenburg, than does anything but the painted arabesque which takes the place of the absent fresco on the nave ceiling at Rohr.

At Schleissheim, however, where Cosmas Damian was painting in 1720–21, there was little evidence of Rococo influence, despite the earlier work of Effner and his associates at Nymphenburg. J. B. Zimmermann's *stucchi*, executed on a contract of 20 August 1720, in the stair-hall over which Cosmas Damian was frescoing the ceiling of the lantern probably followed closely the model for this interior prepared from Effner's designs the previous summer by C.-C. Dubut.[51] In the war-gutted Maximilianskapelle, where Cosmas Damian frescoed the vault with the assistance of J. A. Müller in 1721, the stucco-work may well not have been executed until that year and could hardly have influenced the Asams' work at Aldersbach, if that be of 1720. Yet both Asam and Zimmermann, while working together in the stair-hall in 1720–21, were probably not unaware of the interiors at Nymphenburg in the new mode, though Asam never worked there, and Zimmermann not before 1726.

Moreover, the actual translation into stucco of the sort of Rococo decoration that was, in Germany as in France, first executed in carved woodwork, had not by 1720 been carried very far by Effner's French-trained assistants. There are modest plaster friezes in the Pagodenburg (Pl. 4), completed by 1719, as also in the rooms in the Nymphenburg Schloss that were decorated immediately thereafter, and even some wall-mouldings of plaster in the lower-story lobbies (Pl. 2) of the former. These are presumably the work of the Antwerp-born and Paris-trained sculptor Willem de Groff (*c.* 1680–1742) who carved the Rococo detail over the windows on the exterior. However, the earliest *stucchi* by a German brought up in the native tradition of Wessobrunn that show significant Rococo influence are probably those in the Antecamera on the ground floor of the garden front at Schleissheim.[52] These can be approximately dated between the order for the marble pavement and door-frames of 1723 and that of December 1724 for the grisaille paintings by C. D. Asam that are included in the decoration.

Certainly not by the conservative Dubut, this stucco-work has been attributed to J. B. Zimmermann, as has been also the more restrained and elegantly French gold-on-white ceilings of the Kammerkapelle and the Writing Room in the Electress's apartments on the garden front. The scagliola walls of these two modest interiors, respectively the work of J. G. Bader and of A. and B. Langerbuecher, are of 1724–25, and Nikolaus Stuber's painted ceiling in the lantern over the chapel is dated 1726. The stucco ceilings, therefore, may be assigned to approximately the same date as Zimmermann's larger ceiling of 1725 in the library at Benediktbeuern. The designing, at least, of the *stucchi* at Freising, the next major work of the Asams, could have preceded, then, rather than followed anything comparable by Zimmermann or other stuccoers active at Schleissheim in the early twenties. Certainly it was at Freising that the Asams took the next steps beyond their work at Aldersbach towards a truly German Rococo style of decoration for monumental church interiors.

Before leaving Aldersbach something should be said concerning the colouring there, for that carried into church architecture something of that festive gaiety characteristic of the secular Rococo. This gaiety is considered, by many Protestants, quite inappropriate to religious edifices, but it must be accepted as of the essence of the German Rococo, in contrast to the relative solemnity of the preceding German Baroque even at its richest.

It is difficult to speak with assurance of the colouring of the stucco-work in eighteenth-century German churches. If unrestored, the interiors are often somewhat grimy and the colouring, as a result, has become dimmed and darkened in tone after more than two hundred years of neglect. If the interiors were restored in the nineteenth century the present heavy tonality, whether dull or gaudy, is certainly not authentic; while if lately restored, as at Michelfeld, it often seems today too light and too bright, especially as regards any touches of gilding. In a broad way, however, there seems to have been a significant sequence of change through the first quarter of the century. Before about 1710 stucco decoration was still usually all white, as in many of the finest High Baroque churches in Rome, in strong contrast to the relatively dark tone of the small inset paintings, whether in oil or fresco, but with a vigorous chiaroscuro of its own thanks to the high relief of most of the ornament, quite as in the late seventeenth century in Germany (Pls. 118–123). Then, as the relief gradually grew slighter, the scroll patterns more delicate, and the key of the fresco painting higher, raised work—still white—is set against grounds tinted delicate pinks, greens, and yellows. This was very possibly already true of Freystadt (Pl. 14) where the present colouring—white walls; columns, entablatures, and dome ribs, light blue-grey; background of the stuccos, flesh colour; ornament, golden yellow—dates from the restoration of 1954–59. Here, so to say, is where the young Asams came in, for this is the scheme used in the Dreifaltigkeitskirche in Munich, where C. D. Asam worked in 1714–15, and, not surprisingly, also in the nave of Michelfeld in 1717–18. Then, about 1720, as at Aldersbach and Rohr, the colours are reversed, with the grounds white and the raised decoration standing out distinctly in neutralized pinks and putty colours.[53]

That seems to be the standard sequence in church decoration up to the early twenties. It is somewhat different in German secular decoration. At Pommersfelden Schenk's stuccoed ceilings of 1713–17 are almost all in white relief against pale coloured grounds with only small touches of gilding. In the dining-hall of Effner's Badenburg at Nymphenburg of 1718–20, however, the stucco-work by Dubut is still all white, with colour only in Amigoni's ceiling fresco. So is it again in the great rooms of 1720–24 along the entrance front of Schleissheim that Dubut stuccoed with J. B. Zimmermann's assistance—stair-hall, Festsaal (Pl. 1), and Viktoriensaal—in contrast, as at the Badenburg, to the brilliant colours of C. D. Asam's and Amigoni's frescoes overhead?

The particular combination of gold and white characteristic of Early Rococo *boiseries* in France—which had already been carried over from secular work into church decoration by Pierre Lepautre in the doors and the organ of 1709-10 at the Versailles chapel—had already appeared in Bavaria in the *boiseries* by the Paris-trained J. A. Pichler, presumably of about 1717–18, in the large upper room of the Pagodenburg at Nymphenburg (Pl. 4). Varied with the use of silver instead of gold in most of the Electress's apartments, it is also characteristic of the more domestically scaled rooms along the garden front at Schleissheim that were lined in 1723–25 with Pichler's carved panelling (Pl. 3), and even of the lower walls of the Viktoriensaal. It may well have been in J. B. Zimmermann's already mentioned ceilings in the Electress's suite at Schleissheim, where the walls by exception are not of wood but of scagliola, some of it of seventeenth-century date and brought from the Munich Residenz, that gilding was first consistently used in Germany for the ornament on a palace ceiling carried out in Rococo stucco-work, though the exact sequence of the Schleissheim interiors is a little uncertain.

In church architecture, E. Q. Asam had gilded most of the stucco ornament on the cove at Weltenburg probably two or more years earlier than that (Pls. 25, 27),[54] and there was already gilding on all the bandwork on the intradoses of main arches in the Hofkapelle at Ludwigsburg even before that. The contemporary reversal of the colour scheme of stucco-work from white relief on pastel grounds to semi-neutral tones against white fields at Aldersbach and Rohr, about 1720–21, was already possibly an economical reflection of the gilt-on-white theme of Rococo *boiseries*. The precedent for the extensive gilding at Weltenburg, however, was more probably Roman, like that for the illusionistic 'gilded' coffering on the domed backgrounds in C. D. Asam's frescoes at Weltenburg and earlier in the choir of Weingarten, and even specifically Berninian (Pl. 23).

Another aspect of this ambiguous relationship to the Rococo about 1720 would seem to be the profuse use of gold *mosaïque* (apparently, at least, in the French tradition) in the Maximilianskapelle at Schleissheim, on the intradoses of the ribs at Aldersbach, and even more extensively on the transverse severies and in the cartouches between them at Rohr, as well as in the alternate panels of the Weltenburg cove (Pls. 27, 34, 38). If there seems to be an historical paradox here, it results from the exaggerated assumption that anything tending towards the mature Rococo *must* derive from France. But, as has already been noted, the golden tonality of the whole interior of Weltenburg echoes not Paris but Berninian Rome; and the *mosaïque* of the Rohr vaults, like that used even more profusely a year or so later in the Maximilianskapelle, though suggesting a French origin, is not dissimilar to Cosmas Damian's 'gilded' coffering in several of his principal frescoes of the years 1717–21. It is this very ambiguity that expresses the nascent independence of the German proto-Rococo in these years.

Despite their rather incidental and distinctly tentative character, more tentative on the whole than on many of Schenk's ceilings at Pommersfelden, the various presumptive reflections of the French Rococo at Aldersbach should be recapitulated: the decorative panel-heads on the sides of the wall-pillars; the treatment of many of the transverse severies of the nave vaults; and, most conspicuously, that of the eastern wall above the choir-arch (Pl. 39). There the outlining of the surface by thin mouldings, enriched by scroll-work at the corners and joined by delicate interlaces at the quadrantal points of the arch, is especially worth noting. Yet Egid Quirin, as stuccoer, probably knew of the new mode, as lately introduced into Bavaria, only because his brother was then working for Effner at Schleissheim as well as with him at Aldersbach. The relatively less advanced, or at least less apparently Rococo-influenced, character of most of the stucco-work at Rohr might reflect the absence of Cosmas Damian because of more important commitments elsewhere. But this is novel-writing, and less tenable than the bolder assumption that about 1720 the secular Rococo was merely beginning to play the role of a catalyst in the Asams' modification of German traditions of church decoration rather than providing exclusively the new element in the post-Baroque mode that they were beginning to adumbrate as they moved away from the inheritance of their father and the direct influence of their Roman training.

The Weltenburg and Rohr Altars

The obvious overall superiority of Rohr to Aldersbach lies not in the stucco-work, in both cases somewhat plump and toothpaste-like, but in Egid Quirin's magnificent Berninian high altar (Pl. 37). Here again, however, although the issue has not very much to do with the development in these years towards the German Rococo, there is a question of priority. As has been noted already, several writers have assumed that the Rohr high altar precedes that at Weltenburg; actually it seems impossible to say surely which came first in conception, or even in execution. One of the figures on the Rohr altar carries the date 1723, as stated earlier; yet the sculptural group at Weltenburg was gilded, silvered, and polychromed by the Asams' older sister Maria Salome Bornschlögel only in 1723–24.[55] The date usually accepted for the Weltenburg high altar, 1721, is approximately the same as that of the stucco-work at Rohr, if the inscription at the crossing there be accepted as determinant. The high altar at Rohr was still incomplete, evidently, in the sense that not all the sculpture was executed and in place, at the time of the church's consecration on 27 September 1722, so that there is no strong reason to consider it as earlier than 1721 in conception and basic construction.

Whatever the sequence may actually have been, if indeed the Rohr and Weltenburg high altars were not designed and executed practically simultaneously, both are certainly much more elaborate than the Michelfeld high altar of 1720–21 (Pl. 30), and in both cases the figural compositions that decorate the altarpieces consist of sculptural groups, not oil paintings. With the one at Michelfeld they both have this much in common, however: despite the dominating importance at Michelfeld of Cosmas Damian's fine picture of the Last Supper and at Weltenburg and Rohr of Egid Quirin's sculptures of St. George and of the Assumption of the Virgin, respectively, the setting is in both cases not only solidly architectonic but is also closely coordinated with the architectural elements of the choir (Pls. 36, 37). The entablatures continue those of the side walls and the orders are nearly identical although the altar columns are set much higher. Indeed, the bases of the columns and the stage-like platform for the sculptural composition at Rohr are at the level of the top of the quadrants of choir-stalls that flank the mensa of the altar. Framing the two big altars at the ends of the shallow transepts at Rohr are again columns identical with those at the high altar; and in the side chapels columns, set diagonally as at Michelfeld, also appear but corresponding here to the sub-order of the nave arcade.

At Weltenburg the altar edicule forms a screen in front of the apse and is framed architecturally by the loges on short columns that flank the choir (Pls. 24, 36); at Rohr it fills the entire semicircular area of the apse and is not framed except by the choir-arch at the crossing (Pl. 37). At Rohr the main figural composition is lit principally from windows at the sides of the apse that are hidden by the second pair of columns. Light also descends from behind and above, thanks to a large and quite unconcealed central oculus, and from visible clerestory windows on either side.

Thus bathed in light, the white stucco figures—both of the apostles grouped around the empty, irregularly oval, scagliola sarcophagus below, and of the central floating figure of the Virgin supported by winged angels above, her robes brocaded in gold—stand out against the gold-brocaded dark green curtain immediately behind that fills the segment-topped rear of the edicule. At Weltenburg the contrast is the reverse; for the glittering equestrian figure of St. George on a pedestal, flanked by the dragon and the rescued princess, appears as quite dark under the half-round arch through which is seen the brilliantly lit rear wall of the apse, some distance behind, with its rather pale fresco reflecting the light from high above and from both sides.

The character of these religious tableaux is by no means identical.[56] That at Rohr translates into three dimensions in real, architecturally framed space the sort of Baroque figure composition that goes back to such major sixteenth-century paintings as Raphael's *Transfiguration* and Titian's *Assumption* (Pl. 37). It preserves aesthetic distance, despite all the realism of the astonished apostles' poses and their existence, life-size, in our own space, by the abstract whiteness of the figures as in the present-day work of George Segal. The Weltenburg composition is comparatively static, though even more startingly realistic thanks to the polychromy of the figures and the brilliance of the contrast of light and dark. This is true especially as it is normally seen, remotely, from the dusky and warm-toned nave (Pl. 24); the Rohr composition, on the contrary, terminates a brilliantly lighted, largely white interior (Pl. 35).

There is considerable difference between the treatments of the two edicules. That at Rohr is large in scale and very dark in the tone of its purplish-brown scagliola columns and near-black entablature. Thus it provides a spatial frame of considerable solidity, and even severity, for the dramatic movement of the sculptured figures. Below, the rising gestures of the apostles (who are, all the same, firmly attached to the ground) lead the eye to the ascending figure of the Virgin, which is apparently quite detached physically from the background.

Above, between the widely separated 'horns' of the curved broken pediment, appears a very complex subsidiary figural and spatial composition that is not easy to make comprehensible without detailed plans, sections and photographs (Pl. 37). The space in which this composition exists is defined by a gilded corona of very thin section with elaborately scrolled cresting, supported only by perching and floating angels. This occupies, in plan, the area between the two vertical planes established by the horns of the first pediment and by the pediment frame to the rear over the head of the Virgin. Under this rear frame is a short section of coffered segmental barrel-vault. That is cut in the middle by a circular opening through which white clouds and gilded rays spill downwards quite as does the real light from the large oculus behind and above. Higher up, in front of this glory and in line with the rear of the corona, the dove of the Holy Spirit floats, wings outspread. This bird, apparently floating free, is held in place, like a figure by Reg Butler, by gilded metal rods that provide a second and more tenuous glory. Above and to the rear of the corona, against a much richer glory of gilded stucco rays, clouds, and seraphim that radiate outwards and upwards from the central occulus on the conch of the apse, Christ on the left and God the Father on the right reach out to hold a crown for the Virgin. This is in precise vertical line with her head as it rises towards the opening in the segmental vault at the rear half of the edicule. (The similarity to the elaborate devices of the Baroque theatre is very evident.)

As a setting for a sculptural concept so boldly spatial, so intricate in detail, one may well regret the fussiness of the small-scale stucco decoration on the vault above (Pl. 35). But the contrast seems to epitomize the conflict here between E. Q. Asam's still Berninian aspirations as a sculptor and altar-designer and the very tentative —and even debatable—reflection of Early Rococo ideas in his stucco decoration at this point in his career. Moreover the high altar composition at Rohr so dominates the interior by its great height, the very dark tone of the architectural elements, and the ecstatic upward surge of the sculpture that, as is evident from the illustrations of Rohr usually published, the rest of the interior tends to be forgotten and the significance of the apparent relationship of its decoration to the oncoming Rococo ignored if, indeed, that aspect has been recognized at all.

Despite its considerably more dramatic lighting, the high altar composition at Weltenburg, set at the rear of the narrow choir, is less overwhelming (Pl. 36). The rich intricacy of the elements of which it is composed, if not necessarily closer to the Rococo, is at least less grandly High Baroque than the altar composition at Rohr. A round arch on imposts frames the principal figures. The equestrian statue of St. George, one of the patrons of Weltenburg, apparently advances into the church despite the fact that his horse stands on a pedestal above and behind the small tabernacle on the altar. This equestrian figure is flanked on the left by the writhing dragon that the saint's lance is piercing and on the right by the princess whom he is saving. Despite the animation of her pose, balancing the twisted curves of the dragon, this group is essentially static, without any general sweep of movement like that of the Rohr Assumption. Further to left and right, but in front of the architectural frame of the main composition, are the standing figures of St. Martin, another patron of Weltenburg, and of St. Maurice, the latter with the features of Maurus Bächl, the Weltenburg abbot for whom the church was built and decorated.

With the tall central figure of St. George the two saints form an open triangular group, but they are subordinated to the elaborate architectural framework that defines the spaces in which they are set. Behind the two saints and flanking the central arch are two Salomonic columns of which the helical shafts echo the poses of the dragon and the princess; outside them, both in the lateral and the longitudinal sense, are two more. Between each pair of columns, and providing the immediate background for the flanking figures, are pilasters set on the diagonal. The entablature, identical with that of the choir walls, crowns these elements with an L-shaped block on either side. This is interrupted over the arch by a very large and elaborate gilded escutcheon, supported by angels, carrying the Bavarian electoral arms and encircled by the chain of the Order of the Golden Fleece.

The crowning figures, silhouetted like St. George below against the brilliantly lighted apse, are not linked iconographically with the main group as at Rohr. Angels on the horns of the broken pediment, which is related to the rear pair of columns, adore the Virgin, who ascends in the centre carried on gold-and-white clouds above the coat-of-arms. Over the forward-projecting entablature blocks capping the outer pair of columns are large urns with intricate shapes and delicate floral decorations. These suggest, at least, a Rococo inspiration, though they could just as well derive from Roman Baroque models. Rococo in spirit also, despite Berninian and even Palladian parallels, seem the floral garlands that hang between the column capitals and the pilasters; much more definitely Rococo, if the treatment be original, is the panel-like outlining on the pilaster faces, framing hanging garlands in the upper half and connected by scrolled linkage half way up. Although not clearly seen from the nave, a final element of Baroque richness is provided by the silvered angels who pull back red stucco curtains from the arches over the balconettes in the choir.

The Weltenburg Fresco

Cosmas Damian's vast fresco of the Reception of the Virgin in Heaven and the Community of Saints, painted on the flat surface of the upper ceiling of the nave (Pl. 25), has no more relationship to the Rococo than do his earlier frescoes. In this a *quadratura* colonnade, intended according to its perspective treatment to be appreciated not from the centre of the nave but rather from near the entrance, appears to support a round—not oval—illusionistic dome with a richly ribbed and coffered surface. Within the pictorial space thus created crowds of saints, some standing between the columns of the 'drum', others floating on clouds inside that line, provide a complex yet clearly organized composition well advanced technically beyond even Asam's best work before this at Weingarten (Pls. 32, 33). Acquaintance with Amigoni's frescoed ceilings at Nymphenburg of a year or two before this may explain the lighter, brighter colouring and the greater fluency in grouping the innumerable figures as compared to the Pozzo-like fresco of the Pentecost of two or three years earlier.[57]

It is the stucco decoration of the broad, lower cove below, subdivided by eight ribs into four large and four small sections (Pl. 25), that raises the most difficult questions with regard to the pace of the Asams' movement towards the Rococo in the early 1720s. Instead of the rather clumsy and fat detailing of the stucco-work of 1720 at Aldersbach, the execution here is crisp and metallic, as is appropriate to its largely gilded surface (Pl. 27). The frames of the panels, both the large ones that carry scenes from the lives of St. Benedict and St. Scholastica in relief and the narrower ones with figures of the four Archangels set against grounds of rather elaborate gold-on-green *mosaïque*—now entirely the product of the latest restoration of 1956-62—deserve particular notice. The general spirit of the ornament is perhaps more Rococo than the specific elements of which it is composed, at least in relation to Pichler's *boiseries* of the late 1710s at Nymphenburg (Pl. 4), not to speak of the more properly comparable stucco ceilings by J. B. Zimmermann over the Electress's rooms at Schleissheim, though these are probably some two to four years later.[58] Actually, the foliated bandwork framing the smaller panels has quite an original character, but the use of C-scrolls to truncate the corners of the larger panels, with either double-S-curves at their crowns or concave C-ended 'bites', is remarkably close to Lepautre's work in France of a decade and more earlier when the Rococo first began—closer in fact than it is to the work French-trained craftsmen were carrying out for the Munich court at Schleissheim.

Once more it is tempting to see the Asams as moving parallel to the new Rococo current rather than depending on imported French ideas as a major source of inspiration—more stimulated, that is, than actually influenced at this point by the work of the Effner circle.

A curious feature is the delicate corona (very like that over the high altar composition at Rohr) which appears to float free of the upper edge of the cove (Pls. 27, 28). To this it is actually attached, however, above each of the eight ribs, by small loosely composed groups of white stucco putti and clouds. Very fragile and metallic in design, this corona (which is actually made of iron like the one at Rohr) forms an inner frame of distinctly Rococo feeling for the ceiling painting above. With its relatively miniscule scale and sparkling terminal sunbursts and three-dimensional stars, this is more like an intricate gold necklace than an element of architectural decoration.

At the middle of the south side Cosmas Damian's own figure, in realistically polychromed stucco, bends over the upper border of the cove below the corona in order to look down into the nave, a charmingly informal and personal note (Pl. 28). Immediately above Cosmas Damian in the fresco Egid Quirin as a young angel and Maurus Bächl as Abbot appear between St. Scholastica and St. Martin, the secondary patron of the church, while to his right St. Maurice is again given the features of Bächl. Both the brothers appear very young, though Cosmas Damian was by then thirty-five and his brother twenty-nine. But the first period of their careers was coming to an end in these years of the opening twenties. Despite the high quality of their earliest work as architectural designers at Weltenburg and at Rohr, the years of their main historical contribution to the creation of a German Rococo style of church architecture had, in the interiors at Aldersbach and at Rohr, barely begun.

Recapitulation

The relation of Cosmas Damian and Egid Quirin Asam's work of the early twenties to the Rococo may be summarized thus: their architecture at Weltenburg and Rohr was still almost wholly Roman Baroque; on the other hand, they were already not only evolving a sort of surface ornamentation, especially at Aldersbach, that was not dissimilar to the Early Rococo lately imported into Bavaria by Paris-trained craftsmen but were also introducing some motifs of decoration, at least, that were more probably of French than of Italian or even Austrian[59] origin. Their use of these motifs was, however, still quite incidental.

More significant for the mature German Rococo of later decades was a conspicuous feature of the Asams' church interiors for which there was no current French precedent except in the Versailles chapel: that is, the great enlargement of the frescoed area over the nave, projected at Rohr and carried out at Aldersbach.[60] Characteristic is the employment of a very large panel of fresco on the vault, confined by a stucco frame in relief that may be loosely described as scalloped, and carried through several bays. Curiously enough, however, frescoes framed thus find no place in the Asams' work of the middle years of the twenties at Innsbruck, Freising and Einsiedeln, though all three do have extensive fresco-paintings on the vaults. Almost certainly, this feature had appeared for the first time in a big German church over the choir, rather than over the nave, at Aldersbach, though such scalloped frescoes already existed in the chapel at Pommersfelden (Pl. 5) and at Kreuzpullach, as has been noted earlier.

Probably it was the expansive ambitions of Cosmas Damian as painter, anxious to emulate what he had admired in Rome, that led in the joint work of the brothers to the increase in the extent of the fresco areas rather than the influence of Egid Quirin as sculptor-become-stuccoer wishing to diminish the amount of stucco decoration on ceilings. It must not be forgotten, however, that the latter had been primarily trained as a sculptor, not a stuccoer, during his study with Faistenberger that immediately preceded his debut with his brother at Michelfeld, if not already in Rome. Certainly Egid Quirin had had none of that special craft training, beginning at fourteen or soon thereafter, that such contemporaries as the brothers Zimmermann and the brothers Schmuzer, with their Wessobrunn background, had experienced and from which they would so notably profit. E. Q. Asam's interest, particularly at Rohr and at Weltenburg—and presumably earlier at Michelfeld—must have centred on the figural sculpture. Even the apparent touches of true Rococo influence in the decorative stucco-work at Aldersbach may well have been dependent on preliminary designs by this brother.

Fürstenfeldbruck and St. Jakobi, Innsbruck

It was probably in 1722 that C. D. Asam began the frescoes on the vault of the choir of the church of the Cistercian Abbey of Fürstenfeldbruck, outside Fürstenfeld near Munich, where his father long before had worked on the monastery. Construction had actually been begun by Viscardi in 1701—the cornerstone was laid on 5 August.[61] After Viscardi's death in 1713 and the ending of the War of the Spanish Succession activity was renewed. The old church was demolished in 1716–17 and the new one gradually brought to completion by Ettenhofer, who took charge in 1718. Thus the architectural responsibility was much the same as at the Dreifaltigkeitskirche in Munich where C. D. Asam had worked seven or eight years before. This time, however, the stuccoer was not Bader as in Munich but the elderly P. F. Appiani, who had been responsible for the *stucchi* at Freystadt where the Asams had assisted their father in 1708–10. He began the decoration of the choir in 1718 and, with Asam's help, completed it in 1723. Not surprisingly, the areas assigned to the frescoes are small and their shapes approximately rectangular, so that the result is retardataire for this date though the stucco-work is rather delicate in scale and exceptionally rich.

Much more in the way of novelty might have been expected of another commission of the years 1722–23, when the two brothers were employed together to decorate St. Jakobi, the parish church of Innsbruck in the Austrian Tyrol. This interior is handsomer than the choir of Fürstenfeldbruck, despite the considerable damage the church received from bombing in 1944 and the succeeding restoration completed in 1950, but it does not carry the present story much further forward. St. Jakobi was designed by the Bavarian architect J. J. Herkomer (1652–1717) in the year of his death. The work was carried to structural completion by his nephew and assistant, J. G. Fischer (1673–1747), probably with very little change, and consecrated in 1724 after the completion of the decoration the previous year, though the nine altars, the organ, and the pulpit were installed only over the following five years.[62]

In plan[63] the church has five successive bays, with shallow recesses between the tall wall-pillars in the two bays of the nave. Semicircular transepts flank the crossing bay and, following a slightly narrower choir with loges on either side, there is a shallow rectangular apse. Rather exceptionally, the choir bay (which is square) and not the crossing carries a high dome on a tall drum with windows, so that the east end of the church is flooded with light from above. The other three bays are oblong and covered with transverse handkerchief vaults, that is, low oval domes on continuous pendentives. Nor are the nave and crossing dark, for the side chapels of the nave have large oculi over the altars and there is ample clerestory lighting from above, while each of the transept apses has three tall, rectangular windows.

The nave of St. Jakobi, at least, is not unnaturally quite similar to that of Herkomer's St. Mang at Füssen (Pl. 80) across the mountains in Bavaria, begun in 1701 and not complete as regards the decoration when St. Jakobi was designed, even though the recesses between the wall-pillars, in both cases carrying strongly tectonic pilaster clusters, are much shallower at Innsbruck. This resemblance extends to the basic scheme of decoration, a scheme perhaps hard to avoid in a church consisting of a series of domed bays separated by ribs—here distinctly bolder in section than at Füssen—since there could be no extension of the fresco areas over more than single bays in either case. In the tradition going back in these parts at least to H. G. Asam's choir at Tegernsee of some thirty years earlier (Pl. 16), all the frescoes are round, at Innsbruck as also at Füssen, but in St. Jakobi oval rather than circular except for that on the full dome over the choir. All, moreover, are firmly framed. The decorative stucco-work by Egid Quirin in St. Jakobi is confined to the intradoses of the ribs, both transverse and longitudinal, to the pendentives, and to the choir-arch beyond the crossing. The Asams owed the Innsbruck commission to the priest there, Franz Christoph Mörl, the brother of Cosmas Damian's wife, and negotiations started in the autumn of 1721.[64] But the church was by then structurally complete, and they would have had little more to say about the total design of the interior than Cosmas Damian and Franz Schmuzer had at Weingarten four years earlier.

Except in the choir of St. Jakobi, where relatively large figural frescoes overlap the archivolts, stucco-framed cartouches occupy all the pendentives (Pl. 42). Those in the western bay of the nave and the crossing are of irregular shape, with bold scrolls flanking their tops, while those in the second bay of the nave have rather plain oval frames, like oil paintings, though they are actually filled with frescoes *en camaïeu*. Notable is the relative profusion of figural elements. Putti with inscribed banderoles float above the bottom of the pendentives in the first bay of the nave and are even more prominent at the sides of the oval medallions in the second bay. Firm as are the confining mouldings, the fresco in the westernmost bay does spill out of its frame a bit just above the organ. Palmette motifs, moreover, at the tops of the cartouches and more complicated ornaments including human heads and floral garlands freely break across the frames of the frescoes in all the bays of the nave and crossing. If the details do not have the metallic crispness of the ornament on the lower dome at Weltenburg (Pl. 27), the execution is none the less of a higher order of excellence than E. Q. Asam's work of some two to three years earlier at Aldersbach and Rohr (Pls. 35, 38).

Though the present colour dates from the post-war restoration, it is certainly very attractive and not unplausible. Pink scagliola gives delicate strength, in the Baroque way, to the recurrent pilaster clusters; gilt highlights their white capitals. 'Gold' *mosaïque*, moreover, fills the grounds of much of the stucco-work above the cornice level, though the raised decoration is all white. Yet the total effect today is on the whole considerably more remote from the mature Rococo than are the interior of Aldersbach or the vaults of Rohr, which is rather surprising considering the later date.

Over C. D. Asam's frescoes in St. Jakobi it is unnecessary to linger.[65] They were heavily if tactfully restored in 1947, while the lunette over the altar was then filled with a completely new painting by H. André, replacing one which was in any case not by Asam. The dependence on Pozzo is more consistent here than earlier; as a result the illusionistic spatial effects overhead are solidly Baroque with no Rococo airiness (Pl. 42). But the pace of the Asams' development towards the Rococo, particularly that of E. Q. Asam as stuccoer, would now increase. Well before the work at St. Jakobi was completed the brothers had started on the first of their commissions to which the term 'Early Rococo' may not improperly be applied. This was the redecoration of Freising Cathedral.

Freising

The See of Freising, a town just north of Munich, was in effect the metropolitan diocese of Bavaria since it included Munich, the electoral capital. Today the Bishop of Freising is also Bishop of Munich, but there was no See of Munich in the eighteenth century. The commission, therefore, carried more prestige than any C. D. Asam had had since his early selection to execute the frescoes in the Munich Dreifaltigkeitskirche.[66] But the commission was a difficult one.[67] No new church was to be built; instead the structure of the medieval church of 1164–1205 was to be retained. This had been vaulted in 1481–82 and provided with outer aisles and galleries over the inner aisles in 1619–21, not to speak of a new high altar in 1624 with a painting by no less an artist than Rubens.[68] Moreover, the cloister to the east had been redecorated with frescoes and stucco-work by J. B. Zimmermann in 1716. Now the Prince-Bishop J. F. Ecker von Kapfing und Lichteneck, who had consecrated C. D. Asam's church at Weltenburg five years before, determined to renew the interior in preparation for the *Säkularfeier* planned for 1724 in honour of the 1000th anniversary of the founding of the church by St. Corbinian and the 50th of his own priesthood, and called on the Asams, rather than J. B. Zimmermann and his architect-brother Dominikus, to transform the interior.

For remodelling a medieval church interior, a treatment that emphasized continuity of surface and minimized tectonic or structural features was obviously more viable than one that attempted to create a convincingly Baroque architectural effect. This the Asams seem to have been the first to essay successfully at Freising some years before the Rococo was consistently employed in Germany even for large secular halls, much less for churches. The interiors in Franconia at Pommersfelden, Ebrach and Ellingen mentioned earlier[69] are hardly to be considered more than proto-Rococo; while the larger rooms at Schleissheim—except for the stair-hall and the chapel, little if at all earlier than Freising—are even more definitely Late Baroque, despite certain minor novelties in the membering, the ornaments and, most notably, Pichler's *boiseries* in the Viktoriensaal.

At Freising, as already at Aldersbach, the vaults are for the greater part undivided by transverse ribbing. Thus a broader and more varied visual rhythm could be created overhead in sharp contrast to the dozen identical bays of the exceptionally long nave-arcades below (Pls. 45, 46). One very large fresco of the Glorification of St. Corbinian, apostle to the Bavarians and first Bishop of Freising, unifies the vault surfaces of the fifth, sixth and seventh bays from the west. This C. D. Asam handled not as at Aldersbach—that is, with a scalloped stucco frame—but very much in the manner of Bacciccia's ceiling in the Gesù in Rome, which had possibly influenced already his principal fresco at Weingarten four or five years earlier. Many of the figures to the north-west and south-east spill down out of the illusionistic space of the fresco over the firm, though richly be-garlanded, painted frame into the real space of the church (Pl. 43). Set off by shallow rib-bands to east and west that are, as already at Rohr, more decorative than structural, the next pair of bays to east and to west are each visually merged into a unit in the vaulting by a large, approximately oval, fresco panel out of which again some figures overflow the slightly scalloped frame.

The two westernmost bays at Freising received a similar treatment as did the two easternmost bays in front of the high altar. But the two bays of the choir west of the sanctuary became a sort of 'crossing' that exists only in paint (Pl. 46). *Quadratura* architecture, as already in the choir at Weingarten and, just before this, over the crossing in St. Jakobi, Innsbruck, creates the illusion of a tall dome rising above the Madonna Enthroned such as actually existed over the crossing at Weingarten and over the choir at Innsbruck. What is new here is the way the regular procession of clerestory windows, over which the small cross-vaults cut elsewhere into the base of the continuous barrel of the nave vault (Pl. 47), is interrupted by the illusion of broad segmental lunettes painted on the lower edges of the here unbroken barrel-vault at each side.

Most of the devices employed in the new organization of the vault surface at Freising are still in the Baroque tradition. In their earlier use by C. D. Asam, moreover, these devices had continued to be appropriate elements in an interior architecture that remained Baroque. Here the situation was so different, however, because of the inherited plan and structural system, that they could not produce a plausible Baroque entity. With further modifications, especially as regards ovalized planning and new ways of framing ceiling frescoes—the most important, that already introduced into large-scale church-architecture by the Asams at Aldersbach—many of these novelties at Freising would later become integral elements in mature German Rococo interiors. To the Freising interior as remodelled, on the other hand, there are hardly any eighteenth-century French parallels in executed church interiors.[70]

It is the decorative dissolution of the pseudo-tectonic elements on the nave walls at Freising and the relative delicacy of the ornament on both the nave walls and the subsidiary curved vault surfaces around and below the frescoes (Pls. 43–46) that most closely parallel, if they do not actually emulate, the secular French Rococo that had for some years been gradually infiltrating Bavaria. The panelling of pilaster surfaces, especially conspicuous here because of the coloured scagliola used in the panels, not to speak of the drastic modification of the Corinthian capitals, was not a peculiarity of the Rococo. Originally ancient Roman, such variations on the orders were quite as characteristic of the Italian Quattrocento and by no means unknown in the freer Baroque tradition of such seventeenth-century Italians as Borromini and Guarini. But the special treatment of the broad and shallow pilasters here removes from them almost all their usual slight but real tectonic weight, despite the forward breaks in the entablature above, to a considerably greater extent than at Aldersbach. (In any case Magzin rather than the Asams may well have been responsible there.) The *ressauts* at Freising, moreover, have the actual effect of diminishing the visual weight of the entablature as a continuous horizontal element, quite as does the overlapping of the architrave in between by the broken-curved extradoses of the tribune arches, a treatment already used—though in a more restrained way—above the nave arcade at Rohr (Pls. 34, 46).

The panels of scagliola on the pilaster surfaces, curved top and bottom and broken off in the middle where a cusped oval is inserted, follow at two to three times the usual scale the treatment that had for a decade or more been characteristic for tall narrow panels in French Rococo interiors (Pl. 46). Pichler, who had already used such in the Pagodenburg and in the Schloss at Nymphenburg, was at this very point introducing them in the Viktoriensaal at Schleissheim. The Corinthianesque capitals, moreover, are elaborated to a degree rarely found in the early eighteenth century in France—if indeed they were retained there at all—at the heads of the vertical 'pilasters' subdividing the wall panelling. Here they are broken at the bottom in response to the curved and shell-crowned top of the panel below, while their foliage spreads upward over the architrave of the entablature blocks. The ornamented frieze curves inward in a cyma to reduce the projection of the cornice below the vaulting (Pl. 44).

Exceptionally, this church has tribunes or galleries over the inner aisles that had been added, as was noted earlier, in 1619–21. Therefore no broad blank surfaces had to be coped with between the nave arcade and the clerestory as in most other remodelled medieval churches (Pl. 43). But the wall surfaces above the very plain arches, effectively the parapets of the tribunes, received a treatment very similar to that used for the relief panels, presumably of two years earlier, on the cove at Weltenburg, the only arguably Rococo element of a date earlier than the thirties in that interior. These carry rectangular panels frescoed with scenes from the life of St. Corbinian that are very like the over-doors common in French secular interiors of this period (Pl. 48). Their moulded frames are not only broken by scrolling at the corners and in the centres of the tops but are also overlapped below by the pairs of putti that ride the archivolts of the nave arcade. These putti hold the ends of lettered scrolls, somewhat as over the choir-arch at Rohr. Still more characteristic of the Early Rococo is the panel-like framing used in the intradoses of the tribune arches. These, unlike the ones below in the nave arcade, have no imposts (Pl. 46).

Richer and less French—though approaching the Rococo in relative delicacy of scale and much less clumsy in execution than at Aldersbach—is the ornament on the severies that penetrate the base of the main vault over the clerestory windows; but the paraboloid arrises of the vaulting conoids are still moulded with a vigour that is more Baroque than either Late Gothic or Rococo (Pl. 44). Only in the tribunes do the curving lines of the stucco mouldings ignore the geometry of the cross-vaults they decorate in what one must consider a more truly Rococo way (Pls. 47, 49).

The decoration of these vaults deserves rather detailed analysis. Though they play no part in the general scheme of the monumental nave interior, in the freedom and delicacy of their scrolled and interlaced stucco-work the tribunes present the most advanced aspect of the Asams' work at Freising. The flattened vaults cover passages brilliantly lighted by windows of special curved shape that open over the roofs of the outer aisles (Pl. 47). Thanks to their modest height the scale is almost domestic yet the decoration is, if anything, richer than in the nave. There is no regular division of that decoration into individual bays. As has been noted, moreover, the strongest of the mouldings are very freely curved and do not follow the structural arrises of the severies at the sides. Rather, they are a continuation of the scalloped outer frames of the frescoes. Since these mouldings do not meet at the centre of the vault (Pl. 49) but end in reverse scrolls breaking into rich foliage, the frescoes have also a light inner frame—or liner, as one would say of an oil painting—decorated with very slender bandwork elaborated with scrolls and tendrils that occasionally overlap the surface of the frescoes. This inner bandwork, repeated also on the vault surfaces in the bays which have no frescoes, is the most distinctly Rococo element of the entire decorative scheme.

As in the nave, the regular structural rhythm of the vaults is rephrased by the longitudinal extension of the frescoed panels, each of which spreads out from a single bay over half a bay to east and to west (Pl. 47). In the twelve bays of the total length there are three frescoes separated by unfrescoed bays and two bays also without frescoes at either end. It is clear, I think, that the decorators' ideal for these galleries would have been shorter—and perhaps somewhat taller—spatial elements only five bays long, still quite longitudinal but closer in proportion to the spaces in most major secular interiors of the day.[71]

The stuccoed ceilings by J. B. Zimmermann over the Kammerkapelle in the Electress's suite at Schleissheim and over the library at Benediktbeuern may properly be compared with the ceiling decoration in the tribune at Freising. Not surprisingly, both are closer to the French Rococo than is the Asams' work.[72] Paintings set in scalloped frames, a little like Cosmas Damian's at Aldersbach but much smaller, are included only at Benediktbeuern. Both, moreover, are essentially secular: relatively low rooms with slightly coved, flat ceilings, not tall vaulted spaces like most of the great German church interiors the Asams and others would be redecorating, not to speak of the new churches built over the next thirty or forty years. Thus it is the Asams' work at Freising, rather than J. B. Zimmermann's of probably a year or two later, that should be considered as opening the story of the native German Rococo along lines initiated already on the vaults of Rohr and Aldersbach.

The Asams were now well launched on their career as the leading church decorators of the twenties and thirties. So much were they appreciated at Freising that the bishop not only made Cosmas Damian his court painter (*Hofmaler*) and

Egid Quirin his stuccoer (*Hofstukkateur*), but both of them *Kammerdiener* as well in 1724. C. D. Asam's acquisition in that year of a modest estate at Thalkirchen just outside Munich is evidence, moreover, of his personal prosperity.[73] Egid Quirin began to acquire house property only five years later, but in greater quantity and inside the city. The most relevant mark of general esteem is the fact that in this year 1724 the two brothers were again called on to work, as a few years before in the parish church at Innsbruck, outside Germany, this time for a very large and important abbey in Switzerland.

Einsiedeln

Despite the fact that the monks had all gone over to the Protestant leader Zwingli in the early sixteenth century, the Benedictine Abbey of Einsiedeln, not far from Zürich, founded by the Reichenau monk St. Meinrad in the ninth century, had flourished after its refounding in 1536 under an abbot from St. Gallen. In the seventeenth and eighteenth centuries it became a popular pilgrimage shrine, thanks to its *Gnadenbild*—a fifteenth-century Madonna and Child carved in wood, with faces long blackened by age and garments of real fabric. Though built and rebuilt from the ninth century onwards, today only the lower part of the structure of the two-storied choir of this church—built in 1674–80 by H. G. Kuen (1642–91), an architect from Bregenz on the Bodensee—antedates the eighteenth century.

The vast monastery, almost a Swiss Escorial, was rebuilt in 1704–19[74] to the plans of Brother Caspar Moosbrugger, born in 1656 at Au in the Austrian Vorarlberg, who had become a monk at Einsiedeln in 1682.[75] Next began the building of a new church, for which Moosbrugger had been making successive plans since he first came to Einsiedeln. The execution was in the hands of Michael II Rüf (b. 1667), Moosbrugger's brother-in-law, and later of Michael's cousin Johann II Rüf (1686–1750).[76] The church has a most peculiar plan (Fig. 3). The nave might be considered to be of three bays, but both the first and the second bays are exceptional in character. That at the west end of the church is a sort of octagon, in the centre of

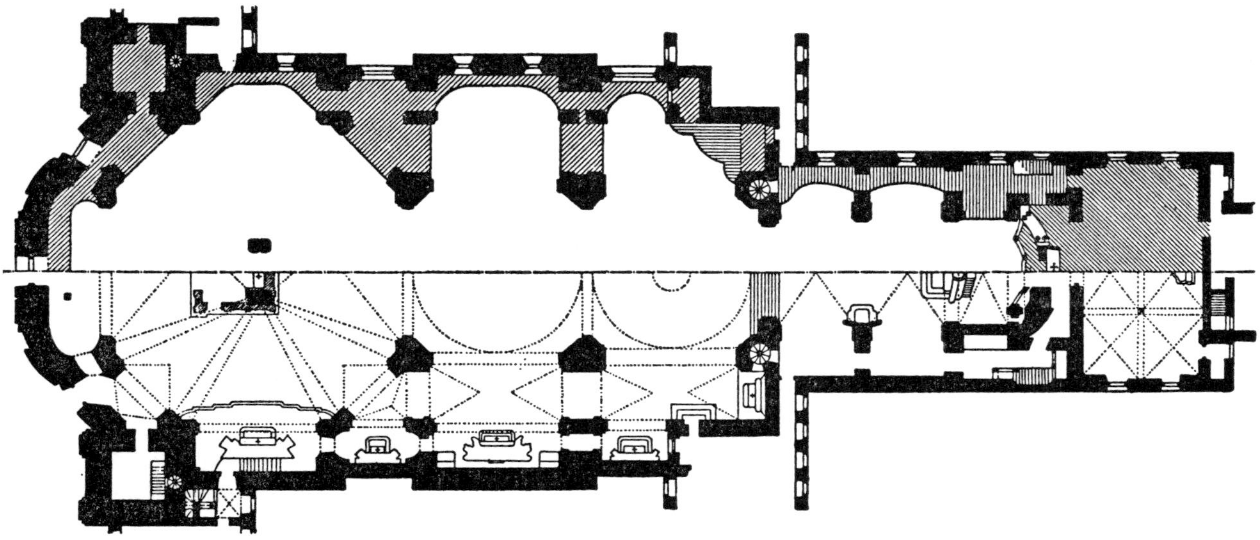

Fig. 3. Einsiedeln, Abbey Church. Plan

which stands the chapel containing the *Gnadenbild*. This is externally of dark grey marble and was thus encased in 1617 by Santino Solari. In 1798, however, the French invaders demolished the chapel. In 1815–17 it was rebuilt a third smaller, using the original materials, by Joseph Singer of Lucerne from designs by the monk Jakob IV Natter (1735–1815) as modified by Luigi Cagnola (1762–1833) from Milan. The rather plain and slick blackish forms of this prominent object, though eye-arresting, are completely out of accord with the sumptuous setting, all white and gold and pink,[77] which the Asams provided in the 1720s (Pl. 53).

One usually speaks of this area as octagonal. Actually it is prolonged transversely; and at its centre not one but two square piers rise over the *Gnadenbild* chapel to carry the inner ends of the radial ribs of the vaulting (Pl. 53). Although there are only very shallow aisles, the wide eastern diagonals of this space are open and connect with the next bay of the nave (Pl. 52). That is, in fact, a sort of crossing with heavy piers set diagonally below a saucer dome and transeptal arms at the sides (Pl. 54). The bay beyond this has side projections also, although somewhat shorter ones, and was to have been capped with a tall pointed dome. To add further to the spatial confusion there is the three-bayed upper choir, considerably narrower than the nave since it is on top of Kuen's lower choir which was retained. This upper choir was rebuilt in 1746 and decorated with stucco-work, reputedly following E. Q. Asam's designs, by Franz Kraus (1716–52), an artist from Augsburg who also redecorated the lower choir at that time and even provided the frescoes there. The frescoes in the upper choir by Giuseppe Torricelli (1716–1808) from Lugano and his twin brother Giovan Antonio were executed in 1748–50.[78]

There are also galleries on either side of the nave. These begin around the octagon and continue across the ends of the transepts of the second bay and along the outer walls of the aisles of the third bay. They also subdivide vertically the arched openings behind the piers separating the second and third bays of the nave (Pls. 51, 54).

As the attempt to describe the organization of the church in simple terms should have made evident, the result has a three-dimensional complexity that a plan can hardly make clear (Fig. 3). This spatial maze is visually more comparable to the illusionistic architecture of the Bibbienas' stage scenery—or even to the ambiguity of Piranesi's *Carceri*—than to space-composition in the main Baroque line of descent from the Renaissance. The interior of Einsiedeln is best appreciated, therefore, when seen in diagonal views without any attempt to establish in the mind's eye a true picture of the actual plan and the continually changing transverse sections. To this effect of gorgeous theatrical profusion the contributions of the two Asams notably added.

It was in the octagon that they began work on 19 February 1724, after Moosbrugger's death the previous year, according to an arrangement that provided, as regards the decoration in the octagon alone, 4,400 gulden for Cosmas Damian's frescoes (with provision for two helpers) and 2,200 for Egid Quirin's stucco-work (with provision for five helpers).[79] The decoration of the two further bays of the nave, the transepts, and the aisles was completed by the Asams in 1726. By that time C. D. Asam, without his brother, was already at work in Bohemia in the big Gothic church Giovanni Santini (1667–1723) had remodelled and extended at

Kladruby, beginning in 1712, and—just possibly—within a year or two elsewhere in those parts as well.[80]

Because of a series of restorations of the interior of Einsiedeln, in 1839–40, in 1909–11 and in 1954–55, there must be some doubt as to the authenticity of certain features of the decoration. The moulded ornament on the pilaster shafts, for example, based on that on the sides of the piers at Aldersbach but considerably richer, is said to be the work of the stuccoers Zotz and Griessl from Zug who were employed in the restoration of 1909–10. Less because of the definite increase in specific Rococo elements—as in the detailing of the vault surfaces over and under the galleries, or the bandwork on the broad and flat intradoses of the ribs—than because of the delicacy, the crispness, and above everything else the profusion of the stucco decoration, the overall effect may seem at first sight almost saturatedly Rococo in a way that the more coherently handled interior at Freising is clearly not (Pls. 45, 54). Such an initial impression, however, is soon modified when the stucco-work and the frescoes are examined more closely.

The Asams' Einsiedeln Rococo (so to call it) is, at the least, distinctly more Germanic than the Asams' Freising Rococo. Comparison with J. B. Zimmermann's almost precisely contemporary ceiling in the Kammerkapelle at Schleissheim, more properly Rococo and also distinctly French in its small scale, its refined elegance, and its gold-on-white bichromy, or with the more original ceiling in the library he decorated in 1725 at Benediktbeuern suggests how much assurance E. Q. Asam still lacked as a post-Baroque stuccoer. One must not forget that he had, unlike Zimmermann, no direct and continuing contact with the Paris-trained craftsmen of the Effner circle; he had also missed, as has been noted several times before, that early training in decorative stucco-work which the Zimmermanns and the Schmuzers of his generation had experienced in their youth at Wessobrunn.

Such comparisons may further suggest, on the other hand, that E. Q. Asam did gain something, as regards the evolution of German Rococo interior architecture, from his independent artistic situation. For one thing, from his background of study in Baroque Rome and from his earlier work in architectural design at Rohr, just reaching completion as regards the sculpture on the altar the year before he came to Einsiedeln, he carried over a more architectonic sense of scale. By this time, moreover, his stucco-work had come to have something of the gusto of his Berninian altars at Rohr and Weltenburg. That is a quality one fails to find in J. B. Zimmermann's much more sophisticated work of these years. (It was to be present a decade or more later, however, from the interiors of the Amalienburg [Pl. 133] he stuccoed in the mid-thirties forward to his latest *stucchi* of the fifties in the Nymphenburg Festsaal.[80a]) But there is also in E. Q. Asam's decorations at Einsiedeln something still of the robust clumsiness of Aldersbach. This may have been an almost necessary ingredient, moreover, if the Rococo in Germany was to develop from a mode suitable primarily for elegant private apartments in Parisian *hôtels particuliers* to a style that could become almost at once—and would remain for centuries—literally popular. That the simple pilgrims who flock to such shrines as Einsiedeln and the Zimmermann's Steinhausen have never ceased to delight in them is evident to this day.

The artistic responsibilities of the Asams at Einsiedeln were certainly less complete than at Freising. The octagon was only completed in the rough when Moosbrugger died on 26 August 1723, almost six months before they were commissioned, but work on the church was proceeding under the direction of the Rüfs.[81] Even though the construction was not as far advanced when the Asams came on the scene here, the situation was not unlike that they had just faced at Innsbruck, where J. G. Fischer had largely finished St. Jakobi from his uncle's designs before they were called in. Moosbrugger left complete designs for the church and it can be assumed that the Rüfs—Michael and later Johann—carried these out except for the intended tall dome over the easternmost bay of the nave. There would have been no occasion here, as at St. Jakobi, to provide additional enrichments for mouldings already executed. The architectural elements of the interior, so much heavier and more conventionally Baroque than at Freising, must be of Moosbrugger's rather than the Asams' design. On the other hand, the very great size of Cosmas Damian's frescoes, filling the main vault surfaces more completely than at Weingarten, St. Jakobi or Freising, may well have been decided on only after consultation with him. As a result little room was left for stucco-work on the main vaults and none at all in the cardinal sectors of the vaulting of the octagon (Pl. 51). On the vault of the second bay of the nave small rhomboidal panels at the base of the pendentives carry stuccoed cartouches though only moulded elliptical frames around insets painted *en camaïeu* were used in the corners of the vault in the third bay (Pl. 50).

These ovals, and the boldly scrolled and scalloped extrados of the choir-arch, which is also executed in stucco, recall St. Jakobi, as does the *quadratura* architecture of the setting of the frescoed Last Supper in the second bay. More novel in Asam's frescoes, but not very happy, is the heavy painted architectural scroll-work at the base of the Nativity in the third bay, one of the richest and most varied of his productions. In this the composition builds up tonally rather than plastically from various relatively dark earthly scenes at the base of the brilliantly lighted figure of God the Father on the domelet of the lantern (Pl. 50).

In terms of decoration, of the close collaboration of painter and stuccoer, the most interesting effects are in the octagon. There cloud-backed figures in fresco stream out asymmetrically across the double rib-bands that frame the eight parts of the vault and over the stuccoed surfaces of the oblique compartments beyond (Pl. 53). But in general one may say that the settings of the frescoes here are much less advanced than over the tribunes at Freising or even in the choir and nave of Aldersbach (Pls. 38, 49).

In considering the stucco decoration at Einsiedeln it is evident that the closest approach to the Rococo is to be found on the vaults of the peripheral areas, the aisles, and the tribunes over them (Pls. 51–54). The membering of the piers remains tectonic despite the very free handling of the pilaster capitals. (The outlining of the pilaster shafts, and perhaps also some of the ornament on the elements of the entablature, is very likely of 1909–10, as has been noted.) The Wren-like segmental arches in the diagonal bays of the octagon, recalling St. Paul's in London, which are repeated above the tribunes in the transeptal arms of the second bay, as also the more freely curved 'horns', likewise consisting only of the cornice member of the vigorously tectonic entablature, above the diagonal piers of the second bay, seem more probably of Moosbrugger's or Rüf's than of E. Q. Asam's invention (Pl. 52). They do, however, provide convenient perches for some of the most charming of his angels. Between them are set delicately festive near-Rococo urns very similar to those—there cherub-flanked—that crown the segmental cornices of the openings in the transepts and the diagonal bays of the octagon. That is a motif Egid Quirin would exploit more conspicuously at St. Emmeram in Regensburg nearly a decade later (Pl. 64).

But it is the treatment of the vault surfaces in the tribunes, as at Freising, that comes closest to the French-inspired stucco-work of J. B. Zimmermann's library ceiling at Benediktbeuern and justifies the general conclusion that the interior of Einsiedeln lies halfway between the late Baroque and the Rococo,[82] partly because of the architectural ordonnance inherited from Moosbrugger, partly because of the moderation with which E. Q. Asam was at this point moving towards the mature Rococo.

C. D. Asam's frescoes executed in churches and chapels where his brother was not called on to provide the stuccos—those of 1726–27 that have been mentioned in Bohemia and those of 1728 which, before bombing, occupied the ceilings of the chapel in the Schloss at Mannheim in the Palatinate and the one at Bruchsal in Baden[83]—can be ignored here. The client at Mannheim was the Elector Palatine Carl Philipp and, at Bruchsal, Damian Hugo Cardinal Schönborn, Prince-Bishop of Speyer and Konstanz. Carl Philipp was a Wittelsbach related to the Bavarian electors; Damian Hugo was the only member of the other great building family of the day to employ one of the Asams—the other Schönborns usually sent to Vienna for their painters as Lothar Franz had done at Pommersfelden.

Heilig-Geist, Munich

The decoration in 1727 of Heilig-Geist in Munich—a late Gothic church whose drastic remodelling had been completed shortly before by Ettenhofer, C. D. Asam's associate at the Dreifaltigkeitskirche in Munich in 1715–16 and again at Fürstenfeldbruck in 1722–23—and of the new church of St. Anna-am-Lehel, built by J. M. Fischer in Munich in 1727–29, proceeded quite directly from the many joint commissions to decorate old and new churches, both of their own and of other architects' design, on which the brothers had been recurrently employed since they first assisted their father at Freystadt twenty years before. That was hardly so true of the two moderate-sized palace chapels in the west of Germany at Bruchsal and Mannheim where Cosmas Damian worked in the late 1720s.

By that time, however, the brothers were being called on more often than earlier[84] to work in the Bavarian capital. Egid Quirin had apparently had no commissions at all in Munich until he became involved with a project for the high altar of St. Peter in 1723 of which he supplied a model two years later. This came to partial execution only in 1732 and Asam's four Fathers of the Church survive. His first executed commission in Munich seems to have been for Heilig-Geist, where Cosmas Damian's frescoes were dated 1727 and signed, curiously enough, by both brothers as 'Maller' (painter) and 'Pildhauer' (sculptor)—not 'Stuckador' as Dominikus Zimmermann described himself a few years later at Steinhausen—but see below.

Heilig-Geist was a late fourteenth-century church much modified in the mid-seventeenth century by the addition of side aisles and a deep choir.[85] On its site it had been proposed in 1710 to erect the Dreifaltigkeitskirche. Later, in 1723 or 1724, Dr. Josef Pachinger, who had become the parish priest in 1722, employed Ettenhofer to undertake a remodelling that almost amounted to total reconstruction. The aisles were raised to the same height as the nave, forming a hall-church, and above the entablature blocks of the slim pilaster-faced piers high-stilted cross vaults without ribs were built (Pl. 55). It was on the flattish upper portions of these vaults that C. D. Asam's frescoes were painted, while the lower vault surfaces, the tops of the pilaster shafts, and the aisle window-heads were richly decorated with stucco-work. Of the six original bays of the nave—the three to the west were added by Franz Löwel in 1885—the second, third and fourth were linked, in the manner of Aldersbach, by a single very large fresco in a scalloped stucco frame. Smaller fresco-panels occupied the remaining vault surfaces of the nave, the aisles, and the choir. The *stucchi*, remarkable for the curious and varied pelmet-like decoration below the quite conventional pilaster capitals, and the frescoes were mostly destroyed by bombing in 1944. Some of the pilaster tops, notably those in the aisles, survive and also much of the decoration that surrounds the scalloped window-heads in the aisles. This flows freely upwards over the architrave into the frieze of the entablature along the side walls. There is little question of considering this interior *architecturally* Rococo or even proto-Rococo; it can barely be called Baroque! The entablature blocks and even the pilaster capitals, moreover, seem to be entirely of Ettenhofer's design and uninfluenced by the Asams.

The other stucco-work, executed not by E. Q. Asam but by Matthias Schmidtgartner, raises critical problems. In its crisp delicacy and in the way it overlaps formal architectural elements above the windows in the aisles, it seems well in advance of most of the stucco decoration at Einsiedeln, the earliest portion of which (in the octagon) it postdates by three years. Should we attribute this to Schmidtgartner, or does E. Q. Asam's signature as 'Pildhauer' on the fresco indicate, as is generally supposed, that he was the responsible designer though not the executant?

St. Anna-am-Lehel, Munich

However that may be, the same problem does not exist in the other Munich church of the late 1720s in which both the Asams worked. At St. Anna-am-Lehel the uncertain element concerns not attribution but priority in relation to the brothers' work with the same architect at Osterhofen. The architects with whom the Asam brothers had worked most closely up to this time—Ettenhofer, Magzin and the Rüfs[86]—were, on the whole, secondary or even tertiary figures except where they themselves functioned as architects at Weltenburg, Rohr and Freising. Now they came in contact, almost at the outset of his career, with J. M. Fischer. Born in 1692, the same year as E. Q. Asam, Fischer was considerably younger than C. D. Asam or the two Zimmermanns. He was destined, however, to be one of the very greatest and, in church work at least, the most prolific of eighteenth-century German architects. To the splendour of Osterhofen,[87] his first major work, the Asams contributed notably. It is their contribution, indeed, that makes it the rival of the Zimmermanns' Steinhausen, built and decorated over the same years of the late 1720s and early 1730s, as the first great new church that may be considered Early Rococo.

A discussion of these two early churches by Fischer properly takes its place here rather than in Chapter V because of the crucial importance of their interiors, and most particularly that of Osterhofen, in the early development of Rococo architecture in southern Germany. In Chapter V, where the work of Fischer is considered as a whole, it will be evident that St. Anna and Osterhofen stand somewhat apart from his first independent works—the reconstructed east end of the church of the Benedictine Abbey of Niederaltaich, undertaken in 1724, and the parish church at Kirchham, begun two years later just as the work at Niederaltaich was completed—not merely on account of their advanced decoration but because of their relationship, which would never in his work be so close again, to the churches of Christoph Dientzenhofer in Bohemia and Moravia that Fischer had known in his youth.

The fall of the fifteenth-century vaults of the Romanesque church outside Osterhofen, on the Danube a little below Niederaltaich, led Abbot Joseph Mair of the Premonstratensian abbey, just south of the town at Altenmarkt, to call on Fischer for advice. It was either the Munich *Stadtmaurermeister* (City Master-Mason) Johann Mayr (1677–1731), whose daughter Fischer had married in 1725, or his own contemporary, Mayr's stepson J. B. Gunetzrhainer (1692–1763)—an 'ingenieur' in the *Hofbauamt* (Electoral Office of Works) under Effner since 1715 and, since 1721, an official of some importance as *Hofunterbaumeister* (Deputy Court Architect)—who actually recommended him to the Abbot. But his own father had been a master-mason of some reputation in north-eastern Bavaria; and, in the early twenties, before his independent career began at nearby Niederaltaich, Fischer had supervised for Mayr and Gunetzrhainer the execution of the tower of the church of Heilig-Grab in Deggendorf, on the Danube just above Niederaltaich to the west, and the completion of the big parish church at Schärding, on the Austrian side of the Inn a little above Passau to the east.

Shortly after visiting Osterhofen in late 1726, Fischer informed the Abbot that repair was impossible and offered instead a plan for a wholly new church at an estimated cost of 13,000 gulden (12 December 1726); later, on 5 March 1727, he raised the estimate to 15,000. Construction started in 1727 and was physically complete by 1728, shortly after which the work of decoration by the Asams presumably began. The chronogram over the choir-arch gives the date of completion, presumably of the *stucchi*, as 1731, however. That seems to indicate a two or three-year campaign, which would have been rather long, even considering the great extent and elaboration of the programme. In any case, C. D. Asam's high-altar painting is signed and dated 1732, two of E. Q. Asam's side altars are dated as late as 1734 and 1735, and the church was not consecrated until 1740.

A nearly identical span of years covers the construction and decoration of St. Anna-am-Lehel.[88] Fischer's surviving accounting of 2 May 1734, for sums advanced to C. D. Asam's assistants, covers the years 1727–33. But his early undated plan of this modest church and monastery for the Hieronymites, preserved in the Hauptstaatsarchiv in Munich, may well date—like the lost original projects for Osterhofen—from 1726, the Hieronymites having moved to Munich from an earlier monastery on the Walchensee in 1725. The cornerstone was laid by the new elector, Max Emanuel's son Carl Albrecht, in 1727 and the church was consecrated in 1737, although E. Q. Asam's high altar was not completed until 1739. The crucial date for the decoration, however, is 1729 which appeared, with C. D. Asam's signature, on the fresco that was destroyed, together with all the stucco on the vaults, in the bombardment of 1944. The same date may be accepted as probable for the completion of the stucco decoration by E. Q. Asam. The comparable date of completion for the stucco decoration at Osterhofen would be 1731 as given by the chronogram there.

The relatively small size of St. Anna readily supports the evidence that its decoration was completed two years earlier than that at Osterhofen; yet the modesty of the decorative programme in Munich could equally suggest that it was begun later and carried out much more rapidly. Thus the closer coordination of the decoration in Munich with the architecture might indicate that here Fischer and the Asams were cooperating for the second time and not the first.

On the grounds that the decoration in the Munich church was completed earlier and that it has been almost totally obliterated, though the church has been physically repaired and the diagonal altars in part survive, St. Anna may be discussed first. The somewhat Guarinian plan, recalling that of the Piedmontese architect's chapel in the Archiepiscopal Palace in Turin, probably derives, not from the plates of Guarini's work published in 1686, but rather from Fischer's knowledge of Christoph Dientzenhofer's Pauline abbey church at Obořiště in Bohemia, built in 1702–12, or that at the castle of Smiřice, probably begun by him about 1700 and completed by Santini in 1713.[89] In both of these, near-oval plans were pinched to a dumb-bell-like shape resembling that of the fresco field in the nave of Aldersbach. One or both of them Fischer had presumably seen while he was in Bohemia, as well as—even more certainly—the similar nave of Svatý Mikuláš Malá Strana in Prague, built in 1703–11 by Dientzenhofer. That has, however, a third bulging bay in the centre.

Cosmas Damian's relatively big ceiling fresco in St. Anna had a heavy scalloped frame with an inner gilded roll moulding, richly reeded and garlanded, that fitted down closely over the arches between the six wall-pillars (Pl. 56).[90] The pendentives round this fresco of St. Anne in Glory, like the vaults of the side chapels, were largely filled with gold *mosaïque*, a decorative motif that had probably made its first appearance in the Asams' work about 1720 at Aldersbach or Rohr and was soon being even more profusely employed in the panels on the cove at Weltenburg. Elaborate stucco-work was largely confined to the rich and intricate pilaster capitals (which have happily survived), to the base of the pendentives, and to the extradoses of the arches. But a very large and plastic achievement of the Bavarian electoral arms, somewhat like that at Weltenburg, overlapped slightly the frame of the fresco above the stilted segmental choir-arch. This was polychromed and supported by floating angels reminding us, like those above the 'horns' over the piers at Einsiedeln, that Egid Quirin was primarily a sculptor.

Here, almost as brilliantly as two or three years later in the Zimmermanns' Steinhausen (Pl. 11)—begun at the same time as St. Anna but frescoed only in 1730–31—the painting on the vault illusionistically extended heavenwards the oval cylindrical space defined by the piers. There was, however, no elaborate development of the stucco-work as 'constructed decoration', such as gives prime novelty to Steinhausen.

Osterhofen

But Osterhofen, because of its greater size and richness, is the real rival of Steinhausen among churches of which the decoration was carried out just before or just after 1730. A very large rectangular structure, Osterhofen is essentially a wall-pillar church, of the type long common in southern Germany, with galleries over the side chapels and a fairly deep choir (Fig. 4). This is dominated by a high-altar composition which quite fills the apse, spatially as well as visually, in the manner of the one at Rohr (Pl. 58). But the so-called Vorarlberg scheme is here modified in several ways that are significant for later Rococo architecture in Germany. Most conspicuously, the side walls of the nave are not straight but undulating, the faces of the pillars being concave while the gallery fronts between are convex (Pl. 59). Such an in-and-out effect, found repeatedly in much more assertive and angular form in Guarini's published projects for longitudinal churches, had been introduced in Bohemia by Christoph Dientzenhofer, who used it in the nave of Svatý Mikuláš in Prague, as has been noted earlier, and also at Břevnov nearby in the Benedictine monastery church of Svatá Markétá in 1709–15, which both C. D. Asam and Fischer presumably knew.

Already, however, Johann Dientzenhofer, later the architect of Pommersfelden, a son of Christoph and a younger brother of J. L. (usually known as Leonard) Dientzenhofer (1660-1707), who had been in charge of the rebuilding of the Benedictine monastery at Banz in Franconia until his death, was far advanced with the building of the great church there, which had been begun in 1710 and consecrated in 1719.[91] This is the most probable source for Osterhofen, not because it was rather nearer but because the wide pillars there, halfway along the nave on either

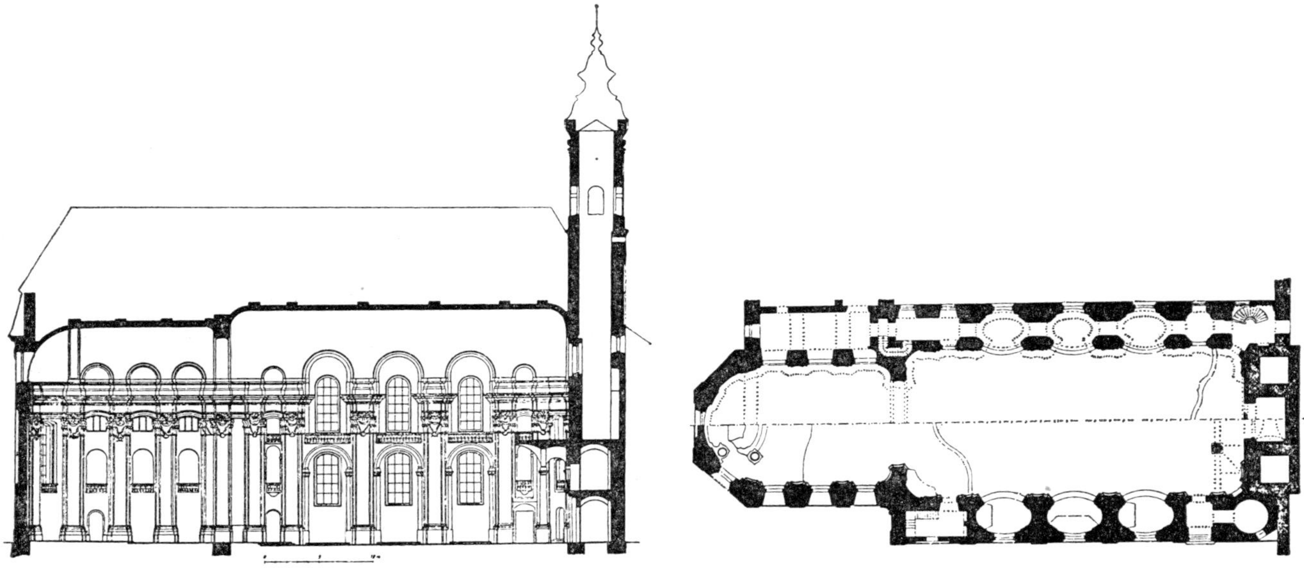

Fig. 4. Osterhofen, Abbey Church. Section and plan

side, are curved in section and concave, whereas in the Bohemian churches, as in most of Guarini's projects, the pillars are angular and convex. The soft undulation of the side walls of the nave at Osterhofen (Fig. 4) is, in fact, un-Guarinian since it minimizes the tectonic articulation generally characteristic of the Turinese architect.[92]

In Fischer's modification of the hitherto straight-sided Vorarlberg plan at Osterhofen, the curved corners at the east and west ends of the nave are equally important for the development towards the Rococo—more important, indeed, as corresponding rather closely to the curved corners often used in early eighteenth-century domestic interiors in France. These quadrants should not be considered Guarinian but Borrominian. They may be traced back at least as far as the vaulting plan of the Roman architect's refectory (now sacristy) in San Carlo alle Quattro Fontane in Rome, although they are more conspicuous in his later church of the Sette Dolori and his chapel of the Re Magi.[93]

But one need not look so far afield for J. M. Fischer's actual models. Even if he is unlikely to have seen the churches in the Allgäu to the south that J. G. Fischer (no relative) had been building since his uncle J. J. Herkomer's death in 1717—several with quadrants at the east end of the nave flanking the choir-arch and one, the modest Feldkirche outside Füssen (Fig. 10) of 1724–25, curved at all four corners—J. M. Fischer may well have known the already mentioned church at Kreuzpullach of about 1710, which likewise has small quadrants in all four corners of the nave. That has even been attributed, rather unplausibly, to Fischer's brother-in-law J. B. Gunetzrhainer—the latter was still less than eighteen years old when it was built—and also to Mayr as well as to Köglsperger. With a later church to the west of Munich, that at Schönbrunn some ten miles north-east of Dachau built in 1723–34, Fischer is even more likely to have been familiar.[94] If this is not by Gunetzrhainer, it is at least likely that Gunetzrhainer executed it from Effner's designs, so that the plans could have been seen by J. M. Fischer, if not the executed building.

Schönbrunn, however, is oval in plan, not a rectangle with corner quadrants and thus actually rather more like two other early churches by J. M. Fischer, those at Kirchham and at Rinchnach.[95] The former was in construction in 1726 before Fischer's first contact with the Osterhofen abbot; the latter was drastically remodelled in 1727, the year Osterhofen was begun, for a Benedictine priory attached to the Abbey of Neideraltaich where Fischer had been working since 1724. Both give even more evidence of Fischer's interest in complex spatial organization than does Osterhofen.

At Kirchham—south of Passau above Austrian Schärding, but on the German side of the Inn—deep niches crowned with semi-elliptical arches house, as at Osterhofen, the altars that flank the very flattened semi-elliptical choir-arch. That curve is repeated in the vault of the choir and also echoed in the shape of the shallow terminal apse. Above the corner niches, the spandrels and the cornices are straight, though at an angle to the rectangle of the nave, not concave as at Kreuzpullach, Schönbrunn and Osterhofen; but overhead the vault is warped into a continuous curved surface that embraces the whole east end of the nave. This configuration is repeated at the west end beyond a short section of elliptical barrel-vault in the central portion of the nave. The present vault is a restoration of 1916 by Franz Rank after a 1914 fire.

At Rinchnach the much deeper corner niches, both to the east and to the west, rise much higher than at Kirchham so that their round arches interrupt the line of the entablature (Fig. 5, Pl. 60). The pilasters and entablature blocks that flank these deep corner niches are, moreover, concave as at Osterhofen, the latter very markedly so. Further curvatures in the plan provide shallower though wider niches on the cross-axis. These curves are more evident in the sharply concave cornice of the *ressauts* of the entablature over the flanking pairs of pilasters—as exaggerated as those at the sides of the corner niches—than in the modest coves above and at the sides of the niches on the cross-axis.

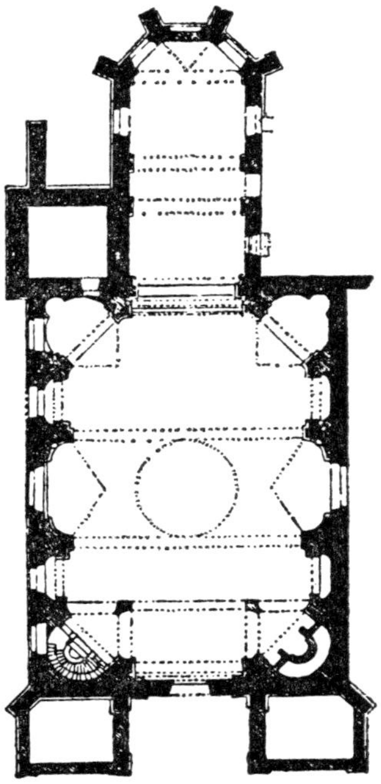

Fig. 5. Rinchnach, Priory Church. Plan

Neither of these churches, of course, rivals Osterhofen in size or in richness of decoration. The stuccoer F. I. Holzinger and the fresco-painter Andreas Haindl, Fischer's collaborators at Rinchnach, both of whom had worked with him earlier at Niederaltaich, were neither of them in a class with the Asams and the decorative work at Kirchham is even feebler and still more provincial. Yet both these early works are, regardless of their relevance to the curved quadrants of the long nave at Osterhofen, more significant than Osterhofen for the main line of Fischer's development—from Unering (Fig. 22), begun in 1730, to Rott-am-Inn (Fig. 28) and Altomünster (Fig. 32), begun respectively in 1759 and 1763—that includes several of his largest and richest churches. He approached the planning of Osterhofen in later life only at Fürstenzell (Pl. 191), where he took over charge of the construction in 1740.

The curvatures in plan at Osterhofen are closely associated with the particular handling of the vaults there and quite different from the more tectonic complexity of the covering of the nave at Rinchnach. There the pointed heads of the severies of the minor cross-vaults above the arches on both the cardinal and the diagonal axes cut sharply into the main curved surfaces overhead much as earlier at Kreuzpullach (Pl. 60). Now the curved elements of the Osterhofen plan serve to adumbrate a rather more novel sort of space. This was a sort of space, however, that had been prefigured on ceilings earlier in the twenties by the scalloped fresco frames at Rohr and Aldersbach, and even more definitely by Waräthi's large fresco over the nave of Metten, as vignetted by F. J. Holzinger's scalloped stucco-work—if that, indeed, antedates Osterhofen. In conformity with the shape and the membering of the nave, the choir at Osterhofen, ending in a rounded apse, is curved in plan at the front corners east of the choir-arch and has close set concave pilaster clusters on the sides (Fig. 4, Pl. 58). In the section one can see, moreover, that the nave ceiling also conforms, for the curve of the corners of the nave to east and west is carried across overhead as a cove (Pl. 57) to terminate the main barrel-vault at each end. Thus this approximates a very much elongated handkerchief vault quite different from the less unified and more conventional vaulting of Kirchham and of Rinchnach.

So rich is the decorative investiture of Osterhofen which the Asams provided that one hardly knows where to begin in describing it. Perhaps it should first be noted that the main ceiling fresco, extending over the three central bays of the nave, is a scalloped rectangle, as at Rohr, rather than a scalloped oval, as at Aldersbach or St. Anna-am-Lehel (Pls. 40, 56, 57). By this time that is hardly novel; but what is novel is the way the ends and sides of the frescoed areas bend, truncate, or are indented by other elements of the decoration. Thus the quadrilobed fresco panels over the bays at the two ends of the nave push east and west, overlapping the transverse coves of the vaulting and also deflecting the very shallow transverse rib-bands on their inner sides (Pl. 57). As a result the latter lose most of their inherited tectonic significance. Analogous indentations in the ends of the frame of the main fresco are also required, thanks to this inward bowing of the rib-bands. Similar rib-bands, likewise almost flush with the vault surface—here wholly of the stuccoer's design, one may assume, and not the architect's—start up from the second and third piers at the sides of the nave, but are cut off by the frame of the main fresco and even mitred to follow its curvature as co-axial outer borders.

Within the fresco itself, which illustrates scenes from the Life of St. Norbert, the founder of the Premonstratensian Order, the particular spatial effect of the *quadratura* architecture, rising from each of the four sides in an independent perspective system to a square of sky, serves to centralize the oblong nave.[96] This suggestion of a square central space, existing only illusionistically within the fresco, is again supported by features of E. Q. Asam's decoration rather than of Fischer's architecture. Yet the central indentations in the sides of the fresco frame, matching those at the ends, reinforced by the mitred elements that join the rib-bands, read in elevation as gentle segmental arch-forms in contrast to the bold S-curves over the bays to east and west. These last serve to ovalize slightly the general shape of the fresco.

The centralizing effect of these shapes overhead is counteracted or balanced by the strongly directional arrangement of the altars. Those in the side chapels are set, as at Aldersbach, against the transverse wall segments that run back from the wall-pillars. In the generous niches of the eastern quadrants of the nave two elaborate altar compositions—far richer than those at Kirchham or Rinchnach (Pl. 60)—emphasized plastically by enormous crowns at their tops held by seraphs below the capitals of the flanking pilasters, provide the setting for polychromed sculptural groups: the enthroned Madonna and Child with Saints to the north and the Holy Kin to the south (Pl. 58). These stunning examples of Egid Quirin's sculpture halt the observer's eyes briefly, well in advance of the spatially complex high-altar composition. At the rear of that, there is Cosmas Damian's oil painting of the Ecstasy of St. Margaret, the patron of the church, set within a rich frame capped by an irregularly scalloped arch, instead of a culminating sculptural composition such as Egid Quirin provided at Weltenburg and Rohr (Pls. 36, 37).

In designing the high altar here, however, even more than earlier at Rohr and Weltenburg, Egid Quirin seems to have sought to improve on Bernini. References to the *baldacchino* of St. Peter's in Rome are as unmistakable (Pl. 58) as in any French seventeenth-century altar project. The four Salomonic columns, two forward and two to the rear, similar to those already used at Michelfeld and at Weltenburg, are as in those earlier instances essentially of the same composite order as the pilasters on the choir and apse walls. To these they are linked, somewhat as at Weltenburg, by floral garlands on which putti merrily swing. But the columns also carry a scrolled superstructure, much lighter and more open than in St. Peter's, enframing the oculus that opens at the base of the glory-filled semi-dome of the apse. This parallels closely the arrangement at Rohr (Pl. 37). The figure of the Agnus Dei over the top of the altarpiece is thus silhouetted, rather in the manner of the St. George at Weltenburg (Pl. 36), against strong light only very slightly obscured by the abstract triangular symbol of the Trinity in the glazing of the oculus.

There is, indeed, hardly any concealed lighting here. Although the side windows in the chapels and galleries are, as at Aldersbach, not normally seen from the nave because of the depth of the wall-pillars, they introduce a very large amount of general illumination, almost as much as in Dominikus Zimmermann's contemporary church at Steinhausen (Pl. 11); while the windows in the apse flanking the high altar to its rear are quite unshielded from the observer in the nave. Fischer, rather than the Asams, must have been responsible for this, since both at Weltenburg and at Rohr the side windows in the apse are hidden by the altar edicule.

One could go on almost indefinitely with the description of this interior, noting specific elements in the stucco decoration and also its general superiority to earlier *stucchi* by E. Q. Asam, including even what was most probably his latest work carried out immediately previous to this in St. Anna-am-Lehel. Yet the Asams' continued independence, as great as Dominikus Zimmermann's at Steinhausen, of the Munich electoral team, whose supervision the more thoroughly Paris-trained Cuvilliés was just taking over from Effner at this point, is at least as significant.

Precisely contemporary with the decoration of Osterhofen, and worth comparing with it, are the interiors of the Ahnengalerie and the Schatzkammer (Pl. 62), of 1728–31 and 1731–32, respectively, in the Munich Residenz. These are not rooms of ordinary residential scale as are most French Rococo interiors and those created earlier for Max Emanuel by Effner's team of Pichler, de Groff, and others in the Pagodenburg and in the Elector's and Electress's suites at Schleissheim; but they are not of monumental size and scale either, as is Osterhofen. Thus the interior of Osterhofen may be considered, more definitely than that of Freising, one of the two or three earliest works of truly German Rococo *architecture*. In the electoral *milieu* the first interiors for which such a claim could as plausibly be advanced are the Spiegelsaal in the Amalienburg at Nymphenburg (Pl. 133), begun in 1734, or possibly the bomb-destroyed Grüne Galerie of 1733 in the Residenz, both by Cuvilliés. In secular work of about 1730 it is more for a notable though rather inaccessible interior at Alteglofsheim—a modest Schloss south of Regensburg on the road to Landshut—that priority may be claimed, despite its small size and private sponsorship.

Noting in passing only, then, the panelling of the pilaster shafts at Osterhofen (Pl. 59), almost identical with that of the pilasters at Freising (Pl. 46) and quite different from the conventional fluting of those in St. Anna-am-Lehel (Pl. 56), the still more extensive use of gold *mosaïque* than in that Munich church, and the bold deployment of floating stucco figures on the ceilings of both nave and choir (Pls. 57, 59), the first element definitely Rococo in derivation, the second ambiguous, and the last still in the High Baroque tradition of Bernini as exaggerated later in such things in Rome as Gherardi's Santa Cecilia chapel in San Carlo ai Catinari and his Avila chapel in Santa Maria in Trastevere, we may now turn to the oval saloon at Alteglofsheim.

Alteglofsheim

For this, dates and solid attributions are sadly lacking or, indeed, any documentary information other than that provided by a letter of the client, Hans Georg Anton Graf von Königsfeld, dated 1 June 1730, in which he mentioned that he was then employing C. D. Asam.[97] Because of Königsfeld's close relations with the Munich court, and on stylistic grounds, other interiors in the south wing of the Schloss are often assigned to the Cuvilliés team.[97a] But C. D. Asam, despite earlier employment under Effner at Schleissheim, was hardly a member of that team, nor had he ever previously been employed for secular work except at Schleissheim. By this time, however, his pre-eminence as a fresco-painter was, not unjustly, recognized as generally as his father's had once been. The mystery is: who provided the remarkable stucco-work covering the two-story height of the walls that vignettes so boldly Asam's Triumph of Apollo on the domed ceiling of the oval saloon (Pl. 61)?

The two most likely possibilities, disregarding questions of style for the moment, would be Cosmas Damian's brother, with whom he so often worked in churches, or J. B. Zimmermann, the stuccoer of the Cuvilliés team. Both may well have been too busy—Zimmermann at Steinhausen, at Beyharting, and in the Ahnengalerie of the Munich Residenz, E. Q. Asam at Osterhofen—to undertake this relatively minor commission. If the vignetting suggests, not J. B. Zimmermann's stucco-work of these years (Pl. 62), but more his brother's at Steinhausen (Pl. 11), much of the detail seems too sophisticated for Dominikus, though not sufficiently so for Johann Baptist at this date. If the somewhat remote relation to the work of the French-trained craftsmen in Munich is more similar to E. Q. Asam's position at this point than to J. B. Zimmermann's, the quality of the figural work seems below E. Q. Asam's standards as a sculptor. The best probability may well be that it is the work of an assistant, either of E. Q. Asam—such as Schmidtgartner, who a few years before executed the stuccos in Heilig-Geist (Pl. 55)—or of J. B. Zimmermann. J. G. Übelherr (1700–63), for example, is a possible candidate. His independent work for the Prince-Abbot of Kempten, Anselm I Reichlin Freiherr von Meldegg, beginning some years after this, is even more original and accomplished; more specifically, he treated the junction of walls and ceilings in most of the rooms there in a somewhat similar way. Most of F. G. Hermann's ceiling paintings in oil there —the earliest dated 1734—are much smaller than C. D. Asam's fresco, however, and are handled more in the manner of those by B. A. Albrecht (1687–1765) in the Grüne Galerie in Munich.[98]

In the treatment of the lower story at Alteglofsheim the principal features are the pilasters, tapered, panelled, and with lambrequin-like elements hanging, as at Heilig-Geist, below the very freely handled capitals. Next comes no full entablature but only a narrow cove that curves upward over the east and west openings—main entrance and middle window—and also over the intervening fireplaces and side windows. Over the north and south doors the cove is bent in a double-S curve below the busts and trophies that mark the cross axis. Elsewhere at this next level there is a continuous attic element broken by pedestals that are very like those below the Salomonic columns of the Osterhofen high altar (Pl. 58). Between these are Donatello-like compositions of playful putti.

The strongest horizontal in the interior is that of the mouldings capping the attic, for the walls have no continuous termination at the top but overlap the edge of the fresco in a series of scalloped crestings. Six of these are nearly identical, but those over the longer north and south walls are stretched out horizontally. Below these last are large oblong oil paintings in frames with much enriched corners. In the other narrower bays, four occupied by windows and two by paintings, the stucco frames rise to bold, inverted volutes at the upper corners linked by pairs of scrolls on either side of the crowning busts. The narrower panels between have convex crowns, sharply outlined against the edge of the fresco, and slender inner bands of moulding around hanging trophies.

Gilt is used in some profusion on the more delicate raised elements, but there is a good deal of plain white as well, so that the general tonality is very light to harmonize with the bright colours of the fresco. The work is coarser than in the contemporary interiors in the Residenz (Pl. 62) and, despite the absence of strongly tectonic elements, there is a gusto here that links this Early Rococo interior backwards to the Baroque and forwards also to the High Rococo of the later years of this decade and the following forties.

Whoever C. D. Asam's collaborating stuccoer was, as a German Rococo decorator he was already the equal of E. Q. Asam at this particular point. The transition between the Late Baroque in Germany and the Early Rococo, to which the Asams had made such notable contributions through the 1720s, was now over but the Asam story is by no means ended. Important works that they initiated in the early thirties shortly after Alteglofsheim and Osterhofen must also be considered.[99]

Minor Work of the Early 1730s

Although Cosmas Damian's fresco at Alteglofsheim is of great significance in the present context because of its association with the anonymous stucco-work, the same is not true of his nearly contemporary paintings on the vaults of the nave at Fürstenfeldbruck.[100] Had the ambitious proposal of the two brothers to undertake together the decoration of the nave for 100,000 gulden been taken up this might well have been their major achievement of 1730–31.[101] However, on 12 July 1729 Jacopo Appiani, the younger brother of P. F. Appiani, with whom Cosmas Damian had worked earlier in the decade here in the choir, provided an estimate, presumably much more modest, for the stucco-work in the nave and this was accepted. Although there is a receipt for a small sum paid to Appiani as late as 24 September 1735, the work was probably completed by the date of the first mass at the high altar, said on 10 June 1731, as the date 1731 appears over the choir-arch and also on the fresco above the organ.

The frescoes in the two western bays of the nave are relatively small and confined within frames of rather plain, though broken, outline. The *stucchi* cover the deeply penetrating severies at the sides with a thick, embroidery-like confusion of ornament quite without Rococo character. The treatment of the next or crossing bay preceding the choir is more interesting. There the much larger fresco, which includes the Christmas Vision of St. Bernard, the Salve Regina, and the Pentecost, has an outline so deeply scalloped that it almost seems vignetted by Appiani's stucco-work rather than actually framed. At the corners of the fresco large stucco-framed cartouches, recalling Egid Quirin's at St. Jakobi in Innsbruck (Pl. 42), contain allegorical figures painted *en camaïeu*. The result is a decorative *tour de force*, somewhat recalling Einsiedeln in its extreme richness, but hardly closer to the Rococo than the elder Appiani's earlier work here in the choir.

It is not easy to arrange the work of the brothers, and particularly that of the more widely employed Cosmas Damian, in an accurate sequence through the early 1730s. It is of minor consequence here that Egid Quirin provided altars in certain churches where the brothers had undertaken major programmes of decoration in the previous decade;[102] nor are those cases where Cosmas Damian worked alone —Ettlingen in Baden in 1732 or Legnickie Pole (then called Wahlstatt) in Silesia in 1733—comparable in significance to the oval saloon at Alteglofsheim.

In the Ettlingen Schlosskapelle, a plain two-storied rectangular room, Cosmas Damian's vast shallow-domed fresco of the Glorification of St. John Nepomuk surrounded by scenes from his life, contracted for on 10 July 1732 and finished by 28 September of that year,[103] completely dominates the interior; while the upper walls have no stucco-work, but only minor architectural elements carried out in fresco. As usual in Cosmas Damian's frescoes these elements and the painted architecture in the main circular area are almost entirely devoid of Rococo character. Only the delicate *boiserie*-like ornament on the semi-elliptical intradoses of the upper windows and the swinging double curves of the balcony suggest the influence of the French-inspired Rococo of the electoral court for the former and, for the latter, the wavy sides of the nave of Osterhofen. Rather than Asam the architect here, J. M. L. Rohrer (1683–1732), who had begun the remodelling of the Schloss for the Margravine Sibylla Augusta of Baden-Baden in 1728, was presumably responsible for the balcony. Rohrer in 1722 had carried out for the Margravine the Pagodenburg at Rastatt, a copy of the one at Nymphenburg, from plans supplied by Effner;[104] thus he had had a very early contact with the incoming Rococo in Bavaria, but this seems not to have influenced him much at the end of his life at Ettlingen.

The architect of the Silesian church—now in Poland as the present place-name indicates—was a far more distinguished figure than Rohrer, and the church itself far larger and handsomer than the Ettlingen chapel. K. I. Dientzenhofer often followed his father Christoph in the exploitation of Guarinian plans for churches[105] and the nave at Legnickie Pole is an irregular oval, with two shallow lobes at either side, thus not unlike the dumb-bell shape of his father's Obořiště and Fischer's St. Anna.[106] A transverse oval vestibule at the front, which received bold external expression in a convex façade, is balanced by a similar transverse oval choir preceding a deep horseshoe-shaped apse. In the apse Asam's fresco is confined within a scalloped frame. Round the fresco the vault surface is richly decorated with *stucchi* that are, like the bandwork on the intradoses of the arches in the nave, of advanced proto-Rococo character. The handling of the nave vault, however, is more tectonic, with Asam's big fresco of the Legend of the Holy Cross brought well down over the crowns of the surrounding arches, as in the third bay of the nave at Einsiedeln

(Pl. 50), except for rising curves on the six vaulting conoids enframing *grisaille* figures of the Four Evangelists. Puffs of cloud overlap the rather stiff and heavily moulded border of the fresco only in two or three places. The fresco on the choir vault is equally firmly framed and has plain cut-off corners over the pendentives. The frescoes on the barrel-vaults of the lobes at each side, however, are confined only by curving mouldings thoroughly Rococo in their delicacy and freedom.

The church was physically complete by 1731 and consecrated in that year. It seems possible—even probable—therefore, that the frescoes, signed 'Cosmas Damian Asam aus Pairisch Minchen' but undated, were mostly painted in 1732 rather than in 1733, the date given by the chronogram in the stucco-work,[107] in spite of Asam's documented employment at Ettlingen through two of the months most suitable for the execution of frescoes in that summer. Thus they could be contemporary also, according to the date generally accepted, with the work of the brothers at St. Emmeram in Regensburg.[108] Neither moving that date backward to 1731, when the preliminary mason's work might have been undertaken in the spring (as was the case in 1723 in the quite parallel situation at Freising), nor moving it forward to 1733 is very satisfactory, and both moves would be hypothetical. Yet it might be, on the one hand, that the relatively large and important commission at Fürstenfeldbruck and, more probably still, that at Osterhofen were effectively completed by the summer of 1731; on the other hand, if the Silesian frescoes, as well as those at Ettlingen, were indeed executed in 1732, Cosmas Damian would hardly have been free before the summer of 1733 to paint the St. Emmeram frescoes. That in Santa Maria de Victoria at Ingolstadt was not undertaken until 1734.

St. Emmeram, Regensburg

Perhaps because we are less well informed concerning his activities, Egid Quirin's schedule in these years seems not to have been as full as his brother's. At least there is no obvious reason why he could not have undertaken the remodelling of St. Emmeram in either 1731 or 1732—his full-time services would hardly have been required in Ingolstadt that early,[109] whether or not he actually designed Santa Maria de Victoria some time before the cornerstone was laid in the spring of 1732 and carried it to physical completion himself the following year. On the strength of this conclusion and, for the moment, regardless of the uncertain sequence of Cosmas Damian's frescoes just before 1734, it will be well to consider Regensburg before Ingolstadt, the remodelled abbey church before the modest new 'praying hall'.

At first sight, the interior of St. Emmeram appears very similar, indeed, to that of Freising except that it is lighter in tone throughout and more dominated by the principal fresco (Pl. 63). Despite the similarity of the Asams' problem here, the redecoration of a great medieval church, there are actually various real differences. Instead of the twelve bays at Freising, there are here only ten (Fig. 6).[110] With no high crypt as at Freising, the vessel is unbroken at floor level except for a single step at the entrance to the choir and another step two bays further east. The proportions are lower and broader, moreover, in part because the vault section is elliptical, whereas the surviving Late Gothic vault at Freising, with its pointed crown filled in, has a roughly parabolic curvature.

There is no tribune, and the relatively broad blank areas between the simply moulded archivolts of the nave arcade and the main entablature are occupied in alternate bays with large paintings by Cosmas Damian of episodes from the life of the martyred St. Emmeram, who had been, according to legend, Bishop of Regensburg in the seventh century. These are set in gilt frames that are concave at the bottom just above the arches and extend upwards across the architrave and frieze of the entablature to the lower edge of the cornice. In the intervening bays there are polychromed stucco figures of Benedictine saints by Egid Quirin standing on rather plain brackets. The entablature is set lower than at Freising, and above it there is a distinct attic that incorporates a convex balconette below each of the big clerestory windows. At Freising the clerestory windows are all identical, with segmental curves at the top and S-curves at the sides that meet across the base; at St. Emmeram nearly identical windows alternate with plain oval ones. The sills of the windows here are all masked by the balusters of the balconettes.

At St. Emmeram, as at Freising, an organ carried on a gallery fills the westernmost bay to nearly its full height, and a tall altar edicule of the 1640s extends across almost the entire width of the eastern wall (Pl. 64). At Regensburg, however, doors[111] with windows over them, as at Michelfeld (Pl. 30), awkwardly squeezed into narrow strips of plain wall, flank the edicule, the heavy dark architectural elements of which dominate the eastern end of the church. The gloomy altar-painting of the Martyrdom of St. Emmeram at nearby Kleinhelfendorf—by Joachim Sandrart and dated 1679—rises over a remodelled fifteenth-century reliquary on the altar.

Equally conspicuous, however, are the big white stucco figures of St. Peter and St. Paul that E. Q. Asam added at the sides. Above he made more considerable emendations. There, between the curved 'horns' of the pediment, the Immaculate Virgin appears enthroned on clouds and the crescent moon above a large clock dial. Over her head are stars, clouds, and the gilded rays of a glory. Some of these rays project so far that they apparently pierce the 'horns', over each of which an angel precariously floats. Behind the angels stucco curtains, pushed aside by the ends of

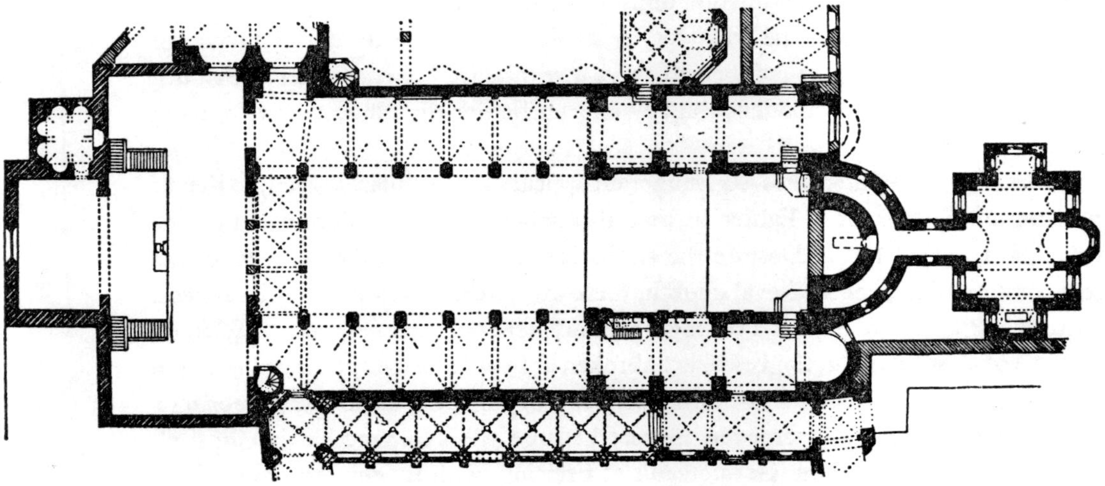

Fig. 6. Regensburg, St. Emmeram. Plan

the altar's entablature, hang from the rear of a circular pelmetted canopy overhead. This canopy partially overlaps the fresco on the choir vault. (The similar stucco draperies that once flanked the seventeenth-century altar edicule at Freising were removed in the nineteenth century.)

The most attractive elements of this elaborate terminal composition at St. Emmeram—which resembles the more modest, and possibly somewhat later, one crowning the Weltenburg altar more than the spatially complex 'vision' over the Assumption of the Virgin at Rohr—are the floral garlands that loop downward on either side, across the gilded capitals of the edicule, with putti swinging on them as jauntily as at Osterhofen. Despite Asam's embellishments, however, the high altar here, so climactic a feature visually at Weltenburg, Rohr and Osterhofen, remains almost as alien to the rest of the interior as that of 1624 at Freising.

Happier by far are the two side altars that project on either side of the church marking the line between the nave and the choir (Pl. 63). Of the thirties, but evidently not by Asam, these are architecturally unpretentious, since they rise only as high as the arches of the nave arcade, but richly decorated with sculpture. Angels with gilded wings, barely attached to the flanking scrolled brackets of scagliola that take the place of an order, pull back gilt curtains to reveal the painted altarpieces. Above, putti perch on the top against small gilded glories, those on the left holding a scroll inscribed AVE MARIA and those on the right holding the papal tiara and keys.

Other incidental features include a pulpit in the nave (Pl. 63)—also of the 1730s and not by Asam—and loges (Pl. 64), which are of Asam's design, at the level of the nave arcade on either side of the walled-in choir. These loges are more like pieces of Rococo furniture than architectural features; while the pulpit is not as interesting or conspicuous as would be usual later in the century. None of these things, of course, considered alone or in combination would justify the conclusion that this is an early masterpiece of the Rococo, well advanced not only beyond Freising but also beyond the two great new churches that had just been completed at Osterhofen and at Steinhausen. It is the frescoes overhead and the handling of the stucco decoration here that are really significant at this point.

First, one should note the great size and the character of the framing of the paintings on the vault. At Freising the largest fresco over the nave extended through only three bays and was not framed at all with stucco-work. Still at Osterhofen the fresco extended only through three bays; but it was surrounded, as earlier at Aldersbach, by a heavy gilded frame of stucco that can be loosely described as scalloped. Now, at St. Emmeram, the principal fresco extends through five of the seven bays of the nave and the shape is an elongated oval, incurved at the sides and with S-curves leading to the bowed ends as at Aldersbach, but without any straight segments (Pls. 65, 66). Moreover, the frame is double, the outer border relatively plain and flat, the inner border in higher relief and also scrolled and foliated with great freedom and richness. As on the tribune vaults at Freising (Pl. 47), some elements of the frame overlap the fresco—the two bold scrolls with their associated leafage on either side and the circular martyrs' crowns at the ends.

The composition of the fresco is so organized in dual perspective that the section at the east end devoted to the Martyrdom of the Christians whom St. Emmeram had converted at Regensburg (Pl. 66) can be properly appreciated only as seen from the western half of the nave and that of the Granting of Exemption to the monastery in the ninth century by Pope Leo IX (Pl. 65) from the choir. In the wide expanses of open sky across the centre this fresco recalls the magnificent one J. B. Zimmermann had just completed at Steinhausen (Pl. 11) more than that surrounded by *quadratura* architecture at Osterhofen that C. D. Asam had painted two years or so before (Pl. 57), his cluttered composition with expressionistically distorted perspective at Legnickie Pole, or the better organized but even more congested one at Ettlingen, both of which last must be of almost the same date. Since this openness is at least as evident on the ceiling of Santa Maria de Victoria, frescoed by Cosmas Damian in 1734 (Pl. 70), these comparisons tend to support the suggestion offered earlier that his work at St. Emmeram is of 1733 rather than of 1731 or 1732. However, his brother may well have begun the remodelling of the church and even the execution of the stucco decoration a year or so before the frescoes were executed.

The smaller fresco on the vault over the choir (Pl. 64), like those in the tribunes at Freising, occupies one bay and the two contiguous half bays. It is slightly overlapped to the east, as has been noted, by the pelmetted canopy high above the head of the Virgin. The other end is bowed like those of the nave fresco, but there is room for only one concave curve in the middle of each side instead of the big double-S curves of the larger frame. Putti, however, straying from the high-altar composition, hover below the vault surface as if to pull the frame downward at either end of these curves. They recall at a more delicate scale the angels floating against the nave vault at Osterhofen (Pls. 57, 59). The subject of the fresco, St. Benedict in Glory, is also handled here far more loosely than the same theme at Weingarten fifteen years before (Pl. 33).

It would be exaggerated to describe these frescoes as specifically Rococo; yet the opening up of the centre and the increasingly informal and asymmetrical character of the figural groupings and landscape settings—the latter already a prominent and attractive feature of J. B. Zimmermann's Steinhausen fresco of 1730–31—do relate to a prime characteristic of Rococo decoration from the first: the preference for using ornament as a frame around more or less bare fields. Moreover, they also approach the freer organization of groups of figures and the more atmospheric handling of landscape in early eighteenth-century French paintings by Watteau and those who were emulating him.[112] This striking modulation away from the solidly Baroque *quadratura* settings of so many of Cosmas Damian's frescoes of ten years earlier is parallel to the change in the character of Egid Quirin's stucco-work, a change initiated at Aldersbach that came to maturity here.

As still in many later German Rococo church interiors, the treatment of the walls of the nave of St. Emmeram is simpler and more conservative than that of the vault surfaces surrounding the frescoes (Pls. 63, 64). The pilaster order, indeed, is more conventional by a good deal than that at Osterhofen or even the one at Freising. Except for the overlapping of the lower members of the entablature by Cosmas Damian's framed paintings and the modest scrolling of the topmost member of the cornice above the pilasters, the entablature is quite plain and unbroken. Thus it provides a strong horizontal band from end to end of the long interior that is barely interrupted by the slight *ressauts* over the pilasters. The double break at the entrance to the choir, associated here with no change in the width of the vessel, is hardly more noticeable than the coupling of the pilasters and the resultant increase in the bay-length from this point eastward.

The pilasters themselves lack the scagliola-panelled shafts of those at Freising and Osterhofen. Plain and white, like the wall surfaces between them, their slight projection is hardly greater than that of the mouldings outlining the panels over the nave arcade against which the polychromed statues are set. For all their simplicity, these panels are very characteristically Rococo thanks to their cut-off and scrolled corners. The gilded frames in the intermediate bays, with their even more elaborately enriched corners, relate not to the plain shafts of the pilasters but to the delicately ornamented capitals. The barely Corinthianesque outline of these is extended downward by a bow in the light moulding at the bottom, as at Osterhofen, and by a naturalistic floral spray (Pl. 67). Like the highlights of the more conventional foliage above and the spiderweb-like netting between the reversed volutes, this is gilded. At the top of the capitals heads of cherubim, set not frontally but freely twisted and in some cases terminating below in the scrolls, rise across the architrave and frieze of the plain entablature blocks.

Above the cornice the surface of the short attic stage, though also plain and undecorated, is varied plastically by slight breaks corresponding to the *ressauts* of the entablature below and also by the convex fronts of the balconettes under the clerestory windows. The simply moulded frames of these windows fill all but completely the tall lunettes of the cross-vaults.

It is in the treatment of the decoration of the severies of these vaults that Egid Quirin's newly acquired command of Rococo design is most apparent (Pls. 63, 64). As in the tribunes at Freising (Pl. 49) the ornament disregards the arrises of the severies. The three-dimensional fields are limited at the sides only by the residual rib-bands, as in the nave of Osterhofen (Pls. 57, 59), and by the curved frames of the frescoes on the main vault. The rib-bands, now wholly devoid of tectonic weight or structural significance, widen where they meet the outer bands at the sides of the frescoed panels; at the ends of the panels they also curve outward to form a third framing band (Pls. 65, 66). This represents a far more drastic transformation of original form and meaning than the mere deflection of the rib-bands by the rounded ends of the nave frescoes at Osterhofen. It was foreshadowed there, however, by the mitring of the rib-bands between the middle bays where they touch the frame of the main fresco. In the half-bays beyond the ends of the frescoes here at St. Emmeram rather extensive fields covered with a brocaded pattern fill the remaining areas across the crown of the vault much as on the terminal coves at the east and west ends of the nave vault at Osterhofen, though there can be no downward coving of the surface of the barrel-vault here since there is no change at this point in the transverse section.

As in the wall panels of the French Rococo, the ornament on all these stuccoed areas is essentially linear, long sweeping curves of slightly foliated mouldings forming elongated C and S-patterns that interlace at the heads of alternate severies. The fields are not entirely bare, for looser and somewhat richer ornament provides a sort of inner frame, as in the Freising tribunes (Pl. 48), defining small round and scalloped areas, here not frescoed but merely tinted in pale colours.

The rib-bands are continuous across the vessel only between the first and second and the sixth and seventh bays of the nave and at the entrance to the choir (Pl. 63); but all of them are identically decorated with narrow panels of gilding recalling a little, despite their very different size, shape and disposition, those on the cove at Weltenburg (Pl. 27). The rectangular frames of those elongated panels are cut by C-curves at the corners and also have concave 'bites' at their ends to provide more space around fair-sized circular rosettes raised against a white ground. These last provide alternating accents with the lozenge-shaped rosettes at the centres of the gilded panels.

To particularize in so much detail the elements of Egid Quirin's stucco investiture of this interior may actually tend to obscure its principal qualities of lightness, brightness, delicacy of scale, and what may be called—for want of a word of specifically religious connotation—its gaiety.[113] These qualities are happily epitomized in certain decorative adjuncts that had evidently appealed to Egid Quirin ever since he executed the high altar at Weltenburg (Pl. 36), but which he had never before used so profusely and so conspicuously; that is, the elaborately shaped urns—gilded, polychromed, and filled with flowers and foliage in natural colours—which he set behind each of the scrolled breaks at the top of the cornice against the plain white surface of the attic (Pl. 64). These remind one of the characteristic delight of the Rococo period, not least in Germany, for small-scale works of decorative art in gold, silver, and porcelain, which—as later in the *art nouveau* of 1900—sometimes seem to have been the happiest, and were certainly the most typical, products of the period.

But if one is therefore tempted to suppose, as some writers have done, that there were determinant influences from the work of French goldsmiths or German designers of porcelain, certain facts should be recalled even though they do not provide negative evidence that can be considered absolute. The designs of J.-A. Meissonier (1695–1750), although dating in many cases from the 1720s, did not begin to be issued in engravings until 1734.[114] Important as these were soon to be for the succeeding *rocaille* phase of the Rococo in Germany, they can hardly yet have been known to E. Q. Asam or even to Cuvilliés in Munich. French plate imported by Carl Albrecht or his father may, however, have been available for emulation.

Although the first European porcelain was produced by J. F. Böttger (1682–1719) in 1709, the great period at Meissen began only much later—after 1731—when J. J. Kändler (*c.* 1706–75) took artistic charge of production. It is just possible that the higher key and the increasing predominance of white highlighted by gold in the decoration of St. Emmeram owed something to this new art-manufacture since the essence of the newly perfected European porcelain was its whiteness—not immediately achieved by Böttger—and the bright tones of colour and gilt with which it was enlivened. But Kändler himself had grown up in the world of interior decoration, having worked as a sculptor from 1723 in the Grüne Gewölbe at Dresden; and the work of the Cuvilliés team in the Residenz in Munich, well under way by 1731, not only included a great deal of white-and-gold stucco-work by J. B. Zimmermann in the Ahnengalerie and the Schatzkammer,[114a] but was being echoed in Zimmermann's Neuer Festsaal of 1731–32 in the monastery at

Benediktbeuern (Pl. 13). He used there much less gold and, moreover, introduced a large fresco in a scalloped frame at the centre of the ceiling, quite as in many of the Asams' church interiors since Aldersbach. The stuccoed ceilings of J. B. Zimmermann seem a more probable inspiration for the Asams and other Bavarians in the early thirties than the porcelain that was being produced in Saxony. (The manufacture of porcelain at Nymphenburg began only in 1761.)

One of the most notable of all remodellings of much earlier churches, familiar to every later visitor to Rome, was what Borromini was able to carry out in St. John Lateran for the Anno Santo 1650. In his ambition to change the long Early Christian nave, with its endless colonnades at the sides, into a more centralized space with broader rhythms he was partially thwarted by the decision to preserve the flat wooden roof rather than to substitute vaulting. Even more serious from his point of view was the refusal of the authorities to permit any changes at the west end of the nave where the wide and tall triumphal arch framed the high altar before the apse. Only at the front was he able to round off one end of the space with characteristic canted and curved elements; but the interior remained excessively long and narrow by post-Renaissance standards. The great aesthetic weakness of the remodelled interior of St. Emmeram, as of the one at Freising, is that the centralization of the enclosed space, so powerfully suggested here by the scalloped oval of the fresco overhead, could not be made real. Each is a tunnel of space, merely chopped off at the ends by the altar to the east and by the organ above its gallery to the west. Thus, for all the great advance towards the mature Rococo in the decoration at Regensburg, it remains true that even Fischer's Osterhofen (Pl. 57) with its curved corners and, above all, the unknown designer's oval saloon at Alteglofsheim (Pl. 61) are more completely Rococo architecturally.

Santa Maria de Victoria, Ingolstadt

Modest as is Santa Maria de Victoria (Pl. 70), designed (if by E. Q. Asam[115]) perhaps just after he began the remodelling at Regensburg,[116] it is also more consistently Rococo considered as interior architecture. A flat-ceilinged room rather than a vaulted church, this praying hall is much closer in spatial character to the secular interiors of the day, and even more to such a saloon in a monastery as the Neuer Festsaal at Benediktbeuern (which is today actually used as a school chapel). Compared to that (Pl. 13), however, Santa Maria de Victoria has the advantage of greater relative height. Compared to French interiors, with the exception of the Salon d'Hercule at Versailles,[117] it still appears very Italianate because of the fresco that occupies the entire ceiling. Although there is a rather solid and symmetrical build-up at the (ritual) 'east' end of the ceiling, with the Virgin, flanked by angels and seated on a globe, set above the Fountain of Life and silhouetted within the arch of a broad columnar edicule somewhat like the high altar at Rohr, the general effect of the composition otherwise, as has been noted earlier, is loose and open, with some landscape elements at the edges and much empty sky around the oval of clouds that frames the floating figure of God the Father. Iconographically, as in the representation of the Four Continents at the sides and of the Fountain of Life, there is considerable similarity to J. B. Zimmermann's Marian ceiling at Steinhausen (Pl. 11). It is to inspiration from that that Cosmas Damian might have owed the freer and airier handling of this fresco, as also of the one over the nave of St. Emmeram painted a year or two earlier (Pls. 65, 66).

It is not easy, in the mind's eye, to see this Ingolstadt interior as it must have been when first completed, probably a year or so before the consecration in 1736, since the rich and dark wooden stalls along the side walls and the similar interior doorways of the late 1740s, as well as the high altar of the 1760s, increase very much the present impression of High Rococo elaboration (Pls. 69, 70).[118] Even more confusing, as modifying the general effect by their dark tones, their extremely ornate gilded frames, and their high placement on the walls, are the oil paintings of various saints, most of them signed and dated in the early 1750s.[119]

As regards the altar of about 1763 by the sculptor J. M. Fischer, a delicate Late Rococo edicule, one may suppose that the pelmetted canopy projecting out of the very shallow altar niche, not dissimilar to the one Egid Quirin introduced at the east end of St. Emmeram (Pl. 64), is original since the frame of the fresco is carried around it and this considerable 'bite' seems to have been taken into account in the contiguous portion of the painted ceiling below the Fountain of Life. Moreover, the brocaded stucco curtains, drawn back by floating putti and of the same bright blue as the canopy above, while doubtless rearranged and even extended by Fischer, recall the more exiguous drapery at the sides of the high altar in Regensburg (Pl. 64) and that Egid Quirin had originally provided earlier at Freising. Certainly of 1734, though perhaps designed earlier while the hall was being built, is all the stucco-work. This includes the rather heavy frame of the fresco, which also serves as a cornice at the top of the walls; the decoration above the tops of the windows on the wall surfaces rising into the cove under the outer member of the fresco frame; the ornament on the jambs and between the upper and lower lights in the tall niches of the twelve pairs of windows at the sides; and that on the fronts of the three shallow balconettes, scalloped in plan, which project slightly from the wall at the west end of the hall (Pl. 69).

Of greatest architectural significance is the handling of the essentially rectangular cornice-frame of the fresco—the plan of the interior is a plain oblong except for the shallow altar niche at the 'east' and the gallery that extends forward over the vestibule to the 'west', and the frame naturally follows that shape. This strongly plastic element consists of an inner moulded band, a heavily reeded roll regularly bound with foliage alternating with ribands, and a narrower outer member forming the lip of the cove at the top of the walls. If this frame can hardly be called either oval or scalloped in the way of those round the frescoes at Aldersbach, Osterhofen, and St. Emmeram, yet the rectangular shape is slightly ovalized by the curved corners. There are also concave 'bites', not only the large one at the 'east', but much smaller ones in the middle of each side that further vary the regularity of the shape of the frescoed ceiling overhead.

Below the slightly curved corners of the fresco frame, asymmetrical scrolled cartouches (Pl. 68), with brief gilded inscriptions and flanking seraphim recalling those Borromini had often used in a similar way,[120] provide a plastic transition to the sharp right angles of the actual plan. Broader features, S-curved in vertical section, also carry the concave 'bites' at the centres of the sides of the frame downward as convex projections.

As seen originally, when the visitor's eyes would have been drawn upwards on entering the hall even more strongly than today, not the real rectangular space at floor level, but the shaped space of the wall areas above the window niches would have made the dominant impression. It is this shaped space, moreover, that is carried indefinitely upward by the open composition of the fresco. Somewhat as the central space of the nave at Osterhofen was made to seem squarish by the rigid *quadratura* architecture of the main fresco there (Pl. 57), the more purely pictorial and less tectonic illusionism of an oval opening in the sky surrounding God the Father serves here to ovalize the space overhead (Pl. 70). This counteracts the strong visual pull of the solider elements of the edicular composition rising behind the enthroned Virgin above the altar. Even so, because of the relatively modest height of this interior, the ceiling is slightly oppressive despite the airy illusionism of its frescoed surface as is seldom true when there is vaulting overhead.

In the absence of a pilaster order and with the wall surfaces broken only by the window-niches, it was possible to treat the areas above the niche-heads continuously (Pl. 70). Moreover, although the substitution of a cove for an entablature had long been characteristic of French Rococo interiors, it is evidence of the originality of the Asams' rapidly maturing style in these years that, in the absence of vaulting—on which hitherto the richest stucco decoration had usually been concentrated—the cove is here so far deepened that most of the *stucchi* are on its curved surface. This band, however, is quite firmly confined both above and below. At the top the down-turning lip outside the heaviest member of the fresco frame is crisp and continuous; at the bottom the scalloped crowns of the window-niches—and now, of course, the tops of the picture-frames in between—provide a somewhat less definite termination. What must originally have served between the tops of the niches as the base-line is now obscured by the intricate cresting of those frames; apparently, broken sections of horizontal moulding were once set somewhat higher than the scrolls of the scalloped archivolts above the niches to link them horizontally.

The motifs in the *stucchi*, almost all now unmistakably Rococo, seem in their loose distribution related to, perhaps influenced by, J. B. Zimmermann's ceilings at Benediktbeuern (Pl. 13) rather than to the more extravagant *stucchi* of the early thirties in the Munich Residenz, executed by Zimmermann but presumably designed by Cuvilliés. (Work on the Amalienburg at Nymphenburg by Cuvilliés and Zimmermann only began in this year 1734 and was not completed until 1739, so that the stucco-work there can have had no influence on E. Q. Asam here.) At the least one may say that, just as Zimmermann's independent work was developing away from the French Rococo in these years, so E. Q. Asam's was moving in the other direction. But one need not hesitate to call either the Neuer Festsaal or Santa Maria de Victoria major examples of a truly German sort of Rococo decoration, however one may feel as to the propriety of calling the Ingolstadt praying hall Rococo *architecturally*.

As at Benediktbeuern (Pl. 13) the decoration on the jambs and soffits of the window-niches is in very low relief and much simpler than that on the walls (Pl. 70). This is also true of the balcony fronts (Pl. 69). However, the rather broad bands between the upper and lower lights carry large and rich rosettes set against scalloped fields of the same gold *mosaïque* that fills the narrow panels on the jambs.

As usual, it is difficult to speak with assurance of the colouring. As at Einsiedeln, and even more at St. Emmeram though not at Freising or Osterhofen, Santa Maria de Victoria, below the brilliantly coloured fresco, seems at first all white highlighted with gold in the early eighteenth-century French way. But what we see, though doubtless correct, is the result of the restoration of 1947–50.[121] The strongest note of colour, outside the fresco, is the blue of the stucco drapery behind the altar, echoing the blue of the Virgin's mantle above in the fresco. Though certainly renewed by J. M. Fischer, as probably also in the two restorations, this may well go back to the Asams. It seems likely, on the other hand, in the light of Egid Quirin's other altars, that his original altar here would have been of warm-toned scagliola with only the capitals gilded and the statuary white, not all white and gold. The *stucchi* of the upper wall are now white against very pale grey, with only some of the smaller shaped fields filled by gilded *mosaïque*. The fields of the corner cartouches are pink, however, and those at the sides, light blue-green. By this time such a gamut is familiar enough in Bavaria and may well follow quite accurately the Asams' original treatment. Even so, the general tonality is much affected by the dark intrusions of the mid-century, as noted earlier; while the appropriate emphasis on the altar has presumably been diminished by the lightness and brightness of the white and gold of Fischer's edicule.

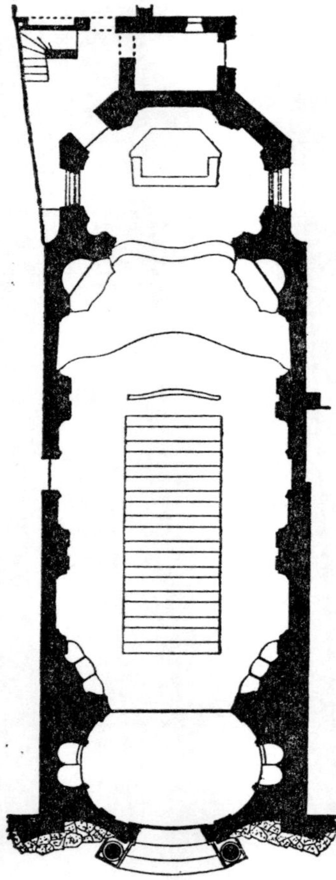

Fig. 7. Munich, St. Johann-Nepomuk. Plan

Since Egid Quirin's responsibility even for the stucco-work of the interior is confirmed by no extant documentation though generally accepted by scholars, there is little hope of establishing whether or not he was responsible for the architectural design of the building, and particularly of its exterior. In the interior the fact that there are two ranges of windows at the sides, joined only by their decorative treatment within the tall niches containing them, as also the way the segmental heads of the niches fail to agree with the tops of the upper row of windows—squared off, but with concave C-cuts at the corners—may suggest that the original architect and the decorator who worked inside were not the same man.[122] But these disparities could be merely the result of changes in Egid Quirin's design between 1732 and 1734.

Many scholars attribute the façade, except for the bell turret added at the top in 1882, to one of the Asams, presumably Egid Quirin, even though no other exterior of his design is known to exist previous to that of the Asamkirche in Munich. The design of this façade, for which the plaster model was made in 1733, would seem on internal evidence to be, if entirely by one man, the work of a Rome-trained artist become a Rococo stuccoer. The *parti* is that of many Roman churches since the sixteenth century; but the use of the familiar scheme is quite arbitrary since the two-story treatment, with broad scrolls flanking a narrower second story, does not correspond here to a tall nave with lower aisles or chapels at the sides. Moreover, the three rows of windows in the flanking bays that were required, at least as regards the two lower pairs, by the two-storied section of the building across the west end, seem to have been almost as unsympathetic to the designer of the façade as the double row of windows in the side walls evidently was to the decorator of the interior. One may surmise that structurally the edifice, begun in the spring of 1732 and roofed by 6 August of that year, was not by either of the Asams. Yet the final design of the façade, as finished and decorated in stucco, might still be by Egid Quirin. For all the slightly retardataire charm of the *stucchi*, mostly bandwork in cream on pink grounds, however, it would not be a notable addition to his architectural *œuvre* as his own church in Munich certainly is.

The Asamkirche, Munich

St. Johann-Nepomuk ought to represent the brothers' major contribution to the Bavarian Rococo. Planned perhaps as early as 1731, begun two years later after the cornerstone was laid by the future elector Max III Joseph on 16 May 1733, it was built, decorated, and furnished during the following fifteen years and more. Though consecrated in 1746,[123] it was not fully equipped with subsidiary fittings even by the time of Egid Quirin's death in 1750. However, as it was physically complete in the rough by the day before Christmas 1734 when it was blessed, and the interior surely in large part decorated before Cosmas Damian's death in 1739, the church may be considered to date in the main from the mid and late thirties. Yet it does not seem, today at least, so consistently Rococo as either St. Emmeram or Santa Maria de Victoria which were decorated just before. Some indication of why the Asamkirche is not a prime example of the Early Rococo—or at least only partially such—may help to define negatively what the true character of the Rococo in Southern Germany was in the thirties as contrasted, on the one hand, with the predominantly Baroque character of most of J. M. Fischer's and J. B. Neumann's contemporary production[124] and, on the other, with the still French-inspired *Reiche Zimmer* in the Munich Residenz and the interiors in the Amalienburg at Nymphenburg (Pl. 133), all by Cuvilliés and his collaborators, as completed late in the decade though begun, respectively, in 1731 and 1734.

In plan and section the Asamkirche is more like a palace chapel than a great abbey church of the order of St. Emmeram or a praying-hall such as Santa Maria de Victoria. Though relatively long and narrow, it does not resemble very closely the most famous German palace chapel of the period, that in the Residenz at Würzburg,[125] designed by Neumann and Hildebrandt in 1731–32 at precisely the time Egid Quirin was presumably making the first plans for his church. Both are two-storied and make play with ovals in plan (Figs. 7, 8); but in the Asamkirche the elliptical shape is used only for the vestibule at the 'west' (i.e. south) end—somewhat like that at Weltenburg where Egid Quirin was working again, precisely in the vestibule, in the mid-thirties—and for the sanctuary, although the nave is slightly ovalized by the in-curving ends of the side walls (Pls. 72, 73).

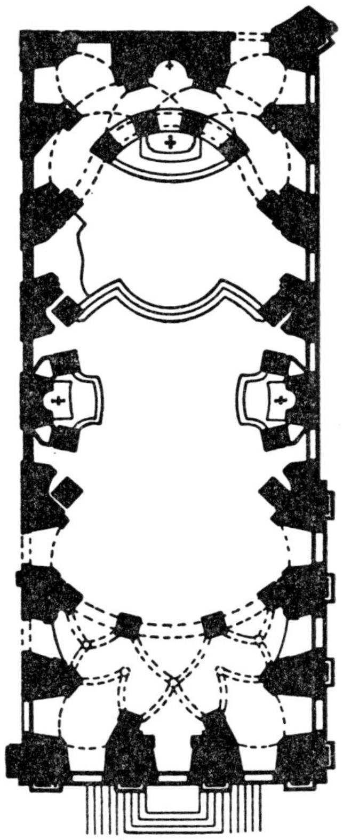

Fig. 8. Würzburg, Hofkirche. Plan

This ovalizing is less extreme in the upper story of the Asamkirche where the side walls are better described as wavy or undulating (Pl. 74); while the shape of the frescoed vault, with Cosmas Damian's fresco extending the entire length of the church from the inside of the front wall to the far end of the sanctuary, may perhaps be called scalloped (Pl. 71). This fresco occupies, in fact, a longitudinal rectangle with deep horseshoe-shaped extensions at the ends and with shallow bulges at the centres of the sides such as Cosmas Damian had first used some twenty years earlier for the large middle fresco over the nave at Michelfeld (Pl. 29). The main fresco over the nave of the Würzburg chapel (Pl. 208), executed in 1736 by J. R. Byss, who had earlier painted the ceiling of the stair-hall at Pommersfelden, has no such firmly framed shape as the one here; rather is it loosely vignetted by the stucco-work that Antonio Bossi (d. 1764) had begun to execute the previous year, almost in the way J. B. Zimmermann's fresco at Steinhausen is by his brother's constructed decoration there (Pl. 11).

Both stories of the Asamkirche have an order; but free-standing columns, which are used in profusion at Würzburg (Pl. 73), appear only at the ends in the upper range (Pl. 77) and there are no engaged columns at all. In the lower order paired pilasters are set on either side of the wide middle bays of the nave, those on the left flanking the very modest door from the ground story of Egid Quirin's contiguous house—there is no corresponding entrance from the priests' house on the right, since the priests were expected to enter more directly into the sanctuary. Each bay in the nave has a shallow arch, semi-circular in those to east and west, semi-elliptical in the centre (Pl. 72). These have coved jambs and intradoses with slight imposts in false perspective, perhaps to suggest a real nave arcade. No entablature joins the pairs of pilasters or connects with the single pilasters, placed diagonally, that terminate the lower walls beyond the niches in the curved corners containing the side altars at the entrance to the sanctuary. Instead, the wall surface of the lower story bends inwards at its top in a cove to support the balcony that runs all around the church. Since the balustrade of this feature is straight along the sides of the nave, except for very slight bulges in the middle bay, and straight across the nave above the vestibule, it provides the strongest horizontal element in an interior predominantly as vertical in expression as in proportion.

Thus, as in the Versailles chapel, the prototype of most eighteenth-century palace chapels, the lower story tells only as a subsidiary space and the meaningful volume is that of the vaulted upper story, which is actually—and even more visually—taller than the one below. Here, flanking the central bay on the left, are the principal doorways from Egid Quirin's house—each with a large round window over it—so that he could enter his chapel, just as kings and electors did theirs, from the *piano nobile* of his modest home.

The upper order is also much richer and more complete than that below (Pl. 74) even though unconventional in handling and in detail. Along the wall the pilasters, their shafts panelled as at Freising and Osterhofen and tapered as at Alteglofsheim, are set against considerably broader flat members between the three shallow niches that occupy most of the side walls. The wider and taller ones in the centre of each wall are completely filled with large paintings.[126] Above the terminal pilasters in the lower story rise free-standing columns. At the front the cornice of the entablature breaks sharply forward in a curve to cap the blocks of architrave and frieze atop these columns. At the other end, however, complete entablature blocks, curved in plan like those at the front, are linked to the walls only by hanging garlands quite like those that run from the free-standing front columns of the Osterhofen altar edicule to the pilasters at either side of the apse (Pl. 58).

The entablature over the pilasters undulates so intricately in three dimensions below the richly decorated cove that rises to meet the frame of the frescoed vault it may almost be said to wriggle (Pl. 74). The *ressauts* over the six pilasters are double-S curved in plan, like the edges of the blocks over the columns, and the entablature is also bent upward in shallow segmental curves in the first and third bays. At the sides of the middle bays, however, the entablature is mitred to follow the flanking coves and also continued illusionistically in the architectural settings within the paintings. The cornice alone rises in a bolder segmental curve above, somewhat like the motif in the diagonal bays of the octagon at Einsiedeln over the openings into the aisles (Pl. 53). The top of the cornice is so high at these points that it is a tangent to the bulges in the sides of the fresco frame, thus interrupting the continuity of the terminal cove. By re-enforcing the emphasis provided by the wide middle bays of the lower story and by the openings, or deep niches, suggested by the architectural settings in the large paintings over them in the upper story, these plastic accents mark a distinct cross-axis. Thereby they help to centralize the spatial composition of the nave, counterbalancing somewhat the strong longitudinal pull that results from the narrow rectangular shape of the interior and the elaboration of the double altar at the far end.

The altar edicule, moreover, is here so completely integrated with the architecture of the church that the whole interior resembles the choir of a pilgrimage shrine almost more than a palace chapel (Pl. 72). One thinks particularly of Dominikus Zimmermann's two-storied choir and altar at Günzburg, designed in 1736, that led the way to his culminating achievement in the choir of Die Wies, carried out a decade later in 1746–49. But the organization of Egid Quirin's terminal feature in the Asamkirche, for all its two stories, is closest—not surprisingly—to the high altar composition at Osterhofen (Pl. 58), completed with the installation of Cosmas Damian's signed and dated picture in 1732 at about the time that the design for the Munich church must have been maturing. The present setting of the lower altar is simple. Seraphic herms by Asam support a pelmetted canopy that follows the curvature of the cove below the balcony, and from this parted stucco curtains, so clumsily modelled that they must be restoration, hang down at the sides. Before the war both herms and canopy were largely hidden by the rays of a very large glory, installed in 1783 above the altar, which was probably the work of R. A. Boos (1730–1810).

The drama of the second story portion of the altar composition was much diminished when Egid Quirin's statue of the titular saint, John Nepomuk, standing in the arch at the rear and silhouetted like the St. George at Weltenburg (Pl. 36) by light from concealed windows behind, was replaced about 1824 with a painting, now destroyed, by Andreas Seidl. That has, in its turn, been replaced since the war with a late eighteenth-century Assumption of the Virgin by T. C. Winck (not yet installed when the photograph reproduced in Plate 72 was made). Fortunately the group of the Trinity above, suspended over an open space defined as at Osterhofen by four Salomonic columns, has survived both the anti-Rococo taste of the early nineteenth century and the bombing of the twentieth (Pl. 77). The *Gnadenstuhl* (Throne of Grace), as this visual presentation of the Trinity is called in German, consists of a large cross bearing the Crucified Christ, supported from behind by the hands of God the Father, and with the Holy Spirit above, the whole surrounded by four cherubim hovering over the entablature blocks of the columns (Pl. 75). Somewhat as at Rohr, the gilded dove representing the Third Person of the Trinity is centred in a metal glory, the whole apparently free-floating but actually supported from the tips of the cherubim's wings. As at Osterhofen (Pl. 58), flowery garlands looping downward to the capitals of the columns provide precarious perches for putti. The two large statues of St. John the Baptist and St. John the Evangelist by Asam in the quadrantal niches at either side are largely masked from the nave by the columns diagonally in front of them.

In this sculptor's church it is not surprising that there should be, as at Rohr, much sculpture and three-dimensional ornament. Seraphic herms beside the crowns of the side altar niches support small pelmetted canopies below the cove of the balcony. Along from the side walls floral garlands hang down the bottom of the balcony (Pl. 72). The centre of each side is again marked by several seraphic figures: two over each of the semi-elliptical arches below and more far above where the cornice of the upper order is tangent to the fresco frame (Pl. 71). There are also small reliefs, not much like those at Weltenburg (Pl. 25), on the cove above the upper entablature. Once, undoubtedly, the great ceiling fresco by Cosmas Damian, with the Presentation of St. John Nepomuk in Heaven as its principal subject and scenes from his life at the base, balanced in visual interest Egid Quirin's sculpture (Pl. 71). Its present condition, despite postwar restoration in 1956–57, is too pathetically ruined to allow a fair judgment. In any case, it had been tampered with in 1860 and then cleaned in 1941–42 as part of a general restoration of the interior.

But Egid Quirin was not only a sculptor and a sculptor practising architecture—as, for example, Michelangelo had been in the sixteenth century—he was also (as Michelangelo was certainly not) a stuccoer. Some examination of the character of his *stucchi* ought to help, at least, to determine how far it is proper, as so many have done, to rate the Asamkirche as even an early masterpiece of German Rococo architecture, much less its culmination.

The lighting of the interior should first be considered. In contrast to the brilliant illumination and high-keyed tonality of the Asam's work since Freising ten years before, this interior is rather dim, dimmer than was intended because of the blocking up of the apse windows in the early nineteenth century. But, compared to the immediately preceding interiors of St. Emmeram and Santa Maria de Victoria, one must suppose it is dark primarily because its designer wished it to be so (Pl. 72). Instead of the predominantly gold-and-white tonality of all the Asams' churches since Einsiedeln, most of the surfaces of the interior, though highlighted with gilding, approximate the warm middle values of the interior of Weltenburg. Indeed, the values are rather lower, as the predominant colour is a muted red. The particular tonality here results, not from any considerable use of real marble as at Weltenburg,[127] but from the scagliola that lines almost the entire interior except for those features that are gilded and the white sculpture. To what extent this scagliola was deepened in tone by the painter Fidel Schabat and the gold dulled by the gilder Joseph Radspieler, who together renewed the interior in 1860, I do not know, nor how successfully the restoration of 1941–42 may have brought back the original eighteenth-century quality twenty-five years ago.[128] One can only say that the whole interior, not merely the badly damaged fresco overhead (Pl. 71), today seems rather gloomy and drab, so that it is difficult to appreciate—or even to see clearly—the variety and the richness of Egid Quirin's ornamentation.

Many, perhaps most, of the elements of the surface decoration, as distinguished from the strictly architectural or sculptural motifs, are unmistakably Rococo, complementing happily the curvilinear spatial organization. Yet there is, overall, a certain plastic boldness: in the free-standing columns; in the projection of the balcony; and also in the firm enframement of the upper cove; as once presumably in the drama of the silhouetted St. John Nepomuk, that contrasts with the similarly galleried two-story interior carried out in 1746–50 by Peter Thumb and J. A. Feuchtmayr in the pilgrimage church at Birnau on the Bodensee (Pl. 161). With more illumination from the 'east' and with the original—undoubtedly brilliant—colours in the fresco overhead, with brighter highlights of gold and a cleaner and possibly lighter tone for the scagliola lining of the walls, this interior (Pl. 72) may well once have had in greater degree that special quality of holy gaiety, or *laetitia*, which is evident still at Birnau—and, for that matter, at St. Emmeram. That this is a dominant characteristic of the most mature German Rococo of the forties and fifties in church interiors all will agree.

Not in intrinsic artistic quality certainly, impaired though the original quality has been by various indignities suffered since, but as regards its position in the development towards the High Rococo of 1740–60, there is today real ambiguity here—some sense that this is not quite the expected following step after those covered thus far in this chapter. It would be ridiculous to presume that there was, in these years of the mid-thirties when the Asamkirche was begun and largely executed, a general *détente* or setback in the progressive development of the German Rococo. Cuvilliés and his associates were producing in the Spiegelsaal of the Amalienburg in 1734–39 what has long been recognized, by francophile foreigners such as Kimball as well as by Germans, as a culminating achievement of the international Rococo (Pl. 133). Yet that is still not remote from French models—though also not, as some have supposed, derived from Boffrand's oval salons in the Hôtel de Soubise in Paris, which were actually initiated a few years later.[129] It is, moreover, a secular interior, approaching but not reaching the monumental scale of the church interiors in which eighteenth-century German architects, stuccoers and fresco-painters made their greatest contribution. On the other hand, Dominikus Zimmermann at Günzburg, in the boldly tectonic treatment of the interior walls of his Frauenkirche,[129a] begun in 1736, may seem, far more definitely than Egid Quirin in his Munich church, to have reverted toward Baroque ideals of vigorous plasticity and structural expression. J. M. Fischer also turned away in the thirties from the proto-Rococo spatial organization of St. Anna-am-Lehel and Osterhofen, in his case towards a more formal kind of centralized planning.[130]

Though exteriors are not very important in the work of the Asams or, indeed, for German Rococo architecture in general, it will be well to illustrate and comment on, not the façade of the Asamkirche alone, but also that of Egid Quirin's house beside it.[131] The façade of the church—above which the modest bell turret, knocked off by bombing in 1945, has not been rebuilt—is, like most eighteenth-century German church façades, Baroque in scale, in conception, and in the tectonic plasticity of its membering (Pl. 76). From the Berninian rustic rockwork at the base, through the free-standing columns that carry the sheltering segmental cornice over the entrance and those that flank the west windows, to the Borrominian outline of the pediment, curved in the centre to follow the circular oculus in the pediment, the elements all belong to the seventeenth-century Roman repertory, even though they are handled with a freedom that recalls a little the façades designed by the Dientzenhofers in Bohemia. Asam's sculpture—St. John Nepomuk silhouetted against the west window, and the angels that rest below and on either side of him and in the pediment of the window above—is likewise still in that Berninian tradition to which Egid Quirin as a sculptor had usually been faithful since the early twenties. Only incidental elements of the ornament are Rococo: the elaborate capitals of the pilasters, concave as in the interior of Osterhofen, with their dangling garlands; the looser garlands that loop down from the sides of the oculus to the pilaster capitals; and, most specifically, the mouldings that outline the wall surfaces just inside the pilasters.

How different is the façade of the house! Except for the rectangular oriel above the entrance, this is a flat a-tectonic surface broken only by regularly spaced oblong windows set in plain moulded frames with simple square ears (Pl. 76). There was still a little rockwork at the base—it has not been restored since the war—echoing that on the church façade and even vermiculated voissoirs over the ground story windows; moreover, the herms that almost seem to carry the oriel are boldly three-dimensional and generously scaled. But the greater part of the wall surface is handled as a painter might have done—but rather more freely than most Rococo external wall-painting that has survived in Bavaria—loosely, atmospherically, asymmetrically, and with no regard for the monumental scale of the church façade to the right.

This, I think, few will question as being Rococo; but is it architecture? No, it is only exterior decoration. Yet, paradoxically, Egid Quirin's quality as an architect —Late Baroque at first, then proto-Rococo, and finally for a time fully Rococo— must be judged by his decorative work in the interiors of a series of churches, from Weltenburg down to the one he built here for himself, carried out usually (except at Rohr) with his brother's collaboration as fresco-painter. Sometimes that brother or he himself was fully responsible for the architecture, as at Weltenburg and in the Asamkirche, at Rohr, and perhaps at Ingolstadt; sometimes other architects were, as at St. Jakobi in Innsbruck, Einsiedeln, St. Anna-am-Lehel and Osterhofen. But most characteristically—and, for the early development towards the Rococo, most significantly—it is the remodelling and redecoration of the medieval churches at Freising and Regensburg that constitute Egid Quirin's greatest architectural contribution.

Other Late Works

There are, however, two more extant architectural works by E. Q. Asam[132] of some consequence, both begun in 1738, that have not yet been discussed. One is modest in size, the Sakramentskapelle in the southerly apse of Freising Cathedral; the other is relatively large, the church of the Ursulines in Straubing, which was completed only after Cosmas Damian's death in 1741. The first is of irregularly oval plan, with flattened sides, a dome overhead frescoed by Cosmas Damian, and a lantern at the base of which a stucco pelmet hangs. Over the altar are statues by Egid Quirin: St. John Nepomuk in the centre with St. John the Baptist to the left and St. John the Evangelist to the right. Above is a glory-framed oculus and, on the S-curved 'horns' of the altar edicule, angels carrying the Cross and the Crown of Thorns.

The Straubing church is circular in plan, with a wide semi-elliptical apse to the east, shallow altar-niches at the sides, and a flattened elliptical bay to the west over which is the organ gallery.[133] Cosmas Damian's large ceiling fresco was completed by his brother. Neither this nor the Freising chapel really represents a further development of Egid Quirin's architecture.

Mention of the terminal work in Cosmas Damian's *œuvre*, completed by him—as the frescoes at Straubing were not—before his death the next year, can well conclude this chapter even though as a *Gesamtkunstwerk* it owes nothing to his brother. The pilgrimage church called Herrgottsruh[134] at Friedberg, just south-east of Augsburg, was rebuilt beginning in 1731 by the architect Johann Benedikt Ettl from Eichstätt with considerable financial assistance from the Elector Carl Albrecht. This curious and rather amateurish many-domed church has one especially notable feature, the large round choir that rises to the east, much higher than the three-aisled nave, and provides both internally and externally the principal feature of the architectural composition. This suffers from the absence of an appropriate high altar. There is, in these post-Vatican-II days, no altar at all against the eastern wall, since that installed in 1870 has been removed. Moreover, Cosmas Damian's frescoes, despite restoration, are in poor condition. But within the grand domed shell provided by Ettl, he and F. X. Feichtmayr (1705–64), of the family[135] that dominated this particular craft from the late thirties down into the sixties, certainly created one of the handsomest Rococo interiors. The dome carries most of the frescoing, with the hemispherical field divided by radial bands into eight segments. There is a very wide one on the west above the choir-arch, a somewhat narrower one above the original location of the altar, and on each side three more. Delicately decorated bands, almost totally devoid of tectonic weight, suggest a sort of radial cage to support the tiny terminal lantern. Between these members the illusory space of the fresco is seen as unified. Below the bands are associated mostly with pairs of pilasters, though only single ones flank the choir-arch. The pink scagliola of these pilaster shafts provides a similar pseudo-structural framework around the walls below. But the intricate elaboration of the capitals and the related enrichment of the frames of the two tiers of windows to the east and of the similar panels at the sides (if not the fresco above the site of the high altar with its rather heavy *quadratura* setting) lighten and blend these conventional elements into a nearly continuous Rococo wall-shell. Characteristic of the Rococo use of decorative and sculptural elements to diminish the vigour of horizontals are the shallow segmental curves at top and bottom of the upper windows and panels, not to speak of the fuller curves of the cartouches flowing upwards across the entablature and also downwards across the arched heads of the lower windows and panels.

More credit here doubtless goes to Feichtmayr as stuccoer than to Ettl as architect or to C. D. Asam. With the late thirties a new generation, brought up with the Rococo, was taking over the decoration, if not the architectural design, of German churches. Of these men, F. X. Feichtmayr and his younger brother J. M. Feichtmayr (1709–72), half a generation younger than Cosmas Damian's stuccoer-brother Egid Quirin, would be the great stars of the High Rococo of the forties and fifties.

Neither of the Feichtmayrs, however, practiced as architects. Important for the Rococo as decoration executed in stucco had been since the early twenties, and would continue to be for forty years longer, significant as were the early contributors of stuccoer-architects such as Dominikus Zimmermann and E. Q. Asam, the progressive evolution of German Rococo architecture in the later years of the Asams' careers had new protagonists. To a greater extent than in the twenties, leadership was in the hands of men who had the practical local background that the Asams, because of their foreign training and their prime interests in painting and in sculpture, necessarily lacked. A few of these architects, moreover, had had in their youth the more specialized and peculiarly German upbringing as stuccoer-architects associated with Wessobrunn, though most were dependent for plastic as for fresco decoration upon the services of collaborators of varying degrees of competence.

CHAPTER II

Johann Georg Fischer of Füssen

IN central Europe in the seventeenth and eighteenth centuries architects and stuccoers of the same family name were likely to be closely related. Thus of the five Dientzenhofers, active particularly in Bohemia but also in the Upper Palatinate and Franconia before and after 1700, four were brothers who had come from Bavaria, and the fifth and most productive, Kilian Ignaz, was the son of the ablest of these, Christoph. These two, and also Johann who worked at Banz and at Pommersfelden, have already been mentioned incidentally in the previous chapter. Around the Bodensee innumerable Beers and Thumbs from the Austrian Vorarlberg were employed through three and four generations; several of them find a place in Chapter IV.

The three most prominent architects named Fischer were not related. Johann Bernard Fischer (1656–1723), known as Fischer von Erlach after he was ennobled by the Emperor Joseph I, was Austrian-born, but trained in Italy and had some first-hand knowledge of Holland and northern Germany. Johann Michael Fischer came from the Upper Palatinate, as has been mentioned earlier. Settling in Munich in 1723, he was employed thereafter largely in Bavaria and Swabia. Several of his churches of the twenties have been discussed in the previous chapter, and there is a further account of most of his mature works in Chapter V. The professional lives of these two Fischers hardly overlapped either geographically or chronologically. The Austrian Fischer died the year before Johann Michael undertook his first commission, the rebuilding of the east end of the abbey church at Niederaltaich on the Danube not far from his birthplace.

The career of a third Fischer, Johann Georg (1673–1747), however, overlapped both Fischer von Erlach's and Johann Michael's, even though he was seventeen years younger than the latter and nineteen years older than the other. Yet his professional activity was more limited than that of either of them and his production largely confined to the Allgäu district of southern Germany, extending only a little into the contiguous Austrian Tyrol. Except for his early employment at Innsbruck and around Reutte and, much later, one rather important church in Dillingen well to the north (as well as some minor works that once existed in and near Augsburg) almost all of his extant *œuvre* is to be found between Ravensburg in southern Württemberg to the west, Kaufbeuren in Bavarian Swabia to the north, and Füssen at the foot of the Alps to the east. There at Füssen he married in 1707 and ten years later bought a house. J. G. Fischer may justly be considered a provincial architect in contrast to the more cosmopolitan Fischer von Erlach, working out of Vienna, and the widely patronized Johann Michael, working out of Munich, whose vast production includes several of the largest and most sumptuous monastery churches in Swabia, in Bavaria, and in his native Upper Palatinate as well as many smaller ones.[1]

Not surprisingly Johann Georg Fischer receives little attention in the two best books in English on the Baroque of Central Europe, John Bourke's of 1958 and Eberhard Hempel's of 1966.[2] Hempel, for example, writing in Dresden, has much more to say about architects active in Saxony and in Poland of considerably less ability. Indeed, he mentions no work of Fischer's own design but only the fact that he carried out J. J. Herkomer's design for St. Jakobi at Innsbruck (Pl. 42) after the latter's death.[3] Moreover, Hempel identifies Fischer merely as Herkomer's 'foreman', i.e. *Palier* in eighteenth-century German terminology, not as his nephew. Bourke, in describing the Innsbruck church, also notes Fischer's responsibility as his uncle's successor for the execution.[4] But he properly includes a brief paragraph also on Fischer's[5] own church at Bertoldshofen (Pls. 90–93) near Oberdorf,[6] his birthplace, which has long been his only well-known work.[7]

That Bertoldshofen should still be Fischer's chief claim to fame results almost as much from the peculiar demand of his client there as to its relatively high standing among the churches of the late twenties and early thirties in which large-scale Rococo interior architecture in Germany was initiated. Although the church at Bertoldshofen is dedicated to St. Michael—not to St. Anthony of Padua as most people suppose—it was the *locus* of a religious *Brüderschaft* devoted to the Paduan saint that the parish priest Johann Lutz had founded in 1685.[8] This lay organization early became an enormous success and counted in its first half-century over 20,000 members. When, in 1720, lightning damaged the tower of the medieval church, Fischer advised Lutz that the whole edifice should be rebuilt. However, only repairs and some enlargement of the existing church were carried out at that time.

A new priest, Johann Ulrich Julius, who took charge of the parish and the brotherhood in 1721, determined in 1727 to build a new church. For this he asked Fischer to provide a design. Julius insisted that the church should follow the model of the Chiesa del Santo in Padua in honour of St. Anthony, and actually took Fischer on a trip to Italy—probably not his first[9]—to see it. The Bertoldshofen church does, indeed, have multiple domes within like the Paduan original,[10] but could hardly be more different otherwise. It was built and decorated over the next six years at a total cost of 14,264 gulden though not consecrated until 5 October 1738.[11]

The highly exceptional model—for an eighteenth-century church—that the architect was expected to follow, rather in the way medieval builders were often called on to imitate the Holy Sepulchre or St. Peter's in Rome, and the unexpectedly effective result, rivalling in richness if not in spacial originality the Zimmermanns' contemporary church at Steinhausen (Pl. 11) and J. M. Fischer's abbey church at Osterhofen (Pls. 57, 59), as decorated by the Asams in the same years, justify up to a point the reputation of Bertoldshofen (Pls. 90–93). Yet it ought not to be considered J. G. Fischer's finest work. St. Katherine at Wolfegg (Pls. 105–110) and the church he built for the Franciscan nuns at Dillingen (Pls. 111, 112), if not those at Marktoberdorf (Pls. 94–96) and Kisslegg (Pls. 99–102), are much more deserving of attention.[12] These illustrate far better the way Johann Georg, despite a very late start, eventually developed as a Rococo designer in the mid-thirties shortly after the completion of Bertoldshofen.

Fischer's late start was originally due to his continued employment by his uncle down to the latter's death in 1717. But even after that date, when he was already forty-four years old, he was chiefly occupied for some years still with churches and monasteries Herkomer had designed if, indeed, these had not already been long under way. Born on 21 January 1673, the son of a prosperous baker, Fischer's relationship to his mother's brother, Herkomer, was much more important for his later career than his apprenticeship to Augustin Stickl, a Marktoberdorf builder. Just where he was—other than probably for a while in Italy—and what he was doing in the late 1690s is not recorded; but on 10 March 1701—two months before the cornerstone of Herkomer's major work, the church of the Benedictine Abbey of St. Mang in Füssen, was laid—he was hired by the St. Mang Abbot Gerhard Oberleitner at 28 kreutzer a day (with free meals and beer) as his uncle's assistant.[13]

Characteristic of the biographies of many architects active in southern Germany in the decades following 1720, though not of Dominikus Zimmermann[14] or J. M. Fischer—and of C. D. Asam only as a fresco-painter—is the fact that their early experience was in association with a relative well established in professional practice. Thus among J. G. Fischer's contemporaries, Joseph Schmuzer[15] (to whom J. G. Fischer was distantly related through one of his grandmothers) had behind him, even at the unusually early start of his own career, some years of assistance to his father Johann, who died in 1701; and Peter Thumb, also an architect's son, had even more relevant experience working under his cousin (and later father-in-law) Franz Beer, who lived until 1726.[16] C. D. Asam inherited, to some extent at least, the reputation of his painter-father Hans Georg; but this must have been enhanced by common knowledge of the two years of study he had spent in Rome and the prize he had won there following on his early collaboration with his father at Freystadt.

The Work of J. J. Herkomer

It will be well at least to outline here Fischer's uncle's career, especially as he was so long directly involved in it. Johann Jakob Herkomer (or Herkommer—even in the family chapel both spellings are found) was born at Sameister near Lechbruck, some ten miles north of Füssen, in 1648.[17] He belonged to that generation which, in Norbert Lieb's words, 'bedeutet die Regeneration am Ende des dreissigjährigen Kriegs'. So did, for example, the Graubündners who then dominated architecture in the Bavarian capital, Viscardi and Zuccalli (who have both been mentioned earlier). More relevant contemporaries, however, were such Vorarlbergers and men from Wessobrunn as Michael Thumb and Johann Schmuzer, both of whom fathered designers of importance in Fischer's own generation.

In his thirties Herkomer spent some time in Venice, returning home in 1685. Over the years 1685–88 he built the small family chapel, dedicated to Our Lady of Seven Sorrows, at Sameister, his birthplace, which had been founded by his brother Isaak (d. 1686).[18] Unfortunately this cruciform domed edifice is now somewhat defaced by the metal sheathing on the 'east' (actually west) end. But the build-up of three-dimensional elements as seen from that direction still has an almost Byzantine air: a small low apse, containing a square Easter Sepulchre, projects from the taller rectangular ambulatory around the eastern arm that leads up to a crowning dome.

Both Isaak and Johann Jakob are buried here and their busts flank the entrance on the inside; while the latter's tombstone, on which he is described as both 'pictor et architectus' and hailed as 'celeberrimus', above a still-life relief of architects' drafting tools, forms part of the pavement. The interior, with its frescoes executed by Herkomer in 1692, has been well restored within the last decade.

After a second visit to Italy in 1694 lasting three years—one must assume he had had financial assistance in his earlier youth from his brother Isaak or some other source and later inherited property—Herkomer was retained by Abbot Oberleitner of St. Mang and worked principally for that monastery in Füssen until his death some twenty years later.[19] His monastic buildings survive, the north wing serving today as the town hall of Füssen. These were planned and started possibly as early as 1697. The church, however, was not begun until 1701, as has been mentioned. This was structurally completed, but not decorated, by 1711 under Leitner's successor, Abbot Dominikus Dierling, though the consecration by Alexander Sigmund Pfalzgraf von Neuburg, Prince-Bishop of Augsburg,[20] followed only in 1717. Herkomer's other surviving works in the Allgäu of these years are not of much relevance here except in so far as several of them were completed by his nephew. The two fifteenth-century churches that he remodelled at Augsburg—St. Moritz in 1714–15 and Heilig-Kreuz in 1716–17—were gutted in the last war.

Better evidence of Herkomer's prestige with contemporaries than much of what survives is the fact that he is known to have provided in 1711 a project for the monastic buildings of the great Benedictine Abbey of Ottobeuren[21] in Bavarian Swabia. Lieb believes that these influenced some, at least, of the interiors of the following years there carried out by Father Christoph Vogt (1643–1725). Surviving records for the years 1711–13 indicate that he also had connections with another great Benedictine abbey, that at Weingarten in southern Württemberg. There he may have been responsible for the buildings serving the abbey's agricultural activities (*Oekonomie-Bauhof*).[22]

Herkomer's present-day reputation, however, depends almost entirely on his two largest churches, St. Mang in Füssen and St. Jakobi over the mountains in Innsbruck. Curiously enough the latter, though actually executed by his nephew, is less relevant to Fischer's own work of the succeeding years than St. Mang. St. Jakobi was described in the previous chapter and need not be discussed again here.[23] The rich decoration in fresco and stucco (Pl. 42) by the brothers Asam was not the choice of Fischer but of the parish priest, Franz Christoph Mörl, who was a brother of C. D. Asam's wife, as was stated earlier. This has little in common with the frescoes and the *stucchi* in the nave of St. Mang from which the decorative treatment of Fischer's own early works largely derives.

Füssen, St. Mang

St. Mang, halfway up the steep slope from the Lech (Pl. 78) to the picturesque medieval Schloss of the Prince-Bishops of Augsburg, occupies the site and makes use of the foundations of a Romanesque abbey church consecrated in 1143.[24] The original plan of St. Mang, with choirs both to the west and to the east of the nave, was retained. The interior, however, was given more directional emphasis by providing at the east a deep, but rather low, monks' choir of horseshoe-shape beyond the rectangular sanctuary and choir. These last are quite similar to the two square bays of the nave and the three of the crossing and transepts (Pl. 80). The vaults of the nave are carried on pendentives. But above these are flattish disks rather than true domes like the hemispherical one that covers the crossing: that rises high over an internal circular gallery and is crowned by a small lantern. The vaults throughout are supported by internal wall-pillars which are not pierced, except by low arches at their base, nor linked by galleries above. Significantly, as will be evident later in connexion with J. G. Fischer's own work, the 'disks' over the sanctuary and the choir are oval rather than round to fit the somewhat elongated shape of these elements of the plan. The identical widths of the nave, the transepts, and the eastern arm were evidently determined by the surviving foundations of the original Romanesque arcades and walls. This restriction, together with the great height of the whole interior except the monks' choir, produced spaces that are, for the period, unusually tall and narrow. These spaces, moreover, are vigorously articulated by the cross-arches between the bays.

Certain features of the church are unmistakably Venetian, indeed specifically Palladian. An arched screen partially shuts off the monks' choir in the eastern apse behind the high altar (Pl. 81) much as in Palladio's S. Giorgio Maggiore and, later, in Longhena's Santa Maria della Salute. More conspicuous from the exterior than from the interior, except at the east end of the sanctuary above the monks' choir, are the wide half-round clerestory windows. Like many of Palladio's these are divided in the ancient Roman way into three by plain vertical mullions (Pl. 78).

The rounded western apse terminates a half-bay covered by a barrel-vault like those set transversely over the subsidiary spatial elements flanking the nave. This vault, unlike those elsewhere in the church, is cut by oval windows at the sides, as is also the half-dome beyond. A large organ of 1752–53, carried on a concave-fronted gallery, fills the upper part of the western apse with a very rich High Rococo composition in three dimensions. This is presumably unrelated to Herkomer's original intentions and long posterior even to Fischer's involvement with the completion of the church.

Exceptionally, as his epitaph indicates, Herkomer was an accomplished fresco-painter as well as an architect; less exceptionally, he was a very able stuccoer also. The frescoes at St. Mang in the choir, the sanctuary, the high-domed crossing and the transept bays are his;[25] while the rich and delicate stucco-work on the pendentives and the circular frames of the frescoes in those eastern portions of the church is from his designs, though certainly not entirely by his hand.[26] The frescoes in the nave of 1720–22 are by F. G. Hermann (1692–1769);[26a] the *stucchi* there, which follow closely Herkomer's in the eastern bays, are by one or more of those who had earlier assisted him, perhaps principally Johann Bader (Pl. 80). As in the later church in Innsbruck, the shafts of the pilaster clusters on the wall-pillars are marbled pink throughout.

Only a very few times in Fischer's own career, after completing St. Jakobi in collaboration with the Asams, did he have the opportunity to see carried out such a sumptuous programme of decoration as at St. Mang. Moreover, he never himself built so large an edifice, since he worked largely in small towns and villages, not for rich monasteries. At the beginning of his career, however, debts to St. Mang are very evident. Even twenty years later in his finest church, St. Katherine at Wolfegg, he was still using Herkomer's Roman-Palladian windows in the clerestory, despite the unsuitability of their antique simplicity to a Rococo interior.

Fischer was already middle-aged when the death of his uncle in 1717 left him free to begin a personal career. Not surprisingly that freedom was only relative: his most considerable commission for some time was the execution of the Innsbruck church from Herkomer's designs. In these same years after 1717, moreover, his work for the Benedictine monastery at Fultenbach south of Dillingen, now destroyed, and much of what he was building in Füssen also followed plans left by his uncle. His principal inherited obligations in Füssen were, of course, to the Abbey of St. Mang. In the church he provided various altars and other fittings, all probably based on designs by his uncle,[27] but there was even more to keep him busy completing the extensive monastery buildings down at least to 1726.[28]

Fischer's Early Works: Churches and Chapels

More relevant to Fischer's later independent production than what he did at St. Mang is the Krippkirche[29] in Füssen, properly called St. Nikolaus. This is a modest town-church set between three- and four-story buildings in the Reichenstrasse, the principal north-south street of the town. A scalloped gable gives the Krippkirche some importance in the skyline though it does not rise above the roofs of some older houses in the street (Pl. 83). But further interest derives from the plastic treatment of the façade. The decorative articulation of the yellow stucco wall below the gable is limited to narrow pilaster strips, painted dark grey, and even thinner window-frames, with only the slightest elaboration at the entrance. But the tall shallow niche rising up into the gable over the doorway in the middle third of the façade is most happily related to the scrolls at the gable's sides and to the double-S-curved cornices both of the entrance and the top of the gable. Whether Herkomer or Fischer was responsible this gable, deriving from those in the court of the monastery, is extremely effective in the *Stadtbild*.

The interior of the Krippkirche is rather dark and the side walls are bleak owing to the absence of windows. Light enters only from the front, from the windows in the rear quadrants and, invisibly, from the sides of the choir. Once the eye is adjusted to this lack of light, the spatial interest of the composition and the elegance of the stucco-work overhead by Seitz, Geyr and Bader, who were in these years still working also at St. Mang, becomes apparent (Pls. 82, 84). To the ritual east a very tall arch, pendant to the convex bulge in the front wall produced by the external niche, opens into an oblong choir of the same width. This choir is covered by a dome on pendentives and carries a fresco dated 1719 by Joseph Obermiller. There are only short side arms and at the rear a shallow rectangular apse; thus the spatial composition of the eastern end of the church somewhat resembles that of Herkomer's chapel at Sameister. The choir here is, however, not circular but oval in shape like Herkomer's sanctuary at St. Mang.

More significant is the way the rectangular shape of the nave is modified (Fig. 9). The unusual convex projection in the front wall Fischer never repeated; but the concave quadrantal curves flanking the choir-arch were henceforth a recurrent feature of his church interiors.[30] Whoever proposed them, the uncle or just possibly the nephew, was adopting here quite early a feature of considerable consequence for the ultimate development of a truly Rococo interior architecture in south German churches. Whether these curved corners, partially ovalizing—at least at one end—the rectangle of the nave, were introduced independently, or rather echo the much bolder quadrants, used in all four corners of the nave of St. Egidien in Nürnberg, built in 1711–18 by Fischer's contemporary Gottfried Trost (1672–1728), or even earlier at Kreuzpullach, need not be decided here. In any case this seems to have preceded its use by other architects by some six years.[31]

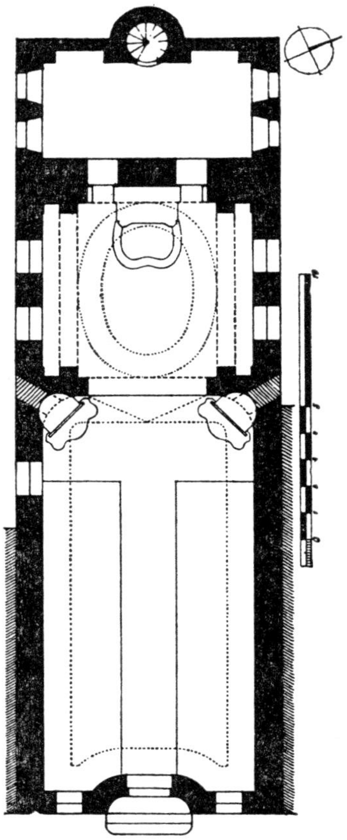

Fig. 9. Füssen, Krippkirche. Plan

Curved corners appear again at Füssen a little later in St. Sebastian, where Fischer rebuilt the nave in 1721–23,[32] and the much smaller church of St. Ulrich and St. Afra, better known as the Feldkirche, to the north of Füssen opposite the entrance to the Neuer Friedhof. As rebuilt by Fischer in 1724–25[33] the Feldkirche has such quadrants at the front as well as at the rear of the nave (Fig. 10). The earliest instance of Fischer's personal adoption of this device would probably be in the cemetery chapel of St. Anna at Kisslegg, near Leutkirch, which was built in 1718–19[34] at almost the same time as the Krippkirche (Pl. 85). There, on a smaller scale and with a change to lower and broader proportions, the planning of the Krippkirche is repeated, though with a circular rather than an oval choir, a gallery across the west end and no bulge at the front.

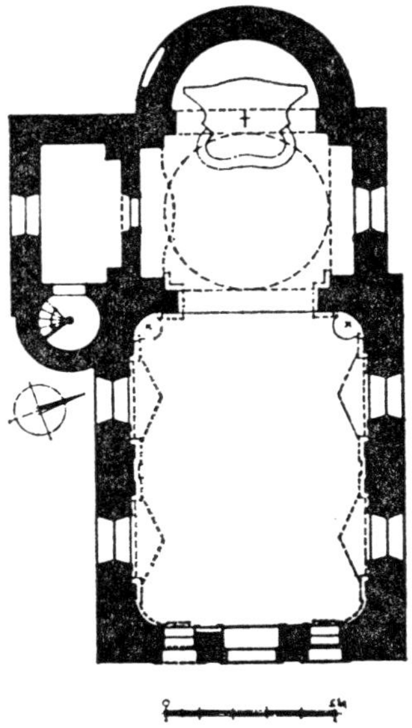

Fig. 10. Füssen, Feldkirche. Plan

Documentary evidence is lacking to connect Fischer with the Kisslegg chapel. But it is not alone the stylistic similarity to known works of his, not to speak of the character of the stucco-work by his relative Hans Herkomer, that supports the attribution. By this date Fischer was being employed by the hereditary Lord High Steward of the Empire (*Reichserbtruchsess*) Ferdinand Ludwig Graf von Waldburg zu Wolfegg—who had probably consulted Herkomer earlier concerning interiors at Schloss Wolfegg—in his other Schloss at Kisslegg. Externally the steep-gabled block of this, dating from the 1560s, was untouched. But under Fischer's general direction the interiors were redecorated, reputedly over the years 1717–21 and principally with stucco-work by Antoni Frast and Nicolas Perte.[35] That was Fischer's first commission from a member of one of the two Waldburg families who would henceforth be his chief patrons. It seems, therefore, all but certain that Ferdinand Ludwig was also the client for St. Anna and Fischer the designer, especially as in 1719 the count had Fischer design the Mariensäule in front of Schloss Wolfegg, a modest column crowned with a statue of the Virgin by Anton Barbacon.[36]

Both the Krippkirche and the Kisslegg chapel have another feature characteristic of most of Fischer's churches of the next fifteen years. The ceilings of the naves are flat—although no advantage is taken of this to introduce very large frescoes, or indeed any at all in the Krippkirche—but they are joined to the walls by a rather deep cove that follows the curves of the quadrantal corners (Pls. 82, 85).[37] Both at Füssen and at Kisslegg the nave arch breaks up through this cove and at Kisslegg the arches of the windows along the side of the nave do so also.

The oval dome over the choir at Füssen carries a good-sized fresco by Josef Obermiller, as has been noted. The capping of the choir at Kisslegg and that of the humble church of St. Georg in Rückholz[38] built in 1719—almost certainly also by Fischer, and with *stucchi* by Hans Herkomer or Johann Bader—follow more closely the treatment of the main vaults of St. Mang (Pl. 80); the frescoes in both are confined to smallish flat disks heavily framed with stucco-work (Pls. 85, 86). The one in the choir at Rückholz is again by Obermiller; the painter of the frescoes in St. Anna has not been identified. Outside the frames of the frescoes, across which foliate decoration scrolls at the cardinal points, much as at St. Mang but more delicately, there is a relatively wider cove than in the bays of St. Mang. These coves are decorated with very free and elegant Corinthian scroll-work that is, as at St. Mang, quite without the heaviness of earlier Wessobrunn work. In both cases the raised decoration is white but set against rich pink grounds. At St. Anna a similar circular fresco, somewhat more luxuriantly framed, also occupies the centre of the flat ceiling of the nave. Around the circle are spandrel-shaped areas of pink, with oval fields at the corners of a pale yellow that appears also in the corners of the surrounding cove. Most of the other stucco decoration on this cove, on the pendentives of the choir, and even on parts of the flat surface of the ceiling of the nave is white on white, as is also true in the Krippkirche.

These are all quite modest interiors, and the rather inaccessible one in the Füssen Feldkirche is little different from that at Kisslegg, though carried out several years later. They may well, moreover, be dependent on earlier designs by Herkomer, though to an extent that is not ascertainable; they certainly owe a good deal to St. Mang. But all four—for one can include the choir of Rückholz as well—have a distinctly proto-Rococo flavour such as is only very rarely found elsewhere in Germany just before and after 1720. In the mid and late 1710s real Rococo design was just being introduced into Germany from Paris at the Bonn Residenz and in the Pagodenburg at Nymphenburg (Pls. 2, 4) by French or at least French-trained artists and then, in 1720, as was stated in the Introduction, first reflected—but rather faintly and uncertainly—by the Asams in the decoration of the churches at Rohr and Aldersbach (Pls. 34, 38).

Oval or ovalized planning, curved corners, broad coves round flat ceilings, delicate continuous patterns of raised ornament: all these things would, within a decade, become characteristic of German Rococo church interiors. Their early use in the Allgäu, out of range of the direct Parisian influence that affected Bonn and Munich or the Viennese influence that preceded and parallelled this in Franconia, gives considerable historical importance in the stylistic morphology of the proto-Rococo, and even the Early Rococo, to Herkomer's immediate followers, his architect-nephew Fischer and the stuccoers who continued for some years to work with him. But there were several years of minor production before Fischer carried the development any further.

Fischer's Early Secular Works

Until Fischer was commissioned in 1727 to rebuild St. Michael at Bertoldshofen and, except for that, down to the rebuilding of the parish church at Marktoberdorf in 1732–33 Fischer's more considerable works initiated after the completion of the Krippkirche were secular. What he may have carried out from Herkomer's designs at Fultenbach in addition to the church there is not clear since nothing remains. Of the work he is supposed to have done about 1720 for another Benedictine abbey, that at Oberelchingen just north-east of Ulm, nothing seems to be extant either, though the big church, as rebuilt in the seventies and eighties by Joseph Dossenberger (1721–85) and frescoed by Januarius Zick (1730–97), survives as a significant and even impressive example of the transition to Neoclassicism in southern Germany. But two *Schlösser*, the modest one for the Wurzach (or Zeil) branch of the Waldburgs at Kisslegg of 1721–27 and the considerably bigger one for the Prince-Bishop of Augsburg at Marktoberdorf of 1722–25, are of a good deal more interest than the priests' houses at Bernbeuren (1724–25), at Altdorf (of the same date), at Rückholz (1729–31) and at Ebershofen (1734)—the last two, in any case, but attributions to Fischer by Neu.[39] Of the prison of 1722–23 at Buchloe little remains and that little much altered; while the Pfeghaus Fischer remodelled in 1725–26 at Sonthofen and the Waltenhofen rectory of 1717 are entirely gone. Moreover, few of these minor secular works that survive are even recognizably of this period except for the Amtshaus at Buchloe of 1728–29, built to house the regional offices of the bishopric of Augsburg.[40] This rather plain rectangular block with simple academic window trim would be recognized in any country as of eighteenth-century date but it has little national or regional, much less individual, character.

Neither the Schloss at Kisslegg of the Counts of Waldburg zu Zeil nor the Jagdschloss at Marktoberdorf correspond very well to one's idea of what a Schloss should be, for both are merely larger, but hardly richer, examples of the eighteenth-century vernacular than the Buchloe Amtshaus. The Kisslegg Schloss[41]—so different from the sixteenth-century one of the Wolfegg branch of the Waldburgs the other side of Kisslegg, where Fischer seems to have been supervising for some years the decoration of the interior—might well be called a 'country house', were it not on the edge of the built-up area of the town with one end of the rectangular block tight against the main road from Bad Wurzach. This end, six windows wide and three stories tall, has no more architectural elaboration than the Buchloe office building. But the location of the chapel is marked by a large half-round window that breaks asymmetrically the ranges of shutter-hung rectangular ones. The façade towards the town, three times the length of that on the street, is quite without incident except for an arch in the centre of the ground story which no longer serves as the entrance—and, to judge from the internal arrangement, probably never did. The garden front, opening on what is now the plain lawn of a public park, is rather more interesting (Pl. 97). Five-windowed wings project at either end and, in the middle of each of these, two-storied dormers with wide shuttered

Fig. 11. Marktoberdorf, Jagdschloss. Front elevation

openings rise to curved gables at the level of the ridge of the main roof. A modest arch, with balconette above, marks the axial entrance.

Reflected in the pool in the park, and with regional character provided by the diagonally striped shutters on the dormers, this simple façade crowned by gable-tops, recalling that over the façade of the Krippkirche, is certainly quite attractive but not in the least monumental, much less palatial. The mode might well be called 'institutional' and the Schloss now houses, appropriately enough, a school. Inside the ceilings have stucco decoration, but most of this is inferior to Hans Herkomer's slightly earlier work in St. Anna.[42] The small chapel of the Schloss, dated 1722, is a square domed chamber, two stories high, with balustraded openings the full width of the arches below the pendentives toward the north-south and the east-west corridors of the first floor. Rather unexpectedly, the dome has a large fresco by J. G. Roth over the whole surface with no surrounding stucco-work cove.

The Marktoberdorf Jagdschloss[43] is an even plainer, but very much more extensive, irregularly quadrangular block set beside and below the church on the high hill above the town to the east (Fig. 11). It was considerably enlarged in 1761–62 by the local builder Franz Kleinhans (1699–1766), who had earlier worked with Fischer in the neighbourhood.

Churches and Chapels of the 1720s and 1730s; Bernbeuren

In the twenties and thirties Fischer built, in addition to the secular works just mentioned, quite a number of parish churches, mostly small, and several even smaller chapels. These are in villages north and west of Füssen and south and north of Sonthofen, as well as two or three across the Alps in a part of the Tyrol that is now Austrian but which was then ecclesiastically dependent on Füssen. Such commissions were not based on plans inherited from his uncle.

St. Nikolaus at Bernbeuren, south-east of Marktoberdorf and north of Lechbruck—hence only a few kilometres from Herkomer's family chapel at Sameister—was the first church for the original design of which Fischer was certainly responsible. This is of considerable size and rather richly appointed inside. Of the original

Romanesque church the 32 m. tower of tufa survives, but this now carries a square belfry stage, chamfered at the corners below a helmet-like Baroque roof, that was added by Fischer. The rest of the church and indeed most of the village had burned on the night of 1 May 1720.[44] The new church, begun shortly thereafter, has a broad five-bayed nave and a deep choir ending in a five-sided apse that repeats the shape and uses the foundations of a Late Gothic choir that had been added to the Romanesque nave (Pls. 88, 89).

The new nave at Bernbeuren is covered with a ceiling of elliptical section into which the arched heads of the very big windows cut at the sides. Bits of fresco of little distinction by Johann Heel from Göggingen, with scenes from the Life of the Virgin, break up rather spottily the surface of the vault; otherwise this is decorated with large-scale proto-Rococo bandwork in pink on a white ground. This stuccowork, executed by J. B. Suiter (d. 1754), is inferior in quality to Hans Herkomer's in St. Anna at Kisslegg, though more advanced stylistically. By 1722 the Asams were working in Fischer's St. Jakobi at Innsbruck (Pl. 42), but there is no evidence of Asam influence here, even though the stucco and fresco decoration was perhaps not executed much before the following year.

The square bay of the choir has one tall window and a similar blind arch on the south side, with matching arches over high-set loges on the north (Pl. 89). The dome over this bay and the pendentives that support it carry unattractive frescoes not of Fischer's day—they are signed by F. X. Benhard and dated 1775. The subject is the Woman of the Apocalypse; that of the fresco on the vault of the apse is the Eucharistic Christ adored by the Four Quarters of the Earth. The sculpture on the three altars has been attributed to Anton Sturm (1690–1757), a Füssener who had been born in the nearby Tyrol. But they were built by a local *Schreiner* named Pfeiffer, son of the better-known altar-builder Jörg Pfeiffer. That on the south carries the date 1739.

Externally the church, for all its considerable size, is of the utmost simplicity, with even less detailing than Fischer's secular work of the period except for the lantern that crowns the tower. But it is not on the exterior that one should, in this period, expect to find evidence of stylistic development. Though the handling of the domed bay of the choir recalls the Krippkirche rather closely, the interior here is also rather disappointing, for it is less advanced in spatial organization than St. Anna at Kisslegg or St. Sebastian (which is more precisely contemporary) since there is no attempt at ovalizing the rectangular nave. Moreover, the dome over the choir is also round, not oval as in the Krippkirche, and the late style of its frescoes quite inappropriate.

Nor is there much to be said in this connexion for the small churches or chapels at Rieden (parish church enlarged 1722–23); Weissensee as remodelled (consecrated 1725); Steinbach near Marktoberdorf (1726); Schöllang (projected 1725; built 1726–31); Rosshaupten (remodelled 1723–29); Reichenbach (1729); Bidingen-Weiler and Buchloe (both 1729–30); Echerschwang (1731); Altstädten (projected 1727, built 1732–34); and St. Urban at Rieden (1734–36). St. Walburga at Weissensee and the Erasmuskapelle at Echerschwang—both Neu's attributions—are especially disappointing in their present dismal condition, as is also tiny St. Blasius at Reichenbach.[45]

Of the work in the Tyrol, I have seen neither the Totenkapelle at Breitenwang of 1724 and the parish church at Unterpinswang, begun the same year and completed in 1727, both near Reutte, nor the Capella di S. Magno at Lana di Sopra near Merano of 1724–25, across the present Italian border. The church at Pfronten-Heitlern, built in 1729–33 by Michael Erdt (as was also the tiny Kolomankapelle dated 1730 at Pfronten-Ösch), was doubtless projected by Fischer, not to speak of the one at Leidershofen, carried out by Franz Kleinhans in 1732, and that at Sulzschneid, erected by Josef Halbritter in 1739–40.[46] Halbritter, who was like Kleinhans a builder rather than an architect, had also been associated earlier with Fischer.

Leeder, Rettenberg and Buchloe

A good example of a comparable project by Fischer of which drawings survive is that dated 1730 for the church at Leeder near Kaufbeuren.[47] The earlier tower, though asymmetrically located on the west front, was evidently to be retained as so generally when medieval churches were rebuilt in the eighteenth century—at Bernbeuren, for example. The nave, almost square in shape, was to have been covered, in the way of almost all these churches, with a flat ceiling above a cove in the manner of the Krippkirche; and Corinthian pilasters were to rise immediately below this cove between the four windows on each side. The choir, of two narrow rectangular bays followed by a three-sided apse—doubtless on medieval foundations if not actually intended to utilize existing medieval walls—would have had seven windows as large as those of the nave, with the severies of the cross-vaults above cutting into the continuous barrel-vault and half-dome overhead. In that a single fairly large panel was provided for a fresco. There is no indication of ornamental stucco-work and the most personal touch is the upper range of oval windows, increasing the light in the nave but blind in the choir, like those in the quadrants of the Krippkirche. The most advanced feature is the lifting of the lower edge of the cove above these oval windows.

Fischer's executed churches do not often have the external pilasters shown in the side elevation for Leeder. It is characteristic, however, that no design for the west front is given and no western doorway provided. The entrance, as in so many English churches, would have been through a modest south porch.

The executed church of St. Stephan at Rettenberg, high in the hills just north of Immenstadt, which was begun in 1727 or 28 and just completed in 1730, may be compared with the Leeder project. The first church at Rettenberg, built before 1300, had been replaced by a second that was consecrated on 4 August 1521. This, together with most of the village, burned on 6 March 1727.[48] The new church that Fischer built, incorporating remains of the medieval structure, has a plan effectively identical with that of the Leeder project though the nave is both longer and lower. Below the cove, which is considerably wider and deeper than that indicated on the sectional drawing of Leeder, a rather heavy cornice associated with the pilaster order of the side walls is carried all around both nave and choir (Pl. 87). The way this cornice is bowed up over the rounded tops of the windows and the arched opening into the choir and echoed by a similar bowing of the architrave under the continuous horizontal cornice in the choir and apse is premonitory—but still in a rather tectonic and Baroque way—of the wavy base-line of the cove in the Leeder project.

The three altars at Rettenberg date from 1735 but were 'renewed' in 1883 when Professor Andreas Miller provided the painting for the high altar. Those over the side altars are by L. K. Weiss (1793–1867) and date from 1841. The frescoes were painted by Professor Johann Turner in 1863–64. Restorations of 1883, 1909–10, and 1954–56 have all left their mark.[49] Except for the dreary frescoes, however, the present condition is good. The walls are white throughout and the flat portion of the nave ceiling pink, with pink medallions also set where the cove—unlike the walls below—is curved at the corners. The rather sparse stucco-work overhead approaches the Rococo quite closely but has little of the exuberance of E. Q. Asam's at Osterhofen (Pls. 58, 59) or Dominikus Zimmermann's at Steinhausen (Pl. 11). Even less does it resemble advanced secular work of this date such as J. B. Zimmermann's in the Ahnengalerie of the Munich Residenz (Pl. 62) or that by some other stuccoer in the oval saloon at Alteglofsheim (Pl. 61). It is, however, not so remote from J. B. Zimmermann's *stucchi* at Weyarn and Beyharting of 1729 and 1730.[50] The relative simplicity of the interior fits well the characteristic exterior, so like that of Bernbeuren, dominated again by a big medieval tower that is here set in a transeptal position and crowned by a bold 'onion'.

It was in 1729, the year he completed the Amthaus at Buchloe, that Fischer was asked to give an estimate for the remodelling and redecoration of the interior of the medieval parish church there.[51] Externally this remains an impressive if somewhat shapeless mass dating from the fourteenth, fifteenth, and sixteenth centuries. Built of rich red brick, the whole is subordinated to a big gabled tower in the north transeptal position probably dating, in its present form, from 1584. Only the generous round-arched windows at the sides of the church suggest on the outside the nearly total remodelling of the interior.[52] The flat ceiling of the nave has, as usual in Fischer's churches, a deep cove carried all the way round into which the top of the choir-arch rather awkwardly breaks. The arcades dividing the nave from the aisles have round arches carried on square piers. To reduce their bulk and doubtless to conform to the medieval pillars that the stuccoed surfaces enclose, these piers are heavily chamfered at the corners. This is a device curiously inconsistent in its 'brutalism' with the extreme delicacy of the Rococo *stucchi* on the intradoses of the arches and can hardly have been intended by Fischer. The diagonal setting of the side altars flanking the choir-arch ovalizes very slightly the rectangular space of the nave, but the cove above is not curved at the eastern corners as at Rettenberg.

The vaulting in the choir is continuous above the cross severies over the clerestory windows. These, surprisingly, retain their pointed Gothic shapes. On the vault surface there is both stucco decoration and an oval central panel painted, apparently, in oil rather than fresco to judge from its dark colouring.[53] Low round arches, carried on alternate piers and columns, now open into the surrounding ambulatory added by Thomas Wicks in 1937.

In the nave, as in the choir, the dark spots of the inset paintings on the flat of the ceiling and in the cove contrast awkwardly with the *stucchi*, which are in exceptionally low relief. As restored, presumably in 1937, the decoration is largely white against white, but small fields here and there are filled with pink and with blue-green. Against this light background the later altars and the earlier pulpit, all in rather dark tones of scagliola with some gilded details, stand out boldly and help to unify the otherwise unrelated spaces of the wide nave and the narrow choir.

Bertoldshofen

Rettenberg and—if he *was* responsible—Buchloe were rebuilt and remodelled by Fischer during the years he was primarily occupied with the design and construction of his first major work, St. Michael at Bertoldshofen. With regard to the earlier history of this church one can be somewhat more explicit than with regard to the original construction of Buchloe, although that earlier history constrained Fischer very little.[54] Despite the fact that Bertoldshofen belonged to the nearby parish of Altdorf until 1443, a church dedicated to St. Michael already existed then of which no trace now survives. In the late seventeenth century the parish priest Johann Lutz was called 'verus restaurator' because he had rebuilt the choir, refurnished the nave, and provided three 'glanzvolle' (glittering) altars. For this work Fischer's first master, Augustin Stickl from nearby Marktoberdorf, provided an estimate in 1684. Fischer came on the scene, as has been stated earlier, only in 1720 when he was called in to advise after lightning had damaged the tower. At that date the master-mason Halbritter—later the builder of Sulzschneid—and the master-carpenter Johann Silcher, both from Marktoberdorf, proposed to restore the tower and enlarge the church, making it longer, broader and higher, at an estimated cost of 2700 gulden. For this Julius, the priest mentioned earlier who succeeded Lutz in 1721, preferred Thomas Windt, a master-mason from Bernbeuren—also nearby—but the church authorities at Marktoberdorf insisted that the work be done by Josef Miller of Rettenbach, who had long before carried out Herkomer's plans at Seeg.

The early history of the Brotherhood of St. Anthony, founded in 1685 by Lutz as has been noted, is obscure since the book of members preserved in the parish archive goes back only to 1737. But it must have been the phenomenal success of the brotherhood that led Julius in 1727 to obtain a plan for a wholly new church from Fischer. Fischer was an obvious choice as architect, since at that point he was still concerned with the completion of the Jagdschloss at Marktoberdorf and well known in any case because of his other work in the neighbourhood, beginning with St. Nikolaus at Bernbeuren. For this project the first ridiculously low estimate of 6000 gulden was based on the assumption that the neighbourhood would donate the necessary timber. On that assumption the work went forward at once, with Fischer as the recognized architect though without a formal contract.

There were many difficulties, for the *Pfleger* (church-trustee) Freiherr von Stain at Marktoberdorf opposed the scheme from the first. But Julius was successful in begging building materials from the Steingaden monastery, from the town of Kaufbeuren and the nunnery there, from the town of Schongau, and from other donors. Called on later to justify his ambitious building activities, Julius offered a detailed accounting, now preserved in the Hauptstaatsarchiv in Munich, of the erection of the church. Thanks to that the names of the craftsmen employed and the specific contracts with them are all known. The *Palier* was Paul Bienz, who had assisted Fischer at Rieden in the early 1720s; the mason and the carpenter were the men who had made the estimate for the enlargement of the church in 1720, Halbritter and Silcher from Marktoberdorf.

It is just possible that Herkomer had provided plans for the work that Lutz had had carried out in the 1680s but more probably it was Stickl, to judge from his estimate of 1684. Of that work Fischer retained the side walls of the choir, substituting a rounded apse for the earlier three-sided one (Fig. 12). The walls of the nave were also retained although the nave was extended from two to three bays, with a new burial chapel under the westernmost, where the ground fell off sharply. This explains the small low-placed western apse, whose pointed roof relates so curiously to the big triple window above in one of Fischer's rare—and in this case hardly successful—west front compositions of any architectural pretension (Pl. 90). The transeptal arms and the tower, rising over the north transept in a façade more carefully organized than that on the west, were entirely new.

Characteristically for Fischer's churches, there is not much to say about the exterior. As in the project for Leeder, prepared just as Bertoldshofen was completed structurally in 1730, the walls have Doric pilasters between the tall arched windows—there are no oval ones above them here—and a continuous entablature that rises slightly in a curve over the west window. This feature is a somewhat Zimmermanian[55] variant of Herkomer's Palladian-Roman lunettes similar to those in the nave of St. Sebastian in Füssen as rebuilt by Fischer a few years earlier.[56] The west gable rises in three steps and except for the middle scallop is like that on the façade of the Krippkirche (Pl. 83).

On the north transept façade the base of the tower breaks forward slightly and rises between the scrolled sides of the gable to a simple panelled shaft with cut-off

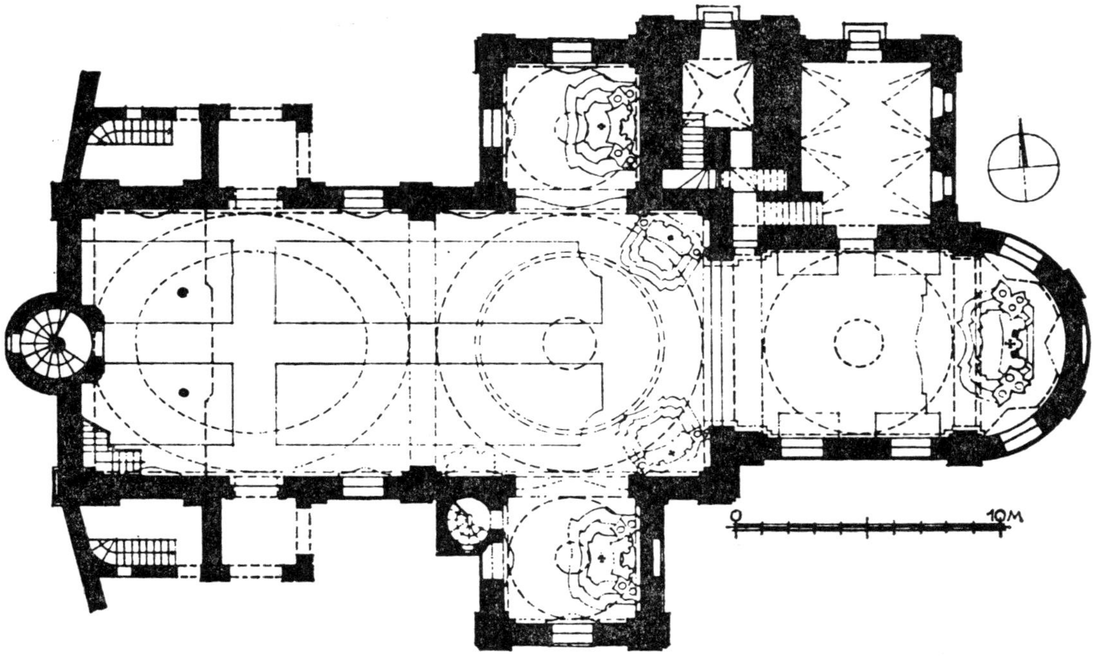

Fig. 12. Bertoldshofen, St. Michael. Plan

corners. As proposed for Leeder two or three years later, there is a clock-face on each side below the belfry arch and a plain domed top with a tiny lantern—like the earlier one at Bernbeuren—rather than the more familiar 'onion' of the Rettenberg tower. (That may, of course, have been a survival or a copy of a favourite local landmark that had existed before the fire.) The most curious thing about the exterior of St. Michael is that, except for the side arms which indicate a cruciform plan, there is no suggestion at all of the exceptional character of the interior. The five domes within are entirely hidden by the tall gable roofs over the nave, the transepts and the choir.

Upon the physical completion of the church, the stuccoer Ignaz Finsterwalder (1708–52) from Wessobrunn with his assistants could set to work. His contract, dated 15 April 1730, was at 1390 gulden. By 1733 the frescoes by Matthias Wolcker were all completed on a 700-gulden contract. (The very crude ones in the sacristy, however, are by J. A. Bergmüller and cost 35 gulden 40 kreutzer). Several of the altars were also in place by St. Anthony's Day in 1733 when the first mass was celebrated; and for two of these Matthias Schäffler (d. 1772) received 200 gulden. For the sculptured figures—and possibly the entire execution—of two more altars and also for the figures on the pulpit Ignaz Hillenbrandt received 285 gulden over the years 1732–37. Leonard Fischer (d. 1751) carried out in intarsia the stalls flanking the choir and the two confessionals, and Gottlieb Dopfer the seating in the nave and the cabinetwork of the pulpit. The organ of 1737 by Georg Ehinger is set on the upper gallery at the west end, where it largely blocks the big triple window that is so conspicuous externally.

Most of the collaborating artists and craftsmen were quite obscure and came from nearby towns. One of the more important, however, Finsterwalder, is much better known, and Hillenbrandt is reputed to have worked just before this in the Magdalena Klause in the gardens of Nymphenburg[57]—the elderly Max Emanuel's rustic hermitage for private devotions—built by Effner in 1723–28. Ignaz Finsterwalder was a member of one of the many families of stuccoers that originated in Wessobrunn near Weilheim in the seventeenth century. At least five relatives of the same name are recorded and, as often in such a situation where several members of one family were on occasion employed together, individual attributions are not always sure. Stephan worked in the Rathaus at Landsberg about 1700; Johann, Gottlieb and Anton assisted Ignaz from time to time, first probably at Klosterlechfeld in 1734 just after the *stucchi* at Bertoldshofen were completed. Bertoldshofen was Ignaz's earliest important commission; a few years later, however, he made an equally notable and much more mature contribution to Fischer's church of 1735–37 for the Franciscan nuns at Dillingen (Pl. 111). Moreover, the interior of Gutenzell, where he executed the *stucchi* and also collaborated on the pulpit with F. X. Feichtmayr in 1755–56, owes rather more to him than to Dominikus Zimmermann who provided the original design for this church of his daughter's convent.[58] His latest work was the stucco decoration dated 1768–69 in the Benedictine abbey church at Scheyern.

Matthias Wolcker, who died young in 1742, is not well known; indeed, this is his only considerable set of frescoes. A Württemberger settled since 1731 in Dillingen, he was a brother of the more active J. G. Wolcker (1700–66)—who was a pupil of J. G. Bergmüller—and a son-in-law of the Dillingen court-painter A. W. Haffe. In Fischer's next important church, that at Marktoberdorf, he fortunately had, for the first time in an interior of his own design, the services of a painter of much greater ability, F. G. Hermann, whom he had known ten years before when Hermann was executing the frescoes in the nave of St. Mang.

So rich is Finsterwalder's incrustation of stucco at Bertoldshofen that at first sight, as in many later Rococo interiors, the eye is distracted by the overall effulgence and incapable of reading clearly the spatial organization (Pls. 91–93). This is, in fact, not very complicated nor even unusual in the way that the curious asymmetry of the external massing might falsely suggest. To speak first of the exterior in relation to the plan once more, the asymmetry is caused by the dislocation of the cross axis at the north side of the church (Fig. 12, Pl. 90). The projection on the north-east is not only much larger than the choir, though the internal transeptal arm is of identical width, but also broader and taller than the nave and crossing, not to speak of the southern transeptal arm. This is because the tall sacristy, opening off the choir to the north, projects as far as does the transeptal arm beside it. This led Fischer to set his tower not at the end of the northern arm but somewhat further to the east. Thus his façade composition is symmetrical but centred on no axis existing inside the church. This curious dislocation of the mass composition, decided on perhaps because it is the north side that faces the village, does not affect the symmetrical organization of the interior. Despite its broader, lower proportions, however, this is closer to St. Mang (Pl. 80) than to its nominal model in Padua. Except that the transept bays and the choir bay are narrower than the nave and crossing and that the nave, considerably shorter than at Padua or Füssen, is treated overhead as a single oblong bay, Fischer has repeated here the scheme of St. Mang of a domed crossing opening into four domed arms (Pl. 92). His treatment of these domes[59] is, however, rather different from Herkomer's at Füssen and evidence of a much less tectonic approach to spatial design.

Least successful, and most remote from Herkomer, is the handling of the nave (Pl. 91). Had it not been lengthened to the west, this could have been covered by a dome of the same dimension as that over the crossing. But the oblong shape, similar to that of the naves of his other churches, required either a division into two bays, as at Padua and St. Mang, or a 'dome' of oval plan, unless he were to content himself here with such a flat rectangular ceiling as he had generally used in his churches. It was doubtless the oval of the sanctuary of St. Mang or that of the choir of the Krippkirche, if not indeed the rather larger library at St. Mang (Pl. 79), that provided the precedent for the oval he used here.

The greater part of the ceiling here is, in fact, as flat as in his earlier naves, thus offering a very extensive area for the principal fresco, but surrounded in his usual way by a cove. The cove, as already at St. Anna at Kisslegg, is proportionately much wider than are Herkomer's in St. Mang (Pl. 80), though it appears to be supported, as those actually are, by the pendentives at the four corners.

This treatment is partially echoed over the crossing (Pl. 93). There the dome, of nearly hemispherical section in contrast to the flat oval of the nave ceiling, does not rise directly from the pendentives but above an intervening coved zone elaborated by twelve frescoed cartouches. The smaller domes of the other three narrower arms rest directly on their pendentives with no such coves; they are, therefore, of exactly the same size as the central dome over the crossing. Doubtless that is the reason Fischer inserted a cove between the latter and its pendentives.

The spatial composition ends in a half-domed apse of which the curved shape corresponds to that of the arches framing the choir and those opening into the transepts. In the way of Fischer's earlier domed choir at Bernbeuren the sacristy opens through a wide arch above a loge on the north side of the choir. This arch is not repeated on the south. There the flat wall of the choir has two big windows, quite as in the Krippkirche, which are identical with the three at each side of the nave and the two that flank the high altar. There are no oval openings; and the one still larger window, that at the west end, is obscured by the organ in front of it, as has been noted, so that it is all but invisible from within the church.

The transverse section of the nave, thanks to the cove at the edge of the ceiling, might be described as 'ovalized rectangular' like that of most of Fischer's earlier churches. Because of the pendentives at the corners, however, the side walls actually terminate above in extended half-ellipses, while the top edge of the west wall and the arch that opens into the crossing are of less elongated semi-elliptical shape. Even so, the broad arch at the end of the nave contrasts with the half-round arches to the east, the north, and the south that open from the crossing into the other three narrower arms. But the cove over the crossing partially ovalizes the section there, though the continuity of the curvature overhead is broken by the higher rise of the central dome (Pls. 91, 92).

Below ceiling level there are no curves in plan except for the terminal apse. But the diagonal placing of the side altars in the eastern corners of the crossing, features nearly as tall and elaborate as the high altar beyond, not to speak of their concave composition with columns set forward at either side, ovalizes the interior at least partially at this point (Pl. 92), somewhat as in his earlier churches at Füssen and Kisslegg, where the eastern corners of the naves are actually curved in plan and the side altars set in niches. Pendant to these altars at Bertoldshofen, on the plain wall areas west of the transeptal arches in the crossing, are the pulpit on the south and, balancing it on the north, the equally rich setting of the statue of St. Anthony.

The foregoing analysis indicates what a complex spatial composition Fischer had created before ever stuccoer or painter was called on to decorate it. It will be obvious, also, that this spatial composition, which owes so much to Herkomer's St. Mang, has little similarity to the Byzantine-Italian interior of the Chiesa del Santo despite its domes—which are here, in any case, only plastered wood-framed shells set well below the high gabled roofs of the exterior. Rather, Fischer elaborated here one of those domed choirs, some of which had side arms, that he had been employing off and on ever since carrying out the Krippkirche from Herkomer's plans ten years before and would continue to introduce in his later churches. Moreover, there is in this modified centralized scheme little that is *more* proto-Rococo architecturally than in his earlier churches.

Negatively, however, the absence of tectonic elements—even the pilasters at the inposts of the arches are minimized in relief and no entablature or cornice crowns the wall surfaces—and, positively, the profusion, the delicate scale, and many of the ornamental elements in Finsterwalder's stucco decoration are significant (Pls.

91–93). The profusion rivals that which Dominikus Zimmermann was providing at this very point at Steinhausen (Pl. 11) and E. Q. Asam for J. M. Fischer at Osterhofen (Pls. 58, 59). Moreover, the delicacy approaches, though it does not equal, that of J. B. Zimmermann's *stucchi* on the ceilings of the Ahnengalerie and the Schatzkammer in the Munich Residenz (Pl. 62) or, more relevantly, in the Neuer Festsaal at the abbey of Benediktbeuern (Pl. 13)—all works of these same years around 1730.

Lacking, presumably, J. B. Zimmermann's and C. D. Asam's direct contact with the Paris-trained craftsmen of Cuvilliés's team in Munich, Finsterwalder in his stucco-work suffers from a kind of obsessive *horror vacui* that blurs the clarity of individual motifs. This is especially apparent in the almost *rocaille* elements flanking the cartouches on the pendentives of the crossing and the recurrent floral sprays and garlands which resemble paper flowers rather more than natural ones (Pl. 93). The colours, moreover, at least as restored—the pinks, the yellows, and the greens—have a sugary quality that contrasts, on the one hand, with the shiny mottled pinks and blues of the scagliola elements of the altars and, on the other, with the darker, duller tonality of many of the frescoes as we see them today.

Fortunately, those on the dome of the choir have stayed lighter and brighter. Some of the less prominent *stucchi*, moreover, on the intradoses of the arches, on the cove below the loge on the north side of the choir, and over the heads of the windows in the nave, are of a more refined and elegant character, rivalling J. B. Zimmermann's at Weyarn[60] and Beyharting of 1729 and 1730, or E. Q. Asam's at St. Emmeram in Regensburg (Pl. 64) which must be almost precisely contemporary with Finsterwalder's.

Before turning from the stucco-work to the frescoes, one should note the way in which the crowning scrolls of the cartouches on the cove of the crossing and on the pendentives of the choir and transepts overlap, and almost seem to scallop, the firm and otherwise rather tectonic cornices at the base of these four domes (Pl. 92). So also, although the main frescoes on the domes and the flat ceiling of the nave are otherwise uninterrupted by stucco intrusions, the stuccoed areas throughout are spotted with innumerable small frescoed cartouches, not only on the pendentives where one might expect them, but all along the coves surrounding the ceiling of the nave and the dome of the crossing (Pls. 91–93). Some similarity to this can be found at just this time in J. B. Zimmermann's treatment of the cove of the Neuer Festsaal at Benediktbeuern (Pl. 13). But Zimmermann was after all the painter as well as the stuccoer there and could balance and harmonize better the two elements, somewhat as Herkomer had done in the monks' choir of St. Mang.

Who the overall designer or co-ordinator of the decorations was at Bertoldshofen is not clear; certainly not Wolcker, more probably Fischer himself. Yet there was evidently no such close collaboration here as one must assume the Zimmermann brothers enjoyed at Steinhausen and the Asam brothers at St. Emmeram or even while they were working in these same years with J. M. Fischer at Osterhofen.

As Wolcker's obscurity and presumptive lack of relevant experience makes not surprising, the frescoes are the weakest part of the *Gesamtkunstwerk* at Bertoldshofen (Pls. 91–93). The altars, the pulpit, and even the choir-stalls and pews are worthy examples of Early Rococo furniture, whether or not their basic design was controlled by Fischer as well as their placing. Unlike J. B. Zimmermann's splendid fresco at Steinhausen (Pl. 11), however, opening up the oval of the nave to the heavens, or C. D. Asam's at Osterhofen (Pl. 57), in which the *quadratura* architecture in the manner of Pozzo centralizes the nave by building up an illusionary square open to the sky high above the oblong nave, Wolcker's painted ceilings play almost no part in the spatial composition of the interior. They are merely particoloured surfaces and their interest, such as it is, only iconographic. To some extent Fischer is responsible for this, for the openings in the tops of the domes, with glimpses of higher painted ceilings above the tiny internal lanterns, emphasize the structural—or at least pseudo-structural—character of the hemispheres overhead at the expense of any pictorial illusion of heavenly space that Wolcker might have attempted.

One further weak point in this church should be mentioned although fortunately the interior is so directional towards the east that one is not much aware of it. The galleries at the west end here, as in so many other eighteenth-century churches, destroy the spatial clarity of the west end (Pl. 91). Sometimes, as with the later Rococo organ at St. Mang, the luxuriance and spatial elaboration of these very big pieces of church-furniture make up for the rather makeshift, or 'afterthought', look of the western galleries on which they are set, but that is not so at Bertoldshofen.

During the years 1727–30 when Fischer must have been busiest at Bertoldshofen, however much he delegated the supervision to Bienz, he was not inactive elsewhere in the neighbourhood, and even further afield. At the church in Leuterschach, built in 1692, he was probably responsible for the new tower added in 1727 as also, in that year, for the now demolished rectory at Waltenhofen.[61] The Amtshaus of 1728–29 at Buchloe and the churches begun at Rettenberg in 1728 and in 1729 at Reichenbach, as well as the remodelling of the Buchloe church in 1729–30 and the project of 1730 for Leeder, have already been mentioned. The Rückholz Pfarrhof of 1729–31[62]—built at a time when he may also have worked on the nave of the church there, inferior though that is to his choir of 1719[63]—is even more modest than the Buchloe Amtshaus. With its five-windowed front and high hip-roof, this might almost be taken for an American 'Colonial' house of the period despite its plain trim of stone and stuccoed walls. The interior, however, has some decorative stucco-work. The chapel of 1730 at Kirnberg near Bernbeuren I have not been able to find.

Marktoberdorf Parish Church

More important, in any case, is the early project of 1728 for St. Katherine at Wolfegg, of which drawings are in the archives there (Fig. A, facing p. 152); but this may better be discussed in relation to the executed church that Fischer began for his old patron Count Waldburg-Wolfegg in 1733, after St. Michael at Bertoldshofen was finished. Just before that, in 1732, Fischer began the big parish church dedicated to the Holy Cross and St. Martin in his native town and completed it within two or three years. The existing fifteenth-century Gothic choir was incorporated in the eastern arm of the new structure, but of this nothing is evident internally except for the relatively great depth (Fig. 13). The whole church, indeed, is on a much larger scale[64] than either Bernbeuren or Bertoldshofen. It is also much more impressive externally, despite the plain treatment of the walls, as it rises beside and above Fischer's massive Jagdschloss and high over the roofs of the town. The characteristic tower—characteristic of the region rather than of Fischer—is especially striking as seen from a distance. But this feature dates from 1680, at least as regards the lower octagonal stage on top of a square trunk that was probably built in the fourteenth century. The uppermost stage, added in 1769, long after Fischer's time, is crowned with an earlier 'onion' of 1722 raised over it at that time.

Broad and without aisles, the nave here at Marktoberdorf, with its elliptical section, is an enlarged version of that at Bernbeuren. The eastern arm, though much longer and more complex spatially, also follows Bernbeuren (Pl. 96). In the nave, though, the pilasters along the side walls are in clusters rather than paired, and their resultant higher relief and more tectonic effect is strongly echoed in the entablature blocks that crown them. However, the cornice only of this entablature continues along the side walls, while above it in each bay are oval windows, like those proposed for Leeder, with cross-severies cutting deep into the main vault. The stucco-work by Abraham Bader of Mindelheim (Pl. 95), dated 1733 in a chronogram, recalls in its rather even distribution J. B. Zimmermann's of 1729 at Weyarn.[65] The big frescoes by F. G. Hermann—that on the dome over the choir is signed and dated 1735—are for the first time in one of Fischer's interiors set within the scalloped stucco frames that had become increasingly characteristic of German interiors during the preceding fifteen years and more. The restoration of the 1930s happily avoided introducing the sugary tones of the Bertoldshofen interior.[66] Moreover, the frescoes, whose iconographic programme relates to the dedication of the church to the Holy Cross,[67] reflect most attractively the greater openness and clearer, fresher colours of J. B. Zimmermann's and C. D. Asam's frescoes of the early 1730s.

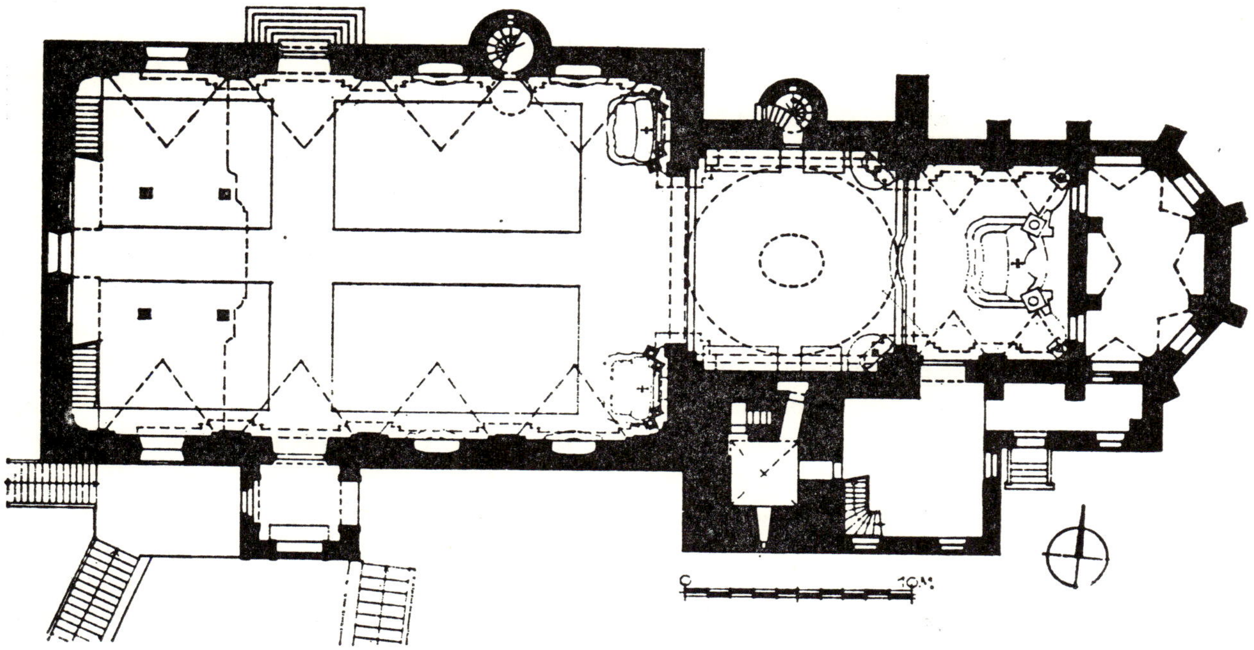

Fig. 13. Marktoberdorf, Heilig-Kreuz & St. Martin. Plan

The result is a light and cheerful if rather shapeless interior. For example, Fischer made here no serious attempt to ovalize the broad rectangular shape of the nave except for the concave bending both of the pilaster shafts at the eastern corners and of the coved band above them (Pl. 94). One thinks of Joseph Schmuzer's St. Martin at Garmisch (Pl. 134), completed just when this church was begun. The nave at Garmisch is, in fact, very little more advanced towards the Rococo than Fischer's, and neither the frescoes there by the excellent painter Matthäus Günther (1705–88), a pupil of C. D. Asam, nor Schmuzer's *stucchi* are as appealing today as what Bader and Hermann provided at Marktoberdorf.

The relation of these collaborators was the reverse of what obtained at Bertoldshofen. The stuccoer Bader, unlike Finsterwalder whose more brilliant career effectively began at Bertoldshofen, was either very unproductive or else his work has been exceptionally poorly documented. Before Marktoberdorf he had perhaps been responsible for the *stucchi* of 1725 in the Liebfrauenkirche in Mindelheim; after Marktoberdorf he worked in the church at Leuterschach with the painter Johann Zick (1702–62) when the nave of that church, built in 1692, was heightened in 1733–37—possibly by Fischer, who built the tower of the church in 1727 as has been noted—and in 1741 he provided scagliola side altars at Hergensweiler.[68]

The painter Hermann, on the other hand, had for some time had a considerable reputation thanks to his frescoes of 1720–22 in the St. Mang nave[69] and, in 1729, he had provided the large fresco in the Festsaal at the Abbey of Weissenau near Ravensburg built by Franz II Beer some twenty years before. Possibly as early as 1734, just before he executed the frescoes at Marktoberdorf, but certainly rather later in the decade or in the early 1740s he also worked in the Prince-Abbot's apartments at Kempten.[70] In addition to many altar paintings in oil, including examples in such great churches as Diessen, Steinhausen, Ettal and Ottobeuren, he was also responsible much later for the frescoes begun in 1752 in the pilgrimage church of Maria Steinbach (Pls. 113–115) and for that dated 1757 over the library at Schussenried, two of the finest Rococo interiors of the mid-century.

How much contact Bader and Hermann may have had with J. B. Zimmermann before they worked for Fischer at Marktoberdorf is uncertain. In the case of Hermann one may note that he had provided the modest—and now badly restored—frescoes in Dominikus Zimmermann's parish church at Buxheim in 1727,[71] when Johann Baptist was evidently not available to collaborate with his brother; and that at Kempten[72] he worked with Übelherr, who had earlier been an assistant of J. B. Zimmermann at the Munich Residenz. Stylistically the joint work of Bader and Hermann is certainly closer to the Zimmermanns than to the Asams. Their redecoration of St. Emmeram in Regensburg (Pl. 63) must have been completed by this time, if not the interior of Santa Maria de Victoria at Ingolstadt (Pl. 70); and St. Johann-Nepomuk (Pl. 72) in Munich was at least begun as late as 1733, even if it was possibly designed a year or two earlier.

Despite Hermann's scallop-framed frescoes and the elegant *stucchi* on the barrel-vault and over the apse in the Marktoberdorf sanctuary, the names of the Zimmermanns and the Asams do not come to mind in relation to the architectonic aspects of Fischer's east end (Pl. 96). The choir-arch, semi-circular and related to the semi-elliptical curve of the nave vault much as at the crossing of Bertoldshofen, rises from bold entablature blocks crowning thin, but quite tectonic, pilaster imposts. The square bay that follows, covered by a dome on pendentives as in several of Fischer's earlier choirs, serves spatially as a sort of crossing here. Even though there are no real chambers to north and south, loges carried, like that on the north side of the Bertoldshofen choir, on generous coves flank the choir. Above and behind these loges there are big triple windows of the type Fischer often used, for example in the nave of St. Sebastian at Füssen and at the west end of Bertoldshofen (Pl. 90)—descendants *via* Herkomer and Palladio from the antique, but possibly influenced by Dominikus Zimmermann also.

The pendentives of the crossing, though not the intradoses of the four arches, are somewhat more simply decorated than at Bertoldshofen, while the scroll-work at the top of the cartouches barely breaks over the thin moulding at the base of Hermann's illusionistic fresco of the Virgin as Intercessor before the Trinity that fills the dome. At the rear of this bay further pilaster clusters carrying the full entablature frame in vigorously tectonic fashion the elaborate high-altar composition that fills the apse spatially (Pl. 96). As in the nave, the cross-severies over the large oval windows above the entablature intersect the main surfaces of the vaults with no mouldings to mark the arrises. Thus above the level of the pilaster order, at least, the eastern arm beyond the domed choir may be considered to be as advanced towards the Rococo as the ceiling of the nave. Yet the general conception of the choir in the Marktoberdorf church is still directly in the line of descent from the Krippkirche.

As regards the major fittings and their location considerable stylistic ambiguity is evident. The side altars of about 1735[73] in the nave, flanking the choir-arch, are not set diagonally, as at Bertoldshofen (Fig. 12), but flat against the east wall, so that they do not serve at all to ovalize the space (Pl. 94). The high altar (Pl. 96), in its openness of construction and complex three-dimensional development, seems to derive from that which E. Q. Asam had provided at Osterhofen (Pl. 58), but this one is much later: 1747. The sculpture on the high altar is by Joseph Stapf (1718–85); the earlier and finer figures of saints by Anton Sturm (1690–1757) and dated 1733, now mounted on brackets at the four corners of the choir, were originally intended for the side altars.[74]

Kisslegg Parish Church

All but precisely contemporary with the Marktoberdorf church are not only several minor works but, as regards the date of their initiation, two others that represent the peak of Fischer's achievement. The simple church of 1732–34 at Altstädten near Sonthofen, projected as early as 1727, has an apsidal east end of horseshoe plan but is otherwise not very interesting. St. Urban at Rieden, remodelled in 1734–36 as was noted earlier, can be ignored also as it is very small and quite featureless. The Amtshaus at Grossdorf of 1733–35, presumably a very modest work, I have been unable to locate.[75] But the parish church at Kisslegg,[76] which was remodelled and much extended over the years following 1734, presumably at the expense of the two Waldburg families—both earlier employers of Fischer at Kisslegg for secular work—deserves more comment at this point. Work there, however, was not in fact started until a year after the construction of St. Katherine at Wolfegg for Count Waldburg-Wolfegg began, even though the result is considerably less advanced in character.

The parish church of St. Ulrich and St. Gallus still dominates the small town of Kisslegg as it must have done in the middle ages. Set at the north end of the main street, it faces the lake and is roughly equidistant from the two *Schlösser* of the Waldburgs (Pl. 98). The west front, turned away from the town, has as usual no other feature than the tall tower, here unusually slender and elegant, even though its shaft is of the twelfth or thirteenth century. The whole church was already raised on a sort of platform and this gives added effect to the complex massing of Fischer's new east end, one of his very few impressive and plastically elaborate exteriors (Pl. 99).

The rectangular apse is blind to the east, but panelled and frescoed; the side arms of the choir, of the same height as the apse, are linked to the sides of the nave by semi-circular chapels whose roofs are no taller than the main roof of the nave where it descends unbroken over the low side aisles. Unfortunately the external frescoes are badly in need of restoration and the stuccoing of the exterior—stone-colour with green trim—is rather dingy in contrast to the fresh paint on most of the nearby buildings that line the streets of the town.

As the exterior suggests, only the eastern portion of the church—and, of course, the upper stories and moulded roof of the tower—are entirely by Fischer. The six-bayed nave with its side aisles is little more than a remodelling of the medieval church, but this remodelling was quite drastic (Pl. 100). Instead of merely encasing the piers of the medieval nave arcades as was done at Buchloe, Fischer substituted new Roman Doric columns. Thus he produced an effect that actually suggests, despite rather stocky proportions, the *quattrocento* more than the middle ages or the eighteenth century. This nave he covered with a barrel-vault—or, at least, a plastered, wood-framed ceiling of that shape. This long semi-cylinder overhead, entirely covered with a fresco by the (justly) little-known painter F. A. Ehrler, receives almost no light. From what one can see of the much darkened fresco, however—it is somewhat more visible in photographs, curiously enough—with its unpersuasive *quadratura* architecture rising over the nave arcades on either side of a rather dim vision of the Triumph of the Church, it seems unlikely that this was ever effective as decoration of the concave surface of the ceiling, much less as an illusionary opening to the heavens.

The stucco-work of the church was entrusted to a far more competent craftsman, Johann Schütz, who came like so many stuccoers from Wessobrunn. He may well have been a brother of Nikolaus Schütz (d. 1785), a pupil and assistant of Dominikus Zimmermann. In any case, like Dominikus, who had been a citizen of Landsberg since 1719, he lived in that town so it is likely that he had some contact with Dominikus, if not necessarily with Dominikus's brother Johann Baptist, who did not. All the same, some believe that Johann Schütz was a pupil of the latter, as his occasional association—probably after the work at Kisslegg—with Übelherr might suggest. However that may be, his first important commission had certainly been the execution of the *stucchi* in St. Katherine at Wolfegg in 1735, two years or so before he worked at Kisslegg, where his altars in the side chapels are dated 1738.[77]

The stucco-work associated with the nave arcade is somewhat ambiguous stylistically (Pl. 100). The cartouches, so to call them, that break up over the crowns of the arches, with their terminal elements silhouetted against the fresco, are truly Rococo in character; the rather boldly projecting sections of down-curved cornice set low in the spandrels, presumably intended to provide visual support for Ehrler's *quadratura* piers and columns in the fresco, are more Baroque though hardly convincingly tectonic.

Far more consistent is the treatment of the flat ceilings of the aisles—flat in the centre, that is, but curving down in a continuous cove around the edges (Pl. 102). The formula is that of most of J. B. Zimmermann's work since his Benediktbeuern library ceiling of 1725: a series of scallop-framed panels in fresco surrounded by crisp and lively Early Rococo elements in relief. The moulding at the base of the cove is more wavy than in Fischer's earlier churches; while modest cartouches, linking the sides of the small frescoes with the crowns of the arches below and the windows in the outer walls, alternate with larger ones that splash downwards into the intervening spandrels.

A western gallery extends across the nave in the first bay. This has a delicately decorated breasting passing just to the east of the first pair of columns and carries an organ completely filling the upper portion of this end of the nave. Against the fourth column on the north is set an elaborate scagliola pulpit (Pl. 100), which was installed sometime within the decade after Fischer's work was completed. The craftsman responsible for it was J. M. Hegenauer from Türkheim. He also supplied the font with its handsome cover, a *tour de force* of *rocaille* shell-work in gilded wood. As usual, these prominent later fixtures much enhance the Rococo character of the whole interior.

Although Fischer was freer in the newly-built east end of the church than in the nave and aisles and could there provide generously the light which is so lacking to the west, the eastward view today is disappointing. A heavy-handed Neo-Baroque high altar of 1938 now occupies rather inadequately the shallow rectangular apse beyond one of Fischer's usual domed choirs (Pl. 101). As in the other parts of the church, Ehrler's frescoes—Last Supper on the hemispherical dome, Adoration of the Shepherds over the altar—are much inferior to Schütz's *stucchi*. These reach a sort of climax here in the settings of the arms of the two branches of the Waldburgs on the north and south walls of the transept of the backs of the two matching loges intended for the families' use. The bulging fronts of these loges, which are carried on coves over the choir-stalls, themselves richly ornamented in intarsia, have extremely delicate and elegant stucco decorations.

These and other subsidiary elements notably increase the total richness of the eastern compartments of the interior and make up in part for the inferiority of the modern elements of the high-altar composition. However, the painting of the Crucifixion on this altar, dated 1738–41 and by J. Th. Sichelbein,[78] who had much earlier in 1722 provided those over the high altar in Franz Beer's church at Rheinau in Switzerland (Pl. 124) and at Schussenried, is of some interest; while the flanking statues of the two patrons of the church, St. Ulrich and St. Gallus, by Ignaz Hillenbrandt and of much the dame date—later, that is, by a year or so than what he was responsible for at Bertoldshofen—are even better. But the handsomest features in this section of the church, though modest in size and some fifteen years later in date,[79] are two reliquary busts of Christ and the Virgin, executed in silver with parcel gilding by F. Ch. Mederl (d. 1765), that flank the entrance to the sanctuary.

It will be only too evident from the preceding description that this church, for all the interest of some of its elements, is no coherent whole, much less consistently Rococo stylistically. In fact the east end, where Fischer was freest, is still very close to the choir he had executed from Herkomer's designs in the Krippkirche twenty years before. Just before he remodelled Kisslegg, at St. Katherine in Wolfegg, where he was much less restricted by the retention of a medieval nave, he had also handled the choir in this, for the thirties, rather conservative manner. The sanctuary at Marktoberdorf, carried out though it was within a medieval shell, seems considerably more advanced (Pl. 96).

Schloss Wolfegg?

Fischer may have known Schloss Wolfegg[80] in his uncle's lifetime, for Herkomer had probably had some contact with the Waldburg-Wolfeggs, even if he had not actually worked in the Schloss. Fischer's first personal employment by Count Ferdinand Ludwig that is documented was for the Mariensaüle in front erected in 1719.[81] In the following years, 1720–21,[82] some rooms on the second story were stuccoed by his kinsman, Hans Herkomer, and with this work Fischer was very likely associated—he had just completed, together with Hans, St. Anna at Kisslegg, for which the Count may well have been one of the clients. The most important interiors of the twenties in the Schloss, unhappily not readily accessible, are on the first story. The date of the ceiling painting by F. G. Hermann in the Roter Salon has been read, perhaps a little doubtfully, as 1721 (Pl. 103).[83] The surrounding *stucchi*, which are of exceptional delicacy for the 1720s, somewhat recall Schenk's at Pommersfelden (Pl. 6) and Roth's at Ellingen (Pl. 7) dating from the previous decade. They could, therefore, just possibly be as early as 1721. But the ceiling of the Blumenzimmer (Pl. 104), where the use of tiles on the walls recalls the lower room in the Pagodenburg as decorated in 1716–19 (Pl. 2), seems closer to J. B. Zimmermann's work of 1729 at Weyarn.[84] Other evidence makes certain that Fischer was working for Ferdinand Ludwig at Wolfegg in 1728. Moreover, Johann Schütz, who was (as has been noted) also employed in the nearby church in the mid-1730s is known from documents to have provided *stucchi* in the Schloss in 1733–34 and in 1743–44.[85] The earlier of these campaigns would be considerably more plausible than the early 1720s for the decoration of the Roter Salon and the Blumenzimmer. Nearer the later date Schütz was also working for that branch of the Waldburgs whose seat was Schloss Zeil, near Bad Wurzach,[86] but there is no evidence of Fischer's employment there.

St. Katherine at Wolfegg

None of the information given above indicates either how much responsibility Fischer may have had in the programmes of redecoration of the 1720s and 30s in Schloss Wolfegg. However, there survive in the archives at the Schloss, among others, five drawings by Fischer of a project for the Wolfegg church indicated as a 'Riszserie von 1728'.[87] The plan in this group (Fig. A, facing p. 152) is inscribed:

'Risz zur all hiesigen löbl. Stüftskirchen soll ohn gefähr mit allen Materialen by 32.000 fl kommen, der andere Risz und 1 Turn by 27.000 fl'. This plan of 1728 for St. Katherine indicates that Fischer was involved in Ferdinand Ludwig's plans for rebuilding the church a good five years before construction started. Fortunately, in those five years Fischer's ideas for the church developed remarkably,[88] so that the result is one of the finest interiors of the opening years of mature Rococo interior architecture in the mid-1730s.[89] It is, indeed, though little visited, superior in some ways to contemporary works by more famous men, such as Hildebrandt's and Neumann's Hofkirche (Pl. 208) at Würzburg or the Asams' St. Johann-Nepomuk (Pl. 72) in Munich, and quite as advanced as such other well known churches begun several years later as Dominikus Zimmermann's Frauenkirche at Günzburg[90] and Joseph Schmuzer's parish church at Oberammergau (Pl. 135).

Except that no tower is yet indicated as rising at the rear of the apse, but rather the retention of the big medieval tower in the south transeptal position, the eastern end of the church in the 1728 plan, with domed choir, flanking loges in the transeptal arms and semicircular apse, is identical with this portion of the executed church. But the proposed nave is very much less advanced in the early project than what was eventually built. The short three-bayed oblong is of the wall-pillar type, which Fischer had never introduced before in a church of his own design, though the naves of both St. Mang and St. Jakobi are of this character. Semicircular chapels were to open off the aisles in the easternmost bay—features that would have affected the exterior more than the interior, as later at Kisslegg.

The very short nave was made necessary by the way the land fell off to the west, a situation Fischer had hitherto usually met—and would eventually meet here—by leaving his west fronts a blank and providing entrances into the naves only from the north and the south. Here, however, he proposed in 1728 a west door, as well as the usual side doors in the aisle walls, and even flanked his façade with towers set at the ends of the aisles. This might well have produced a rather monumental composition of the sort generally reserved in the eighteenth century for the grander abbey churches. There was no attempt at all to ovalize the rectangle of the nave; the principal side-altars, even, were to be set, not diagonally, but in niches flanking the choir-arch in a flat eastern wall.

In the executed nave, which extends so far to the west that its blank front all but overhangs the cliff and is partly masked by a contiguous house at lower level, the three wall-pillared bays were retained, but the space was given a wholly different character (Pls. 106, 107).

Of the advanced plan-types of the second quarter of the eighteenth century in Germany, two related ones are of particular importance: the oval, first employed perhaps at Schönbrunn in 1723–24 and, most notably, in Dominikus Zimmermann's Steinhausen (Pl. 11), which had just reached completion at this point; and what may be called the 'ovalized rectangle', possibly first introduced at Kreuzpullach in 1710 and much used in various different versions by J. M. Fischer in the twenties.[91] Toward the latter, of course, J. G. Fischer's planning had been tending ever since he built the Krippkirche from Herkomer's designs fifteen years earlier, but it was here that he first employed it on a large scale when the construction of the church actually began in 1733.[92]

The most important earlier example in Germany of a monumental interior that combined the wall-pillar type of structural organization with ovalizing elements[93] is J. M. Fischer's Osterhofen (Fig. 4), just completed internally with the execution of the Asams' frescoes and stucco-work. The Asams were inhibited by an inherited medieval plan in their other major work of the early thirties, the redecoration of the interior of St. Emmeram in Regensburg (Pl. 63). But they were at this time developing the ovalized rectangular scheme, though in a somewhat limited and special way, in Egid Quirin's own much smaller church in Munich (Fig. 7), which was begun, like St. Katherine, in 1733. Thus the nave of J. G. Fischer's Wolfegg church has effective priority in maturing a spatial form which quite a few other Germans had for several years been approaching without as yet realizing that form in a large church interior.

The modification of the conservatively rectangular plan of 1728 was carried out very simply, though the ovalizing was only fully effected overhead in the vault. By omitting the pair of projected towers at the front and moving the three bays of the nave westward, room was made for very generous quadrants between the easternmost bays of the nave and the choir-arch (Pl. 107). Thus the east end of the nave was continuously curved. There was no space, however, for such quadrants at the other end and they would, in any case, have much reduced the area of the western galleries (Pl. 106). Thus the actual ground plan of the nave is not so unlike that of the Krippkirche (Fig. 9), except for the absence of an internal bulge at the front. A major difference there is, however.

Because of the very much greater width of this nave, wall-pillars were provided at the sides, as proposed in 1728, to support a vault which is here unbroken by the transverse arches that subdivide the domed bays of Herkomer's wall-pillared naves in St. Mang and St. Jakobi. Roughly semi-elliptical in section, though geometrically more of a three-centred arch, this barrel-vault combined the unifying effect of the unribbed vault of Marktoberdorf (Pl. 94) with the single coved oval of the ceiling over the nave at Bertoldshofen (Pl. 91). Indeed, at the eastern end the very broad pendentives over the corner quadrants carry what is in fact a semicircular half-dome terminating the main vault (Pl. 107).

The plan made it impossible to provide such a semicircular termination at the west end, however. There the pendentives in the corner are much narrower and the main vault above ends between their tops in a straight line toward which its surface curves down in a deep cove (Pl. 106). Thus at vault level the plan is at least partially ovalized at all four corners; but the resultant shape is unsymmetrical in relation to the placing of the three great arches below that connect the wall pillars at either side.

Looking eastward, which is the normal direction even though the church must be entered at the side, one sees only the continuously curved end of the vaulted space. This is echoed beyond by the circular dome of the choir and the half-dome of the apse, both of the exact dimensions of the choir-arch (Pl. 107). Looking westward, on the other hand, one sees a rectangular space only slightly modified overhead by the pendentives at the corners. Two galleries, however, projecting into the nave up to half the depth of the westernmost bay, occupy this end, and these mask to a considerable degree the actual termination of the space; indeed, they also confuse one's apprehension of the space below the level of the vault at this end of the church (Pl. 106).

Western galleries had ever been a problem for Fischer as for most other architects of the period. Thus far Dominikus Zimmermann had perhaps handled that carrying the organ at Steinhausen more happily than anyone, but his bolder solutions still lay ahead. Here, however, Fischer was more successful than in any of his other churches. The front of the lower gallery is projected slightly eastward at the centre, turns the corners to left and right, and is then continued on brackets across the side bays between the wall-pillars. Thus it serves, together with the inner faces of the pillars, to provide a sort of interior shell surrounding the main ovalized rectangle of space, and helps as well to subordinate the shallow subsidiary spaces between the wall-pillars at the sides which might otherwise detract seriously from the effective unity of the nave.

The upper gallery crosses into the easternmost side bays less comfortably, since it is set just below the springing of the side arches (Pl. 106). But the wider central section of its front, flanked by S-curves, provides visual support for the elaborate, but relatively small, organ. The organ also partially hides the straight section at the base of the vault in the middle of the west end, thereby enhancing the ovalizing effect overhead of the pendentives in the corners and the quadrants of vaulting above them.

The strictly architectural detailing, largely confined to the pillars and the arches they support, is as in most Rococo church interiors of the 1730s quite simple but still somewhat tectonic. The archivolts of the arches, overlaid with ornament only at their crowns, are very narrow and in low relief. The curious handling of the pilasters, most notably of the choir-arch, diminishes their tectonic significance. Under the intradoses of the arches they serve as imposts without intervening entablature blocks and are of normal width for their height. But towards the nave, they present only a narrow edge, no wider than the archivolts above. On the broad wall-pillars at the sides of the nave the pilasters are coupled and, with their paired capitals, the inner faces of the piers seem like vertical wall-strips flanked by flat fillets and with decoration only across the top. At the choir-arch, unfortunately, these curious pilasters seem pinched and arbitrary, particularly if they are considered to be pendants in some degree to the compound piers beyond under the pendentives of the choir at the entrance to the sanctuary (Pl. 105). At the sides, however, the treatment very effectively reduces the pseudo-structural articulation of the wall-pillars in contrast to Herkomer's boldly plastic pilaster clusters at St. Mang and St. Jakobi. Indeed, one might almost say that these are not pilasters in the Roman tradition at all but rather Rococo versions of Greek antae.

Very Roman still, however, are the large three-part windows under the side arches that introduce even more light into the nave than do Herkomer's at St. Mang. As at St. Sebastian, these are related to oval windows below, but not so closely, and the crowns of these smaller openings push up the string-courses over them at the base of the big lunettes. These string-courses correspond here to the thin abacuses of the pilaster capitals and not, as in several of Fischer's earlier interiors, to the cornice of an entablature.

In the eastern portion of the church, though that was little changed from what had been projected in 1728 (Fig. A), certain emendations were introduced that make it more harmonious with the nave (Pl. 105). The apse, as is rare in Fischer's churches, is round and strongly lighted by big side windows like that at Bertoldshofen (Pl. 92), not flat and blind as at the Krippkirche and later at Kisslegg. The side arms of the choir, though not as deep as they would be at Kisslegg, are more generous and better lighted than in Fischer's earlier churches and chapels. But for the general spatial composition of the interior it is the recurrent introduction of minor curved elements that is more important. Thus the fronts of the loges above the choir-stalls continue the line of the lower gallery at the west end that also extends across the side bays of the nave, while their double-S curves in plan echo the central portion of the upper western gallery just below the organ. The concave vertical elements at the corners of the choir between the antae—so to call them—under the archivolts of the surrounding arches are a minor refinement. These are no more noticeable in the plan than those at the eastern corners of the Marktoberdorf nave (Pl. 94), but here they play at least a small part visually in producing that effect of effortless juncture of rectangular and curved spatial elements which is of the essence of Rococo design at architectural scale.

The decorations in this church, the finest Fischer had so far obtained from his various collaborators, also help to make it one of the exemplary works of the early maturity of German Rococo interior architecture in the 1730s. The painter, responsible here for the largest and finest fresco in any of Fischer's churches, was Franz Josef Spiegler; the stuccoer was Johann Schütz, concerning whom something has been said in connexion with his slightly later work at Kisslegg. F. J. Spiegler (1691–1757) came from nearby Wangen and had been a pupil of J. K. Sing (1651–1729) in Munich. He began in the 1720s as a painter in oils. One of the side altars in the great Benedictine abbey church at Weingarten that were erected in 1723–25 has a painting by him, probably of that early date. Following this came his frescoes —of very low quality, at least in their present condition—in Peter Thumb's abbey church at St. Peter in the Schwarzwald (Pl. 157). These are dated 1727. At the abbey of Salem he provided the frescoes under the gallery in the south transept in 1730.[94] His most famous works, the frescoes in J. M. Fischer's abbey church of the forties at Zwiefalten (Pl. 194) and in the vast medieval one at Säckingen, mentioned in the Introduction, were painted only much later, in the early fifties. The Wolfegg frescoes are, in fact, his first works of large scale and high quality.

The enormous fresco over the nave carries the date—presumably of completion —1736. This includes several subjects. At the centre is St. Katherine as the patron saint of the Wolfegg Schloss and church; both are represented, the latter curiously enough without its big medieval south-west tower (Pl. 108). But the principal theme is the legendary duel fought near Roveredo in the Graubünden between Count Johannes von Sonnenberg, an ancestor of the Waldburgs, and the Cavaliere Anton Maria di San Severino that occasioned the founding of the church.[95] The fresco, in the dome of the choir, of St. Katherine Disputing with the Learned Men of Alexandria has been much repainted.

The organization of the fresco over the nave, framed by earthly scenes[96] at the base that are relatively dark, and then opening up in the whole central area through passages transitional in key to the paler tonality of the heavens, owes much one would assume[97] to J. B. Zimmermann's fresco at Steinhausen, completed in 1731

(Pl. 11), and something possibly to slightly later ceiling frescoes by C. D. Asam, either in St. Emmeram at Regensburg (Pls. 65, 66) or in Santa Maria de Victoria at Ingolstadt (Pl. 70). The painter, very likely as a result of close consultation with the architect such as must have occurred between the Zimmermann brothers at Steinhausen and recurrently between the Asam brothers, supported and enhanced the spatial composition created by the architect.

Above the base moulding, which is tangent to the crowns of the arches below and over which cartouches and loose clusters of clouds and seraphs' heads in stucco break upward, the painter surrounded his field with earthy constructions. These provide the equivalent to Asam's *quadratura* settings in the big fresco over the nave of Osterhofen (Pl. 57), for four separate perspective systems are used, one at each side and one at each end. To the east, the normal and principal view, a rocky landscape builds up above and behind the elaborate armorial achievement of the Waldburg-Wolfeggs, in polychrome stucco atop the choir-arch, to a skyline roughly coincident transversely with the second of the wall-pillars below. On both sides the rectangularity of the nave is definitely suggested in the fresco, but most firmly and arbitrarily on the south. The shape of the east end, squared off but with small quadrantal corners, is also echoed by the painter as a sort of landscape frame for the two knightly combatants on horseback. Thus the earthly and earthy substructure around the fresco provides the equivalent of the coves that surround so many of J. G. Fischer's flat ceilings, while the centre is much brightened so that its relatively shallow curvature shall suggest the open heavens. The colouring is not as clear and singing as in J. B. Zimmermann's fresco at Steinhausen nor the grouping of the many figures as masterly as in C. D. Asam's frescoes of about this date at Legnickie Pole in Silesia and at Břevnov outside Prague, but this is certainly one of the most impressive, and also one of the least-known, large German frescoes of the thirties.

Further frescoes, rather lighter in tone, fill the pendentives and the spandrels (Pl. 107). Their markedly Rococo framing, with C-scrolls cutting off the upper corners and cartouches breaking and overlapping their horizontal elements, together with their lighter colouring, may even suggest, as in the case of the landscape elements and the loose composition of Asam's fresco over the nave of St. Emmeram (Pls. 65, 66), that there was influence here, at second or third hand, from French Rococo painting.

In the stucco-work, richest in the transepts and apse (Pl. 105), most delicate on the fronts of the balconies, the French decorative elements that had reached Schütz presumably via J. B. Zimmermann's *stucchi* of a few years earlier, especially those at Weyarn dated 1729 and those in the Neuer Festsaal (Pl. 13) at Benediktbeuern of 1731–32, are employed with a thoroughly German vigour and flourish. This is particularly true of the 'antae' capitals—which may, of course, be of Fischer's own design. Thanks to a late restoration, the stucco-work is all clean and fresh, though the accuracy of the colouring here cannot, as at Marktoberdorf, be vouched for. The background is, of course, white and much of the raised work is white also. Small fields of light blue-green and somewhat larger fields of a still lighter pink—used in fact as the ground colour on the vaults of the transepts and the apse—contrast with the more varied and semi-naturalistic hues of the floral sprays and garlands. A bright yellow, suggesting gold, is introduced chiefly for highlights, but rather more recurrently than usual, at least as interiors of this period have generally been restored. There are also many small touches of real gilding. Although the tones of the frescoes, except at the east, seem slightly too dark in relation to the pale *stucchi* surrounding them, an interesting example of close collaboration between painter and stuccoer is the use of the pink, green and yellow of the stucco for the small frescoes *en camaïeu* on the vaults of the side bays of the nave.

It is impossible to cover in detail all the accessories.[98] As at Bertoldshofen, the altars of shiny scagliola, highlighted with gold and including white statuary as well as oil paintings,[99] are important adjuncts to the total effect. The intarsia choir-stalls are of 1755 and the pulpit, crowned with the figure of St. Paul, must also be of about that date. The altars may well be somewhat later than the wall and vault decoration, but hardly as late as these other features. It is probably significant that the church was not consecrated until 1742, well after Ferdinand Ludwig's death in 1735, the year before Spiegler's main fresco was completed. By that time, however, one may suppose that Schütz's work, at least, was nearly done and the altars designed if not yet executed and in place.

The location of St. Katherine on the site of a pre-existing church imposed, as usual, certain conditions on the design of the exterior. Since the west front was even more unapproachable than that at Bertoldshofen once the nave had been lengthened—it can only be seen rising as blankly as that of Bernbeuren from quite a distance across a broad valley—the entrances had to be at the sides. But Fischer made no attempt to elaborate the side façades; the doorways are not even protected by side porches while the curious pattern of the fenestration, understandable from the interior, seems merely wilful from outside (Pl. 109). The view of the east end of the church, however, which projects diagonally toward the entrance front of the Schloss was obviously the most important. As the image of the church in the fresco indicates—and also that on the relief portrait of Ferdinand Ludwig set into the lower wall on this side—this was considered the main façade, somewhat as later at Kisslegg. It is indeed—and most exceptionally—entirely executed in stone, although the medieval tower at the south is stuccoed; for that element was, in the end, retained as originally proposed in 1728. Fischer capped the old shaft with a pilastered belfry stage like that on his earlier towers, adding here also clocks. These are set above arches that push up the cornice of the pilaster order at the base of the squared 'onion' of the roof (Pl. 110).

One can well believe, however, that this retention was not to Fischer's taste, for the greater bulk and height of the old tower dwarfs the new tower, rising at the rear of the apse, that he must have intended to provide the climax of the composition. Even so, the massive quadrants of the apse walls flanking this more modest vertical accent are most happily related in scale to the rear walls of the transepts on either side. Bold and simple, with the big plain arches of the windows framed by Fischer's usual heavy Doric pilaster order set on a high podium, the plastic interest of the composition is much increased by the way the lower cone-shaped roof of the apse, behind the clock-stage of the eastern tower, intersects both the attic, masking the roofs of the transept arms, and the higher roof of the main body of the church.

There is no ornament and very little sculpture, in part doubtless because of the coarse texture of the stone. However, two carved stone figures, dated 1736 and by M. A. Stapf (1704–75) from Pfronten, stand on the outer corners of the attic and others are set, one above another, in niches on the blank lower wall of the tower. Probably not intended for its present position is the rather retardataire portrait relief—somewhat like a tomb slab, and executed in darker and finer-grained stone—of Ferdinand Ludwig in armour with his right hand touching the top of the model of the church that has been mentioned earlier. This is certainly not a work of any of the artists who collaborated on the interior of the church, for its decorative frame shows no evidence at all of contact with the Rococo; nor does it seem to be by Stapf.

Franciscan Convent Church, Dillingen

When I first saw the Franziskanerinnenkirche at Dillingen (Pls. 111, 112) six or seven years ago, long before visiting Wolfegg, I was at once struck by the great interest of the spatial organization of the interior. As generally with Fischer, the exterior is dull. Here it is no more than a rectangular wing projecting from the south transept of the vast parish church, built by Albertalli in the 1620s, and backing on to the convent occupied by the nuns. Although I know now that the Dillingen church is little more than a reduced version of St. Katherine at Wolfegg, what I wrote then is still applicable: 'The most mature of Fischer's churches of the mid-1730s followed [after the Kisslegg church]. The nave is again rectangular but the quadrantal curving of all four corners assimilates the shape more nearly than at Wolfegg to . . . [an] oval, with which shape [Dominikus Zimmermann] at this point was in fact experimenting further at Günzburg,[100] where the sides of the oval nave [also] have short straight segments. But the . . . spaces between the wall-pillars . . . are much deeper than at Günzburg, so that the result spatially is closer to the scalloped oval of J. B. Neumann's Schlosskapelle at Werneck (Pl. 207), possibly designed in 1738 though not completed before the mid-40s . . . The stucco-work . . . by Finsterwalder as at Bertoldshofen . . . is more advanced in style, with *rocaille* elements of the High Rococo as in Cuvilliés's, Dietrich's and J. B. Zimmermann's *boiseries* and plasterwork going forward in these years at the Amalienburg.'

In the nave of the Dillingen church,[101] which is shorter than that of St. Katherine, asymmetry along the 'east-west' (actually south-north) axis was readily avoided by locating the two bays at the sides midway between the semicircular ends. This somewhat superior regularity of plan is contradicted, however, by the very deep nuns' gallery that cuts off almost the whole of the rounded north end of the nave. Perhaps to make up for this, as also for the absence both of an apse beyond the domed choir and of transeptal arms—there is really no 'crossing', as at Wolfegg or Kisslegg, but merely, as in the Krippkirche, a domed sanctuary—the niches in the eastern quadrants where the side altars are have greater relative importance than at Wolfegg (Pls. 107, 111). There, their tops are below the string-courses that continue the line of the abacuses of the main pilaster order; here the imposts at the base of the arches over the niches are at that level. However, the archivolts are even narrower than those of the main arches and do not rise as high, since the tops of the niches are semicircular, while the arches at the sides of the nave are not only wider but stilted as well. As a result a different treatment of the pendentives below the rather heavy moulding outlining the ovalized rectangle of the vault became necessary. In each of them there are here two frescoed panels of irregular shape, framed and separated by *stucchi* of semi-*rocaille* character. The smaller pendentives in the choir carry richer *rocaille* cartouches filled with relief-like grisailles rather than the larger and plainer frescoed areas in the domed choirs of Wolfegg and Kisslegg.

Over the years 1733–35, just before Fischer was called to Dillingen, the contiguous parish church had been extensively redecorated. Matthias Wolcker, who had worked at Bertoldshofen, executed the frescoes there. The Rococo stucco-work, which is rather similar to Bader's at Marktoberdorf of about the same date, is by a local craftsman, Joseph Feistle.[102] Neither of these men worked with Fischer in the Franziskanerinnen. Rather than Wolcker, the inadequacy of whose earlier work at Bertoldshofen must by now, after Spiegler's frescoes at Wolfegg, have been only too apparent to Fischer, the painter employed here was Christian Thomas Scheffler (*c.* 1700–56), like Günther a pupil of C. D. Asam.

Scheffler's first important commission had been the frescoes in the Jesuit (now Evangelical) church built at Ellwangen in northeastern Württemberg in 1724 by the lay-brothers Jakob Amrhein and Josef Güldimann.[103] These he painted with the assistance of Joseph Fiertmaier (1702–38), another pupil of C. D. Asam, in 1726. In 1733 he provided the ceiling frescoes in the Benedictine abbey church at Unterliezheim,[104] near Dillingen to the north-east; and shortly before he began working in Fischer's church he had in 1736 frescoed the great hall and chapel in the Deutschordenskommende in Mainz, just built by A. F. von Ritter zu Grünstein[105] (*c.* 1695–1765). In the early forties he would work in two of Neumann's churches, Heusenstamm near Offenbach in 1741 and St. Paulin at Trier in 1743 (Pl. 206). None of this work is very attractive. His masterpieces came later: these are the frescoes of 1751 in the Jesuits' Studienkirche[106] in Dillingen, the church in which Albertalli had introduced the so-called 'Vorarlberg scheme'—the nave with wall-pillars—early in the seventeenth century, and those of a few years later in the Alte Kapelle in Regensburg[107] and in Heilig-Kreuz, the Jesuits' church in Landsberg.[108] In the Studienkirche his frescoes are the most important element in the Rococo redecoration, and they are even more profuse and conspicuous, if perhaps somewhat less distinguished, at Landsberg.

The fresco on the ceiling of the Franziskanerinnen, however, though quite Asamesque in organization if not in colouring, is hardly one of his best works (Pl. 112). *Quadratura* architecture of a distinctly un-Rococo character builds up from each of the four sides with none of that subtle ovalizing Spiegler employed in his ceiling at Wolfegg. The subject matter, however, cannot have been very inspiring to the artist. Scenes from the history of the nunnery itself, dated in painted cartouches at the base, occupy the four sides; the Foundation in 1241 by Count Hartmann and his bishop son; the Fire of 1438; the Rebuilding of the Convent in 1464; and the Exposition and Adoration of the Host in the church in 1550. In the sky above and between the *quadratura* edifices, all identical, that provide the settings for these events, what might be called a 'Franciscan Heaven' is revealed, with St. Francis and St. Clare most conspicuous among the hosts who kneel in clouds below the Trinity. This fresco is signed and dated 1737.

The eight panels in the pendentives of the nave are devoted to scenes from the Life of the Virgin; the Descent of the Holy Ghost is on the dome over the choir; and the Four Cardinal Virtues, in grisaille on gold grounds, occupy the pendentives below. The oil paintings on the altars are also by Scheffler: the Assumption of the Virgin on the high altar; a Miracle of St. Anthony on that to the left of the choir-arch; and St. Francis's Vision at Portiuncula to the right. The altars were built by Einsle of Göggingen and marbled by a local craftsman named Wolkner. The pulpit, executed by Franz Kleinhans, an old associate of Fischer's, carries a figure of St. John Nepomuk by Hörlein, a woodcarver from Pfronten.[109]

The church is lighted entirely from the 'south' (west) through grouped windows. Above, the curious Michelangelesque or Zimmermanian version of the Palladian triple-window with lobes at the base of the side openings that Fischer had used in the nave of St. Sebastian at Füssen and on the west front of Bertoldshofen is repeated in each bay; below, the large windows of oval or, more accurately, ovalized rectangular shape, like the plan of the nave, are better related to these than at Wolfegg but not as closely linked as at Füssen. For a J. G. Fischer church, this side façade is not uninteresting: a pilaster order, coupled between nave and choir, defines the bays and a kidney-shaped depression painted in fresco is introduced at entablature level over each of the window groups. Finally a modest belfry, square with cut-off corners and simply panelled, recalling the characteristic tops of Fischer's earlier church towers, rides the gable at the 'east' end.

Despite its smaller size, inferior frescoes, and over-large nuns' gallery that blocks almost a third of the nave, the Dillingen church represents in some respects an advance beyond the larger and grander church at Wolfegg in the clarity with which the spatial concept of the ovalized rectangle—or should one not rather say here, 'rectangularized oval'?—is realized. Finsterwalder's *stucchi* (Pl. 111), moreover, represent a very considerable advance over what he had provided earlier at Bertoldshofen (Pls. 91–93), and their generally white and off-white colouring, relieved chiefly by gilded highlights, is very superior to the confectionery tones of that church as restored, and even perhaps to the more authentic and varied colouring of the interiors at Marktoberdorf and Wolfegg.

The Problem of Maria Steinbach

Was this rather modest church in Dillingen, then, the culmination and the effective end of Fischer's career? That is difficult to answer. In 1739 he provided a project for the big church of the Benedictine Abbey of Ottobeuren;[110] and in 1744 he may have designed the modest parish church at Arnach,[111] not far to the north-east of Wolfegg, which was completed only in 1749 two years after his death. Restored in 1837 and again in 1930, this is of little interest, though very similar to his more modest village churches of twenty years earlier.

The really important question is whether he could have been the architect responsible in 1746 for the original design of Maria Steinbach,[112] near Memmingen, one of the grandest of all south German pilgrimage churches. Since he died the following year, he would have had little chance to do more than begin the construction. Moreover, the interior (Pls. 113–116) owes a great part of the impression it makes to the twenty-seven fine frescoes, late masterpieces of Fischer's old associate Hermann (of which the principal one is dated 1752, as has been noted earlier), and to the equally climactic stucco-work of Übelherr, completed after his death while on this job in 1763, by F. X. Feichtmayr just before he also died. Thanks to the last restoration of 1953–54, the frescoes and the *stucchi* are all clean and fresh.

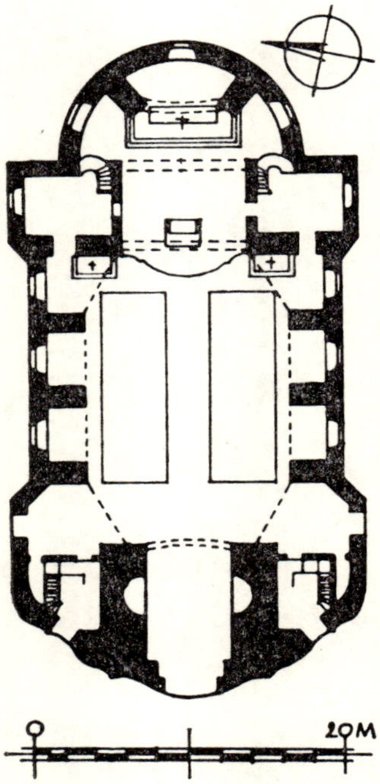

Fig. 14. Maria Steinbach, Pilgrimage Church. Plan

The spatial invention of this church, however, and the originality of the plan (Fig. 14) are of an order comparable to that of J. G. Fischer's at Wolfegg and Dillingen, and only an architect of high calibre could have been responsible, however much the total effect is enhanced by the frescoes and the *stucchi*.[113] Some profess to see in the shapes of the window tops and in the galleried choir with its double high altar evidence of Dominikus Zimmermann's hand. But the elaborate altar composition (Pl. 116), which was probably not included in the original designs and only executed—perhaps by Übelherr—in the late 1750s, is at least as similar to E. Q. Asam's in St. Johann-Nepomuk (Pl. 72) in Munich of the mid-1730s as to Zimmermann's of 1746–49 at Die Wies, not to speak of his less advanced one at Günzburg,[114] designed in 1736 at much the same time, probably, as Asam's in Munich.

The bowed façade (Pl. 117) recalls to some extent several by J. M. Fischer (Pls. 179, 190, 197); so do the curved balcony fronts between the boldly tectonic wall-pillars (Pl. 115). But such a domed choir with transeptal projections as there is here is characteristic neither of Zimmermann nor of J. M. Fischer, while this feature had been used over and over again by J. G. Fischer. Admittedly, the diagonal setting of the pilastered piers at the rear of the choir is hardly approached even at Wolfegg (Fig. 14). Moreover, the whole organization of the apse beyond, here considerably wider than the choir and with what amounts to diagonal wall-pillars flanking the altar (Pl. 115), has no precedent at all in his work. When one looks upward in the nave, however, the rectangular shape of the great fresco of the Virgin in Glory with its curved corners, though softened by the swerving *rocaille* curves of the stucco frame (Pl. 114), distinctly recalls the upward view at Wolfegg, particularly at the west end there (Pls. 106, 108).

Forty years ago, Max Hauttmann[115] was ready to assign the authorship of the church to J. G. Fischer; but Hugo Schnell, while recognizing that possibility, is now inclined, not towards Mayr's theory that Anton Lacher, who supervised the construction, was responsible for the design, but rather to give credit for the design —and it is very considerable credit indeed—to the man who was later abbot of the Premonstratensian Abbey of Rot-an-der-Rot that administered the Steinbach church.[116] Mauritius Moritz, before becoming Abbot of Rot in 1760, was for many years vicar of Steinbach—he even added the Sorrowing Mother of Steinbach to his arms—and, as abbot, he was very actively engaged in building at Rot.[117] There he almost certainly designed the new choir of 1777 and also demolished the rest of the church, except for the medieval towers, before his death in 1782 in preparation for the rebuilding of the nave. For that work again no designer from outside was employed by the next abbot who carried the work to completion. But to consider Moritz the originator of this remarkable church is to make of him a sort of Rococo Suger.

On that uncertain note must end this account of J. G. Fischer's architecture. At the least one may say that Steinbach is as Fischeresque as it is Zimmermanian, while in the years of its designing and construction Dominikus Zimmermann must have been fully occupied with Die Wies, which was begun in 1746 like Steinbach and consecrated in 1754, the year before Steinbach. Moreover, although Zimmermann had employed Hermann twenty years before for the frescoes in the Buxheim parish church, with results that can hardly have satisfied him once he saw his brother Johann Baptist's mature frescoes in their church at Steinhausen, he would not—being a stuccoer himself—at all probably have employed Übelherr for *stucchi*, busy though he was at Die Wies in the late 1740s and early 1750s. There can be no greater compliment to Fischer, however, than that Maria Steinbach, a church rivalling Die Wies in distinction, may—and not too implausibly—be attributed to him.

Johann Georg Fischer: List of Work

The less certain attributions are marked with a ?; projects are in parentheses; demolished buildings are in square brackets. Projects for executed works are not entered separately unless more than a year earlier than the beginning of construction. Other architects involved with particular works are noted in parentheses, J. J. Herkomer by initials only.

1717–22	Füssen, Benedictine Abbey Church of St. Mang (begun by J.J.H., 1701)
1717–26	Füssen, Benedictine Abbey of St. Mang (begun by J.J.H., 1697; Festsaal and main stair-hall by A. Maini, 1721–23)
1717–24	Innsbruck, St. Jakobi (J.J.H., 1717)
1717–	[Fultenbach, Benedictine Abbey and Church] (J.J.H., 1716–17)
1717–21	Kisslegg, Wolfegg'sches Schloss, interiors
1717–19	Füssen, Krippkirche (J.J.H., 1717)
1718–19	?Kisslegg, St. Anna
1719	?Rückholz, St. Georg, choir
1719	Wolfegg, Mariensäule
c. 1720	[Oberelchingen, Benedictine Abbey, additions]
c. 1720	?Augsburg, St. Margareth, remodelled
c. 1720	?Augsburg, St. Ursula, remodelled
1720/1–3	Bernbeuren, St. Nikolaus
1721–5	Füssen, St. Sebastian and St. Rochus, nave
1721–3	Rieden, Pfarrkirche, enlarged
1721–7	Kisslegg, Zeil'sches Schloss
1722–3	Buchloe, Prison
1722–3	(Project for Pfarrhof, Denklingen)
1722–5	Marktoberdorf, Jagdschloss (enlarged by Franz Kleinhans, 1761)
1723–7	Rosshaupten, St. Andreas
1724	(Project for Pfarrkirche, Sulzschneid: see 1736)
1724	Breitenswang, Totenkapelle
1724–5	?Weissensee, St. Walburga
1724–5	Füssen, Feldkirche
1724–5	Bernbeuren, Pfarrhof
1724–5	Lana di Sopra, Capella S. Magno
1724–7	Unterpinswang, Pfarrkirche
1725	?Altdorf, Pfarrhof
1725–6	[Sonthofen, Pfeghaus, remodelled]
1726	?Steinbach, Chapel of St. Magnus & St. Wendelin
1726–31	Schöllang, St. Michael
1727	[Waltenhofen, Pfarrhof]
1727	(Project for St. Peter & St. Paul, Altstädten: see 1732–4)
1727–8	Leuterschach, St. Johann Baptist
1728	(Project for St. Katherine, Wolfegg: see 1733–36)
1728–9	Buchloe, Amtshaus
1728–9	?Wolfegg, Schloss, interiors (see 1734–5)
1728–30	Rettenberg, St. Stephan
1728–33	Bertoldshofen, St. Michael
1729	Reichenbach, St. Blasius
1729–30	?Weiler, Kalvarienbergkapelle
1729–31	?Rückholz, Propstei

J. G. FISCHER

1729–33	?(Pfronten-Heitlern, St. Leonhard) (Michael Erdt)
1730	?(Pfronten-Ösch, Kapelle St. Koloman) (Michael Erdt)
1730	Kirnberg, Kapelle
1730	(Project for Marienkirche, Leeder) (Stefan Socher, 1740)
1731	Echerschwang, Kapelle St. Erasmus
1732	?(Leidershofen, St. Oswald) (Franz Kleinhans)
1732	Helmishofen, St. Nikolaus, tower
1732–3	Marktoberdorf, Heilig-Kreuz & St. Martin
1732–4	Altstädten, St. Peter & St. Paul
1733–5	Grossdorf, Amtshaus, enlarged
1733–6	Wolfegg, St. Katherine
1734	(Project for Wallfahrtskirche auf dem Lechfeld)
1734	?Ebenhofen, Pfarrhof
1734	(Project for Amtshaus, Pfaffenhausen)
1734	(Project for Schloss Wellenburg)
1734–5	?Wolfegg, Schloss, interiors
1734–6	Rieden, St. Urban, remodelled
1734–8	Kisslegg, St. Ulrich & St. Gallus, remodelled and enlarged
1735–7	Dillingen, Franciscan Convent Church
1736–8	(2nd Project for Sulzschneid) (Josef Halbritter, 1739–40)
1738	Göggingen, Kapelle
1739	(Project for Ottobeuren)
c. 1740	?[Augsburg, Café Fronhof]
c. 1740	?[Augsburg, Palais Greifenklau]
1744–9	?Arnach, St. Ulrich & St. Margareth
1746–55	?Maria Steinbach, Wallfahrtskirche

CHAPTER III

The Schmuzers: Johann, Franz Xaver and Joseph

IN southern Bavaria the hamlet then called Gaispoint, beside the great Benedictine Abbey of Wessobrunn near Weilheim, produced notable inter-related groups of stuccoers and stuccoer-architects from at least as early as 1600.[1] There originated the Zimmermanns[2] and also the Feichtmayrs[3] with whom the mature Bavarian Rococo of the mid-eighteenth century is so closely associated. But in the late seventeenth century the principal Wessobrunn figure was Johann Schmuzer, born there in 1642 and dying there in 1701.[4] Like other Wessobrunners, he was brought up as a stuccoer and in his turn brought up his sons Franz Xaver (I, more usually known as Franz, 1676–1741) and Joseph (1683–1752) as stuccoers. In the next generation Franz Xaver (II, 1713-75), a son of Joseph, continued the family tradition; while G. B. Übelherr (1700–63), originally an assistant of J. B. Zimmermann and later associated with the Feichtmayr brothers, having married Joseph's daughter in 1741, became a brother-in-law of Franz Xaver II and assisted his father-in-law at Ettal. But Johann was an architect as well as a stuccoer and so in the next generation was Joseph, just as was Joseph's contemporary Dominikus Zimmermann, born at Gaispoint two years later than he.

Two of the greatest south German churches of the end of the seventeenth century are that of the Premonstratensian Abbey of Obermarchtal in southern Württemberg,[5] begun in 1686 by the Vorarlberger Michael Thumb (*c.* 1640–90), and that at Friedrichshafen on the Bodensee[6]—then Hofen, a Priory of the Benedictine Abbey of Weingarten—which was begun in 1695 by Michael's presumably younger brother Christian (*c.* 1640–1726). The latter also supervised and completed Obermarchtal after Michael's death in association with their cousin Franz II Beer (1660–1726). On both of these (Pls. 118, 120) Johann Schmuzer collaborated, providing all the stucco decoration and producing, at Hofen, one of the most richly decorated interiors of its day, though architecturally Obermarchtal is more impressive. The contract for Johann's work at Obermarchtal is dated 7 May 1689; his employment at Hofen began nine years later, late enough so that he could be assisted by his sons Franz, then twenty-two, and even—before the work was completed in 1701, the year of Johann's death—by Joseph, seven years younger. (Craftsmen were usually apprenticed at fourteen in eighteenth-century Germany; indeed they often are still today.)

On the vaults at Hofen the extremely rich yet rather provincial flood of ornament in high relief, with gawky putti, Corinthian scroll-work and naturalistic flowers (Pl. 122), illustrates the immediate family tradition in which the younger Schmuzers were raised. Characteristic is the *horror vacui* on the vaults over the crossing and the choir, and the restriction of the paintings to small dark squares and circles overwhelmed by their elaborate three-dimensional framing. The vault of the nave (Pl. 120) is somewhat less crowded with ornament and it is from that the brothers Franz and Joseph would take off in their own ecclesiastical work of the next few years.

But Johann's independent work as an architect had begun a good deal earlier. In 1673 he was already providing a project for reconstructing the whole of the Wessobrunn monastery and, from 1680, he was building the Fürstentrakt, intended for the reception of princely visitors, which his sons completed after his death.[7] Other work of his of the 1680s that exists or existed at Kappel near Unterammergau, Schiessen, Pfreund, Oberostendorf, Ziemetshausen and Ettelried—most of it minor and some of it insecurely attributed—can be ignored here. But his pilgrimage church of 1687–92 at Vilgertshofen,[8] between Wessobrunn and Landsberg-an-der-Lech, is at least as impressive as Obermarchtal or Hofen, though not rivalling them in size. The plan is a square from which project four narrower arms with rounded ends, those to east and west being considerably more prolonged than in Pietro da Cortona's somewhat similarly planned Ss. Luca e Martina in Rome of fifty years earlier. Unusual, and influential later on Dominikus Zimmermann (who may possibly, at the age of fifteen, have been working under Schmuzer here by 1700), was the two-storied treatment of the long narrow choir with its side galleries—probably suggested by that of the nearby Augustinian church at Polling[9] as remodelled in 1621–26—and a double altar supplied later by Johann's son Franz in 1721 (Pl. 119). The very heavy scale of the *stucchi* with tiny fields of interpolated fresco—those in the choir were executed as late as 1734 by J. B. Zimmermann—is characteristic of Johann Schmuzer's generation (Pl. 121). But in quality it is inferior to his own contemporary work at Obermarchtal (Pl. 118) and at Wessobrunn, or to that which surrounds H. G. Asam's frescoes in the Tegernsee church (Pl. 16), which was built at much the same time by Antonio Riva. Even Franz was probably too young to have worked with his father here.

The early death of Johann Schmuzer made it possible, and even necessary, for both sons to begin their independent careers relatively young. Moreover, Franz may possibly have worked on his own already at Stötten in 1698–99 at the same time as he was assisting his father at Hofen. It was Johann's close association with the Vorarlbergers, particularly Franz Beer, that brought the sons immediately after his death most—indeed perhaps all—of their employment as stuccoers. Joseph's career as architect, still as executant for Beer, began only around 1720; Franz seems never to have been so employed, but, like Dominikus Zimmermann he often turned his hand in these decades to the design and execution of scagliola altars and such: notably the altar at Hofen of 1711–12 (Pl. 120), the pulpit at Bergatreute of 1718, and the altars at Vilgertshofen of 1721 and Donauwörth of 1724 (Pls. 119, 129). At Hofen and Vilgertshofen Franz added focal interest to churches which had been decorated or designed by his father and, at Donauwörth, to a church designed by Franz Beer that was most probably built, and almost certainly stuccoed, by his brother Joseph. A few words concerning Franz Beer and his work seem appropriate at this point.

Early Work for Franz Beer

Franz II Beer,[10] born at Au in the Vorarlberg, had begun his architectural career as assistant to his already-mentioned Thumb cousins, Michael and Christian, at the pilgrimage church rebuilt by the Jesuits on the Schonenberg outside Ellwangen in northern Württemberg in 1682–83. From the opening of the new century down to his death in 1726 he was perhaps the foremost architect active in the districts just north and south of the Bodensee, with his headquarters in Konstanz. The first church he designed, at least the first of real consequence, was that for the Benedictine nuns at Holzen, north of Augsburg in Bavarian Swabia. The confessor of this convent, Father Christoph Vogt (1648–1725), built the church in 1698–1704 and it was consecrated in 1710.[11]

Beer had already in 1702 employed Franz Schmuzer in the chapter house at Obermarchtal and, reputedly, Joseph in the church at Irsee,[12] near Kaufbeuren, which he had begun in 1699 and which was consecrated in 1704.

The character of the *stucchi* at Irsee is already rather different from the slightly earlier ones at Hofen, designed by Johann (Pls. 122, 123). Instead of the *horror vacui* of the decoration in the choir there, the principal elements are now rather widely spaced, although the choir again received a somewhat richer treatment than the nave. The shells and the garlands on the nave, both found earlier at Hofen (Pl. 120), are cleanly set off against the plain surface of the vault, while the heavy Wessobrunn scroll-work, so conspicuous before 1700 (Pl. 121), has been entirely omitted. The oil paintings by a lay-brother of the monastery, Magnus Remy (d. 1734) from Graz in Austria, very dark today in contrast to the white stucco of the rest of the interior, are little larger than those over the choir at Hofen however. For the most part they have equally simple shapes; only the one over the crossing is somewhat elaborated by cut-off concave corners and convex bulges to east and west (Pl. 123).

The freer and more delicate ornament on the vault of the apse, especially that surrounding the MD and CCII above the altar, seems more advanced than the rest of the *stucchi*. Perhaps the separate hands of the two brothers are to be distinguished here and that alone in the apse is the work of Joseph—but this is so uncertain it may in fact be the reverse of the truth.

At Beer's Rheinau near Schaffhausen[13] in Switzerland the stuccos by Franz Schmuzer (Pl. 124) show similar differences from Johann's work of 1700 (Pl. 120). The fresco fields are still larger both in the nave and in the choir; and these fields, alternately circular and square with concave curved corners, display to advantage the relatively light-coloured paintings that the Rome-trained F. A. Giorgioli (*c.* 1655–1725), a Swiss artist from the Ticino, initiated in 1707. The stucco-work itself, executed over the two following years, is again for the most part very restrained and geometrically ordered, with rather large plain surfaces as at Irsee (Pl. 123).[14] Both the garlands flanking the frescoes on the main vaults in alternate bays of the nave and choir and the shells used on the severies at the sides in the intervening bays are nearly identical in outline, but somewhat freer and more naturalistic in execution here.

More similar to the ornament on the apse vault at Irsee is the light scroll-work on the alternate severies. Similar scroll-work, terminating in naturalistic sprays of foliage, is also used in the intervening bays where the circular frescoes are set in larger square panels with in-curved corners, identical with the frames of the frescoes in the other bays, in place of the looped garlands. This aspect of the *stucchi* is closer to the delicacy that apparently already characterized P. F. Appiani's precisely contemporary stucco-work on the ceiling of the Bürgersaal in Munich.[15] It has really nothing to do with the Rococo except in so far as it breaks away from the earlier Wessobrunn tradition in which the younger Schmuzers had been trained. At this early date, however, when Lepautre was only introducing tentatively the new Rococo mode into church decoration in the Versailles chapel,[16] it would be surprising to find any influence of the new French mode at such a distance from Versailles and Paris.

The treatment of the vault over the crossing, however, is quite remarkable for the date (Pl. 124). The frescoed area on the cross-vault is so large that its four lobes are all but tangent to the arches that define this bay; moreover, the moulded frame is distinctly scalloped. Below, on the vaulting conoids, are pairs of cartouches, asymmetrically leaf-shaped, with the surrounding voids filled with rather free scroll-work that is carried across the unmarked arrises. Landolt finds these shapes 'unwessobrunnisch' and suggests, not very plausibly, that they reflect up-to-date Italian influence. On the other hand, their similarity to such proto-Rococo vault decoration as the Asams provided a decade later at Aldersbach and Rohr (Pls. 34, 38) is probably not significant, for these innovations were not, as far as is known, carried further by Franz Schmuzer in the intervening years.

St. Urban

There is no identified work by Franz Schmuzer of a date between the completion of the Rheinau commission and his contract of the spring of 1718 to execute the *stucchi* at Weingarten. In Bavaria the first half of the decade was generally unproductive because of the Austrian occupation during the War of the Spanish Succession. In the work of the Germans who took the lead in assimilating French influence and adapting the imported Rococo mode to execution in stucco in the next decade, J. B. Zimmermann and E. Q. Asam, there was very little to suggest their awareness of the work of the men who built and decorated the Pagodenburg in 1716–19 before Zimmermann and C. D. Asam were called to work with Effner at Schleissheim in 1720. A nearly unique example of church decoration in these years with *stucchi* as well as frescoes, executed in 1714–15, is the interior of Dreifaltigkeitskirche in Munich (Pl. 15). Crisply delicate stucco ornament, as carried out there in white against pale pink and yellow grounds, had by that time been common for some six or seven years, although this use of colour was not yet emulated by Franz Schmuzer in the all-white interior of Rheinau. More significant in the Munich church, perhaps, is the close involvement of stucco-work and fresco in the dome, towards which the treatment of the crossing-vault at Rheinau was certainly leading a few years before.

It would be helpful in dealing with the early development of the Schmuzers of the second generation if the hiatus of 1710–18 could be made shorter by even a year or two, especially as this hiatus is, in fact, even longer as regards our knowledge of the work of Joseph than in the case of Franz. Landolt, moreover, noting that the *stucchi* over the crossing at Rheinau are not specifically assigned to Franz Schmuzer in the surviving documents, is ready to query his authorship. His authorship is even less certain for the stucco-work in another rather grander Swiss church by Beer which is more closely related to new developments elsewhere in Europe in this decade.

For the *stucchi* in the church Beer built in 1711–15 for the Cistercian Abbey of St. Urban (Pl. 125)[17] in Canton Luzern no stuccoer's name is recorded. A certain resemblance to Rheinau in the relative openness of the treatment, however, has suggested to some an attribution to Franz Schmuzer. In the absence of documentation, and with no knowledge of what he may have done in the preceding five years, such an attribution is hazardous. But whoever was responsible—and no other names have been proposed—may be credited, presumably about 1716–17, with what seems to have been the very earliest reflection of the French Rococo in large-scale church architecture, since Lepautre's work in France was restricted to accessories.

The pilasters on the wall-pillars at St. Urban, which are coupled rather than single as at Rheinau, are neither plain nor fluted as in earlier churches but are decorated, rather like those in many French secular interiors of the previous ten or fifteen years, with panels outlined by mouldings ending in scroll decoration at top and bottom and framing blank oval cartouches at mid-height. A few years later, in 1720, the Asams[18] were to take up this idea in the treatment of the sides of the wall-pillars at Aldersbach (Pl. 38) and elaborate it further in 1723–24 on the pilasters in Freising cathedral (Pl. 46), filling the panels there with scagliola and using somewhat more specifically Rococo detailing.

The doubling of the pilasters, with the consequent widening of the solid areas walling the nave, taken together with their surface decoration—which is echoed somewhat sketchily on the west wall below the organ gallery—reduces notably the tectonic importance of the order. It also suggests, if rather remotely, the French sort of panelled *boiseries* Pichler was executing in the Pagodenburg at Nymphenburg in these same years (Pl. 4).

Weingarten and Weissenau

If Franz Schmuzer was, indeed, responsible for this innovation in church decoration, he had little opportunity to carry it further in his next major commission for which the contract is dated 31 March 1718. This was the execution of the stucco-work at Weingarten (Pls. 32, 33), which he began two months later in May. The link with Franz Beer, who had been briefly in charge of the building of this church at its initiation in 1715–16 and may still have been responsible for the completion of the vaulting in 1717, is probably not significant here, for by 1718 Frisoni was in control, as was noted in Chapter I. In any case the Vorarlberg scheme of the interior, almost Roman in scale and majesty, offered little opportunity to the stuccoer, especially as the vaults were soon receiving C. D. Asam's frescoes which were commissioned later in 1718 and completed by 1720. Franz Schmuzer's work is quite swamped by that of Asam as fresco-painter, as was never the case when Asam collaborated in succeeding years with his brother Egid Quirin. But the delicate bandwork on the intradoses of the ribs is already proto-Rococo in a way Franz's documented *stucchi* had not been hitherto.

The balance was soon restored in the church of the Premonstratensian Abbey of Weissenau,[19] not far south of Weingarten, rebuilt (except for the choir of 1628–31) by Franz Beer on a contract signed 18 February 1717, just as his association with Weingarten was coming to an end. The oil paintings overhead by J. K. Stauder (d. 1751), dated 1719, are hardly larger than Giorgioli's frescoes at Rheinau of ten years earlier and their shapes are mostly plain circles or transverse rectangles with rounded ends (Pls. 126, 127). These rather dark paintings have little of the illusionism, suggesting an opening to the sky, of C. D. Asam's principal fresco of St. Benedict in Glory in the nave of nearby Weingarten (Pl. 33). The stucco-work here, however, though it does not extend downwards as at St. Urban on to the shafts of the coupled pilasters on the wall-pillars, nonetheless does have a distinctly new character.

Beer's architecture at Weissenau is nearly as tectonic in emphasis as the interior of Weingarten. The east end must be ignored since it is a survival (Pl. 127); moreover, the large fresco over and around the choir-arch on the eastern wall is later, 1743, and not by Stauder but by J. A. Hafner, who also frescoed, in an advanced Rococo manner, the entire vault of the older choir. Despite the (by now) usual absence of a high dome, Beer gave strong emphasis to the broad—but not quite square—crossing bay by introducing marbled engaged columns into the piers at the four corners. Curiously enough, he also suggested a sort of second crossing by widening as well the third bay of the nave (Pl. 126). In these two bays, in which the vaults are domical over slightly oblong compartments, the paintings are large and round overhead and smaller paintings are introduced in the pendentive areas below. In the true crossing the latter are enclosed in scalloped cartouches rather modestly framed; but those in the third bay of the nave are triangular with concave corners and their diagonal edges echo the lines of the arrises of the intersecting severies at the sides of the other bays.

The white stucco-work is of a delicacy hardly equalled hitherto in south German churches, and much of its detailing displays a rather more specifically Rococo character than at Weingarten (Pl. 33). These *stucchi* must date from 1719, or thereabouts, perhaps a year later than the latter. Except at the crossing, the very broad rib-bands between the bays, corresponding in width to the coupled pilasters below, are flat and include much Rococo lattice-work as well as larger tinted areas carrying rather coarse rosettes (Pls. 126, 127). In the normal bays cartouches filled with lattice-work link the peaks of the cross-vaults and the curved ends of the frames of paintings. The filigree-like ornament surrounding these cartouches spreads loosely out over the tinted surfaces at either side in a much freer and more elegant way than ten years earlier at Rheinau (Pl. 124).

The result lacks, perhaps naturally (since the stuccoer probably worked here more or less independently of the architect), the bold assurance and the architectural effectiveness of E. Q. Asam's stucco-work on the vaults at Rohr, which can hardly be much later than this (Pls. 34, 35). But it is further evidence of a general movement towards the Rococo around 1720 among the Wessobrunners.

Pielenhofen

At Pielenhofen, north of Regensburg, in the church built for the Cistercians by Franz Beer for Abbot Rogerius I Röls, of which the west front carries the date 1719,[20] Stauder's paintings,[21] reputedly of 1720, on the vault—in fresco this time—are still relatively small (Pl. 128). These occupy the tops of the domed handkerchief vaults that are consistently used here in place of the ribbed barrel-vault, with transverse severies in each bay, common to Beer's earlier churches at Rheinau and St. Urban.

The stucco-decoration—in white against pink grounds—is undated and its designer unrecorded. But the double pilasters have ornamental panelling very like that at St. Urban (Pl. 125) and one may hazard a guess that the stuccoer was the same. There is also considerable resemblance to Weissenau (Pls. 126, 127), where Franz Schmuzer also worked together with Stauder in a church by Beer, presumably just before this. The resemblance somewhat strengthens, but hardly confirms, the theory that he was the stuccoer earlier at St. Urban. Yet the general effect, though considerably richer, is not so much more Rococo than at Weissenau. One must conclude that, compared to the Asams, whose work at Aldersbach (Pl. 38) is dated 1720, even by that year Franz Schmuzer—if the *stucchi* at Pielenhofen, indeed, be his work and about 1720 their date—had not advanced as far along the road to a German mode of Rococo church decoration as they, though considerably further than the Zimmermanns at Mödingen (built 1716–18), where one of the frescoes by Johann Baptist is dated 1719 and Dominikus' stucco-work is probably very little earlier.[22]

Heilig-Kreuz, Donauwörth

Interest now shifts from Franz to Joseph, who had already in 1717 been given charge of the execution of the plans—or so it is believed—that Beer had made for Heilig-Kreuz, the church of the Benedictine Abbey at Donauwörth (Pls. 129, 130).[23] Since the paintings here, by Stauder as at Weissenau and Pielenhofen, were executed in 1720–21, it seems plausible, even though Franz Schmuzer's high altar is dated 1724, to assign Joseph's stucco-work to *c.* 1720 like that, possibly by Franz, at Pielenhofen.

One need hardly suppose that the basic architectonic qualities of this church derive from modifications of the original design—whether Beer's or another's—that Joseph made during the execution. In this typical example of the Vorarlberg scheme there are three oblong bays in the nave preceded by a shallower bay containing a western gallery, a flat-domed crossing with transeptal arms that do not project externally, a two-bay choir with the second bay shallower than the standard dimension of the first, and a semicircular apse. The side galleries are concave-fronted as at Weingarten and set well behind the pilaster clusters decorating the wall-pillars through which passages are cut at both ground and gallery level. Thus from the nave these pilaster clusters, like those at Weingarten, have almost the look of free-standing piers and are very vigorously tectonic (Pl. 130). Neither the longitudinal nor the transverse ribs have much projection, while their under-surfaces are emphasized by delicate decoration quite similar to Franz Schmuzer's at Weissenau.

Not surprisingly, it is to that church, decorated by his elder brother probably just before this, that Joseph Schmuzer's work at Donauwörth comes closest. But there are notable differences. The east end of Weissenau (Pl. 127), with its narrow early seventeenth-century choir which was never rebuilt and the vast later fresco by Hafner on the upper part of the east wall of the nave, contrasts with the wholly consistent Beer-Schmuzer choir and apse, as broad as the nave, of Heilig-Kreuz (Pl. 129). Moreover, the present fresco (which is actually not by Stauder but modern) on the flat dome of the crossing occupies the entire space above the pendentives, and these are also almost completely filled by frescoes confined in slightly scalloped triangular frames of stucco, one of the most advanced features of the whole scheme of decoration.

Whatever the sources of Joseph's inspiration—certainly not alone Franz's work at Weissenau—the general character of the vault decoration here, in sharp contrast to that of the architecture, is almost Early Rococo rather than proto-Rococo (Pl. 130). The delicate scale, the large areas of tinted *mosaïque* and the predominance of scalloping generally, taken together with the handling of the surfaces of the severies more specifically, are well in advance of what J. B. Zimmermann, restrained by Dubut, was executing at Schleissheim at about this time (Pl. 1). Simple mouldings following the arrises subdivide the vault surfaces on either side of the circular frescoes overhead into three curved triangular surfaces in each bay. On the other hand, each of the flanking severies in the middle of the bays contains a large palmette that is still rather boldly Baroque in size and relief.

More significant, however, is the inner frame that provides the chief decoration on the surfaces of the severies, for this is not only intricately curved inward and outward but terminates at the base in foliated C-scrolls. These are echoed, moreover, in other tendril-like elements curling outward at various points along the edge of the frame. Even more strikingly Rococo is the treatment of the panels at the sides on the main vault. In each of these the inner frame is of necessity markedly asymmetrical, but it is also much lighter in weight and still more freely elaborated by foliated C-scrolls around the edges continuing the scalloped moulding with little change in dimension.

In comparison to the stucco-work of E. Q. Asam of approximately this date at Rohr and Aldersbach (Pls. 34, 35, 38), Schmuzer's is distinctly more refined and sophisticated.[24] Yet, unlike theirs, it does not modify effectively the architectonic character of the interior; for Joseph was still little more than a decorator here, despite his probable responsibility for the total execution of the church.

As an architect Joseph made a respectable, if conservative, debut at Donauwörth and for the rest of the decade he continued to be employed, now on his own, chiefly for rather small commissions. For the historian this is regrettable, since these were the years in which others, particularly those like Schmuzer who were stuccoer-architects, rapidly advanced—if that is the proper word—from the proto-Rococo of 1720 to the Early Rococo of 1730. Joseph seems to have had no such splendid opportunities as the Asams at Freising (Pls. 43–49) in 1723–24 or those with which J. M. Fischer provided them at the end of the decade at St. Anna-am-Lehel in Munich and at Osterhofen (Pls. 56–59). One need, therefore, only enumerate here the items in Joseph's modest but fairly active practice in these years.

Pfaffenhofen near Donauwörth is a rather simple church without aisles. The decoration is very similar to that in Heilig-Kreuz, which it follows very closely in date since it was built in 1722–23. In the new nave Schmuzer built at Pähl in 1723–24 the fresco by Johann Bader (1709–79), once a pupil of Martin Knoller in Rome, is of 1772 and the stuccos of the same date, so that the interior has already a somewhat Neoclassic look and is irrelevant in this account. Commissions began to pile up only in 1727 with the building of the small church at Mertingen, also near Donauwörth, dominated now by the ceiling fresco painted by J. B. Enderle (1725–98) in 1785. But there is also the decoration of the Prälatur of the Irsee monastery, where Joseph's career as a stuccoer had begun, and (probably) the rebuilding of the nave at Kohlgrub, near Murnau—where the fresco dates from 1927 (!)—both of 1727–29.

Prälatur, Irsee

The stair-hall at Irsee[25] with a large fresco by F. A. Ehrler overhead, has perhaps the finest and certainly the most advanced *stucchi*, on the cove at the edge of the ceiling, that either of the brothers had yet executed (Pls. 131, 132). The fashion in which the moulding at the top of this cove is bowed inward in the middle of the sides and at the corners of the fresco, while still rather timid, provides for the first time in his work that interlocking of painting and stucco characteristic already of the major interiors decorated by the Asams in this decade. The fresco, moreover, overlaps the frame in places, as often in the Asams' church interiors. The relief of the elements of the stucco is higher than at Donauwörth and the gusto of the whole closer to the exuberance of E. Q. Asam's work at Einsiedeln of 1724–26 (Pls. 51–54) than to the more French refinement of J. B. Zimmermann, with whose library ceiling of 1725 at Benediktbeuern (Pl. 13) this monastic interior may more appropriately be compared. Significant architecturally is the curving of the corners of the square shape below the base of the cove over eagles in high relief, employed like Borrominian seraphs to make a plastic transition (Pl. 132), but not more significant than the use of a cove instead of an entablature to provide a curving plane of transition between walls and ceiling.[26]

St. Martin, Garmisch

Finally, in the late twenties, there is the small north chapel, rather broadly dated 1727–34, of the church at Mittenwald, where Joseph a few years later—in 1738–40—was to rebuild most of the rest. The stucco decoration here was executed not by Schmuzer but by Benno Peghofer and the fresco on the vault is by Josef Dieffenbrunner. This is an attractive if somewhat rustic interior, but the decoration of Joseph's much more important new church at Garmisch was presumably completed earlier.

However, even this first big commission of his, St. Martin at Garmisch[27]—despite frescoes by Matthäus Günther (1705–88), signed and dated 1733, and sculpture on the high altar by Anton Sturm (1690–1757), two of the most accomplished artists of the period—is disappointing if compared to contemporary Osterhofen (Pls. 57–59) and Steinhausen (Pl. 11), or even to Freising (Pls. 43–49) as redecorated by the Asams in 1723–24. As has been suggested, a fairer comparison would be with J. G. Fischer's Marktoberdorf church (Pls. 94–96). The estimate for St. Martin was accepted in 1729 by the client, who was Marquard Schmid, the parish priest. But the Augustinians of Rottenbuch assisted financially, and their Prior Patritius Oswald laid the cornerstone on 18 July 1730. Schmuzer and his *Palier*, who was to supervise the construction, had arrived at Garmisch ten days earlier. The church was consecrated on 23 September 1734.

The three-bay nave is of ungainly breadth, so that the handkerchief 'vaults' appear precariously[28] stretched between the shallow double ribs; the crossing is barely differentiated from the preceding nave bays; and the vaulting of the narrow squarish choir accords neither with that of the bays of the nave and crossing nor with the low dome over the apse (Pl. 134). The illumination seems excessive thanks to the tall arched windows in each bay of the nave, all quite unshielded, and the wide kidney-shaped windows above them. Somewhat similar combinations of arched windows and irregularly shaped openings above flank the high altar and flood the apse also with rather too much light.

But all these elements and characteristics may be seen positively as well as negatively, for each of them conduces towards an interior that is rather consistently un-Baroque, and hence already quite Rococo. Notable is the way tectonic elements are omitted or weakened throughout. The paired pilasters barely break the wall surface; the entablature blocks above them are thin and tall; and the transverse ribs are even more like the vertical bands in contemporary *boiseries* than the similar elements at Weissenau (Pls. 126, 127).

The curious shapes of the upper windows clearly recall Dominikus Zimmermann, who had already used such forms earlier at Siessen and Buxheim in the mid-1720s, but they are more conspicuous internally here and introduce far more light than do his at Steinhausen (Pl. 11).

In distinct contrast to the round-arched vaulting in near-square bays and the conventional spatial geometry of the earlier interiors decorated by Franz or Joseph Schmuzer in churches designed by Beer is the semi-elliptical section of the vault here, broad and flattened like J. G. Fischer's at Bernbeuren and Marktoberdorf even though marked off in bays. Thus, if the oval or the ovalized rectangle made no appearance in the planning of St. Martin, the section of the nave and, as a result, the outline of its eastern wall falls, as in Fischer's churches (Pls. 89, 94), somewhere between the two shapes (Pl. 134) and the whole organization of the vaulting of the nave is geometrically very irregular by Renaissance and Baroque standards.

More recognizably Rococo, however, is the stucco ornament on the vault. There the particular treatment of vertical *boiserie* panels that Lepautre had evolved a generation earlier in France and Pichler had introduced in Germany at the Pagodenburg is enlarged to near-monumental scale[29] and curved to follow the vault surface (Pl. 134). In each bay, on either side of the relatively big but simply framed frescoes, the whole concave area is outlined by a light moulding that breaks into scroll-work at the corners, while in the middle of each tinted field there also floats an elaborately scalloped cartouche filled with *mosaïque* and linked top and bottom to the bounding mouldings. This stress on the homogeneity of all the curved surfaces overhead, phrased not by vigorously structural ribs but only by thin decorative bands between the bays, is characteristically Rococo, even though it has here been much enlarged in scale and also translated, as generally in advanced south German work for ten years or so, from walls to ceilings and from carved woodwork to moulded stucco. Yet there is little to suggest any close familiarity with J. B. Zimmermann's stucco-work—so much more elegant, so much more inventive in detail—of these years in the Munich Residenz, the churches at Weyarn and Beyharting, and the Neuer Festsaal of the Abbey of Benediktbeuern (Pl. 13). Even the work of a fellow Wessobrunn architect-stuccoer, J. B. Zimmermann's brother Dominikus at Steinhausen (Pl. 11), on the other hand, while less replete with specifically Rococo elements, has a German gusto that is lacking here, as does that of E. Q. Asam at this point in Fischer's Osterhofen (Pls. 58, 59), if not in his St. Anna-am-Lehel in Munich (Pl. 56). In two words, the Garmisch church is advanced but provincial, as was not so true of Schmuzer's secular work at Irsee a few years earlier (Pls. 131, 132).

Oberammergau

Other things by Joseph Schmuzer of the early thirties—the stuccos in the entrance hall of the Wessobrunn monastery, where he was now working half a century after his father; the small pilgrimage church of Maria-Aich at Peissenberg nearby of 1732–34, again with frescoes of 1734 by Günther on the flat-domed vaults; and the nave of Gablingen near Augsburg—prepare one no better than the rather larger but quite dreary church of Maria-Hilf outside Bad Tölz, executed from Schmuzer's designs by the local builder Lorenz Reiter in 1735–37, for the very positive achievement represented by his parish church at Oberammergau,[30] with its splendid dome-fresco by Günther in the nave, signed and dated 1744. This church was begun in 1736, the year before Schmuzer undertook his first masterly transformation of a medieval church, that of the Augustinians at Rottenbuch, who assisted financially here as also at Garmisch. Still provincial, but even for its later date much more advanced than Garmisch, Oberammergau is his first really memorable production and the earliest, properly enough, to which most scholars and visitors have usually paid any attention.

As is so often—and by no means unhappily—the case with eighteenth-century German churches, the present effect of the interior at Oberammergau is much enhanced and made more saturatedly Rococo by the presence of various fine later furnishings (Pl. 135). The altar that all but fills the apse, executed in scagliola with much gilded detail, white statues, and an oil painting of the Assumption of the Virgin by Günther, was completed by F. X. Schmädl (1705–77) only in 1762 though the painting is dated 1759 and his fresco overhead, 1761. The side altars are by Schmädl too, with an oil painting of St. Anthony dated 1756 by J. J. Zeiller (1708–83) over that on the south. However, the pulpit by Paul Zwink, also of 1756, is not especially large or rich.

Not handsome later accessories, but certain specifically architectonic qualities of Schmuzer's original design here, are very relevant to the problem of distinguishing Rococo from Baroque interior architecture. There is, first, the restriction of the pilaster order to the east end of the nave, where almost all but the capitals are in fact now hidden by Schmädl's side altars, and to the choir, where the shafts have characteristic Rococo panelling. Even more significant, however, is the related omission of a heavy entablature at the sides of the nave. But these are only negative aspects of this interior, evidence that tectonic elements have been still further reduced than at Garmisch or in J. G. Fischer's slightly earlier churches at Wolfegg and at Dillingen (Pls. 106, 111). More important is the avoidance, on the one hand, of heavy mouldings on the arrises where surfaces of different curvature meet, except at the base of the domes above the pendentives, and, on the other, the depression of the curvature of all the vaults. Equally significant, but by this date not unusual, is the rounding of the corners of the nave and choir. These quadrants, carried transversely across nave and choir as generous coves, are echoed above and behind the gallery at the west end and also in narrower concave chamferings at the 'transept' openings. Different from interiors by J. G. Fischer of the mid and later thirties is the use of the dome on pendentives over the square central portion of the nave, but Fischer had used domes rather consistently over his choirs from the first.

The rather specifically German Rococo device of framing large ceiling frescoes with scalloped mouldings over which other freer elements of the stucco-decoration break is reflected here only in the handling of the frescoed cartouches on the pendentives of the domes and the smaller ones over the choir-arch and the side windows, for the larger scalloped fresco field at the west end is rather firmly confined. In all cases, however, the element at the top of these subsidiary features rises in a double-C-curved clamp, so to call it, across the otherwise unbroken horizontal mouldings of the frescoes overhead in a way that was becoming quite common by 1740.

Emphasis on continuity of even-tensioned surfaces, in opposition to the Baroque emphasis on tectonic elements of structure or pseudo-structure, is further increased by the profusion of delicate, almost underscaled, stucco ornamentation by Joseph Schmuzer and his son Franz Xaver II (Pl. 135). This not only surrounds all the cartouches, as has been mentioned, but also fills the broad cove at the choir-arch and outlines the smaller coves and chamfered intradoses elsewhere. The side windows, which flood the church with even light as at Garmisch, cut awkwardly into the walls and the scale of the whole is barely monumental; yet the total effect is more consistently Rococo than anything greater German architects of the period such as J. M. Fischer or J. B. Neumann had so far produced (see Chapter V).

Filling the tops of saucer domes with frescoes was no novelty in Germany. Stauder must have provided originally such a dome fresco for Joseph Schmuzer twenty years before this over the crossing at Donauwörth where the modern fresco is today (Pl. 129). Thanks to the relatively broad and low proportions of Oberammergau, however, hardly domestic yet modest by the standard of such large Late Baroque churches as Heilig-Kreuz at Donauwörth, the frescoed vault produces an effect not altogether unlike J. B. Zimmermann's at Steinhausen (Pl. 11).

Rottenbuch

Of the ovalized oblong plan of Oberammergau, with its wide though shallow transeptal bays merged into the central space by coved framing and with its domed central space echoed in the smaller square choir ending in a flattened and coved apse, there could be no equivalent at Rottenbuch because of its surviving medieval plan and structure. But the stuccoer-decorator in Joseph came here to the fore, so that he was able to produce an interior of a gorgeousness unequalled in Bavaria up to this time (Pls. 136–142). If Hofen (Pls. 120, 122) perhaps best exemplifies the German decorative style of about 1700, this interior illustrates the style of about 1740 in its ecclesiastical version quite as notably as the slightly earlier interiors of Cuvilliés's Amalienburg do the secular version. But even the one large room at the Amalienburg, the Spiegelsaal (Pl. 133), only *approaches* impressive spatial creation at architectural scale; here the monumental dimensions of the vessel existed before Joseph Schmuzer was called on to undertake the redecoration. He could not much modify the basic proportions, any more than could the Asams at Freising cathedral (Pl. 45), but he could go well beyond their redecoration of a large medieval fabric, St. Emmeram in Regensburg (Pl. 63), by extending much more richly the Rococo investiture of stucco-work from the ceiling downwards over the side walls and the nave arcades almost to the floor.

The church of the Augustinians at Rottenbuch, on the main road from Schongau to Garmisch in southern Bavaria, was built in the late eleventh or early twelfth century as a cruciform basilica with a free-standing campanile.[31] Damaged and restored after fires in the late thirteenth and again in the early fourteenth century, the church received a new choir and transept in the mid-fifteenth century and was reconsecrated in 1468. A Late Gothic remodelling of the Romanesque nave followed, with consecration in 1477. In 1737 Prior Oswald, who had already in 1715–16 renewed most of the altars damaged in the War of the Spanish Succession, began the redecoration of the interior. Joseph Schmuzer was already the monks' appointed architect and had been working for them at Garmisch and Oberammergau, as has been noted. In that year and the next the fifteenth-century choir and transepts were stuccoed by him with the assistance, as at Oberammergau, of his son Franz who supervised their helpers. The frescoes, again by Günther, illustrate the life of St. Augustine and other related subjects of Augustinian import. (The less conspicuous ones are by assistants working from Günther's designs.)

Structural changes were minor, although the windows were given round heads and the ribs of the vault either removed or buried under the new stucco lining of the vault. As a result the original pointed crown of the vault was quite hidden[32] above the flattened concave surfaces of the large fresco panel (Pls. 138, 142). Only the severies over the windows retained the pointed form at their intersection with the main vault; but that was quite characteristic also of many of the new vaults erected in Germany in the eighteenth century. The ghostly flat pilaster clusters and attenuated entablature blocks at the base of the vaulting conoids are repeated from Garmisch, as indeed they were still in the work of most German architects in this period. But the pilasters are even more deprived of tectonic significance than in the apse of Oberammergau by the free elaboration of their capitals. This is in the line of descent from the Asams' treatment of the pilasters at Freising and Osterhofen (Pls. 45, 59) and is much enhanced by the Asam-like decorative panelling on their shafts.[33] This Joseph's brother Franz may have first used in church decoration twenty years earlier at St. Urban (Pl. 125).

The detailing of the stucco-work on the vaults (Pls. 138, 139, 141, 142) is as Rococo as at Oberammergau. But instead of the almost French delicacy and restraint of the ornamentation at Oberammergau (Pl. 135), there is here a vitality, an exuberance, that almost rivals now the superb stucco-work in the Amalienburg (Pl. 133) by J. B. Zimmermann and the *boiseries* there by Joachim Dietrich.[34] One might even guess that Cuvilliés's first book of designs, the *Livre de cartouches*, was eagerly studied on its appearance in 1738 by the Schmuzers, father and son, even though their first campaign of redecoration here began a bit earlier and was in that year brought to completion.

Considered as an independent T-shaped space, the three-bay choir and the nearly square bays of the crossing and the transepts, for all their much greater inherited height and steeper vaulting, were not without some similarities to the interior of Oberammergau. The visitor's eye is drawn almost as strongly upwards to the fresco of St. Augustine's Reception in Heaven on the flat dome over the crossing as eastwards to the high altar (Pls. 137, 141, 142). This fresco is relatively smaller than the one over the nave at Oberammergau (Pl. 135), but it is strongly supported visually by unusually large and rich cartouches containing minor frescoes on the pendentives. The choir is unified overhead by a large fresco of the Four Quarters of the Earth paying Homage to the Virgin. This is set in a frame of scalloped oval shape that extends through all three bays of the choir (Pl. 138).[35]

The eastward view is naturally dominated by the elaborate high altar (Pl. 142). At the sides this overlaps the apse windows, while its columns project so far into the choir that it effectively occupies, as an almost independent edicule, the whole space of the shallow three-sided apse somewhat in the way of E. Q. Asam's high altar at Osterhofen (Pl. 58). The main altar as well as the side altars, the pulpit and organ case were, like those at Oberammergau, the work of Schmädl and considerably later: the six side altars are dated 1745–46; the pulpit and the organ, 1747 (Pls. 136, 140). The high altar is perhaps as late as 1750.

Before Prior Oswald's death in 1740 Joseph and his team in 1739 also built and decorated the sacristy. The next prior, Clemens Prasser, undertook the decoration of the nave in 1741. But two years later the work was held up by the War of the Austrian Succession and only brought to a conclusion at the time the side altars were begun and the nave and aisle frescoes completed by Günther and his assistants after the war was over. The Josephskapelle was, however, completed first in 1744.

The total length of the church, with six bays in the nave to the west of the crossing and three to the east in the choir, was about the same as the ten bays, there unbroken by a crossing, with which the Asams had to cope in St. Emmeram at Regensburg (Fig. 6). Such long narrow spaces were always difficult for eighteenth-century architects to deal with, and Schmuzer made rather less of an attempt than had the Asams to centralize the composition of the nave. He gave up, however, the even rhythm of his Garmisch ceiling, which by this time must have seemed distinctly old-fashioned (Pls. 134, 136, 137), and grouped the six bays of the nave overhead, 1, 1, 2, 1, 1. These areas all have large frescoes that fit well down between the vaulting conoids on either side. The double one in the middle of the nave is a convex-scalloped oval, the others are squarish with concave sides. Very loose cartouches, mostly without inset frescoes, mask the vaulting conoids of which the arrises are marked only by very light double mouldings.

The ornament moves throughout as with a life of its own, overlapping the frames of the frescoes at the centres of their sides and other relatively rigid boundaries. All this is fairly comparable—and slightly inferior in quality—to what the Asams had done a decade earlier on the vault of the nave of St. Emmeram. But the great difference here is the way the decoration is equally elaborate on the sides of the nave below (Pls. 136, 137) in contrast to the simple treatment of the walls at St. Emmeram (Pl. 63).

Certain structural changes were not difficult to make in transforming a medieval interior. As in the choir here, so also in the nave, large new windows in the clerestory, similar in their irregularly oval shape but smaller than those at Garmisch, flood the nave with a clear bright light that makes the gilded highlights sparkle. The medieval piers are simply sheathed; but thanks to the broad bevel which continues round the arches—modified in shape from pointed to paraboloid, like the vaults overhead, by hiding the apex of each under a sprawling cartouche—they tell not as structural elements of tectonic vigour but as a partial extension downwards of the walls above (Pl. 137).

The blank band above the nave arcade, usually present in early medieval churches of basilican section except where, as at Freising (Pl. 45), there were original or later galleries, was always awkward to handle in transformations, but the result here is far more successful than an analytical description might lead one to suppose. Large fresco panels of scalloped outline fit down over the heads of the nave arches, somewhat as in the alternate bays at St. Emmeram but here clamped —as it were—to the bevel of the arches by the three-dimensional curve of the cartouches mentioned above (Pls. 136, 137, 140). These panels rise so high that the ornament at their crowns similarly overlaps and clamps on to the base of the clerestory windows, quite ignoring the horizontal line of the cornice of the pilaster order.

The frescoes in these panels are light and bright, in that airy Rococo tonality which J. B. Zimmermann seems to have first introduced into German church decoration in his great fresco of 1730–31 at Steinhausen. For all their atmospheric illusionism these rather firmly, even if freely, framed fresco panels take their place between the wider nave arches below and the narrower clerestory windows above in a way that serves to unify the wall-decoration vertically, much as the combination of high-keyed illusionistic frescoes and surrounding stucco-work unifies the vaults longitudinally. Their colouring is almost as light in tone as the surrounding white and gold stucco-work with its pink and blue grounds.[36]

Curiously enough, between the bays panelled pilasters carrying modest entablature blocks were introduced as in the choir, doubtless partly out of habit and partly to link the vaulting conoids visually with the piers of the nave arcade below (Pls. 136, 137). Yet, except for the short sections of cornice—here very stiff and seemingly out of place—that are set at the base of the vaulting conoids well below the heads of fresco panels between, this much flattened and interrupted order hardly provides even the 'ghost' of a conventional framework of tectonic architectural elements. For one thing, the capitals are so dissolved, as in the choir, into the freest sort of Rococo ornament that they all but merge with the scroll-work at the deeply concave sides of the fresco panels; while the straight outlines of the shallow shafts are much weaker visually than the ornamented panels on their surfaces.

Thus to a degree unequalled up to this point in newly built churches—relevant comparisons would be with Dominikus Zimmermann's parish church at Günzburg of 1737–41[37] or J. G. Fischer's contemporary Franziskanerinnen at Dillingen (Pl. 111)—this monumentally dimensioned interior has become as total an example of Rococo decoration as the richest secular works of its day, Cuvilliés's Spiegelsaal (Pl. 133) or J. B. Neumann's Weisser Saal (Pl. 209) at Würzburg as stuccoed in 1744 by Antonio Bossi. At Nymphenburg, however, if not so much at Würzburg, the links with the French Rococo are still close, even though the Spiegelsaal probably does not derive (as has sometimes been supposed) from Boffrand's salons in the Hôtel de Soubise in Paris. Here at Rottenbuch the line of descent from the French Rococo is more completely severed, both by the great increase in scale and by the characteristic German use of large frescoed areas and exuberant stucco-work in contrast to the modest dimensions, delicate *boiseries* and flat plaster ceilings, usually ornamented only at the edges and centres, of contemporary Parisian interiors.

On account of the existing medieval shell within which he had to work at Rottenbuch Schmuzer did not carry further here the development of a new and truly German sort of Rococo spatial composition in the way he had done just before this at Oberammergau (Pl. 135). The elongated oblong space of the nave could not be much ovalized, except insofar as the particular shape of the largest fresco over the two middle bays of the nave has a certain centralizing effect. That effect is far less, all the same, than in the work of the Asams even as early as 1720 at Aldersbach (Pl. 38) since this fresco occupies absolutely and, above all, relatively to the length of the nave so much less space. To some extent the organ and its setting eventually rounded off the west end, though this very partial rounding was not strengthened visually by making the front of the gallery below boldly concave or double-S-curved, as was frequently done in similar instances elsewhere, instead of nearly straight (Pl. 136).[38]

The east end of the nave opened into the crossing and the best that could be done to suggest any sort of spatial enclosure there was to provide a round arch, inevitably somewhat tectonic in expression, descending well below the vault surface and supported at the sides by clusters of pilasters (Pl. 137). By setting these vertical elements diagonally, however, as the probable shape of the underlying medieval piers may have suggested, and bevelling the face of this big arch like those in the nave arcade, this end of the long rectangle of the nave was, in fact, very slightly ovalized. The curvature of the apse, of course, rounds off the remoter east end of the whole interior in a long familiar way that has nothing to do with the Rococo, and overhead the transept ends are also rounded despite their square corners below (Pl. 139).

Irrelevant to the space composition of the nave as a whole, but very effective in its own right, like the Asams' decorations in the tribunes at Freising (Pls. 47, 49), is the treatment of the side aisles (Pl. 140). Here the vaulting conoids descend low between the aisle windows and the bits of entablature on which they rest are supported, not by pilaster strips as in the nave, but by modest consoles consisting merely of Rococo ornament. On the vault surfaces of the aisles stucco-work vignettes the frescoes and further decoration surrounds—almost in the way mid-eighteenth-century mirrors were framed by Chippendale even in England—the scallop-arched window-openings. But here the actual height is not great and the scale of the decoration rather closer to that in secular interiors both French and German.

To appreciate how far Joseph Schmuzer had by now moved away from the Baroque architectural traditions of the opening of the century in which he was brought up, one need not go back to Hofen (Pl. 120) or even to Irsee (Pl. 123). The contrast to Donauwörth (Pl. 130) is strong enough at Rottenbuch, and it is much enhanced by the superior quality and light airy colouring, including much of the pink and blue that are used in very pale tints for the grounds of the *stucchi*, of Günther's frescoes as compared to Stauder's rather dark and dull oil paintings there. One would therefore expect that the church which was newly built by Schmuzer at Mittenwald[39] in 1737–40, the same time as the earlier campaign of redecoration at Rottenbuch and three years after his Kreuzkapelle there was consecrated, would have a Rococo interior of real distinction since it was the work of the same team as before—Joseph Schmuzer, his son Franz Xaver II, and Matthäus Günther.

Mittenwald

Perhaps the parish priest Ludwig Schmid could not obtain sufficient financial support from the Prince-Bishop of Freising, a brother of the Elector Carl Albrecht, to whom Mittenwald belonged territorially. Unhappy at any rate, though not unusual, was the decision to preserve the narrow Gothic choir of the earlier church. But the very flat handkerchief vault over the wide eastern bay of the nave provides a most unsatisfactory transition to this choir since it exposes the blank east wall with its hard rectangular corners; while the entrance arches of the side chapels are too low to provide effective transeptal extensions of this spatial element. As at Oberammergau, the rest of the nave is covered with a shallow dome which is entirely filled with Günther's Triumph of the Church over the Synagogue and Heathenism. This provides, somewhat in the Asam manner, the illusion of a much higher dome with a small oculus at its top open to the heavens.

To the west, against the front wall with its exceptionally delicate and elegant stucco-work, there is a shallow cove beneath the pendentives, and this is echoed to the east in the chamfer of the broad rib that crosses the nave. But these minor curved surfaces do not have the generosity and space-shaping virtues of those at Oberammergau, nor are they echoed here at the window openings in the side walls. The whole church has, indeed, a somewhat unprofessional, even makeshift, look architecturally that is unworthy of its *stucchi*, presumably largely Franz's work, and Günther's frescoes; while the accessories, which include an earlier pulpit dated 1716, are not as at Oberammergau intrinsically interesting enough, despite an oil painting by Günther over the high altar, to intensify the Rococo quality of the whole. Thus, as at Garmisch, one may feel that Mittenwald has lost most of the quality of even modest Baroque architecture without exemplifying with any distinction the new Rococo as an architectural style as well as a decorative mode.

St. Anton, Partenkirchen; North Quadrangle, Weingarten

In St. Anton[40] above Partenkirchen the rotunda of the nave was built in 1738–39, probably but not certainly by Joseph Schmuzer, as an enlargement and extension of a chapel begun in 1704 by the master-mason Fabian Meyr for the Partenkirchen parish priest Dr. Matthias Samweber. The magnificent fresco, dated 1739, shaping the entire domed space—thanks to its setting of simple yet vigorous *quadratura* architecture—is all but the last work of J. E. Holzer (1709–40). This provides effectively the entire visual interest of the broad low cylinder since there is almost no stucco decoration. Hardly characteristically Rococo, the fresco seems to look forward as much to the frescoes of Goya in San António de la Flórida in Madrid in their cool Neoclassic setting as back to the Baroque.

Whether or not Joseph Schmuzer worked in 1738–39 at St. Anton, immediately after redecorating the east end of Rottenbuch he took on the construction of the north quadrangle of the Weingarten monastery.[41] His contract is dated 11 April 1740. For the entire monastery an unusually large and elaborate symmetrical scheme, projected presumably by Frisoni in 1723 at the time of the completion of the church, exists in a drawing of 1724 by Father Beda Stattmüller still preserved at Weingarten. Construction began in 1727 and Joseph Schmuzer, in taking over the job so much later, departed very little from the 1723 scheme in the portion he executed. This was so far advanced by 1743 that Franz Xaver II could then carry out the stucco-work in the middle and upper stories; for the job he was paid 1100 gulden on 10 December. There are no really notable interiors remaining today, although the Audienzsaal has a fresco by G. B. Goez (1708–74), and some of Franz's *stucchi* survive both inside and out. These display a delicacy and restraint, particularly on the corridor ceilings, that is even greater than what he was presumably responsible for at Mittenwald and in strong contrast to the bolder relief and more ebullient curves of the nearly contemporary stucco-work in the nave of Rottenbuch.

Steingaden

Already in these years Franz, apparently without his father, was also undertaking the redecoration of the nave of the Romanesque church of the Premonstratensian Abbey of Steingaden, near Rottenbuch but on the so-called Romantische Strasse.[42] The deep four-bay choir here had been vaulted and decorated in an unusually crisp and restrained manner in 1663 (Pl. 144). Now it was the two square double bays of the nave, covered with much flattened handkerchief vaults, that received very large frescoes of scalloped outline devoted to the principal events in the life of St. Norbert, the founder of the Premonstratensian Order, as usual in that Order's churches. The paintings by J. G. Bergmüller (1688–1762),[43] including here the Saint's Visit to the Site of the Abbey and the Founding of Steingaden by Duke Welf, are very richly vignetted by lacy *stucchi* above modest cartouches in the pendentives.

Here, as at Rottenbuch, one may suppose that the work was interrupted by the War of the Austrian Succession not long after it was begun. No doubt it was again delayed by the considerable financial obligations this abbey accepted in 1745–46 by undertaking the construction of the pilgrimage church at nearby Die Wies, the largest work of Dominikus Zimmermann and his brother Johann Baptist.[44] However that may be, Bergmüller's fresco under the organ gallery is signed and dated 1751, providing a terminus for the interior as a whole, but his other frescoes in the nave have usually been assigned to the war years of the early forties.

The side walls at Steingaden are treated much as at Rottenbuch, though the pilaster clusters and their entablature blocks are more strongly tectonic. Moreover, the curved tops of the frescoed panels[45] over the round arches of the nave arcade—though they rise above the cornices of the entablature blocks, thus overbalancing their slight horizontal emphasis with a strong vertical movement—do not, as at Rottenbuch, overlap the horizontal sills of the broad clerestory windows that fill the lunettes of the double bays. If one looks backward, away from the earlier choir (Pl. 143), the general effect of the stucco-work surrounding Bergmüller's very high-keyed frescoes is intricate, crisp, and almost blindingly brilliant, with the decorative elements silhouetted in white against pale blue grounds and sparkling with gilded highlights in the strong light from the big clerestory windows.

If this interior does not stand comparison as a whole (Pl. 144) with the almost exactly contemporary nave of Rottenbuch (Pl. 137), there are nonetheless aspects of it that are well worth noting, such as the very large size and the airiness of the frescoes and, even more characteristically for this period, their vignetted rather than moulded borders. These are considerably more vigorous and architecturally integral than the elegant *stucchi* similarly surrounding the frescoes in the aisles of Rottenbuch (Pl. 140). Even though the decorative treatment of the nave here has little effect on the total spatial composition as determined by the existing Romanesque structure—which is much affected as well by the earlier remodelling of the choir—the concave scalloping of the organ gallery in plan and the broad coved area beneath, twisted in three dimensions, on which Bergmüller frescoed the Decollation of St. John Baptist (Pl. 143), are architecturally as well as decoratively more positively Rococo than in Joseph's contemporary west end at Rottenbuch (Pl. 136), perhaps because this portion was completed so much later, to judge from the date 1751 on the fresco.

Ettal

The masterpiece among the interiors built or remodelled by one of the Schmuzers is that of the church of the Benedictine Abbey of Ettal,[46] located between Oberammergau and Garmisch, as restored and redecorated by Joseph, beginning in 1745, after a fire of 1744. (Franz Xaver II was not employed here.) From the exterior Ettal is wholly Baroque. After Viscardi's church at Freystadt of 1700–10, it is the largest and most impressive church of centralized plan in southern Germany erected earlier than d'Ixnard's St. Blasien of the 1770s (Pl. 146). The plan of its twelve-sided nave and aisles is, moreover—and most exceptionally—an inheritance from its founding in the Gothic period (Fig. 15).[47]

The cornerstone was laid on 28 April 1330 by the Emperor Louis the Bavarian in accordance with a vow made in Italy shortly after his coronation in Rome, and the original church was consecrated in 1370. Always a very unusual establishment, since it accommodated according to the founder's stipulation twelve knights and their wives as well as twenty monks, Ettal took on a new role—still maintained—when Placidus Seitz (who became abbot in 1709) opened a school there that at once became, if not the Eton, at least the Downside or the Portsmouth Priory of Catholic Germany. For this new use the monastery buildings were vastly enlarged and the church remodelled according to plans prepared in 1709[48] by Zuccalli.

What one sees of the exterior of Ettal today, both of the monastery and of the church, is much affected by various later changes (Pl. 145). There was a total reconstruction of the conventual and school buildings in 1753 just after Joseph Schmuzer's death. This was followed by the demolition of considerable portions of them after secularization in 1822. Then came the building of the north tower in 1853–54 and the restoration of the church façade in 1894–1901. Finally the present school and conventual buildings were built in 1903–12 and the south tower erected in 1905–07. Yet the grandiose façade with its engaged columns, following the curve of the round plan and leading up to the heavy radial buttresses of the rotunda behind only to surge forward on either side in concave wings and end in tall flanking towers, is essentially what Zuccalli intended and partially executed (Pl. 146). No bolder or more imposing version of the High Baroque scheme of Sant'Agnese in Agone in Rome probably exists. Even vast Loyola in Spain, as executed at much the same time from the designs of Carlo Fontana, is hardly as impressive, being towerless, though much elaborated with very Spanish decoration both inside and out. But the plain and rather crudely executed exterior of Ettal hardly prepares one for what Joseph Schmuzer and his collaborators were able to achieve here on an inherited Gothic plan within an existing Baroque shell in the middle decades of the century.

The fire of 29 June 1744 was a very serious one, gutting the church and its new-built choir and destroying the conventual buildings, including a library of 30,000 books. Abbot Benedict II Pacher, however, was able to enlist generous financial support for an institution that was already educating so many noblemen's sons; while the cult statue of the Virgin (possibly by Giovanni Pisano, but more probably by Tino di Camaino), originally set against the central pier of a rotunda vaulted radially like an English chapter-house, had made it a goal for pilgrims from the very first. The shrine reached its peak of fame in the eighteenth century, moreover, when 70,000 pilgrims a year were coming to Ettal and innumerable instances of miraculous favours were recorded—1930, it is said, between 1600 and 1761.

Of the surviving Gothic aisle (Fig. 15), compartmented by the deep radial buttresses, nothing can be seen from Schmuzer's nave. Moreover, the twelve angles of this are so masked internally by pilaster clusters both in the main story and in the clerestory that the interior appears to be cylindrical rather than dodecagonal (Pls. 147–150). But these much flattened vertical elements have hardly more tectonic weight than the plain and very shallow blind arches between them; while the cornice is broken off below each of the big upper windows to increase further the effect of vertical continuity. Under the arches areas of gilt *mosaïque* are enclosed and compartmented by delicate *stucchi*, while bolder asymmetrical cartouches splash upward across the continuous architrave and frieze to overlap the sills of the clerestory windows as at Rottenbuch.

The pilaster order in the clerestory is even more freely treated than that below. The panels of gilt grille-work which flank the clerestory windows are much stronger visually than the pilaster clusters, and the arches of the tall windows bend the architrave of the entablature upward, thereby considerably diminishing its horizontal force. The frieze of this upper entablature, furthermore, is but a shallow cove and its cornice hardly more than a frame for the enormous fresco

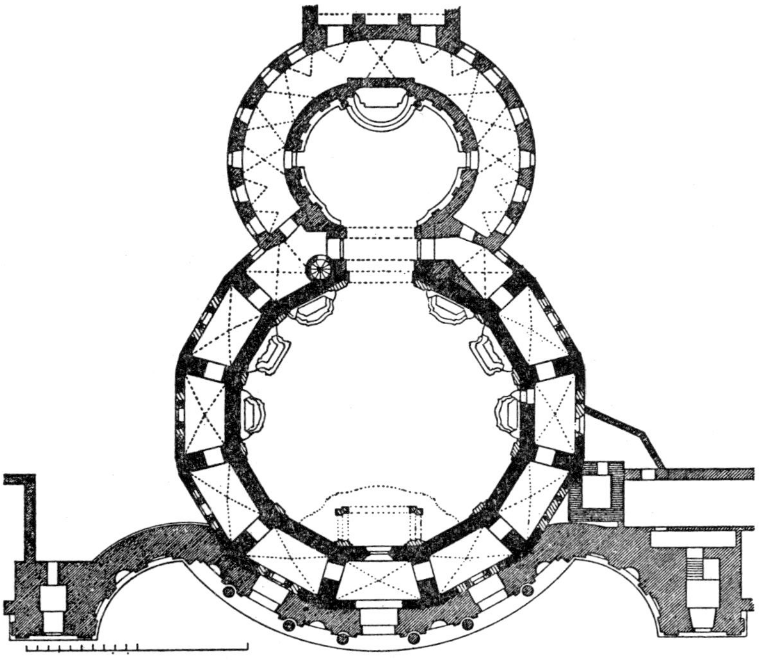

Fig. 15. Ettal, Abbey Church. Plan

covering the entire surface of the dome.[49] This fresco is dated 1752, the year of Joseph Schmuzer's death, and signed by J. J. Zeiller (1708–83) (Pl. 150).[50]

Somewhat unexpectedly, not stucco but painted *quadratura* elements of extremely free character vignette the fresco. In intention this illustrates Isaiah 8: 18, but more obviously the subject is the Glorification of St. Benedict, who receives the Ettal Madonna from angels in a Heaven full of Benedictines, Cistercians and Celestines, saints, popes, Fathers of the Church, etc. Even more than in the Zimmermann's churches at Steinhausen (Pl. 11) and Die Wies, the main spatial illusion is of a cylinder, in this case circular rather than oval, which opens up to the heavens through the centre of the dome. Here, however, there is a small terminal lantern, frescoed internally, of which the real but confined space unfortunately contradicts to a degree the grand spatial effect of the main fresco.

The architectonic effect of this interior, as in most Rococo churches both new and remodelled, is not created or modified merely by the general decorative scheme of the walls and the principal fresco overhead. There is also a second relatively large fresco by Zeiller over the choir-arch, also signed and dated 1752, of the foundation of Ettal by Louis the Bavarian. This is set in a magnificent gilded *rocaille* frame (Pl. 147), which corresponds at this point in the clerestory to the windows that occupy each of the other eleven bays. There are further minor touches that are of architectonic, if not spatial, significance as well. For example, the gilt cornice of the upper entablature is curved downward behind the elaborate openwork crown of the frame of this fresco. That curvature serves to suggest a slight bulge in the circular plan at this eastern axial point. It also acts as a respond to the sharp outward curve of the entire entablature of the lower order as it rises, in this bay only, over the tall arch of the choir entrance. Thus a strong eastward 'pull' was created within the round space of the cylindrical nave without any actual modification of the inherited circular plan.

Additional eastward emphasis is provided by prominent features eventually introduced in the three easternmost side bays of each range of six in contrast to those on the western side. There are only relatively small light-coloured balconettes in the three bays to the west and these are all horizontal in emphasis (Pl. 149). The smaller rectangular ones to left and right rest on coved brackets, while that in the centre carrying the much later organ is of convex scalloped plan and coved out over tiny coupled Ionic columns. But to the east the accents are as vertical as the central choir-arch, and all dark golden in tone into the bargain (Pl. 147). The six tall altars are largely of a tawny-coloured scagliola that contrasts with the pale pinks and greens of the pilaster clusters; but there is also much gold, echoing the recurrent gilt highlights of the capitals and the panels of *mosaïque* on the stuccoed walls. These altars occupy the bays to left and to right of the choir-arch to which they lead by the gradual increase in their elaboration.

As so often in eighteenth-century churches, the altars are considerably later in date than the frescoes and the *stucchi*. They were executed only after Schmuzer's death, from 1756 onward, by J. B. Straub (d. 1784) and include oil paintings by T. C. Scheffler completed by his brother F. A. Scheffler (1701–60); by Zeiller; by F. G. Hermann; and by Martin Knoller (1725–1804)—this last painted in Rome in 1763–65.

Straub's pulpit is also late. This pulpit and the six altars are all somewhat coarser in scale and more three-dimensional as well as darker in value than the *stucchi* on the walls. In the execution of the latter Joseph Schmuzer was assisted not by his son Franz, as has been noted earlier—then quite possibly still, or again, busy at Steingaden—but by his son-in-law J. G. Übelherr. That perhaps explains their relative delicacy in contrast to the bolder relief and coarser detail of the stucco-work at Rottenbuch and Steingaden (Pls. 137, 143).

It was in the later period after Joseph Schmuzer's death, to which the rich confessionals of dark wood also belong, that the church was consecrated in 1762. The organ by Georg Herterich above the western balconette is still later, being dated 1768 (Pl. 149). The confessionals, two to each side of the entrance bay, and even the altars might perhaps be considered furniture rather than essential elements of the interior architecture. It is notable that the former and four of the latter (Pl. 148) include no 'ghosts' even of tectonic elements, while the 'order' of the other two altars, despite fairly conventional pairs of entablature blocks set diagonally, is as distorted as anything in the engraved plates of garden fabricks by Meissonier. Even though not begun until four years after Joseph Schmuzer's death in 1752, the presence of the altars and their general character must have been foreseen by Schmuzer, as they would surely have been by any other German architect of the day. Considering their great size and prominence, these features are quite as essential a part of the Rococo interior he set out to create here as in the newly built churches of the period.

Very different, and reinforcing by contrast the essential homogeneity of the nave as rebuilt and largely decorated between the mid-forties and the mid-fifties—the same years in which the Zimmermanns were building and decorating the great new pilgrimage church at Die Wies, the other most notable example of German Rococo interior architecture of these decades[51]—is the choir of Ettal (Pl. 147). The decoration of this smaller chamber, dating in its circular plan back to Zuccalli, began only in 1769 when Knoller, returned from his third stay in Rome, executed the ceiling fresco in a style that already began to reflect the early Neoclassicism of his friend A. R. Mengs (1728–79) and the other Northern painters active in Rome in the mid-century. Even more Neoclassic—or at least what is usually called Louis XVI—is the decoration of the walls and the high altar with real marble and rather severe *stucchi* by Josef Lindner, from 1778, and with reliefs of 1788 and 1790 by R. A. Boos.

Hohenpeissenberg

One or two minor late works attributed to Joseph Schmuzer may now be mentioned. The big parish church at Tapfheim[52] between Donauwörth and Dillingen, dated 1747 by an inscription, has a squarish flat-vaulted nave narrowed by concave quadrants flanking the choir-arch, the whole decorated with rather sparse stucco-work, probably not by Joseph, and a fresco signed by Anton Enderle. The more attractive Gnadenkapelle, originally built in 1514, which is attached to the church at Hohenpeissenberg, near Schongau and Wessobrunn, was frescoed by Matthäus Günther, Schmuzer's frequent collaborator, in 1748 (Pl. 151). The delicate Rococo stucco-work there, executed during the extension and redecoration of this chapel the previous year, may well be by Joseph even though in these years he was leaving most of the stucco-work to Übelherr at Ettal, a far more important commission. It would be appropriate for his career to have concluded not far from his birthplace and with so characteristically Rococo an interior.

But the relevant cycle of Joseph's achievement as a Rococo architect—his brother and his son[53] having never been more than stuccoers—lies between what he carried out as executant of Franz Beer's plans at Donauwörth about 1720, still almost wholly Baroque architecturally, and the post-Rococo choir of Ettal, decorated more than half a century later, for which he was not responsible. This was for the most part an ascending curve that began, as regards relevant architectonic innovation, with St. Martin at Garmisch about 1730 and culminated some twenty years later, just before his death, with the decoration of the nave of Ettal. He was not, even to the extent of his brother Franz Xaver I, one who played a significant part in the early acclimatization of the Rococo in German interior architecture in the way of the Asams or J. B. Zimmermann; he never built a new church of the importance and distinction of several of J. G. Fischer's—Oberammergau is his best—but at Rottenbuch and, above all, at Ettal in transforming two medieval edifices he produced interiors that epitomize, almost better than any others of the second quarter of the eighteenth-century in southern Germany, most of the potentialities of Rococo architecture.

CHAPTER IV

Peter II Thumb

THUMB'S architectural career opened in the first decade of the eighteenth century and ended fifty years later with the building of his library for the Benedictine Abbey of St. Gallen in Switzerland, designed in 1757 and completed without his supervision in 1767, the year of his death.[1] He began practice some years before French Rococo influence first reached Germany and continued as a Baroque architect for twenty years and more. His finest work, however, the pilgrimage church in Baden at Birnau on the Bodensee (Pls. 159–166) of 1746–50, is a superb example of Rococo architecture with an interior from which almost all inheritance from the Baroque has been purged or melted away. One may leave unsettled for the moment the degree of his responsibility for the vast abbey church at St. Gallen (Pls. 167–172). This building looks back in some respects to the German Baroque of 1700; yet it may also be thought to look forward towards the Neoclassicism of the later eighteenth century. This is not altogether surprising, since construction of the church began only in 1755, and much of the decoration throughout and even the actual structure of the eastern arm—not by Thumb—date from after 1760. Thus his career, stylistically, is characteristic of the general modulation of German architecture from the Baroque towards the Rococo, and then away from the Rococo, during the half century that runs from before 1720 to the end of the sixties.[2]

Certain questions of attribution in eighteenth-century Germany are probably unanswerable, since the thoroughly studied archives of the monasteries have not as yet provided the information. Weingarten is much less convincingly assignable to any one architect than St. Gallen; Wiblingen and Frauenzell are usually assigned either to no namable designer or, hypothetically, to rather too many alternative ones.[3] Dating, moreover, is not always absolutely certain, particularly for the stucco decoration which is so important a part of the interior architecture of this period. (Frescoes, on the other hand, are quite often signed and dated.) Yet the general historical picture is less affected by gaps in documentation than in most other periods. This is especially true as regards Thumb—there is, goodness knows, no lack of dates for St. Gallen. Those before 1715, however, for the initiation of work at two of his earliest churches, St. Trudpert in Baden and Ebersmunster (Haut-Rhin) in Alsace, are not very significant for the buildings, largely carried out later, which survive today. Moreover, in the case of his library at St. Peter in Baden there were two campaigns separated by more than a decade, one of construction and a second for the decoration.

The unsettled questions that most concern Thumb might be considered psychological. How did it come about that an artist capable of three or four of the finest interiors of his period also produced so much mediocre or at least very conventional work? and why were these masterpieces all designed late in his career? The library at St. Peter was begun in the mid-thirties, when he was fifty-six, and not completed for fifteen years or more; he was sixty-four when he started to build Birnau, and he was seventy-seven when he designed the St. Gallen library. One may think of Frank Lloyd Wright, hardly uninventive in his early years, who was—if anything—still more inventive in his seventies and eighties, though relatively unproductive in his fifties and sixties. But Wright's reputation hardly rests on a mere three or four works. More comparable are certain of Thumb's close German contemporaries: Dominikus Zimmermann, four years younger than Thumb, began his first great church, that at Steinhausen, when he was forty-one; but his other masterpiece, Die Wies, in a range of production considerably smaller than Thumb's, was built at the same time as Birnau, so that he was seventy when it reached completion in the mid-fifties. Joseph Schmuzer undertook his greatest work, the transformation of Ettal, when he was sixty-two. For this notable achievement only his remodelling of medieval Rottenbuch, undertaken in his fifties, and up to a point, his new church at Oberammergau offer any persuasive premonition. The career of J. G. Fischer offers similar problems, since his major works are as few as the Schmuzers' and the finest of them (unless he can be credited with Maria Steinbach), St. Katherine at Wolfegg and the Franziskanerinnen at Dillingen, were built when he was in his sixties.

However impossible plausible explanations of such situations may be, it is still worthwhile to examine the works that preceded the rare masterpieces of artists like Thumb in order to see if the former may not, after all, have led up in some significant respects to the latter. At the very least such an examination exposes the matrix in which the jewel took form and throws some light on the differing contexts that conditioned the masterpieces and the run-of-the-mill work the same men produced.

Peter Thumb, called 'II' to distinguish him from his grandfather of the same name, was born into one of the leading builder-families of the Austrian Vorarlberg.[4] From that district, after about 1650, many masons who later became architects had set out to work throughout southern Germany, Switzerland and Austria, dominating the field particularly in the lands around the Bodensee. Thumb's grandmother, Barbara Beer, belonged to another such family, and various relatives of his mother, Christiana Feuerstein, were architects or stuccoers. Peter's father Michael was a prominent architect. But he died in 1690 at the age of fifty, leaving his greatest works, Obermarchtal and Hofen (Friedrichshafen), to be completed by his brother Christian and their cousin Franz II Beer.

Born at Bregau in 1681, Peter Thumb became an apprentice at Au in 1697 under Michael Herbig, a mason and stone-carver, for the usual term of three years. In 1709 he was taken into the famous Au Zunft (masons' guild). But he had already begun to work in architecture under other men. Moreover, in that year 1709 he was actually commissioned by the Benedictines of St. Trudpert in Baden—and

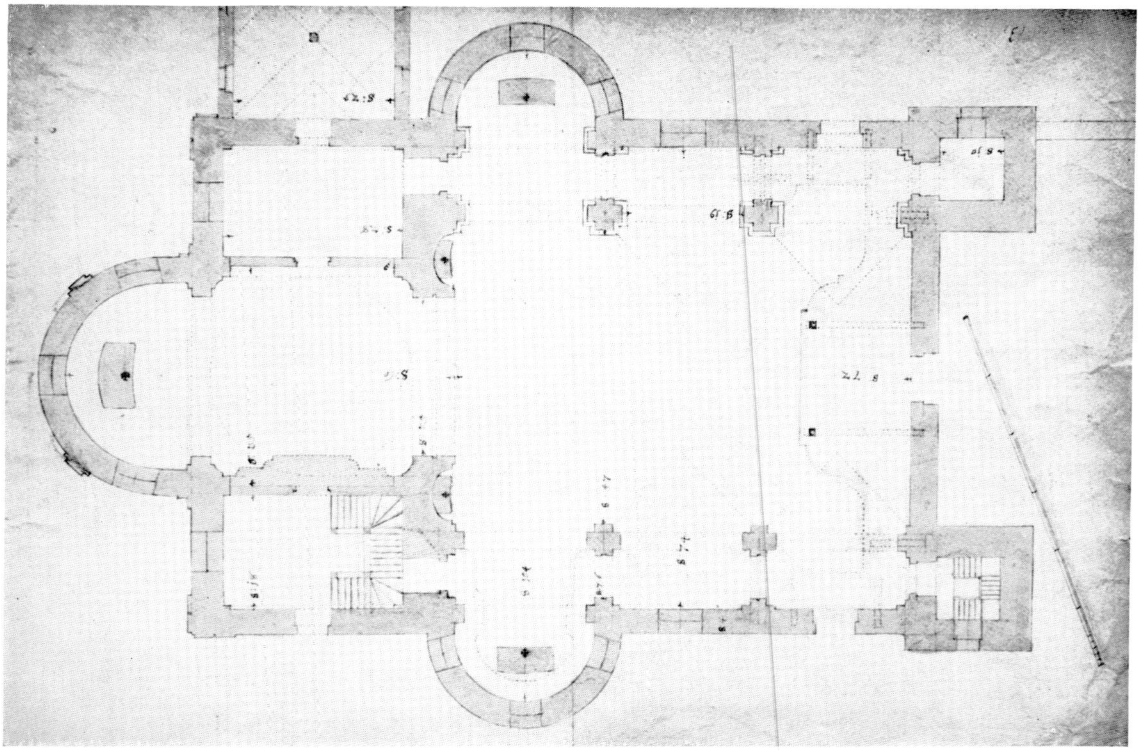

Fig. A. Project for St. Katherine, Wolfegg, 1728

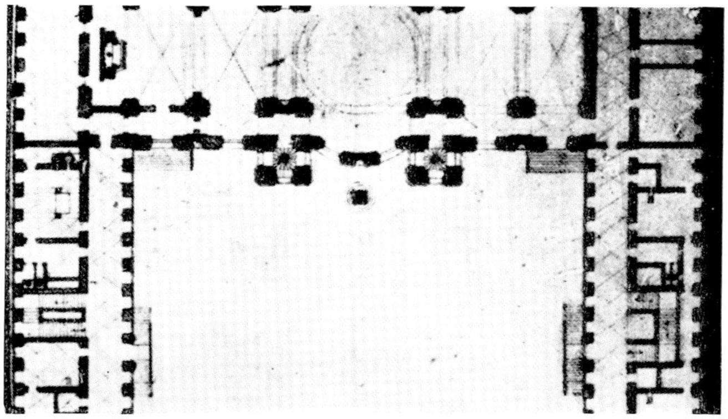

Fig. B. Frauenalb, Nunnery Church. Plan

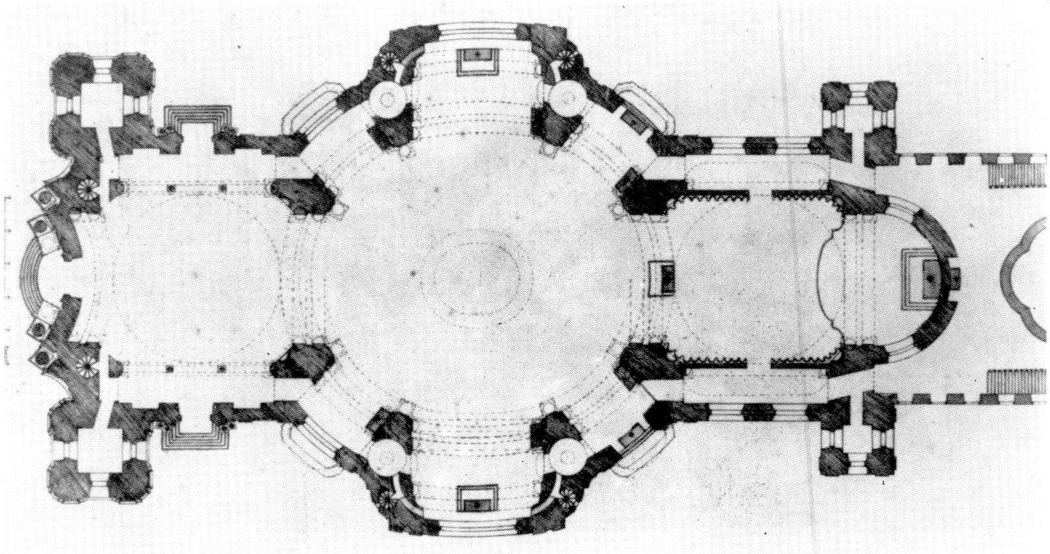

Fig. C. Dominikus Zimmermann's 1732 project for Ottobeuren

possibly also by those of Ebersmunster in Alsace—and the following year he vaulted the surviving Gothic choir there.[5]

In 1707 Thumb married Anna Maria Beer, the daughter of his cousin, Franz II, and between 1704 and 1711 he supervised the construction of Beer's big church at Rheinau (Pl. 124) in Switzerland just as, a decade later, Joseph Schmuzer would supervise Beer's Heilig-Kreuz at Donauwörth at the opening of his architectural career. Unlike Schmuzer and his brother, Thumb was not a stuccoer. Indeed, the stucco-decoration at Rheinau was executed by Franz Schmuzer, as may have been that at St. Urban (Pl. 125),[6] another Beer commission supervised by Thumb from 1711 to 1715. In 1707–11 he was also engaged, together with his considerably older brother Gabriel (b. 1671), in carrying out a project, initiated in 1703 by Caspar Moosbrugger, for the parish church at Lachen in Canton Schwyz. In Thumb's later career most of his churches were to be built in southern Germany, particularly in the region of the Austrian-ruled city of Freiburg-im-Breisgau and in contiguous Baden. These districts north-west of the Bodensee were in easy reach of Konstanz, where he settled in 1720 and was made a citizen in 1726.[7] He was perhaps fortunate in these years (1704–14) of the War of the Spanish Succession to be so largely employed in Switzerland and across the Rhine in Alsace.[8] The earliest work of his own design carried to completion after the church at Ebersmunster, built about 1710–15 but rebuilt 1719–27, was probably the modest tower of the church at Erstein, also in Alsace, dating from 1715–16.[9]

St. Trudpert

Next, doubtless, came the execution of the nave of St. Trudpert over the years 1715–22.[10] A four-bayed wall-pillar church with galleries (Figs. 16, 17; Pl. 152), the interior of St. Trudpert is chiefly appealing because of the *stucchi*, reputedly executed in 1716 by the Italians Carpoforo Orsati and Michelangelo de Prevostis, which surround rather large frescoes by F. A. Giorgioli completed in 1722. Thumb

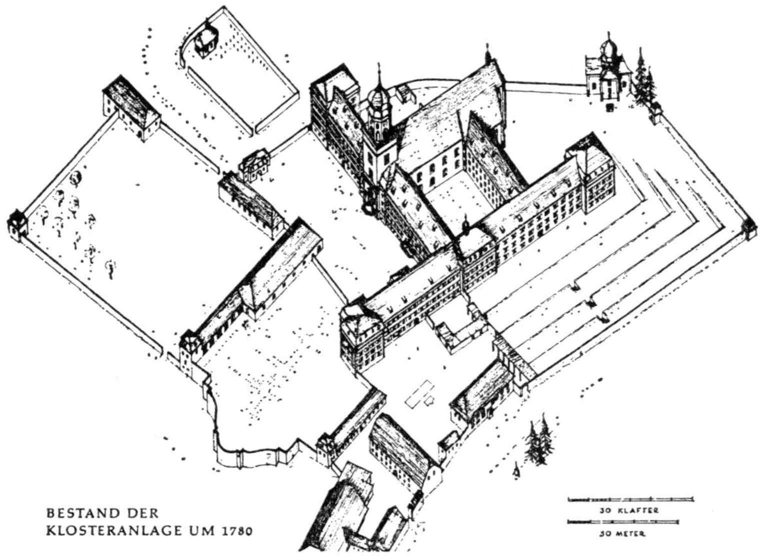

Fig. 16. St. Trudpert, Abbey, about 1780

had worked earlier with Giorgioli when he was supervising Rheinau for Franz Beer, but the frescoes at St. Trudpert play a far more important part in the decoration. If the stucco-work that surrounds them is actually of 1716 the large size of the areas provided for the frescoes overhead, made possible by the continuous surface of the unribbed barrel-vault, and the scalloped framing of the big cartouche-like frescoes at the sides of the vault must be considered quite advanced in character. In the choir, on the vault Thumb had built in 1710, the principal fresco extends over two of the narrow bays in the manner of C. D. Asam's fresco of 1720 in the choir of Aldersbach (Pl. 38). That in the middle of the nave is even longer since it extends through three of the wider bays of the new construction (Fig. 17). The shapes of these frescoes, however, remain relatively simple compared to Asam's and the *stucchi* include no proto-Rococo elements. Moreover, the flanking sections of the eastern wall, made necessary by the disparity in width between the inherited choir and the new nave, break the interior space into two unrelated parts, and the richly coloured stucco drapery over the choir-arch, against which light-toned figures in high relief are set, visually separates rather than joins these parts.

Ebersmunster

A more considerable opportunity came to Thumb before St. Trudpert was completed[11] when the Benedictines of Ebersmunster called him back across the Rhine to rebuild the church he had completed for them in 1715 after it had been largely destroyed in a fire set by a stroke of lightning in 1717.[12] Into the new church he incorporated several important surviving elements of the earlier one (Fig. 18): the choir with its seven-sided apse, of which the shape and the plain external buttresses recall the church consecrated in 1155 whose foundations were retained; the square crossing, of the same width as the choir, with its wide transeptal arms; and the tall shafts, at least, of the three towers, two flanking the west front, conventionally enough, and a third at the rear of the apse. Thus the remarkable external composition, recalling Carolingian churches, belongs to the church of 1710–15, though the crowning elements of the towers, particularly that to the east, were elaborated in the rebuilding (Pl. 153).

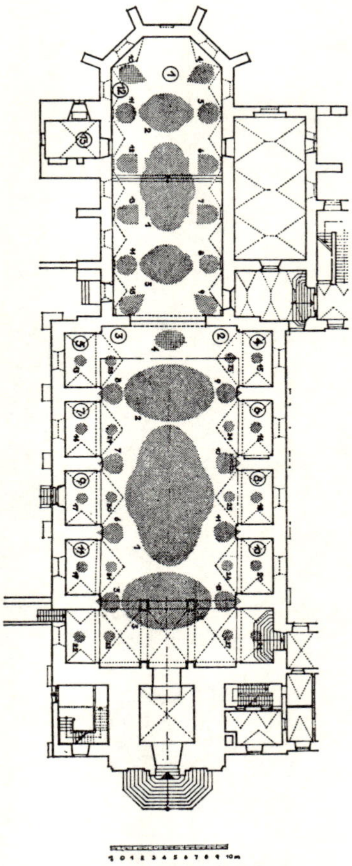

Fig. 17. St. Trudpert, Abbey Church. Plan

That rebuilding began in 1719, and Thumb brought with him no less than 200 assistants and workmen to carry out his design under the direction of two *Palier*, his brother Gabriel and J. G. I Feuerstein, probably a relative of their mother. In 1728 Heinrich Kohler and another Feuerstein, Leopold, took charge. Caspar Wöllfel was the master-carpenter in 1727; by that date, according to an inscription behind the organ, the structural work in the church was complete and the decoration already begun. In 1731, after the stucco-work and many of the frescoes were finished, Johann Vogel was called in to build the spiral stairs leading up to the organ. In 1727 Georg Machoff (or Machauff) received 300 livres for the *stucchi* in the nave and forty-five for those in the choir. He had two assistants, Peter N. (?) and Anton Blanck. The fresco-painters active in 1728–29 were Joseph Matter, Joseph Sibert or Siffert, and (?) Collet, the first two, at least, coming from Strasbourg. They executed, respectively, the frescoes in the first, second, and third bays of the nave. The fresco over the crossing is by Joseph Magges from the Tyrol and was not executed until 1759. The furnishing of the church with altars, confessionals, and organ was effectively completed in 1733–35 with the gilding by Edmond 'der Fasser' of the high altar; but for the sculpture in the composition Leonard Meyer of Sélestat had already received fifteen livres on account in 1728. The work of other minor craftsmen need not be itemized here.[13]

In most respects a typical Vorarlberg church of its slightly uncertain date,[14] Ebersmunster is exceptionally romantic as seen from a distance (Pl. 153), not because of its site, which is not remarkable, but for its silhouette. Seen in varied relation to the two conventional west towers with their solid octagonal belfry stages and lantern-crowned 'onions' covered with green glazed tiles, the axially located eastern tower, taller and more varied in shape, always dominates.

The interior rivals in size and grandeur not only the Swiss churches Thumb had supervised for Beer, Rheinau and St. Urban, but also Beer's churches in southern Württemberg, Weissenau of 1717–23 and even Weingarten, begun in 1715 and approaching completion internally in 1719 when the rebuilding of Ebersmunster started (Pl. 154). Like Weingarten (Pl. 33), Ebersmunster has handkerchief vaults over the broad oblong bays of the nave as well as a flat dome over the square crossing like Weissenau (Pl. 127). The grand effect is actually enhanced by the way the pilasters on the pillars here in Alsace are painted to look like ashlar masonry[15] —irregularly banded in two colours, moreover—although the vaults are treated in the German manner with stucco-work and large frescoes.

The contrast with such a great church in north-eastern France, as Saint-Jacques at Lunéville, is striking.[16] This was begun in 1730 by a French architect, Romain, probably to the designs of a more distinguished one much employed by German clients—Germain Boffrand—and completed by Héré de Corny in 1747. Saint-Jacques follows the medieval hall-church scheme, at this time little used in Germany but very popular in the eighteenth century in northern France. For all its size and fine masonry, inside as well as out, the Lunéville church quite fails to match either the still truly Baroque scale and tectonic vigour of Thumb's interior or the more advanced sort of richness, already approaching the Early Rococo, of that interior's stuccoed and frescoed vaults. It is notable, nonetheless, that the vaults of the narrow bays of the long nave of Saint-Jacques as well as those of the aisles are of the handkerchief type, even though only that of the dome over the square crossing carries Rococo decoration. Héré's towers, on the other hand, above a lower stage based on Borromini's at Sant'Agnese in Agone in Rome, are of an elaboration and a Rococo fantasy never rivalled by the western towers of south German churches,[17] even those of as late a date as these must be.

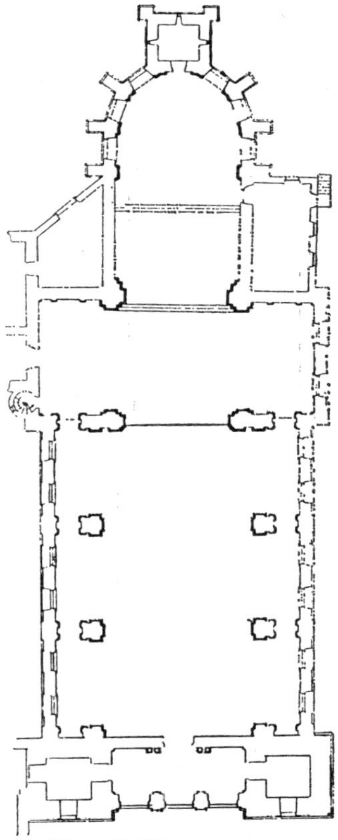

Fig. 18. Ebersmunster, Abbey Church. Plan

Considered in relation to contemporary south German architecture, however, Ebersmunster is not advanced, for it does not have the overall Early Rococo character of the Asams' church interiors of the mid-1720s at Freising (Pl. 45) and Einsiedeln (Pl. 51), much less of Osterhofen (Pl. 59) or Steinhausen (Pl. 11), with which the Ebersmunster stucco-work and frescoes of 1727–29 are more closely contemporary. Nonetheless the frescoes[18] in the four bays of the nave are very large and airy in composition, even if no larger than C. D. Asam's at Weingarten of ten years before (Pl. 33). Their frames, moreover, if hardly to be considered scalloped, are of distinctly varied outline, especially that of the one above the organ. Machoff's *stucchi* have quite lost the Italianate fullness of those which Orsati and De Prevostis executed at St. Trudpert (Pl. 152), somewhat over a decade earlier, but there is in the dry and somewhat sparse bandwork no close approach to J. B. Zimmermann's French-derived ceiling decorations of the mid-twenties at Schleissheim and Benediktbeuern (Pl. 13).

However, the interior of the church at Ebersmunster, like its far more exceptional exterior, is nonetheless truly impressive, carrying the characteristics of the Vorarlberg masters' mature style farther westward than it had ever been seen before. It provides a Late Baroque monument unique in French territory and complete down to the side altars, executed by Mathias Wurtzer and Antoine Kettler with paintings by André von Will, and the church doors, the ten confessionals, and the frames of the altarpieces carved by Rupert Haagel.[19]

St. Peter

Unfortunately at St. Peter in the Schwarzwald, where Thumb was commissioned on 1 May 1724 to build the new church of the Benedictine abbey, he seems not to have had the same opportunities as in Alsace. This church, begun in 1724, was completed and consecrated in 1727.[20] The somewhat later altars of 1728–31, with rich sculpture by J. A. Feuchtmayr (1696–1770),[21] only serve to emphasize its otherwise rather barren appearance so awkwardly do those at the east end of the nave overlap the pilastered piers supporting the arch at the entrance to the narrower choir (Pl. 157). Even so, in certain respects this interior approaches the Early Rococo architecturally in ways that Ebersmunster does not, if with a rather unhappy result.

As at St. Trudpert, a continuous barrel-vault serves to unify the three bays of the nave and the slightly wider crossing bay (Fig. 19); indeed a similar vault carries on the vista through the two bays of the deep choir and the terminal square sanctuary, interrupted only by the range of frescoed medallions surrounding the choir-arch. As later in Joseph Schmuzer's St. Martin at Garmisch (Pl. 134), however, the effect of spatial continuity is weakened visually by the ribs, here of fairly vigorous profile, between the bays of both nave and choir (Pl. 157). The pilaster clusters are less tectonic in effect, thanks both to their conjunction with the segmental arches carrying the balconies and, theoretically at least, to the panelling and the dry proto-Rococo ornamentation, in the tradition of St. Urban (Pl. 125), on their shafts. This stucco-work by the Swiss G. B. Clerici, from Mendrisiotto in the Ticino, and the relatively small and tightly-framed frescoes by F. J. Spiegler do little to complement the relative novelty of the spatial organization.[22] Fortunately a later interior by Thumb in the monastery at St. Peter (Pl. 158) and the way the group of buildings crowns this romantically rural site (Pl. 155) make up for the marked inferiority of the interior of the church.

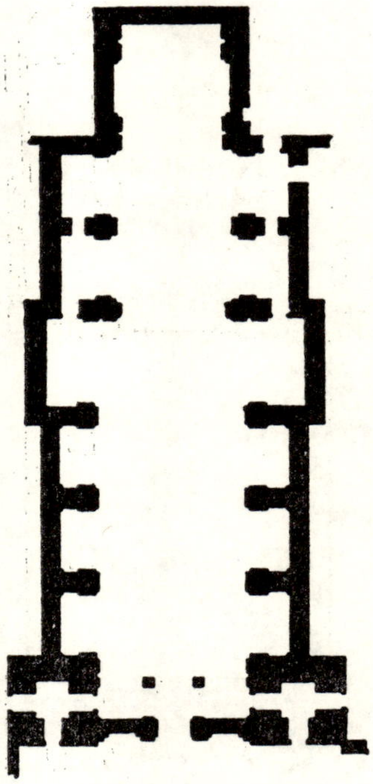

Fig. 19. St. Peter, Abbey Church. Plan

The west front is very tall and strong, following closely but improving upon that of Ebersmunster. The belfry stage of the towers is shorter and the double-onion terminals, small above large, are at once more boldly and more gracefully curved. The arcade at the base between the towers is blind since there is no porch as on the Alsatian church, and statues fill three niches in the crowning story below a double-curved central pediment and flanking scrolls. The result is far more Baroque than the rather flat and dry arrangement of the comparable elements at Ebersmunster.

The small onion-topped belfry over the sanctuary to the east, however, is no rival to the splendid terminal tower in Alsace (Pls. 153, 155).

Minor Works of 1725–35

Franz II Beer died in 1726. Henceforth for the next thirty years his son-in-law's architectural services were almost as much in demand as his had been, even if the earlier results were not comparable to Beer's best works in size and in quality. In the following ten years, before Bürgi, the abbot who had commissioned the church at St. Peter, called on Thumb to build the library there—completed and decorated only under the next abbot, P. J. Steyrer, who succeeded Bürgi in 1749—, he built the church and the Cistercian nunnery at Friedenweiler near Freiburg (1725–31); the church and a wing of the Benedictine nunnery at Frauenalb near Karlsruhe (1726–31)—largely erected from 1704 on by Franz Beer; subsidiary buildings at Rheinau (1726) carried out in association with his brother-in-law Johann Michael II Beer (1700–67); the Cistercian monastery at Tennenbach near Freiburg, begun in 1726; work in Cistercian nunneries and churches at Günsterstal near Freiburg (1728) and Lichtental outside Baden-Baden (1724; 1728–34); the remodelling of the church and buildings of the Cistercian nunnery at Königsbruck in Alsace (1728);[23] the parish church at Biengen near Freiburg (1730); the priory at Wipperskirch (1731–32); the Augustinian church and priory at Waldkirch (1732–34); and the choir and tower of the parish church at Rust (1733), all four near Freiburg. He also remodelled the Rhine Mill at Konstanz, a work of engineering rather than architecture (1737). From 1732 he was responsible, as supervising architect of the medieval Münster in Konstanz, for the maintenance of the fabric, but this entailed no new construction in his day.

Such a volume of production was rivalled in the period only by that of J. M. Fischer in Bavaria and Franconia,[24] and it is not surprising that Thumb had little chance to develop stylistically when his clients were content with—in fact, may even have dictated—familiar solutions of the monastery-and-church problem when he was building or rebuilding for them.

Friedenweiler is small and has little decoration; but for Frauenalb, commissioned in 1725, an interesting scheme was evolved. The church, placed across one end of a quadrangle, had a $2\frac{1}{2}$-bay choir and a $2\frac{1}{2}$-bay nave to left and right of a domed crossing (Fig. B, facing p. 152). Towards the quadrangle a bowed aisle, serving as a vestibule inside the main entrance, was flanked by two towers that composed with the dome somewhat as at Sant'Agnese in Agone in Rome. This is clearly premonitory of St. Gallen (Fig. E, facing p. 168) as actually built, though even Thumb's earliest project dates from some twenty-five years later. But the Frauenalb church is a ruin today, having been burned together with the convent in 1853. The Tennenbach monastery was demolished in 1807. Extant is the attractive church (now serving the parish) at Waldkirch. This has a large round ceiling fresco by F. B. Altenburger over the fourth of the five bays of the nave which is wider than the others and has short transeptal arms. The altars of 1738–41 are by J. M. Winterhalter, and that must be the approximate date of the *stucchi* also. The rather curious plan and the spatial organization of Waldkirch is, however, of some significance as a premonition of Birnau.[25] It is unnecessary here to deal further with these minor works beyond noting the exceptional amount of monastic construction of which St. Peter offers the largest and most impressive surviving example. Most of this is very plain in character, though often surprisingly monumental in bulk, even at minor foundations such as St. Trudpert (Fig. 16).

Library at St. Peter

The libraries in monasteries of the eighteenth century in Germany, Austria and Switzerland are among the most striking architectural interiors of their day, rivalling the churches in richness of decoration, if not in size, and the great halls of palaces in the variety of their spatial composition. The Austrian monasteries set the pace in Thumb's day: Jakob Prandtauer's at Melk, completed after his death in 1726 by Josef Munggenast (1680–1741) and frescoed by Paul Troger (1698–1762), and Munggenast's at Altenburg, begun in 1740, and at St. Florian, carried out by Gothart Hayberger in 1744–50. But in the early eighteenth century some fine ones were built and decorated in southern Germany such as those that J. B. Zimmermann stuccoed at Ottobeuren[26] and Benediktbeuern. The libraries at Ottobeuren, at Melk and at St. Florian all had galleries round the walls, and so do both of those that Thumb built, the earlier one at St. Peter (Pl. 158) and the later one at St. Gallen (Pl. 174). Of the two, the earlier is the more interesting architecturally though much less well known or readily accessible.

Since the libraries usually occupied portions of the monastery complex[27]—though that at Benediktbeuern is free-standing—they were almost necessarily rectangular in basic plan. In order to provide as much space as possible for books they were two stories tall, except for that at Benediktbeuern which is relatively low. The ceilings in the more elaborate examples were usually vaulted and decorated, like those in the churches, with *stucchi* and frescoes. As with the churches, the furnishings are frequently later than the architecture and not always harmonious or worthy of their setting, as is unfortunately true at St. Peter.

The date of construction of the St. Peter library is given by the authorities of the present-day seminary there as 1734–39. But the plan was not formally accepted until 1737,[28] and the decoration was executed after 1750. Although the architectural design belongs to the mid-thirties, the large fresco overhead by Benedikt Gamb is signed and dated 1751 and the Rococo stucco-work is by J. G. Gigl (d. 1765), who also worked in the Fürstensaal and the House Chapel when the monastery was rebuilt from 1752 on.[29]

To a greater extent than in most churches of the day, the rectangular shape of the St. Peter library was 'ovalized' spatially by Thumb (Pl. 158), partly by his ingenious treatment of the vaulting and partly by the waving outline of the gallery, so different from the straight lines of the galleries in many other libraries. The vault is very flat at the crown and Gamb's big fresco that now extends across it helps to strengthen the ellipsoid spatial effect by its scalloped shape.

The vault rises from ten vaulting conoids. Those at the corners are minimized, as in Wren's St. Stephen Walbrook or the crossing of St. Paul's, while the single ones at the middle of the ends and the pairs in the middle of either side, though they are triangular continuations downwards of the main vault surface, are so masked by their decoration with large frescoed and stucco-framed cartouches[30] that they hardly appear to constitute tectonic elements in the composition overhead. As in Early Gothic vaulting, the severies over the cross-bays, which are wider in the middle of the sides than at the corners, vary in curvature in order to keep their crowns the same height. But the still usual pointed intersections of such cross-vaults with the main handkerchief vault are here indicated only by the slightest of mouldings on the arrises. Similar arrises rise from each of the corners, though the observer's eye is drawn rather to the stronger arched mouldings that cross the corners diagonally. These last approximate in length, and even in curvature, the arrises with which the broader cross-vaults above the central bays of the sides meet the main vault. The latter are, however, pushed far outward in effect by the bulging sides of the frame of the main fresco; the nearly flat surface of the fresco, indeed, actually distorts the underlying handkerchief vault at these points, as was presumably already intended by Thumb in his original design of the thirties. The result, one may claim, is almost the most exemplary, as it is one of the most extreme, examples of Rococo vaulting,[31] even if the memory of certain of Borromini's vaults, ribbed though most of those are, must for many hover in the background. These Roman vaults could probably have been known only at third or fourth remove, if indeed at all, to Thumb. Certainly he never saw the ceiling of the refectory, now sacristy, at San Carlo alle Quattro Fontane in Rome that Borromini built a hundred years earlier, which comes so close to this vault in spirit.

The gallery bends in and out, loosely following the shape of the overhead fresco (Pl. 158). Bold convex bulges, crowned with pairs of wooden figures of the Arts and Sciences by Christian Wenzinger, marbled to look like alabaster, mark the centres of the two ends and flank the middle bays at the sides, with deep concave curves at the corners. The swinging Rococo rhythm is further enhanced by the slighter bulges in front of the first and third bays on the sides, as also by the absence of articulated supports below. In the two most nearly comparable libraries, the one by the Wiedemans at Wiblingen, built just before this in the early thirties, and that carried out by Jakob Emele in the fifties at Schussenried following, to a considerable extent at least, a design of Dominikus Zimmermann's of 1748, the surrounding galleries are carried on columns. These clutter the edges of the interior space in the lower story. Since such columns serve a structural purpose, moreover, they introduce a tectonic element that may be considered somewhat alien to the spirit of the mature Rococo of these decades in southern Germany. It should be noted, however, that Thumb returned to the use of columns in the library at St. Gallen (Pl. 174).

One can hardly suppose that any of the detail executed in stucco is an integral part of the design of the late thirties. Certainly the predominant colouring, so delicate in its very slight contrast of creamy off-white against white as to appear monochromatic in photographs, dates from the fifties. But the visual emphasis that the space-defining balcony receives, thanks to the blue-grey scagliola of its balustrade, as also the contrast provided by the curious panels that take the place of pilasters below the bulges in the cove under the balcony, also of deep-toned scagliola, may well have been intended from the first. These vertical elements recall the equally curious scagliola panels against which the tapered pilasters on the upper wall of E. Q. Asam's St. Johann-Nepomuk in Munich are set (Pl. 74). The winding cove-supported balcony might also have been suggested by that in Munich, for the balusters are of similar shape here, though not so richly decorated, and the swings only exaggerate the slight curvatures in plan of the balcony in the Asamkirche.[32]

Following the original designing and the beginning of the construction of the St. Peter library, Thumb, though then only in his fifties, was somewhat less active than earlier during the twenty years that intervened before the construction of the great church of St. Gallen finally got under way in 1756. But in the middle of this period came his masterpiece, the pilgrimage church and summer residence of the Abbots of Salem at Birnau, on the north side of the Bodensee east of Überlingen, which occupied him over the years 1745–50. Before describing Birnau a few minor works should be briefly mentioned.

Minor Works of 1735–45

In 1738–39 Thumb built the monastery beside his church at St. Trudpert (Fig. 16). In 1738 he also provided the designs for the Piaristenkolleg (now the Gymnasium) founded by Margrave Ludwig Georg of Baden-Baden in 1731 at Rastatt. This was executed in 1739–45 by the younger Rohrer, J. P. E., the son of J. P. L. Rohrer who had died in 1732. In addition he advised Rohrer on his project of 1740 for the Stadkirche at Rastatt; this was erected much later in 1756–64.[33] In 1739–42 he built the very modest church and priory at St. Ulrich (Pl. 156) south of Freiburg, a dependency of the Abbey of St. Peter, and in 1739–42 he worked in the parish church at Mengen near Sigmaringen in southern Württemberg. His slight connexion with the building of the church of St. Peter at Bruchsal in Baden in 1742, designed by J. B. Neumann for Damian Hugo Cardinal Schönborn, Prince-Bishop of Speyer and Konstanz, and his related activity at the Neues Schloss at Meersburg on the Bodensee in 1743, also for the Cardinal, can be ignored;[34] while at St. Ulrich the *stucchi* and the frescoes in the church by F. L. Hermann, who had worked in the fifties in the Abtskapelle at St. Peter, date from 1767, after Thumb's death. The Mengen parish church is Gothic and his work there only a modest remodelling and redecoration as a setting for frescoes executed in 1740 by G. W. Vollmer and Joseph Sautter. Even less than what he had carried out in the late twenties and early thirties does any of this compare in interest with the library of St. Peter or the church at Ebersmunster. The church of the Priory of Petershausen at Mengen, built in 1741–46 but destroyed by fire in 1810, was apparently of considerably greater interest since it seems to have been in plan even more premonitory of Birnau than Waldkirch.[35]

Birnau

Eighteenth-century monastery and pilgrimage churches, the most characteristic architectural monuments of the age in Germany and exceeding in number the palaces of secular and ecclesiastical princes, are usually impressive externally because of their bulk, dominating by their great height the massive ranges of monastery buildings or residential quarters for the attached priests. These churches are very often picturesque as well as bulky, thanks to their double towers, their occasional tall domes—rare after 1720—their gables and their heavy roofs. Thus Ebersmunster, though the monastery buildings are small and plain, profits from its striking cluster of onion-topped towers, an unexpectedly Middle European sight on the French side of the Rhine (Pl. 153). Many churches, unlike Ebersmunster, have superb hilltop or valley-bottom sites, backed with broad cultivated fields and dark, well-maintained forests, as in the case of St. Peter (Pl. 155). Sometimes, moreover, a single tower takes the place of the more usual pair at the west front. When, as at St. Ulrich (Pl. 156), this occupies a transeptal position—usually because it has, so to say, medieval roots if not a medieval trunk, as in the case of several of J. G. Fischer's churches—the composition can be picturesquely asymmetrical almost in the High Victorian way. When the tower is centred on the west front as it is (to take an especially distinguished example) at J. B. Neumann's St. Paulin in Trier, designed in the thirties and completed in the forties, the great height of the tower usually overshadows the church behind. Even Neumann's great plastic ingenuity hardly achieved at St. Paulin a satisfactory relationship between the very narrow portions of the west front of the nave extending to left and right and the central projecting shaft of the tower above the main entrance.

It is in this connexion that Birnau[36] deserves more comment than most of Thumb's earlier exteriors (Pls. 159, 160). Taking his cue, doubtless, from the largest monasteries—though here the residential element, being only summer quarters for the abbot and monks of Salem, is relatively small, as at Zimmermann's contemporary Die Wies—such as Weingarten and Einsiedeln, where two-towered church façades are set between long monastery wings to left and right, he flanked his single west tower by massive three-storied square blocks, setting back slightly the plain elements between, but without attempting otherwise than by the greater richness of treatment of the front of the tower to indicate that the central portion is actually the façade of a church. To the rear the taller roof of the nave of the church extends backwards behind the middle stage of the tower, while the double roofs of the segmental 'transepts' at either side echo those of the corner blocks in front.

From the rear (Pl. 160), also, it is the handling of the roof that provides the major plastic interest rather than the thin pilaster order with its entablature bent upward in segmental curves over the upper windows. The choir roof is higher than those of the transepts and the front corner blocks because this portion of the church, though narrower than the nave, is still quite wide; behind that the even narrower apse is again crowned with a double roof, the upper portion of which is a continuation of that of the choir. Such thorough and unconventional study of the plastic composition of a church exterior was rare at the time and contrasts happily with the episodic fashion in which Dominikus Zimmermann, for example, strung out the comparable elements of his great church and its adjuncts at Die Wies.[37]

Whether Thumb's achievement in the design of the exterior of Birnau should be considered Rococo is not easy to say. The upper stage of his tower (Pl. 159), with its diagonally set pilasters and its curved capping above and below the tiny lantern, is certainly unusually rich for the period, yet hardly Rococo in the sense of the tops of Héré's towers on Saint-Jacques at Lunéville. The exotic window shapes and painted bandwork on the flanks of Die Wies are certainly a good deal less academic than the pilaster order and the two ranges of windows, one above the other, consistently used for both the front and the sides of Birnau. All of this is really more in continuity with Baroque principles—and even international Baroque practice

—than consistent with the originality of his interior here or that of the earlier St. Peter library. But the Rococo in the Germany of the mid-eighteenth century, as from its beginnings in France, was primarily an interior style or mode, not one ever formulated and elaborated for exteriors.[38]

The Birnau pilgrimage dates from the fifteenth century, unlike that to Die Wies, Birnau's contemporary architectural rival, which was built to house a new object of devotion. Here a medieval Madonna was enshrined, but the original church at 'old' Birnau, burned in the Thirty Years War, had been rebuilt in the late seventeenth century. The shrine was an apanage of the Cistercian Abbey of Salem to the north, to which land at Birnau had been given by the lords of Bodman in 1241. But in the eighteenth century, when the popularity of the pilgrimage began to increase, the monks had difficulties with the neighbouring city of Überlingen and so decided to build further to the east along the north shore of the Bodensee on their own property, combining with the new church a summer residence as was being done at the same time by the Abbey of Steingaden when building Die Wies.[39] A natural terrace, well above the level of the lake, provided a superb site to which, as has been noted, Thumb responded most worthily.[40]

In 1741 the monastery had obtained plans from J. G. Stahl, the architect of Cardinal Schönborn, whose seat nearby at Meersburg has been mentioned. At Meersburg Stahl, with considerable advice from Neumann if not from Neumann's actual designs, was building the stair-hall of the Neues Schloss. Nothing came of Stahl's project for Birnau. But it will be recalled that Thumb was architect of the Münster of Konstanz and was even being consulted by the Cardinal at this point about the work at Meersburg and also in connection with the execution by Stahl of Neumann's church of St. Peter at Bruchsal. It was not surprising that in 1745 the new Abbot of Salem, Stephan Euroth, who actually came from Meersburg, should call in Thumb, for he had already done a great deal of work for Cistercians in Switzerland, in Baden, and in Alsace, beginning with his supervision of St. Urban for Franz Beer thirty years before.

On 17 March in that year there was what would today be called a design-conference at Salem, and five days later the exact site was fixed. The next year, on 4 March, the old church was given up and, on 12 April, the cornerstone of the new one was laid. Then, on 17 June 1746 an agreement with Thumb was signed by Euroth's successor as Abbot of Salem, Anselm II Schwab,[41] elected only eleven days earlier, including a rather low estimate of 7,800 gulden, and in August of that year the cornerstone of the priests' house at the front was laid. The structural work went forward with no breaks so that already on 10 March 1748 the first payment, not covered by the contract with Thumb, was being made to the stuccoer J. A. Feuchtmayr.[42] The payments made in 1748 were for two pairs of side altars, sixty-one stucco capitals and, on 23 November, for a design for the high altar.[43] In 13 July 1749 he was further paid for eighty-eight carved keystones used on the sides of the church and three window-frames on the tower. The Augsburg painter G. B. Goez (1708–74), who like Feuchtmayr had worked in the chapel of the Neues Schloss at Meersburg in 1741, was commissioned to execute the frescoes in this year 1748 and they were carried out in 1749.[44] On 20–21 September 1750 the church, by then effectively complete, was consecrated.

Feuchtmayr still continued to provide various fittings. In this year 1750 he was asked to provide six confessionals and the Stations of the Cross, of which only eight survive, and was paid for ninety-six pew-ends, as also for already executed *stucchi* and gilding on the galleries. Payment for his other work came later, so that his last bill, for the statues of St. Windelin and St. Blasius on the side altars, is dated as late as 1 June 1758. But despite the late date of some of the payments to Feuchtmayr—for the sculpture on the organ, 7 April 1752; for the confessionals and the Stations of the Cross commissioned in 1750, 17 May and 1 December 1753; and for the busts, putti and flower vases on the gallery, 20 April 1757—the interior, with the exception of these last on which he had the assistance of F. A. Dirr, must have been completely finished and furnished within a year or two after the consecration. Fortunately very few changes have occurred since. But the present high altar is not as Feuchtmayr and Dirr designed it, for it was modified by J. G. Wieland in 1790; the small lantern that originally rode the ridge of the apse roof was removed in 1810; and the original organ, taken out in 1824, was replaced with the present one only in 1950.

The interior of Birnau is so original that it is very possibly unique in church architecture (Pl. 161); certainly there are no close parallels in eighteenth-century Germany before this time and what leads up to it is the library at St. Peter (Pl. 158) rather than any of Thumb's extant churches.[45] The nave is neither basilican nor yet of the wall-pillar type that Thumb had inherited from Franz Beer and used so far for all his larger churches.[46] The nave approaches most closely such a 'praying-hall' as Santa Maria de Victoria in Ingolstadt, probably built and certainly decorated by the Asams in the mid-thirties (Pl. 70). Yet it is unlike this in its generous dimensions, especially that of height, and is perhaps almost as closely related to the deep choirs of such churches as Polling, Vilgertshofen (Pl. 119), and Günzburg.[47] The quadrantal corners at the east end, balanced here by a narrower diagonal truncation of the corners at the west end, had already had a long history in eighteenth-century Germany,[48] though Thumb had never used them before this (Fig. 20).

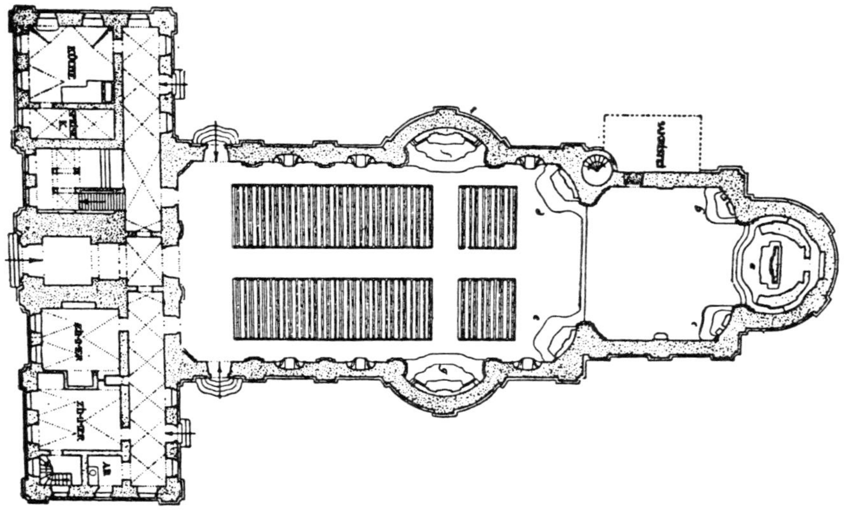

Fig. 20. Birnau, Pilgrimage Church. Plan

The transeptal chapels of curved outline, placed not halfway along the nave nor at its east end but in the fourth of its five bays as at Waldkirch and Mengen, might have been suggested by the half-round side chapels at St. Urban. But by carrying these chapels up the full two-story height of the interior, Thumb made of them here important features of the space-composition echoing, as in the two later examples, the broader but equally tall spaces of the choir and the sanctuary to the east. The vault is very much flattened to a semi-elliptical curve,[49] which the choir-arch conspicuously repeats, and the vaulting conoids round the edge barely have independent existence visually so far does the vast ceiling fresco extend down into them (Pls. 161, 165) as in the St. Peter library (Pl. 158).

Beyond the nave to the east the plan is telescopic as the exterior massing clearly indicates (Fig. 20). The square choir is somewhat narrower than the nave and the apse still narrower. The circle of the shallow dome of the choir, therefore, which is filled with a large round fresco in the fashion common since H. G. Asam painted the dome at Tegernsee sixty years earlier, rests not on four equal pendentives as usual but on six (Pl. 166). These are unevenly disposed round the sides between the wide elliptical opening of the choir-arch to the west and the narrower opening, also semi-elliptical, of the sanctuary arch to the east. The handling of the vault elements here is thus as free (not to say freehand) as in the St. Peter library (Pl. 158). The membering in the eastern corners of the choir repeats effectively that in the curved eastern corners of the nave, even though the vault segments above them are quite different (Pl. 162).

Finally, over the small horseshoe-shaped sanctuary, which the open edicule of the high altar completely fills spatially, there is not another dome but instead a handkerchief vault. This is penetrated at its sides by the severies of the sub-vaults above the flanking windows in much the same way as the severies over the arches and the side windows of the choir fit between the pendentives below the dome. Thus there is overhead along the central axis a sequential development from the broad, practically flat, ceiling of the nave, flanked though it is by rather boldly pointed intersecting vaulting elements above the side and corner bays, through the shallow-domed choir with its pendentives, to the tighter and more confining curvature of the vault that crowns the easternmost compartment (Pls. 161, 162). This is Rococo space-composition at its richest and most subtle in contrast to the effectively unbroken rectangle of Santa Maria de Victoria, with which the nave, if considered by itself, may not improperly be compared (Pl. 70).

Galleries were constituent features of the wall-pillar type of church and occasionally, as for example at Einsiedeln in the twenties, they had constituted important elements in the total spatial effect. Such galleries, however, had almost always been subordinated hitherto to a giant order or its equivalent except in libraries. Here, however, there are no continuous vertical elements of structure. The balcony continues unbroken round nave and choir and even passes, diminished in breadth, behind the tops of the altars in the transeptal projections (Pl. 163). The gallery provides, moreover, the only continuous horizontal below the plane of the nave fresco overhead, for entablatures and even entablature-blocks are consistently omitted, except in the edicule of the latar which is not of Thumb's period. Yet, surprisingly enough, pilasters are used in great profusion (Pls. 161–163). Clusters of them below the balcony separate all the bays, both longitudinal and oblique, and upon them rest the bases of the coved elements, similar to those supporting the balcony at St. Peter and echoing at smaller scale the vaulting conoids that rise from an upper order of pilaster-clusters.[50] But these pilasters, with their very freely designed capitals, can hardly be considered tectonic elements, at least not in the Baroque sense (Pl. 173). Rather they articulate the wall surface in the manner of the tall panels which so often, but by no means always, replaced pilasters in the *boiseries* of French Rococo interiors; while the flanking elements of the clusters are associated with the 'wall-arches', so to call them, that outline the bays above the concentric segmental heads of the windows.

Of the profuse but delicate stucco-work, here incidental yet complementary to Thumb's architecture, it is hardly necessary to speak in detail. This is neither the 'constructed decoration' of Dominikus Zimmermann's precisely contemporary choir at Die Wies[51]—a total substitution of *rocaille* elements for inherited architectural forms—nor yet the almost unrelated overgrowth which, for all its high intrinsic quality, seems to submerge and confuse J. M. Fischer's original architectonic intentions in several of his grandest churches (Pls. 192, 198).

The interior of Birnau is generally white, though varied here and there by pale pastel tones; even the accents in this interior, provided by the somewhat stronger pink and blue marbling of the posts in the balcony railing, are high in key and restricted in quantity.[52] The altars are also of a relatively light pink and blue though executed in hard, shining scagliola (Pl. 164). The statuary, here of the highest quality, is also mostly white, with stronger colour on the draperies in some cases —for example, the famous *Honigschlecker*, a putto holding a beehive and licking honey from his finger. Only the small figures in the Stations of the Cross are fully and naturalistically polychromed.

All the more curious and unfortunate, therefore, in this interior that otherwise represents the highest Rococo accomplishment of the mid-century, is the retardataire character of Goez's frescoes. Despite the greater freedom of its painted architecture, that of the Woman of the Apocalypse in the dome of the choir still follows the Pozzo-derived formula of C. D. Asam's choir fresco of 1718–20 at Weingarten (Pl. 166). This is not a serious anachronism, since it affects very little the total spatial composition of the interior and the tonality of the whole is light and even gay. But in the nave, where one might have expected an open aerial composition such as J. B. Zimmermann had used as early as 1731 over the oval nave of Steinhausen (Pl. 11) and was providing at this very point again for his brother at Die Wies,[53] Goez started out by breaking the ceiling into two areas. One, occupying the western two bays of the nave, is almost square; the second more extensive one, centred on the transeptal axis, fills the other three bays (Pls. 161, 165). Fortunately Goez's broad painted rib, though darker in tone than the largely white architecture below, is so closely related to the tonality of the fresco as a whole that it is not conspicuous. But the two independent systems of perspective in the two parts of the fresco tend to break up the spatial unity of the nave and work against the carefully graded succession of spaces Thumb had provided in his architecture. Finally, the brownish parapet of heavy painted *quadratura* architecture which Goez stretched across the vaulting conoids, somewhat in the manner of Michelangelo's

Sistine ceiling, made impossible that easy, freehand grace in the handling of vault-intersections which is such a notable example of the Rococo transformation of an inherited Baroque architectural device in the library at St. Peter (Pl. 158).

Following once more the manner of C. D. Asam—in this case most specifically that of his ceiling fresco in the nave of Osterhofen (Pl. 57) of twenty years earlier—the principal fresco over the eastern bays of the nave (which is devoted to the Glorification of the Virgin as Queen of Heaven) has conspicuous *quadratura* architecture so handled perspectively that it seems to extend upward a Baroque sort of nave that has no physical existence below, thus providing only a minimal area of open sky in the centre (Pls. 161, 165). The architectural elements are, however, so organized as to suggest at the base an ovalized rectangle that rises to a circle of sky in the centre; while in the western half of the nave the clouds that carry the trumpeting angels largely obscure the simpler architectural setting.

So great, however, is Thumb's achievement here as a Rococo architect, so happy the embellishment provided by his other collaborators, the sculptor and stuccoer Feuchtmayr and his assistant Dirr, that one can only be surprised he never again produced anything at all similar to this interior in the way that the nave of Birnau is similar to his library at St. Peter.[54] Younger architects, particularly the Dossenbergers,[55] would move in this direction in the fifties and sixties, but Thumb did not, even in his latest work, the St. Gallen library (Pl. 174), designed a decade later than Birnau. Although the degree of Specht's responsibility for the church at the Abbey of Wibligen outside Ulm, which he began to execute in 1771, is not certain[56] it may be relevant to note, despite the stylistic ambiguity of its curious interior, that J. G. Specht (1721–1803) was associated with Thumb at Birnau.

St. Gallen

Although Thumb was even less active[57] after the completion of Birnau than just before, his association with one of the largest and grandest churches of the second half of the eighteenth century, that of the Benedictine Abbey of St. Gallen in Switzerland, and his designing of the library there fill the last years of his productive career with major interest down to his retirement in 1758. The story of the design and construction of St. Gallen is more complicated even than that of Weingarten or of Wiblingen, but from this story can be deduced more conclusive evidence for assigning it to Thumb than Weingarten to either Franz Beer or Caspar Moosbrugger, or Wiblingen to J. M. Fischer or Specht.[58] As at Weingarten and at Einsiedeln, Caspar Moosbrugger's name appears early in the sequence at St. Gallen, where he provided projects for a new church in 1720–21. Next came, a few years later, projects by a local Benedictine, Gabriel Hecht (1664–1745), for a partial reconstruction of the medieval church or, more accurately, churches. Then, in 1730, Thumb's brother-in-law, Johann Michael II Beer, made a report on the state of the old edifice, medieval successor to that of which the famous pre-Romanesque plan is still preserved in Thumb's St. Gallen library.

In 1749, on 27 February, Thumb first offered a project for the church. This had presumably been prepared the previous year, just after Birnau was structurally complete. On 14 April he, together with another Beer, Johann Michael I (1696–1780), and J. C. Bagnato, made another report on the old church, as did also J. M.

II Beer on 13 September. In 1749–50 another Vorarlberger, Johann IV Rüf (1686–1750),[59] provided a project, as did Bagnato again in 1750. The following year Thumb once more prepared a project and, probably the year after that, a young Benedictine lay-brother, Gabriel Looser, who was employed as a cabinetmaker at St. Gallen, constructed a handsome wooden model that happily survives. It largely follows Thumb's ideas, though to some extent those of Bagnato.

In 1752, however, the chapter of the abbey decided to keep the old eastern church as their choir, rebuilding only the western one as a nave. Two years later further projects were offered by J. M. I Beer and by J. J. Rüscher (1662–1755), a Vorarlberger active in the Palatinate. Finally in 1755, after Thumb had further modified his design of 1751, the demolition of the old western church began. At that point Thumb was finally commissioned by Abbot Coelestin Gugger von Standach to build the present nave and central domed area, though the eastern church on the site of the present choir was still to be kept.

Before proceeding further with this account of St. Gallen something should be said about Thumb's responsibility for the design, since Boerlin, in discussing the question at length,[60] refuses to give full credit to him as most scholars have hitherto done. First the evidence provided by the surviving plans I–XIV,[61] most of them preserved at St. Gallen, should be noted. The earliest, the Moosbrugger projects of 1720–21 (I and II),[62] both include *two* domed crossings but nothing approaching a central rotunda. His next project (III),[63] which retains the medieval church to the east, has a more or less centrally planned nave with a heavily framed ovalizing fresco indicated over the crossing. Nothing at all relevant is to be found in the plans of Hecht, Rüf, or the earliest of J. M. I Beer's (IV, V, VI).[64] Beer's next projects (VII, VIII, IX, X),[65] however, propose a domed crossing where the new nave joins the choir, but with no attempt at symmetry in the treatment of the eastern and western arms. Significant in these schemes, however, are the bulging transept façades, as at Thumb's Frauenalb (Fig. B, facing p. 152). In VII[66] the bulge is even flanked by towers on the north side. If the project belongs to the year when Beer's name is first mentioned in the records as making a report on the condition of the old church, 1749, it is later by nearly twenty-five years than Frauenalb and contemporary with Thumb's first project for St. Gallen.

The surviving projects most relevant to the design of the church as finally built are those numbered XII, XIII, and XIV.[67] Of equal relevance is Looser's model of 1752.[68] Closest of all to the church as built is a plan found in Lucerne by Adolf Reinle in 1950 (Fig. F, facing p. 168).

Project XII (Fig. H) proposed a rotunda as wide as the nave and aisles and slightly projecting transepts, again with central bulges. This Boerlin attributes to Moosbrugger on the basis of the resemblance of the eastern pair of towers to those in Moosbrugger's project (III) of 1721[69] and details of the north elevation that resemble elements of the west front of Einsiedeln. The attribution is not persuasive, both because of Moosbrugger's death two years after his 1721 project was submitted and because of the marked superiority of the draughtsmanship to his other surviving drawings. Lieb and Dieth[70] propose more plausibly Thumb's brother-in-law J. M. II Beer as the author and a date not earlier than 1730 for this crucial project which once more suggests—though not very definitely—influence from Thumb's Frauenalb plan as in the case of J. M. I Beer's projects (VII and VIII).

Project XIII, of 1750 and by Bagnato,[71] is much less similar to the church as executed, although the diagonally placed eastern towers may well have provided the model for those finally executed by J. M. I Beer. But Thumb's project, XIV (Fig. D), incorporates similar towers, as does the Looser model.[72] The model, however, is closer in plan[73] to project XII, since nave and choir each have only two bays instead of three as in the executed church. The scalloped plan of the transepts, moreover, corresponds to Thumb's project of 1751 (XIV) rather than to the plain bulges of the Lucerne plan (assigned to Thumb by Lieb-Dieth as well as by Reinle)[74] and the executed church (Figs. E, F). But the surviving plan that is closest to the nave and rotunda Thumb actually built, since it shows the medieval choir retained, is one found at Au (Fig. G) by Franz Dieth in 1956 that must certainly be by Thumb. The model, however, has an internal elevation in two stories with—as shown on the southern side only[75]—no entablature above the lower order of coupled pilasters, but rather a cove supporting a shallow balcony that is very similar to the one at Birnau. Despite the abbot's close relations with Bagnato, of which Boerlin makes much in his 'Conclusio',[76] there seems to be little more reason at St. Gallen than at Birnau to transfer the major credit for the design of the nave and rotunda as executed from Thumb to Bagnato. Nor do Lieb and Dieth,[77] who were familiar with Boerlin's contentions from an article,[78] give his attributions as much attention as they have received here.

What is really significant, regardless of variant attributions of surviving projects, is that the basic idea of a church with a central domed area flanked by matching nave and choir goes back some thirty years before the construction of St. Gallen actually began in 1755 to Thumb's Frauenalb. Thus in German lands, as often elsewhere, such an architect as Thumb can be seen to have taken up again, in the third quarter of the century, certain formal aspects of the pre-Rococo decades early in the century with the result that the Baroque—which had reached full maturity only belatedly in the north—came almost full circle within the lifetime of a generation.

Work on the foundations at St. Gallen began in 1755 and on 29 August 1756 the cornerstone was laid. The following year the raw construction was complete and the stucco and fresco decoration begun by Christian Wenzinger, whom Thumb had known at St. Peter thirty years before. The work was completed by 1760 when the church was consecrated on 15 November.

Peter Thumb had retired to Konstanz on 26 October 1758, his career already ended. When the decision was finally made to reconstruct the east end of the church, apparently about the time of the consecration in 1760, the chapter therefore turned to J. M. I Beer, who provided on 20 December a two-towered project with a shallow segmental apse. The following 19 February the changes he was proposing in the existing designs of 1750–51 for the east end by Bagnato and by Thumb (as represented in Looser's model of 1751) were accepted, and very soon demolition of the old eastern church made possible the building of the new choir. This was probably completed structurally by 1764 when the stuccoers, in this case J. G. Gigl who had been working at St. Peter in the fifties and his brother Mathias, began to execute the *stucchi* inside.

Fig. D. Thumb's 1751 project for St. Gallen

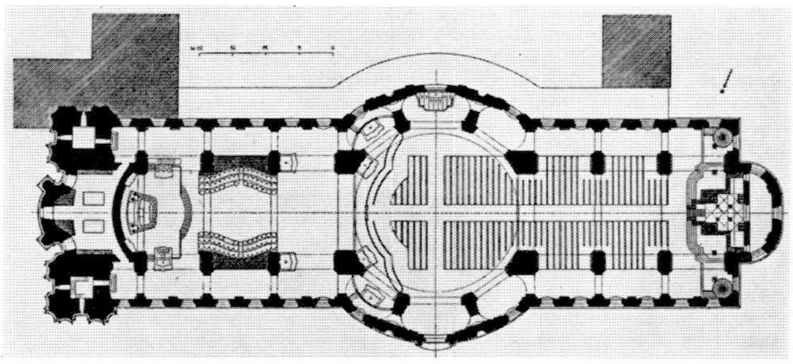

Fig. E. St. Gallen, Abbey Church. Plan

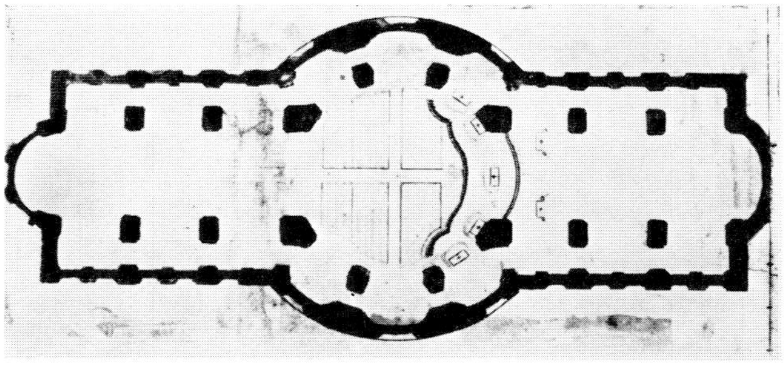

Fig. F. Project for St. Gallen, now at Lucerne

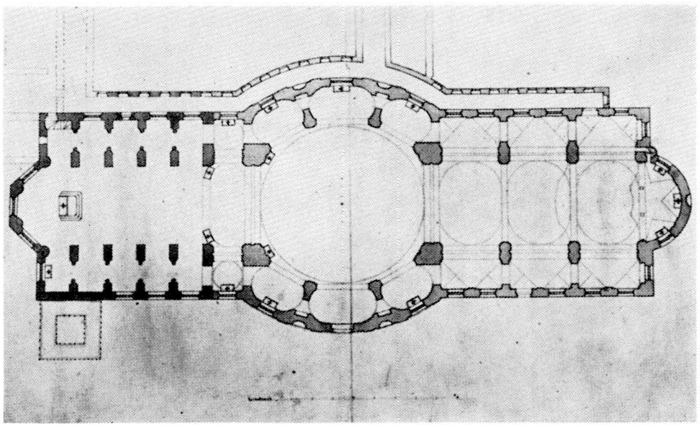

Fig. G. Project for St. Gallen, now at Au

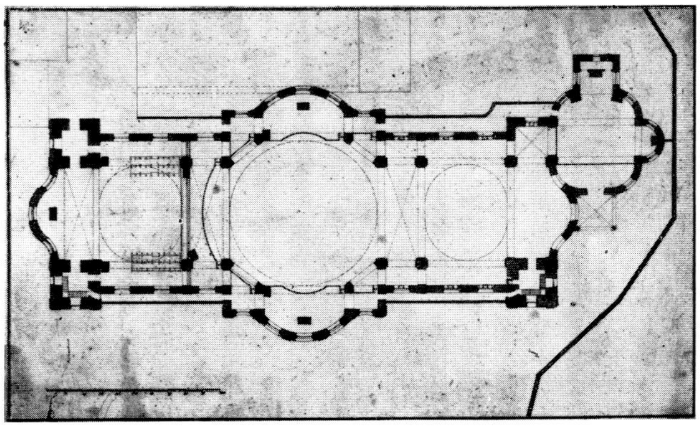

Fig. H. Anonymous project for St. Gallen

In some respects St. Gallen must be accepted as a culminating point in eighteenth-century Germanic architecture. Behind it lay the line of great churches that had begun in the 1680s and 90s with Obermarchtal in Swabia, by Peter Thumb's father and his uncle Christian, and in Switzerland with the Jesuit church at Solothurn, sometimes attributed to a member of another Vorarlberg building family, H. G. Kuen (1641–91); ahead lay international Neoclassicism, initiated in this part of Europe by the French architect P.-M. d'Ixnard (1723–95), at St. Blasien near the Titisee in the Schwarzwald, a few years after the old church there burned in 1768. Because of its great size and the particular character of its plan and spatial organization, moreover, St. Gallen has an almost equally prominent place in the international sequence of great post-Reformation churches that began some two hundred years earlier in Milan and Rome. Yet, paradoxically, it does not represent the culminating point in Thumb's architectural career, much less a culminating example of Rococo architecture, as does his church at Birnau.

The long history of the commission for St. Gallen helps to make its position in Thumb's *œuvre* clear. One cannot say that St. Gallen was actually the result of committee-design, notoriously a method likely to produce weak solutions; but the sequence of designs by so many different men over thirty-five years; the six years of study by Thumb in successive projects intended to meet various objections of the abbot and the monks; and the decision—eventually negated—to retain the medieval eastern church (which can hardly have been sympathetic to any of the architects involved, but which they had to take into account even in making projects for a totally new church)—all this set up limitations that would have been more thwarting than stimulating to any architect.

All the same, the edifice that was finally produced after the old eastern church was eventually replaced in the sixties by Beer's new choir does represent essentially what Thumb had all along been working towards. That was a church dominated spatially by a central area so placed, as earlier in 1726–31 at Frauenalb, that the nave and the choir extended symmetrically to east and west on either side (Fig. E). Such a plan, probably first seriously proposed for St. Gallen in project XII (Fig. H), whatever its precise date and whoever its designer, was arrived at conceptually by moving the characteristic crossing-dome of the post-Reformation church-formula westward. This had in fact already been done quite early in the seventeenth century by Jacques Le Mercier in designing his Eglise de la Sorbonne in Paris, presumably because that church, like Frauenalb, lay across the end of a quadrangle and therefore required a major entrance on the cross-axis.

Le Mercier's domed crossing, however, being very little wider than his nave and his choir, is no rotunda. This was also true of Frauenalb; but there the end of the transept was bowed outward to make the existence of the circular *pièce centrale* more apparent from the exterior and to provide a dominant element where the main entrance was to be set. This tower-flanked bulge could hardly be more different from Le Mercier's temple portico in Paris. An early German approach to such planning is found in the church of Stift Haug in Würzburg, built in 1670–91 by Antonio Petrini (d. 1701).

The closest any architect had come to the St. Gallen scheme in a major executed work was, curiously enough, Christopher Wren's St. Paul's in London as finally designed in 1675 and completed in 1710. After a characteristic struggle, of the sort that goes back to Bramante's difficulties in planning St. Peter's, between an architect set on creating an edifice of a central type and a clergy determined—partly for functional reasons and partly out of respect for local tradition—to have a church with a longitudinal axis, the moderately long nave for the worshipping public was balanced against what is, for the period, a very deep choir that echoes the plan of the earlier medieval church. Thus Wren arrived at a scheme that was effectively symmetrical on the cross-axis. However, the pair of towers at his west end—at St. Gallen they were eventually provided at the east end—and the paired chapels behind them (not to speak of the relative unimportance of the transeptal entrances, compared at least to Le Mercier's temple-fronted north façade at the Sorbonne) diminished the external effect of symmetry on the transverse axis. All the same, the high-drummed dome over the crossing of St. Paul's clearly revealed the centrality of the rotunda underneath it. Moreover, the broadening of the core-space internally beyond the width of the nave and choir, so that the aisles run into the rotunda through diagonal bays while the dome rises as a result over not four but eight pendentives, ensured that the rotunda would dominate the spatial composition of the interior.

In the long struggle between centralized and longitudinal church plans, some of the most interesting Baroque examples had been those in which the two conceptions were merged into a space that was—roughly but not yet precisely—oval in shape as, probably for the first time, in Borromini's San Carlo alle Quattro Fontane in the 1630s. Such merging in eighteenth-century German architecture had, in several characteristic churches from as early as the 1720s, taken either the form of an oval more or less rectangularized or of a rectangle more or less ovalized. At the mid-century the nave of Zimmermann's Die Wies[79] is an example of the first, that of Thumb's Birnau of the second (Fig. 20), and both are climactic examples of Rococo interior architecture. Other German architects had been working along rather different lines.

Josef Greising (1664–1721), a Vorarlberger active in Franconia who built a great deal for the Schönborns, had provided in 1711–21 at the west end of the Neumünster in Würzburg an octagon the full width of the surviving Romanesque nave and aisles that followed beyond. This was masked externally, however, by a typical Roman Baroque façade of concave rather than convex plan. After producing several projects for Einsiedeln that included oval choirs with annular aisles, Caspar Moosbrugger eventually worked out quite a different plan with a western octagon centred on the existing small shrine of the Madonna, and this is what was finally executed by the Rüfs in the 1720s (Fig. 3). The curious and confused sequence of interrelated spaces at Einsiedeln could hardly be expected to appeal to Thumb or to any other well-trained and experienced architect and hardly supports the theory that the crucial project XII for St. Gallen (Fig. H) is by Moosbrugger. Yet familiarity with Benedictine Einsiedeln, also in Switzerland, may have helped to make the idea of a rotunda acceptable to the Benedictines of St. Gallen from the first.

The preoccupation of another architect family not of Vorarlberg origin, the Dientzenhofers, who were from Bavaria but chiefly active in Bohemia, with longitudinal plans made up of intersecting ovals—as suggested by many of Guarini's published projects and more especially that of 1679 for the church of Our Lady of Altötting in Prague—was represented in southern Germany by Johann Dientzenhofer's Banz at the opening of the century. This line of plan-development reached a climax in J. B. Neumann's Vierzehnheiligen (Fig. 33), across the Main from Banz, a great church projected a few years earlier than Thumb's design of 1749 for St. Gallen though carried out over an even longer period.[80] In this the nave was widened and enlarged to provide the setting for the shrine of the fourteen *Nothelfer*, but this hardly constitutes a definite rotunda. Neumann's later church at Neresheim, (Fig. 35), also designed in the forties but only executed long after his death in 1753, is probably even less relevant to Thumb and St. Gallen because of its date, although the rotunda-like dominance of the principal spatial element of the interior is carried considerably further than at Vierzehnheiligen. But the interest of the most productive of Bavarian church-architects among Thumb's close contemporaries, J. M. Fischer, in flanking a round, or more usually an octagonal, *pièce centrale* with longitudinal elements to west and east certainly is relevant (Figs. 24–26).[81]

It was only at Rott-am-Inn, however, designed in 1759 a decade later than Thumb's earliest project for St. Gallen, that Fischer was finally able to realize his formal aspirations (Fig. 28). Even so, the main subsidiary spaces of nave and choir to east and west of the very big octagon there remained single dome-covered bays of square plan, not the three-bayed arms of Thumb's nave and Beer's choir.

Thumb's solution, which is considerably larger dimensionally than Fischer's, was also more traditional than that and most of the others that have been mentioned. His nave (Pl. 170), at the outer end of which is a galleried western apse,[82] remained of the wall-pillar type so long a favourite of the Vorarlbergers, and each of the three oblong bays that replaced the two proposed in project XIV and in the Looser model is covered by a handkerchief vault, as in his nave at Ebersmunster thirty years before (Pl. 154). So large are the arches behind the pilaster-clusters, so open the subsidiary spaces between them, thanks to the absence of side galleries, that the effect is notably multi-spatial and tectonic in the Baroque way rather than in the Rococo tradition of a unified and decoratively walled space. The frescoes executed by Wenzinger,[83] begun in 1757 just before Thumb left St. Gallen, are extraordinarily aerial and open, especially that over the rotunda (Pls. 169–171)—just the sort one would have liked to see at Birnau (Pls. 161, 165). Yet the nave vaults, here separated by rather plain and quite tectonic ribs, might more appropriately have carried frescoes of the Pozzo-like order of C. D. Asam's of forty years earlier at Weingarten (Pl. 33).

The *stucchi* in the nave of St. Gallen, also by Wenzinger, are extremely bold and plastic, with more use of figures than is usual in Rococo decoration (Pl. 172). Yet they seem almost as much an afterthought as those J. M. Feichtmayr was executing at this point in Fischer's Ottobeuren (Pl. 198), with none of the inevitability of the *stucchi* at Birnau which resulted, one may presume, from close collaboration between the architect and the stuccoer there (Pls. 163, 173). This is especially true in the rotunda where the pendentives are almost as firmly articulated tectonically as are Viscardi's of half a century earlier at Freystadt (Pl. 14) and carry groups of stucco figures in relief (Pl. 171). They rise, moreover, above alternate half-round and stilted arches, quite as at Freystadt or Borromini's Sant'Agnese in Agone, so that there is here none of that freehand curvature of vaulting surfaces characteristic of the St. Peter library and Birnau. Indeed the rotunda is not altogether improperly considered proto-Neoclassic by some scholars. How truly Baroque it really is, all the same, if academically and traditionally so, the advanced Neoclassicism of the high altar to the east, of 1810 and by J. S. Moosbrugger, makes the more evident by contrast.

The Rococo character of the Wenzinger stuccos in the nave and the rotunda was maintained in those executed a decade later in the choir by the Gigls, but the frescoes there by A. O. Moretti of 1819–21 naturally have nothing in common with the original style of the rest of the church, whether that be considered Baroque, Rococo, or even proto-Neoclassic. Happily, however, Thumb's able collaborators at Birnau—Feuchtmayr and Dirr—had been called on in the sixties to carve the confessionals in the aisles of the church and the magnificent organ-crowned choir stalls to the east, so that the nave is not without rich furnishings appropriate to a Rococo interior despite the rather late date of their execution.

A disappointing aspect of St. Gallen used to be that the interior appeared slightly dingy, despite the light from the tall side windows, in comparison to Birnau and most great interiors of the mid-eighteenth century. This doubtless meant no more than that the restoration of 1866–67, which altered the original colour-scheme—white walls with green stucco decoration and gilded highlights—to near-monochrome, should have been followed by a new and more accurate restoration of the interior at the time the exterior was renewed in 1928–38. Such a restoration finally began in 1964.[84]

As the imposing two-towered east façade (Pl. 168), which still recalls Moosbrugger's project III of 1721, is definitely not by Thumb, it seems unnecessary to discuss it here in detail. Thumb's project XIV of the early fifties shows towers placed diagonally (Fig. D), as earlier proposed by Bagnato in his project XIII of 1750 and as seen in the Looser model. That provided, however, no side entrance directly into the rotunda. Such an entrance in the centre of the bulge appeared first in the plan surviving at Au (Fig. G). The executed north façade gives a rather different sort of emphasis to the rotunda externally than Thumb proposed in project XIV (Pl. 167). Instead of a two-pitched roof of the sort used over the transepts and apse of Birnau, rising above a continuous entablature related as at Birnau to a continuous pilaster order, and with a blocking course and a pediment to give emphasis to the cross-axis, there are in the executed church long ranges of plain wall broken only by very tall arched windows (Pls. 167, 168). Over the bulge of the rotunda, however, the cornice line is considerably raised. Even on this bulge there is no order, only flat projections with plain sunken panels and niches between the three still larger and taller windows. The centre is accented by a modest portal below and a freely curved gable rising against the roof. This, though still two-pitched, is less boldly modelled than in the project. The statues in the niches are by Wenzinger, as is presumably also the scroll-surrounded armorial achievement in the gable. This portion of the façade was evidently erected from the amended design of Thumb as represented by the Au plan (Fig. G). The comparable feature of the Looser model differs both from project XIV and from the executed work since it follows externally the scalloped plan of the interior, thus recalling slightly Bagnato's project XIII of 1750. Beer reverted to a far richer treatment in executing the east front though he continued the design of Thumb's nave along the side walls of the choir (Pl. 168).

If Thumb left St. Gallen in 1758 and retired to Konstanz with the largest architectural work of his long career still far from finished and, stylistically, more Baroque than Rococo, he did not leave before initiating the previous year, in the latest of all his productions, the monastery library,[85] a Late Rococo interior of very high quality. This, like the church, was carried out and decorated only in his absence and over the next ten years, though the raw construction was complete by 1758. At the least, however, one may assume that the ceiling paintings of the early sixties by Joseph Wannanmacher (1722–80), dark though they have become, and the delicate stucco decoration of the Gigls which vignettes them—not to speak of Looser's rich cabinet-work and marquetry floor—would have met with his approval. Thumb's second son, Michael Peter Franz Xaver (1725–69), supervised the completion of the library at St. Gallen as also of the nave and rotunda of the church.

The library (Pls. 174, 175) is considerably longer than the one at St. Peter (Pl. 158) and it seems much lower since the vaulted ceiling, carried on the solid cores of broad bookcases that function like wall-pillars in churches, is so low-pitched as to be nearly flat. The continuous gallery, supported by red scagliola columns and entablature blocks set diagonally at the corners of the stacks in the lower story, winds in and out. With its alternating curves and straight sections, however, this feature is less continuously flowing, and hence less truly Rococo, than the one at St. Peter. In part because of the colouring of the St. Gallen interior—all reddish and golden in tone below the ceiling in contrast to the predominant white of St. Peter—this library, considered as a whole, is distinctly less characteristic of the Rococo. Here, as more strongly in the rotunda of the church, one senses not so much some sort of proto-Neoclassicism as a slightly bored reaction against the light-hearted exuberance of the High Rococo.

Thus the conclusion, like the early stages of Thumb's career, leaves still a mystery the sources of the originality and the assurance of the major Rococo achievements of his middle years in the library at St. Peter and at Birnau. But the late works at St. Gallen round out a picture that is very characteristic of the stylistic ebb and flow of the forty years between the twenties, when Thumb was building his first considerable churches at St. Trudpert and Ebersmunster, and the mid-sixties when he died. He had been the most prolific major architect of his time in the lands round the Bodensee. No other Vorarlberger, moreover, had mastered so fully as he the Rococo mode that had been introduced into Germany in his early youth and come to maturity in Bavaria in the twenties and early thirties. He and several of his contemporaries then developed the Rococo into a consistent style of monumental interior architecture that flourished into the fifties. Like most of his German contemporaries, Thumb seems to have worked quite without theory, following for a while whole-heartedly a stylistic current that more famous architects such as J. M. Fischer and J. B. Neumann accepted only occasionally and with some diffidence, and then returning to the main international stream of mid-eighteenth-century evolution towards Neoclassicism.

The story of this later development, most familiar perhaps in the particular case of A.-J. Gabriel in France, underlines the curious fact that certain of the more original artistic manifestations of the eighteenth century, such as Chinoiserie and the Rococo, were historically culs-de-sac, without relevant succession in the following period. The particular course that architectural doctrine followed in the early and mid-eighteenth century helps to explain this phenomenon, for the theorists seem never to have concerned themselves positively with the Rococo. Most of them, indeed, consistently condemned it while not disdaining, if they were themselves designers, to employ *rocaille* decorative motifs freely well through the mid-century.[86] This is certainly the case with J. M. Fischer and J. B. Neumann, so that some discussion of a selection of their works should help to give an idea of the stylistic limits of the Rococo even in southern Germany where it flourished longer —at least at a high level of quality—than anywhere else.

CHAPTER V

The Limits of the Rococo: The Work of Johann Michael Fischer and J. B. Neumann

FROM Gurlitt in the 1880s to Hempel in the present decade, writers on eighteenth-century German architecture, especially that of Bavaria, have always given considerable attention to the work of J. M. Fischer.[1] Before, or immediately after, J. B. Neumann he is today the best-known German architect of the period. Moreover, most writers consider either him or Neumann the greatest, rivalling the somewhat older Austrians, Fischer von Erlach and Hildebrandt.

Much of the critical ambiguity concerning the stylistic identity, so to put it, of church architecture in Bavaria and the lands around the Bodensee through the half century 1720–70 resides in the difficulty of making one major decision. Was Fischer's work Baroque, or was it, at least more consistently, Rococo? There is also a third alternative that sounds more plausible than either near-absolute. Did Fischer's churches gradually change from being the one to being the other? Lane Faison's proposed name for Fischer's ambiguous style—and, for that matter, for the style of Fischer's German contemporaries—'Barococo' is hardly satisfactory. Such a coinage would logically exclude much fine work in Germany that is as completely anti-Baroque as the secular interiors of the French Rococo were demonstrated by Kimball[2] to have been.

A sequential account of Fischer's work, or at least of the more significant examples of an *œuvre* stated on his grave in the Frauenkirche in Munich to have included 32 churches, 23 monasteries, and 'very many' secular works, may help to locate the uncertain borderline between the Rococo stylistic enclave, so to call it, and the Late Baroque ambience. At the least, that enclave provided a far from isolated area of extraordinary vitality of which the material presented in earlier chapters has already offered much evidence.

Provided Rococo architecture in southern Germany is granted to have had at least quasi-independent existence, it is not difficult to outline its history. After the initial importation of the new French decorative mode into Germany in the second decade of the eighteenth century, there followed in the early and mid-twenties a short period of regional interpretation—acclimatization, one might call it—after which an increasingly autochthonous development began. That development led during the thirties to stylistic maturity, a maturity that lasted with little loss of vigour at least through the fifties and even into the early sixties.

In terms of political history the Rococo period, starting immediately after the Peace of Rastatt in 1714, was broken in two in Bavaria by the War of the Austrian Succession in the early forties. No political event or development, however, neatly coincides with the gradual acceptance of the post-Rococo mode, usually though inaccurately called Louis XVI, that followed about a quarter century later.[3] When the change occurred in the years just before and after 1770, it was led by French architects who had settled permanently in Germany, as only a few had done earlier at the initiation and during the high florescence of the Rococo there. Most of these Frenchmen were well aware of the revolution in taste that was already occurring elsewhere. Largely initiated by their compatriots in Rome in the forties, this had very soon thereafter been supported by anti-Rococo critical writers in France such as Laugier and Cochin, not to speak of the German Winkelmann in Rome. There is probably also some social coordination with the gradual rise of the middle class in Germany in these decades.[4] At least there was a relative diminution in the building activities, hitherto so extensive, of feudal magnates, whether secular or ecclesiastical.

Fischer's professional career, well documented from his arrival in Munich in 1718 to his death there in 1766, parallels the entire length of the Rococo story. From the very early Rococo—or even proto-Rococo—of his great church at Osterhofen of before and about 1730, where he had provided the structural framework for an interior more superbly decorated by the Asams than most for which they were wholly responsible (Pls. 57–59), to the mature Rococo of his Anastasiakapelle (Pls. 201–203) of the fifties, attached to the late seventeenth-century abbey church at Benediktbeuern, his own contributions were of the highest order. But these two interiors are not as typical of his work as the more famous abbey churches of Zwiefalten and Ottobeuren (Pls. 192, 198), both designed in the forties, nor do they exemplify very well his characteristic interest in combining centralized with longitudinal planning (Figs. 22, 24–26, 28, 32).[5]

After Osterhofen that interest was largely independent of the contemporary preoccupation of other south German architects—architects whose churches, discussed in earlier chapters, were much more thoroughly inspired by non-Baroque, i.e. Rococo, architectural aims than Fischer's—with plans of ovalized-rectangular or rectangularized-oval form. Nonetheless Fischer's earliest churches of the twenties, already described in Chapter I,[6] were not unrelated to the development of such plans (Fig. 5). His personal familiarity with the Guarinian plans of Christoph Dientzenhofer's churches in Bohemia, evident both in St. Anna-am-Lehel in Munich (Pl. 56) and at Osterhofen (Fig. 4), was certainly significant in the general Bavarian picture around 1730. Fischer's biography to some extent provides the explanation for this aspect of his early work. So also various local situations, most notably the fact that he was several times called on to take over the construction of great abbey churches already planned and begun by others, help to explain the somewhat exceptional importance for the period of rectangular wall-pillar schemes in his *œuvre* (Figs. 23, 27).

Fischer's Youth

From Fischer's sophisticated interest in centralized planning one might suppose that he had had in his youth a period of travel and study in Italy, or at least such relations with leading French and Austrian contemporaries as certainly affected Neumann's early development; actually his background, up to his arrival in Munich in 1718, was more provincial than J. G. Fischer's despite his years in Bohemia and Moravia. Johann Michael Fischer was born at Burglengenfeld, a small town in the Upper Palatinate about fifteen miles due north of Regensburg.[7] His like-named father was a master-mason there, and Fischer must have received his earliest training from him and from other local craftsmen. After reaching the age of twenty Fischer worked for several years in Bohemia, and about 1715–16 he was supervising building construction at Brno in Moravia.

Then came a most important step in his career. In 1718 he moved to Munich and worked as *Palier* for the Munich *Stadtmaurermeister* (City Master-Mason), Johann Mayr (1677–1731), the third of that name active in the building business in Munich. Mayr had been employed in his youth as *Palier* by the then *Stadtmaurermeister*, Martin Gunetzrhainer (d. 1699)—himself the successor of another Mayr (Kaspar, d. 1673)—whose widow Mayr married and whose architect-sons, the earlier-mentioned Johann Baptist (p. 61) and Ignaz Anton (1698–1764), he trained.[8]

In 1723, as has been noted, Fischer became a citizen of Munich and a *Maurermeister*. Then, marrying Mayr's daughter two years later, he became a step-brother-in-law of the Gunetzrhainers. Thus, as was true of none of the architects to whom previous chapters were devoted, he established himself early in the traditional builder-architect hierarchy of the Bavarian capital. Moreover, thanks to J. B. Gunetzrhainer's position as assistant to Joseph Effner, he was indirectly associated also with the dominating architect of the court circle in those years before Cuvilliés—in effect, but not in title—succeeded as *premier architecte* of the Electors of Bavaria about 1730.

Fischer's first job under Mayr was probably the supervision over the years 1718–24 of the monastic buildings of the Augustinian Priory of Schlehdorf where, ten years later, he was to design and at least begin the church. Schlehdorf is in Upper Bavaria on the Kochelsee near the larger town of Murnau. Whoever actually designed the big church at Murnau, begun in 1717 and rising slowly through much the same years as the Schlehdorf priory though not consecrated until 1734, it is probable that Mayr, or possibly J. B. Gunetzrhainer, was involved in the commission.[9] In any case Fischer will hardly have been unfamiliar with this church since it was so near Schlehdorf. The rounded octagonal shape of the Murnau nave (Fig. 21), with the low-domed vault carried on eight compound pillars of concave section, is certainly premonitory of much of his own later planning, though not the cruciform layout of the very extended choir. That, however, is later than the nave by some years and probably by a different architect.

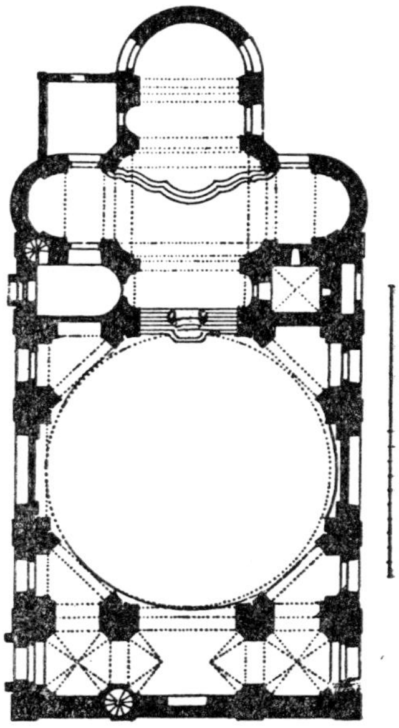

Fig. 21. Murnau, Parish Church. Plan

Already in 1721 Fischer was also building on his own the stables of the electoral Schloss Lichtenberg near Landsberg, a minor job doubtless assigned to him by Gunetzrhainer. In 1723 he was still probably supervising for Mayr the Brigittine monastery buildings at Altomünster, not far to the east of Augsburg, where he would rebuild the great church at the end of his life, and more certainly (as noted in Chapter I) the tall and elegant tower of the Heilig-Grabkirche at Deggendorf on the Danube, designed by Gunetzrhainer with some assistance from Mayr. Two years later Fischer was still working with them on the completion of the parish church at Schärding, on the Austrian side of the Inn above Passau, a large and rather dull wall-pillar church, as has also been mentioned earlier.

Niederaltaich

In 1724, his independent career began at the Benedictine Abbey of Niederaltaich, where Mayr had earlier rebuilt the monastery's living quarters. In 1718 Jakob Pawagner from Passau had begun for Abbot Joscio Hamberger a rather complete reconstruction of the abbey church within the fourteenth-century walls of the nave.[10] This work was completed by 1722; but the old choir still stood beyond a temporary wall at the east end of the nave behind the high altar. Several architects, including Fischer, who were then asked to inspect the choir reported that its condition was structurally precarious, and Fischer specifically recommended total reconstruction. Pawagner was then dismissed by the Abbot and Fischer took over, as would occur several times in his career in such situations.

The cornerstone of Fischer's new east end was laid on 28 September 1724. Externally it followed the semi-circle of the medieval ambulatory, but internally the space was articulated with unexpected originality, prefacing to some extent his churches of 1726 and 1727 at Kirchham and Rinchnach that followed immediately after its completion. Above a crypt new-built by Fischer the broad apsidal area is subdivided horizontally into a low-vaulted sacristy below and a taller upper story intended to serve as a monks' choir (Pls. 176, 178). At both levels the space is divided into three uneven parts by arches, segmental in the sacristy, half-round in the choir, that continue the lines of Pawagner's nave arcades. The central portion is in both cases a squarish longitudinal rectangle covered by a dome. The very low one below is on continuous pendentives and decorated with a very large scalloped fresco by Andreas Haindl (1683–1757) from Wels, a painter who had been working in the nave and aisles of the church since 1719. This is surrounded by delicate *stucchi* of Early Rococo character in white and yellow against pale pink that were executed by J. I. Holzinger. The freshness and openness of the decoration contrasts with the heavy *stucchi* by the Italians G. B. and Sebastiano Allio in the nave of the church whom Holzinger had been assisting over the previous four or five years.

In the choir the much bigger fresco by Haindl is quite differently handled. A heavy, cornice-like stucco border of ovalized rectangular shape sets it quite apart from the spandrels. These are decorated with heavy cartouches framing paintings rather than the elegant oval reliefs introduced in these positions in the sacristy below. The whole effect is considerably more tectonic and less proto-Rococo, since in the sacristy even the ribs defining the central space are broader, flatter, and lightly decorated with bandwork. Moreover, the heavy cornice blocks in the upper choir, continuing those over the pillars of Pawagner's nave and presbytery to the west, seem over-scaled and even alien intrusions; Fischer's own rather delicate archivolts spring from simple imposts at a higher level.

In this central space there is no evidence internally of the curve of the outer wall, except that a coved arch carried on concave imposts rises over and around the semi-elliptical top of the big east window in the choir and its richly stuccoed crown. Both in the sacristy below and in the choir above, however, the side compartments, defined on their inner sides by straight ribs, follow on the outside the curvature of the original ambulatory walls and are therefore asymmetrical in relation to the transverse axis. Fischer—or Holzinger—disguised this asymmetry with considerable success by ingenious handling of the severies of the cross-vaults over the window heads—three in the sacristy below and two in the choir above—and by the character of their decoration. This decoration consists principally of small-scale *stucchi* but also includes a few restricted areas frescoed by Haindl.

Ranges of wooden cabinets with gilded Rococo crestings and appliqués, made in 1727 by the lay-brother Pirmin Tobiaschu (b. 1669), furnish the sacristy (Pl. 178). The monks' choir above is now empty since the stalls the monks use are in the presbytery. The view toward the west into the main body of the church from the choir is almost completely blocked, as it must always have been, by the rear of the upper stage of the vast high altar. That had been constructed by Jakob Schöpf in 1703, ten years before Pawagner's remodelling of the church began.

Rinchnach

The two interiors at Niederaltaich (Pls. 176, 178), completed just before Osterhofen was designed, and more particularly the sacristy, suggest how ready Fischer must have been to accept the novel ideas of the Asams for the decorations when they joined him there as collaborators a few years later (Pls. 58, 59). As spatial exercises, however, the Niederaltaich interiors are more closely related to the modest church commissions he undertook in 1726 and 1727 at Kirchham and Rinchnach (Fig. 5; Pl. 60). The latter was for the same client, the Niederaltaich abbot, since Rinchnach was a priory subsidiary to the abbey.

These two churches have already been described in Chapter I.[11] I need now only note the way in which, at Rinchnach, the bigger frescoes, rather dim and greyish today compared to the brilliant colouring of those at Niederaltaich, consist of two scalloped half-circles at the west and east ends separated by a section of barrel-vault out of which rises the small frescoed dome over the centre of the nave. Thus there is still lacking the unity provided at Osterhofen two years or so later by C. D. Asam's vast scalloped rectangle over the nave with its powerful illusion of space centralized and extending upward (Pl. 57). On the other hand the *stucchi*, with raised work in white against grounds so very pale in their pastel tones as to appear monochrome in photographs, are both more profuse than at Niederaltaich and more distinctly Early Rococo, somewhat in the manner of J. B. Zimmermann's at Weyarn[12] of 1729, the same year in which the decorations here at Rinchnach were completed. The *stucchi* may well be by Holzinger as at Niederaltaich; but it is difficult to explain, except by physical deterioration and poor restoration, the low quality of the frescoes, if they are indeed by Haindl. This underlines the great importance for Fischer of his collaboration with the Asams at St. Anna-am-Lehel and Osterhofen soon after this.[13]

Other Early Works

Of the three less important churches next designed by Fischer, the biggest, that at Schlehdorf—which is said to have been begun by Fischer in 1727 but is more largely very much later in date, 1770–80—can be ignored here. Probably by Balthasar Trischberger, a former assistant of Fischer's, or Matthäus Kramer, Schlehdorf is wholly characteristic of that decade in its dry proto-Neoclassic character.[14] The village church at Bergkirchen, just west of Dachau, built in 1731, is a slightly larger version of that at Kirchham.[15] The lengthened octagon of the nave is there apparent externally, however, and the choir is ovalized in plan. In its present largely denuded state the church is not very attractive except for its fine hill-top site.

Unering

Unering, north-west of Starnberg near Seefeld, must be almost precisely contemporary with Bergkirchen—Lieb calls it 1730,[16] but Hagen-Dempf evidences a receipt of 4 February 1732 for a payment to Fischer for his assistants[17] and the date inscribed in the church itself is 1731. This modest church in a tiny village is of some significance in Fischer's development since, within the irregular octagon of the nave here, he gave up the triplex organization of the vaulting at Niederaltaich and in the small churches from Kirchham through Bergkirchen in favour of a much simplified version of the Murnau plan—a square that is elaborated by shallow niches in the diagonal planes cutting off the corners (Fig. 22). The plan, which shows no curves other than the section of the niches and the layout of the triconch choir, does not make plain what happens in the vaulting zone. There broad pendentives rise in a slightly concave curve over the diagonal cornices of the corners and the rectangular entablature blocks flanking them (Pl. 177). Above the arches on the cardinal axes there are also warped coves. These expand as they go upward to make the adjustment from the straight plane of the archivolts to the curved surface of the dome. A heavy stucco moulding of sharp double-S curvature separates the broad spandrel areas, painted in grisaille, from the main fresco overhead. There is, however, in this interior little Early Rococo 'feeling', so to say, for no ornamental stucco-work at all was introduced except in the heads of the niches. Moreover, the frescoes, at least as lately restored, are quite undistinguished. Yet this not very attractive small church seems to be the connecting link between Murnau and Fischer's much larger and finer churches at Ingolstadt and Aufhausen that followed in the middle of the decade.

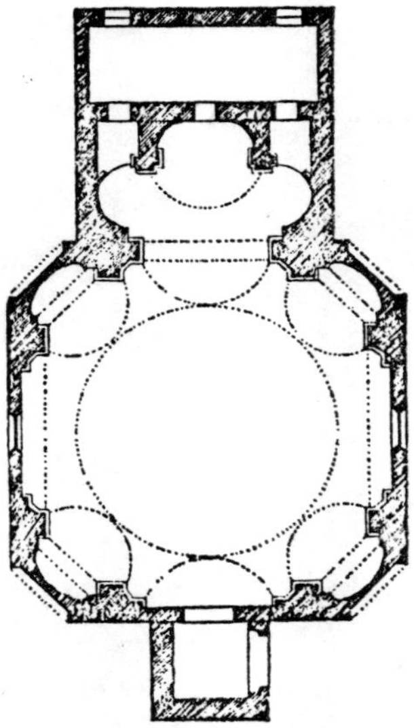

Fig. 22. Unering, Parish Church. Plan

Diessen: Architecture

By this time Fischer was already involved in a much bigger commission comparable to that of 1727 for Osterhofen. This produced a church that is rightly one of the most famous of all eighteenth-century German works. As at Osterhofen, where the decoration was just reaching completion in the early thirties, the church of the Augustinian Priory of Diessen, beside the south end of the Ammersee south-west of Munich, owes almost as much to Fischer's collaborators as to his own contribution.[18] Eventually these included: for the altar-paintings (1739), the two greatest Venetians of the day, G. B. Pittoni and G. B. Tiepolo; for the frescoes on the vaults (1736), rivalling C. D. Asam's at Osterhofen in size and splendour, the highly reputed J. G. Bergmüller, since 1730 director of the Augsburg Akademie; for the high altar (*c.* 1738), Cuvilliés and Joachim Dietrich; and, above all, for the *stucchi* (1736–38), the brothers F. X. and J. M. Feichtmayr, to mention only the most distinguished elements in this very successful example of *Gesamtkunstwerk*.

Yet, strictly architecturally, Diessen is not one of Fischer's happiest works largely because (one must suppose) of the circumstances under which he became involved with it.[19] In October 1720 the cornerstone was laid for a new church here —the monastic buildings had already been rebuilt in 1681–88 by Michael Thumb. This new church was probably from the design of Magnus Feichtmayr, a modest builder-architect from Weilheim. The work advanced slowly and in 1729, a year after Herkulan Karg succeeded on the death of Prior Ivo Bader, who had begun the reconstruction, Fischer was called in to advise as he had been earlier at Niederaltaich and at Osterhofen.

Fischer accepted the existing layout, but proposed that the walls, which had risen as yet only a few feet, should be demolished and a new start made. Persuasive as ever with abbots and priors, he and Karg set off two years after this, in the late summer of 1731 on a trip to visit relevant churches, including several built or building by Fischer himself. On 16 April 1732 the construction of the church, this time according to Fischer's design, began again and, by the early autumn of the next year, was so far advanced that Karg set off on another trip through the Tyrol as far as Bolzano to look at church fittings. However, it was only three years later that the edifice was physically complete enough—or perhaps that sufficient funds had been gathered—to permit the employment of Bergmüller and the Feichtmayrs, and the church was not consecrated until 7 September 1739.

Since this campaign was so prolonged and complicated, running through many years during which Fischer was building several other churches in which he had a freer hand than at Diessen, it may not be inappropriate to discuss first the architectonic aspects of Diessen and then—after describing the three churches he began in the mid-1730s—the decoration which was finally brought to completion only some ten years after Fischer was first called in in 1729.

The church as begun in the spring of 1732, presumably as the result of definite instructions by Karg to Fischer after their trip the previous year, is for the most part of the conventional 'Vorarlberg' order as regards plan, structural articulation, and spatial organization (Fig. 23). Shallow rectangular chapels with no tribunes over them flank the four easternmost of the five bays of the nave between the wall-

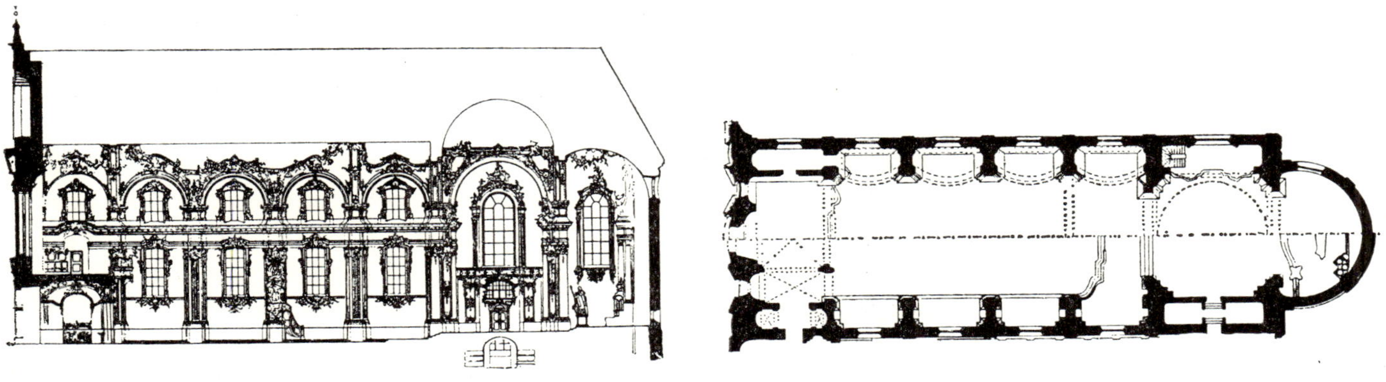

Fig. 23. Diessen, Priory Church. Section and plan

pillars. The crossing, of the same width as the nave, has transeptal arms that do not project beyond the outer walls of the nave and are further shortened by solid walls supporting galleries. To the east there is a half-round apse, the only curved element in the whole plan.

Fluted pilasters and tall entablature blocks give strong tectonic character to the wall-pillars, and this tectonic emphasis is even stronger at the choir-arch, which is narrower than the nave, and either side of the choir, where pairs of engaged columns reinforce the piers (Pl. 181). Above the main entablature the relatively tall attic below the springing of the vaults has a quite exceptional outward curve immediately over the cornice followed by a tall cyma—the latter perhaps more associated with the stucco decoration of the vaults than an element in Fischer's original architectonic treatment of the interior. Though the easternmost and westernmost bays of the nave—the latter above the organ gallery over the entrance lobby—are set off by fairly bold ribs, the decorative rib-bands of the Osterhofen nave (Pl. 59) a year or two earlier and of the Asam's redecoration of St. Emmeram (Pl. 63), probably precisely contemporary with the construction of Diessen, are entirely omitted. This again might be the result of the decorators' later programme rather than the architect's original intention, yet certainly no *structural* ribs ever interrupted the continuity of the three central bays of the vault. Furthermore, thanks to the high curvature of the main barrel-vault, effectively stilted by the attic member, the cross-vaults over the side bays intersect the main vault minimally, meeting it in modestly moulded arrises that follow, as at Osterhofen, an inward-bending three-dimensional curve. Thus the vault overhead was from the first largely devoid of tectonic articulation, in conscious or unconscious preparation for the Rococo decorative programme that followed.

Somewhat exceptional is the omission of tribunes over the side chapels. This strongly emphasizes, as compared to Osterhofen (Pl. 59) and later churches by Fischer such as Fürstenzell (Pl. 191) and Zwiefalten (Pl. 192), the wall-pillars as important structural elements. The western organ gallery, however, is echoed by loges set against the wall-pillars in the second bay of the nave (Pl. 182) and by the wider galleries that run across the transept ends below the very large round-arched windows that flood the crossing with light (Fig. 23). Except for the windows flanking the apse, also round-arched, the other windows, both in the chapels below the main entablature and above in the clerestory, are segment-headed. The chapels and the transepts are so deep, however, that these windows like those at the sides of the apse—masked by the engaged columns at the crossing—are not visible in a general view of the interior, though conspicuous in the longitudinal section (Fig. 23).

The absence of a drum cut by windows above the pendentives of the crossing and below the hemispherical dome might be mentioned; after the one Frisoni built at Weingarten in 1718–20, however, that element of the standard Counter-Reformation organization of church interiors had generally gone out of use in Germany, doubtless as much to bring the frescoed interior surface of the dome nearer to the worshippers as to simplify the visual articulation of the interior space at the crossing. Although the executed altars belong, of course, to the later campaign of decoration and are not part of the structure of the church, their location on the western sides of the wall-pillars at right angles to the axis of the nave was probably intended from the first, for this placing was by now common in German churches.

Unlike Osterhofen, where the front of the church is masked externally by the surviving medieval towers at the west end, Diessen has a handsome façade, presumably designed in 1732 (Pl. 179). The wavy Guarinian interior walls of the nave of Osterhofen here appear on an exterior, another echo of the Bohemian churches by the Dientzenhofers that Fischer had known in his youth, but a rather restrained one. As the plan indicates (Fig. 23), the plain outermost bays are slightly convex, while the next slightly narrower bays, cut by oval windows below and by tall segmental-topped ones above, are concave. The wider central bay is once more convex. This central convexity is visually increased by the raised curve of the sill of the central window over the rather modest entrance doorway[20] and by the way its segmental top pushes upwards the architrave of the main entablature. Similarly, higher up, above the plain concave elements that rise at either side of the attic, the up-curved cornice, broken by a central concave niche, suggests (as a hundred years before Borromini's had done at the top of the façade of the Oratorio di San Filippo Neri in Rome) contrasting convexity. This inward and outward play is resolved only at the crown by the terminal cornice that follows the curvature of the plain arch framing the niche.

Despite the plastic enrichment of this façade—a bust set in a small oval niche above the entrance door, a coat of arms in a rich cartouche below the pediment of the central window (the one element that seems to be specifically Rococo), and a statue on a pedestal in the crowning niche—the relative simplicity of this façade sets it apart, as is the case with most contemporary exteriors, from the elaborately decorated nave inside. There is not much reason, moreover, to consider this or any other façade by Fischer Rococo—though that of Aufhausen represents a sort of abortive proto-Rococo—rather than Late Baroque, as must on the whole have been true of the interior before it received its *stucchi* and its frescoes from 1736 on.

Berg-am-Laim

By that time, however, Fischer was involved in three other commissions that are clearer expressions than any aspect of Diessen of his personal ambitions as an organizer of interior space. In August 1735 there was published an engraving of a church,[21] flanked by residence quarters for the attached religious brotherhood, to be erected at Berg-am-Laim, just outside Munich to the east, on the site of a chapel built in 1692 by Max Emanuel's brother the Elector Joseph Clemens of Cologne. Since then the associated Archfraternity of St. Michael, founded in 1693, had grown in numbers and in importance. For them, Clemens August, Joseph Clemens's nephew and successor, who was a brother of the Elector Carl Albrecht, had employed Fischer, rather than Cuvilliés (who had been working for him at Brühl since 1728), to prepare this project earlier in the year. The history of the building of the church[22] is very complicated owing to Clemens August's employment of P. J. Köglsperger (b. 1707), the son of Philipp Köglsperger, in 1737–38 to undertake the actual construction, and then of Cuvilliés to adjudicate between Köglsperger and Fischer. The latter was finally put in charge of the construction only in the summer of 1739, though he had been paid earlier that year for his plans and other help. The church was physically complete by 1742 and J. B. Zimmermann's contract for the frescoes and the *stucchi* is dated 31 January 1743 (Pl. 187).

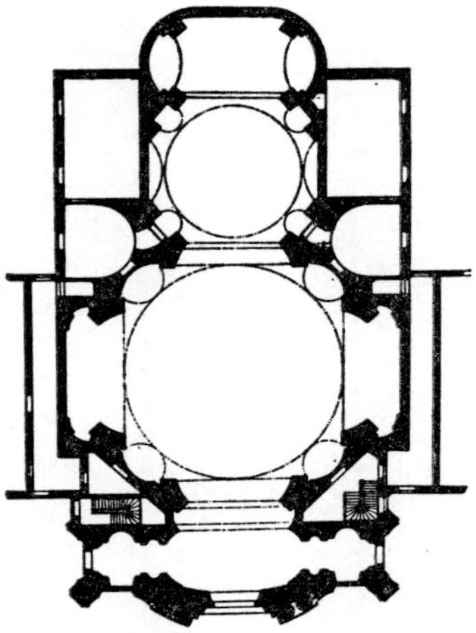

Fig. 24. Berg-am-Laim, St. Michael. Plan

The published plan of 1735 was considerably modified as the church rose over the years 1738–42, so that the details of the spatial organization Fischer originally proposed are not entirely clear. Evidently, however, there was to have been a nave of centralized plan. Its basically octagonal shape, recalling Unering (Fig. 22)—and, behind that, presumably Murnau (Fig. 21)—would have been irregularly defined at the sides by eight curved lobes, wide to east, west, north and south, narrow on the diagonals. Beyond this was to follow a transverse rectangular choir of which the bowed ends would be continued horseshoe-wise into a rounded apse. Passages were to surround the whole except on the north and south. A relation to Murnau can also be recognized in the church as built (Fig. 24), though the organization is less regular than in the project. The surrounding passages were all omitted, though a shallow transverse lobby with rounded ends occupies the convex bulge of the west front Köglsperger had begun; the choir is a domed square with cut-off corners echoing the wider column-flanked concave corners of the nave, and the apse repeats at slightly larger scale the shape of the lobby.

Ingolstadt and Aufhausen

Between the preparation of the early design for Berg-am-Laim published in 1735 and the beginning of construction there in 1738 Fischer designed in 1735–36 and started to build two other churches which, while somewhat smaller[23] and never so sumptuously decorated, are more successful as expressions of his spatial ideals, and certainly much less tectonically Baroque than this interior (Pl. 187), with its eight pairs of engaged columns in the nave, four more pairs in the choir, and a further pair flanking the high altar. The Franciscans' church in Ingolstadt[24] (originally commissioned by the Augustinians) was badly damaged in the last war and has since been demolished. Designed presumably in 1735, the cornerstone was laid on 11 May 1736; J. B. Zimmermann's frescoes were painted in 1739–40 after the building was complete and consecration followed on 27 September 1740.

Fischer's name first appears in the account book of the Oratorians of Aufhausen[25] when he was paid 6 gulden 40 kreutzer on 12 July 1735. His first plan, therefore, may actually be as early as the 1735 project for Berg-am-Laim. In 1736 he received 90 gulden for his assistants—probably to cover the following year—and, in 1738, 45 gulden 45 kreutzer for his assistants' work through 1739. Thus the dates of construction seem to be effectively identical with those of Ingolstadt—1736–39—though Aufhausen was not consecrated until 22 March 1751. Three undated plans[26] by Fischer for the church and the associated monastic buildings survive in the parish archives.

The naves of both Ingolstadt and Aufhausen followed much more closely than Berg-am-Laim the domed octagonal plan Fischer used first at Unering (Figs. 22, 25, 26). Both have, however, more generous choirs of square plan—that at Ingolstadt with incurved corners and aisle-like side passages; at Aufhausen, but not at Ingolstadt, this is balanced—not quite symmetrically—by a lobby to the 'west'. This is a smaller square under the organ gallery, but is extended transversely and provided with corner niches. At Ingolstadt the transept ends were slightly bowed and the relatively large diagonal chapels—absent at Unering, but already present at Rinchnach (Fig. 5)—were scalloped ovals in plan. The much smaller corner chapels at Aufhausen are hexagonal and fit within the straight walls that flank this church. Ingolstadt revealed more of its plan externally, thanks to convex-segmental cut-off corners and bulges between them on the north and south. In both cases the choir externally is narrower than the element that encloses the nave.

What must have been the most significant difference at Ingolstadt was that the eight piers in the nave, decorated with very tectonic fluted pilasters in pairs, are quadrantal in plan, somewhat like the curved corners of the nave of Murnau (Fig. 21). As at Rinchnach (Pl. 60), this was most evident in the bold, but here not exaggerated, curvature of the entablature elements above (Pl. 185).[27] This led to a different handling of the vault surfaces in the two churches, otherwise near-twins. At Ingolstadt over the wide arches on the east-west and north-south axes, there identically treated, wide coves carried across, somewhat as at the east and west ends of the nave of Osterhofen (Pls. 58, 59), but more like the narrower coves at Unering. These three-dimensionally curved elements, being semi-elliptical though in effect stilted by the attic at their base—here less heavy and idiosyncratic than the one at Diessen (Pl. 181)—rose no higher than the tops of coves of the narrower, but semi-circular, arches that cross the corners. These latter coves, starting flat in the attic above the relevant entablature blocks, were warped into concavity towards their crowns. As with Unering (Figs. 22, 25) the plan gives little idea of what went on overhead.

The surface of the domed vault, like that at Unering, has no structural break over the eight pendentives rising between the wider and the narrower coves; it was, in any case, almost entirely filled by Zimmermann's fresco. In shape this fresco was again, like the plan of the nave below, an irregular octagon, with four long concave sides coaxial with the crowns of the wide coves at the cardinal points and, across the diagonal corners, broken, convex curves—a much more unified treatment than at Unering. As at Osterhofen (Pl. 59) the fronts of the tribunes over the corner chapels, as also that of the broad organ gallery which fills the western arch at the same level, were convex. Their convex-curved surfaces, though not in the same plane, were in a sense, pendants to the convex curves of the fresco frame above and below the concave counter-curves of the coves of the arches.

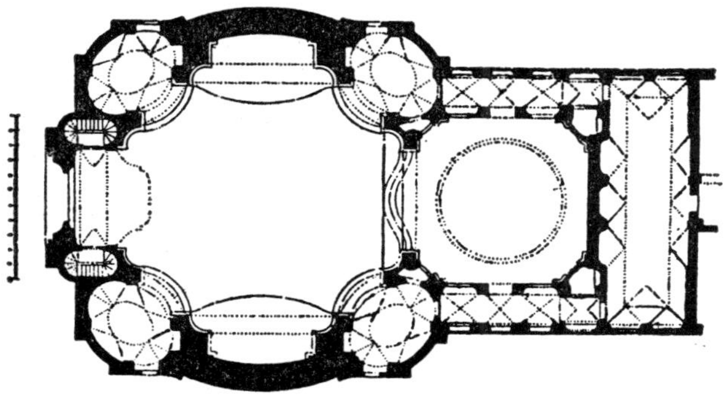

Fig. 25. Ingolstadt, Franciscan Church. Plan

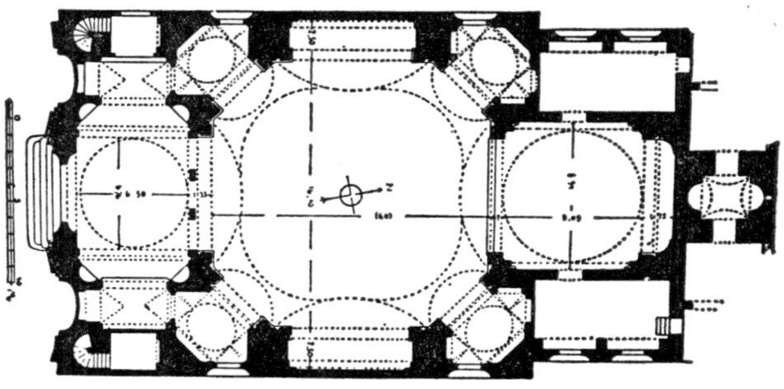

Fig. 26. Aufhausen, Pilgrimage Church. Plan

Ingolstadt must have been much more sumptuously furnished than Aufhausen. There the re-use of earlier altars and the late date of consecration suggest that money ran out early in the campaign. Perhaps because the decoration is somewhat later, however, Aufhausen realizes more consistently—or so one may judge from surviving photographs of Ingolstadt—the Rococo implications of its twin, especially above the level of the entablature (Pls. 184, 185, 188). Below that level this is not so true. On the one hand, the narrower piers at Aufhausen are not concave in plan and their entablatures, therefore, do not curve but are bent at an angle as at Unering. On the other hand, the applied pilasters are less tectonic than they were at Ingolstadt since they are unfluted and have capitals that are far more dissolved into Rococo ornament from the inherited Corinthian model, quite in the manner of those the Asams had introduced into Fischer's earlier interior at Osterhofen (Pl. 59). Above the entablature and the here totally undecorated attic, the concave surfaces of the vault around the base of the dome are more consistently warped. Round both the wide semi-elliptical arches at the cardinal points and the narrower arches across the diagonals the coves between the eight pendentives start as narrow vertical elements, continuing the flat plane of the pilasters below, and widen as they are warped upward into deep concavities below the broad stucco frame of the fresco to which all eight are tangent. This frame, basically, is of the rounded-square shape of that of the fresco over the central portion of the choir at Niederaltaich (Pl. 176). It has, moreover, a slightly entablature-like character suggesting a frieze with triglyphs. At each of the cardinal points, however, this frame bites inwards into the fresco, so that the shape as a whole, if not exactly scalloped, is distinctly wavy like the surfaces of the vault immediately below.

The relatively larger fresco over the square choir, likewise coaxial with the four arches below (Pl. 188), is pinched upwards and inwards at the corners by fresco-filled cartouches, somewhat as the wider armorial achievement over the choir-arch seems to push inwards the frame of the nave fresco at that point. Although there is no concave curvature in the pilaster clusters at the corners of the choir, a wide cove unbroken by imposts frames the fresco on the flat wall behind the high altar.[28] This serves to emphasize the semi-elliptical shape that echoes the choir-arch. The loges at the sides are likewise framed by a continuous narrow cove. These loges are set very high, just below the main entablature of the pilaster order, like those above the corner chapels and the organ gallery over the 'western' lobby (Pl. 184).

Curiously enough at another point, where one might expect to find right-angled corners softened by coves as in several of Fischer's later works—the junction of the wall-pillars with the side walls—they are absent (Fig. 26). Such coves seem, however, to have been intended according to Fischer's surviving plan.[29] That also indicates large transeptal altars, bow-fronted in shape and flanked by columns; these were never executed any more than the rounded apse proposed for the 'east' end of the church. Such omissions seem additional evidence of that lack of funds which inhibited the early and adequate furnishing of the church and postponed the consecration until eleven years after that of the church at Ingolstadt.

Neither the *stucchi* nor the frescoes at Aufhausen are dated, and the artists who executed them are unidentified. At least as lately restored, the quality of the *stucchi* is higher than that of the paintings and their delicacy suggests a date in the early forties rather than one nearer the time of consecration in 1751. On the other hand, to judge from surviving photographs, the stucco-work in the Ingolstadt church,[30] whether or not by J. B. Zimmermann like the frescoes there, was distinctly less Rococo in character (Pl. 185). Here at Aufhausen (Pl. 184) the fine lines that make separate panel-like fields of each of the coves over the eight arches and the pendentive areas between, the former filled with pale blue-green, the latter with pale pink, enhance the a-tectonic character of the vaulting by emphasizing the continuity of the surfaces. Thus, of this interior above the cornice line, one may say that it is wholly Rococo in contrast to the Baroque structuralism of the piers below.

In the lower zone there is very little stucco or other decoration (Pl. 188), though the Corinthian capitals of the pilasters have undergone, as has already been noted, considerable modification from any Classical norm, and the coved under-surfaces of the bowed loges in the diagonal bays and the organ gallery carry relatively rich Rococo decoration that is warped in three dimensions. These have fields of pale blue enframed by a rather strong yellow—the restorer's substitute for gold?—that is echoed at the tops and bottoms of the flanking pilaster capitals. Naturalistic pinks are used for the seraphs' heads over the clamp-like motif at the head of the arches and greens for the foliate branches that extend to left and right of them.

Had this church received the usual complement of contemporary or slightly later altars instead of retaining those of the previous century, the general effect might well have been more consistently Rococo, despite the coupled columns that were intended to flank the apse. But this inconsistency underlines what is henceforth characteristic of all J. M. Fischer's larger churches; on the one hand, a firmly Baroque substructure, as clearly revealed usually in the plans, and then overhead a free Rococo organization of the vaulting. His vaulting[31] is generally quite devoid of tectonic elements and depends for its positive Rococo character upon the distribution—whether that was determined by Fischer or by the collaborating stuccoers—of the stucco decoration around the big frescoes in their scalloped or wavy frames. Probably some years before Aufhausen was complete as regards its decoration, this inconsistency was spectacularly illustrated at Diessen (Pls. 181–183).

But first there should be a few words concerning the façade of Aufhausen, since façades were one aspect of J. M. Fischer's churches to which he gave rather more attention than any of the architects considered in earlier chapters. Though narrower and lower than that of Diessen (Pl. 179), presumably completed before the building of the Aufhausen church began, the concept of the design is quite similar. The side bays are concave and there are no outer bays beyond them. The central portion is flanked by Doric pilasters of which the higher relief requires *ressauts* in the entablature at either side of the arch of the central 'west' window. The slight convexity of this bay is increased visually by the steps that bow out before the entrance below and by the warping of the very plain terminal cornice of the gable above. In all three bays, however, the three-dimensional variation of the surface is greatest in the niches within which the relatively small windows are set. This can, fortunately, be appreciated even in the plan (Fig. 26). It is the coves[32] forming these niches—coves repeated round the entrance and also round the windows on the sides of the nave—rather than the curvature of the entablature that provide the chief plastic interest of the exterior.

Doubtless the façade was intended by Fischer to receive more elaboration of one sort or another than the monks' financial situation eventually allowed. However that may be, the only sculpture is a statue of the Virgin set in the very plain central niche that rises into the gable. The external colouring here as restored—two tones of cream with the shafts of the pilasters light grey—lacks the positive character of the pink walls and stone-coloured trim of Diessen, not to speak of any elements executed in marble, while the way the land falls away immediately beyond the narrow road in front makes the façade difficult to see except in sharp perspective and all but impossible to photograph.[33]

Diessen: Decoration

Interesting and significant as Aufhausen is as a step in Fischer's development of the centralized plan, its modest interior is completely overshadowed by that at Diessen as decorated in 1736–39. Indeed, in the first impression of grandeur combined with splendour that it provides Diessen outshines any church that had been built and decorated up to that time in southern Germany, except perhaps Osterhofen (Pls. 57, 59) and the Zimmermanns' Steinhausen (Pl. 11). The actual dimensions are very large—70.30 × 21.70 m. overall; nave vault 21.40 m. high; crossing some 25.40 m.—and the succession of spaces is as dramatic as the plan and section suggest (Fig. 23; Pls. 181, 183). When one enters the church through the lobby under the organ gallery the low vault overhead displays a sample of the stuccoers' Rococo virtuosity at its richest and most delicate. But ahead one can already see most of the interior, framed from here by a low semi-elliptical arch and screened by the iron lace-work of the grille that Marx Kriner from Munich wrought in 1739 following a design supplied by J. B. Straub (Pl. 180).

From this initial point the series of side-altars are of almost as great visual importance as the structural wall-pillars against whose near sides they rise. Their large—and in two cases extremely fine—paintings are set in structures of a curious mustard-yellow scagliola, highlighted with gilt, and they are flanked by brilliantly white statuary. From the lobby, however, the large fresco that occupies the three central bays of the nave is not yet visible, though the long vista toward the high altar in the apse makes the whole interior clearly apprehensible as articulated space. At the further end of the central bays the spatial continuity is already slightly interrupted; overhead, by a transverse rib of moderate projection and tall semi-elliptical profile above the curved stilting of the attic; and, below, rather more subtly by two steps capped by a low balustrade that serves in this fifth bay to separate the laymen's nave from the eastern elements of the church that are reserved for the monks. Beyond that slight barrier there follows a much sharper break in the space of the interior, for the eastern termination of the nave is emphasized by a pair of engaged columns at the choir-arch and these are flanked by altars wider and taller by a good deal than the ones in the western bays of the nave (Pl. 181). The visual effect of the columns is, of course, tectonically Baroque.

Above the choir-arch, however, which is semi-circular, not semi-elliptical, and firmly framed by a broad and rather plain archivolt, the stuccoers attempted to soften in a Rococo way the sharp rectangular juxtaposition of east wall and nave vault by introducing drapery held by floating putti, much as Orsati and de Prevotis had done a good deal less elegantly in Peter Thumb's church at St. Trudpert a score or so of years before (Pl. 152).

As seen through the opening into the choir the piers that support the pendentives at the far side of the crossing are quite conspicuous. In them there is a characteristic conflict between Baroque structural expression and Rococo emphasis on continuous surface framed by decoration (Fig. 23; Pl. 181). Between the engaged columns below the arches there are diagonal elements treated like the vertical panels in Rococo *boiserie,* but at several times the French scale. This is an elaboration of the motif which the Asams had used on the pilaster-shafts in Fischer's Osterhofen ten years before (Pl. 58) but here there are no crowning capitals. Instead, an elongated cartouche is warped upwards across the entablature of each of the compound piers, all but touching the clusters of clouds that overlap the cornice under the putti who tumble about in front of the attic. Still higher there are larger cartouches with figural reliefs against grounds of gilded *mosaïque* and these all but fill the pendentives, spilling upwards as well across the elaborate frame at the base of the painted dome. Scrolling clamps at the cardinal points also bind the extradoses of the arches to this frame and further break up in a Rococo way its Baroque circularity.

Beyond this, terminating the view, is the high altar. This occupies, visually, the whole of the apse, though it is actually set well back against the curved rear wall. Further steps beyond the two in the fifth bay of the nave elevate the choir and sanctuary floor. Four run straight across at the choir-arch, raising the level there to that of the top of the balustrade further west, and three more bow forward immediately in front of the mensa. The high altar, as has been noted earlier, is of about 1737 or 1738. It was designed by the most famous of all Rococo decorators outside France and executed by one of the most virtuoso wood-carvers in the very years that these same men, François Cuvilliés and Joachim Dietrich,[34] were producing the most famous of German Rococo secular interiors, those in the Amalienburg at Nymphenburg (Pl. 133). Its distinctly academic character is, therefore, somewhat unexpected, especially in contrast to the altars that E. Q. Asam was providing for St. Johann-Nepomuk in Munich (Pl. 72) and Dominikus Zimmermann for Günzburg[35] in those years of the late thirties. Rather it recalls somewhat in its style, as more definitely in its iconography, the one E. Q. Asam had erected at Rohr some fifteen years before (Pl. 37).

Columns of the same golden-brown scagliola as the side altars are set diagonally in groups of three at either side. These are not of the same order as that of the engaged columns around the crossing but considerably smaller. The crisp cornice of their entablature blocks is at approximately the same height as the modillioned cornice that surrounds the whole interior, while their bases are raised on high podia behind and above the mensa. As usual, painting and sculpture both play important parts in the total composition. B. A. Albrecht's Assumption of the Virgin occupies a tall gilded frame wreathed with foliage, presumably carved by Dietrich; soft curves at its base and a semi-elliptical crown over small S-curved breaks introduce the only Rococo touches in the whole lower part of the composition. But the arched crown does rise across the entablature below the cornice of the order, and that cornice links the entablature blocks at either side in a shallow concave curve in what is at least a proto-Rococo way.

Above the cornice of the altar there are no architectural elements. The figures of Christ and God the Father look down with welcoming gestures on the ascending Virgin at the top of the painting, while on the conch of the apse behind them the Holy Ghost appears framed by gilded stucco rays, seraphs' heads, and clouds. Higher up, touching the half-dome, a pelmetted canopy is sustained by floating putti. If this composition can hardly be considered specifically Rococo, it is at the least distinctly Asamesque.[36]

The preceding description of the interior of Diessen was assumed to cover all that can be seen from the entrance lobby before entering the nave; actually, various details—as of the high altar—not likely to be apprehended in detail at so great a distance, have been included also. Nonetheless the description is a very partial and imperfect one. As soon as the worshipper or visitor advances[37] into the nave the 'pull' of the side altars, leading the eye forward to rest finally on the high-altar composition at the far end of the church with its four great white statues of the Fathers of the Church (Pls. 180–181), is more than counter-balanced by the visual demands of the richly decorated vault. Once one looks up at that, the stylistic ambiguity of the interior seems resolved in a thoroughly Rococo way. Here, as earlier at Osterhofen (Pl. 57), the entire vault is occupied by a single composition. In the manner introduced by the Asams at Aldersbach and developed by them at Osterhofen a vast fresco, extending here through the three middle bays of the nave, provides the illusion that the heavens are opening upwards through the barrel-vault (Pls. 182, 183). Around its frame, here considerably more boldly waved and scalloped than in earlier examples, a great deal of stucco-work is loosely distributed over the spandrels and at the ends. To this the treatment of the easternmost and westernmost bays is coordinate but subsidiary (Pls. 180, 182).

The extensive area of the principal fresco gave Bergmüller[38] plenty of room to deal with more than one subject, quite as C. D. Asam had done at St. Emmeram (Pls. 65, 66) and Spiegler was doing at this point in St. Katherine at Wolfegg (Pl. 108). At the east end, above a simple *quadratura* construction of dark steps that are echoed at the west end, the subject is the Refounding of the Monastery in 1132 on its present location by the Augustinians, with a drawing of the new church, complete even to its actually unexecuted towers, held up for admiration below their prior on his throne (Pl. 183). The fresco glorifies the Virgin, St. George, the patron saint of the original foundation, St. Augustine, the founder of the order, and others.[39] Solid *quadratura* walls at either side, on to which the crowns of the stucco cartouches at the heads of the arches over the middle bays spill upwards, enframe the central group of saints floating on clouds—illusionistically at approximately the level of the crown of the vault—below the painted heavens. For all its ingenious organization, this fresco of Bergmüller's and those he painted to east and to west over the end bays of the nave—illustrating the original foundation by St. Rathard at nearby St. Georg and the taking over of that monastery by the Augustinians in 1013—lack, even to the degree of Spiegler's of the same date at Wolfegg, the brilliant colours of J. B. Zimmermann's and C. D. Asam's frescoes, as also that freer, more open sort of composition which the former had introduced at Steinhausen and the latter carried even further at St. Emmeram earlier in the decade (Pls. 11, 65, 66).

There is no such lingering academicism in the *stucchi* the Feichtmayrs and Übelherr provided (Fig. 23; Pls. 181–183). While the urns over the two middle piers a little recall J. B. Zimmermann, under whom Übelherr had worked in the early thirties, and the seraphic herms above them those by E. Q. Asam in St. Johann Nepomuk, for the most part this team of stuccoers established themselves here as quite independent and fully mature masters of the High Rococo. Asymmetrical motifs are repeatedly used and shell-like elements, deriving from the latest French prints of *rocaille* ornament, are actually more conspicuous than in the Amalienburg (Pl. 133). Altogether this represents, at the bold scale of the German Rococo, as close a parallel to what was then called the *genre pittoresque*, the successor in the thirties to the earlier Rococo of the Régence in Paris, as what Cuvilliés and his team were providing at Munich and Nymphenburg in these years.

In contrast to the rather dark and dull frescoes the tonality of the stucco-work is very high-keyed, at first sight almost pure white throughout, with modest but recurrent touches of gilding. Actually, though this is hardly visible even in colour photographs, there is some variation in the whites, notably considerable areas of very pale violet-grey; but, except at the crossing, there are none of those small patches of pink and blue-green that were so commonly present in earlier German Rococo interiors and which can produce—often, perhaps, because of poor restoration—a rather sugary effect.

Here there are only three tonal keys: the very pale one of the *stucchi*, the quite heavy one of the frescoes—especially that on the dome over the crossing, devoted to the saints associated with the nearby Abbey of Andechs across the Ammersee, which receives little light—and the middle tone, much stronger in hue than anything else, of the golden-brown altars. This last is the more striking because of the contrasting sort of brightness of the associated white sculpture. The Venetian colour of the altarpieces by Pittoni and by Tiepolo, to left and to right in the third bay of the nave, provide other brilliant visual incidents. Unfortunately the high-altar painting of Albrecht and most of those that he, Bergmüller, F. G. Hermann, and others provided over the remaining side altars do not vie with these Italian works but rather echo the dull tones of Bergmüller's frescoes.

Bergmüller had, by this time, been painting altarpieces in oil for some twenty years. After his first in the Herz-Jesu at Ehingen and that of 1716 over the high altar at Tannheim, he supplied them to many more churches, including Buxheim (1718), Donauwörth (1724), and Aldersbach (1728–29), to list only those mentioned in earlier chapters which antedate the work at Diessen. His career as a fresco-painter began, perhaps as much as ten years after his first altarpieces, with the frescoes in the nave of Ochsenhausen, where he had earlier (1718–19) provided the altarpiece in the Antoniuskapelle; but his production included, among the churches that have been described in this book, only Steingaden (Pls. 143, 144) though he was not inactive elsewhere.

Johann Michael Feichtmayr was already thirty when the work at Diessen was completed, but no earlier *stucchi* have been plausibly attributed to him. His brother Franz Xaver was four years older, and the redecoration of the fifteenth-century church at Walleshausen (Pl. 186), north-east of Landsberg, carried out about 1732 gives a good idea of his earlier work.[40] Not surprisingly this resembles the *stucchi* by Ignaz Finsterwalder of about the same date at Bertoldshofen (Pls. 91–93). The motifs, however, are in this modest but charming church less crowded together and the lightness of Franz Xaver's touch is closer to the elegance of J. B. Zimmermann's contemporary *stucchi* in the Neuer Festsaal at Benediktbeuern (Pl. 13). Probably without benefit of architect-collaborator, Feichtmayr remodelled this small Late Gothic parish-church into a consistent Early Rococo interior with a minimum of structural alteration, though the new windows he provided were given round arches and the ribs of the vaulting were removed. The profile of the vaults was also modified, as in the big medieval churches at Freising and at Rottenbuch remodelled by the Asams and by the Schmuzers, respectively, to an irregular paraboloid curve. Except for the introduction of pilasters carrying entablature blocks in the polygonal choir and very simple imposts below the bases of the vaulting conoids in the nave, there are no conventional Baroque elements.

With the general assistance of his younger brother Johann Michael and the well-trained Übelherr—more particularly for the execution of the seraphs and the putti—Franz Xaver was obviously ready by 1736 to collaborate as effectively with Fischer at Diessen in the creation of a Rococo interior as the Asams did at Osterhofen. Yet the Asam-like capitals, the rich enframements of the aisle and transept-windows, and the even richer fronts of the galleries at the west end and in the transepts, being merely decorative interpolations, could not for all their virtuosity transform the Baroque structural elements of the church. Nor were these brilliant stuccoers from Wessobrunn able to do so when they worked with Fischer at Zwiefalten (Pls. 192–194) a decade later and at Ottobeuren in the mid-fifties (Pl. 198). In both these vast and sumptuous churches and most of his others the result is the same: the naves and choirs are Rococo overhead but Baroque below the entablatures, whether they follow the octagonal scheme of Aufhausen or the longitudinal plan of Diessen. To this, however, there is at Fürstenzell, where the Feichtmayrs did not work with him, one exception or near exception among Fischer's larger churches, and there are several others also among his minor works.

Zwiefalten and Fürstenzell

The building histories, in both cases rather complicated, are almost parallel for Zwiefalten and for Fürstenzell. The work at these abbeys was undertaken by Fischer very soon after his churches at Ingolstadt and at Diessen—though not that at Berg-am-Laim, nor presumably the one at Aufhausen—were quite complete with all their frescoes, *stucchi*, and altars in place. Fischer's intervention at Fürstenzell came a year earlier than at Zwiefalten. The Cistercian Abbey of Fürstenzell is a short distance south-west of Passau in the Upper Palatinate and not far from Fischer's earliest church at Kirchham. In 1738 Abbot Stephan Mayr, who came from Schärding in Austria across the Inn where Fischer had worked even before he built Kirchham, called on the master-mason Joseph Wolf from Regensburg-Stadtamhof, who was then working at nearby Aldersbach, to design a new church for the abbey, since the physical condition of the medieval one was too bad to justify its retention.[41] The following year, doubtless from distrust of Wolf's artistic capacity, Mayr turned to the sculptor-architect J. M. Götz (1696–1760) from Passau to supply a second project, and construction according to that went forward at once under the master-mason Thomas Gärtler, also from Passau. After one year's building operations the abbot once more lost confidence in his designer and his builder, broke the contract with Götz, and called in Fischer who was, he wrote, 'famous from *vieler Experience*'.

Accepting most of what had thus far been built by Wolf and Gärtler, but modifying considerably the design of the interior, Fischer was able to push the work forward rapidly under the supervision of his *Palier* Martin Wöger. Though the War of the Austrian Succession interrupted the work briefly in 1742, the nave was vaulted in 1743 and the façade erected in 1744, so that the decoration and furnishing of the church with frescoes, *stucchi*, and altars could proceed in 1744–45. The church was blessed in the latter year and consecrated three years later on 27 October 1748. The south tower, however, was completed only in 1774.

At Zwiefalten, north-west of Biberach in Swabia (eastern Baden-Württemberg today), the cornerstone for Fischer's work there was not laid until 1 June 1744 and the decoration of the church, by J. M. Feichtmayr for the *stucchi* and by F. J. Spiegler for the frescoes, only began at the east end three years later.[42] In 1749 the nave was extended westwards and the façade was begun the following year. Further work on the interior went on intermittently for fifteen years until the church was consecrated in 1765. But before the laying of the cornerstone—that is, in the years when Fürstenzell was reaching physical completion—there had been considerable building activity at Zwiefalten that limited, even more than had the early building history of Fürstenzell, Fischer's freedom in designing and executing the church. In 1738 Abbot Augustin Stegmüller of this Benedictine abbey decided to proceed with the reconstruction of the twelfth-century church. A new guest-wing (*Gastbau*) of the abbey had been completed the previous year by the master-masons of the abbey, the brothers Josef and Martin Schneider (1689–1763; 1692–1760), extending the monastery buildings that had been begun by Tommaso Comacio in 1668 and carried out by Michael Thumb in 1684–90 with the assistance of Franz II Beer. Beer's association with the monastery, moreover, continued down to 1710, and he even provided a project for the rebuilding of the church. But it was according to plans of their own that the Schneiders began the construction of the east end of a new church, with extended choir, square crossing, and flanking towers, after the old choir was demolished in 1739. The following year the old nave was also demolished and a cornerstone for a new one, still intended to be built according to the plans of the Schneiders, was laid on 11 July 1740.

Then in 1741, followed one of those episodes that had been from the days of Niederaltaich so important for Fischer's career as an architect of abbey churches. Stegmüller, evidently doubtful like Mayr of the competence of the craftsmen he was employing, had the work that the Schneiders had thus far executed assessed by Father Bernard Stuart from the Schottenkloster in Regensburg. Stuart's report was negative and it was at this point that Fischer was called in. He prepared new plans and these were accepted, though some of the work the Schneiders had already carried out, notably the towers flanking the choir, were retained and they were even allowed to remain in charge of the construction. When, in 1744, the second cornerstone was laid, building activity had thus been going on for five years, and for the last three according to Fischer's plans, at the same time as building proceeded rapidly at Fürstenzell. But the campaign of construction at Zwiefalten was to be considerably more prolonged. All the same 1745 saw the vaulting of the east end and nave; 1746, the vaulting of the transepts; and 1747, the vaulting of the crossing. The westward extension of the nave two years later and the erection of the façade in 1750 may, perhaps, be considered afterthoughts; but this further building activity delayed the execution of the decoration in the nave to 1751, four years after that in the choir, but still at the hands of Feichtmayr and Spiegler. Spiegler also provided the high-altar painting in 1753, the year after the blessing of the church on 18 October 1752. That, however, rather than the considerably later date of the consecration in 1765, represents the point at which the church, its decoration, and its furnishing were effectively complete.

The very history of the two churches, similar though it is in the late arrival of Fischer on both scenes, suggests the reasons for some of the differences between them, though it does not entirely explain the disparities. Fürstenzell is inevitably the more consistent *Gesamtkunstwerk* (Pl. 191) since it was built and decorated in the four years 1741–45. At Zwiefalten, where construction started at the same time, the execution of the decoration began only in 1747, two years after the frescoes and *stucchi* at Fürstenzell were finished, and was not carried to completion before the early fifties. It is perhaps of less importance that the collaborators were different. Zeiller,[43] who executed the frescoes at Fürstenzell, was at least as capable as Spiegler, who worked at Zwiefalten; but J. G. Funk (d. 1772), although a Munich *Hofstukkateur* on the Cuvilliés team and hence associated with J. B. Zimmermann, did not have then, nor has he had since, the high reputation of J. M. Feichtmayr. Funk's *stucchi* lack the virtuosity of Feichtmayr's and are, of course, several years earlier; but they do play an important part in producing at Fürstenzell an interior more consistently Rococo than any other major church of Fischer's except Osterhofen (Pls. 58, 59), and one that represents a much more mature sort of Rococo than the Asams had helped so notably to evolve at the latter church fifteen years earlier.

Fürstenzell in plan and structural organization is a four-bay wall-pillar church with no crossing and a square-ended two-bay choir. The nave is 30.20 × 14.70 m. and the choir 20.25 × 12.80 m., so that the whole is much shorter than Diessen or, above all, Zwiefalten. Two features, familiar from Osterhofen, play their part in making this interior, on the whole, more Rococo than Baroque. On the one hand the corners of the nave are rounded and above the east and west end the barrel-vault curves down in a generous cove (Pl. 191). This cove is echoed at smaller scale at the east end of the choir, as also in a more complicated way in the flattened ovals of the side chapels.

Above the side chapels the parapets, much more richly decorated than the plain balustrades of Osterhofen and here crowned with *rocaille* grillwork, are slightly convex. The faint waviness of the side walls that results is not, however, continued on the faces of the wall-pillars. Instead of the concave clusters of pilasters of Osterhofen (Pl. 59), decorated by the Asams with Rococo panelling in scagliola, the wall-pillars here are more tectonically articulated by pairs of fluted pilasters crowned with relatively conventional Corinthian capitals. It is, therefore, almost as true still of Fürstenzell as of Diessen that the interior is consistently Rococo only above the cornice line. But there is much less here that remains Baroque than at Zwiefalten despite the great superiority of Feichtmayr's Rococo *stucchi* there.

The very length of Zwiefalten and the related articulation of the interior changes the spatial emphasis from the short, partially ovalized rectangle of the Fürstenzell nave, followed by a proportionate choir—a two-part sequence—to a five-part one (Fig. 27). Thus it recalls the very long and relatively narrow spaces the Asams and the Schmuzers had to cope with when they redecorated the medieval churches at Freising, Regensburg, and Rottenbuch. Whether or not the Schneiders in their plan of 1739 echoed in part that of the preceding medieval church, the great depth of the monks' choir and the presbytery beyond, as also the marked development of the crossing with transepts that extend well beyond the side walls of the nave—which Fischer accepted in 1741—would have been, in the work of these masons attached to a monastery, traditional and hence vestigially medieval. The deep 'fore-church' of 1749 extended the nave then, as at Fürstenzell, of four bays divided by wall-pillars the equivalent of two further bays—at least above the organ gallery at vault level. Thus the entire interior was stretched out to 93.50 m. in length, more than twice the total length of Fürstenzell.

The proportions, on the other hand, are rather low compared with Diessen or Fürstenzell, not to speak of the remodelled churches mentioned just above. The nave, including side chapels, is 27 m. broad; the choir and presbytery—their breadth limited in any case by the Schneiders' towers—only 14 m. and with no collaterals. But excluding its side chapels, the nave is only some 3 m. wider than the eastern arm and the crossing the same, so that there is only a very slight telescopic effect in contrast to the marked closing-in of the space of the nave by the choir-arch at Fürstenzell (Pl. 191). The height of the crossing at the centre of the dome is 27 m., that of the barrel-vault of the nave 21 m.

If anything, these lower proportions, so contrary to what one might expect from the plan, are more Rococo than Baroque. Rococo in effect also, as at Osterhofen and Fürstenzell, are the bowed arches of the side chapels between the wall-pillars, here closer in their simple treatment to the former than the latter, but with curious

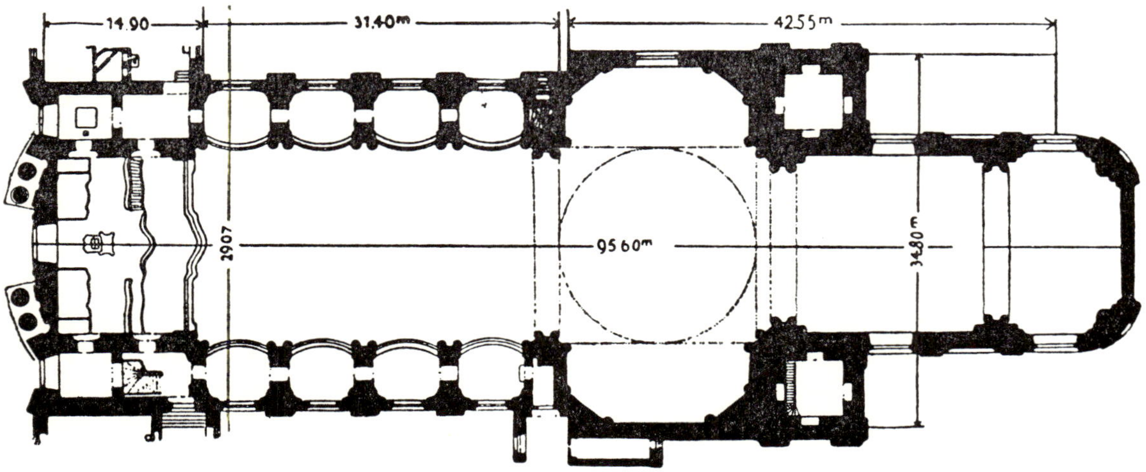

Fig. 27. Zwiefalten, Abbey Church. Plan

warped intradoses which rise from diagonally set imposts carrying characteristic Rococo decoration (Pl. 193).

These Rococo touches are, however, contradicted below the cornice level by a treatment of the wall-pillars that is more vigorously tectonic than Fischer had ever employed previously except at Berg-am-Laim. The pairs of engaged columns on the wall-pillars, carried out in pale blue-grey and pink scagliola with gilded capitals, together with the identical ones that are grouped in threes and fours at the corners of the crossing and introduced singly as well in the apse and the transepts, are by far the most conspicuous feature of this interior, except for Spiegler's enormous fresco of 1751 overhead (Pl. 194). Filling all four bays of the nave even more completely than Zeiller's at Fürstenzell, thanks to the absence of deep coves at the ends of the barrel-vault,[44] this is more striking in its organization, if not in its colouring, than any of C. D. Asam's. Within the scalloped frame, over which *rocaille* ornament breaks like ocean froth, the composition is vigorously ovalized. At both ends *quadratura* staircases of semi-circular plan, set asymmetrically, frame the open heavens somewhat as at Diessen. There, in an ellipse sharply outlined by bands of cloud, St. Benedict leads mankind in homage to the Virgin and the Trinity.[45]

Nowhere, perhaps, is the aptitude of the abler eighteenth-century German fresco-painters at collaborating with—indeed, even on occasion over-riding—the architects in the creation of ovalized interior space more evident than here at Zwiefalten. And in no church is the dichotomy, so characteristic of Fischer, between articulated Baroque structure—or pseudo-structure—of considerable tectonic vigour below and fluid unification of space above by the use of illusionistic painting and of profuse, but relatively delicate, surface ornamentation sharper than at Zwiefalten. To this the particular range of the colouring definitely conduces. The strong though cloudy hues of the scagliola columns, repeated in the altars,[46] bring these elements forward in contrast to the white and near white, highlighted with gold, of the *stucchi* and the yellowish or 'golden' tonality of the frescoes.

Both these churches have impressive façades that are almost entirely in the Baroque tradition. The one at Fürstenzell is dominated by the tall flanking towers with their elaborately articulated terminal lanterns. These recall somewhat the onion-shaped crowns of the regional tradition still, but they also approach Rococo sophistication in their scalloped silhouettes (Pl. 189). At Zwiefalten, however, the towers are where the Schneiders began them, behind the transepts and flanking the choir, so that they play little part in the view from the front. But the façade, by exception entirely executed in stone, is perhaps the most powerful Fischer ever built (Pl. 190). As in the interior, columns give great vigour and scale to the whole, yet the basic scheme is the double-S-curve of his earlier façades, here made bolder in plan and simpler in detail. Behind the sections of broken pediment above the pairs of columns at the centre the front of the gable is appropriately much flatter in treatment; on the other hand, the big double scrolls at the sides and the double-S-curved terminal entablature repeat against the sky the basic shape of the main story in plan.

By the time Fürstenzell was consecrated in 1748 Fischer had taken on what was to be the biggest commission of his career, that for the church of the Benedictine Abbey of Ottobeuren. In the following score of years before his death in 1766 he was certainly responsible for two more major churches, Rott-am-Inn and Altomünster; quite probably, indeed almost certainly, for two others, Haigerloch and Schäftlarn; and possibly or in part (though not at all probably) for two others, Maria Steinbach and Wiblingen; not to speak of about ten smaller churches and chapels, several remodellings, and a few secular works. It is manifestly impossible in this summary account of his *œuvre* to deal with these in even as much detail as has been provided for most of his earlier works from Kirchham to Zwiefalten. Maria Steinbach, where it is the façade that is most suggestive of his hand (Pl. 117), has been briefly discussed at the end of Chapter II;[47] Schäftlarn I have covered elsewhere;[48] and that church, as well as Ottobeuren, Rott-am-Inn, and Wiblingen[49] are described in considerable detail and thoroughly illustrated by Lieb. The last, as executed by J. G. Specht (1721–83) in 1771–77 and decorated in 1778–81 under the direction of Januarius Zick (1730–97), has little or nothing to do with Fischer's project of a decade or more earlier, however.

Rott-am-Inn

Among the churches most certainly designed by Fischer, three are in varying degree examples of his preoccupation with centralized planning. Of these Rott-am-Inn, near Wasserburg across the Inn from Austria in eastern Bavaria, is all but the latest of his churches, having been begun only in 1759.[50] Fischer here carried to a sort of theoretical perfection the plan-scheme he had first employed on a large scale at Ingolstadt and Aufhausen. The central rotunda—actually, as usual with Fischer, not a circle but an octagon with corner chapels—is flanked by identical square elements to east and west (Fig. 28). Thus it rivals in proto-Neoclassic formality of organization, as noted in Chapter IV,[51] the great church at St. Gallen begun by Thumb four years earlier (Fig. E, facing p. 168), which had yet to receive, in fact, its eastern arm balancing Thumb's nave. Only in the early to mid-sixties were both St. Gallen and Rott brought to completion.

Of special significance at Rott is the provision of an additional plan element to the west, a more modest 'fore-church' than at Zwiefalten, with a lobby below and the organ gallery above; for Fischer thus avoided any horizontal break in the western chamber that repeats in plan—and here also in section—the choir to the east. Unlike most of his churches with octagonal naves, the dimensions of this approach, as earlier at Berg-am-Laim, those of his wall-pillar churches. The total internal

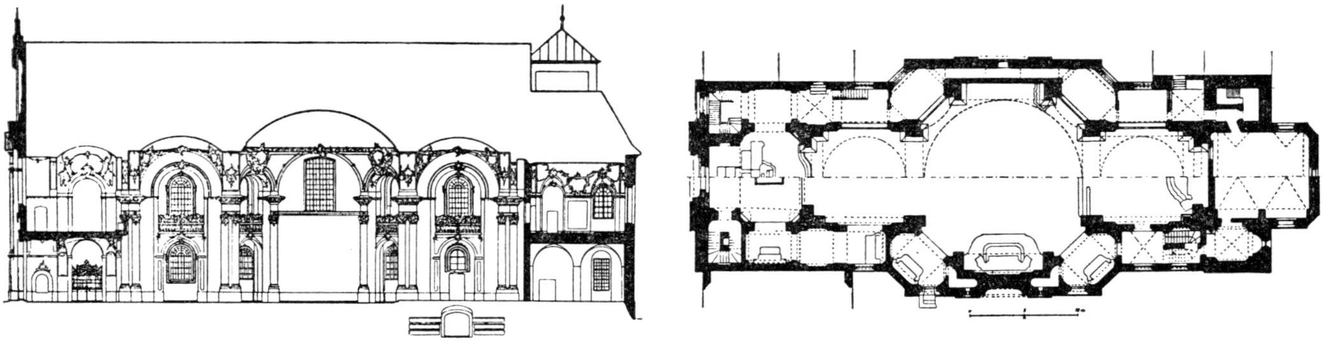

Fig. 28. Rott-am-Inn, Abbey Church. Section and plan

length is 46.10 m. and the height of masonry dome over the octagon 18.10 m. The other dimensions can be read, at least approximately, from the plan (Fig. 28).

As at Zwiefalten, there is again at Rott a contrast between the tectonic expression of the major structural elements, still distinctly Baroque up to the cornice level, and the Rococo treatment overhead (Pl. 195), especially the coving of the diagonal arches and the irregularity of the double pendentives over them. Large *rocaille* cartouches, moreover, filled with fluttering putti modelled presumably by Jakob Rauch—F. X. Feichtmayr's son-in-law, who undertook the stucco decoration in 1760—rise above the crowns of the eight arches to overlap, as over the crossing at Diessen, the somewhat tectonic circular frame of the fresco. This Matthäus Günther painted sometime in the years before the consecration in 1763 with his usual distinction.

Despite the fact that Abbot Benedict Lutz of Rott had first obtained in 1758 designs for the redecoration of the existing Romanesque church by Feichtmayr and Rauch, from the time Lutz visited Fischer in Munich later that year the architect seems to have had for once a free hand here, uncomplicated by earlier plans and even material beginnings by other masons and architects such as had affected adversely most of his major works from Diessen to Zwiefalten. Less than two months after Fischer had brought his plans to Rott on 26 April 1759 the contract was signed on 2 June and two days later the cornerstone was laid.

Ottobeuren

Ottobeuren, where Fischer had first come on the scene a decade before, is the largest and grandest, but by no means the most satisfying of Fischer's works. There the situation was quite different although—considered in somewhat over-simplified terms—the result was much the same; for this is again a distinctly Baroque structure of centralized plan, extended longitudinally, that is almost as distinctly Rococo overhead, thanks to the decorations in fresco and stucco. At Ottobeuren, however, these adjuncts are considerably later than the actual construction of the church. The *stucchi* executed by J. M. Feichtmayr on a contract of 1754 were only started two years later and not completed until 1764; the frescoes by J. J. Zeiller are of 1763; and most of the altars and other fittings were not finally installed until 1767, a year after the consecration. That, however, was arbitrarily timed to coincide with the millenial celebration of the founding of the abbey in the eighth century.

The reconstruction of the monastery buildings of this especially large and important abbey, situated a few kilometres northeast of Memmingen in Bavarian Swabia,[52] was begun by Abbot Rupert Ness shortly after his succession in 1710 from the designs of the monk Christoph Vogt. Father Vogt had earlier—in 1704—made the plans for the Benedictine abbey church at Holzen north of Augsburg and in 1709 those for the church of the Damenstift at Edelstetten, south of Günzburg, both also in Bavarian Swabia. He now provided also the first plan for rebuilding of the Ottobeuren abbey church, but nothing came of this project then or later.

Ten or fifteen years passed before anything more of consequence occurred. Then the stuccoer-architect Andrea Maini, originally from northern Italy, who had designed and carried out the library[53] in the monastery with J. B. Zimmermann's cooperation in 1715–18 and, in 1721–23, the Festsaal in the Abbey of St. Mang at

Füssen, offered new designs for the church. One of these was for a lobed and domed hexagon elaborated by no less than three towers and a squarish, oval-domed choir to the east. The whole was organized geometrically on overlapping equilateral triangles, with the apex of one of them at the centre of a triangular altar.[54] This conception is distinctly Borrominian; and so is his other design, which was almost as close to S. Carlo alle Quattro Fontane as the first is to Sant' Ivo. The second scheme[55] included additional elements to the east: beyond a domed choir, again of square plan, there was to be a smaller square sanctuary, also domed, and finally a modest semicircular apse. Both plans provided side passages flanking the choir and leading to the monastery buildings behind.

Late in 1732 Dominikus Zimmermann, presumably at the request of Abbot Ness, also offered two plans for the church, one of them of special interest here (Fig. C, facing p. 152). With its big rotunda, flanked east and west by aisled and domed squares, this scheme was distinctly premonitory of Thumb's St. Gallen (Fig. E, facing p. 168) and Fischer's Rott-am-Inn (Fig. 28). Zimmermann also proposed western towers beyond the line of the aisles to frame a concave façade that would be decorated with columns rather in the discreet way of Carlo Fontana's S. Marcello in Rome. Thus far actual construction had not started. Now, in 1736, Simpert Krämer, then in charge of the work on the other buildings of the monastery[56] offered the first of a series of projects[57] for the church, and on 27 September 1737 a cornerstone was laid.

Krämer's plans of 1736–39 retain something of the centralization of Maini's and Zimmermann's. But he reduced the width of the rotunda at the same time that he extended all four arms—western nave, eastern choir, and transepts—and finished them off with apsidal ends. Krämer also retained Zimmermann's western towers, pulling them inward slightly, but to fit his western apse he proposed a convex instead of a concave façade. In an early scheme this was to be scalloped; in a later one it is linked to the towers by counter-curves like that at Weingarten as completed in the twenties by Frisoni.

There was evidently some dissatisfaction with these projects of Krämer, for in 1739 certain 'architecti in vicinia' were called in. Plans that Joseph Schmuzer produced at this time survive, but they had no effect on the actual construction of the church. Five years later Joseph Effner, the electoral *Oberhofbaumeister*, was called in to modify the Krämer plan on which construction had finally started in the late thirties. Effner did not suggest many changes in the main body of the church,[58] perhaps because the foundations were already in place, but he did propose setting four great columns against the convex west façade. He also wished to substitute a square domed sanctuary, like that in one of Maini's schemes, for Zimmermann's choir, thus destroying the symmetry along the north-south axis which both Zimmermann and Krämer had proposed.

While it is not clear how much had actually been built by 1748 when Fischer was called in—Krämer was, indeed, not dismissed until the following year—the plans he offered over the years 1748–50[59] and the one he thenceforth gradually carried to completion six or seven years later (Fig. 29) did not differ much more than Effner's proposals from Krämer's of ten years earlier. He brought back Zimmermann's domes over the western arm and over the choir, but because of the limited dimensions of these elements the domes had to be slightly ovalized transversely. He also, somewhat less happily, provided two chapels of equal width, rather than a broad one and a narrow one, on each side of the nave, and repeated the pairs of arches through which these opened into the nave over the loges that he introduced on top of the side elements flanking the choir. His sanctuary with its rounded eastern corners is a sort of compromise between Krämer's half-round apse and Effner's square chamber. On the west front he retained the two towers of Zimmermann's design and the convex façade, with a curve bolder than that at Zwiefalten, that had possibly already been begun by Krämer (Pl. 197).

It is thus evident that the church executed by Fischer over the years 1748 to 1755—when the dome over the crossing was completed—is by no means even predominantly of his design. His most significant contribution was the widening of the crossing and the introduction there, as also in the three apses, of engaged columns projecting by three-quarters of their diameter. These took the place of the half-columns proposed by Krämer and the square pilaster-piers of Effner. As at Zwiefalten they much increase the Baroque vigour of the interior. So also does the treatment of the surfaces of the piers at the crossing between the engaged columns, for these are here neither diagonal nor concave, as at Diessen, Ingolstadt and Aufhausen, but convex.

On the other hand, nowhere in Fischer's work is there more Rococo decoration below the cornice line (Pl. 198). The capitals are notably virtuoso features, as is also the treatment of the lower arches and their spandrels, both in the western arm and in the choir. There the arches at the sides open above the magnificent Rococo stalls of 1755–64 which were carved in wood by Martin Hormann (1688–1782) and have much associated wooden sculpture by Joseph Christian (1706–1777). Moreover, both Fischer's surviving sectional drawings for the church, especially

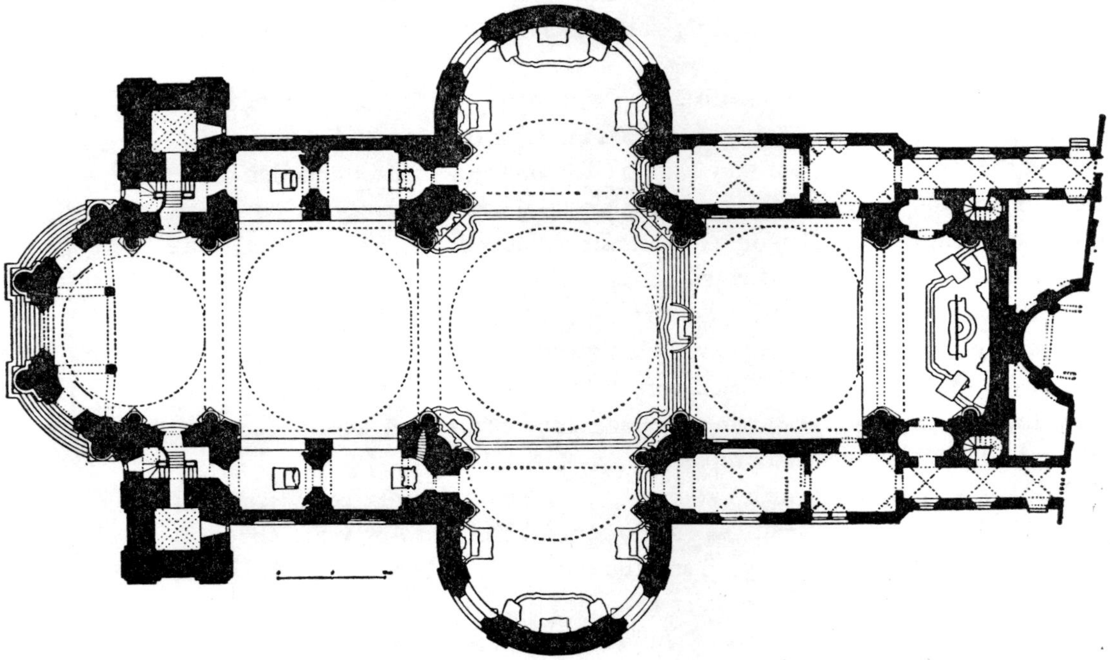

Fig. 29. Ottobeuren, Abbey Church. Plan

one that Lieb dates 1748–50,[60] give evidence that such elaborate *stucchi* as Feichtmayr eventually supplied were intended by Fischer from the first.

The exterior of Ottobeuren, even more than the interior, must be considered as much the design of Krämer as of Fischer who brought it to completion (Pl. 197). On the façade, the great columns, more evenly disposed than at Zwiefalten, were evidently derived from Effner's revision of Krämer's project; but the bold, apse-like bowing of the whole front may go all the way back to Maini. On the other hand, the treatment of the gable above the main order is pure Fischer and follows closely that of the relatively simple one at Fürstenzell rather than the bolder pattern of that at Zwiefalten (Pls. 189, 190). Unfortunately the Ottobeuren towers lack the grace and variety of outline of those at Fürstenzell. Those still recall somewhat the one designed at Deggendorf by Johann Mayr and J. B. Gunetzrhainer, of which Fischer had supervised the construction thirty years or so earlier.

Partly because of its high location, open to the north, but more because of the great plastic interest of the façade and the transeptal apses, not to speak of the enormous monastery behind and to the right, this is one of the grandest Baroque masses in Germany (Pl. 196). In contrast to the giant scale of the whole, the modest Rococo decoration on the façade, added by Feichtmayr in 1761–62 and concentrated over the main portal and higher up over the central western windows, seems even less relevant than at Diessen (Pl. 179). But it was not on exteriors that a German Rococo architecture came into being. Whatever the ambiguity of Fischer's interiors stylistically, there is no denying the essentially Baroque character of all his façades, his towers and, here, of his whole mass-composition, though he was quite as much controlled by the plan inherited from Krämer in organizing the exterior of the churc h as he was within, and he had nothing to do with the monastery buildings.

Schäftlarn

At Schäftlarn, whose completion is very nearly contemporary with Fischer's work at Ottobeuren, the exterior is of no great consequence. The interest lies almost entirely in the interior, brilliantly decorated by J. B. Zimmermann with both frescoes and *stucchi*.[61] There is an even greater difficulty here than at Ottobeuren, however, in determining the extent of Fischer's architectural responsibility—if, indeed, he actually had any as is generally accepted. Reconstruction of the Premonstratensian Abbey of Schäftlarn at this lovely site, deep in the Isar Valley some twelve miles south of Munich, began at the opening of the eighteenth century—a cornerstone was laid on 16 March 1701—from the design of the then electoral *Hofbaumeister* G. A. Viscardi and with the financial support of the Elector Max Emanuel.[62]

By 1712 a new west tower had been completed to replace the old one that had fallen two years before, but twenty years passed before reconstruction of the church began. Viscardi was by then long dead, and for the new church, of which the cornerstone was laid on 5 July 1733, Cuvilliés rather than Effner, his superior in the electoral service, provided the plans. Demolition of the old church and the laying-out of the foundations of the new one followed in 1734–35. But the work, directed for Cuvilliés by Franz Ronninger, proceeded very slowly and after the outbreak of the War of the Austrian Succession came to a total halt in the early forties. (Max Emanuel's son and successor as Elector, Carl Albrecht, had become Emperor as Charles VII in 1740, but he soon saw his lands overrun by the Austrian troops of his rivals, Maria Theresia and her husband Francis of Lorraine.)

The end of the war on the death of Carl Albrecht did not lead to an immediate revival of the project under his son and successor as elector, Max III Joseph. It was only in 1751 that work began again following a revised and reduced plan nominally provided by J. B. Gunetzrhainer, Effner's successor as *Oberhofbaumeister*. The documents indicate, however, that control of the work (and probably of the designs for it) was in the hands of a 'Herr Fischer', whom it is plausible to suppose was Gunetzrhainer's step-brother-in-law, J. M. Fischer, certainly a far more experienced and highly reputed church architect than he. Moreover, Melchior Streicher (d. 1772), who was supervising the Anastasiakapelle at Benediktbeuern that Fischer had designed the year before and was to assist Fischer at the end of the decade at Rott-am-Inn, was the *Palier* here. Under Streicher's direction the work now proceeded rapidly. By the following year the choir vault was completed and in the year after that the vault of the nave, so that Zimmermann—now seventy-four years old—could execute with the assistance of his son Franz Michael the frescoes and the stucco-work. B. A. Albrecht's painting on the high altar is dated 1755; the altar itself, with its sculpture by J. B. Straub, is of 1756. Services were being held in the effectively complete, but undecorated, church by 1753, though consecration did not follow until seven years later in November 1760.

The relative rapidity, as compared with the contemporary situations at Zwiefalten and Ottobeuren, with which Schäftlarn was brought to structural completion in two or three years and then decorated over the next three, doubtless explains the greater consistency—or one might use Minguet's word, homogeneity—of character in this interior (Pls. 199, 200), overshadowed though it is in size and richness by Fischer's more famous churches from Osterhofen to Rott-am-Inn (Pls. 58, 59, 195). Zimmermann had had decades of experience as a decorator of churches and even, probably, real architectural responsibilities in the remodelling of Andechs[63] in these same years of the early and mid-fifties—perhaps also, though very much less successfully, just before that at St. Blasius in Landshut. It is difficult, however, to believe that he could have had much influence on the planning and the spatial articulation of this church (Fig. 30), for which an architect of the highest contemporary reputation was presumably fully responsible, with little or no advice even from Gunetzrhainer.

What is surprising, considering the priority of the plan of Cuvilliés according to which the foundations were laid out in the thirties, is the highly original, yet still quite Fischeresque, organization of this interior. Even so, Schäftlarn recalls Pietro da Cortona's Santa Maria in Campitelli in Rome as much as any of Fischer's own earlier churches. The transepts, shortened from those proposed by Cuvilliés, have the same curved corners as those in the Roman church; but this is, of course, a characteristic Rococo device and one Fischer had recurrently exploited in one way or another ever since the twenties. Here this curvature is repeated at the choir-arch and also at the west end, somewhat as at Osterhofen and Fürstenzell (Figs. 4, 38; Pl. 191). The relatively generous coves overhead related to these curvatures in plan are peculiarly characteristic of Fischer, but these are associated here only with the main axis, not with the cross-axes of the nave and the choir as in his churches of central plan (Pls. 185, 188).

The interior organization of the nave is, indeed, longitudinally rectangular, with bays of barrel-vaulting to east and west of the low dome over the wide middle bay of the nave, not octagonal as at Ingolstadt, Aufhausen or Rott-am-Inn. Structurally, indeed, this is a variant of the wall-pillar church, though the spacing of the piers is by no means even thanks to the varying widths of the bays of the nave. Beyond the choir-arch the next spatial compartment, however, is a true square. This is covered with a dome that is smaller, and hence lower, than that over the nave, much as at Santa Maria in Campitelli or, even before that, Ricchino's San Giuseppe in Milan. The telescoping continues no further, however, for the apse is as wide as the choir. This terminal spatial compartment is nearly as deep, moreover, and of horseshoe plan, somewhat like that proposed by Fischer for the east end of Berg-am-Laim in 1735. It had, therefore, to be covered with a three-quarter dome rather than the usual half-dome, and one nearly as tall as that over the choir.

The proportions of the interior, within an overall length of 49.20 m., are almost as low and broad as those of the much longer interior of Zwiefalten (Pl. 192). The barrel-vaulted sections of the nave are 13.50 m. wide; the domed central portion, 14.70 m.; the choir, 10.50 m.; and the apse at its broadest point, a metre wider. The dome in the middle of the nave rises to 19 m. and the barrel-vaulted sections flanking it to east and west are 16.70 m. high. The dome of the choir is a little lower, 16.60 m., and the floor here rises three steps at the choir-arch; a further step at the entrance to the apsidal sanctuary reduces the actual height of its three-quarter dome to 16 m.

Two things particularly differentiate this interior from the much more impressive but less homogeneous one at Zwiefalten (Pls. 192, 193). These are the centralizing of the relatively short nave—a characteristic aspiration of Fischer's, though carried out here in a fashion unique in his *œuvre*—and the restraint in the

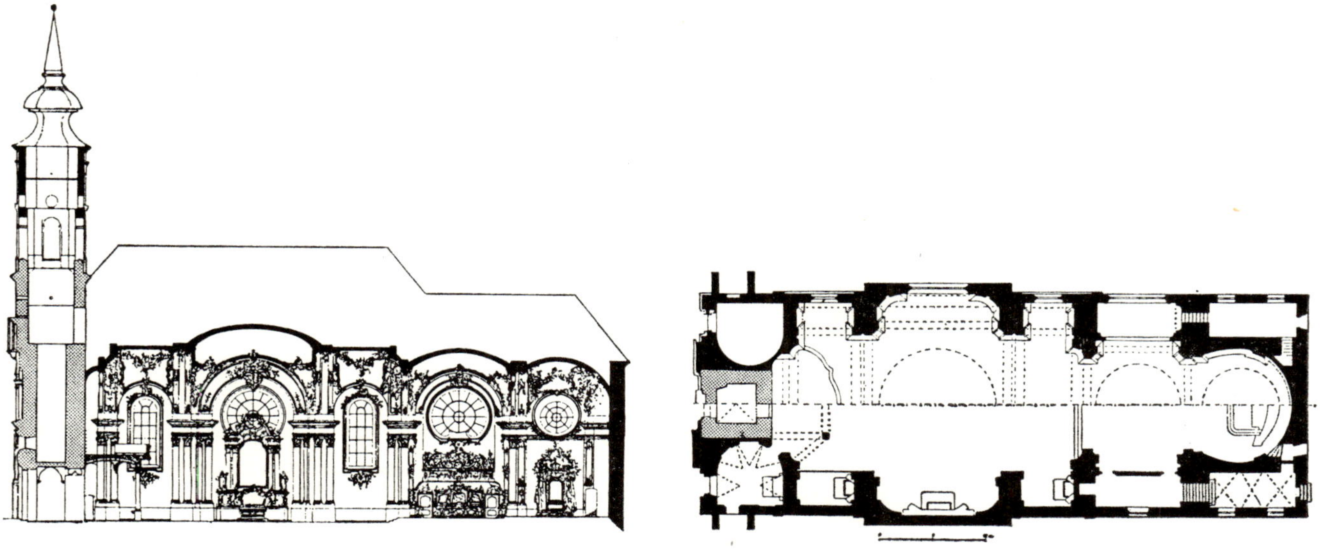

Fig. 30. Schäftlarn, Abbey Church. Section and plan

modelling of the wall-pillars. Instead of the boldly tectonic engaged columns of Zwiefalten, which were repeated somewhat less recurrently at Ottobeuren (Pl. 198), with their rotundity further emphasized in both cases by shiny coloured surfaces, there are below the entablature here at Schäftlarn, just as at Osterhofen and Fürstenzell (Pls. 59, 191), only shallow pilasters. Moreover, these have quite plain shafts though they are crowned by delicate Rococo capitals that carry the gold-and-white[64] theme of the *stucchi* overhead down into the wall-plane below the entablature.

As usual in Fischer's churches and those of others as well in this period, there is also stucco-decoration around the windows and on the fronts of the loges flanking the choir and of the organ gallery. This last projects into, but does not as at Diessen fill, the first narrow bay of the nave. As first at Diessen and later at Ottobeuren, the characteristic Rococo decoration of the coves and the barrel-vaults of the side chapels is echoed in the diagonal panels between the pilasters of the piers at the corners of the choir and, most notably, on the barrel-vaults of the short side arms of the choir. The walls of these side arms like those in the apse, moreover, are not set apart from the vaults by the strongly tectonic entablature of the pilaster order used on the wall-pillars.

Not since Osterhofen where, a quarter of a century earlier, Fischer had worked in close collaboration with two major decorative artists responsible for the frescoes and *stucchi*—though brothers, rather than a father and a son as here—had Fischer produced such an interior, not even at Fürstenfeld. At Schäftlarn the Rococo elements truly outweigh what may well be considered the last considerable vestiges of the Baroque: the pilaster order and its entablature rather than the coincidental, but presumably not consciously derivative, similarities to Ricchino's or Pietro da Cortona's churches of the previous century in Italy. Those vestiges had survived in all his churches and, of course, almost as universally in the work of several architects far more consistently Rococo than he, as has been noted in earlier chapters.

In the apse of Schäftlarn the order is at least partially melted away; only the architrave of the entablature extends all the way round and, even so, it is curved downwards under the great round windows at the sides. Below the entablature blocks that flank the altar, moreover, the pilaster strips terminate, not in capitals, but like the panels of French *boiseries* only in swatches of *rocaille* ornament, as was usually the case only in very modest contemporary churches (Pl. 199). So also the entire entablature is omitted on the outer walls of the nave and the choir as well as in the transept arms. In the latter, at least, the big round windows provide visual links between the Rococo decoration of the vault and the openwork *rocaille* cresting above the loges at the sides; elsewhere similar windows serve as backgrounds for the elaborately Rococo elements that crown the side altars.

Benediktbeuern, Anastasiakapelle

But if Schäftlarn establishes at one end of Fischer's career, as Osterhofen does at the other, a high-ranking position for him among the architects of large Rococo churches, his minor works of the fifties illustrate almost equally well his special capacities, even though he did not in them usually have the services of collaborators of the calibre of the Asams, the Feichtmayrs, or the Zimmermanns. The Anastasiakapelle, attached to the north-east corner of the seventeenth-century abbey church at Benediktbeuern, which H. G. Asam frescoed in the 1680s is, for a chapel, quite large, larger indeed than many of Fischer's village churches (Pl. 201); but in plan it is a true oval, as none of them are however much some approach that shape, and therefore not unlike Schönbrunn-bei-Dachau of thirty years before.

The contrast between the German Late Baroque before the arrival of the Rococo in church architecture and the High Rococo could hardly be better illustrated than by comparing these two interiors. What the chapel of 1750–58[65] still shares with the church of 1723–24, beyond the basic oval plan of the nave of the latter, is the use of a pilaster order broken off by arches rising high into the domed vault of the four cardinal points. But the whole spatial effect is modified in the chapel at Benediktbeuern by the fact that, except for the shallow bulge of the apse,[66] these breaks in the oval are no deeper than the thickness of the pilasters (Pl. 202). Moreover, though the pilasters and their entablature are emphasized by their pink scagliola surfaces, they lack the academic fluting of those at Schönbrunn and in Fischer's much later church at Fürstenzell, while their capitals are translated from the conventional Corinthian of Schönbrunn into delicate compositions full of *rocaille* asymmetry in detail.

Overhead, the fresco in the Anastasiakapelle by Zeiller (Pl. 203), executed in 1752, is remarkably fresh and open, almost as if the influence of Tiepolo's ceiling over the stair-hall at Würzburg, begun in 1750, had already reached Upper Bavaria (which is, of course, by no means impossible). The delicately multi-scalloped frame of this fresco fits well down over the eight arches, alternately wide and narrow, that intersect the base of the dome. Across that frame the *rocaille* flourishes in the stucco-work,[67] predominantly white in contrast to the scagliola of the pilaster order below and the bright hues of the fresco above, splash up recurrently. Thus these serve almost to vignette Zeiller's great version of the Trinity in Heaven awaiting St. Anastasia. The fresco effectively dominates the interior colouristically, since only the fields of the larger cartouches that flank the arches at the sides are also frescoed. It should further be noted as significant in the detailing that all the openings, whether round or segmental-arched, are surrounded by coved frames lightly touched with stucco ornament. Above all the interior, though blind on the southwest, is flooded with light from the many big windows, so that the contrast with the relatively dark Baroque interior of the seventeenth-century church to which the chapel is attached, strikes the visitor at once on entering and must for the worshipper, quite change the devotional atmosphere.

Minor Late Works

Compared to this extremely rich and by no means small chapel, many of Fischer's village churches, early and late, seem very modest. Among his minor works the pilgrimage church of St. Anna at Haigerloch in Hohenzollern—carried out reputedly from Fischer's designs by the local builder Christian Grossbayer for Prince Joseph Friedrich of Hohenzollern-Sigmaringen in 1752–55,[68] just as the Anastasiakapelle was reaching completion—is the most comparable in the profusion of the decoration. This church, moreover, is not very large—internal length 25 m. as compared to about 13 m. for the Anastasiakapelle—nor is it characteristic of

Fischer's planning at this point in his career as that is exemplified in his major works.

The nave of St. Anna, squarish but divided into three bays, is covered with a very much flattened semi-elliptical ceiling. This carries the main fresco by Meinrad von Aw—a painter who was actually born in Sigmaringen—within a stucco frame that is roughly rectangular in shape but varied by free curves, especially at the corners. Beyond lies a slightly narrower square choir covered with a dome on pendentives. From this, however, there open to left and right, through semi-elliptical arches identical with the choir-arch, very short transeptal arms. These are rather like those that flank the middle of the nave of Schäftlarn, which was then being brought to completion. Their flat ends and curved corners, beneath deeply coved ceilings, indeed, are not unlike the compressed semi-domes over the transept ends at Zwiefalten. The narrower arch leading into the apse is semi-circular and the apse itself is also rounded in plan.

The modest size of this interior, the profusion of the *stucchi* by no less a stuccoer than J. M. Feichtmayr and, above all, the complicated *rocaille* structure of the very tall side altars in the eastern corners of the choir, masking all but completely the conventional pilaster clusters below the pendentives, create an effect of congestion unusual in Fischer's churches, large or small, and not at all Baroque in effect. Yet the result is, in some sense, a sort of parody of the Rococo.

The cornerstone of the small church at Bichl, just north of Benediktbeuern, was laid on 15 May 1751 and it was blessed and in use from 1753, though not consecrated until 1758.[69] Not surprisingly the Benediktbeuern abbot, Leonhard Hohenauer, for whom Fischer was building the Anastasiakapelle, called on him to provide the design. The nave is, in plan, one of Fischer's characteristic irregular octagons, here with curved corners and modest coves carried round the arches at the four sides. Beyond is a narrower square choir that is an echo of the nave. At the west a low oval lobby precedes the nave. Despite the various curves in the plan and the low pitch of the main arches and the domical ceilings, this interior is far more Baroque than Rococo in general effect. There are no *stucchi* at all here, and overhead the frescoes by Zeiller, signed and dated 1752 like those in the Anastasiakapelle, are surrounded by heavy painted architectural elements that are quite without Rococo elegance and grace instead of scalloped frames and delicate decoration in stucco. In this interior only J. B. Straub's big statue of St. George over the high altar and, more specifically, the canopied scagliola setting that J. Geiger provided for it, dated 1753, have distinctly Rococo character in scale, in colour, and in detail.

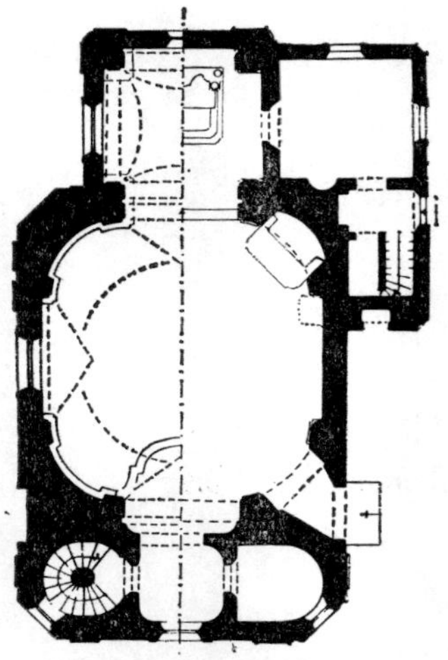

Fig. 31. Sigmertshausen, Pilgrimage Church. Plan

The small pilgrimage church at Sigmertshausen near Schönbrunn, a few kilometres north of Dachau, was built by Fischer in 1755. This is very similar to Bichl, except for the location of the tower over the west front and the omission of the lobby set under the organ gallery in the earlier church. The Bichl tower is a survival, dating from 1671, related to the original medieval church demolished in 1751; the tower at Sigmertshausen required rectangular support below and the church is entered, in any case, not from the west, but through the south-west corner (Fig. 31). Sigmertshausen can actually be considered a sort of Rococo twin of Baroque Bichl. As is hardly apparent in the published plan, the curved quadrants at the corners are broader than at Bichl, so that the nave tells spatially as a rounded square rather than as an octagon. Then, in place of the distinctly tectonic Doric pilasters of Bichl, carrying a heavy entablature of considerable height, there are merely shallow pilaster-strips here, without capitals but with small *rocaille* flourishes above them —the only stucco decoration in the whole interior—on the *ressauts* of a much compressed architrave. The frescoes overhead are signed by F. J. Degle and dated 1755. Degle also supplied in paint the equivalent of Rococo stucco decoration, none too happily on the dome over the square choir, where little space was available on the pendentives, but in the nave very effectively. White *rocaille* scroll-work, varied with green fronds of palm, surrounds the large cartouches in the corners with their grisaille figures; while the four generous quadrants of a painted frame in the general shape of a rounded square provide a gilt border for the main fresco. Across this, stucco-like decoration flourishes in white paint, rising from the cartouches at the corners and over the coats-of-arms at the choir-arch, break upwards in the usual Rococo way.

Altomünster

The church at Rott-am-Inn, completed in the early sixties and generally considered Fischer's final masterpiece, has already been discussed. The church of the Brigittines of Altomünster near Aichach, which he began four years later on 22 May 1763, is posthumous as regards all the decorations in fresco and in stucco. Brought to physical completion by Fischer's assistant Balthasar Trischberger on 9 July 1766, two months after Fischer's death, the *stucchi*—as at Rott the work of F. X. Feichtmayr's son-in-law Rauch—were executed over the following years, according to some evidence down even to the consecration of 29 August 1773.[70] The frescoes by Josef Magges, who had worked in the crossing at Ebersmunster in Alsace in 1759 long after the original construction of that church in the twenties by Peter Thumb, are signed and dated 1768.

The peculiar interest of Altomünster lies in the exceptional spatial complexity of the east end, made necessary by the retention of the walls of the deep double choir that had replaced the Romanesque apse in the Gothic period, and utilized here to provide three separate choirs for the nuns of the Brigittine Order, for the monks, and for the lay-brothers (Fig. 32).[71] Though the nave of the church is, on the whole, a large but inferior copy of that at Rott with sparse and inferior stucco-work, the next spatial compartment under the nuns' choir is, despite the great restraint of Rauch's *stucchi*, a splendid example of the very latest Rococo (Pl. 204).[72]

The plan of this portion of the church is that which Fischer had used recurrently since the twenties, a square with cut-off corners covered by a domical vault, here so much flattened that it must be of wooden construction. But the imposts, as at Sigmertshausen, are reduced to a minimum, as are the archivolts of the four main arches; while the arrises, where the diagonal fenestrations cut into the domical surface, are of a paraboloid curvature almost as free-hand as the swatches of *rocaille* ornament that flank their heads. Unlike the fresco in the nave, solidly encircled by an architrave tangent to the crowns of the eight arches below, the one overhead here, while also basically circular, has a multi-scalloped frame recurrently linked to the surrounding plain surface of the dome by modest clamps and sprays. Much

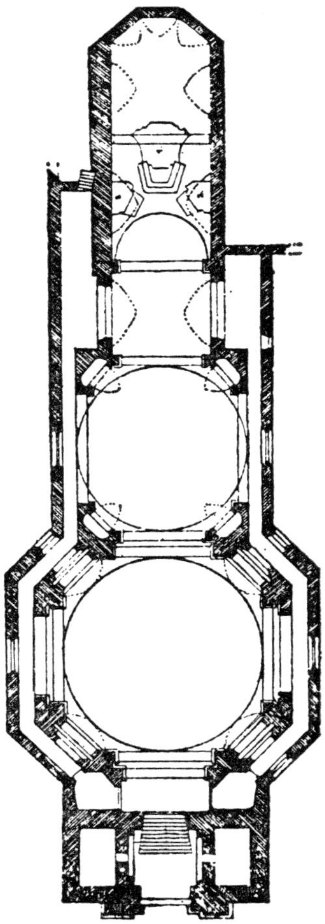

Fig. 32. Altomünster, Abbey Church. Plan

of the vitality of the High Rococo had by now been lost, yet linkage with the Baroque was more completely severed than even in the Anastasiakapelle (Pl. 202) or at Sigmertshausen.

In this, Fischer's final exercise in the creation of meaningful interior space, one need no longer say that it is Baroque below and Rococo only overhead. Admittedly, however, this choir is only a part of the whole church and quite lacks the grander scale of Osterhofen and Fürstenzell, though it is certainly one of Fischer's 'purest' Rococo achievements.

Like the nave at Rott, on the other hand, the nave of Altomünster must be considered in Fischer's more usual way a mixture of Baroque and Rococo. For all its size it is not, as regards quality, however, the equal of the naves of his earlier major works in the long roster that began with Osterhofen in the twenties and effectively ended nearly forty years later with the completion of Rott just before his death. The space beyond the nave ranks much higher, for it provides not the least of the evidence that Fischer *could* be a consistently Rococo architect.

J. B. Neumann

Equal to Fischer's, if not ahead of his, has long stood the reputation of J. B. Neumann.[73] Even less than in the case of Fischer can Neumann be considered to have been either consistently—much less primarily—a Rococo architect. In discussing here the 'limits of the Rococo' his *œuvre* can be dealt with a good deal less extensively than Fischer's, for he played little part in the early development of the Rococo in the twenties and his fully Rococo interiors of the forties are few though exemplary. There are, moreover, even greater ambiguities in his major churches than in Fischer's, particularly as regards the most famous, that at Vierzehnheiligen, which many, perhaps most, writers consider more Rococo than I. Unlike the situation with Fischer, Neumann's secular commissions rival his churches in interest and importance. Moreover, several of the most famous are open to interpretation either as Late Baroque or as Rococo. In fact they are mostly rather a mixture of the two, somewhat like Fischer's major churches, though less plausibly describable by any such simple formula as 'Baroque below and Rococo above'.

Five years older than Fischer, and by 1718 a captain of engineers, Neumann began his serious association with architecture with his early involvement in the planning of the Residenz at Würzburg, on the upper Main in Franconia, for Johann Philipp Franz Graf von Schönborn, who became Prince-Bishop of Würzburg in 1719.[74] Throughout most of Neumann's life the Würzburg Residenz continued to be his principal professional preoccupation. At first, however, he was distinctly subordinate to several older architects: to Maximilian von Welsch and Johann Dientzenhofer, whom Johann's uncle, Lothar Franz, had been employing at Pommersfelden, and to Lukas von Hildebrandt, whom Johann's brother Friedrich Carl had employed for his palaces in Vienna and his Schloss near Göllersdorf in Lower Austria.[75] In 1723, moreover, Neumann was sent to Paris to consult with Germain Boffrand and Robert de Cotte about the Prince-Bishop's building projects in Würzburg. It was then that he probably first came into direct contact with the French Rococo, more than a decade later than the Wittelsbach electors of Cologne and Bavaria and the latter's architect Joseph Effner. The following year Germain Boffrand came to Würzburg, as was mentioned in the Introduction, and provided designs for certain interiors that have not survived.[76]

Holzkirchen and Wiesentheid

In 1726 and in 1727 Neumann planned the first two churches for the design of which he was solely responsible: that for the Priory of Holzkirchen,[77] between Würzburg and Wertheim, and that of the parish church at Wiesentheid,[78] a Schönborn seat somewhat farther away and to the east of Würzburg. Wiesentheid is wholly Baroque, with interior walls and ceiling all painted by the Italian G. F. Marchini, who had worked earlier at Schloss Weissenstein. His clumsy *quadratura* architecture is as unpersuasive illusionistically as it is there and not as entertaining, since there is no pretence of ruination.

Holzkirchen is very French, but most academically so, following closely the corner chapels of the Dôme des Invalides in Paris in plan and section (Pl. 205). The very delicate *stucchi* by J. P. Castelli on the frieze of the unbroken entablature, the surface of the dome, and the coved intradoses of the windows have a transitional character that is more French than German, and not much like the proto-Rococo of the previous decade in Franconia (Pls. 5–8). But Castelli came from Bonn, where he had worked with Hauberat for Joseph Clemens,[79] and had also been associated with Boffrand in the Würzburg Residenz in 1724. Holzkirchen was completed in 1730; Wiesentheid a year or two earlier.

Würzburg, Hofkirche

The Hofkirche in the Würzburg Residenz was designed and built over the years 1731–43 for Friedrich Carl von Schönborn, Prince-Bishop of Würzburg and since 1729 also of Bamberg, from plans that had been modified by Hildebrandt.[80] It was begun only a very little earlier than the Asams' church in Munich, with which almost precisely contemporary work it was earlier compared in Chapter I.[81] There, perhaps, too great emphasis was given, by contrast, to its un-Rococo aspects.

In these years there arrived in Würzburg a stuccoer who was later to be responsible for the decoration of all of Neumann's most consistently Rococo interiors. Antonio Bossi (d. 1764), an Italian-Swiss from the vicinity of Lugano, had worked at Ottobeuren in 1718–19 and possibly longer. Neumann brought him to Würzburg in 1733 from Mainz, where he had been working under Welsch for Friedrich Carl's uncle Lothar Franz. His services were needed primarily to execute the *stucchi* in the Schönbornkapelle attached to the Dom. Two years later Bossi undertook the stucco decorations in the Hofkirche, a year before the Swiss-born painter J. R. Byss began the frescoes overhead. Byss had earlier executed the ceiling in the stair-hall at Schloss Weissenstein for Lothar Franz, as has been noted earlier, and was invited to Würzburg two years before Bossi.

This interior, as already stated, is dominated visually by a multitude of free-standing scagliola columns carrying a heavy entablature (Fig. 8; Pl. 73). Bossi's *stucchi*, therefore, largely based in any case on Hildebrandt's designs, do not play a very important part in the general impression the visitor first receives. Yet there is—if one looks closely at such details as are not derived from Hildebrandt—considerable advance beyond Holzkirchen as completed five years earlier (Pl. 205).

This is especially true of the distinctly Rococo ornament on the cross-severies that penetrate the edges of the interlocking oval domes and on the flat rib-bands that mark—rather in the manner of those Johann Dientzenhofer introduced at Banz some twenty years before—their three-dimensionally curved intersections (Pl. 208). Moreover, the irregular framing of the main frescoes at the base of the vault is, in effect, scalloped, since its more architectural elements are overlapped by many putti, and even by some Rococo ornament. There is, as a result, some resemblance to the Zimmermanns' dome at Steinhausen with its frame of 'constructed decoration' (Pl. 11). Yet the contrast with the decorations overhead in Fischer's Diessen (Pls. 181, 182), carried out by the Feichtmayrs only a year or two later, is very striking. It is even more difficult to realize that this church is almost precisely contemporary, at least as regards its decoration, with Cuvilliés Amalienburg (Pl. 133). The Hofkirche, it might be said, has a distinctly Baroque interior in which the Rococo elements, though present in the *stucchi*, are still incidental.

Yet, if one forgets the remarkable plan of intersecting ovals, echoing at least indirectly the Bohemian churches of the Dientzenhofers, and ignores the lower story with its tectonic order—of which the importance seems to have been increased beyond Neumann's original intentions by Hildebrandt, especially at the ends (Fig. 8; Pl. 73)—and focuses the attention on the upper story of the middle bay of the interior, this curiously shaped central space has a good deal in common with the ovalized rectangles and rectangularized ovals that other architects were creating in the thirties (Pl. 208). In this space, moreover, the contributions of Neumann's associates Byss and Bossi play almost as important a part as did those of the collaborators of J. M. Fischer at Diessen or J. G. Fischer at Wolfegg. Indeed, difficult as it is to define at all precisely the special character of Rococo—as distinguished from Baroque[82]—painting on vaults, the extreme openness of Byss's Assumption and the total absence of *quadratura* architecture or other earthly elements overhead here in the nave—though not in the choir to the east—is advanced beyond most other ceiling frescoes of the thirties. Even the stunted and tapered pilasters, essentially of Hildebrandt's design, are at least as proto-Rococo as is his work in Vienna (Pl. 10) and at Schloss Schönborn (the latter for the same client as here) twenty years earlier—as proto-Rococo, yes, yet surprisingly still no nearer to the real Rococo that was already entering Germany from Paris at that time.

St. Paulin, Trier

For the extensive range of Neumann's production, consisting to an unusual degree in this period in southern Germany of large secular works, it is difficult to provide a strict chronological succession, for the construction and related decoration of German palaces usually continued over several decades. At Bruchsal in Baden, for example, the magnificent interiors, destroyed in the last war, were first planned as early as 1731; but the frescoes by Johann Zick and the Rococo *stucchi* by J. M. Feichtmayr (Pl. 213) were not completed until the mid-fifties, after Neumann's death.[83] So also among Neumann's churches, St. Paulin in Trier,[84] planned in 1733 and begun the next year, received Scheffler's frescoes, with their curious enframement of dark and heavy painted *rocaille* forms that merge into clouds, only in 1744, and was not consecrated for another decade (Pl. 206). Käppele (Pl. 218), across the river from the town at Würzburg, commissioned in 1740, was begun only in 1748; and Matthäus Günther's frescoes—as presumably the anonymous associated *stucchi*—date from 1752, the year before Neumann died. At Schloss Werneck, first projected in 1733, the building of the chapel[85] to a modified plan began in 1741, and the *stucchi* were completed by Bossi some four years later (Pl. 207).[86]

Sequentially, then, St. Paulin follows the Würzburg Hofkirche and precedes Käppele and the Werneck chapel, provided its major architectonic characteristics are considered apart from its decoration and its furnishing. In two respects these may be considered Rococo, the curved elements in plan that make the transition from the un-aisled nave to the narrower apsidal-ended choir—with which is associated a generous cove at the east end of the nave vault—and the smaller coves that enframe the tall arched windows at the sides of nave and choir (Pl. 206). The omission of ribbing on the nave vault may have been decided only when Scheffler executed the frescoes, but even in the choir and apse the ribs are devoid of tectonic emphasis.

On the other hand, the treatment of the piers that divide the nave into bays is as vigorously structural in expression, thanks to their academic entablature blocks, as that of the wall-pillars in Fischer's contemporary Diessen (Pl. 182) despite the later decoration of the pilaster heads here. This gives them a distinctly Rococo flavour, especially to the pairs of concave ones at the east end of the nave. The stylistic ambiguity of this interior is further increased by some of the late furnishings, not so much the very open columnar high altar with its crowning scrolls, designed by Neumann in 1745 but executed by Ferdinand Dietz (1708–77) only in 1755–61, as the solid panels flanking the choir grille of 1767, which already resemble the rather Louis XVI ones flanking the altar at Altomünster that probably date from the early seventies (Pl. 204).

Analysis tends, alas, to distort the totality of any *Gesamtkunstwerk*. Thanks to Scheffler's *rocaille*-framed frescoes overhead, Neumann was able to create here a part-Baroque, part-Rococo interior that has considerable consistency. To the observer who views it, not piecemeal but as a whole, St. Paulin is at least less discordant than are Fischer's great churches of the same years of the late thirties and early forties. It must be admitted, however, that these churches of Fischer's are superior to St. Paulin as regards their much handsomer frescoes and their very grand scale.

Würzburg, Weisser Saal

In the late thirties and forties, down to the death of Friedrich Carl von Schönborn in 1746, construction proceeded quite steadily on the Würzburg Residenz,[87] unaffected by the War of the Austrian Succession, since the Prince-Bishop, unlike the Wittelsbachs, was on the Austrian side. Plans for the principal interiors, the stair-hall and the Kaisersaal, the latter projecting on the garden front, were prepared in 1735.[88] The stair-hall was begun two years later and by 1741 the entire garden front was completed. The following year the vaults over the Kaisersaal, the Weisser Saal in front of it, and the stair-hall were finished and ready for decoration.

Neumann's sectional drawing of the stair-hall and the Weisser Saal[89] indicates that by the early forties he had come to accept Rococo decoration of an advanced *rocaille* character for monumental secular interiors; moreover, he knew that Bossi could execute it with distinction.[90] In the drawing of the stair-hall the balustrades of the flights of stairs and the landings consist of large-scale *rocaille* elements organized as an open-work cresting. These balustrades would have been very like those Neumann's one-time assistant, Johannes Seiz (1717–79), executed in stone in the electoral palace at Trier nearly twenty years later.[91] Overhead the Würzburg vault was to be decorated at the base with even bolder *rocaille* patterns in stucco; a similar treatment is also shown for the vault of the Weisser Saal, but not for the Kaisersaal.

As is well known, however, the vault of the stair-hall was finally completely filled in 1750–51 with the culminating masterpiece of Tiepolo, while the stairs and walls below did not receive their decoration until the sixties, when Antonio Bossi's son Materno (1735–1802) provided a scheme of decoration already post-Rococo in character.[92] But the decoration of the Weisser Saal entirely in stucco was completed by Antonio Bossi in 1744 and produced what is perhaps the most perfectly homogeneous of all monumental Rococo secular interiors up to this date (Pl. 209), not even excepting Cuvilliés's more modestly dimensioned Spiegelsaal at the Amalienburg (Pl. 133) or his earlier Grüne Galerie in the Munich Residenz that was destroyed in the war.[93]

How much credit Neumann should receive for the Weisser Saal it is hard to say —essentially this was the work of Bossi as stuccoer. Yet the framework, the rectangular plan and the high cloister-vault, were certainly provided by the architect, though several years before the *stucchi* were executed. Perhaps the pilaster-strips and the entablature—and more certainly the very plain door-frames—would have been of Neumann's design originally. Except for the last, however, these conventional elements were all but completely transmuted by the stucco-decoration. The pilasters, for example, have no capitals; and their shafts carry tall Rococo panels, characteristically elaborated decoratively at top and bottom, and with even more ornament clustered around the candle-holders at mid-height. The entablature has no architrave; and the frieze is a cove across which decorative elements scroll upwards, somewhat like modillions, under the moulded cornice. Extremely elaborate cartouches with asymmetrical borders of the richest and wildest *rocaille*, moreover, fill the panels above the doors, while even bolder *rocaille* decoration, interspersed with putti, provides a broad and loose band rising high on the vault (Pl. 209).

Except for the outlines of the doorways and the pilasters, straight lines and right angles are avoided—especially notable is the rounding of the entablature at the corners, with the cornice rising in a horn-like curve below elaborate flag-bedecked trophies on the surface of the vault. These last are, curiously enough, perhaps the most definite vestiges of a Baroque sort of decoration in an interior otherwise a translation from wood into stucco of the *genre pittoresque* of Pineau and his Parisian contemporaries at roughly twice the conventional French scale. But everything is exaggerated here by French standards. Though the corners of the vault where the trophies rise are softened to suggest a French coved ceiling, the vault is tall; the relief of the *stucchi* is high, especially on the vault; and the details of the *rocaille* decoration are slightly nightmarish, or should one here say 'oneiric'?[94] On the other hand, the tonality is of extreme delicacy, true white against a milk-white so pale that the difference is invisible in most photographs.

In this room Bossi reveals himself as a Rococo decorator of the highest order, and with a distinctly personal touch in the consistent crinkliness of his surfaces and the bold assurance of his asymmetrical curves. The great refinement of J. B. Zimmermann's *stucchi* following Cuvilliés's designs in the Amalienburg (Pl. 133) is perhaps more attractive to most visitors; but the Weisser Saal, as much as any of the great contemporary church interiors, is more idiosyncratically Germanic, despite the fact that the stuccoer was Italian-Swiss by birth.

Evidently, through the late thirties and early forties, Antonio Bossi, by that time settled in Germany for twenty years and more, had gradually mastered quite fully the High Rococo mode. One must suppose, however, that his personal style depended more on the published designs of the French, so often pirated by Augsburg engravers, and—after they began to appear in 1738—those of Cuvilliés than on first-hand knowledge of the work of the Feichtmayrs and other German stuccoers.

There had been, down to about 1740, a certain geographical limitation to the spread of the Rococo north-westwards from Bavaria into Franconia, as also south-westwards beyond Swabia into Württemberg, despite the early and increasingly active sponsorship of the Wittelsbach electors of Cologne still further west in the Rhineland. The Franconian proto-Rococo—so to call it—of the second decade of the century had no real succession after 1720. But during the next two decades, and chiefly in the lands of the Wittelsbach electors of Bavaria, the early Rococo advanced to a maturity that architects such as Neumann, working elsewhere, seriously emulated only after 1740.

To recapitulate, there is about the Weisser Saal little or nothing that can be considered *architecturally* Rococo, largely devoid though it is of Baroque inheritances. As a sort of over-scaled translation of a characteristic French Rococo room it is not a close parallel to the monumental church interiors of the Bavarian architects. The architect's part here was largely neutral, or even negative; yet Neumann must have encouraged Bossi to carry out here in stucco decorations similar to those proposed for execution in carved wood in contemporary and slightly earlier books of designs, such as had already been exploited with real virtuosity in the Paradezimmer of the Residenz.

Werneck, Chapel

However, at Werneck,[95] in the chapel there, which must be almost precisely contemporary with the Weisser Saal, Neumann achieved—despite the Corinthianesque capitals of the piers and their bold entablature blocks—a more truly Rococo spatial effect in the scalloped oval of a plan very like those towards which Bavarian architects had been working in their many churches since the twenties (Pl. 207). Relevant, also, are the curved shapes[96] of the entablature blocks, Baroque though these remain in their tectonic vigour, and also the delicacy shown in the handling of the intersections where the half-domes over the lobes meet the main oval dome, not to speak of the upward *rocaille* splashes at the bases of the undifferentiated pendentives and those running across the crowns of the arched arrises. Especially effective is the way the convex gallery fronts in the three bays on the entrance side play against the deep concavity of the lobes above and behind them. Then, though the Doric columns that support the gallery are of a positively High Renaissance directness of structural expression, there is the typically Rococo handling of the decoration on the jambs and intradoses of the openings behind them.

Würzburg, Sala Terrena

In Neumann's next interior there are again Doric columns that play an even more definitely structural role. All the same the Sala Terrena on the garden front below the Kaisersaal in the Würzburg Residenz (Pl. 210) is almost as exemplary a Rococo work as the Weisser Saal, though it resembles it hardly at all. From as early as 1730[97] Neumann had intended its shape to be a very elongated ellipse—in fact really a rectangle with diagonal or rounded corners—with the space fully ovalized only overhead as in so many Bavarian churches. This near oval was to be surrounded by isolated supports and these are, as executed, slight shafts of strong marble carrying simple cubic impost blocks.

The drawings indicate no scheme of decoration, in contrast to the elaborate treatments proposed already for the great hall above, the stair-hall and the Weisser Saal in the early forties. For this interior as executed, however, Bossi provided in 1749 a continuous band of stucco-work. This is irregularly intersected below by the arches carried by the columns, which are of uneven widths, and very freely scalloped above in order to provide a Rococo sort of frame for the fresco that Johann Zick painted the next year. (It was Friedrich Carl's dissatisfaction with that, incidentally, which is supposed to have led to his calling the great Tiepolo from Venice at that point to paint the frescoes in the stair-hall and the Kaisersaal.)

Würzburg, Kaisersaal

But if the Weisser Saal in front of it and the Sala Terrena below it are, despite the columns in the latter, among the most totally Rococo of large German palace interiors, the architecture of the Kaisersaal overhead, despite the profuse Rococo *stucchi* that frame Tiepolo's frescoes of 1752–53, is distinctly Baroque (Pls. 211, 212). The plan is not ovalized, even though the vault is a high oval dome, and a powerful range of fluted scagliola columns, more tectonic even than Fischer's plain ones at Zwiefalten and Ottobeuren (Pls. 192, 198), defines an elongated octagon or, more accurately, a transverse rectangle with the corners cut-off on the diagonal. One may perhaps say of this particular Neumann interior, as of so many of Fischer's churches, that it is Baroque below and Rococo above; yet the strong lines of the relatively wide marbled mouldings on the arrises of the vault and the firm and relatively simple shape of the main fresco[98]—perhaps dictated by Tiepolo—contrast with the rather looser handling of the decoration on the vaults in Fischer's churches.

It is at least worth remarking that Tiepolo's earlier fresco here, the one begun in 1750 over the stair-hall, occupies the entire vault leaving no room for *stucchi*; while that on the centre of the vault in the Kaisersaal (Pl. 211) overflows the scalloped frame in the old Bacciccian way to a degree rarely seen in Germany since C. D. Asam's fresco over the nave of Freising Cathedral (Pl. 43).

Bruchsal and Brühl

In comparison to the Würzburg Kaisersaal, the circular stair-hall at Bruchsal (which was destroyed in the war) must have seemed considerably less Baroque, thanks to the shallow pilasters, the flattened entablature, and the continuous cove with *stucchi* by F. X. Feichtmayr that surrounded the fresco that Zick painted on the domed ceiling (Pl. 213). But the Marmorsaal[99] there, on the other hand, with its paired engaged columns was evidently rather more Baroque, despite the thoroughly Rococo handling of the vault overhead. The decoration of these interiors was finally completed only in 1754, the year after Neumann's death, as has been noted. But the earlier, and happily surviving, stair-hall in Schloss Augustusburg at Brühl for Clemens August, the Archbishop and Elector of Cologne—planned in the early forties and largely built in 1743–48 but finally completed as regards the decoration only after Clemens August's death in 1761[100]—is almost as Baroque as the Würzburg Kaisersaal or the Bruchsal Marmorsaal, even considering the profuse Rococo *stucchi* on the walls and on the flat portions of the lower ceiling. The brilliantly coloured scagliola, moreover, used as a ground for the white *stucchi* also has a more Baroque than Rococo flavour.[101]

Vierzehnheiligen

The ambiguity of Neumann's architecture in terms of the stylistic antithesis, Baroque-Rococo, is perhaps more acutely felt in his major churches—only a very few of his smaller churches are touched on at all in this condensed account of his *œuvre*—than in his monumental secular interiors. Nowhere is the issue more difficult to resolve than at Vierzehnheiligen. This big pilgrimage church on the Main, north-west of Bamberg and across the river from Banz, if not Neumann's abbey church at Neresheim, over the Württemberg border towards Schwäbisch Gmünd, is as famous an example of eighteenth-century German church architecture as the Asams' St. Johann-Nepomuk, J. M. Fischer's Ottobeuren, or the Zimmermanns' Die Wies.

The building history of Vierzehnheiligen is almost as complicated as that of Ottobeuren,[102] but the result is more completely Neumann's than Ottobeuren is Fischer's. In 1735 Stephan Mösinger, who had the year before become abbot of the Cistercian establishment at Langheim in the diocese of Bamberg, applied to his bishop, Friedrich Carl von Schönborn,[103] who was at that time Neumann's employer at Würzburg, for permission to replace with an impressive new church the modest chapel dedicated to the Fourteen *Nothelfer* (a sort of heavenly witness, or even guardian angel) that the shepherd Hermann had seen four times in 1445–46 at the Frankenthal farm belonging to the Langheim Abbey.[104] Three years later, after various negotiations concerning the financing of the project, a first set of plans for a church of centralized design was obtained from G. H. Krohne (1703–56)[105] in the winter of 1738–39. Further negotiation followed; then, in 1742, Neumann prepared a more conventional design which survives. This is signed and dated 26 July.

On 23 April 1743 the cornerstone was laid and work on the foundations and the east end of the church was begun by the master-mason Thomas Niestler (d. 1768) and his stepsons, not according to Neumann's project, but following a new, long-naved design by Krohne.[106] By the end of the year Mösinger had informed Friedrich Carl of his dissatisfaction with Krohne's plans, however, and in 1744 Neumann set to work again in earnest on a series of alternative designs for the church. The elderly Maximilian von Welsch also provided on 15 April that year a plan[107] for which the abbot thanked him, but this probably had no influence on Neumann. Finally, later in that same year, construction according to Neumann's latest design began under the direction of J. J. M. Küchel. As the regular architectural adviser of the Langheim monks Küchel had been in the background from the first.

Two years later Friedrich Carl died and, as a result, Küchel took full control as architect of the Bamberg diocese under the new Prince-Bishop, Joseph Anton Philipp Freiherr von Frankenstein, who was not, like Friedrich Carl, also Prince-Bishop of Würzburg. Then, in succession, Mösinger died in 1751; Neumann died in 1753; and over most of the years of the Seven Years' War, 1756–63, construction was in abeyance while Küchel served as an engineer-officer. He came back on the job in 1761, however, and in 1762–63 the vaulting of the church was completed, ten years after Neumann's death and twenty since he first became involved with Vierzehnheiligen. At that point, in 1763, came the contract for the stucco decoration with the Feichtmayrs and Übelherr, still undoubtedly the leading German stuccoers. However, Übelherr died that year and F. X. Feichtmayr the next, so that the execution of the work, carried out over the next six years, was almost entirely J. M. Feichtmayr's responsibility. At the same time Giuseppe Appiani (d. 1786) was painting the frescoes. Consecration by the then Prince-Bishop of Bamberg[108] followed on 14-15 September 1772.

From this summary of the building history it is evident that Neumann never saw the Vierzehnheiligen church physically complete and that he had nothing at all to do with the programme of decoration. Even the remarkable free-standing Shrine of the Fourteen (*Gnadenaltar*), a virtuoso *rocaille* construction of 1764 that occupies the centre of the nave, is entirely of Küchel's design.[109] The latter also died in 1769, moreover, shortly before the work of J. M. Feichtmayr and Appiani was at last completed. Only the spatial and structural organization of the church can be considered Neumann's, and even that was affected by the location, already determined by existing plans, of the all-important *Gnadenaltar*, well forward in the middle of the nave. But that the essential architectonic qualities of the church as ultimately executed are of Neumann's devising in the mid-forties is established by the existence of a model probably dating from 1744—carved in wood, but with some minor details in cast tin—now in the Fränkisches Heimatmuseum in Bamberg, not to speak of various plans that document the development of Neumann's ideas over the years 1741–44.[110]

The Baroque of Vierzehnheiligen is of a rather special sort, carrying much further the Guarinian planning of the Dientzenhofers—Christoph's in Bohemia even more than that of Johann, who had worked for the Schönborns and also across the Main at Banz—than does the Würzburg Hofkirche. (This had been consecrated only in 1743, at just the time Neumann was becoming seriously involved with

Vierzehnheiligen.) Such planning ideas had certainly influenced J. M. Fischer, who knew the Bohemian work of Christoph Dientzenhofer at first hand, at St. Anna-am-Lehel and at Osterhofen in the late twenties (Fig. 4). Fascinated as Fischer was, on the one hand, by centralized planning and, on the other hand, forced by circumstances to use rectangular plans of the Vorarlberg type for his largest works at Diessen, Fürstenzell, Zwiefalten, and Ottobeuren (Figs. 23, 27, 29), he did not pursue this direction—in any case only tangent to the incipient Rococo even in the twenties—any further.

The architects most deeply involved in the development of Rococo architecture in south Germany were interested in unified space-creation, merging most characteristically the longitudinal demands of their ecclesiastical clients with the centralizing ideals they themselves, like so many others since Brunnelleschi, espoused in ovalized rectangles and rectangularized ovals, as has been discussed in earlier chapters. Such a Dientzenhofer-like succession of oval units as Neumann—with Hildebrandt's encouragement, if not at his suggestion—used in the Hofkirche and expanded to monumental size here was hardly ever approached further south.

The Hofkirche scheme, essentially Baroque in the ultimately Piedmontese tradition of linked ovals, was enlarged and made more complex at Vierzehnheiligen by the conventional addition of transepts,[111] actually not oval but three-quarters circular, and even of a secondary cross-axis, marked by oval elements in the aisles, at the point where the smaller and the larger ovals of the nave meet (Pl. 216). Even more Baroque is the emphatically tectonic handling of the structural elements (Fig. 33). The free-standing columns and their engaged counterparts in the Hofkirche play no important structural role though they do support galleries and provide aesthetically a sort of large-scale plastic ornament, as in several of Fischer's major interiors. Here, at Vierzehnheiligen, however, the piers with their engaged columns circumscribing the eastern half of the first oval of the nave and flanking the sides of the second one, not to speak of their responds at the far side of the crossing, are major structural elements that visibly support, as in medieval architecture, the various vaults above (Pls. 214, 215).

Even so, as so often in Fischer's churches, the Baroque organization controls chiefly below the main cornice. Overhead, thanks to the later decoration—both the large frescoes in nave and choir, characteristically set in scalloped ovalized rectangles,

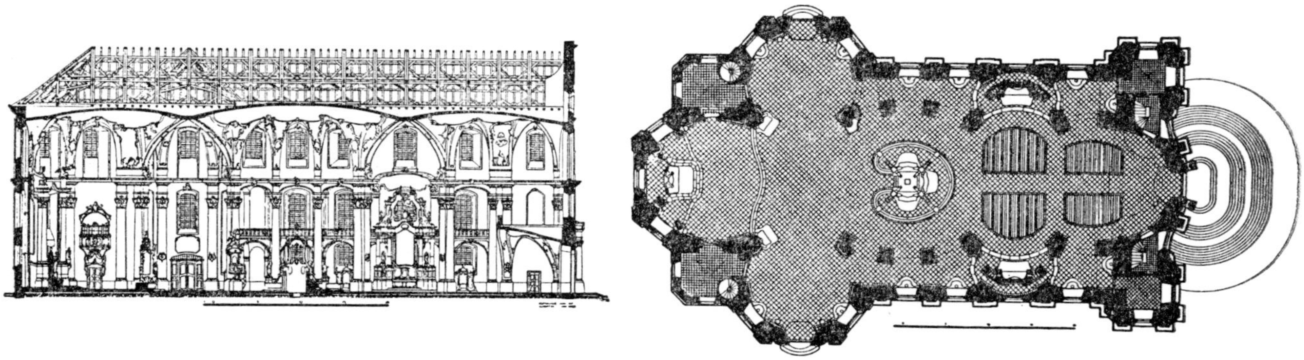

Fig. 33. Vierzehnheiligen, Pilgrimage Church. Section and plan

and the very large and open cartouches at the sides, emphasizing the continuity of surface rather than the structural articulation of the vaulting conoids—the effect is predominantly Rococo. Even at the crossing, where shallow rib-bands, recalling those at Banz, follow the three-dimensional curves of the arrises at the intersections of the nave, choir, and transept vaults, the almost freehand look of the apparently warped surfaces belies the basic regularity and structural logic of the complicated visual pattern (Pl. 216).

Thus the proper comparison of Vierzehnheiligen is with the hybrid Baroque-Rococo churches of Fischer, not with the Baroque, untouched by Rococo ideas, of the early years of the century nor with the great churches, from Steinhausen and Osterhofen in the late twenties to Birnau and Die Wies of the years when Vierzehnheiligen was rising, that best illustrate the earlier and the later Rococo. This is not the whole story of Neumann and the Rococo as, above all, the Weisser Saal, completed in the same year that Neumann arrived at the final plan for Vierzehnheiligen, the Werneck chapel of 1741–45, and the Sala Terrena in the Residenz of 1749–50 make evident. But since Vierzehnheiligen is his most famous church, it is important to see it correctly in relation to the work of his contemporaries.

Käppele, Würzburg

The latest church that Neumann saw brought to completion and decorated before his death is the good-sized pilgrimage chapel known as Käppele, high on the Nikolausberg across the Main from the main portion of Würzburg. At this location a modest chapel had been built in 1653 to house an early seventeenth-century *Vesperbild* (a sculpture of the Pietà) that had been set up here some dozen years earlier.[112] The popularity of this shrine led to the enlargement of the chapel, with the addition of a tower, in 1684 and twice more in 1690 and in 1713. The curious silhouette of Neumann's chapel, which is so conspicuous from across the river, is more Slavic than either Baroque or Rococo, thanks to its various slated domical roofs and onion-topped towers. This is doubtless a survival of a favourite aspect of the earlier conglomerate.

However that may be, it was in 1740 that the Prince-Bishop Friedrich Carl obtained from Neumann the first project for a new and grander edifice. Only after Friedrich Carl's death in 1746 was any action taken. Then, on 15 February 1747, the Capuchins responsible for the services in the chapel were empowered by the new Prince-Bishop, Anselm Franz Graf von Ingelheim, under whom the construction of the Residenz had halted, to erect a small habitation (*Hospiz*) beside the existing chapel. On 5 April the cornerstone was at last laid for Neumann's new edifice which was to rise beside the existing one. The construction was completed by Balthesar Trexler as builder in the following year and, on 6 April 1750, the new Prince-Bishop, Carl Philipp von Greiffenklau, sanctioned the employment of Matthäus Günther, a Bavarian painter from Unterpeissenberg more respected by posterity than most of those (except for Tiepolo) who had worked elsewhere with Neumann and who was Bergmüller's successor as director of the Augsburg Akademie, to execute the frescoes. These were completed in 1752, the year before Neumann's death, and so also must have been the *stucchi*. Who was responsible for the latter is not known. They are almost certainly not by Antonio Bossi, but close rather to the work of the Feichtmayrs and Übelherr who, more than a decade later, were to undertake the decoration of Vierzehnheiligen.

The plan of Käppele is a domed square, with corner piers set diagonally, out of which open four rounded arms (Fig. 34). The apse and the galleried eastern lobe are slightly prolonged and those to north and south somewhat flattened so that the plan a little recalls—though the result does not at all resemble—Borromini's San Carlo alle Quattro Fontane, and even more E. Q. Asam's church at Straubing. More relevant comparisons are with Fischer's small churches from Unering to Sigmertshausen (Figs. 22, 31), but its relative complexity rather contrasts with the plain oval of Fischer's contemporary Anastasiakapelle at Benediktbeuern (Pl. 202). The real prototype, however, was the Schönbornkapelle attached to the Würzburg Dom. Of the construction of that Neumann had early been put in charge at the opening of his career in 1721–24 by Johann Philipp Franz von Schönborn and he had completed it for Friedrich Carl in 1729–36. The original plan, according to which this chapel was begun, had been provided by Maximilian von Welsch after earlier studies by the cathedral architect Georg Bayer and the stuccoer Georg Hennicke; but this was modified by Neumann in 1722, and further 'corrected' by Boffrand in Paris when Neumann visited him there the following year.[113] As brought to completion in the thirties, the Schönbornkapelle—not yet reopened since the war when it was much damaged—offered considerable evidence both of the relatively early date of its original designing and redesigning and of its multiple parentage, while Käppele, for the most part, is a homogeneous work of the mid-century (Pl. 218).

But not, unfortunately, wholly so. The unity of the interior is seriously damaged by the very large, more or less Louis XVI—rather than truly Neoclassic—high altar which was erected, probably from a design by J. G. Winterstein (1743–1806), in 1797–99. This fills the rear of the apse and rises well up into the zone of the

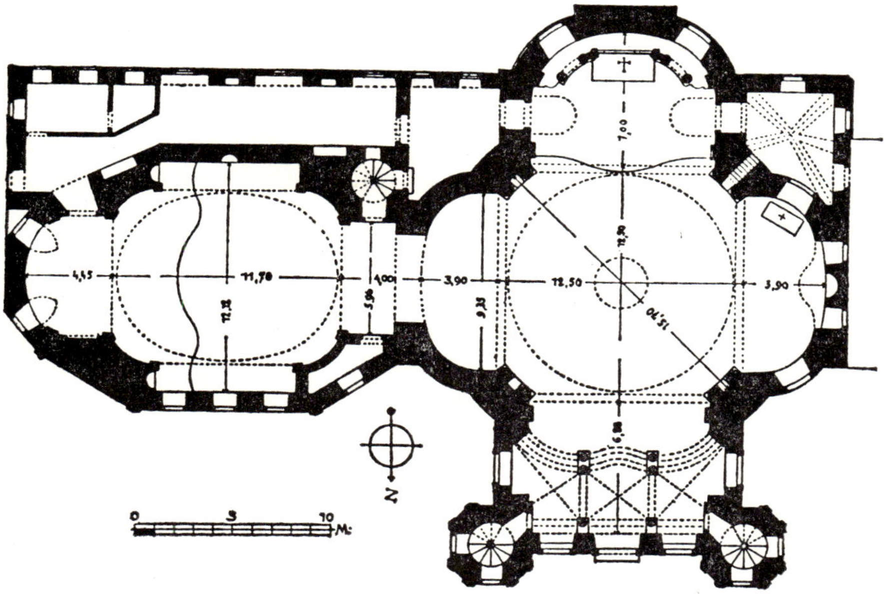

Fig. 34. Würzburg, Käppele. Plan

vaulting. To the left, moreover, a large arch opens out of the northern lobe into an equally Louis XVI secondary chapel on the site of the original seventeenth-century shrine. This was erected in 1778 by Dominikus Ickelsheimer and decorated over the next three years. The pulpit, also, is late, having been designed by the younger Bossi, Materno, in 1800. To appreciate Käppele properly, therefore, one should look towards the right into the southern lobe or towards the ritual west, where a double-S-curved balcony supports an elaborate Rococo organ.

As in so many of Fischer's churches, the Rococo decoration of the vaults here—extended downwards across the *ressauts* by swatches of *rocaille* ornament to pilaster capitals of free design, and complemented by original fittings, such as the prominent organ and the side altars to the right—dominates the interior. The only Baroque elements are the coupled engaged columns at the corners below the pendentives; the continuous full entablature (though the architrave of that is actually pushed upwards by the tops of the window arches); and, perhaps, the rather bold, though unmoulded, square-sectioned rebate that marks, instead of Rococo coving, the intersections of the vaults of the four arms with the pendentives under the central dome. Thus, like Fischer in his contemporary chapel at Benediktbeuern (Pl. 202), an architect who never lost touch with the Baroque produced late in life a High Rococo interior of great richness and considerable distinction.

Neresheim

The situation at Neresheim, the last of Neumann's major works to be built, was entirely different; and the very different result points up Neumann's somewhat unexpected ability to produce the fine Rococo interior of Käppele. In 1745 Abbot Aurelius Braisch of the Benedictine Abbey of Neresheim, near Aalen in northern Württemberg, where Johann Schmuzer had built the library shortly before his death in 1701 and Dominikus Zimmermann had decorated the Festsaal[112] in 1719, started work on the foundations for a new church to the north of the existing Romanesque building.[114]

Two years later Neumann was called in to prepare an estimate of the cost of a new church; this he worked out at 45,791 gulden, without the furnishings. In this year 1747 he also prepared his first project, and further foundations were then laid at the west end by the newly appointed *Palier* Dominikus Wiedemann. Wiedemann came, like Braisch, from Ehingen and was probably Braisch's choice rather than Neumann's since the latter had never employed him elsewhere. A younger man, Leonhard Stahl (1730–74), had been in charge up to this time. On 24 March 1749 Neumann's more developed plans were received by the abbot and on 4 July 1750 the cornerstone was laid. In the last years of Neumann's life, 1750–53, construction proceeded slowly. Six days after his death, on 25 August 1753, Neumann's son Franz Ignaz Michael (1733–85) asked to be appointed as architect to continue the construction according to a plaster model[115] that Neumann had had made. A week later, on 1 September, J. M. Fischer applied for the job, as did also another unknown architect on 10 November.

The building of the church continued to proceed very slowly so that on 2 June 1755, when Braisch was succeeded as abbot by Benedikt Maria Angehr, the outer walls had only reached a height of 40 schuh (about 40 ft.). Two months later, on

1 August, Franz Neumann signed the working drawings for the vaulting. But only in 1758 did the walls finally reach the height of the main cornice. By that time two new men had appeared on the scene: first J. G. Conradi, from 10 May 1757 to 5 February 1758, and then another Wiedemann, Johann Baptist, who finally brought the work to conclusion in 1773.

Doubtless at the suggestion of the last, Angehr decided on 28 June 1759 to substitute plastered wooden vaults for those of masonry that Neumann had originally projected and for which Franz Neumann had provided working drawings six years before. These were completed by 1764. It was five years later still, on 23 November 1769, that Martin Knoller signed the contract for the frescoes which were executed over the next five years.[116] Only then, on 19 May 1775, was a stuccoer, Antonio Giuseppe Sartori, from Sacco in the Italian Tyrol, called in to complete the decoration. But he was dismissed the following January and, on 30 March 1776, a new contract was made with Thomas Scheithauf (1741–1807) from Bavaria who completed his work on 27 September 1778. Next came the furnishing, mostly under Scheithauf's direction. Before that was far advanced the monks moved into the new church in 1782 and began the demolition of the old one. The new church was finally consecrated on 7 September 1792, nearly half a century after Neumann provided his first project.

It is apparent from this summary of the unusually prolonged and complicated story of its construction that only the plan and the structural organization of Neresheim, as at Vierzehnheiligen, represent Neumann's intentions.[117] Comparison makes plain, however, that his final intentions differed quite distinctly (Fig. 35; Pl. 217). This was partly the result of different circumstances—for example, there was no shrine to be centrally placed here in the nave, and the monks would need a deep choir. Yet it was at least equally the result of a shift in his own formal ideals in these years of the late forties, and this shift was in a direction that would also be evident in the next decade in Thumb's planning of St. Gallen and J. M. Fischer's of Rott-am-Inn (Figs. E, 28).

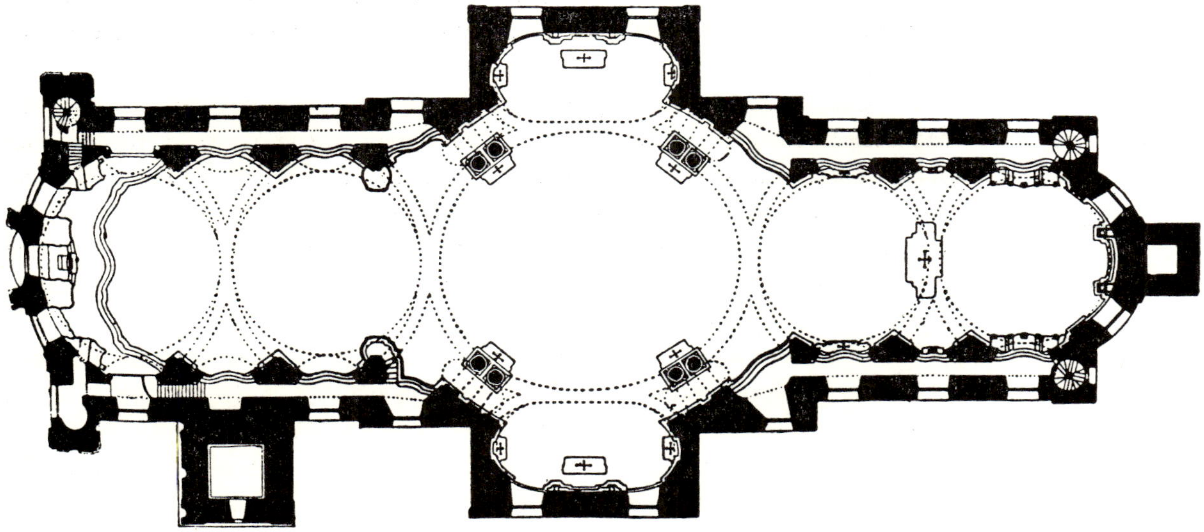

Fig. 35. Neresheim, Abbey Church. Plan

As in these later churches, the Neresheim crossing is a real rotunda, even though it remained a longitudinal oval, not a circle or an octagon. Still more significantly nave and choir are of equal length, each divided into two domed bays, and both are apsidal-ended. The structural organization of this plan, especially in the rotunda, is vigorously tectonic (Pl. 217). The pairs of columns[118] at the corners of this vast space carry the pendentives above with Roman grandeur; while overhead there is throughout that sort of muscular articulation of the elements creating the vaulted spaces that Soufflot, influenced by his study of Gothic vaulting, was to essay in the Paris Panthéon a decade later.

Thus in the architectonic elaboration of the church, as distinguished from its decoration—over which Neumann had no control whatsoever twenty years after his death—there is something not merely anti-Rococo but, in relation to the international architectural scene in the late 1740s, distinctly forward-looking. On the one hand the diagonally-set pilaster clusters that line the sides—almost as tectonic as the columns at the rotunda, but in a different way—look back to the Dientzenhofers, and thus to Guarini, as do the scissors-like patterns of the ribbing between the domed bays of nave, crossing, and choir. In contrast to all this that is High Baroque, on the one hand—and very late Baroque, if not actually proto-Neoclassic—on the other, certain elements are still rather in the tradition of the intervening decades of the Rococo florescence: the transverse oval shapes of the transepts, for instance, and the semi-elliptical curvature of all the arches overhead. This last, however, was *not* Neumann's intention, for his drawings[119] make plain that his masonry domes would have been semi-circular in section, though their intersections would necessarily have been of lower curvature.

The present rather proto-Neoclassic appearance of the interior is far more due to the absence, or at least the drastic shrinkage, of Rococo elements in the *stucchi*, however, than to Neumann's architectural intentions, which continued here to be predominantly Baroque. Scheithauf's handling of the decoration remained as transitional as that which he had just provided in the church at Dischingen, built in 1769–71[120] by Joseph II Dossenberger (1721–85). His stucco-work is in both cases more notable for its dryness and its paucity than for positive Neoclassic flavour.

The frescoes by Knoller—a painter who in 1755 and again over the years 1760–65 had been in contact with Winkelmann and Mengs in Rome—are of much higher quality than Scheithauf's *stucchi*. Moreover, they also maintain, even this late, the eighteenth-century German traditions of fluidity and openness of composition at least as well as do Wenzinger's of ten years earlier at St. Gallen. Even in the figures there is as yet little of the stiffness already characteristic of early Neoclassic painting elsewhere in Europe.

Later vicissitudes at Neresheim, therefore, explain more than Neumann's intentions the very great differences between his two last churches, both of which were designed and begun in the forties. No one is likely to consider the interior of Neresheim as Rococo; while Vierzehnheiligen, at least overhead, is more Rococo than Baroque; and such a smaller late work as Käppele is almost as consistently Rococo perhaps as most of Fischer's interiors or even several of the mature works of the Schmuzers and Peter Thumb, if not of J. G. Fischer. This so very evident contrast between a church of which the decoration was finally completed in the early seventies and one where the decoration began in those years helps to define, somewhat more closely than was attempted in the Introduction, the chronological terminus of the Rococo in the same way that the preceding discussion of a considerable portion of the *œuvres* of both J. M. Fischer and J. B. Neumann has attempted to sketch, at least, its stylistic boundary.

Conclusion

At much the same moment the first major Neoclassical church in Germany began to rise from the designs of P.-M. d'Ixnard (1713–95) at the Abbey of St. Blasien in the Schwarzwald after the burning of the old church there in 1768. D'Ixnard's Pantheon-like project for the church, dated 1771, began to be executed

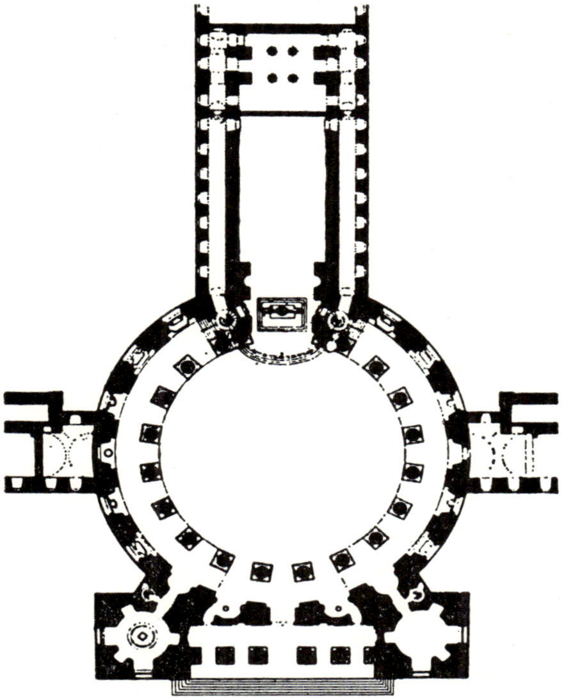

Fig. 36. St. Blasien, Abbey Church. Plan

by Franz Joseph Salzmann the following year and was carried to completion, with Nicolas Pigage's collaboration, over the years 1774–76.[121] Here the interior is, except for the deep and narrow monks' choir to the east, a closed circle 46 m. in diameter beneath a dome[122] of 36 m. span that appears to rest on a ring of twenty free-standing columns (Fig. 36). Dating the end of the Rococo flatly in the early seventies implies, however, a disregard for certain significant biographical facts that indicate that the end was already approaching some years earlier in the late sixties.

South German Rococo architecture was the creation of a group of talented architects and stuccoers utilizing the abilities of a smaller number of generally less able painters. Most of these men were born before 1700. Here, however, their death-dates are more meaningful than their exact birth-dates, which extend over more than thirty years from J. G. Fischer's in 1673 to J. M. Feichtmayr's in 1709.[123] When J. B. Neumann died in 1753 several of the men associated with the earlier stages of the Rococo in Germany were already gone: C. D. Asam died in 1739, Effner and Welsch in 1745, J. G. Fischer in 1747, E. Q. Asam in 1750, Joseph Schmuzer in 1752, and probably also in these years F. J. Roth, the exact date of whose death is not known. Later, in the fifties, the stuccoer and fresco-painter J. B. Zimmermann died in 1758, preceded by two other painters who had been especially active since C. D. Asam's death, Scheffler in 1756 and Spiegler the next year. Among less important men the architects Bagnato and Krämer died also in 1757 and 1758, respectively.

In the early and middle years of the next decade the losses were more serious. The painter Bergmüller died in 1762, but he was succeeded by the rather more accomplished Matthäus Günther, a pupil of C. D. Asam's, not merely as head of the Augsburg Akademie, but also as the leading south German fresco-painter. J. B. Gunetzrhainer, among the architects, died in 1763; and in that year and the next two of the finest stuccoers, Übelherr first and then F. X. Feichtmayr. J. M. Feichtmayr, however, survived to complete the *stucchi* at Vierzehnheiligen, dying only in 1772. The year 1766 saw even greater losses: Dominikus Zimmermann, Peter Thumb, and J. M. Fischer, the first two already retired since 1758, but the last still working at Altomünster. The death of François Cuvilliés followed in 1768.

Thus by 1770 none of the great men survived except the younger Feichtmayr brother; nor did most of them, except perhaps for the elder Feichtmayr and Bossi, leave successors of at all comparable calibre. C. D. Asam, Joseph Schmuzer, J. B. Neumann, J. B. Zimmermann, Peter Thumb, Antonio Bossi, and Cuvilliés all had sons, and F. X. Feichtmayr, both a son and a son-in-law, who practised their elders' professions. In several cases they collaborated on the late works[124] of these elders or carried them to posthumous completion. But none of the artists of the next generation achieved a high personal reputation, nor did most of them ever receive commissions of any great importance.[125] Only in painting did the curve of achievement continue for a while to rise, or at least not notably to sink. Zeiller, living until 1783, Günther, living until 1788, and even Knoller, who died only in 1804, on occasion equalled, if they did not surpass, the men they succeeded. But except for Knoller, their best work was done well before 1770.

As regards architecture, there followed after the losses of the fifties and sixties almost a vacuum of German talent. However, this vacuum was already being filled by Frenchmen[126] who, when they arrived, were already in many cases converts—as most notably d'Ixnard, who reached south-west Germany, probably via Strasbourg, in 1764—to Neoclassicism. More often, perhaps, in the way of Nicholas Pigage (1723–96), at Mannheim, Schwetzingen near Heidelberg, and Benrath outside Düsseldorf,[127] or P.-L.-P. de la Guépière (*c.* 1715–73), at Monrepos near Ludwigsburg and Solitude near Stuttgart,[128] they made the shift gradually and gracefully in the early sixties away from the Rococo after they had—at least in Pigage's case—produced in the previous decade work in the earlier style that was still of the highest international quality. For the most part it had not been the

French who had brought the French mode of the early eighteenth century to Germany;[129] but it was—ironically—to a very considerable extent French architects settling in Germany in the third quarter of the century (as they had not so often done earlier[130]) who played an important part in providing a substitute as that mode began to lose its vitality in the sixties.

German architects of a distinction comparable to the great men of the Rococo decades hardly appeared before the end of the century. And, when they did, the Gillys and Weinbrenner, not to speak of Schinkel and Klenze after 1815, retained no link whatsoever with the Rococo. So the story with which this book has been concerned came, if not abruptly, at least by the late seventies all but totally, to an end. Yet production of Rococo *stucchi* continued in rural areas of Austria and Switzerland for another quarter of a century, and the vestigial use of Rococo painted decoration on house-fronts in Alpine lands has lasted, almost without a break or a programmatic revival, down to the present.

NOTES

NOTES

INTRODUCTION

[pages 1–6]

1. The latest and best general account in English of the Rococo, succinct but remarkably complete, is the article 'Rococo' by Hans Sedlmayr and Hermann Bauer in the *Encyclopedia of World Art*, XII, New York, [1966], cols. 230–269, with extensive international bibliography, cols. 269–274. This article, which had appeared a few years earlier in the Italian edition of the work, is cited henceforth as Sedlmayr-Bauer ('Rococo').
2. See F. Kimball, *Le Style Louis XV*, Paris, 1949, Ch. II. The original edition is *The Creation of the Rococo*, Philadelphia, 1943. As the later French edition has significant additions, the work is cited henceforth as Kimball (*Louis XV*).

2a. Plate 1 is a sort of Frontispiece; it shows the transition from the Baroque after the early introduction of the Rococo in Bavaria.

3. Blenheim is today spelled Blindheim in German, but the event on the Continent is known as the Battle of Höchstädt.
4. Liselotte, as she was known, was the first and the eldest of some half-dozen Wittelsbachs who were major clients for the Rococo over the next half-century. They were rivalled only by the Schönborns (see especially Chapter V, pp. 208–220).
5. Kimball (*Louis XV*), p. 108, Pl. 100–101.
6. See Max Hauttmann, *Der kurbayerische Hofbaumeister Joseph Effner*, Strasbourg, 1913, henceforth cited as Hauttmann (*Effner*).
7. *Op. cit.*, pp. 31–36. Effner was entirely controlled here by Boffrand's advice, however: . . . 'le Sr. Oeffner n'étant chargé que de l'execution de ce que led^{t} Mr. Boffrand aura jugé faisable pour porter le dessein de S.A.E. [Max Emanuel] à sa perfection . . .', p. 34.
8. Kimball (*Louis XV*), pp. 132–133; Pl. 140–147 (de Cotte's designs of 1716–17).
9. See pp. 224–225 below.
10. No interiors of this date survive at Bonn.
11. L. Hager, *Nymphenburg Schloss, Park und Burgen*, Munich, n.d., pp. 30–34, henceforth cited as Hager (*Nymphenburg*).
12. Pichler's life-dates are not known; probably Tyrolean-born, he trained in Paris.
13. Perhaps by the sculptor Willem de Groff (*c.* 1680–1742), Antwerp-born but Paris-trained, who executed the decorative details of the exterior. The ceiling paintings are late work of the Austrian J. A. Gumpp (1654–1719): Hager (*Nymphenburg*), *loc. cit.*
14. See p. 128 below.
15. See H. R. Hitchcock, *German Rococo: The Zimmermann Brothers*, London, 1968, henceforth cited as *Zimmermann*.
16. See Chapter I.
17. Kimball (*Louis XV*), *loc. cit.*
18. See Chapter V.
19. N. Lieb and F. Dieth, *Die Vorarlberger Barockbaumeister*, Munich, [1960], pp. 59–60. However, later citations of Lieb-Dieth (*Vorarlberger*) refer to the 2nd ed., Munich, 1967.
20. See pp. 6–8 below.

20a. See pp. 6–7 below.

21. Kimball (*Louis XV*), pp. 68–86.
22. See *Zimmermann*.
23. See Chapter I.
24. See A. M. Zendralli, *I Magistri grigioni*, Poschiavo, 1958; Lieb-Dieth (*Vorarlberger*).
25. See H. Schnell, 'Die wessobrunner Baumeister und Stuccatoren', in N. Lieb, H. Schnell and J. Stadler, *Wessobrunn* (Grosse Kunstführer Nr. 13), 2nd ed., [Munich, 1960], pp. 13–21, henceforth cited as *Wessobrunn*.
26. See Chapter III.
27. See Chapter III, Note 3.
28. See H. Kreisel, *Das Schloss zu Pommersfelden*, Munich [1953], pp. 15, 17–19, 24, henceforth cited as Kreisel (*Pommersfelden*) and R. Teufel, *Schloss Pommersfelden*, 15th ed., [Munich, 1967], pp. 14–16.
29. According to Dorothee Trepplin, *Bau und Ausstattung des Klosters Ebrach in 17. und 18. Jahrhundert*, Berlin, 1937, p. 77, henceforth cited as Trepplin (*Ebrach*), Schenk had been called from Silesia—presumably Breslau—in 1713; according to Kreisel (*Pommersfelden*), p. 26, he came from Bayreuth. He began receiving payments for work at Schloss Weissenstein in 1714 and was appointed electoral *Hofstuccateur* by Lothar Franz on 23 February 1715. But what is especially significant is the fact that, already in 1713, Lothar Franz had sent Schenk to Vienna, recommending him to his nephew, Friedrich Carl, as 'einen admirablen Kerl', in order 'was neues zu sehen und davon zu profittieren', as he certainly did: Hilde Rosenmayr, 'Die Grotesken des Jonas Drentwett im Belvedere', in *Prinz Eugen und sein Belvedere*, Vienna, 1963, p. 107, henceforth cited as Rosenmayr ('Grotesken'). Maximilian von Welsch, who began the stables opposite the Schloss the next year, was also sent to Vienna by Lothar Franz in 1713.

The design, 'samb Zieratten', was the joint work of Johann Lukas von Hildebrandt (1668–1745), the Genoa-born architect of Prince Eugene and of his own nephew, the Vice-Chancellor of the Empire, Carl Friedrich von Schönborn, and of the painter whom both the prince and the prelate were employing, Jonas Drentwett. It was not followed at all closely by Schenk and Cignani according to the description of the design sent from Vienna that Rosenmayr ('Grotesken'), p. 108, quotes.

30. The fresco by the Italian-trained Swiss J. R. Byss (1660–1738) over the stair-hall at Pommersfelden is at least as large as the one at Ebrach. That fresco is not all that relevant here, however, since it occupied the entire ceiling with no framing except for the *quadratura* architectural elements painted by the Italian G. F. Marchini.
31. Trepplin (*Ebrach*), pp. 68–83.
32. Rosenmayr ('Grotesken'), pp. 100–102, provides some background in Hildebrandt's work of the previous decade for the interiors in the Lower Belvedere and Schloss Schönborn that are here discussed. There is also mention of Jonas Drentwett's older brother, Abraham (1647–1729), who published engravings of ornament inspired by French designs of Bérain and others: *idem, loc. cit.* See also Kimball (*Louis XV*), pp. 62–65, and L. Vanuxem, 'Note sur les contrefaçons de gravures et ornements français au XVIIIe siècle à Augsbourg et sur leur influence en Souabe', *Bulletin de la Société de l'histoire de l'art français*, 1952 [1953], pp. 29–35.
33. B. Grimschitz, *Johann Lukas von Hildebrandt*, Vienna, 1932, pp. 94–95, 69–72, Pls. 109, 110, henceforth cited as Grimschitz (*Hildebrandt*); Rosenmayr ('Grotesken'), pp. 97–98, 109–110; Gerhart Egger, 'Das Konzept der Innenräume des Belvedere', *Prince Eugen und sein Belvedere*, Vienna, 1963, pp. 19–22. Both Rosenmayr and Egger give more attention to the interiors in the Upper Belvedere of the twenties than to the earlier work that is alone relevant here.
34. Grimschitz (*Hildebrandt*), Pl. 62.
35. Kreisel (*Pommersfelden*), Pls. 30–47.
36. Perhaps J. M. A. Temcalla, whom Carl Friedrich later recommended to his brother, Johann Philipp Franz, the Prince-Bishop of Würzburg, in a letter of 18 March 1724: W. Boll, *Die Schönbornkapelle am Würzburger Dom*, Munich, 1925, n. 102, p. 142, henceforth cited as Boll (*Schönbornkapelle*). Temcalla is not mentioned by Rosenmayr ('Grotesken') nor is any other stuccoer's name given.

36a. Friedrich Wolff, *François de Cuvilliés, 1695–1768*, Munich, 1967, henceforth cited as Wolff (*Cuvilliés*), pp. 41–42.

37. Grimschitz (*Hildebrandt*), pp. 75–78, Pls. 75–76.
38. *Op. cit.*, p. 76.
39. There were a certain number of French architects already working in Germany in the first decades of the century: see Note 117 to Chapter V. Of those who came a bit later, L.-R. de La Fosse (*c.* 1666–1726) and J. C. Froimont may be mentioned, especially for their work on the Versailles-like Schloss of the Electors Palatine at Mannheim, though what they were responsible for there does not seem to have had much to do even with the beginnings of the Rococo in Germany: P. de Colombier, *L'Architecture française en Allemagne au XVIIIe siècle*, 2 v., Paris, 1956, 122–131, henceforth cited as de Colombier (*Architecture française*); and L. W. Böhm, *Das Mannheimer Schloss*, Karlsruhe, [1962], pp. 4–7, henceforth cited as Böhm (*Mannheimer*).
40. W. Kalnein, *Das Kurfürstliche Schloss Clemensruhe in Poppelsdorf*, Düsseldorf, [1956], pp. 145–150, henceforth cited as Kalnein (*Poppelsdorf*).
41. Born probably about 1688; P. de Colombier, *L'Art française dans les cours rhénanes*, Paris, [1930], pp. 59–61. Hauberat carried out also the very considerable extensions of the electoral Residenz in Bonn in these years following de Cotte's designs. To quote de Colombier: 'En somme, en 1723, quand Joseph Clément mourut, les projets de Robert de Cotte étaient executés ou fortement amorcés: l'amélioration des extérieurs déjà construits par Riva, la redistribution de l'intérieur du palais et sa décoration, la construction d'appartements particuliers pour l'électeur, ou *buen retiro*, et l'édification de la galerie vers le Rhin.' All the interiors in the palace were destroyed in the great fire of 1777.
42. Kimball (*Louis XV*), Pl. 191.
43. This is least true of the group of stuccoers who worked first at Bonn for Joseph Clemens and then for his nephew and successor, the Elector Clemens August, at Brühl, Bonn, and in Westphalia from the twenties down to the middle of the century. Giuseppe Artario—or Artaria—(1697–1769), who later worked for James Gibbs in England, came like Bossi from Lugano. According to F. Hermanini, *Gli Artisti italiani in Germania*, Rome, n.d., Vol. II, p. 67, the two younger Castelli, Karl Peter and Dominikus, were the sons of Giovanni Pietro, an Italian, though they themselves may well have been German-born. K. P. Castelli moved from Bonn to Würzburg in 1724 at the time of Boffrand's employment there. C. P. Morsegno (d. 1754) was either Italian or Italian-Swiss.
44. See Chapter I, *passim*.
45. See Chapter II, Note 9.

46. See Max Hauttmann, *Geschichte der kirchlichen Baukunst in Bayern/Schwaben und Franken 1550–1780*, 2nd ed., Munich, 1923, p. 41, henceforth cited as Hauttmann (*Geschichte*).
47. See Chapter V, pp. 224–225.
48. Lieb-Dieth (*Vorarlberger*), p. [134].
49. *Op. cit.*, pp. 119, 122.
50. *Op. cit.*, p. 120.
51. For various reasons, but particularly because most of the architects to whom the following chapters are devoted were more concerned with ecclesiastical than with secular architecture, these palace interiors are little discussed in this book; but for several of those by J. B. Neumann, see pp. 211–215 and Pls. 209–213 below. For one in which J. B. Zimmermann provided the stucchi and the frescoes, see *Zimmermann*, Pl. 56.
52. It is evident in some cases that the monasteries hoped to preserve part or all of their existing churches, but were eventually persuaded by the reports of experts who examined the ancient fabrics that drastic rebuilding was necessary for safety's sake. J. M. Fischer, particularly, thus obtained two of his major commissions. See pp. 61, 178.
53. See *Zimmermann*, Pls. 2, 3.
54. See Chapter V.
55. See Chapter I, pp. 51–55.
56. It can only be hypothesis that C. D. Asam actually knew the earlier work of these men at Nymphenburg. Moreover, the priority of the ceilings of the Kammerkapelle and the Electress's Writing Room at Schleissheim to the Asam's *stucchi* at Freising is by no means certain. See p. 41 below.
57. See two late accounts: Sedlmayr-Bauer ('Rococo') and P. Minguet, *Esthétique du rococo*, Paris, 1966, especially his third chapter: 'Le style rococo dans l'architecture en Allemagne du sud au XVIIIe siècle', pp. 123–175, henceforth cited as Minguet (*Esthétique*).
58. Sedlmayr-Bauer ('Rococo'), cols. 235–6.
59. Rather ironically the clearest eighteenth-century descriptions of the Rococo were provided not by its supporters but by its enemies. A rather too simple definition of the Rococo would be 'everything that the Abbé Laugier most disapproved in the work of his contemporaries'.
60. Legeay is a rather mysterious figure, even his birth-date being unknown. Disappointingly, John Harris in the latest article concerned with him, 'Legeay, Piranesi and International Neo-classicism in Rome 1740–1750', in *Essays in the History of Architecture presented to Rudolf Wittkower*, London [1967], p. 190, n. 10, merely remarks of his work for Frederick the Great: 'Because these two buildings [the Hedwigskirche and the Communs of Sanssouci] are not central to the hypothesis put forth in this article, they are not discussed here . . . This will form the substance of a subsequent article'. See, however, de Colombier (*Architecture, française*), I., pp. 60–62. Sedlmayr-Bauer ('Rococo'), col. 232, also note: 'As well as in Paris . . . the Rococo came under fire in Germany, specifically in Saxony', mentioning an attack by Reiffenstein in 1742.
61. The principal accounts are: S. Sitwell, *German Baroque Art*, London, 1927; J. Bourke, *Baroque Churches of Central Europe*, London [1958], 2nd ed., London [1962]; N. Powell, *From Baroque to Rococo*, London, 1959; E. Hempel, *Baroque Architecture and Art in Central Europe*, [Harmondsworth, 1965]. A new translation (with a Preface by Hans Scharoun, surprisingly), Pierre Charpentrat, *Living Architecture: Baroque*, London [1967], devotes pp. 56–92 to German Baroque and Rococo architecture, with excellent photographs and many plans. Sedlmayr-Bauer ('Rococo') list only the poorest of these, Powell's, in their bibliography; but Hempel's volume in the Pelican History of Art had not appeared when they prepared their article. The most useful of these works are henceforth cited as: Bourke (*Churches*) and Hempel (*Central Europe*).
62. Like Gurlitt (*Geschichte*) in 1889, Hempel breaks up the architectural story not only chronologically into four periods but, within each of these, into as many as ten or a dozen geographical sub-sections. Moreover, his overall picture is somewhat affected by the fact that he was writing in Dresden and had readier access to the countries of eastern Europe than to western Germany, Austria and Switzerland.
63. See pp. 4–5.
64. P. Minguet (*Esthétique*), p. 303.
65. See *Zimmermann*, Pls. 14, 42.
66. See below, pp. 211–212.
67. For example: Bernhard Rupprecht, *Die bayerische Rokoko-Kirche*, Kallmünz, 1959, henceforth cited as Rupprecht (*Rokoko-Kirche*) and, much earlier than that, what is still after 45 years perhaps the best brief account of the south German Rococo as manifested in all the arts: Adolf Feulner, *Bayerisches Rokoko*, Munich, [1923], henceforth cited as Feulner (*Bayerisches*). Rupprecht is valuable especially for his iconological approach, neglected in the present work; Feulner, for his splendid plates, including works damaged or destroyed in the last war.

CHAPTER I

[pages 19–21]

1. The painting and sculpture of the Asams are here considered, not for themselves as painting and sculpture, but for the part they play in the *Gesamtkunstwerk*, the total artistic effect of the interiors in which they worked, especially those where they worked together. The exteriors of these buildings also are hardly touched on here, since neither at Weltenburg nor at Rohr can they be considered at all probably to have been executed according to C. D. or E. Q. Asam's designs. The existing literature predominantly approaches the work of the Asams from other angles, as is perhaps not surprising: P. M. Halm, *Die Künstlerfamilie der Asam*, Munich, 1896; Alois Mitternieser, *Herkunft, Aufstieg, und Niedergang der Künstlerfamilie Asam*, Munich, 1936; Erika Hanfstaengl, *Kosmas Damian Asam*, Munich, 1939, henceforth cited as Hanfstaengl (1939); Carl v. Lorch, *Die Brüder Asam, sechzig Bilder*, Königsberg, [1943]; Erika Hanfstaengl, *Die Brüder Cosmas Damian und Egid Quirin Asam* [Munich], 1955, cited as Hanfstaengl (1955); H. L. Zollner, *Die Dioskuren des süddeutschen Barock* (Beiträge zur Geschichte der Stadt Ettlingen, 3), Karlsruhe, [1964].

   As regards their architectural activities the contribution of Ottmar Endres, *Untersuchungen zur Baukunst der Brüder Asam*, Munich, 1934, henceforth cited as Endres (*Untersuchungen*), is only a 51-page dissertation with plans of Rohr and St. Johann-Nepomuk in Munich and a diagram of the ceiling of Freising, but with no plates. Another dissertation, by Carl Lamb, *Zur Entwicklung der malerischen Architektur in Südbayern in der ersten Hälfte des achtzehnten Jahrhunderts*, Würzburg, [1935], henceforth cited as Lamb (*Entwicklung*), is somewhat more important, but quite without illustrations of any sort. The most useful secondary source for information concerning the Asams' work in churches, other than monographs devoted to individual buildings, is Norbert Lieb *Barockkirchen zwischen Donau und Alpen*, Munich [1953], henceforth cited as Lieb (*Barockkirchen*), especially pp. 33–60, 145–154, 166–168.

2. Cornerstone laid at Weltenburg 29 June 1716; consecration 9 October 1718: Lieb (*Barockkirchen*), p. 150. The old church at Mödingen was demolished in 1716; the new church must have been designed and begun that year or the next. The inscription over the choir arch—*Templum hoc ex integro restauratum MCCXIIX*—indicates the date of completion as 1718, and the first mass was celebrated on 7 October 1718, though the consecration was three years later, on 25 July 1721: Julius Schöttl, *Die Klosterkirche Maria-Medingen*, 2nd ed., [Munich, 1961], (Kunstführer Nr. 509), pp. 3–4.

3. It may not be irrelevant that Egid's middle name was Quirin, though nominally he was so christened, on 1 September 1692, not after the abbot but for the saint to whom the Tegernsee church is dedicated. E.Q. was actually born at Tegernsee, where his father was working in 1692, and both brothers grew up there. C.D. was baptized at Benediktbeuern, where he was born, on 28 September 1686. The documented biographical information concerning the Asams is conveniently summarized in Lieb (*Barockkirchen*), pp. 148–149.

4. 'Pier Leone, whose frescoes and altarpieces are now all but forgotten', 'At [Maratti's] death in 1713 his pupils were in full command of the situation': R. Wittkower, *Art and Architecture in Italy, 1600–1750*, 2nd ed., Baltimore, 1966, pp. 222, 323.

5. On 21 July 1721 C. D. Asam signed a receipt for 800 gulden for the frescoes he had executed or was still executing in the Maximilianskapelle and 600 for that over the stair-hall; his work in the chapel was completed by 7 September 1721 though the chapel was not consecrated until three years later: Hanfstaengl (1939), p. 53. J. B. Zimmermann's contract for the stair-hall was dated 20 August 1720.

6. There is a résumé of documented dates for the Asamkirche in Lieb (*Barockkirchen*), p. 151. The cornerstone was laid 16 May 1733, but the evidence suggests that it was planned two or three years before that, presumably just after Egid Quirin brought all the necessary property together in 1729–31. In May 1731 he had asked for the bishop's permission to build and, in August and September, for that of the elector.

7. Cornerstone laid 1 May 1732; roofed 6 August 1733; plaster model of façade 1733; beginning of the execution of stuccos and frescoes of the interior 1734; consecration 1 July 1736. C. D. Asam was given 10,000 gulden for his fresco, half of which he returned, and he reputedly completed the work in eight weeks. There is no documentary evidence that his brother executed the stucco-work; and the responsibility for the design of the exterior, which carries a good deal of Early Rococo stucco decoration, is quite uncertain: Franz Koislmeier, *Maria de Victoria/Ingolstadt*, 3rd ed., Munich, 1961 (Kunstführer Nr. 582), pp. 3–4, henceforth cited as Koislmeier (*Maria de Victoria*). See also pp. 77–81.

8. The remodelling of the interior of St. Emmeram for Abbot Anselm Godin, who had just been raised to princely rank by the emperor, began in 1731. This included the opening up of the choir before the high altar and the vaulting of the nave, as well as

elaborate redecoration in the nave, with much stucco-work and frescoes on walls and vault and modification of the Early Baroque high altar. The date *c.* 1732 usually accepted for C. D. Asam's main fresco is hypothetical since that is only signed 'Cosm. Dam. Asam pinxit', but not dated: B. H. Röttger, *St. Emmeram/Regensburg* (Kunstführer Nr. 573), 2nd ed., [Munich, 1960].

In these years of the early 1730s Cosmas Damian was very busy. In 1730–31 he was working in the nave of the Fürstenfeldbruck abbey church. The chronogram over the organ there reads 1731. The chronogram over the choir-arch at Osterhofen also reads 1731, suggesting that date for the completion of the Asams' decorative work on the vaults (see next note). On 10 July 1732 Cosmas Damian contracted to fresco the chapel of the Schloss at Ettlingen in Baden for 4,000 gulden, giving a receipt on 20 July for a payment of 500 and completing the work by 28 September 1732. In that year he also signed and dated the oil painting that provides the principal altarpiece at Osterhofen. From mid-July to early October 1733 he was executing the frescoes at Wahlstatt (now Legnickie Pole) in Silesia, of which the completion is indicated by a chronogram reading 1733. Hanfstaengl does not attempt to fit the Regensburg frescoes into this rather tight sequence at any particular point but merely states that the decoration of St. Emmeram was completed by 1733: Hanfstaengl (1939), pp. 111, 115, 118, 129, 132; Hanfstaengl (1955), pp. 41, 43, 49.

9. Lieb (*Barockkirchen*), p. 154. The side altars of St. Norbert and St. John Nepomuk by Egid Quirin are dated, respectively, 1734 and 1735. Hanfstaengl (1939), p. 106, assigns the frescoes by Cosmas Damian here to 1730–31, which is very plausible.

10. Magzin probably began the reconstruction of the nave in 1718. Over the choir-arch the date 1720 is included in the stucco decoration: Lieb (*Barockkirchen*), pp. 150–151. See the discussion of the date of execution of this work in relation to Rohr, p. 40 below.

11. See pp. 24ff. and 35ff.

12. A. Bauch, *Die Wallfahrtskirche Mariahilf Freystadt* (Kunstführer Nr. 722), 2nd ed., [Munich, 1963], pp. 3–6. Viscardi had begun the Schloss at Helfenburg for Count Tilly in 1699 and H. G. Asam decorated it with frescoes before its completion in 1707. Asam's contract for the Freystadt frescoes was dated 26 July 1708 and these were finished by that October. The frescoes were cleaned and patched up by Erwin Vogt during the restoration by Hans Mayerhofer in 1954–9. The original cost was some 17,000 gulden; cornerstone laid 26 August 1700; consecration 3 August 1710. (It is curious that Hempel [*Central Europe*], p. 180, attributes the frescoes at Freystadt to C. D. Asam with no mention of the father, who is not even listed in his index.)

In 1716 C. D. Asam provided frescoes and an altarpiece for Count Tilly's chapel at Schloss Günching: Hanfstaengl (1939), p. 33. Of Viscardi's Dreifaltigkeitskirche in Munich, begun in 1711, where Cosmas Damian worked in 1714–15 something will be said later (pp. 23–24). In his vast church at Fürstenfeldbruck, begun in 1701, C. D. Asam worked twice—but only after Viscardi's death—in the choir in 1722–3, and again in the nave in 1730–31. See pp. 49, 69–70 below.

13. The Gesù Nuovo in Naples was begun by the Jesuit Giuseppe Valeriani in 1584. The crossing at Freystadt, as at Sant'Agnese in Rome, is an irregular octagon with the arches in the narrow diagonal bays stilted to carry them up to the same height as the other four arches. The exterior more than the interior justifies the characterization of Freystadt as the most 'imposing' centrally planned church of the Bavarian Baroque: Hauttmann (*Geschichte*), p. 160. Entirely free-standing, as few Italian—and, above all, Roman—churches of the Baroque period ever were, the dome is flanked by four towers over the corners of the main square mass from which the four arms, uneven in length but identically treated, project. It recalls such a major work of the High Renaissance as San Gallo's Madonna di San Biagio outside Montepulciano more than Longhena's seventeenth-century Santa Maria della Salute in Venice. Wittkower, orally, has suggested a relationship to the Baroque sanctuary at Mondoví as it existed before 1700.

14. There exists, curiously enough, a signed portrait dated 1711 by E. Q. Asam. In that year, more expectedly since H. G. Asam had just died at the age of 62, C. D. Asam, before leaving for Italy, completed the altar-painting begun by the former for the church at Helfenburg: Lieb (*Barockkirchen*), p. 148.

15. H. Batzl, *Ensdorf Oberpfalz* (Kunstführer Nr. 724), [Munich, 1960], pp. 3–5. The stucco-work in the 'crossing', however, was executed by Ph. J. Schmutzer and Thomas Aicher at the time C. D. Asam was working here.

16. J. Popp, *Geschichte der hl. Dreifaltigkeitskirche*, Munich, n.d., pp. 11–14.

17. Lieb (*Barockkirchen*), p. 149; Hanfstaengl (1939), p. 31.

18. There are various differences in plan. The very short nave has a three-sided front identical with the apse at the end of the much deeper choir; the transepts are also short but flat-ended; and the crossing is distinctly ovalized along the longitudinal

axis with the pendentives above warped to carry the circular dome.

19. *Abtei- und Pfarrkirche Weltenburg* (Kunstführer Nr. 360), 9th ed. [Munich, 1963], pp. 4–8, henceforth cited as *Weltenburg*. See also Lieb (*Barockkirchen*), pp. 150, 167, where the established facts are conveniently summarized. Lieb, p. 40, gives the dimensions in more detail and doubtless more accurately.

20. *Weltenburg*, pp. 10–11. Even the irregularly oval shape may well be considered High Rococo. It is unclear whether this was established when the church was first built or in the 1730s, as seems on the whole much more likely.

21. This is the ultimate treatment of these cross-axial bays. There is no evidence as to how they were filled, if at all, when the church was first built. Both the large picture, on axis to the south, of the Arrival of the Benedictines with Columbus in the New World and the one to the north—where the pulpit is set—of St. Benedict Preaching were painted by C. D. Asam in 1734–6. He was paid 260 gulden in 1735 and 100 more in 1736. The fresco of the Foundation of the Monastery by Tassilo III on the choir ceiling was completed in 1740 after Cosmas Damian's death by his son Franz in accordance with the original contract: Hanfstaengl (1939), p. 59. The marble-work of the confessionals and the pulpit is by Jakob Kürschner and contemporary with the paintings. The space-framing coronas over Egid Quirin's quadrantal altars, also of this date, completing the circles suggested by the conches of the niches in which they are set, come forward almost to the plane of the main pilaster order, while Bernini's side altars at Sant' Andrea are architectonically framed in the usual Roman manner: *Weltenburg*, pp. 11–13.

The piecemeal fashion in which Weltenburg is discussed in this account is quite inadequate to suggest the total effect of the interior with all its later decorations installed. Many have attempted a description; one of the latest and best is that in Lieb (*Barockkirchen*), pp. 38–46.

22. Giorgioli's marble balustrade before the high altar is dated 1720 and the paving of the church floor 1723; this doubtless represents the *terminus* for the marble-work and also of this campaign of decoration: Lieb (*Barockkirchen*), p. 150. The marble on the walls is unlikely to be of the original period of construction, 1716–18, though such a lining may well have been intended by Cosmas Damian from the first and even executed well before 1721.

23. It is unfortunate that nowadays during services the church is brilliantly illuminated by artificial light, all but completely wiping out the subtle effects intended by Asam and well described by Lamb (*Entwicklung*), p. 21.

24. Lieb (*Barockkirchen*), p. 167, believes the altar was designed by Cosmas Damian—but when?—and only executed by his brother in 1721; Hanfstaengl (1955), p. 16, merely gives the date 1721 as that when 'Egid Quirin hat den Hochaltar aufgestellt'. But see Notes 55 and 56.

25. The palace, begun for Count Mansfeld-Fondi in 1697, was sold to Prince Adam Franz von Schwarzenberg on 12 June 1716 by Mansfeld's daughters after his death in 1715; by that time the western half, which includes the chapel, had been completed: Grimschitz (*Hildebrandt*), p. 33.

26. The stucco-work on the cove at Weltenburg is most probably of 1721—certainly not of 1716–18—and hence no argument, properly speaking, either against or in favour of earlier inspiration from the Vienna prototype, even if the *stucchi* there were previous to 1721 as is extremely unlikely. Even a date later in the 1720s, when Fischer von Erlach was in charge of the completion of the palace for Prince Schwarzenberg in 1720–22, or when his son completed the work in 1723–8, would be hard to accept stylistically. It could, perhaps, be significant that the Marmorgalerie was stuccoed in 1725, the year before Daniel Gran executed the frescoes there; but those *stucchi* seem distinctly less advanced: Hans Sedlmayr, *Johann Bernhard Fischer von Erlach*, Vienna [1956], p. 61. John Harris, orally, would associate the *stucchi* in the chapel in date with those at Schönbrunn that belong to Pacassi's campaign of decoration in the principal apartments beginning in the mid-1760s.

27. Hanfstaengl (1955), p. 16: 'im gleichen Jahr 1721 hat Egid Quirin . . . wohl auch die Stuckierung mit Ausnahme der Vorhalle vollendet' (the 'wohl' admits the absence of exact documentation). Lieb hazards no date for this stucco-work, nor does the anonymous author of *Weltenburg*.

28. Hugo Schnell, *Amberg* (Grosse Kunstführer XVI), 2nd ed., Munich, 1962, p. 18; Hanfstaengl (1939), pp. 34–37; Hanfstaengl (1955), pp. 13–14.

29. Of a vast fresco by C. D. Asam that seems once to have existed in the choir of St. Georg at Amberg, presumably executed in 1718, no trace remains. The Asamesque frescoes on the nave walls and vaults of 1718–23 are by J. A. Müller, who signed the one under the gallery, possibly working together with other Asam pupils: Karl Hof, *Die Stadtpfarrkirche St. Georg in Amberg* (Kunstführer Nr. 615), Munich, 1955, pp. 5–6.

30. Heribert Batzl, *Michelfeld Oberpfalz* (Kunstführer Nr. 747), Munich, 1962, pp. 3–4, henceforth cited as Batzl (*Michelfeld*).
31. The exact dates, extending for only 72 days, were from 29 April to 10 July 1720, the consecration following four days later: Hanfstaengl (1939), p. 48.
32. Batzl (*Michelfeld*), p. 4, believes the stuccoing was begun in 1716 before the Asams were called to Michelfeld. Hanfstaengl (1955), p. 14, says of Egid Quirin only 'dem die Stuckierung der Kirche zugeschrieben wird'; but all the same she describes the total decorative programme at some length with the implication that it is collaborative work by the two brothers.
33. Actually there are no masonry vaults, but a high masonry dome may originally have been intended over the choir. All the ceilings are of plastered wooden construction though of slightly curved section to suggest vaulting.
34. Hanfstaengl (1939), p. 37.
35. Richard Schmidt, *Schloss Ludwigsburg*, Munich, [1954], pp. 8–9, henceforth cited as Schmidt (*Ludwigsburg*).
36. Hanfstaengl (1939), p. 41.
37. Hugo Schnell, *Weingarten* (Grosse Kunstführer V), 2nd ed., [Munich, 1959], pp. 9–17, 31, 37, henceforth cited as Schnell (*Weingarten*). The demolition of the old church began on 14 June 1715 and the cornerstone of the new one was laid on 22 August of the same year. The contract with J. A. Feuchtmayr (1696–1770) for the splendid carved and inlaid choir-stalls is dated 19 January 1720. The altars, designed by Frisoni and executed by Corbellini with sculpture by Diego Carlone over the years 1720–23, were all installed before the consecration on 10 June 1724. The overall cost was 210,969 gulden; toward that cost Frisoni at one point personally loaned the abbey 20,000 gulden: Schmidt (*Ludwigsburg*), p. 9.

    These dimensions give some idea of the exceptional size of Weingarten: length 101.74 m.; breadth of nave 29.32 m.; breadth at transept 44.14 m.; height of nave vaults 28 m.; height of dome about 60 m.: Lieb (*Barockkirchen*), p. 21.

    One may wonder why, as has been noted, Frisoni did not in 1718 employ, or urge the monastery to employ, Carlone or Retti rather than Schmuzer, and L. C. Colomba (1661–1737), Württemberger *Hofmaler* since 1711 and since 1715 in general charge of the fresco decorations at Ludwigsburg, instead of C. D. Asam. This may be the explanation: Schmuzer was already favourably known to ecclesiastical authorities in southern Württemberg (see Chapter IV). The employment of the Ludwigsburg *stuccatori*, on the other hand, had thus far been entirely secular, and Retti continued in these years with such work. C. D. Asam had had, almost exclusively, monastic clients, mostly Benedictines: at Weltenburg, which he had just completed as architect; earlier at Ensdorf; and still in 1718 at Michelfeld, as well as for Maria-Hilf at Amberg. In 1718, moreover, Frisoni was making the arrangements for the decorations in the lately vaulted Hofkapelle at Ludwigsburg which he had begun in 1715. Undoubtedly he planned from the first to employ there Carlone as sculptor and stuccoer, Corbellini for the scagliola, and Colomba as the principal painter, even though the contract with Colomba was not signed until 26 August 1718, two months later than Asam's first Weingarten contract but well before his second and more important one. Actually Carlo Carlone (1696–1775), Diego's younger brother, called from Vienna where he already had a high reputation, provided the largest fresco in the Hofkapelle, that on the dome, as well as the altarpiece. Both Diego Carlone and Colomba—Carlone perhaps until 1721, Colomba until 1720—already working at Ludwigsburg in any case, were thus soon occupied on a project much more important to Frisoni than Weingarten since the work was being done for Duke Eberhard Ludwig: Schmidt (*Ludwigsburg*), pp. 50–51. Later, probably in 1722 or 1723, Diego Carlone did provide the sculptured figures for Frisoni's altars at Weingarten, of which Corbellini executed the scagliola, and Carlo Carlone an altarpiece for the altar of St. Joseph, but only in 1731: Schnell (*Weingarten*), p. 36.
38. The contract called for four principal frescoes on the main vaults; four more on the pendentives at the crossing; and 36 smaller ones, mostly over the side chapels. The work was to be completed within two years and the payment was 7,500 gulden: Schnell (*Weingarten*), p. 26.
39. There seems to be no documentary evidence for the theory that the young E. Q. Asam was employed for a time by Fischer von Erlach in Salzburg and Vienna between his Roman stay and his study with Faistenberger, much less after he left Faistenberger in 1716 when he began very shortly to work at Michelfeld with his brother.
40. As Cosmas Damian's familiarity with the churches of Rome was probably selective, it seems better to cite the most conspicuous rather than the earliest Roman example.
41. Later, of course, work of the mature, and even the late, Rococo found a fairly prominent place here as in most earlier German churches. This was not yet true of Frisoni's high altar—designed in 1718 or 1719 but executed only in 1720–23 by Corbellini and Diego Carlone, as has been noted—that

dominates the east end; but the great organ of 1737–50 at the west end by Josef Gabler and the pulpit of 1762–65 by Fidelis Sporer (1733–1811) are of distinctly High Rococo character: Schnell (*Weingarten*), pp. 36, 41. For that matter, J. A. Feuchtmayr's choir stalls, begun in 1720, approach the Rococo more closely than Schmuzer's stucco-work.

42. Beda Menzel, *Die Abteikirche in Rohr*, Regensburg, 1962, pp. 7–9. The few facts given in Lieb (*Barockkirchen*), pp. 149–167, are more complete than what is supplied by Father Menzel: he even omits the date of consecration!
43. So called because it was generally used by the architects who came from the Austrian Vorarlberg, even though this German variant of the characteristic Counter-Reformation pattern was apparently initiated in the Jesuits' Studienkirche at Dillingen in 1610–17 by Johann Albertal, i.e., Giovanni II Albertalli (d. *c.* 1657), of a Swiss architect-family from the Grigioni, and not by an Austrian Vorarlberger: Lieb-Dieth (*Vorarlberger*), pp. 28–33.
44. As regards the plan and section of Rohr Endres points out interesting dimensional relationships. The three bays of the nave taken together, but without the western half-bay; the height of the crown of the vault; and the total width, including side chapels, are in each case, he says, 18.90 m. The side chapels are half the height of the crossing, which is 20.7 m., and the crossing is nearly square, 12.30 × 12.40 m.: Endres (*Untersuchungen*), pp. 25–26. Lieb (*Barockkirchen*), pp. 33–34, gives what are presumably slightly more accurate figures for these dimensions.
45. See pp. 39–40.
46. Byss, who was born in Solothurn in Switzerland, was called from Prague and appointed electoral *Kabinettmaler* by Lothar Franz in 1713. He completed the ceiling of the stair-hall in 1717 within the *quadratura* balustrade painted by G. F. Marchini (who came from Como) that forms a border above the cornice. Rottmayr reached Pommersfelden only in December 1716, painting the fresco in the Marmorsaal the following year while Byss was at work in the stair-hall: Kreisel (*Pommersfelden*), pp. 25–26, 30.
47. See p. 41.
48. In addition to that in the chapel at Pommersfelden (Pl. 5), which is rather large in relation to the total area of the vault, there is a still earlier though much smaller one in the village church at tiny Kreuzpullach, south of Munich not far from Wolfratshausen. The paintings on the gallery front here are signed and dated J.G.B. 1710, but other information concerning the date and the artists responsible for this very remarkable edifice is lacking. Possibly the initials stand for the painter J. G. Bergmüller (1688–1762), but some surmise they are rather those of the stuccoer J. G. Bader who was responsible at just this point for the *stucchi*—now no longer extant—in the Munich Bürgersaal. The architect must certainly have been from Munich, and Lieb's attribution to Philipp Köglsperger (b. 1673) has not been contested: N. Lieb, *Münchener Barockbaumeister*, Munich, 1941, pp. 104–105, henceforth cited as Lieb (*Münchener*). Construction presumably began not more than a year or two before the inscribed date.
49. Michael Hartig, *Aldersbach* (Kunstführer Nr. 698), [Munich, 1959] pp. 3–6; Lieb (*Barockkirchen*), pp. 46–49, 150–151, 167–168; Hanfstaengl (1955), pp. 29–31. Plates 20–22 in Hanfstaengl are especially valuable for showing details of the stucco-work. The nave is 40.07 × 14.20 m., with side chapels 3.55 m. deep; the choir 24.25 × 10.40 m.; the vault of the nave is 20.62 m. high: Lieb (*Barockkirchen*), p. 47.
50. Much earlier, on 30 September 1715, Asam had been paid 1,500 gulden for the painting over the high altar at Metten. He is also known to have been invited to fresco the vault of the nave and had already executed, some time after 1715, frescoes on the vault and the north wall of the presbytery as well as the oil painting for the Marienaltar. The subject of the fresco was changed eventually by Abbot Roman II Märkl and the commission given to Waräthi: Wilhelm Fink, *Abtei Metten an der Donau* (Kunstführer Nr. 97), 2nd ed., [Munich, 1957], pp. 9–12; Baumeister, 'Zeichnungen des Cosmas Damian Asam', *Das Münster*, vi, 1953, pp. 245ff. Hanfstaengl does not mention C. D. Asam's connexion with Metten nor the drawing in either of her books.
51. C.-C. Dubut (1687–1742) was a Frenchman, but one who came to the Munich court from Berlin, where he had been associated with Andreas Schlüter (*c.* 1660–1714). Hence he was out of touch with the latest Parisian developments; in any case, his original training had been more Italian than Parisian.
52. Neither at Schleissheim nor at Weltenburg can all the individual parts of the decoration that were certainly, or almost certainly, carried out in the early 1720s be precisely dated, though for Schleissheim Hauttmann (*Effner*), especially pp. 117–124, gives considerable information, and the death of Max Emanuel in 1726 provides a *terminus* for the major campaign of decoration there. J. B. Zimmermann's ceiling of the previous year in the library at Benediktbeuern had already given handsome evidence of the early acceptance of French-inspired Rococo decoration in the monastic world.

Various known facts, such as the date 1723–4 of Maria Salome Bornschlögel's execution of the gilding, silvering, and polychroming of her brother's St. George and his companions at Weltenburg and that of the completion of the marble pavement there (see Note 22) suggest a fairly definite term, *c.* 1723, for the second campaign of these years at Weltenburg, including presumably the *stucchi* on the cove. The contract of 20 June 1723 for the redecoration of Freising Cathedral by the Asams seems further to confirm this conclusion; while their work in St. Jakobi at Innsbruck—as has been noted earlier, Egid Quirin was not employed with his brother at Fürstenfeldbruck in 1722–23—which began in 1722, may be thought to push the term of both the brothers' early work in Bavaria back a year further. The date 1723 on Cloudy's statue in the Rohr high-altar composition, for example, need not imply that Egid Quirin himself was still occupied there after the church had been consecrated on 27 September 1722.

53. The interior of Aldersbach was last restored in 1911–14; that of Rohr in 1956; Lieb (*Barockkirchen*), pp. 149, 151. There is no reason to suppose the colours used are not essentially correct although one may suspect that the tones are a bit off. Hanfstaengl (1939), p. 49, gives the date 1913–14 for the restoration of the frescoes at Aldersbach.
54. See Hauttmann (*Effner*), Pl. XIX, C.
55. The distinctly poor fresco of the Glorification of the Immaculata on the apse wall behind, projected doubtless by C. D. Asam but largely executed by his son Franz, dates from as late as 1734–6. The subject refers to Carl Albrecht's revival, specifically in honour of the Immaculate Conception, of the Bavarian knightly Order of St. George in 1729: Hanfstaengl (1939), p. 60. The fresco on the choir ceiling of the Foundation of the Monastery by Tassilo III dates from 1740, as has been noted, just after Cosmas Damian's death and that, like the ceiling painting in the vestibule of 1745, must also be by Franz: Lieb (*Barockkirchen*), p. 150. Lieb's assumption, p. 167, that the altar at Weltenburg was projected, not by Egid Quirin, but by Cosmas Damian, might imply an earlier date than 1721 for its original conception, however. On the other hand, Gerhard Hojer, in a Munich doctoral dissertation of 1967, would date the altar as late as the apse fresco on the basis of iconographic considerations. This might apply to the crowning figure of the Immaculate Virgin, but seems unlikely for the St. George who was, after all, one of the patrons of Weltenburg.
56. The great difference between the two compositions, most probably designed and executed at much the same time, suggests that two different original designers were involved. Stylistic considerations might seem to support the conclusion that the composition at Rohr was the idea of a painter and that at Weltenburg of a sculptor. Other considerations lend weight to the opposite hypothesis: Cosmas Damian, as the architect of Weltenburg, may well have planned the high-altar arrangement there from the first and might, therefore, have provided, either in 1716–18 or more probably later, a design for the sculptural composition his brother eventually executed. That Cosmas Damian never executed frescoes in the fields provided on the vaults at Rohr and is, indeed, represented there only by the large oil painting of the Martyrdom of Sts. Peter and Paul which serves as an altarpiece in the transept—the several altarpieces over the altars in five side chapels, of somewhat inferior Asamesque character, are presumably the work of pupils—flanked by stucco figures of saints of Egid Quirin's design, suggests he was not long, if at all, at Rohr. However, he need not have been present in order to provide his brother with a sketch project for the group of the Assumption or to paint his altarpiece. This is an interesting problem in the history of the figural arts that has little to do with the particular subject of this book.
57. Amigoni's ceilings over the Festsaal and the Viktoriensaal at Schleissheim are several years later, but both were completed well before 1726.
58. The resemblance to the stucco-work in the Schwarzenberg chapel (Pl. 21) is at least as close, but the date of that remains uncertain and is probably much later (see Notes 25 and 26).
59. Except for the employment of the Austrian painter J. A. Gumpp (who died in any case in 1719) for the ceilings in the Pagodenburg, the Munich court around 1720 seems to have had no significant artistic links with Vienna. But see p. 8 above.
60. Rather than Italian or Austrian models, the Versailles chapel, since it also was a palace chapel, may well have provided the prototype for the frescoes on the vault of the Maximilianskapelle at Schleissheim that C. D. Asam executed in 1720–21. Only at Freising, however, can this relationship be traced further today—if, indeed, even there —though Asam's ceiling of 1728 in the chapel at Bruchsal, now destroyed, was evidently of somewhat similar character.
61. The date for the execution of the frescoes is unsupported by documentary evidence but assumed by most scholars to precede shortly the completion of the choir in 1723: Hanfstaengl (1939), pp. 69–70.

62. H. Schnell, *Fürstenfeldbruck* (Kunstführer Nr. 6), 4th ed., [Munich, 1963], pp. 3–4.
63. Josef Weingartner, *Die St. Jakobskirche zu Innsbruck* (Kunstführer Nr. 287), 4th ed., [Munich, 1959], pp. 2–4. For further discussion of Herkomer's and Fischer's work, see also Chapter III.
64. *Op. cit.*, p. 5. A letter of 19 October 1721 from Mörl is in the Hauptstaatsarchiv in Munich; another dated 30 October calls for a visit and preliminary sketches. A note of 20 June 1722 has to do with the execution of the *stucchi* by Egid Quirin, particularly requiring that he should enrich the mouldings already executed—make them 'zierlicher'. The agreement of 8 August 1722 provided for the payment of 3,500 gulden to Cosmas Damian for the frescoes and 2,400 to his brother. The fresco over the organ was begun on 8 July 1722 and the rest were executed between 5 June and 6 August 1723: Hanfstaengl (1939), p. 61.
65. They are described in their pre-war condition in considerable detail by, among others, Hanfstaengl (1939), pp. 62–64.
66. See pp. 23–24.
67. Sigmund Benker, ed., *Der Mariendom zu Freising* (Kunstführer Nr. 200), 4th ed., [Munich, 1961], pp. 2–4. Hanfstaengl (1939), p. 65, and Hanfstaengl (1955), p. 31, give several relevant dates more precisely than Benker. According to the contract of 1723 the scaffoldings were to be down by the Feast of St. James in 1724 and all that remained was to be completed by the Feast of St. Bartholomew. The masons started to cut away the vault ribs in April and went on to remake the Gothic window openings in the clerestory. This preparatory work was well advanced by May, and on 20 August Cosmas Damian began his frescoes and Egid Quirin the stucco-work. But before April, when the structural changes began, the Asams must have given instructions of an essentially architectural character —the contract mentions 'vorliegende Risse' —since no architect's name is mentioned and their own architectural competence was well known to the bishop, thanks to his familiarity with Weltenburg and doubtless also with Rohr. The fresco of the Virgin as Queen of Heaven on the pseudo-dome is dated MDCCXXIV. This and the other frescoes were restored in 1919–21 and the entire interior again in 1951: Ernst Gall, *Handbuch der deutschen Kunstdenkmäler/ Oberbayern*, 3rd. ed., Munich, 1960, henceforth cited as Gall (*Oberbayern*), p. 69.
68. Since 1926 in the Alte Pinakothek, with a copy in its place at Freising.
69. See pp. 6–7.
70. The church built, or rebuilt, in 1719–27 at Ebersmunster in Alsace (Pl. 154) by Peter Thumb is hardly in this context to be considered French; nor was it much more than faintly proto-Rococo.

    Saint-Jacques at Lunéville, like so many northern French edifices of the eighteenth century a hall-church in plan and section, is Rococo only in its ornamental details, presumably to be attributed for the most part to Emanuel Héré de Corny (1705–1763), who completed it in 1747, rather than to Germain Boffrand (1667–1754), who provided the original design, or Romain who undertook the construction, probably in 1730. Hautecoeur attributes the church flatly to Boffrand, with no mention of Romain as executant and no date for the towers; of it he writes, 'un des exemples achevé du style rococo en France': *Histoire de l'architecture classique en France*, III, Paris, 1950, pp. 355, 368. The dates 1730–45 for the church were long ago given by W. H. Ward in *The Architecture of the Renaissance in France*, 2nd ed., London, [1927], pp. 402, 405, without documentation and have been generally, if uncritically, accepted since. The bare name of Romain as the builder and the date 1747 of completion are found, without supporting documentation, in *L'Eglise Saint-Jacques de Lunéville*, [Lunéville], n.d., p. 3.
71. The great length of the Galerie Dorée in the Hôtel de Toulouse in Paris—redecorated, according to Kimball (*Louis XV*), pp. 117–118, in 1718–19 by F. A. Vassé (1681–1736)—was inherited, as was its compartmented ceiling; such interiors as the Grosse Galerie at Pommersfelden (Pl. 6) of 1713–14 or Frisoni's slightly later Spiegelgalerie at Ludwigsburg are at most only proto-Rococo.
72. The latter is signed and dated 1725; the former, as has been noted, is possibly a year or so earlier, and hence almost exactly contemporary with the redecoration of Freising: *Zimmermann*, p. 85.
73. Nothing apparently now remains of this house nor of the small chapel beside it that Cosmas Damian built and decorated. Curiously enough, the house is not mentioned in the pre-war guide by Georg Dehio, *Handbuch der deutschen Kunstdenkmäler*, III, Süddeutschland, 2nd ed., Berlin, 1920, p. 351, under 'Thalkirchen'. Hanfstaengl (1939), pp. 102–103, describes this 'Schlösschen', as she calls the house, and notes that it still survived then with some remains of frescoes on the exterior walls. Cosmas Damian named it 'Maria Einsiedeln' in reference to the brothers' next major commission, which overlapped their work at Freising. The chapel was demolished in the early nineteenth century.
74. Rudolf Henggeler, *Die Abteikirche Einsiedeln* (Kunstführer Nr. 538), 10th ed.,

[Munich, 1964], pp. 2–7, henceforth cited as Henggeler (*Einsiedeln*); Hanspeter Landolt, *Schweizer Barockkirchen*, Frauenfeld, [1948], pp. 65–71, 102–103, 111–112, henceforth cited as Landolt (*Schweizer*).

75. Caspar Moosbrugger has been mentioned earlier as one of the older architects associated with Weingarten—in the estimation of some scholars, at least, the principal designer of that church.
76. Lieb-Dieth (*Vorarlberger*), pp. 103–104.
77. That is the general effect of the colouring. It actually includes green and violet, as well as Venetian red which, in small quantities used with much white, gives an impression of pink. Landolt (*Schweizer*), p. 103, warns that the actual tones are now the result of the restoration of 1910.
78. Landolt (*Schweizer*), p. 134.
79. Hanfstaengl (1939), p. 70–71.
80. Santini is often called Johann Aichel, or Santin-Aichel, by Germans; whether there is a Czech as well as an Italian and a German form of his name I do not know: Heinrich Gerhard Franz, *Bauten und Baumeister der Barockzeit in Böhmen*, Leipzig, [1962], pp. 105, 115–116, henceforth cited as Franz (*Böhmen*). At Kladruby the retention of the elaborately ribbed vaults in the nave and their imitation in Santini's new east end meant there was no space for frescoes overhead except on the pendentives below the lantern of the new dome at the crossing. Most of C. D. Asam's work, therefore, consisted of providing a series of large paintings set in plain rectangular frames occupying the solid wall areas below the clerestory windows in the nave and the choir. There are twelve scenes from the Life of the Virgin in the one and eight illustrations of the verses of the *Te Deum Laudamus* in the other. As to the date of the frescoes—certainly after Santini's death when K. I. Dientzenhofer (1689–1751) was in charge of the work—Hanfstaengl (1939), p. 76, merely says, '1726 war die Innenausstattung vollendet'; others give the date of the frescoes as 1726–27.

   Hanfstaengl (1955), pp. 38–39, dates C. D. Asam's great ceiling fresco devoted to a Miracle of the Blessed Günther, apostle to the Hungarians, in the Prälatensaal of the Benedictine monastery at Břevnov just outside Prague immediately after the work at Kladruby and made mention earlier, (1939), pp. 84–85, of frescoes nearby in Schloss Weisserberg, assigning them to 1728. By that she probably meant the monastery attached to the Weisser-Berg pilgrimage church. Hempel, pp. 88–89, the latest writer to mention the fresco at Břevnov, dates it 1731, giving no authority. The building of the monastery at Břevnov was begun by P. I. Bayer (1684–1733); however, the magnificent church, Svatá Markétá, of 1709–15 is by Christoph Dientzenhofer (1655–1722), and his son Kilian Ignaz was still working at the monastery as late as 1740 when he built the entrance gate: Franz (*Böhmen*), pp. 47, 222, n. 122; Karl M. Swoboda, ed., *Barock in Böhmen*, Munich, [1964], p. 319. Franz gives no date for the Asam fresco, being concerned only with architecture; Erich Hubala in *Barock in Böhmen*, p. 327, when describing the fresco also gives no date. On page 215, however, he hazards 'um 1735' and also notes that 'Asams Anwesenheit auch 1735 und 1736 in Prag dokumentarisch bezeugt ist'. (Incidentally, it is Hubala who gives the dates 1726–27, instead of 1726 alone, for Asam's work at Kladruby.) Despite Hanfstaengl, therefore, it would seem that the fresco at Břevnov is, at the least, not earlier than 1730.

   Stylistically the fresco is ambiguous: the solid oval dome shell is an illusionistic equivalent of the real cove at Weltenburg and seems therefore to look backward; the oval opening to the sky in the centre, on the other hand, so empty and so asymmetrically peopled, looks forward. Whatever its date, the Veronese-like scene of the miracle, with the gorgeous roast peacock coming to life again on the King of Hungary's table at the Blessed Günther's behest, is one of the most attractive of Cosmas Damian's works, in its Venetian luxury almost prefiguring Tiepolo's frescoes of twenty years later at Würzburg.

80a. *Zimmermann*, Pls. 56, 57.
81. Landolt (*Schweizer*), p. 133, mentions only Johann Rueff (*sic*), crediting him personally with the north-west wing of the monastery without specifically noting his supervision of the church. Henggeler (*Einsiedeln*), p. 5, gives Thomas Meyer as the architect or master-mason responsible for completing the church after Moosbrugger's death.
82. Further support for this stylistic conclusion is the similarity between the handling of the diagonal compartments of the vault of the octagon and the ceiling of Dominikus Zimmermann's great church at Günzburg, begun ten years later and generally recognized as fully Rococo above the level of the entablature: *Zimmermann*, Pls. 31, 32.
83. That at Mannheim was signed and dated 1728: Hanfstaengl (1939), p. 90; Böhm (*Mannheimer*), pp. 10, 13–15. In the necessarily drastic restoration after the last war this was replaced by a copy. The *stucchi* also are almost entirely new and do not much suggest, as restored, Egid Quirin's hand, though he is reputed to have worked here.

   On 30 May 1728 the two brothers Asam were paid 100 gulden for a trip to Bruchsal.

The frescoes were painted by Cosmas Damian between June and October that year but Egid Quirin did not in the end work there: Hanfstaengl [1939], p. 92.

Cosmas Damian's newly uncovered frescoes at Gotteszell and the joint work of the brothers in the northerly Johanniskapelle in Freising Cathedral—their work in the southerly Sakramentskapelle is late (see p. 00)—both presumed to be of 1729 or shortly thereafter, need not be considered here either, for what survives is in both cases of minor importance in these years of profuse production: Alexander von Reitzenstein and Herbert Brunner, *Reclams Kunstführer . . .* Bd. I, Bayern, 4th ed., Stuttgart [1961], pp. 279, 307, henceforth cited as Reitzenstein-Brunner (*Bayern*).

84. In 1730, moreover, both brothers—already Freising *Kammerdiener* since 1724—were made electoral *Kammerdiener*. C. D. Asam had received electoral *Hofschutz* as early as 1719 even before he was called in 1720 to work for Max Emanuel at Schleissheim: Lieb (*Barockkirchen*), p. 149. There is no point in attempting to translate these modest distinctions of rank at episcopal and electoral courts.

85. Walter Brugger, *Heilig-Geist-Pfarrkirche München* (Kunstführer Nr. 264), 2nd ed., [Munich, 1962], pp. 3–5.

86. J. G. Fischer ranks higher, of course, and so do several of the architects with whom Cosmas Damian alone had on occasion been associated: notably Frisoni at Weingarten and Effner at Schleissheim. Santini had died before Cosmas Damian came to Kladruby, but he probably worked there with K. I. Dientzenhofer, as he certainly did later at Legnickie Pole (see Note 80).

87. Max Heuwieser, *Damenstift Osterhofen* (Kunstführer Nr. 291), 3rd ed., [Munich, 1959], pp. 3–5; Lieb (*Barockkirchen*), pp. 55–60, 154–168.

88. Sigfried Grän, *Die Klosterkirche St. Anna* (Kunstführer Nr. 42), 2nd ed., [Munich, 1960], pp. 2–5; Felicitas Hagen-Dempf, *Der Zentralbaugedanke bei Johann Michael Fischer*, Munich, [1954], pp. 6–12, henceforth cited as Hagen-Dempf (*Zentralbaugedanke*).

89. Franz (*Böhmen*), pp. 65, 222, n. 119. Smiřice may be entirely by Santini rather than by Dientzenhofer, however, as its star vault certainly suggests: *op. cit.*, pp. 70–71.

90. Photographs of the interior before bombing are preserved in the Klosterarchiv at St. Anna: Grän, *op. cit.*, ill. pp. [4], [6]. The church is now too denuded of decoration to be worth illustrating in its present post-war state.

91. *Angelicum Banz* (Kunstführer Nr. 221), 6th ed., [Munich, 1961], pp. 3–6.

92. Guarini's church of A Divina Providencia in Lisbon, destroyed in 1755, came closest to Banz and Osterhofen.

93. Such curved corners were probably first used by Borromini, as assistant to the aged and feeble Maderno, in the Chapel of the Sacrament at San Paolo fuori le Mura in Rome in the late 1620s: Paolo Portoghesi, *Borromini nella cultura europea*, [Rome, 1964], p. 33, n. 1.

94. Gall (*Oberbayern*), pp. 99–100.

95. For Fischer's earlier work of the twenties, see pp. 177–180.

96. At Rinchnach at the same time Fischer introduced instead a small central dome above the barrel-vault that covers the middle bay of the nave.

97. Hanfstaengl (1939), p. 99.

97a. Wolff (*Cuvilliés*), p. 41.

98. See Hugo Schnell, *Die fürstäbtliche Residenz zu Kempten und ihre Prunkräume*, Munich, 1947, pp. 13–15. Übelherr assisted J. B. Zimmermann in the Munich Residenz in 1730–33.

99. There are also frescoes of these years by Cosmas Damian in the Schloss at Mannheim, where he had frescoed the ceiling of the chapel in 1728, over the stair-hall (signed and dated 1730) and in the Rittersaal. Spendid though these interiors are, and much more successfully restored than the chapel, the frescoes are associated, particularly in the stair-hall, with very handsome Early Rococo *stucchi* by Paul Egell (1691–1752) from Dresden, a pupil of Balthasar Permoser, that are not very closely related to current developments in Bavarian church architecture: Böhm (*Mannheimer*), pp. 10–12.

100. Lieb (*Barockkirchen*), pp. 28–32, 147–148, 166–167. Cosmas Damian's first wife died in 1731 and the following year he married again, this time the daughter of the merchant J. B. Ettenhofer.

101. Hanfstaengl (1939), p. 110. Egid Quirin was, however, later employed to provide the side altar of St. Sebastian (contract of 1 January 1737) for 1,500 gulden and that of Sts. Peter and Paul in 1746, also for 1,500 gulden: Lieb (*Barockkirchen*), p. 148.

102. Altars of St. Norbert and St. John Nepomuk, Osterhofen, 1734 and 1735; altar of St. Sebastian, Fürstenfeldbruck, 1737; high altar, St. Anna-am-Lehel, 1738–39.

103. Hanfstaengl (1939), p. 115. The contract mentions a fee of 4,000 gulden, and a receipt from Asam survives for 500 gulden, dated 20 July 1732, suggesting that the client was very prompt in paying her artists. Stemmermann in Zollner (*Dioskuren*), provides many illustrations of the frescoes, including one excellent colour plate, and a detailed discussion of the iconography.

104. Herbert Brunner, *Reclams Kunstführer*, II, Baden-Württemberg, Pfalz, Saarland, 3rd ed., Stuttgart, [1960], pp. 136, 416, henceforth cited as Brunner (*Baden-Württemberg*).

105. His chapel for the convent of the Elisabethinerinnen in Prague of 1724–5, for example, although only two bays long, has the curved corners and the concave pilaster clusters Fischer used at Osterhofen: Franz (*Böhmen*), p. 147, Pls. 123–124.

106. *Op. cit.*, pp. 147–148, Pls. 125–126. Legnickie Pole was built in 1727–31.

107. Hanfstaengl (1939), p. 122.

108. See Note 8.

109. The possibility, indeed the probability, that his earliest designs for the Asamkirche date from at least as early as 1731, when he first applied to the Bishop of Freising and then to the Elector Carl Albrecht for permission to build, has been mentioned above, p. 20.

110. Bernh. Hermann Röttger, *St. Emmeram zu Regensburg*, (Kunstführer Nr. 573), 2nd ed., [Munich, 1960]. There were originally (that is, surviving from the Romanesque period) ten bays, but those of the choir were longer than those in the nave, particularly the easternmost, preceding the minor apses that flank the Carolingian ambulatory. In the remodelling, which included the opening up of the choir, the decorative bay-length as marked by the pilasters could be made to differ from the true bay-length in the choir aisles since the aisles were here quite closed off except for the hidden entrances to the loges. The choir-bays became longer, at least the first and second from the west did, thanks to the use of double pilasters instead of single ones as in the nave. But because of the location of the new wall closing off the Carolingian east end the last unit is only a half bay deep and the order terminates with a mere quarter-pilaster jammed in beside the ambulatory doors and the wider windows over them that flank the high altar. It is not easy to understand why Egid Quirin chose this solution, but as a result the relationship between the inherited altar-edicule and the present ordering of the choir is distinctly awkward. This is in sharp contrast to Asam's usual practice, as at Weltenburg, Rohr and Osterhofen, of using the same order for a newly built altar-edicule as that on the walls of the choir at the rear of which it is set.

111. These lead into the surviving Carolingian ambulatory, which was walled off when the church was redecorated in the early 1730s.

112. Models were probably not available to Germans in engravings by and after Watteau's paintings and projects for wall decoration, however, until the publication of the *Répertoire de Julienne*, Paris, 1734. All the same, there were even more evident secular echoes of Watteau, Lancret or Pater in the vignetted paintings by B. A. Albrecht on the ceiling of the Grüne Galerie in the Munich Residenz designed by Cuvilliés in 1733. These were unfortunately destroyed in 1944 but are known from photographs.

113. Perhaps the Latin word *laetitia* would serve.

114. Kimball (*Louis XV*), p. 160.

114a. See Wolff (*Cuvilliés*), pp. 37–40, for the work of the thirties in the Residenz.

115. Or might C. D. Asam again, as at Weltenburg, have been just possibly both 'pictor et architectus' here at Santa Maria de Victoria? This is probably not worth serious consideration.

116. For the dating, see Note 7.

117. The Salon d'Hercule was decorated originally by Pierre Lepautre in 1712–14 and the sculpture was provided by Vassé from 1729. The ceiling by François Lemoyne (1688–1757), designed in 1732 and completed in 1736, was 'the first of all those at Versailles to be undivided into compartments. It was, also, in the French decoration of the time. to be the last of the painted vaults of figural subjects': Kimball (*Louis XV*), pp. 88–89, 141. This was, of course, no novelty at all in Bavaria for secular interiors, the first such having been provided by Amigoni in the Badenburg at Nymphenburg nearly fifteen years earlier.

118. Of marquetry in various cabinet woods with inlay of silver, tin, gilded brass, ivory, and mother-of-pearl; each cost 500 gulden: Koislmeier (*Maria de Victoria*), pp. 3, 11.

119. Among others on the left wall: St. Bernard by J. G. Wolcker, 1753; the Blessed Peter Forrerius of Chaumousey by M. Puechner, 1753; St John Nepomuk by Scheffler, 1752; then St. Joseph, to the left of the altar, and St. John the Evangelist, to the right, both by G. B. Goez (1708–1774), 1749. On the right wall: St. Henry (the Emperor Heinrich II) by Wolcker, 1752; St. Stephen (King of Hungary) by Puechner, 1753; St. Wenceslas (Duke of Bohemia) by Scheffler, 1752; and the Blessed Andochius of Autun by Wolcker, 1753: Koislmeier (*Maria de Victoria*), pp. 11–14.

120. First, probably, in the refectory (now the sacristy) at S. Carlo alle Quattro Fontane in Rome, but also in the aisles at St. John Lateran.

121. Koislmeier (*Maria de Victoria*), p. 3. There had been an earlier restoration in 1866.

122. On the outside these windows are similarly linked vertically, but there they are separated by pairs of pilasters of the same order as on the front.

123. For the dating, see p. 20 above. The Asamkirche is, of course, mentioned in every book on German eighteenth-century architecture and in many general works as well.

CHAPTER I

[pages 81–88]

124. See Chapter V.
125. The history of the Würzburg Hofkapelle is conveniently summarized by Hans Reuther, *Die Kirchenbauten Balthasar Neumanns*, Berlin, 1960, pp. 101–103, henceforth cited as Reuther (*Kirchenbauten*).
126. These are both late. That on the left by T. C. Winck is dated 1794; that on the right is by Franz Asam, hence presumably after his father's death in 1739, but undated: Lieb (*Barockkirchen*), p. 168.
127. In 1736 the Elector Carl Albrecht presented some grey marble from the Munich Residenz for door-frames in the church: *idem*, p. 151.
128. Such photographs as the one from which Plate 74 was made, of which several were published by Hermann Popp in *Die Architektur der Barock- und Rokokozeit in Deutschland und der Schweiz*, Stuttgart, 1913, p. 54, suggest how much lighter and cleaner the church may have been before World War I. The illustrations of the Asamkirche provided by Werner Hager, *Die Bauten des deutschen Barocks, 1690–1770*, Jena, [1942], especially that on p. 127, all presumably made after the restoration of 1941–42, reinforce this impression. In both cases, however, allowance must be made for the photographer's presumptive use of very long exposures or skilful artificial lighting.
129. See *Zimmermann*, pp. 59–62.
129a. *Op. cit.*, Pls. 29–34.
130. See Chapter V, pp. 180, 183–188.
131. The façade of the church was reputedly erected in 1735, the year after the raw fabric of the church was blessed on 24 December 1734. Though the final design had presumably been established by that date, it must have been a good many years in construction, for as late as 13 August 1740 Egid Quirin was asking the Munich City Council for 'einige weisse Steine zum Kirchenantritt', usually interpreted to mean for the façade. One may assume, however, that it was complete by 1746 when the church was consecrated.

    Although Egid Quirin acquired the house next door to remodel for his own use in the spring of 1733, there is no evidence as to the date of the external *stucchi* on the façade, which could have been carried out very much later. The priests' house to the left of the church was rebuilt in 1771–3 and is not of Egid Quirin's design: Lieb (*Barockkirchen*), p. 151.
132. Two drawings by Egid Quirin published by Hanfstaengl (1955), Pls. 2 and 58, both in the Stattliche Graphische Sammlung in Munich, add little to his achievement as a specifically Rococo designer. One, undated, is of an oval edifice that resembles Weltenburg, curiously enough, more than anything for which he was personally responsible as architect; the other, of 1740, was for the high altar at Maria Dorfen which was executed by another hand in 1748–9: *op. cit.*, p. 47. This resembles most closely the one at Osterhofen of ten years earlier (Pl. 58).
133. Hanfstaengl (1955), pp. 59–60, Pls. 56, 76–80. The plan resembles that of J. B. Neumaun's Käppele (Fig. 34).

    E. Q. Asam's quite incidental work in the Jesuit church in Mannheim, begun only in 1749 the year before his death in that town, was destroyed in the war; *loc. cit.*
134. Reitzenstein-Brunner (*Bayern*), pp. 287–289.
135. See Chapter III, Note 3.

CHAPTER II

[pages 89–90]

1. See Chapter V, pp. 175–208.

    There are still more South-German Fischers of varying degrees of prominence that may, at least, be mentioned here: in the eighteenth century J. M. Fischer (d. 1801) —called 'of Dillingen'—who was a sculptor; then Karl von Fischer (1782–1820), who built so much in Munich for King Max I Joseph at the opening of the nineteenth century; and finally, very much later, Theodor Fischer (1862–1938), the architect of the Ulm Garnisonkirche and the teacher of Bonatz, Gropius, and Oud. More relevant here, however, are Franz Karl, Johann Georg's not very active son and successor, and the much more productive stuccoer Josef Fischer, called 'of Faulenbach' (near Füssen) to distinguish him from Johann Georg. Fischer von Erlach also had an architect son, Joseph Emanuel (1693–1742), who completed several of his major works.
2. See Note 61 to the Introduction.
3. Hempel (*Central Europe*), p. 103.
4. Bourke (*Churches*), pp. 246–247.
5. *Op. cit.*, p. 163.
6. Since 1898 called Markt Oberdorf and since 1953 Marktoberdorf to distinguish it from four other Oberdorfs, several nearby, and henceforth so written in this work. The Augsburg Hochstift owned considerable Marktoberdorf property from the fourteenth century, so that at least as early as the fifteenth century the Prince-Bishops of Augsburg had a Schloss here.

7. The latest and most complete account of the life and work of J. G. Fischer is by Martin Dömling, 'Johann Georg Fischer (1673–1747)' in *Lebensbilder aus dem bayrischen Schwaben*, Band 8, Munich, 1961, pp. 256–276, henceforth cited as Dömling ('J. G. Fischer'). The article is without illustrations except for Fischer's portrait, now hanging in the Marktoberdorf Rathaus, and a facsimile of his signature as 'Baumaister'; but it includes a bibliography, p. 276, and a list of works, beginning with his activity as assistant to his uncle Johann Jakob Herkomer (1648–1717). A later article by Wilhelm Neu, 'Beiträge zum Werk des Füssener Baumeisters J.G.F.', *Das Münster*, October 1965, pp. 345–350, henceforth cited as Neu ('Beiträge'), adds quite a few minor works, several of them illustrated, to Dömling's list. Most of Neu's attributions are based on documents he has found in the Hauptstaatsarchiv in Munich, Hochstift Augsburg, Neuburger Abgabe, henceforth referred to, in the way he does, as HANA. My own list, nearly twice as long as Dömling's, is given on p. 125.
8. Hugo Schnell, *Bertoldshofen* (Kunstführer Nr. 647), [Munich, 1957], p. 3, henceforth cited as Schnell (*Bertoldshofen*); Michael Petzet, *Landkreis Marktoberdorf*, Munich, [1966], pp. 33–34, henceforth cited as Petzet (*Marktoberdorf*).
9. According to Dömling ('J. G. Fischer'), p. 258, Fischer had in his youth joined his mother's brother J. J. Herkomer in Italy after his pupilage with the Marktoberdorf master-mason Augustin Stickl. This last is documented for 6 June 1694, though it probably began a year earlier, and ended on 18 May 1695.
10. Bertoldshofen has, in effect, five domes; the Chiesa del Santo seven—or eight, counting that over the later chapel behind the domed choir. The Paduan church was built 1231–1308: John White, *Art and Architecture in Italy, 1250–1440*, [Harmondsworth, 1966], pp. 17–18, with plan, Pl. 7.
11. See pp. 102–108.
12. See pp. 108–123.
13. Dömling ('J. G. Fischer'), pp. 256–262.
14. The Zimmermanns' father and stepfather were, however, both Wessobrunn stuccoers, though minor ones, and J. M. Fischer's father was a provincial master-mason. More important for Fischer was the professional position in Munich of his father-in-law, Johann Mayr. See Chapter V, p. 177.
15. See Chapter III, pp. 127–128.
16. See Chapter IV, pp. 152–153.
17. Hildebrand Dussler, *Der allgäuer Barockbaumeister Johann Jakob Herkommer*, Kempten, 1956. Herkomer's birth-date is sometimes given as 1652.
18. Michael Petzet, *Stadt und Landkreis Füssen*, Munich [1960], pp. 151–153, henceforth cited as Petzet (*Füssen*).
19. *Op. cit.*, pp. 7–44.
20. Füssen, like Marktoberdorf, was closely linked with Augsburg. From the fourteenth century the bishops of Augsburg had possessed the castle there, ruled the city as feudal lords, and exercised some authority over the monastery of St. Mang, founded by St. Magnus in the eighth century.
21. Norbert Lieb, 'Die barocke Architektur und Bilderwelt des Stifts Ottobeuren', *Ottobeuren Festschrift zur 1200-Jahrfeier der Abtei*, Augsburg, 1964, pp. 310–338.
22. Lieb (*Barockkirchen*), p. 146.
23. See Chapter I, pp. 49–51.
24. Petzet (*Füssen*), p. 7.
25. That in the monks' choir is signed and dated 1709: *op. cit.*, p. 10.
26. Among those who assisted J. J. Herkomer with the *stucchi* may be noted a nephew or great-nephew with the same name, less confusingly referred to as 'Hans'; Johann Bader; Thomas Seitz; and Paul Geyr: they all worked later with J. G. Fischer, *op. cit.*, p. 13.
26a. For further information concerning Hermann, see Note 69.
27. The following can be specifically cited: marble cupboards in the choir, installed 1719; antependium of the high altar, 1719–20, of which the mensa only was in place at the time of the consecration in 1717; Brüderschaftsaltar and altars in the eastern and western side chapels, completed in 1723; Heilig-Grab-Kapelle, finished 1735, with fresco dated 1734 by Hermann and *stucchi* of the same years by Josef Fischer: *op. cit.*, pp. 13–25.
28. The buildings were all roofed by the time of Herkomer's death in 1717, but the interiors were carried out, presumably mostly from his uncle's designs, by J. G. Fischer, except for the Festsaal and main stair-hall, for which Andrea Maini was brought over from Ottobeuren in 1721–23. There are nearly 150 rooms, many of them with frescoes by Hermann. Most have some stucco decoration, in certain sections executed as late as 1764: *op. cit.*, pp. 27–44. Dömling ('J. G. Fischer'), p. 276, believes a campaign of remodelling undertaken in 1749 was based posthumously on Fischer's designs. For the handsome library, see Note 32.
29. So called from the painting over the high altar of the Nativity, which naturally includes a manger (Krippe). The church was built for the Franciscans. Construction began on 8 August 1717 and was almost certainly not complete—as Dömling, p. 274, supposes—when Herkomer died on 27 October. The fresco on the choir ceiling by

Joseph Obermiller is dated 1719, as also presumably the *stucchi* by Bader, Seitz and Geyr, who had all been assisting Herkomer earlier in St. Mang. The scagliola high altar has been attributed to Dominikus Zimmermann: Petzet (*Füssen*), pp. 50–53. Zimmermann married in 1708 in Füssen, but by 1716 he had settled further down the Lech at Landsberg so that there is not much basis for the attribution.

30. Though the church at Fultenbach is long gone, Herkomer's plan, preserved in the Klosterarchiv at Ottobeuren, indicates that the crossing there had diagonal corners, thus approaching the quadrantal flanking of the choir-arch in the Krippkirche: *Barock am Bodensee/Architektur*, Bregenz, 1962, henceforth cited as *Barock am Bodensee*, No. 108 and Pl. 16.
31. See p. 64.
32. St. Sebastian was built in 1507 and retains its Gothic choir with *stucchi* of 1687 by Johann Schmuzer and frescoes of the following year by Herkomer. In 1701, at the same time as he began St. Mang, Herkomer provided plans for a new church. As early as 1721 a new nave was begun by Fischer, possibly following his uncle's design of twenty years earlier. This was only consecrated, however, at the same time as the Feldkirche in 1725 and by the same bishop. At St. Sebastian, as in the Krippkirche, the eastern corners of the nave curve inward to meet the arch at the entrance to the narrow choir. The nave received its decoration twenty years later when Josef Fischer provided the *stucchi* and Bartholomäus Stapf the frescoes in 1745 and 1746: Petzet (*Füssen*), pp. 54–56.

Considered as a whole, with the later decoration, St. Sebastian is not as relevant at this point in the story as the Feldkirche with its four quadrants in the nave (see Fig. 10). However, if the handling of the ceiling overhead is of the early twenties and not of the forties, that does deserve particular comment. In the library of the abbey of St. Mang (Pl. 79)—a curious spatial composition of oval plan extending up through the equivalent of four storys—Herkomer had raised a small oval dome over the centre of the flat ceiling of the third level above the gallery. At St. Sebastian the ceiling is similarly divided, but the lower section is a deep cove and the upper a broader domical area than in the St. Mang library.

Unfortunately St. Sebastian is at present—summer 1967—in restoration and inaccessible, so that exactly how this cusped shape is adapted to the rectangular west end of the nave is not clear to me. This ceiling, if designed either by Herkomer or by Fischer and not a later emendation, is a step in the direction of Fischer's cusped dome over the crossing at Berholdshofen (Pl. 91).

33. Petzet, *op. cit.*, pp. 57–59; not in Dömling's list of Fischer's work. This chapel-like edifice opposite a cemetery is easily confused with St. Sebastian, which is associated with a different cemetery, the Alter Friedhof laid out in 1528.
34. Friedrich Piel, *Handbuch der deutschen Kunstdenkmäler/Baden-Württemberg*, [Munich], 1964, p. 250, henceforth cited as Piel (*Baden-Württemberg*); Dömling ('J. G. Fischer'), p. 274. Though the chapel was not consecrated until 1723 its construction must precede that of the nave of St. Sebastian. It is, of course, possible that Herkomer as at St. Sebastian had prepared plans for this chapel which Fischer used.
35. Piel (*Baden-Württemberg*), p. 250; Brunner (*Baden-Württemberg*), p. 269.
36. Piel, *op. cit.*, p. 550; Brunner, *op. cit.*, p. 639.
37. The formula was still in use by J. C. Bagnato almost a generation later in his churches at Altshausen, begun in 1748, and Unterwachingen, begun in 1754.
38. This is all but identical except that the rear half fits exactly the curve of the apse, with pendentives only at the western corners: Neu ('Beiträge'), p. 347–348. The ceiling fresco is by Obermiller, who painted that in the choir of the Krippkirche. The one here, of the Lamb of God, is now largely restoration of 1958–59. Petzet (*Füssen*), pp. 149–150, does not mention Fischer as the designer of the Rückholz choir, but the attribution is highly plausible and generally accepted.
39. Neu ('Beiträge'), pp. 347–348. Petzet, *op. cit.*, pp. 150–151, does not mention Fischer in describing the Rückholz Pfarrhof (or Propstei) which he calls a 'Schlösschen' because of its size and decoration.
40. Tilmann Breuer, *Stadt und Stadtkreis Kaufbeuren*, Munich, [1960], pp. 76–77, henceforth cited as Breuer (*Kaufbeuren*).
41. Usually called either the Zeil'sches or the Wurzach'sches Schloss: Brunner (*Baden-Württemberg*), p. 269; Piel (*Baden-Württemberg*), p. 250.
42. Piel, *loc. cit.*, speaks of the decoration as the work of 'eine grosse Zahl von Künstlern und Handwerkern, under denen J. M. Feichtmayr' (1709–72) and attributes the stuccoed Sibyls in the stair-hall to his workshop. Brunner, *loc. cit.*, attributes these to J. A. Feuchtmayr (1696–1770).
43. An original fifteenth-century Schloss had been rebuilt in the early sixteenth century and enlarged in 1598–99. In 1722 the Prince-Bishop of Augsburg, Sigmund Alexander von Neuburg, had this demolished, and on 27 April 1723 the accounts indicate

that the sum of 2,200 gulden was allotted initially for the construction by Fischer of a new building. Further detailed accounts, which survive, cover the story of its completion at a total cost of 17,813 gulden. The enlargement of 1761–62 was undertaken by Franz Kleinhans (1699–1776), a former assistant of Fischer's, for Prince-Bishop Joseph Leonard Graf von Hessen-Darmstadt and cost 3,993 gulden: Petzet (*Marktoberdorf*), pp. 145–152.

44. It is generally assumed that construction of the new church started later in that year or early in the next and was completed by 1723 even though it was not consecrated until 1725: Dömling ('J. G. Fischer'), pp. 265, 274; Sigfrid Hofmann, *Bernbeuren Pfarrkirche St. Nikolaus*, [Neuburg (Donau)], n.d., p. 3; Gall (*Oberbayern*), p. 273.

Hugo Schnell, *Bernbeuren in Allgäu* (Kunstführer Nr. 216), [Munich, 1937], has long been out of print and some of its information corrected by later researches. For instance, Neu ('Beiträge'), p. 345, n. 6 and n. 7, provides evidence for Fischer's responsibility for the design of the church deriving from documents (HANA Nos. 1419/I and 1313/II) in the Hauptstaatsarchiv, Munich. These also establish Johann Baltasar Suiter (or Suitar) from Dillingen as the stuccoer, not Josef Fischer to whom others have attributed the *stucchi*. The latter appears in the documents only later in 1735. A drawing for St. Nikolaus survives in the Plansammlung of the Munich Hauptstaatsarchiv (No. 5846): Neu, *op. cit.*, p. 349, n. 11. The church was restored in 1936.

45. Weissensee, Schöllang, Rosshaupten, Reichenbach, Echerschwang and Altstädten are none of them listed by Dömling ('J. G. Fischer'), pp. 274–275. Neu, however, found in the documents in the Munich Hauptstaatsarchiv evidence for Fischer's connexion with Reichenbach (HANA 6017) and also with Rosshaupten (HANA 9643): ('Beiträge'), p. 340, n. 14, and p. 349, n. 11. He also notes, pp. 347–348, that Weissensee was consecrated in October 1725 at the same time and by the same bishop as Fischer's new nave of St. Sebastian and the Feldkirche in Füssen as well as his churches at Rieden and Bernbeuren, but that is hardly serious evidence of his intervention there. For Echerschwang Neu, p. 348, n. 24, found mention of Fischer's name in the Bernbeuren parish records, however. For the enlargement of the Rieden parish church a drawing (No. 5884) survives in the Plansammlung of the Munich Hauptstaatsarchiv.

46. There are projects for this by Fischer of 1724 and of 1736. The builder, a Marktoberdorf master-mason, was doubtless influenced by these existing designs. The tower was added in 1742: Dömling ('J. G. Fischer'), p. 275.

47. The project for Leeder (HANA 12013–12015) was offered in competition with one by Joseph Schmuzer. The church, as built in 1740 by Stefan Socher, follows Fischer's plans more closely than Schmuzer's. Fischer was paid 20 gulden for his unused plans: *loc. cit.*; Neu ('Beiträge'), pp. 345–346, n. 11.

48. [Alfred Randelzofer], *Die katholische Pfarrkirche St. Stephan in Rettenberg*, [Ottobeuren, c. 1965], pp. 2–5.

49. *Ibid.*, pp. 8–15.

50. *Zimmermann*, Pl. 21.

51. Neither Brunner (*Baden-Württemberg*) nor Dömling ('J. G. Fischer') mention Buchloe at all and E. Gall in *Handbuch der deutschen Kunstdenkmäler / Östliches Schwaben*, Munich, 1954, p. 153, henceforth cited as Gall (*Östliches Schwaben*), has very little to say about it. T. Breuer, *Stadt und Landkreis Kaufbeuren*, Munich, [1960], pp. 72–76, henceforth cited as Breuer (*Kaufbeuren*), also gives no architect's name, but records the date on the choir-arch, MDCCXXX, and illustrates the plan, p. 73. Neu ('Beiträge'), pp. 346–347, n. 15, reports finding in the Hauptstaatsarchiv in Munich a descriptive estimate for this work in a letter of 1729 (HANA 5838) from the parish priest to the Prince-Bishop of Augsburg. Apparently 200 gulden was all that was then available and the work was carried out only in much simplified form in the following summer of 1730.

52. Illustrated by Neu ('Beiträge'), p. 348.

53. Breuer (*Kaufbeuren*), p. 73, suggests Johann Georg Lederer from Augsburg as the author of the ceiling paintings and a date of about 1730. The advocation to the *Göttliche Mutter* explains the largely Marian iconography. No stuccoer has been even tentatively identified.

54. Schnell (*Bertoldshofen*), pp. 3–5; Petzet (*Marktoberdorf*), pp. 33–47. Petzet's account is later and rather more detailed. It also provides the plan (p. 35) and two elevations (pp. 38–39).

55. In southern Germany it seems not improper to call this modification of the Roman window Zimmermanian; actually Michelangelo had introduced it in Santa Maria degli Angeli.

56. There, however, oval openings elaborate the window pattern below the central section and between the lobes at the sides.

57. Mentioned in Thieme-Becker but not confirmed by Hager (*Nymphenburg*).

58. *Zimmermann*, p. 91; Pl. 58.

59. These are, of course, not domes structurally but merely plastered shells constructed

of timber. Each, moreover, has an open oculus at the top, surrounded by a balustrade and revealing a glimpse of a higher plastered surface just under the peaks of the roofs. The non-structural character of all the 'vaulting' is most apparent in the nearly flat-ceiled nave and also explains the statical peculiarity of the central dome above its lower-pitched cove. At Padua the domes as seen from the outside are, like those of St. Mark's in Venice, of timber construction; but there these fifteenth-century emendations of the thirteenth-century church are emphasized as picturesque features of the silhouette instead of being hidden, as here, beneath gabled roofs and therefore suggest at least the masonry vaults below them.

60. *Zimmermann*, Pl. 11.
61. Dömling ('J. G. Fischer'), p. 276, accepts the Leuterschach attribution; for Waltenhofen a document survives, HANA 2345: Neu ('Beiträge'), p. 349, n. 21.
62. A fifteenth-century wooden building erected when the land came into the possession of the Benedictines of St. Mang in Füssen was replaced by a residence for the prior, hence its superiority to ordinary priests' houses in villages: Petzet (*Füssen*), pp. 150–151. As has been noted, Petzet does not assign the Pfarrhof to Fischer.
63. The tower was renewed in 1732. The stucco work of 1741 in the nave is perhaps by Josef Fischer: *op. cit.*, pp. 149–150. Petzet does not mention J. G. Fischer in connexion with the nave, nor even with the choir of 1719, though he does note the latter's close resemblance to Herkomer's work.
64. Petzet (*Marktoberdorf*), pp. 131–143, including sections, pp. 133–34, and plan, p. 135. The original contract at 2,817 gulden calling for an edifice of 112 by 70 schuh was with the master-masons, the local Halbritter and Bienz from Rieden, and with the local master-carpenter Filser, all three of whom had been working with Fischer at Bertoldshofen. That the architect was really Fischer, who is not mentioned in this contract, is known from a letter of 1739 written by the priest at Leeder in which he states that Fischer went over his estimate for the Marktoberdorf church by 2,000 gulden: Neu ('Beiträge'), pp. 345–346. By the time of the consecration, 28 September 1738, the church had in fact cost some 15,000 gulden. The contracts for the stucco-work and the frescoes are dated 7 February 1733 and the remodelling and redecoration of the choir followed in 1734. The church was restored in 1936–38. Petzet's account supersedes that of Georg Lill, *Katholische Pfarrkirche Markt Oberdorf* (Kunstführer Nr. 468), [Munich, 1940], which has long been out of print.
65. Zimmermann, Pl. 12.
66. Petzet (*Marktoberdorf*), p. 137, states that the original colouring—green, yellow, pink, violet and blue on a white ground—was 'nur conserviert', which doubtless explains this superiority.
67. *Ibid.*, pp. 136–137, gives the programme in detail. The largest fresco is devoted to Constantine's Victory over Maxentius.
68. Reitzenstein-Brunner (*Bayern*), p. 471; Gall (*Östliches Schwaben*), p. 221; E. Gall, *Handbuch der deutschen Kunstdenkmäler/ Westliches Schwaben*, Munich, 1956, p. 144, henceforth cited as Gall (*Westliches Schwaben*).
69. See p. 94 and Pl. 80.
70. Schnell (*Kempten*), p. 15. F. G. Hermann was the son of the Kempten painter Franz Benedikt Hermann. The Benedictines of St. Mang in Füssen, about 1710, gave the younger Hermann 900 gulden so that he could study in Venice with G. A. Pellegrini (1675–1741). In 1713, in Rome, he received the same prize from the Accademia di S. Luca that C. D. Asam had won two years before. In 1725 the Prince-Abbot of Kempten appointed him *Hofmaler*.
71. *Zimmermann*, Pl. 12.
72. Schnell (*Kempten*), p. 14–15. Hermann's wall-painting in the Arbeitszimmer is signed and seems to be dated 1734. The *stucchi* and the ceiling painting here, however, are probably several years later, as is also the joint work of Hermann and Übelherr in the other rooms at Kempten. These are usually assigned to the early forties.
73. Petzet (*Marktoberdorf*), p. 138.
74. *Ibid.*, p. 137.
75. Concerning the tower of Helmishofen, rebuilt in 1732, Neu reports ('Beiträge'), p. 347, n. 16, a surviving document (HANA 5992) in the Munich Hauptstaatsarchiv. Helmishofen, also, I have not seen.
76. Brunner (*Baden-Württemberg*), pp. 268–269; Gall (*Westliches Schwaben*), pp. 130–131; Piel (*Baden-Württemberg*), p. 250. The pamphlet by Emil Wahr, *Die Kirchen von Kisslegg* (Kunstführer Nr. 336), [Munich, 1938], has long been out of print.
77. Gall (*Westliches Schwaben*), p. 131.
78. *Loc. cit.*, but Piel (*Baden-Württemberg*), p. 250, says 'um 1740'.
79. Gall (*Westliches Schwaben*), *loc. cit.*, says 'um 1753–55'.
80. Johannes Graf von Waldburg-Wolfegg, *Schloss Wolfegg* (Grosser Kunstführer 36), Munich, [1961], does not throw much light on this question.
81. Piel (*Baden-Württemberg*), p. 550.
82. Waldburg-Wolfegg, *op. cit.*, p. 26.
83. *Ibid.*, p. 27.
84. *Zimmermann*, Pl. 12.
85. Waldburg-Wolfegg, *loc. cit.*

86. Rudolph Rauh, *Schloss Zeil* (Kunstführer Nr. 731), [Munich, 1962], p. 13; Piel (*Baden-Württemberg*), p. 552.
87. *Barock am Bodensee*, Nos. 125a and b. 'Von Fischers Hand sind viele Projekte mit unterschiedlichen Lösungen vorhanden. Die Planung erstreckte sich auf mehrere Jahre'. Mention is also made of an article by Waldburg-Wolfegg (who was, incidentally, a descendant of the client), 'Johann Georg Fischer als Architekt eines schwäbischen Adelgeschlechtes', with the notation that this would be published in *Das Münster*. Unfortunately Count Waldburg has since died and the article has never appeared.
88. Another surviving plan by Fischer dated 1733, *Barock am Bodensee* No. 126, is effectively that of the church as executed.
89. Now, at last, handsomely restored and once more open. No new publication, showing the present condition, is yet available other than postcards and colour-slides. There is also, most unfortunately, no publication devoted solely to St. Katherine at Wolfegg: but see Brunner (*Baden-Württemberg*), pp. 637–638; Piel (*Baden-Württemberg*), pp. 549–550; and Gall (*Westliches Schwaben*), p. 130.
90. *Zimmermann*, Pls. 31–34.
91. See Chapter V, pp. 179–180.
92. Of course, the interior of the Feldkirche was already an ovalized rectangle, but that was only a modest chapel.
93. St. Egidius in Nürnberg had no wall-pillars.
94. Piel (*Baden-Württemberg*), p. 414.
95. There exists at Schloss Wolfegg a sketch by Spiegler in oil on paper, now mounted on canvas, for this portion of the fresco: *Barock am Bodensee*, No. 128. This is dated 1735, a year earlier than the fresco.
96. The duel occupies only the west end of the fresco. What the subject or subjects are of the remaining portions of the base of the fresco is not clear, presumably additional episodes related to Waldburg family history. This is the sort of information which might well have reached print in Count Waldburg's unpublished article as well as specific attributions and dates for various furnishings in St. Katherine.
97. Spiegler probably knew Steinhausen as it is not far from Wolfegg. He is less likely to have seen the frescoes at Regensburg and Ingolstadt.
98. See Note 96.
99. The oil painting on the high altar is a Coronation of the Virgin by Jasper de Crayer (1584–1669). Piel (*Baden-Württemberg*), p. 550, gives the date on this, curiously enough, as 1696, presumably a misprint.
100. *Zimmermann*, Pls. 31–34.
101. Adolf Layer, *Dillingen an der Donau*, Dillingen, 1961, pp. 26–27; Reitzenstein-Brunner (*Bayern*), pp. 209–210; Gall (*Östliches Schwaben*), p. 80.
102. Layer, *op. cit.*, pp. 22–25.
103. Piel (*Baden-Württemberg*), p. 105; Brunner (*Baden-Württemberg*), p. 112.
104. Reitzenstein-Brunner (*Bayern*), p. 803.
105. [G] Dehio/[E] Gall, *Pfalz und Rheinhessen*, Munich, 1951, p. 28.
106. Layer, *op. cit.*, pp. 15–18.
107. Reitzenstein-Brunner (*Bayern*), p. 680.
108. Gall (*Oberbayern*), pp. 276.
109. Most of this information comes from a printed description mounted on a card in the church.
110. Lieb (*Barockkirchen*), p. 157.
111. Brunner (*Baden-Württemberg*), p. 19; Piel (*Baden-Württemberg*), p. 15. This is not listed even as an attribution by Dömling ('J. G. Fischer'). He does mention, however, p. 276, as possible late works of Fischer the Café Fronhof and the Palais Greifenklau in Augsburg, the one destroyed in the last war, the other since restored, and both of the early forties; also (without date) Herrgottsruh outside Friedberg near Augsburg. According to most others the last was built in 1731–33 by Benedikt Ettel (or Oettel) from Eichstätt: Reitzenstein-Brunner (*Bayern*), p. 287; Gall (*Östliches Schwaben*), p. 25. This has a big fresco of 1738 over the domed choir by C. D. Asam and very fine *stucchi* by F. X. Feichtmayr as noted above (pp. 87–88).
112. Hugo Schnell, *Maria Steinbach* (Kunstführer Nr. 205), [Munich, 1955], pp. 3–4.
113. This makes quite implausible L. Mayr's suggestion in *Memminger Geschichtsblättern*, January 1923, No. 1, that the master-mason Anton Lacher (1705–1777) was responsible for the design as well as the execution of the church.

CHAPTER II

[pages 114–125]

114. *Zimmermann*, Pls. 31–34.
115. Hauttmann (*Geschichte*), pp. 50, 187.
116. Schnell, *Maria Steinbach*, p. 4.
117. Brunner (*Baden-Württemberg*), p. 440; Piel (*Baden-Württemberg*), p. 402.

CHAPTER III

[pages 127–135]

1. H. Schnell, 'Die Wessobrunner Baumeister und Stukkatoren', in *Wessobrunn*, pp. 13–21.
2. See *Zimmermann*, p. 37.
3. Franz Xaver Feichtmayr (I, 1705–64) and Johann Michael Feichtmayr (1709–72) were brothers. Joseph Anton Feuchtmayr (1696–1770), born in Linz in Austria, was not a close relative. F. X. II Feichtmayr was a son of F. X. I. He became an assistant and associate of J. B. Zimmermann in 1752 and, on Zimmermann's death in 1758, married the widow and succeeded his former master professionally. Jakob Rauch was a son-in-law of F. X. I.
4. Over twenty Schmuzers are mentioned in Thieme-Becker. Eight of them, however, belong to a separate Tyrolean branch; and four, who are associated with Vienna, may not have been related to the Wessobrunners.
5. Lieb (*Barockkirchen*), pp. 16–20, 145, 166.
6. Badly damaged by bombing in 1944, some of the decoration of the vaults in the nave and the choir now is restoration of 1949–50, but most plausible in character. The monastic house was originally a priory attached to the Benedictine Abbey of Weingarten. In 1824–30 the priory buildings were remodelled as a summer residence for the Dukes of Württemberg and the church is today Protestant: Gall (*Westliches Schwaben*), p. 137f.; Brunner (*Baden-Württemberg*), p. 166f.
7. *Wessobrunn*, p. 23. Lieb, in Thieme-Becker, cites an estimate made in 1671 for work at Schwangen near Füssen as Johann Schmuzer's actual debut.
8. Michael Hartig, *Wallfahrtskirche Vilgertshofen* (Kunstführer Nr. 484), new ed., Munich [1956], pp. 3–6.
9. Gall (*Oberbayern*), 190–192. The architect was probably Hans Krumpper from Weilheim and the stuccoer Georg Schmuzer, who also took charge of the construction. The latter was very likely a cousin, if not an uncle, of Johann Schmuzer.
10. Lieb-Dieth (*Vorarlberger*), pp. 77ff. This Franz Beer was usually known to contemporaries as 'von Bleichten'. His portrait serves as frontispiece in the cited book.
11. The *stucchi* at Holzen are of exceptional richness. Though doubtless by a Wessobrunn stuccoer, they do not resemble the work of either of the Schmuzers at this date.
12. Norbert Lieb, *Die Pfarrkirche Irsee* (Kunstführer Nr. 562), 2nd ed., [Munich, 1964], p. 3, henceforth cited as Lieb (*Irsee*).
13. Landolt (*Schweizer*), pp. 49–52, 100f., 111. The church of the Benedictine Abbey of Rheinau was rebuilt by Beer in 1704–11. Only the Late Gothic south tower was retained but, curiously enough, Beer imitated this closely in his north tower of 1706–11 in order to produce a symmetrical west front.
14. This similarity reinforces the suggestion that Franz designed the Irsee *stucchi*, even if his brother executed them. It seems extremely unlikely that the elder brother would be imitating the younger brother some six or seven years later, despite the common source at Friedrichshafen where both had worked.
15. Anton Koerbling and Hugo Schnell, *Der Bürgersaal in München* (Kunstführer Nr. 95), 3rd ed., [Munich, 1961], pp. 4–5, 8–10.
16. Kimball (*Louis XV*), pp. 80–84. The choir-stalls of Notre-Dame in Paris, designed by Lepautre, and the altar there by Vassé followed within a year or two: *ibid.*, pp. 84–88.
17. Landolt (*Schweizer*), pp. 52–56, 101f.
18. The Asams will hardly have known St. Urban, but might possibly have seen and been influenced by Pielenhofen (Pl. 128), where the St. Urban scheme of pilaster decoration was repeated.
19. Hugo Schnell and Otto Thimme, *Pfarrkirche Weissenau* (Kunstführer Nr. 151), 3rd ed., [Munich, 1963], pp. 1–5.
20. Herbert Batzl, *Pielenhofen* (Kunstführer Nr. 760), [Munich, 1962], pp. 3f. Lieb-Dieth (*Vorarlberger*), p. 78, give the date of construction of the church as 1719–35; Reitzenstein-Brunner (*Bayern*), p. 645, give the date of the frescoes as 1720.
21. The fresco of the Pentecost over the crossing recalls C. D. Asam's in the choir of Weingarten; that over the following bay to the east, the Glorification of the Trinity, is framed by a *quadratura* balustrade such as Asam used both at Weingarten and at Aldersbach in the principal frescoes in the naves.
22. *Zimmermann*, p. 83.
23. F. X. Traber, *Die ehemalige Benediktinerabteikirche zum Heiligen Kreuz in Donauwörth*, Donauwörth [1950], pp. 8f, 16–22. Lieb-Dieth (*Vorarlberger*), p. 78, give the date of construction as 1717–20 and attribute the design to Beer; Reitzenstein-Brunner (*Bayern*), p. 219, give the date of the frescoes as 1720–21. The Gothic church on the site had been demolished in 1717 except for its tower.
24. E. Q. Asam approaches the quality of Joseph Schmuzer's *stucchi* at Donauwörth most closely on the cove at Weltenburg, the decoration of which is usually dated about 1721 (Pl. 27).
25. Lieb (*Irsee*), p. 14: 'erbaut 1727/29 (von Joseph Schmuzer?) . . . bemerkenswerte stuckierung von den Brüder Schmuzer'.
26. Of course, J. G. Fischer in the Allgäu, working at first from his uncle J. J. Herkomer's plans, had begun using such coves consistently in his churches as early as 1717 as has been detailed in Chapter II, pp. 94–97.

27. Hugo Schnell, *Pfarrkirche St. Martin Garmisch* (Kunstführer Nr. 20), 2nd ed., [Munich, 1958], pp. 2–5. The roof was raised on 22 October 1732 and a year later the scaffolding was removed.
28. And indeed they would be precarious were this ceiling of masonry vaulting rather than plastered wooden construction.
29. Of course this had been true up to a point earlier in interiors with stucco-work by Franz and by Joseph Schmuzer. But the resemblance is much closer here and the rib-bands are now no more tectonic than the coupled pilasters below. It should also be noted how identical bands are used in the vertical plane to outline the east wall of the nave and in place of a moulded archivolt over the choir-arch. As a decade earlier at Aldersbach this and the handling of the surfaces of the barrel-vaults in the transepts seem especially significant here.
30. Franz Bogenrieder, *Pfarrkirche Oberammergau* (Kunstführer Nr. 21), 3rd ed. [Munich], pp. 2–6. The church was a dependency of the Abbey of Rottenbuch and Schmuzer had already been employed to build the Pfarrhaus here in 1731.
31. Hugo Schnell, *Pfarrkirche Rottenbuch* (Kunstführer Nr. 8), 17th ed., [Munich, 1961], pp. 2–6.
32. This was a common treatment of such surviving pointed vaults as the Asams had been confronted with at Freising. By this time it was used wherever churches with Gothic arcades or vaults were redecorated. The result is roughly parabolic in section, but this rather strange shape is less noticeable than usual at Rottenbuch thanks to the very rich decoration of the vault surface.
33. The resemblance is closest to those at Osterhofen, but the shafts here are not concave.
34. Completed in 1739, the Amalienburg interiors must be almost precisely contemporary with the decoration of the choir and crossing of Rottenbuch.
35. This would seem to be the first use by one of the Schmuzers of this most characteristic feature of German Rococo church architecture. In general, indeed, it was at Rottenbuch that Joseph Schmuzer left his provincialism behind and joined the main stream of Bavarian development in the thirties, even though the spatial organization of his earlier church at Oberammergau is more notable. The rounding of the vaults over the square transept ends is especially significant (Pl. 139).
36. The latest restoration of 1961–63 has lightened and neutralized somewhat the colouring of the *stucchi* so that the harmony with the frescoes is not now so close.
37. *Zimmermann*, Pls. 31–34.
38. But then the Asams had done little more at the west ends of Freising and St. Emmeram than Schmuzer here, and far less than Borromini in the late 1640s at the 'west' end in remodelling the interior of St. John Lateran in Rome.
39. Gall (*Oberbayern*), p. 212.
40. Humilis Fischer and Hugo Schnell, *Die Votiv und Wallfahrtskirche St. Anton in Partenkirchen* (Kunstführer Nr. 128/129), 3rd ed., [Munich, 1950], pp. 3f.
41. Lieb (*Barockkirchen*), p. 146.
42. Hugo Schnell and F. S. Ringmeier, *Steingaden* (Kunstführer Nr. 5), 5th ed., [Munich, 1954], pp. 4–10. The original Romanesque church was consecrated in 1176. This seems to be the point at which Franz Xaver II's independent career began if his father was not at all involved in the Steingaden commission. The nave 'vaults' of wood and plaster may well be the work of Franz Xaver, though he seems never otherwise to have practiced as an architect.
43. Bergmüller is thought to have studied in Rome under Carlo Maratti before Maratti's death in 1713 in the years when C. D. Asam was with Ghezzi, Maratti's god-son. In 1730 Bergmüller became director of the Augsburg Stadtakademie, to which position Matthäus Günther succeeded on Bergmüller's death in 1762.
44. *Zimmermann*, p. 89.
45. They illustrate miracles attributed to various members of the order.
46. *Ettal* Ettal, n.d. The Abbey publishes two pamphlets, neither of them very scholarly, one with sixteen small black-and-white plates, the other with sixteen slightly larger colour plates and three line-cuts. As usual, however, the facts are best given by Lieb (*Barockkirchen*), pp. 98–106, 160, 171f.
47. Wolfgang Götz, 'Die gotische Klosterkirche in Ettal', *Das Münster*, March–April, 1965, pp. 115–122.
48. Ground was broken on 21 July 1710 and the cornerstone of the new façade laid on 7 August. The new choir was complete by 1718 and it was consecrated on 15 September 1726. The monastic buildings had been finished by 1721. Lieb (*Barockkirchen*), p. 160.
49. The carpentry work of the 'dome'—for there is no masonry vault—was carried out by Johann Pföderl in 1747.
50. Pius Fischer, *Der Barockmaler Johann Jakob Zeiller und sein ettaler Werk*, Munich [1964].
51. *Zimmermann*, Pls. 41–48.
52. The attribution to Schmuzer is not always accepted. Some features suggest rather the hand of Dominikus Zimmermann. Unfortunately, I was not allowed to have photographs taken in the interior, which certainly has considerable interest whoever designed it.

CHAPTER III

[pages 135–149]

CHAPTER III

[pages 149–150]

53. It would seem that after working still with his father at Weingarten in the early forties Franz Xaver II, already aged 30, had an independent career. In 1750–51, even before his father's death, when the nave of Heilig-Blut at Kappel near Unterammergau was vaulted he carried out the *stucchi*—the choir there had been built by his grandfather Johann in 1680. At the same time, 1750–53, he remodelled the nave of the parish church at Schongau, probably following a design by Dominikus Zimmermann, who had redecorated the choir in 1748. The frescoes in the choir (1748) and the nave (1761) there are by Matthäus Günther. The high altar was probably executed by F. X. Schmädl, but from a design by Ignaz Günther (1725–1775) now preserved in the Staatliche Graphische Sammlung in Munich. This is signed and dated 1758. The following year, 1759, Franz executed in scagliola the altars of St. John Nepomuk and St. Francis Xavier at Obermarchtal, where his own career had begun.
At Ziemetshausen, where Johann had built the nave of the parish church in 1686–94, the remodelling in 1754 of the pilgrimage church 'Auf dem Vesperbild', built in 1725 by Simpert Krämer, has been attributed to Franz, but is more probably by J. G. Hitzelsberger with *stucchi* by Tassilo Zöpf, both of whom were working in 1749–50 in the parish church there. Other attributions are no more plausible, so that the last twenty years of Franz Xaver II's life remain a blank.

CHAPTER IV

[pages 151–153]

1. The latest list of Thumb's work, at least of his 'wichtigsten Bauten' is that given by P. H. Boerlin, *Die Stiftskirche St. Gallen*, Bern, [1964], pp. 83–84, henceforth cited as Boerlin (*St. Gallen*). Boerlin's list includes nineteen commissions only. Boerlin, however, discusses Thumb's career before St. Gallen at some length, *ibid.*, pp. 84–89. J. L. Wohleb, 'Peter Thumb oder Thum?', *Schau ins Land*, 1956, pp. 141–147, and Lieb-Dieth (*Vorarlberger*), pp. 118–119, offer many more works in their lists, including supervision of buildings designed by others, some unexecuted projects, and even a few attributions. The latter also make many references to details of Thumb's life and to particular buildings and projects in their introductory text: *op. cit.*, pp. 7, 10–13, 16–22, 24–27, 33–38, 40, 52–57, 62–65, 67. Their treatment of the subject, being the latest except for Boerlin's more restricted account, supersedes Wohleb's as well as the one in Thieme-Becker. Moreover, many of Thumb's minor as well as major works are there illustrated by Dieth's—unfortunately unprocurable—photographs.
2. A loosely chronological summary of this stylistic modulation in Germany as arbitrarily periodized by various scholars in the last fifty years was given in the Introduction (pp. 4–5). Thumb played no part in the earliest stage of formulation of a German Rococo interior architecture in the twenties and early thirties, for he was a latecomer to the Rococo compared to the Asams and the Zimmermanns, or even to J. G. Fischer and Joseph Schmuzer. His major works, however, are exemplary at the same time that they are all but unique in the German High Rococo of 1735–55.
3. The problem of the responsibility for the design of Maria Steinbach has been briefly discussed in Chapter II, pp. 123–125.
4. This summary account of Thumb's life is largely based on Lieb-Dieth (*Vorarlberger*), *loc. cit.*
5. See W. Sebert, *Die Klosterkirche St. Trudpert* [Freiburg], n. d., p. 6; Piel (*Baden-Württemberg*), pp. 418–419.
6. This matter was discussed in Chapter III, p. 131.
7. In that year he bought the 'Haus zur Leithern' for 2,370 gulden: Lieb-Dieth (*Vorarlberger*), p. 21.
8. In the ten years between the Battle of Blenheim and the Treaty of Rastatt, Bavaria was occupied by the allied troops as was noted in Chapter I; it is not clear just what the situation was to the west in the Austrian enclave round Freiburg and in French Alsace. Evidently this area cannot have been too much disturbed by the war since the Benedictines of St. Trudpert and of Ebersmunster were able to begin the renewal of their medieval churches then.
9. See W. Holtz, *Handbuch der Kunstdenkmäler im Elsass*, [Munich, 1965], henceforth cited as Holtz (*Elsass*), pp. 40–42, Ebersmunster; p. 4, Erstein. The tower was replaced in 1861.
10. Piel (*Baden-Württemberg*), pp. 418–19. The cornerstone of the nave was laid in 1715. However, the core of the west tower is probably tenth century, with terminal octagon and spire of 1720–22. The monastery building was carried out after 1737 by Thumb. The frescoes offer legends

of St. Peter, St. Paul and St. Margaret as well as the story of St. Trudpert. The high altar of 1780–84 is by F. J. Christian, a brother of the then abbot.

11. The large monastery, also in Baden, that Thumb built over the years 1718–31 and enlarged in 1738–40 for the Benedictine Abbey of Ettenheimmünster, north of Freiburg, was demolished in the nineteenth century. Several handsome Rococo doorways from the abbey buildings survive in various locations in nearby Lahr, Riegel, and Ettenheimweiler. The surviving church was altered and enlarged by F. J. Salzmann in 1765: *Ettenheimmünster Wallfahrtskirche und ehemaliges Kloster*, Stuttgart [1963], pp. 3, 16.
12. G. Metken, *Ebersmünster* (Kunstführer Nr. 821), [Munich, 1965], p. 6; X. Ohresser, *Eglise et abbaye d'Ebersmunster*, Sélestat, 1961, pp. 18–20, henceforth cited as Ohresser (1961); *idem*, *Histoire de l'abbaye d'Ebersmunster*, Sélestat, 1963, p. 48. Abbot Bernard Roethlin undertook the building of the church, which was finished in 1715. According to Boerlin (*St. Gallen*), p. 83, the work was begun as early as 1708, but that seems unlikely: see Note 10. Abbot Jean V. Sengler began the new church in 1719 and Prior Ildefonse Beck carried it nearly to completion before his death in 1730.
13. Metken, *op. cit.*, pp. 6–7; Ohresser (1961), pp. 20–22.
14. Some have wondered if the church completed in 1727 was that designed and begun in 1719. It may be noted, however, that the campaign of 1719–27 would have been only a little longer than that of 1715–22 for the construction of St. Trudpert.
15. Actually, except for the incorporation of some medieval stone masonry in the lower walls of the choir, the church is almost entirely built of bricks made by the monks on the site. However, the base courses of the piers and the decorative trim of the exterior are in sandstone from the Vosges, some of it beige but mostly pink. The external brickwork, like that inside, is entirely covered with stucco: Ohresser (1961), p. 22. The stiff Ionic pilasters in the choir, all of beige stone, contrast with the later and more elegant Corinthian pilaster order of the nave.
16. [Pourel and Gérardin], *L'Eglise Saint-Jacques de Lunéville*, [Lunéville?], n.d.
17. There are comparable towers of this period, however, in Bohemia.
18. The frescoes, whitewashed during the French Revolution, were cleaned in 1866.
19. '. . . Aidé', Ohresser (1961), p. 21, notes, 'de trois compagnons dont la conduite donna lieu à des plaintes pour des fréquentes escapades nocturnes et qui se virent infligés des retenues de salaires . . .' One wonders whether these lively woodcarvers were Swiss, Tyrolean, or natives of Alsace. Will, like Meyer, came from nearby Sélestat; Matter and Siffert were from Strasbourg; Kettler came from Colmar; but Magges was a Tyrolean.
20. H. Ginter, *St. Peter/Schwarzwald* (Kunstführer Nr. 561), 6th ed. [Munich, 1966], pp. 3–6. Abbot Ulrich Bürgli was responsible for the rebuilding of the church, the surviving medieval edifice having been merely repaired after a bad fire in 1678. Jakob Felger supervised the construction in a short campaign of three years that included the execution of much of the decoration.
21. See Note 42 below.
22. Since Spiegler's frescoes were twice whitewashed, once in 1824 and again in 1874–5, their present poor condition is not surprising. The restoration of 1964–5, moreover, has exaggerated the contrast between the very pale stucco-work and the dark, hard tones of the frescoes. The result is today the least attractive of Thumb's larger works. In detail, however, Clerici's thin and wiry *stucchi* approach the Early Rococo somewhat more closely than Machoff's of perhaps a year or two later at Ebersmunster. In addition to Clerici, Spiegler, and J. A. Feuchtmayer, Christian Wenzinger (1710–97), later responsible for both the frescoes and the *stucchi* at St. Gallen, worked at St. Peter, providing the sculpture on the baptismal font in 1733; and J. C. Stoner, Gossman, and Pellandella painted altarpieces. The choir gates by Michael Reinhardt from St. Trudpert are dated 1728, the pulpit 1729, the organ 1730, and the choir-stalls as late as 1770.

    The monastery buildings at Schwarzach near Bühl in Baden, also begun by Thumb in 1724, were completed in 1736, but little remains of them today.
23. See Holtz (*Elsass*), p. 88. The buildings were destroyed in the French Revolution.
24. See Chapter V, p. 175.
25. See pp. 160–166.
26. *Zimmermann*, Pl. 4.
27. At St. Peter the library occupies the central portion of the wing separating the west and east courts of the extensive monastery buildings. The library was probably always incorporated in such a range, but the rest of the monastery was rebuilt in 1752–7 for Bürgi's successor Steyrer by the minor Vorarlberger Hans VI Willam.
28. Lieb-Dieth (*Vorarlberger*), p. 118.
29. Piel (*Baden-Württemberg*), p. 418.
30. It is surprising to note the close similarity of the fresco-filled cartouches of a good generation earlier on the nave vault of St. Trudpert to these thoroughly Rococo features in the St. Peter library.

31. In 1738–9 Schmuzer was, however, rounding the square ends of the transepts at Rottenbuch in the vaulting somewhat more simply (Pl. 139).
32. As construction of the Asamkirche began in 1733 features of its interior could have been known to Thumb when he designed the St. Peter library (see Chapter I, pp. 81–83). The unusually long period over which in both cases construction and decoration continued makes it difficult to date precisely particular elements of the interiors. By the fifties, of course, one may suppose that the interior of the Asamkirche was well known to Gigl, if the balusters of the St. Peter balcony and the scagliola panels below are, in fact, of his design rather than Thumb's. Whether or not influenced by E. Q. Asam's church in Munich, the cove-supported balcony and its curved plan must almost certainly be integral to the original design of the mid to late thirties. The vaulting in Willam's modest Abtskapelle (now Hauskapelle) of the fifties at St. Peter, with fine Rococo *stucchi* by Gigl and frescoes by F. L. Hermann (1710–97), is very similar to that in the library. This interior has little spatial interest, however, because of its crypt-like proportions in contrast to the two-story height of the library.
33. Lieb-Dieth (*Vorarlberger*), p. 118. Piel (*Baden-Württemberg*), p. 382, does not mention Thumb in connexion with these works of J. P. E. Rohrer.
34. Both at Bruchsal and at Meersburg J. G. Stahl (1687–1755), rather than Thumb, was responsible for executing Neumann's designs: Piel (*Baden-Württemberg*), pp. 69/70, 314.
35. See Note 45 below.
36. Birnau is sometimes called Neubirnau, but writers seem to prefer the simpler form, as do current map-makers. See Mauritius Linder and Leodegar Walter, *Birnau das Barock-Juwel am Bodensee*, Birnau, n.d.; H. Ginter, *Birnau am Bodensee* (Kunstführer Nr. 435, Farbdruckausgabe), [Munich, 1962], henceforth cited as Ginter (*Birnau*); and H. Schnell, *Birnau am Bodensee Marien-Wallfahrtskirche* (Grosser Kunstführer Nr. 10), 2nd ed., [Munich, 1955]. Linder-Walter as well as Ginter provide many colour plates both of the exterior and the interior but these are outdated thanks to the restoration of 1965–7. Externally the wall surface is now pink and the pilasters and other trim stone-colour.
37. *Zimmermann*, Pls. 41–48.
38. This statement brushes off an interesting question, the answer to which—if there is one—must be sought internationally rather than just in south Germany. I suspect it was in Belgium that an exterior architecture which might be considered Rococo developed most successfully, but the roots, presumably, were French. See, however, Sedlmayr-Bauer ('Rococo'), cols. 238–239.
39. Ginter (*Birnau*), pp. 2–5.
40. Thumb intended to build a wide staircase leading to the lake. He also proposed a generous circular landing around an elaborate fountain half-way down that would be fenced with a tall iron fence between stone posts carrying urns. In *Barock am Bodensee*, No. 156, the drawing for this, now in the Generallandesarchiv, Stuttgart, is attributed to J. A. Feuchtmayr, who was responsible for the *stucchi* in the church. In this same catalogue Pl. 26 reproduces a contemporary portrait of Thumb.
41. Certain notations by Schwab dated 26 August 1746 on this agreement have led Boerlin (*St. Gallen*), pp. 86–87, to query Thumb's responsibility for the design of Birnau as executed. But the fact that the executed church does not follow the scheme described in the earlier agreement, of which the abbot noted that it should be 'cassirt und ein neuer errichtet worden', certainly does not seem to exclude the probability that a new contract was made with Thumb, according to which the construction of the church was soon carried forward. Boerlin, however, suggests J. C. Bagnato (1696–1757) as the designer of the existing church, noting certain stylistic resemblances to his Deutschordensschlosskirche at Mainau of 1733–9 and his parish church of 1738–41 at Merdingen. Neither the fact that Bagnato may have been associated in some capacity with work of the forties at Meersburg, as was also true of Thumb, nor his later employment by Schwab at Salem on the remodelling of the choir of the church there in 1752–7 seems to strengthen much this rather surprising attribution. Neither Schnell in Grosser Kunstführer Nr. 10 nor Lieb in his excellent account of Birnau in (*Barockkirchen*), pp. 128–135, 163–164, 173, mentions Bagnato's name in connexion with Birnau.

Johann Caspar (not Giovanni Gaspare) Bagnato was not Italian-born. He came from the Palatinate and was principally employed by the Deutschorden for work at their various *Schlösser* in Baden and for churches they controlled. His other work does not suggest he had the ability to produce such a church as Birnau.
42. This Feuchtmayr was a son of J. F. Feuchtmayr (1659–1718) who had worked with Franz Beer at Salem on the stucco decoration of the Kaisersaal there in 1708–10. Joseph Anton had himself provided the altars for Thumb's church at St. Peter shortly after its consecration in 1728–31 as

has been noted earlier: Wilhelm Boeck, *Feuchtmayer Meisterwerke*, Tübingen [1963], pp. 18–19; Pls. 23–28 (St. Peter); pp. 25–28, Pls. 61–81, 84, 86–89 (*Birnau*).

The elder Feuchtmayr spent most of his life working for the Abbey of Salem and the son, though born at Linz in Austria, was brought up in a nearby village, so that he was well known to the Salem monks. These Feuchtmayrs were not related—at least not at all closely—to the brothers Franz Xaver and Johann Michael Feichtmayr from Wessobrunn: see Note 3 to Chapter III.

43. Drawings for various elements of the stucco decoration by Feuchtmayr survive in the library at St. Gallen as well as for the altars: *Barock am Bodensee*, Nos. 148, 150–154, Pls. 29, 30. No. 149 is a drawing by Feuchtmayr's assistant F. A. Dirr for the high altar, signed and dated 1757, which was developed from Feuchtmayr's earlier design (No. 148).

44. It is worth underlining that the initiation of the decoration of Birnau by Feuchtmayr and Goez antedates by three years the comparable work in the St. Peter library by Gigl and Gambs.

45. The nave of Mengen-Petershausen, built by Thumb in 1741–6 just before Birnau and destroyed by fire in 1810 as has been mentioned, was evidently quite similar as regards the surrounding gallery, continued there at the sides of the deep rectangular choir, and the placing and shape of the quasi-transeptal chapels. The corners of the nave were not rounded, however, nor the choir domed. Two plans by Thumb of *c.* 1741 survive in the Generallandesarchiv, Karlsruhe: *Barock am Bodensee*, Nos. 142, 143, Pl. 27. This church is not included by Lieb-Dieth (*Vorarlberger*) in their 1960 list of Thumb's works.

46. Thumb, of course, had built several modest aisleless churches before this. That of 1732–4 at Waldkirch, with its transeptal chapels, as well as Mengen, is already somewhat premonitory of the Birnau nave as has been noted.

47. *Zimmermann*, Pl. 29.

48. See Chapter I, pp. 63–65, and Chapter II, pp. 95–97.

49. The barrel-vault of St. Trudpert was already oval in section, but not as wide or as much flattened in the centre. Once more the resemblance to the quite flat frescoed ceiling of Santa Maria de Victoria is notable. In the St. Peter library the vaulting rises higher than here and the frescoed area is more restricted and by no means so flat. But Goez's fresco in the chapel of the Meersburg Schloss occupies an even flatter ceiling provided by Stahl in 1741: Joachim Holz, *Das Barockschloss in Meersburg*, [Weissenhorn], n.d., p. 10, Pl. 17–18.

50. The gallery at Birnau, carried on a cove, recalls even more distinctly than that of the St. Peter library the similar feature in E. Q. Asam's St. Johann-Nepomuk in Munich, where the pilasters of the lower story are also without entablature (Pl. 72). Even the rib-like curved members over Asam's pilasters that break the surface of the cove are omitted by Thumb. Moreover, the continuity of the cove at Birnau is interrupted in each bay above the lower range of windows by shallow transverse severies that correspond, in a more delicate and less structural way, to those above the upper range of windows. The closest prototype in Munich of the spreading elements above the pilasters at Birnau are the warped three-dimensional facets of Asam's cove flanking the entrance to the choir of St. Johann-Nepomuk.

51. *Zimmermann*, Pls. 45, 46.

52. In 1966 the *stucchi* at Birnau were repainted, but there is no assurance that the decisions then controlling the choice of tones were correct. However that may be, the walls remain white, the upper pilaster shafts are marbled in pale pink, and those below are of a warm but light grey, a sort of putty colour. The raised ornament is creamy, with some fields of very pale blue, pale pink, or pale green. Gold is introduced only for the highlights of the white scroll-work of the balcony railings; but the solider elements of this balustrade, lining up with the pilasters above and below, are marbled in blue and pink. Elsewhere, equally strong tones are used only in the severies above the upper windows, evidently as a transition to the deeper tones of the *quadratura* elements that frame the ceiling fresco.

One may assume that the high key of the tonality throughout is proper for *c.* 1750. One may query, however, whether modern taste has not reduced the liveliness of the general effect by making the relatively stronger notes of blue and pink and green too pale, if not the beige of the raised ornaments. The livelier contrasts at Santa Maria de Victoria seem closer to Rococo colouring as it has survived unfaded in porcelain, but sharp accents of colour are generally less characteristic of the forties than of the previous decade.

53. *Zimmermann*, Pl. 48.

54. The St. Peter library is of a distinctly bolder and more Rococo character: this is more, I suspect, because J. G. Gigl was from Wessobrunn and probably younger than J. A. Feuchtmayr—though his birth date is not known—than because the stucco-work there was initiated at least three years

later than at Birnau. Contrary to the usual situation in churches of the mid-century, the architecture of Birnau is more Rococo than the *stucchi*, which are here distinctly subordinated to the handling of the architectonic elements. One can imagine this interior as existing as an effective spatial entity without Feuchtmayr's stucco work or Goez's frescoes. This is, of course, not the case at Die Wies, where architect and stuccoer were the same man and the fresco-painter his brother.

55. A. Wohlhaupter, *Die Brüder Hans Adam und Joseph Dossenberger*, Munich (1950), henceforth cited as Wohlhaupter (*Dossenberger*).
56. Lieb (*Barockkirchen*), pp. 136–144, 164–165, 173–174.
57. His church at Hilzingen, near Singen in southern Baden, built in 1747–9 while Birnau was in construction, deserves mention, however. It is a charming country-cousin, so to say, of Birnau, lacking the galleries and, except for the transeptal chapels, the curves in plan. The pilaster order carrying heavy entablature blocks still has strongly tectonic character in the Baroque tradition.

    Overhead the *rocaille* stucco-work is delicate in scale and widely spaced. The frescoes by Benedikt Gambs, set in cartouches at the sides of the ceiling and in larger scalloped frames along the centre of nave and choir, are rather dark, but this may have been exaggerated by poor restoration.
58. Boerlin (*St. Gallen*) identifies and illustrates fourteen different projects produced by various architects before the reconstruction of the church at last actually began. It is impossible here to do more than summarize Boerlin's thirty pages (35–65) of discussion of these successive projects of 1720–55. Shorter accounts of the history of the church as rebuilt in 1756–64 by Thumb and J. M. I. Beer are provided by J. Duft, *Kathedrale St. Gallen* (Kunstführer Nr. 550), 7th ed., [Munich, 1962], pp. 3–14, henceforth cited as Duft (*Kathedrale*); and by Landolt (*Schweizer*), pp. 74–81.
59. Together with his brother Michael II (1667–1726), Moosbrugger's brother-in-law Johann Rüf had been in charge of the construction of Einsiedeln from Moosbrugger's designs since 1720, and had himself designed and built in 1746 the north wing of that monastery.
60. Boerlin (*St. Gallen*), pp. 79–114.
61. *Ibid.*, Pls. 1–44. The Roman numerals are those used both by Boerlin and by Lieb-Dieth (*Vorarlberger*).
62. *Ibid.*, Pls. 1–3.
63. *Ibid.*, Pls. 4–7.
64. *Ibid.*, Pls. 9–14.
65. *Ibid.*, Pls. 15–22.
66. *Ibid.*, Pl. 15.
67. *Ibid.*, Pls. 27–35.
68. *Ibid.*, Pls. 36–42.
69. *Ibid.*, Pls. 7, 8.
70. Lieb-Dieth (*Vorarlberger*), p. 51.
71. Boerlin (*St. Gallen*), Pls. 31–34.
72. *Ibid.*, Pl. 36.
73. *Ibid.*, Pl. 38.
74. Lieb-Dieth (*Vorarlberger*), p. 53.
75. Boerlin (*St. Gallen*), Pls. 37, 41.
76. *Ibid.*, p. 117.
77. Lieb-Dieth (*Vorarlberger*), pp. 51–53.
78. *Schweizerische Zeitschrift für Archäologie und Kunstgeschichte*, 1953, pp. 223ff.
79. See *Zimmermann*, Pl. 40.
80. Neumann's design was developed in the mid-forties; the church was structurally complete and ready to receive the frescoes and the stucco decoration only in 1763. The *stucchi*, therefore, are contemporary with the work of the Gigls in the choir of St. Gallen: see Chapter V, pp. 215–218.
81. For detailed discussion, see Chapter V and also Hagen-Dempf (*Zentralbaugedanke*). Also relevant is Dominikus Zimmermann's project of 1732 for Ottobeuren (Fig. C).
82. This is a shrunken survival of the church associated with Otmar, the eighth-century abbot who founded St. Gallen. Most of the early projects (I–VIII) for the reconstruction of the abbey retained it, while the designer of project XII proposed instead to substitute a small chapel to the south of the western apse. Such a chapel, this time larger and more nearly detached, also appears in Bagnato's project (XIII) of 1750 and even in Thumb's of 1751. It is significant that neither the Lucerne nor the Au plan provide any such chapel, but in the latter three altars are indicated in the western apse, which is semi-circular rather than flattened as in the executed church (Figs. D–H).
83. Wenzinger had studied in Rome in 1731 and after that in Paris from 1737 on; indeed, he even received an award from the French Académie. Perhaps because of this foreign training, he responded early to the international currents leading towards Neo-classicism in the fifties. This hardly explains the extreme openness of his composition on the dome of the rotunda. That seems rather an attempt to emulate Tiepolo's fresco, completed in 1753, over the stair-hall in the Würzburg Residenz or, more probably, J. J. Zeiller's on the dome at Ettal, painted in 1752 (Pl. 150). Fortunately the stiffening of the figures in the fresco was not echoed in those executed in stucco, not altogether unworthy rivals of J. A. Feuchtmayr's more famous ones at Birnau, and no premonitions of Neoclassicism restrained the exuberance of the *rocaille* elements in the stucco-work (Pl. 172).

CHAPTER IV

[pages 171–174]

84. Since the church has been filled with scaffolding for several years and the re-painted interior has been revealed as yet only in the nave, it would be premature to attempt to describe in detail the present colouring of the *stucchi*. Glimpsed here and there in the summer of 1966, the green of the raised decoration appeared to be quite pale.

This very light tone may well be correct, providing further evidence of Wenzinger's somewhat academic taste, and in any case was not unusual even in the mid-century decades. On the other hand, much stronger colours were being introduced around the figural groups on the pendentives of the rotunda, access to which was at that time difficult.

85. Duft (*Kathedrale*), pp. 16–23.

86. Not the consistent condemnation, more characteristic of French architects of the mid-century who wrote treatises and contemporary critical writers, but as regards the former their willingness to introduce considerable Rococo decoration in the interiors they designed.

CHAPTER V

[pages 175–186]

1. Gurlitt (*Geschichte*), pp. 298–299, 305–306, discusses only Ottobeuren and Zwiefalten as works of Fischer, though he mentions also, without giving Fischer's name, Freising Neustift and Wiblingen. It is interesting that he knew Zwiefalten only from drawings! Hempel (*Central Europe*), pp. 233–237, with several other passing references, has lately given a much more continuous account; and he provides plans of St. Anna-am-Lehel in Munich, Fischer's church at Ingolstadt, Ottobeuren, and Rott-am-Inn. The best single account, perhaps, is still that by Feulner (*Bayerisches*), pp. 44–56. For a good Fischer bibliography as also for a summary list of his works, see Lieb (*Barockkirchen*), pp. 152–154.
2. This both Sedlmayr-Bauer ('Rococo') and Minguet (*Esthétique*) accept as axiomatic.
3. Although much of the fighting in Europe during the Seven Years' War—'French and Indian Wars' to Americans—took place on Bavarian territory, there seems to have been no such general hiatus in the years 1756–63 as in 1704–14 or 1740–45. See, however, pp. 223–224.
4. See W. H. Bruford, *Germany in the Eighteenth Century: The Social Background of the Literary Revival*, Cambridge, 1935, Part III, pp. 131–269.
5. See Chapter I, pp. 64–65.
6. See Chapter I, *loc. cit.*
7. For the known dates of Fischer's life, etc., see Lieb (*Barockkirchen*), *loc. cit.*
8. For brief accounts of the careers of Johann Mayr and the Gunetzrhainers, see Lieb (*Münchener*), pp. 60, 72–83, 117–126.
9. For a detailed discussion of Murnau, see Lieb (*Münchener*), pp. 83–91.
10. See A. Heufelder, *Niederaltaich* (Kunst-Niederaltaich. Pawagner also began Schärding. führer Nr. 120), 8th ed., [Munich, 1964], pp. 2–4. The author is the Abbot of
11. See pp. 64, 65.
12. *Zimmermann*, Pl. 21.
13. See pp. 60–68.
14. Reitzenstein-Brunner (*Bayern*), pp. 741–742; Gall (*Oberbayern*), pp. 200–201.
15. Hagen-Dempf (*Zentralbaugedanke*), pp. 61–62, with plan.
16. Lieb (*Barockkirchen*), p. 152.
17. Hagen-Dempf (*Zentralbaugedanke*), p. 62.
18. N. Lieb, *Diessen Ammersee* (Kunstführer Nr. 30), 5th ed., [Munich, 1966], p. 3.
19. *Ibid.*, p. 2.
20. The door-frame with its crowning feature is, exceptionally, of real pink marble, now much faded, as are the pilaster capitals. This 'structural polychrome' is overwhelmed by the stronger pink of the painted stucco of the walls. The pilaster order and other framing features are painted pale beige—a sort of stone-colour. The inferiority of the carved detail to the quality of the stucco inside is typical and helps to explain why stone or marble was so little used, even on exteriors.
21. Hagen-Dempf (*Zentralbaugedanke*), Pl. opp. p. 16; plan p. 29.
22. Lieb (*Barockkirchen*), pp. 155–156, gives a long list of documented dates and a bibliography.
23. The principal internal dimensions of Berg-am-Laim are: length, 44.8 m.; breadth, 24.8 m.: Hagen-Dempf (*Zentralbaugedanke*), p. 29. Lieb, *op. cit.* p. 68, gives more detailed measurements. The comparable dimensions for Aufhausen are 35 × 22 m. and for the Ingolstadt church 23.6 × 28.55 m.: *idem*, pp. 13, 21.
24. *Ibid.*, pp. 21–28.
25. *Ibid.*, pp. 13–20.
26. *Ibid.*, Pl. opp. p. 32.
27. *Ibid.*, Pls. opp. pp. 49 and 56 further illustrate the interior before the last war.
28. According to the surviving plan by J. M. Fischer (see Note 26) the executed east end represents a marked simplification of what he originally intended: a roughly parabolic

apse with pairs of columns set diagonally flanking the altar.

29. See previous Note.
30. See Note 27.
31. To judge from the thickness of the external walls and the sturdiness of the corner piers that function like wall-pillars, the vaulting of these fair-sized churches of the mid-thirties is of masonry. From the first the smaller churches, Kirchham, Rinchnach, Bergkirchen and Unering, with their thin walls, presumably had wooden 'vaults'. This is manifestly true of Rinchnach, where a domelet rises above the central barrel section of the 'vaulting' overhead. Among the small later edifices, Sigmertshausen, which has thick walls and heavy corner piers, is very likely vaulted in masonry and also the Anastasiakapelle, which is also quite thick-walled. The large longitudinal churches from Osterhofen to Zwiefalten, with naves flanked by wall-pillars, certainly have masonry vaults, as does Ottobeuren. The character of the vaulting at Rott-am-Inn and Altomünster is not quite so clear. The very large spans associated with relatively slight supports might suggest that the vaulting is in wood, more particularly at the former; in fact, I understand the vaults are of masonry. The real point is that, whatever the actual structure employed, the visual emphasis in these interiors is not on the material of which the vault is made but on its aesthetic value as the upper boundary of the enclosed interior space in contradistinction to the manifestly structural character of the supporting piers below.
32. These coves, such a characteristic feature of Rococo interiors, suggest a mode by which a Rococo sort of church façade might have been adumbrated. The fact that characteristic French façades of the Rococo period are generally flat and rather plain, with ranges of segmental-topped windows, is not relevant since they are secular works. But the matter is not very important, since a Rococo exterior architecture in Germany was barely even immanent, except perhaps in Cuvilliés's *Schlösser* at Haimhausen and Wilhelmstal, unless one accepts as of more than vernacular significance such façades as are richly decorated with applied Rococo *stucchi*. The best-known example is the Falkenhaus at Würzburg, but the Asamhaus properly belongs to this genre also (Pl. 76).

    Such covings, not uncommon on Fischer's exteriors and ubiquitous in his interiors, are certainly French in origin. They are, for example, found in Boffrand's grand-ducal chapel in the Lunéville château of Leopold of Lorraine and in the church that he designed, Saint-Jacques, also at Lunéville, as well as in very many secular interiors of the High Rococo decades in France. But Boffrand's coves around church windows, such as those at Lunéville, have a much richer and more academic apparatus of imposts and archivolts than Fischer's.
33. It would not appear from the plan (Fig. 25) that Fischer's Ingolstadt church ever had a façade of the Diessen-Aufhausen type (Figs. 23, 26). Three-dimensional interest there must have been deflected to the cut-off corners and the bulges of the side-walls. These elements would surely have created a full-round plastic mass of distinctly Baroque character.
34. The attribution of the sculpture to Joachim Dietrich is generally accepted by most scholars, including Norbert Lieb. Curiously enough, however, in Lieb (*Barockkirchen*), Pl. 77, the caption notes: 'Meister der Figuralskulpturen unbekannt'. The painting on the high altar of the Assumption of the Virgin, dated 1738, is definitely by B. A. Albrecht, who had been collaborating with Cuvilliés and Dietrich in the Reiche Zimmer in the Munich Residenz for some years. Albrecht provided also the painting on the Joseph-Altar the following year at the same time Pittoni did that on the Stephan-Altar and Tiepolo the one on the Sebastian-Altar: *ibid.*, p. 155.
35. *Zimmermann*, Pl. 34.
36. Compare the high altars by E. Q. Asam at Rohr (Pl. 37) and at St. Emmeram (Pl. 64).
37. A Rococo interior does not actually discourage movement, and there are often subsidiary features of interest in transepts, side chapels, and so forth; but the totality is best appreciated from a point not far beyond the western entrance. Despite all the fascinating variety and profusion of detail that architects and collaborating decorators provided, they worked together towards a unity that should not be apprehended piecemeal, however much it must so be described. Enjoyment of the individual elements of the whole, not to speak of response—in the case of statuary or paintings—to their religious significance, follows and is subordinate to this impression of unity.

    Here at Diessen, very evidently, it is the relative independence and the unmistakable structural significance of the wall-pillars, the most conspicuous inherited Baroque elements, that interfere with the homogeneity of the interior. To speak of stylistic ambiguity, in other words, is not a mere hypercritical reaction to a mixture of intentions; this ambiguity definitely lessens the value of the whole as a consistent aesthetic, or even religious, experience. Thus it may be claimed that there is absolute inferiority here as compared with such more modest contemporary churches as J. G. Fischer's at Wolfegg or the later one at Dillingen that are more coherently Rococo architecturally (Pls. 107, 111). There are few styles to whose monuments the adjective 'pure' might seem less applicable than the Rococo, but the weakness of Diessen and many other major works of J. M. Fischer is what might be called their 'impurity'.

38. Lieb (*Barockkirchen*), p. 155, suggests that Bergmüller may have been assisted by J. E. Holzer.

39. The western end of the fresco, contrary to what was said in Note 37, can only be appreciated when looking back from the fourth bay of the nave.

40. Indeed, this is F. X. Feichtmayr's earliest known work. The interior has surviving inscriptions of 1466, 1478, and 1732. The frescoes are signed by Peter Wolcker from Augsburg: Gall (*Oberbayern*), p. 281.

41. See N. Lieb, *Fürstenzell* (Kunstführer Nr. 690), 2nd ed., [Munich, 1965], pp. 3–6, henceforth cited as Lieb (*Fürstenzell*).

42. Kath. Pfarramt Zwiefalten, *Ehemalige Benediktinerabteikirche zu Zwiefalten*, [Stuttgart], n.d., pp. [2]–[6]. (There is another, presumably earlier, edition with title *Reichsgotteshaus zu Zwiefalten.*) E. Kreuzer, *Zwiefalten*, [Berlin, 1964], is a doctoral dissertation without illustrations, chiefly concerned with the iconographic progamme of the decorations; R. Zürcher, *Zwiefalten*, Constance, 1967, is a more general work and very fully illustrated. Convenient, as usual, is the summary of documented dates in Lieb (*Barockkirchen*), pp. 157, 169–170.

43. Fischer proposed that J. B. Zimmermann, who was working in 1743–4 in his church at Berg-am-Laim, should execute the frescoes. The abbot preferred painters then of high repute in Austria. His first choices were Paul Troger (1698–1762) or Bartolommeo Altomonte (1702–1783), but in the end he settled for Zeiller, Austrian-born like himself and Troger, and once Troger's pupil: Lieb (*Fürstenzell*), pp. 5–6. Presumably, as at Berg-am-Laim, Zimmermann would also have been preferred by Fischer for the *stucchi;* doubtless he chose, or accepted, Funck because of the latter's employment with Zimmermann at Nymphenburg a few years earlier.

44. Though not very apparent in photographs, there are very slight coves at both ends of the nave vault, however. More conspicuous are the broader ones at the chancel arch and the east and west ends of the choir. Progressively narrower ones on the north and south arches of the crossing and at the outer corners around the big windows in the tribune provide further evidence of Fischer's addiction to such Rococo devices for softening spatial transitions and partially ovalizing right-angled shapes. A larger-scaled example here is the curving of the vaults over the diagonal corners at the ends of the transepts, producing not really a coving, in this case, but a sort of half-dome with a slice off the circumference. The semi-octagonal ends of the transepts he modified thus were perhaps already begun when Fischer took over.

45. Spiegler's frescoes to the east of the nave are earlier in date than the principal one: those over the choir and presbytery, 1747; those over the transepts, 1748; and that on the crossing dome, 1749. Feichtmayr's stucco-decoration in the eastern portions of the church is also dated 1747–9 and that in the nave 1751. The fresco over the organ gallery and those on the oval vaults of the side chapels are by Meinrad von Aw (1712–92) and dated 1760; those in the tribunes are also by von Aw and four years later. The ones in the fore-church under the organ gallery were painted by the Viennese artist Franz Sigrist (1720–87) in 1760, and that is when the wrought-iron grille there by J. G. Jüngling was installed. The grille at the entrance to the choir is earlier, 1751–7, and by Joseph Büssel.

46. Work began on the high altar in 1748–9. But the sculpture by Joseph Christian (1707–77) from Redlingen is later, 1754, executed at the same time as he was working on the altars in the nave and on the west front. In the absence of other information, one may suppose that the general design of the altars and the colouring of the scagliola with which they are covered were a part of Fischer's general artistic responsibility here.

47. See pp. 123–125.

48. *Zimmermann*, pp. 80–82; Pls. 54, 55.

49. Lieb (*Barockkirchen*), pp. 93–98, 159–160, 171 (Schäftlarn); pp. 79–87, 158, 170–171 (Ottobeuren); 88–92, 159, 171 (Rott-am-Inn); 136–144, 164–165, 173–174 (Wiblingen). For Schäftlarn and Ottobeuren, see also below, pp. 201–204 and 198–201, respectively.

50. N. Lieb, *Rott-am-Inn* (Kunstführer Nr. 14), 6th ed. [Munich, 1967], pp. 2–6, and Lieb (*Barockkirchen*), *loc. cit.*, give the history of the building and decorating of this church.

51. See p. 171.

52. H. Schnell, *Ottobeuren* (Kunstführer Nr. 73), 10th ed., [Munich, 1959], pp. 2–4; *Ottobeuren Kirche Kloster Museum* (Grosse Kunstführer 2), 4th ed., Munich, [1962]. The latest and most complete account of the designing, building and decorating of Ottobeuren, however, is Lieb's article, 'Die barocke Architektur- und Bilderwelt des Stifts Ottobeuren', in Ae. Kolb and H. Tüchle, eds., *Ottobeuren Festschrift zur 1200-Jahrfeier der Abtei*, Augsburg, 1964, pp. 307–378. In preparation for the twelve-hundredth anniversary of the founding the church was carefully restored outside and in, as also was the monastery.

53. *Zimmermann*, Pl. 4.
54. Lieb (*Barockkirchen*), Pl. 23.
55. *Ibid.*, Pl. 22.
56. In the main he followed Father Vogt's plans, possibly incorporating some suggestions made by Herkomer. The principal dimensions, mostly established earlier in the complex story of the church before Fischer took over and completed it, may be given now: length 89 m.; nave 20.90 m. broad, with chapels at the sides 6.80 m. deep; breadth at crossing 53.30 m., with transepts 18.20 m. wide. The crossing dome is 35.60 m. high at the crown. Other dimensions can be read from the plan and section (Fig. 29).
57. Lieb, *op. cit.*, Pls. 25 (*c.* 1736–7), 26 (1738–9).
58. *Ibid.*, Pl. 27.
59. *Ibid.*, Pls. 28–33.
60. *Ibid.*, Pls. 30–31.
61. *Zimmermann*, pp. 80–82; Pls. 54, 55.
62. Lieb, *op. cit.*, pp. 159–160, lists the documented dates for the construction and decoration of the monastery and the church. See also B. Moschick, *Kloster Schäftlarn* (Kunstführer Nr. 537), [Munich, 1951], which is earlier and less authoritative.
63. *Zimmermann*, p. 90; Pls. 51–53.
64. There is in this interior, as restored, not much gilding. The raised *stucchi* are painted in neutral, rather putty-like, colours, more delicate in tone than most photographs suggest; thus they contrast only slightly more than at Diessen or Zwiefalten with the white ground. The visual emphasis is on the bright colouring of the frescoes as Zimmermann, if not Fischer, must have intended.
65. Gall (*Oberbayern*), p. 223 (with plan, p. 222), gives the dates thus; Reitzenstein-Brunner (*Bayern*), p. 152, give 1751–58. Lieb (*Barockkirchen*), p. 153, says 1750, with no date of completion, as do Hagen-Dempf (*Zentralbaugedanke*), p. 93, and Mindera (*Benediktbeuren*), p. 35. The date of the cornerstone-laying—15 May 1751—of the small nearby church at Bichl, built for the same Abbot of Benediktbeuern as the Anastasiakapelle, Leonhard Hohenauer, suggests that the chapel, the designing of which brought Fischer to the abbey, had at least been commissioned, if not begun, the previous year: Mindera (*Benediktbeuern*), p. 41. It must have been completed structurally by 1752, since that is the date of the frescoes and the *stucchi*, so that the date 1758 for the completion is not very meaningful. The slight priority of the Anastasiakapelle—possible as regards the start, certain as regards the effective completion—to the work at Schäftlarn is, however, not very relevant here. They are not much alike and neither need be considered more 'advanced' at this date than the other.
66. Even that element of the plan is taken up within the thickness of the wall and does not appear on the exterior (Pl. 201). The plain stuccoed walls with their flat stone quoins are broken below the crowning cornice of stone only by the deep window apertures—arched below, segmental-topped above—and a very slight and flat projection in the middle of the north side; the south side is set against the north wall of the choir of the church. The evident thickness of the walls in relation to the modest span suggests that the vault is of masonry, as noted earlier.
67. The identity of the stuccoer is uncertain. Gall (*Oberbayern*) suggests Thomas Sporer, but notes the unrevealing initials 'J.B.' and the date 1752 in the blind window. The main altarpiece of the Reception of St. Anastasia in Heaven is much earlier than the date of the chapel, 1726, and by Amigoni, whose Immaculata is on the northern side altar. All three altars are probably by Ignaz Günther or his workshop, including the associated sculpture. A special feature is the silver-gilt reliquary bust of St. Anastasia designed by E. Q. Asam that stands on the mensa of the high altar.
68. Piel (*Baden-Württemberg*), p. 181; Brunner (*Baden-Württemberg*), pp. 190–191. Lieb (*Barockkirchen*), p. 153, accepts more definitely than these scholars the attribution to Fischer. The church was restored in 1955 with a somewhat gaudy result that looks provincial beside contemporary Schäftlarn and the Anastasiakapelle.
69. Mindera (*Benediktbeuern*), pp. 41–42; and *Bichl*, n.d., pp. [1]–[2], (a folder, with no author or place of publication, available in the church). Neither this church nor the Anastasiakapelle are discussed by Hagen-Dempf (*Zentralbaugedanke*), though she lists them both on p. 93.
70. See M. Hartig, *Altomünster* (Kunstführer Nr. 589), 5th ed., [Munich, 1966], pp. 5–8; Hagen-Dempf (*Zentralbaugedanke*), pp. 52–59.
71. The plan alone (Fig. 32) can hardly make clear the exceptional sequence of spatial elements at Altomünster. Since no sectional drawings seem to be available to provide a more adequate diagrammatic explanation, a verbal description must be essayed. The octagonal nave has two sets of galleries around it, the upper at entablature level; through the next spatial element (Pl. 204) the lower galleries continue on either side, but overhead this area is much reduced in height by the screened-off nuns' choir at the level of the upper gallery of the nave. The following presbytery is very tall once more and the retrochoir only slightly lower. But this section is cut off at the base by a semi-circular screen behind the high altar. This rises to the height of the galleries at

the sides that continue to the east those of the forward areas. The easternmost element is partially cut off, above the screen and a little farther back, by a large free-standing altar in the centre—much more prominent than the one below immediately in front of the screen—and by diagonally-placed altars at either side that are nearly as tall.

Neither Hartig, *loc. cit.*, or Hagen-Dempf, *loc. cit.*, give dimensions or even provide a scale to go with the plan. The former, however, states (p. 5) that the total cost was 44,096 gulden.

72. The spatial vista into the taller spaces beyond is fascinating but hardly characteristic of either the Baroque or the Rococo—anachronistically it might be called Corbusian! The rather Louis XVI character of the panels of the screen flanking the altar should be noted, for their decorative treatment is already characteristic of the post-Rococo seventies, when the church was consecrated.
73. The literature concerning Neumann and his principal work, the Residenz at Würzburg, is very extensive, but two books are of the greatest value here. There is a good bibliography in Reuther (*Kirchenbauten*), pp. 112–114, following accounts of all his churches. Each of these provides a sort of compressed monograph comparable to the treatment in Lieb (*Barockkirchen*) of the major churches south of the Danube, among which there is none by Neumann. The more general treatment in M. H. von Freeden, *Balthasar Neumann Leben und Werk*, 2nd ed. [Munich, 1963], henceforth cited as Freeden (*Neumann*), includes a most useful list of biographical dates, pp. 66–71. This was first published in the catalogue of the exhibition held in 1953 in the Residenz at Würzburg on the 200th anniversary of Neumann's death.
74. Freeden (*Neumann*), pp. 5–18, 66. Neumann was also involved very early with the Schönbornkapelle attached to the Würzburg Dom which he eventually carried to completion. See Walter Boll, *Die Schönbornkapelle am Würzburger Dom*, Munich, 1925, henceforth cited as Boll (*Schönbornkapelle*), and Note 113, below.
75. See Introduction, pp. 6–8.
76. Kimball (*Louis XV*), Pls. 100–101.
77. Reuther (*Kirchenbauten*), pp. 64–65, Pls. 21, 22. Johann Dientzenhofer before his death in 1726 had provided plans for Prior Bonifatius Freiherr von Hutten, a brother of Johann Philipp Franz von Schönborn's predecessor as Prince-bishop of Würzburg, Christoph Franz von Hutten. After Prior von Hutten's death Neumann made a new plan unrelated to Dientzenhofer's. This was executed in 1728–30.
78. *Ibid.*, pp. 99–100; Freeden (*Neumann*), Pls. 28, 29. The client was Rudolf Franz Erwein Graf von Schönborn. Not a churchman, he was the founder of a surviving Schönborn line. The church was completed in 1728 by the time the construction of Holzkirchen started. The frescoes were executed in that year and the next, the furnishing followed in 1730, and the church was consecrated 2 November 1732. It is hard to realize that this is contemporary with Steinhausen, Osterhofen and Bertholdshofen.
79. See Note 43 to the Introduction.
80. Reuther (*Kirchenbauten*), pp. 101–105; Grimschitz (*Hildebrandt*), pp. 140–142, Pls. 107, 210, 220–222, 242. The story of the designing, building, decorating and furnishing of the Hofkirche, which extends—as regards the executed church—for more than a decade, is extremely complicated. The early projects by Maximilian von Welsch, 1720–21, and by de Cotte and by Boffrand, 1723, can be ignored here. In 1730 Neumann first proposed the present location at the south-west corner of the complex and this was then discussed in Vienna, since Friedrich Carl continued as Imperial Vice-Chancellor until 1735. Early in 1731 Friedrich Carl informed Neumann that Hildebrandt had prepared plans for the church; in March Neumann offered a new project of his own; and in April he received Hildebrandt's. Early the following year Neumann prepared his semi-final plans and sent them to Vienna. He then accepted some changes, proposed presumably by Hildebrandt, before beginning actual construction in that spring of 1732, and the work advanced so rapidly that the vaulting was completed by July 1733. In 1734 certain further changes proposed by Hildebrandt were incorporated and the following year Antonio Bossi began to execute the stucco-decorations, following in the main designs by Hildebrandt, while Byss executed the frescoes and J. W. von der Auvera (1708–56) the sculpture. The inappropriate pulpit is of 1774–75 and by Bossi's son Materno (1739–1802).
81. See pp. 81–82.
82. See Rupprecht (*Rokoko-Kirche*), Chapter I.

83. Freeden (*Neumann*), pp. 68, 71. Zick began the frescoes in 1751 and completed them in 1754. Neumann was at Bruchsal in 1751 and again in 1753, shortly before his death, the last of no less than twelve visits during the course of construction there.
84. Reuther (*Kirchenbauten*), pp. 88–89. The client was another Schönborn, Franz Georg, Archbishop and Elector of Trier, Prince-Bishop of Worms, Prince-Prior of Ellwangen, and Prior of St. Paulin. Shortly after the cornerstone was laid on 26 March 1734 French troops entered Trier and

remained until the end of the War of the Polish Succession in 1737. Neumann provided the design for the entrance portal in 1744 and that for the high altar the next year. His plans for the sacristy are dated 1747 and his projects for the side altars 1752. The consecration of 1754 was preliminary; the final consecration by Franz Georg's successor, Johann Philipp Graf von Walderdorff followed three years later on 6 March 1757.

85. *Ibid.*, pp. 109–110.
86. *Ibid.*, pp. 97–98.
87. Freeden (*Neumann*), pp. 67–70. Friedrich Carl's successor as Prince-Bishop of Würzburg, Anselm Franz Graf von Ingelheim, was no builder; Neumann's various works at Würzburg got under way again only after the latter's death in 1749.
88. To the late thirties belonged the magnificent suite of Rococo apartments—the Paradezimmer—that before their destruction in the last war rivalled the Reiche Zimmer in the Munich Residenz and the apartments of the Prince-Abbot of Kempten in the profusion and the quality of their rich decoration. But these were in size and shape ordinary rooms, not great interiors of monumental dimensions, so that they are hardly relevant here. Moreover, Neumann probably had little to do with their decoration: Freeden, *op. cit.*, Pls. 18–20.
89. *Ibid.*, ills. on p. 30. The location of the drawings is given as 'Ehem. Staatl. Kunstbibliotek, Berlin'. I am not sure where they are today, if indeed they survive.
90. Bossi had been associated with the sculptor J. W. von der Auvera (1708–56) in the decoration of the Paradezimmer: *ibid.*, p. 33.
91. Karl Lohmayer, *Johannes Seiz*, Heidelberg, 1914, Pl. 31, Pl. VI.
92. This Louis XVI treatment of the walls below does not go badly with Tiepolo's fresco; in fact, few visitors note that the decoration is more than a decade later than the fresco they came to admire! The same is not true of Materno Bossi's other contributions to Neumann interiors of the Rococo decades. See p. 220 and Pl. 218.
93. See Feulner (*Bayerisches*), Pls. 20, 49, 63.
94. There is no such word to be found even in the largest English dictionaries.
95. Freeden (*Neumann*), p. 68; Reuther (*Kirchenbauten*), pp. 97–99.
96. These recall Fischer's, notably that at Rinchnach (Pl. 72).
97. Freeden (*Neumann*), illustrations on pp. 30, 31.
98. It even breaks up Bossi's gilded *rocaille* enframement of the cartouche on one of the vaulting conoids.
99. Freeden (*Neumann*), Pl. 42.
100. H. Kisky, 'Die Baugeschichte des Brühler Schlosses', in *Kurfürst Clemens August, Ausstellung in Schloss Augustusburg zu Brühl, 1961*, Cologne [?1961], pp. 118–119, Pl. 5–8. Freeden (*Neumann*) pp. 69–70, lists six trips to Brühl by Neumann over the years 1740–45.
101. Kisky, *loc. cit.* Most of the *stucchi* are of the late forties and by Giuseppe Artario (d. 1770), but G. A. Brillie (d. 1794) carried out those on the north wall, with the big trophy, in the sixties after Clemens August's death, and the gilt bust of Clemens August over that was installed only in 1775. The fresco overhead is by Carlo Carlone (1686–1775). Artario is usually called Artaria in England, where he worked as stuccoer with James Gibbs, most notably in St. Martin-in-the-Fields, as has been noted earlier.
102. For a bibliography of the very extensive literature about Vierzehnheiligen, see H. Reuther, *Vierzehnheiligen* (Grosser Kunstführer 20), Munich, [1957], p. 26. Reuther (*Kirchenbauten*), pp. 90–96, gives a more succinct account, which has been followed here. R. Teufel, *Vierzehnheiligen*, 2nd ed., Lichtenfels [1957], henceforth cited as Teufel (*Vierzehnheiligen*), provides the best illustrations.
103. Langheim was in the diocese of Bamberg, but Carl Friedrich held that see as well as Würzburg.
104. Already in January 1736 J. J. M. Küchel (1703–69), an employee of the Bamberg diocesan authorities who was Neumann's representative in Bamberg and also, in some sense, titular architect of the Abbey of Langheim, picked a site, high above the Main, where the church could be built with its axis in line with Johann Dientzenhofer's great church of the Abbey of Banz, clearly visible on the other side of the river. For Küchel's association over the years with Vierzehnheiligen, see Joachim Holz, *Johann Jacob Michael Küchel*, Lichtenfels, 1963, pp. 42–44, and *passim.*
105. See H.-H. Möller, *Gottfried Heinrich Krohne und die Baukunst des 18. Jahrhunderts in Thüringen*, Berlin, 1956, pp. 79–82, Pls. 78–80. Krohne's project of 1739–40 was for a church of centralized plan. Krohne had already in 1735 provided a project for rebuilding the Abbey of Langheim, *ibid.*, pp. 75–79.
106. Möller, *op. cit.*, Pl. 82. Prepared in 1742, this later design by Krohne has much in common with Neumann's plan of 1742, *ibid.*, Pl. 81. Küchel also prepared plans in 1741–2. The priory building went up rapidly in 1743–4 to the north-east of the site selected for the church, presumably from a design by Krohne.
107. Teufel (*Vierzehnheiligen*), Pls. 18–22. His Pls. 23–24 illustrate designs by J. C. Haass,

the master-carpenter who eventually erected the roof of the church in 1761.

108. Adam Friedrich Graf von Seinsheim. Appropriately, he was a Schönborn on his mother's side and, like Carl Friedrich, he was Prince-Bishop both of Würzburg (from 1755) and of Bamberg (from 1757).

109. Teufel, *op. cit.*, Pls. 76, 88, 89. *Ibid.*, Pls. 15–16 show his 1741–2 plan and elevation with the proposed central location of the Shrine. This is not indicated on the Neumann and Krohne plans of 1742 mentioned in Note 106.

110. *Ibid.*, Pls. 49 (model), 28–47. Pls. 51–52 show plans by Neumann's son made in 1753–54 after Neumann's death. These are, in effect, working drawings for the execution of the church by Küchel.

111. 'Addition' is not really correct for the transepts. Transepts are already present in Neumann's earliest plan of 1742—Möller (*Krohne*), Pl. 81—as in most of the plans by other architects.

112. H. Schnell, *Das Käppele/Würzburg*, (Kunstführer Nr. 306), 4th ed., [Munich, 1960], pp. 2–6; Reuther (*Kirchenbauten*), pp. 109–110. The advocation is *Mariä Heimsuchung*.

113. Boll (*Schönbornkapelle*), especially Pls. 10–13 (Hennicke); 16–19 (Welch); 23–26; 28 (Hildebrandt); 29 (Boffrand); 31–33 (Neumann); Reuther (*Kirchenbauten*), pp. 106–108. There is some resemblance also in the plan to the tri-lobed east end of Neumann's modest church at Gaibach, designed in 1740 and built in 1742–5 for Friedrich Carl. It is worth remarking that in this interior small swatches of *rocaille* ornament replace pilaster capitals, as in J. M. Fischer's later church at Sigmertshausen, but the church at Gaibach is otherwise almost devoid of decoration. Notably, there are no frescoes at all. Reuther (*Kirchenbauten*), pp. 54–56; Freeden (*Neumann*), Pl. 60.

114. G. Neumann, *Neresheim*, Munich-Pasing, 1947, pp. 80–174; Reuther (*Kirchenbauten*), pp. 78–84. For a full range of views of the interior of the church, see P. Weissenberger, *Neresheim*, Königstein in Taunus, n.d.; for (not very satisfactory) colour plates, K. Setz, *Neresheim Gottesburg über Walden und Zeiten*, Aalen, 1966.

115. This was promised on 10 March 1748 but seems to have represented the final project of the following year.

116. Knoller put in, all told, 21½ months on the work.

117. As for Vierzehnheiligen, a very considerable number of Neumann's drawings for Neresheim survive, so that the development of his ideas through successive stages can be followed in great detail: Neumann, *Neresheim*, *loc. cit.*, and more especially Pls. 27–41. *Ibid.*, Pls. 1–26 and 43–47, offer correlative plans and interior views of churches by Borromini and Guarini; the Dientzenhofers; Hildebrandt; Welsch; and earlier works by J. B. Neumann, in Italy, Bohemia, Austria, and Germany, respectively.

118. These columns are of granite and quite strong enough, like the small marble columns in the Werneck chapel and the Würzburg Sala Terrena, to provide the necessary support if the vaults had been carried out in masonry as Neumann intended. Even more than in the piers at Vierzehnheiligen is it apparent that these columns can—and do—perform a major structural function. Neoclassic theorists must have approved, however much the Guarinian vestiges in Neumann's planning might shock them.

119. See Note 117.

120. Wohlhaupter (*Dossenberger*), pp. 39–40. Most of the work of the Dossenbergers is Zimmermanian, but in the seventies they moved rather consistently towards Neoclassicism.

121. De Colombier (*Architecture française*), pp. 191–208; Piel (*Baden-Württemberg*), pp. 415–416.

122. When the church was consecrated in 1785 the ribbed dome had only painted coffering. The present truly coffered surface dates from the reconstruction of the dome after a fire in 1874. This, of course, exaggerates the Pantheon-like look of the interior.

123. That is, among the architects and stuccoers who have had important roles in this book. Some men who were a good deal younger such as Joseph II Dossenberger, born in 1721, and K. A. von Lespilliez, born two years later, have been mentioned, but only very incidentally. They are of the same generation as the French who arrived in time to rival them in the sixties and seventies. See p. 224 below.

124. Particularly, one may believe J. B. Zimmermann's son Michael and F. X. Feichtmayr's son-in-law Franz Rauch were important in this respect, for the former was responsible —and possibly very largely—for the decorations in the abbey church at Schäftlarn and in the Great Hall at Nymphenburg, and the latter even more completely for the *stucchi* at Rott-am-Inn and at Altomünster.

125. Here again Rauch is perhaps an exception, but hardly on the score of quality.

126. De Colombier (*Architecture française*) breaks down the story regionally, which quite obscures the chronological picture.

127. More accurately 'de' or 'von' Pigage, since he was ennobled in 1768. He came from Lunéville in Lorraine and was called to Mannheim by the Elector Palatine Karl Theodor in 1749: de Colombier (*Architecture française*), pp. 162–177; E. Renard,

Das neue Schloss zu Benrath, Leipzig, 1913, pp. 8–14. For his splendid interiors in the Mannheim Schloss, the tall galleried library destroyed in the war—which was the finest of all the more functional secular Rococo rooms—and the somewhat too rich Bibliothekkabinett, which survives, see Böhm (*Mannheimer*), pp. 7–8, Pls. on pp. 11, 24; for Benrath, see Renard, *op. cit.*, pp. 27–47, Pls. I–XXVII.

Pigage's later fame rests principally on the echoes of the new English gardens his associate Ludwig Sckell introduced peripherally at Schwetzingen in the sixties and seventies and the fantastic fabricks the former built to go with them. That is hardly relevant here. French academic theorists, however, have always been fascinated by the plans of Benrath.

128. H. A. Klaiber, *Der württembergische Oberbaudirektor Philipp de la Guépière*, Stuttgart, 1959, pp. 81–94 (Monrepos); 94–109 (Solitude); G. Kleemann, *Schloss Solitude bei Stuttgart*, Stuttgart, 1966.

129. See the Introduction, p. 2.

130. There were not unimportant exceptions even well before the Rococo period. Jean de Bodt (1670–1745), who had been in Holland and England, was called to Berlin in 1699 by the Elector Friedrich Wilhelm III. Paul du Ry (1685–1724) entered the service of the Landgrave Karl of Hessen-Kassel in 1685. His son Karl Ludwig, born in 1692, and his grandson Simon Ludwig, who died in 1799, built most of eighteenth-century Kassel. Unfortunately the greater part of their work was destroyed in the war. Neither the second nor the third du Ry need be considered French. A fourth du Ry, another Karl Ludwig, predeceased his father Simon Ludwig. See O. Gerland, *Paul, Charles und Simon Louis du Ry*, Stuttgart, 1895, and also Note 39 to the Introduction.

THE PLATES

1. Schleissheim, Neues Schloss. Festsaal (p. 1)

By Joseph Effner, *c.* 1723-25, with *stucchi* by C.-C. Dubut and J. B. Zimmermann, and ceiling fresco by Jacopo Amigoni

2. Nymphenburg, Pagodenburg. Lower room (p. 2)

3. Schleissheim, Neues Schloss. Elector's bedroom (p. 2)

4. Nymphenburg, Pagodenburg. Upper room (p. 2)

5. Pommersfelden, Schloss Weissenstein. Chapel (p. 7)

6. Pommersfelden, Schloss Weissenstein. Grosse Galerie (p. 6)

7. Ellingen, Schloss. Stair-hall (p. 7)

8. Ebrach, Abbey. Kaisersaal (p. 7)

9. Munich, Palais Preysing.
Façade (p. 8)

10. Vienna, Lower Belvedere. Goldkabinett (p. 7)

11. Steinhausen, Pilgrimage Church. Interior to east (p. 12)

12. Augsburg, Schäzler Haus. Festsaal (p. 14)

13. Benediktbeuern, Abbey. Neuer Festsaal (p. 21)

14. Freystadt, Pilgrimage Church. Dome over crossing (p. 22)

15. Munich, Dreifaltigkeitskirche. Dome over crossing (p. 23)

16. Tegernsee, Abbey Church. Vaults of nave and crossing (p. 23)

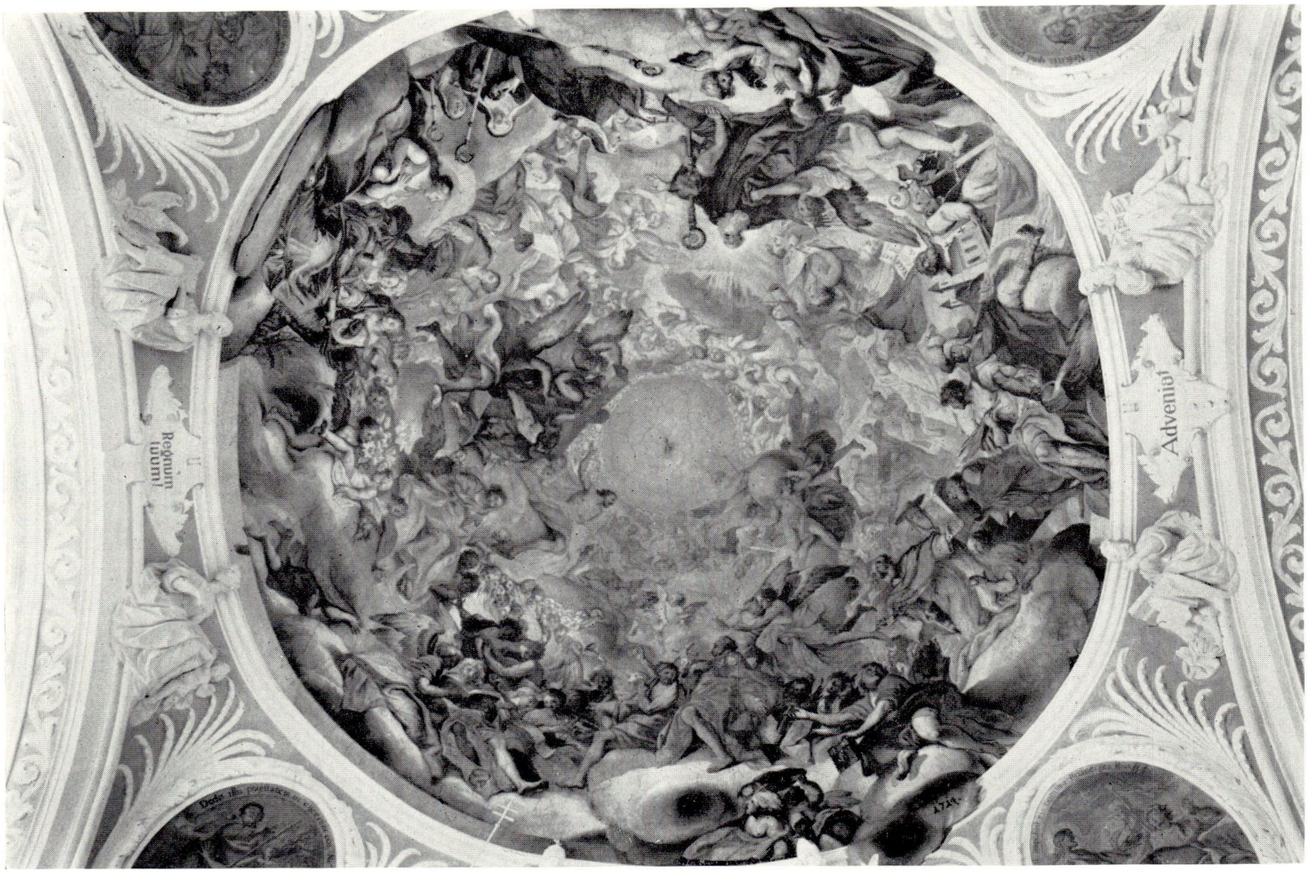

17. Ensdorf. Abbey Church. Dome over crossing (p. 19)

18. Ensdorf. Abbey Church. Interior to east (p. 23)

19. Weltenburg, Abbey Church. West front (p. 27)

20. Weltenburg, Abbey. General view (p. 19)

21. Vienna, Palais Schwarzenberg. Chapel (p. 27)

22. Rome, San Carlo ai Catinari. Capella di Santa Cecilia (p. 27)

23. Rome, Sant' Andrea al Quirinale. Interior to 'east' (p. 26)

24. Weltenburg, Abbey Church. Interior to east (p. 24)

25. Weltenburg, Abbey Church. Interior looking upwards (p. 47)

26. Weltenburg, Abbey Church. Interior to west (p. 25)

27. Weltenburg, Abbey Church. Detail of cove (p. 47)

28. Weltenburg, Abbey Church. Detail of corona with portrait of C. D. Asam (p. 48)

29. Michelfeld, Abbey Church. Middle bay of nave (p. 30)

30. Michelfeld, Abbey Church. Interior to east (p. 29)

31. Michelfeld, Abbey Church. Interior to west (p. 30)

32. Weingarten, Abbey Church. Interior to east (pp. 31, 131)

33. Weingarten, Abbey Church. Nave vaults (p. 34)

34. Rohr, Priory Church. Interior to west (p. 35)

35. Rohr, Priory Church. Interior to east (p. 35)

36. Weltenburg, Abbey Church. High altar (p. 44)

37. Rohr, Priory Church. Choir (p. 44)

38. Aldersbach, Abbey Church. Interior to east (p. 38)

39. Aldersbach, Abbey Church. Choir (p. 38)

40. Aldersbach, Abbey Church. Nave vault with fresco (p. 39)

41. Ceiling fresco project by C. D. Asam (p. 40)

42. Innsbruck, St. Jakobi. Nave vaults (p. 49)

43. Freising, Cathedral. Nave vaults (p. 51)

44. Freising, Cathedral. Clerestory (p. 53)

45. Freising, Cathedral. Interior to west (p. 52)

46. Freising, Cathedral. North side of nave and choir (p. 52)

47. Freising, Cathedral. North tribune (p. 54)

48. Freising, Cathedral. Fresco on wall of nave (p. 53)

49. Freising, Cathedral. Vault of tribune (p. 54)

50. Einsiedeln, Abbey Church. Vault of third bay of nave (p. 58)

51. Einsiedeln, Abbey Church. Interior to east (p. 55)

52. Einsiedeln, Abbey Church. South transept (p. 55)

53. Einsiedeln, Abbey Church. Octagon at west end of nave (p. 55)

54. Einsiedeln, Abbey Church. Crossing (pp. 55)

55. Munich, Heilig-Geist. Interior to west (before bombing) (p. 59)

56. Munich, St. Anna-am-Lehel. Interior to east (before bombing) (p. 60)

57. Osterhofen, Abbey Church. Interior to west (p. 63)

58. Osterhofen, Abbey Church. East end of nave and choir (p. 63)

59. Osterhofen, Abbey Church. Interior to south-west (p. 63)

60. Rinchnach, Priory Church. Interior to east (pp. 65, 179)

61. Alteglofsheim, Schloss. Oval saloon (p. 68)

62. Munich, Residenz. Schatzkammer and Ahnengalerie (p. 69)

63. Regensburg, St. Emmeram. Interior to east (p. 71)

64. Regensburg, St. Emmeram. Choir (p. 71)

65. Regensburg, St. Emmeram. Nave fresco to west (p. 73)

66. Regensburg, St. Emmeram. Nave fresco to east (p. 73)

67. Regensburg, St. Emmeram. Pilaster capital (p. 75)

68. Ingolstadt, Santa Maria de Victoria. Cartouche (p. 78)

69. Ingolstadt, Santa Maria de Victoria. Interior to 'west' (p. 77)

70. Ingolstadt, Santa Maria de Victoria. Interior to 'east' (p. 77)

71. Munich, St. Johann-Nepomuk. Fresco on vault (p. 81)

72. Munich, St. Johann-Nepomuk. Interior to 'east' (p. 81)

73. Würzburg, Residenz, Hofkirche, interior to 'east' (p. 82)

74. Munich, St. Johann-Nepomuk. Upper wall of nave (p. 82)

75. Munich, St. Johann-Nepomuk. The Trinity (p. 83)

76. Munich, Asamhaus and St. Johann-Nepomuk (p. 85)

77. Munich, St. Johann-Nepomuk. Upper altar (p. 83)

78. Füssen, Abbey of St. Mang. Exterior from the south (p. 93)

79. Füssen, Abbey of St. Mang. Library (p. 244)

80. Füssen, St. Mang. Vaults of crossing and nave (p. 93)

81. Füssen, St. Mang. Choir screen (p. 93)

82. Füssen, Krippkirche. Interior to 'east' (p. 94)

83. Füssen, Krippkirche. Façade (p. 94)

84. Füssen, Krippkirche. Interior to 'west' (p. 94)

85. Kisslegg, St. Anna. Ceiling of nave and choir (p. 96)

86. Rückholz, St. Georg. Choir (p. 96)

87. Rettenberg, St. Stephan. Interior to east (p. 100)

88. Bernbeuren, St. Nikolaus. Interior to west (p. 98)

89. Bernbeuren, St. Nikolaus. Interior to east (p. 98)

90. Bertoldshofen, St. Michael. Exterior from north-west (p. 102)

91. Bertoldshofen, St. Michael.
Interior to west (p. 105)

92. Bertoldshofen, St. Michael. Interior to east (p. 105)

93. Bertoldshofen, St. Michael. Dome over crossing (p. 107)

94. Marktoberdorf, Heilig-Kreuz & St. Martin. Interior to east (p. 108)

95. Marktoberdorf, Heilig-Kreuz & St. Martin. Nave ceiling (p. 109)

96. Marktoberdorf, Heilig-Kreuz & St. Martin. Sanctuary (p. 108)

97. Kisslegg, Wurzach'sches (or Zeil'sches) Schloss. Garden front (p. 97)

98. Kisslegg: St. Ulrich & St. Gallus in centre, Wolfegg'sches Schloss to left and Wurzach'sches Schloss below (p. 112)

99. Kisslegg, St. Ulrich & St. Gallus. Exterior from the north-east (p. 111)

100. Kisslegg, St. Ulrich & St. Gallus. Interior to east (p. 111)

101. Kisslegg, St. Ulrich & St. Gallus. Crossing (p. 111)

102. Kisslegg, St. Ulrich & St. Gallus. North aisle (p. 111)

103. Wolfegg, Schloss. Roter Salon (p. 114)

104. Wolfegg, Schloss. Blumenzimmer (p. 114)

105. Wolfegg, St. Katherine. Choir and apse (p. 114)

106. Wolfegg, St. Katherine. Interior to west (p. 114)

107. Wolfegg, St. Katherine. Interior to east (p. 114)

108. Wolfegg, St. Katherine. Nave vault (p. 118)

109. Wolfegg, St. Katherine. Exterior from south (p. 120)

110. Wolfegg, St. Katherine. Exterior from south-east (p. 120)

111. Dillingen, Franciscan Convent Church. Interior to east (p. 121)

112. Dillingen, Franciscan Convent Church. Nave fresco (p. 122)

113. Maria Steinbach, Pilgrimage Church. Interior to east (p. 123)

114. Maria Steinbach, Pilgrimage Church. Nave fresco (p. 124)

115. Maria Steinbach, Pilgrimage Church. Interior to south-east (p. 123)

116. Maria Steinbach, Pilgrimage Church. Apse (p. 124)

117. Maria Steinbach, Pilgrimage Church. West front (p. 124)

118. Obermarchtal, Abbey Church. Interior to east (p. 127)

119. Vilgertshofen, Pilgrimage Church. Interior to north-east (p. 128)

120. Friedrichshafen, Hofen Priory Church. Interior to east (p. 127)

121. Vilgertshofen, Pilgrimage Church. Scroll-work in stucco (p. 128)

122. Friedrichshafen, Hofen Priory Church. Choir vault (p. 128)

123. Irsee, Abbey Church. Interior to east (p. 129)

124. Rheinau, Abbey Church. Interior to east (p. 129)

125. St. Urban, Abbey Church. Interior to north-west (p. 130)

126. Weissenau, Abbey Church. Interior to west (p. 132)

127. Weissenau, Abbey Church. Interior to east (p. 132)

128. Pielenhofen, Abbey Church. Interior to east (p. 133)

129. Donauwörth, Heilig-Kreuz. Interior to east (p. 133)

130. Donauwörth, Heilig-Kreuz. Interior to south-west (p. 133)

131. Irsee, Prälatur. Stair-hall (p. 135)

132. Irsee, Prälatur. Stair-hall, corner of stucco cove (p. 135)

133. Nymphenburg, Amalienburg. Spiegelsaal (p. 139)

134. Garmisch, St. Martin. Interior to east (p. 135)

135. Oberammergau, Parish Church. Interior to east (p. 137)

136. Rottenbuch, Abbey Church. Interior to west (pp. 138)

137. Rottenbuch, Abbey Church. Interior to east (p. 138)

138. Rottenbuch, Abbey Church. Choir vault (p. 139)

139. Rottenbuch, Abbey Church. North transept vault (p. 142)

140. Rottenbuch, Abbey Church. South aisle (p. 142)

141. Rottenbuch, Abbey Church. Vault of crossing (p. 140)

142. Rottenbuch, Abbey Church. Apse (p. 140)

143. Steingaden, Abbey Church. Interior to west (p. 144)

144. Steingaden, Abbey Church. Interior to east (p. 144)

145. Ettal, Abbey. General view (p. 146)

146. Ettal, Abbey Church. West front (p. 146)

147. Ettal, Abbey Church. Interior to east (p. 145)

148. Ettal, Abbey Church. Interior to north-east (p. 148)

149. Ettal, Abbey Church. Interior to west (p. 145)

150. Ettal, Abbey Church. Fresco over nave (p. 147)

151. Hohenpeissenberg, Gnadenkapelle. Interior to east (p. 149)

152. St. Trudpert, Abbey Church.
Interior to east (p. 153)

153. Ebersmunster, Abbey Church. Exterior from east (p. 154)

154. Ebersmunster, Abbey Church. Interior to east (p. 154)

155. St. Peter, Abbey.
Exterior in landscape (p. 156)

156. St. Ulrich, Priory Church. Exterior in landscape (p. 161)

157. St. Peter, Abbey Church. Interior to east (p. 156)

158. St. Peter, Abbey. Library (p. 158)

159. Birnau, Pilgrimage Church. Exterior from south-west

160. Birnau, Pilgrimage Church. Exterior from north (p. 160)

161. Birnau, Pilgrimage Church. Interior to 'east' (p. 160)

162. Birnau, Pilgrimage Church. Choir and apse (p. 162)

163. Birnau, Pilgrimage Church. Interior to north-west (p. 160)

164. Birnau, Pilgrimage Church. Side altar and pulpit (p. 165)

165. Birnau, Pilgrimage Church. Interior to 'west' (p. 160)

166. Birnau, Pilgrimage Church. Fresco over choir (p. 165)

167. St. Gallen, Abbey Church. Exterior from north-west

168. St. Gallen, Abbey Church. East end (p. 172)

169. St. Gallen, Abbey Church. Interior of nave to east (p. 166)

170. St. Gallen, Abbey Church. Interior of nave to north-west (p. 171)

171. St. Gallen, Abbey Church. Rotunda (p. 171)

172. St. Gallen, Abbey Church. *Stucchi* in south transept (p. 171)

173. Birnau, Pilgrimage Church. Pilaster capitals and cove above (p. 165)

174. St. Gallen, Abbey. Library, interior to south (p. 173)

175. St. Gallen, Abbey. Library, interior to south-west (p. 173)

176. Niederaltaich, Abbey Church. Retrochoir (p. 178)

177. Unering, Parish Church. Interior to east (p. 180)

178. Niederaltaich, Abbey Church. Sacristy (p. 178)

179. Diessen, Priory Church. West front (p. 183)

180. Diessen, Priory Church. Interior from entrance (p. 188)

181. Diessen, Priory Church. Interior to east (p. 180)

182. Diessen, Priory Church. End of nave (p. 180)

183. Diessen, Priory Church. Large fresco over nave (p. 190)

184. Aufhausen, Pilgrimage Church. Detail of vaulting (p. 187)

185. Ingolstadt, Franciscan Church. Interior (p. 185)

186. Walleshausen, Parish Church. Interior to north-east (p. 191)

187. Berg-am-Laim, St. Michael. Interior to east (p. 183)

188. Aufhausen, Pilgrimage Church. Interior to 'east' (p. 184)

189. Fürstenzell, Abbey Church. West front (p. 196)

190. Zwiefalten, Abbey Church. West front (p. 196)

191. Fürstenzell, Abbey Church. Interior to east (p. 192)

192. Zwiefalten, Abbey Church. Interior to east (p. 192)

193. Zwiefalten, Abbey Church. Side of nave (p. 196)

194. Zwiefalten, Abbey Church. Fresco over nave (p. 196)

195. Rott-am-Inn, Abbey Church. Interior to west (p. 197)

196. Ottobeuren, Abbey. Air view (p. 201)

197. Ottobeuren, Abbey Church. Exterior from north (p. 200)

198. Ottobeuren, Abbey Church. Interior to east (p. 198)

199. Schäftlarn, Abbey Church. Interior to east (p. 201)

200. Schäftlarn, Abbey Church. Interior to west (p. 201)

201. Benediktbeuern, Abbey. Anastasiakapelle, exterior from east (p. 204)

202. Benediktbeuern, Abbey. Anastasiakapelle, interior to east (p. 204)

203. Benediktbeuern, Abbey. Anastasiakapelle, fresco on vault (p. 205)

204. Altomünster, Abbey Church. Choir (p. 207)

205. Holzkirchen, Priory Church. Interior (p. 209)

206. Trier, St. Paulin. Interior to east (p. 210)

207. Werneck, Chapel. Interior to west (p. 213)

208. Würzburg, Residenz. Hofkirche, vaulting (p. 209)

209. Würzburg, Residenz. Weisser Saal (p. 211)

210. Würzburg, Residenz. Sala Terrena (p. 214)

211. Würzburg, Residenz. Kaisersaal, vault (p. 214)

212. Würzburg, Residenz. Kaisersaal (p. 214)

213. Bruchsal, Schloss. Stair-hall (p. 215)

214. Vierzehnheiligen, Pilgrimage Church. Interior to east (p. 215)

215. Vierzehnheiligen, Pilgrimage Church. Interior to east and fresco over nave (p. 215)

216. Vierzehnheiligen, Pilgrimage Church. Crossing (p. 218)

217. Neresheim, Abbey Church. Interior to east (p. 220)

218. Würzburg, Käppele. Interior to east (p. 218)

LIST OF PLATES

PLANS AND SECTIONS

GLOSSARY

a-tectonic—avoiding structural expression
Ahnengalerie—Gallery of Ancestors
anta—a square pilaster on either side of a door or at the corner of a building
architectonic—qualities peculiar to architecture as contrasted with 'pictorial' or 'sculptural' qualities
architrave—lowest member of entablature; moulded frame of a rectangular opening
archivolt—the curved frame of an arch from impost to impost; the band of mouldings defining this curve
arris—the sharp edge formed by the angular contact of two plane or curved surfaces
ashlar—regularly coursed masonry of rectangular blocks of stone

balconette—small balcony, often more symbolic than actually usable
banderole—a flat band with an inscription
bandwork—proto-Rococo decoration consisting of narrow intersecting raised bands
baroquize—redecorate an earlier, usually medieval, church in Baroque style, often with some actual remodelling
barrel-vaulting—continuous vaulting of semicircular or semi-elliptical section
basilican—church plan with nave and continuous side aisles of lesser height terminating in a rounded apse
boiseries—carved wooden panelling
Brüderschaft—religious organization of pious laymen

centralized plan—a plan based on a circle, an octagon, or a Greek cross
chamfering—easing a rectangular edge or corner by a diagonal, concave, or even convex cut
chronogram—inscription giving date by capitalizing relevant letters to provide a roman numeral
cloister-vault—square vault covered by broad unbroken severies rising from the four sides of a square or rectangular bay
conoids (vaulting)—lower portions of a main vault between intersecting cross-vaults
console—bracket, usually of scrolled section
corona—light, crown-like, circular frame apparently detached in space
cove—relatively narrow concave surface providing a transition between perpendicular walls and horizontal ceilings
cross-vaults—vaults in which 'barrel' shapes of the same height intersect
crossing—where nave and transepts meet
cyma—a projecting moulding whose profile is a double curve

dessinateur—draughtsman, but with subordinate responsibility for design
drum—the upright cylinder under a dome

edicule—relatively small feature of edifice-like character
Elector—one of the ecclesiastical or hereditary secular princes who, rather than the Emperor, were the real rulers in the Holy Roman Empire
en camaieu—painting in two tones suggesting a cameo
engaged column—column partially incorporated, one-quarter or one-half usually, into the body of a wall or pier
entablature—that part of an order which is above the column, including the architrave, the frieze and the cornice
extrados—the upper or exterior curve of an arch

fabrick—garden pavilion
Festsaal—Great Hall
foliated—similar to, or incorporating, plant elements

Gesamtkunstwerk—a work of architecture in which the other arts, notably fresco-painting and stucco-decoration, play an integral part
glory—rays, usually gilded, shooting out radially from a central symbol such as the dove representing the Holy Spirit
Gnadenbild—painting or sculpture serving as the focus of the cult of a religious pilgrimage
grisaille—monochrome painting, not necessarily in neutral tones
Groteskensaal—hall with arabesque decorations
Grüne Gewölbe—literally, green vaults
gulden—equivalent to 18th-century English shilling

hall-church—church with aisles of same height as nave
handkerchief vault—dome on continuous pendentives over oblong bay, hence usually irregular, not to say freehand, in curvature
herm—figural element terminating in abstract rectangular pier below the level of the breast or waist
Hofbaumeister—court architect
Hofmaler—court painter
Hofstukkateur—court stuccoer
hôtel particulier—private mansion

impost—element, usually moulding-crowned, supporting an arch
intrados—the underside of an arch

jochverschleifend—extending through several bays

Kammerdiener—appointed member of a court
Kammerkapelle—private chapel
Klassicismus—Neoclassicism in German lands
kreutzer—'penny'; monetary subdivision of *gulden*

Landesbaudirektor—supervising architect in Württemberg
loge—high-placed balconette, usually in the choirs of churches, for the use of distinguished persons

Marmorgalerie—marble gallery
Marmorsaal—marble hall
modillion—bracket under a cornice
mosaïque—checkered or diapered pattern, usually gilded

Neuer Festsaal—New Hall
Nothelfer—heavenly witnesses called on by the pious for help in need: the patrons of the shrine at Vierzehnheiligen

Oberhofbaumeister—head of electoral 'Office of Works' in Bavaria
oculus—a circular window
'onion'—characteristic Central European bulbous termination of a church tower
order—range of pilasters or columns with associated entablature

Palier—foreman or supervising assistant for an architect
pendentive—triangular portion of a sphere providing the transition between a square plan below and a circular dome above; usually, therefore, one of four, but over some plan-shapes there may be more
piano nobile—main floor
pièce centrale—dominating central feature of a cross-axial plan, usually circular or octagonal
pilaster clusters—single pilasters flanked by half pilasters in a rear plane
premier architecte—head of French Royal 'Office of Works'
putto, putti—cherub, cherubs

quadratura painting—wall or vault decoration of architectural elements organized in illusionary perspective

rebate—cut, usually of rectangular section, at the edge of a projecting architectural member
reeded—convex-fluted
ressauts—projections in the line of an entablature over pilasters or engaged columns
retardataire—stylistically belated
rib—projecting member between two bays of a vault or between meeting severies, as in some cross-vaults
rib-band—low relief member substituted for a rib
rocaille—advanced Rococo decoration after the mid-1730s with much use of shell-forms and recurrent asymmetries

Sala terrena—Garden Room
Salomonic columns—columns with a helical twist
scagliola—stucco marbled and polished
Schatzkammer—Treasure Room
Schuh—unit of measure, roughly a foot
severy—compartment of a vault
soffit—underside of top of an opening
Spiegelgalerie—Gallery of Mirrors
Spiegelsaal—Hall of Mirrors
Stadtbild—general visual effect of a town
stucchi—stucco-decoration
stuccoer—master-plasterer

tectonic—structurally expressive
titular saint—saint to whom a church is dedicated
tribune—gallery above side aisle or side chapel
triconch—three-lobed

Vesperbild—cult painting or sculptural group, usually a Pietà
Vorarlberg scheme—naves flanked by wall-pillars that support the vaulting
Vorarlbergers—architects and other building craftsmen from the Austrian Vorarlberg province

wall-pillar—a sort of internal buttress flanking a vaulted nave and separating the side chapels that provides the principal support of the vaulting
Wessobrunner—stuccoers born and trained at Wessobrunn in Upper Bavaria

WORKS CITED

Abbreviations and full titles of works cited recurrently

Barock am Bodensee: *Barock am Bodensee/Architektur*, Bregenz, 1962

Batzl (*Michelfeld*): Heribert Batzl, *Michelfeld Oberpfalz* (Kunstführer Nr. 747), Munich, 1962

Boerlin (*St. Gallen*): P. H. Boerlin, *Die Stiftskirche St. Gallen*, Bern [1964]

Böhm (*Mannheimer*): L. W. Böhm, *Das Mannheimer Schloss*, Karlsruhe [1962]

Boll (*Schönbornkapelle*): W. Boll, *Die Schönbornkapelle am Würzburger Dom*, Munich, 1925

Bourke (*Churches*): John Bourke, *Baroque Churches of Central Europe*, London [1958], 2nd ed., London [1962]

Brunner (*Baden-Württemberg*): Herbert Brunner, *Reclams Kunstführer*, II, *Baden-Württemberg, Pfalz, Saarland*, 3rd ed., Stuttgart [1960]

de Colombier (*Architecture française*): P. de Colombier, *L'Architecture française en Allemagne au XVIIIe Siècle*, 2 v., Paris, 1956

Franz (*Böhmen*): Heinrich Gerhard Franz, *Bauten und Baumeister der Barockzeit in Böhmen*, Leipzig [1962]

Gall (*Oberbayern*): Ernst Gall, *Handbuch der deutschen Kunstdenkmäler / Oberbayern*, 3rd ed., Munich, 1960

Gall (*Östliches Schwaben*): E. Gall, *Handbuch der deutschen Kunstdenkmäler / Östliches Schwaben*, Munich, 1954

Gall (*Westliches Schwaben*): E. Gall, *Handbuch der deutschen Kunstdenkmäler / Westliches Schwaben*, Munich, 1956

Grimschitz (*Hildebrandt*): B. Grimschitz, *Johann Lukas von Hildebrandt*, Vienna, 1932

Hagen-Dempf (*Zentralbaugedanke*): Felicitas Hagen-Dempf, *Der Zentralbaugedanke bei Johann Michael Fischer*, Munich [1954]

Hager (*Nymphenburg*): Luisa Hager, *Nymphenburg Schloss, Park und Burgen*, Munich, n.d.

Hanfstaengl (1939): Erika Hanfstaengl, *Kosmas Damian Asam*, Munich, 1939

Hanfstaengl (1955): Erika Hanfstaengl, *Die Brüder Cosmas Damian und Egid Quirin Asam*, [Munich] 1955

Hempel (*Central Europe*): Eberhard Hempel, *Baroque Architecture and Art in Central Europe*, [Harmondsworth, 1965]

Kalnein (*Poppelsdorf*): W. Kalnein, *Das Kurfürstliche Schloss Clemensruhe in Poppelsdorf*, Dusseldorf [1956]

Kimball (*Louis XV*): Fiske Kimball, *Le Style Louis XV*, Paris, 1949

Landolt (*Schweizer*): Hanspeter Landolt, *Schweizer Barockkirchen*, Frauenfeld [1948]

Lieb (*Barockkirchen*): Norbert Lieb, *Barockkirchen zwischen Donau und Alpen*, Munich [1953]

Lieb (*Münchener*): Norbert Lieb, *Münchener Barockbaumeister*, Munich, 1941

Lieb–Dieth (*Vorarlberger*): Norbert Lieb and Franz Dieth, *Die Vorarlberger Barockbaumeister*, 2nd ed., Munich, 1967

Petzet (*Füssen*): Michael Petzet, *Stadt und Landkreis Füssen*, Munich [1960]

Petzet (*Marktoberdorf*): Michael Petzet, *Landkreis Marktoberdorf*, Munich [1966]

Piel (*Baden-Württemberg*): Friedrich Piel, *Handbuch der deutschen Kunstdenkmäler/Baden-Württemberg*, [Munich] 1964

Reitzenstein–Brunner (*Bayern*): Alexander von Reitzenstein and Herbert Brunner, *Reclams Kunstführer*, I, *Bayern*, 4th ed., Stuttgart [1961]

Reuther (*Kirchenbauten*): Hans Reuther, *Die Kirchenbauten Balthasar Neumanns*, Berlin, 1960

Schmidt (*Ludwigsburg*): Richard Schmidt, *Schloss Ludwigsburg*, Munich [1954]

Sedlmayr–Bauer ('Rococo'): Hans Sedlmayr and Hermann Bauer: article ('Rococo') in *Encyclopedia of World Art*, XII, New York [1966]

Wessobrunn: H. Schnell, 'Die wessobrunner Baumeister und Stuccatoren', in N. Lieb, H. Schnell and J. Stadler, *Wessobrunn* (Grosse Kunstführer Nr. 13), 2nd ed., [Munich, 1960]

Zimmermann: H. R. Hitchcock, *German Rococo: The Zimmermann Brothers*, London, 1968

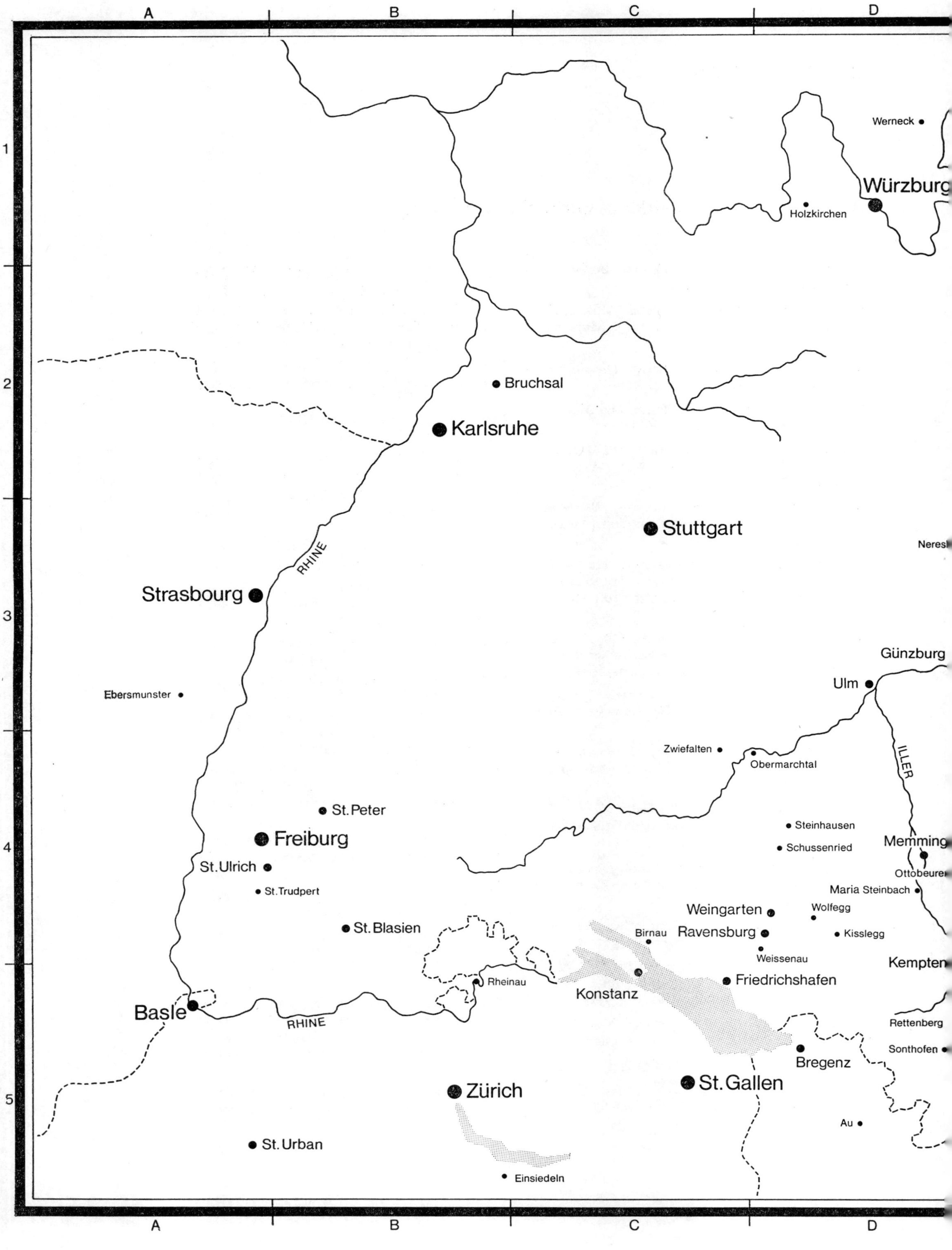
A
B
C
D
1
2
3
4
5
Werneck
Würzburg
Holzkirchen
Bruchsal
Karlsruhe
Stuttgart
Neres
RHINE
Strasbourg
Günzburg
Ulm
Ebersmunster
Zwiefalten
Obermarchtal
ILLER
St. Peter
Freiburg
Steinhausen
Memming
Schussenried
St. Ulrich
Ottobeure
St. Trudpert
Maria Steinbach
Weingarten
Wolfegg
St. Blasien
Birnau
Ravensburg
Kisslegg
Weissenau
Kempten
Rheinau
Friedrichshafen
Konstanz
Basle
RHINE
Rettenberg
Bregenz
Sonthofen
St. Gallen
Zürich
Au
St. Urban
Einsiedeln

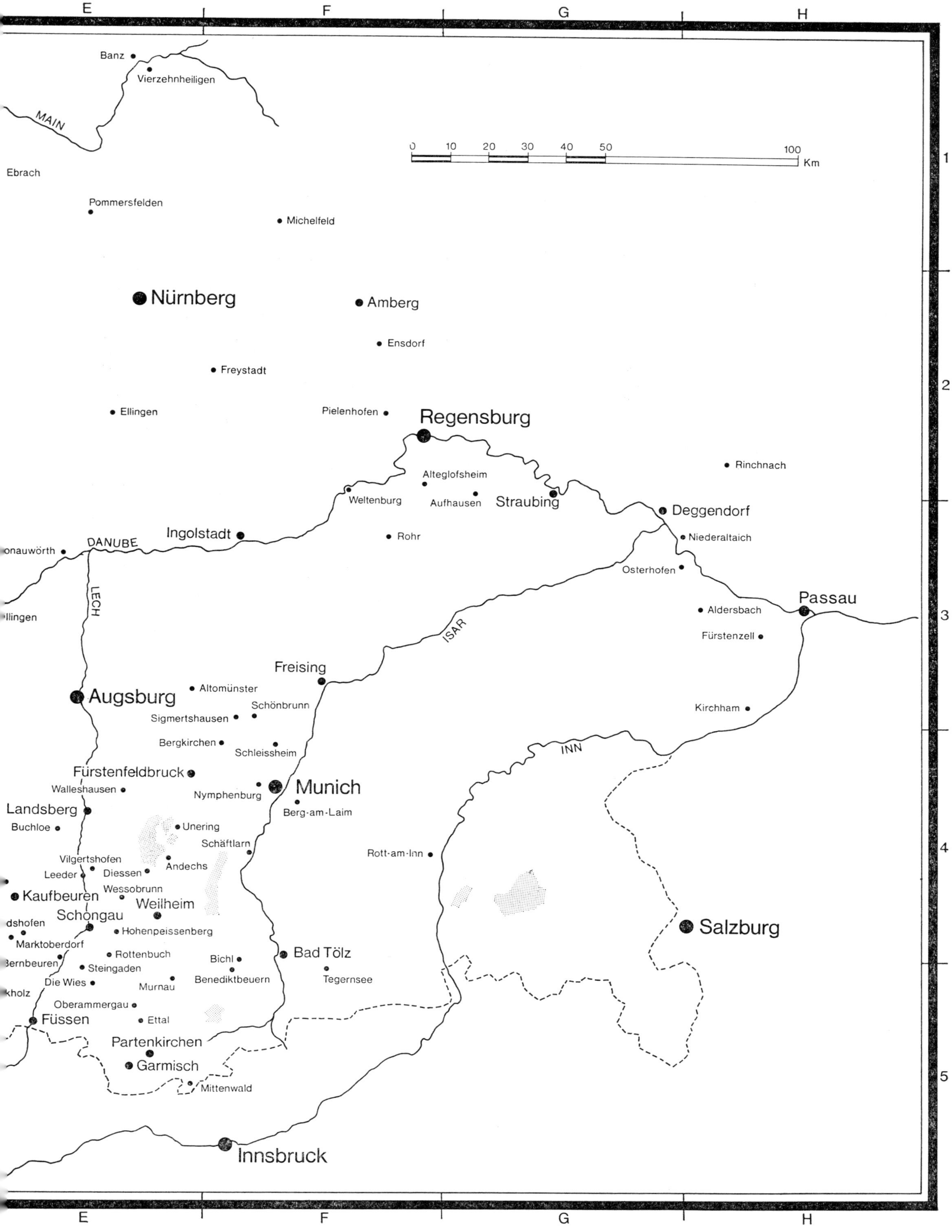
E
F
G
H
Banz
Vierzehnheiligen
MAIN
0 10 20 30 40 50 100 Km
1
Ebrach
Pommersfelden
Michelfeld
Nürnberg
Amberg
Ensdorf
Freystadt
2
Ellingen
Pielenhofen
Regensburg
Rinchnach
Alteglofsheim
Weltenburg
Aufhausen
Straubing
Deggendorf
Ingolstadt
DANUBE
Rohr
Niederaltaich
onauwörth
Osterhofen
LECH
Passau
llingen
Aldersbach
3
ISAR
Fürstenzell
Freising
Augsburg
Altomünster
Schönbrunn
Kirchham
Sigmertshausen
Bergkirchen
Schleissheim
INN
Fürstenfeldbruck
Walleshausen
Munich
Nymphenburg
Landsberg
Berg-am-Laim
Buchloe
Unering
Schäftlarn
Rott-am-Inn
4
Vilgertshofen
Andechs
Leeder
Diessen
Wessobrunn
Kaufbeuren
Weilheim
Schongau
dshofen
Salzburg
Hohenpeissenberg
Marktoberdorf
Rottenbuch
Bichl
Bad Tölz
Bernbeuren
Steingaden
Tegernsee
Die Wies
Murnau
Benediktbeuern
kholz
Oberammergau
Füssen
Ettal
Partenkirchen
Garmisch
5
Mittenwald
Innsbruck

ACKNOWLEDGEMENTS

The plates are reproduced from photographs from the following sources:

AKO 176; Lala Aufsberg, Sonthofen 25, 32, 33, 36, 44, 45, 47, 48, 75, 77–84, 87–90, 93–96, 99–102, 113, 116, 117, 122, 123, 129, 130, 132, 146, 150, 165, 173, 179, 181–183, 197–199, 201; Alinari, Florence 22, 23; Wayne Andrews, Detroit 57, 58, 162, 211; Abtei Neresheim 217; Bayr. Landesamt für Denkmalpflege, Munich 40, 65, 66, 71, 72; E. Burda, Freiburg 155; Calig, Freiburg 156; CIM, Macon 153; Deutscher Kunstverlag, Munich 3; Lotte Eckener, Konstanz 160; Th. Finckenstaedt 12; Dr. Greiff, Garmisch-Partenkirchen-Wamberg 147; Gross, St. Gallen 167, 168; Photo-Verlag Gundermann, Würzburg 8, 205, 208, 209, 213, 218; Walter Hege, Munich 210; Martin Herpich & Sohn, Munich 28; Hermann Hessler, Frankfurt am Main 30; Josef Heutle, Memmingen 114, 115; Hildenbrandt, Göppingen 20; Hirmer Fotoarchiv, Munich 2, 4, 5, 6, 11, 27, 34, 35, 38, 118, 145, 148, 163, 180, 182, 192–194, 200, 215, 216; Cramers Kunstanstalt, Dortmund 196; Photo-Verlag H. Kronburger, Oberammergau 140; Verlag Fritz Lauterbach, Fürth 69; P. Ledermann, Vienna 10; Bildarchiv Foto Marburg, Marburg 15, 56, 119; Rudolf Merz, Baldham, Munich 19; Gebr. Metz, Tübingen 190; Erich Müller, Kassel 207; Oberfränkischer Ansichtskartenverlag, Bayreuth 214; Verlag A. Ohmayer, Rothenburg ob der Tauber 73; Österreichische Nationalbibliothek, Vienna 21; U. Pfistermeister, Artelshofen 17, 18, 37, 39, 63, 64, 67, 188; from Popp, *Architektur der Barock- und Rokokozeit*, Stuttgart (1913) 74; Erhard Pöppel, Freiburg 152; O. Poss, Regensburg 187; Helga Schmidt-Glassner, Stuttgart 1, 7, 61, 206; Robert Schmitt, New York 85, 86, 109, 110, 138, 139, 177, 184, 186, 189; Dr. Hugo Schnell, Munich 43, 49, 55, 59, 68, 91, 92, 120, 121, 169, 185; Verlag Schöning & Co., Lübeck 212; Th.u. H. Seeger, Egg 50–54, 124, 125, 164, 170–172, 174, 175; Staatliche Sammlung, Munich 41; Eugen Spaninger, Kisslegg 97; Dr. Johannes Steiner, Munich 13, 14, 16, 24, 29, 31, 42, 46, 70, 103–108, 111, 112, 126–128, 131, 134–137, 141–144, 149, 151, 154, 157, 158, 159, 161, 163, 166, 178, 191, 195, 202–204; Strähle, Schorndorf 98; Fritz Thudichum, Munich 9, 24, 26, 62, 76; Verlag H. Tschernich, Rosenheim 60; Verlag R. Zerle, Munich 133.

The plans and sections in the text are taken from the following sources:

Tilmann Breuer, *Stadt und Landkreis Memmingen* 14; B. Grimschitz, *Johann Lukas von Hildebrandt* 8; Hagen-Dempf, *Zentralbaugedanke* 5, 22, 25, 31, 32; Max Hauttman, *Geschichte der Kirchlichen Baukunst 1580–1760* 21, 33; Photo Peter Hütter, Ravensburg A; *Kunstdenkmäler von Bayern* 1, 2; Schnell & Steiner, *Grosse Kunstführer 10* 20; Schnell & Steiner, *Kunstführer 561* 19; Schnell & Steiner, *Kunstführer 573* 6; Landolt, *Schweizer* 3, E; Lieb, *Barockkirchen* 4, 7, 15, 23, 24, 27–30, C; Lieb–Dieth, *Vorarlberger* 26, B, G; X. Ohresser, *Église et abbaye d'Ebersmunster* 18; Petzet, *Füssen* 9, 10; Petzet, *Marktoberdorf* 11–13; Piel, *Baden-Württemberg* 36; Reuther, *Kirchenbauten* 34, 35; W. Sebert, *Die Klosterkirche St. Trudpert* 16, 17; courtesy of Schweizerisches Landesmuseum, Zürich D, H, F.

INDEX OF PERSONS

INDEX OF PERSONS

INDEX OF PLACES

The numbers in brackets refer to the Map (pages 416–17) and those in italics refer to the Plates.